Cases in Advertising and Promotion Management

THE IRWIN SERIES IN MARKETING
Gilbert A Churchill, Jr., Consulting Editor
University of Wisconsin, Madison

Cases in Advertising and Promotion Management

Fourth Edition

John A. Quelch
Professor of Business Administration
Graduate School of Business Administration
Harvard University

Paul W. Farris
Landmark Communications Professor of Business Administration
The Darden School of Business Administration
University of Virginia

IRWIN

Burr Ridge, Illinois
Boston, Massachusetts
Sydney, Australia

Senior sponsoring editor: *Stephen M. Patterson*
Editorial coordinator: *Lynn Nordbrock*
Marketing manager: *Scott J. Timian*
Project editor: *Lynne Basler*
Production manager: *Ann Cassady*
Art coordinator: *Heather Burbridge*
Art studio: *Laser Graphics, Inc.*
Compositor: *J.M. Post Graphics, Div. Cardinal Communications Group, Inc.*
Typeface: *10/12 Times Roman*
Printer: *R. R. Donnelley & Sons Company*

Library of Congress Cataloging-in-Publication Data

Quelch, John A.
    Cases in advertising and promotion management/John A. Quelch,
Paul W. Farris.—4th ed.
        p. cm.
    Includes bibliographical references and index.
    ISBN 0-256-12272-5
    1. Advertising—Case studies.   2. Sales promotion—Case studies.
I. Farris, Paul.   II. Title.
HF5823.Q44   1994
659.1—dc20   93—5170

Printed in the United States of America
1 2 3 4 5 6 7 8 9 0 DOC 0 9 8 7 6 5 4 3

Preface

This book is designed to provide students of advertising and promotion management an opportunity to gain "real world" experience through the analysis of case studies. The book has been designed primarily for courses in advertising management, promotion management, and marketing communications. The cases are almost all written from the perspective of an advertising manager, product manager, or marketing manager addressing one or more problems in advertising and promotion management. The companies and organizations represented include manufacturers of consumer package goods and durables, industrial products manufacturers, retailers and other service marketers, and nonprofit institutions. All of the cases have been successfully classroom tested and many have also been taught in executive development programs.

In addition to providing a thorough coverage of advertising issues, special attention is paid to the management of sales promotion programs which are becoming an increasingly important component of many marketing budgets. Other communications approaches are also addressed—including direct mail, telemarketing, and point-of-purchase merchandising. The value of this integrated collection of case studies lies in the richness and diversity of the management problems which they collectively present.

LEARNING WITH THE CASE METHOD

The principal objective of the case study method is to develop student skills in problem solving and decision making. In studying a case, the reader's task is to assume the role of the decision maker and consider all of the information available to the decision maker at the time of the case event. Alternative solutions to the problem must be evaluated, and finally, a recommended course of action must be decided upon.

The quality of a case analysis as a surrogate for experience depends on the same factors as the quality of an experience in the real world. The manager who is not fully involved in a decision is unlikely to learn much from it. Even worse, the manager may misunderstand the situation and justify a decision for the wrong reasons. Cases are much the same. The student must review the case thoroughly to derive maximum benefit from the discussion. To base an analysis of a case on one or two isolated facts may enable a student to make a "contribution" to the discussion, but it is hardly likely to constitute a worthwhile learning experience.

Although there is rarely a single "right" answer to a case problem, there may be several wrong ones—at least, "wrong" in the sense that it is difficult to convince anyone else that the decision proposed is reasonable. Experience will tend to show that bringing an opinion to a case is not the same thing as bringing an analysis that is based on logic, the case facts, and assumptions which other members of the class are willing to accept as reasonable. In addition, be careful to avoid looking for a single message in a given case. You may find only the one that you forced yourself to see.

Do not be disappointed if a class ends with more uncertainty about the decision than was apparent when it began. A group consensus is in no way necessary for learning to occur. Indeed, confusion is sometimes a higher state of knowledge than ignorance. And, in any case, making decisions in the face of uncertainty is the manager's raison d'être. Once a decision-making task can be routinized, it belongs to a clerk.

ORGANIZATION OF THE BOOK

We have summarized below the principal objectives of each group of cases in the book. Please note that the classification of a particular case in one chapter rarely means that the issues it raises pertain *only* to the subject of that chapter. The planning and design of advertising and promotion programs require that each element of any program be integrated with the others. It is not possible, for example, to discuss media selection sensibly without considering target markets and messages. Nor is it possible to consider the promotion budget independent of the advertising budget. Please be aware that the inclusion of a case in a specific chapter reflects the *relative* rather than exclusive emphasis of the issues it raises.

The learning objectives for each group of cases are as follows:

1. Advertising, Promotion, and Marketing Communications
   a. To establish the diversity of the marketing communications mix, with emphasis on advertising and promotion, and to explore the different roles of each element of the mix.
   b. To show the relationship of communications policy to the marketing mix, to push and pull marketing strategies, and to product positioning, differentiation, and segmentation.
   c. To present the development of advertising and promotion programs as a logical six-stage process involving the definition of program objectives, target markets, messages, media, a budget and its allocation, and a measurement and evaluation program.
   d. To emphasize the dependency of advertising and promotion management on a thorough understanding of consumer behavior and consumer information needs.

2. Advertising, Branding, and Positioning
   a. To discuss the product-market circumstances which enhance the brandability and advertisability of a product.
   b. To explore the advantages and disadvantages of umbrella branding.
   c. To examine the linkages between product positioning, branding strategies, and marketing communications.

3. Message Strategy and Copy Testing
   a. To emphasize that copy strategy and execution must be developed consistent with campaign objectives, product positioning, and target markets.
   b. To explore models of "how advertising works," both at the strategic level and at the level of the individual consumer.
   c. To evaluate particular types of message appeal such as comparison advertising.

    d. To illustrate how advertising testing and research can contribute to the formulation of effective advertising and promotion campaigns.

    e. To expose students to a variety of measurement techniques and criteria in order to permit discussion of how to select and design measurement systems for advertising and promotion.

4. Media Strategy
   a. To introduce students to the concepts used to evaluate individual media vehicles and combinations of media vehicles.
   b. To give students experience in applying target-group weighting, cost-per-thousand, reach-frequency trade-offs, and other concepts, to actual media selection and scheduling decisions.
   c. To link the science and art of media planning to the other elements of advertising and promotion decision making.

5. Budgeting
   a. To explore problems both in setting the level of the advertising and promotion budget and in allocating it efficiently.
   b. To present a variety of advertising and promotion budgeting techniques, including controlled experiments, econometric models, and consumer simulation models.
   c. To demonstrate the importance of integrating advertising and promotion budgeting into the strategic planning process.

6. Sales Promotion
   a. To expose students to the scope and variety of consumer and trade promotion options available to the manufacturer.
   b. To contrast the roles of advertising and promotion and to permit discussion of the circumstances under which different advertising and promotion mixes are appropriate.
   c. To explore the design and implementation of cooperative advertising and promotion programs in which manufacturers share costs with trade accounts.

7. Point-of-Purchase Merchandising
   a. To emphasize the importance of managing communications at the point-of-purchase.
   b. To demonstrate the intimate link between distribution effectiveness and advertising effort.
   c. To illustrate techniques used by distributors to extract more merchandising support from their suppliers.
   d. To highlight the importance of trade policy to manufacturer-trade relations.

8. Agency Relations and Management
   a. To illustrate how marketing management evaluates and selects suppliers of advertising and promotion services.
   b. To identify the difficulties which often arise in agency-client relations and the reasons why they occur.
   c. To provide institutional information on the advertising agency industry to facilitate discussion of agency organizational structure, management style, and positioning.

9. Social and Ethical Issues
    a. To highlight the range and diversity of ethical issues that can arise in advertising and promotion decision-making.
    b. To explore the legitimacy of advertising by public agencies.
    c. To illustrate the role of pressure groups in countering controversial advertising and promotion programs.
10. Projects and Exercises in Advertising and Promotion Management
    a. To develop student skills in the mechanics of media planning.
    b. To improve student understanding of the factors which underlie both overall advertising and promotion expenditure levels by industry and by company and their allocation among advertising media and promotion programs.

ACKNOWLEDGMENTS

Books are always more work than they appear to be. Books are also the work of more people than they appear to be. For a casebook this is especially true, and there are many colleagues whose help and contributions we wish to acknowledge.

We both studied advertising and promotion management under the direction of *Professor Stephen A. Greyser* of the Harvard Business School to whom this book is dedicated. His thoughts will be spread throughout the book because they guided our thoughts. In addition, Steve supervised the first cases that either of us wrote. We learned much from his high standard of case writing, his judicious attention to detail, and his perceptive understanding of how a case should be developed and organized to translate into an effective and exciting classroom experience.

We have also been privileged to be able to include cases written by some of our other close colleagues and friends. N. Craig Smith, now associate professor at Georgetown University, helped prepare three cases on social and ethical issues. V. Kasturi Rangan, professor at Harvard Business School, contributed an exciting case on advertising copy testing—Ad Council's AIDS Campaign (A). Three other Harvard faculty, William Bruns, Frank Cespedes, and Nitin Nohria, contributed valuable cases on the management of advertising agencies and media companies (Actmedia; Hill, Holliday, Connors, Cosmopoulos, Inc.; WPP Group). Mark Parry, assistant professor at the University of Virginia, updated the U.S. Postal Service message strategy case, while Kusum Ailawadi, now at Boston College, worked with Paul Farris on a new case on Carnation's infant formula. David H. Maister, a specialist in the marketing of professional services, provided us with a case on the management of advertising agencies (Francis, Berther & Allfreed). Christopher Gale of the University of Virginia allowed us to include his computerized promotion-planning exercise based on the Procter & Gamble Company (B) case.

Thanks are due to our research assistants for their diligence, patience, and professionalism. At Harvard Business School, they included Cynthia Bates, Greg Conley, Alice MacDonald Court, Tammy Bunn Hiller, Ron Lee, Penny Pittman Merliss, Elisa Morton Palter, Susan Smith, Melanie Spencer, Aimee Stern, and John Teopaco. Research assistants at the University of Virginia included Lisa Axel, Robert Carraway, Bette Collins, Frank Conley, James Culley, Rod DeVar, Anne Kroemer, Valerie Lester, Nischal Rajey, Kenneth Smith, and Nancy Trap.

We are grateful to our many colleagues whose comments and suggestions in response to a lengthy survey questionnaire helped determine the blend of cases presented in the fourth edition. We express our thanks and appreciation. Taking one step back in the case-writing process, we must acknowledge the many executives of the companies and organizations discussed in the case studies for the trust and time which made this book a reality. In similar vein, we gratefully recognize the financial support and encouragement for our case writing efforts furnished by the Divisions of Research at the Graduate School of Business Administration, Harvard University, and The Darden Graduate School of Business Administration, University of Virginia. In addition, we would like to acknowledge the efforts of Steve Patterson, Senior Sponsoring Editor, and Lynn Nordbrock, Editorial Coordinator, for their sustained efforts in gathering market feedback and developing the fourth edition revision strategy.

Somehow, even with all of the help already acknowledged, there remained enough yet to be done that we often tried the patience of our wives with last-minute homework that was accomplished only with their goodwill and understanding. Many thanks to Joyce and Kate.

John A. Quelch
Paul W. Farris

Survey Respondents

Jonathan Barsky
University of San Francisco–
San Francisco

Alexandra Blake
University of Tulsa

Sheri Bridges
Wake Forest University

Terry Bristol
Oklahoma State University–
Stillwater

Dodds Buchanan
University of Colorado–
Boulder

Roy Busby
University of North Texas

Simeon Chow
Boston University

David Eppright
University of West Florida

Judy Foster
Michigan State University–
East Lansing

David Gardner
University of Illinois–
Champaign–Urbana

Susan Jones
Ferris State University

Ronald Kaatz
Northwestern University

Karen King
University of Georgia–
Athens

R. Monroe League
University of Missouri–
Kansas City

Thomas Leigh
University of Georgia–
Athens

George Low
University of Colorado–
Boulder

Scott MacKenzie
Indiana University

Russ Merz
Eastern Michigan University

Loretta Nitschke
Milligan College

Glen Nowak
University of Georgia–
Athens

William Peters
American University

Stephen Pharr
University of Idaho–Moscow

Bonnie Reece
Michigan State University–
East Lansing

Doug Robideaux
Georgia Southern College

Marla Royne
University of Georgia–
Athens

Susan Rozensher
Iona College

Bennett Rudolph
Grand Valley State
University

Cliff Schultz
Columbia University

W. Shambroom
Iona College

Edward Stephens
Syracuse University

Rollie Tillman, Jr.
University of North
Carolina–Chapel Hill

Russell Wahlers
Ball State University

Fred Zandpour
California State University–
Fullerton

Contents

PART 1

Advertising, Promotion, and Marketing Communications

Warner-Lambert Ireland: Niconil*

Declan Dixon, director of marketing for Warner-Lambert Ireland (WLI), examined two very different sales forecasts as he considered the upcoming launch of Niconil, scheduled for January 1990. Niconil was an innovative new product that promised to help the thousands of smokers who attempted to quit smoking each year. More commonly known simply as "the patch," Niconil was a transdermal skin patch that gradually released nicotine into the bloodstream to alleviate the physical symptoms of nicotine withdrawal.

Now in October of 1989, Dixon and his staff had to decide several key aspects of the product launch. There were different opinions about how Niconil should be priced and in what quantities it would sell. Pricing decisions would directly impact product profitability, as well as sales volume, and accurate sales forecasts were vital to planning adequate production capacity. Finally, the product team needed to reach consensus on the Niconil communications campaign to meet advertising deadlines and to ensure an integrated product launch.

COMPANY BACKGROUND

Warner-Lambert was an international pharmaceutical and consumer products company with over $4 billion in worldwide revenues expected in 1989. Warner-Lambert consumer products (50 percent of worldwide sales) included such brands as Dentyne chewing gum, Listerine mouth wash, and Hall's cough drops. Its pharmaceutical products, marketed through the Parke-Davis division, included drugs for treating a wide variety of ailments including heart disease and bronchial disorders.

Warner-Lambert's Irish subsidiary was expected to generate £30 million in sales revenues in 1989: £22 million from exports of manufactured products to other Warner-Lambert subsidiaries in Europe and £4 million each from pharmaceutical and consumer products sales within Ireland.[1] The Irish drug market was estimated at £155 million (in manufacturer sales) in 1989. Warner-Lambert was the 16th largest pharmaceutical company in worldwide revenues; in Ireland, it ranked 6th.

---

*Research Associate Susan P. Smith prepared this case under the supervision of Professor John A. Quelch as the basis for class discussion rather than to illustrate either effective or ineffective handling of an administrative situation. Copyright © 1992 by the President and Fellows of Harvard College. Harvard Business School case N9–S93–008.

[1]In 1989, one Irish pound was equivalent to $1.58 U.S.

Dixon was confident that WLI's position in the Irish market would ensure market acceptance of Niconil. The Parke-Davis division had launched two new drugs successfully within the past 9 months: Dilzem, a treatment for heart disease, and Accupro, a blood pressure medication. The momentum was expected to continue. The Irish market would be the first country launch for Niconil and thus serve as a test market for all of Warner-Lambert. The companywide significance of the Niconil launch was not lost on Dixon as he pondered the marketing decisions before him.

SMOKING IN THE REPUBLIC OF IRELAND

Almost £600 million would be spent by Irish smokers on 300 million packs of cigarettes in 1989; this included government revenues from the tobacco sales tax of £441 million. Of 3.5 million Irish citizens, 30 percent of the 2.5 million adults smoked cigarettes (compared to 40 percent of adults in continental Europe and 20 percent in the United States.)[2] The number of smokers in Ireland had peaked in the late 1970s and had been declining steadily since. Table A presents data from a 1989 survey that WLI had commissioned in 1989 of a demographically balanced sample of 1,400 randomly chosen Irish adults. Table B shows the numbers of cigarettes smoked daily by Irish smokers; the average was 16.5 cigarettes.

TABLE A Incidence of Cigarette Smoking in Ireland (1988–1989)

Of adult population (16 and over)	30%	(100%)
By gender		
Men	32%	(50%)
Women	27	(50)
By age		
16–24	27	(17)
25–34	38	(14)
35–44	29	(12)
45–54	29	(9)
55+	27	(19)
By occupation		
White-collar	24	(25)
Skilled working class	33	(30)
Semi- and unskilled	38	(30)
Farming	23	(17)

Note: To be read (for example): 27 percent of Irish citizens aged 16–24 smoked and this age group represented 17 percent of the population.

---

[2]*Adults* were defined as those over the age of 15, and *smokers* as those who smoked at least one cigarette per day.

TABLE B   Number of Cigarettes Smoked Daily in Ireland (based on 400 smokers in a 1989 survey of 1,400 citizens)

More than 20	16%
15–20	42
10–14	23
5–9	12
Less than 5	4
Unsure	3

Media coverage on the dangers of smoking, antismoking campaigns from public health organizations such as the Irish Cancer Society, and a mounting array of legislation restricting tobacco advertising put pressure on Irish smokers to quit. Promotional discounts and coupons for tobacco products were prohibited, and tobacco advertising was banned not only on television and radio, but also on billboards. Print advertising was allowed only if 10 percent of the ad space was devoted to warnings on the health risks of smoking. Exhibit 1 shows a sample cigarette advertisement from an Irish magazine.

SMOKING AS AN ADDICTION

Cigarettes and other forms of tobacco contained nicotine, a substance that induced addictive behavior. Smokers first developed a tolerance for nicotine and then, over time, needed to increase cigarette consumption to maintain a steady, elevated blood level of nicotine. Smokers became progressively dependent on nicotine and suffered withdrawal symptoms if they stopped smoking. A craving for tobacco was characterized by physical symptoms such as decreased heart rate and a drop in blood pressure, and later could include symptoms like faintness, headaches, cold sweats, intestinal cramps, nausea, and vomiting. The smoking habit also had a psychological component stemming from the ritualistic aspects of smoking behavior, such as smoking after meals or in times of stress.

Since the 1950s, the ill effects of smoking had been researched and identified. Smoking was widely recognized as posing a serious health threat. While nicotine was the substance within the cigarette that caused addiction, it was the tar accompanying the nicotine that made smoking so dangerous. Specifically, smoking was a primary risk factor for ischemic heart disease, lung cancer, and chronic pulmonary diseases. Other potential dangers resulting from prolonged smoking included bronchitis, emphysema, chronic sinusitis, peptic ulcer disease, and for pregnant women, damage to the fetus.

Once smoking was recognized as a health risk, the development and use of a variety of smoking cessation techniques began. In *aversion therapy,* the smoker was discouraged from smoking by pairing an aversive event such as electric shock or a nausea-inducing agent with the smoking behavior, in an attempt to break the cycle of gratification. While aversion therapy was successful in the short term, it did not prove a lasting solution as the old smoking behavior would often be resumed. Aversion therapy was now used

EXHIBIT 1 Cigarette Advertisement from an Irish Magazine

infrequently. *Behavioral self-monitoring* required the smoker to develop an awareness of the stimuli that triggered the desire to smoke and then to eliminate systematically the smoking behavior in specific situations by neutralizing those stimuli. For example, the smoker could learn to avoid particular situations or to adopt a replacement activity such as chewing gum. This method was successful in some cases but demanded a high degree of self-control. While behavioral methods were useful in addressing the psychological component of smoking addiction, they did not address the physical aspect of nicotine addiction that proved an insurmountable obstacle to many who attempted to quit.

NICONIL

Warner-Lambert's Niconil would be the first product to offer a complete solution for smoking cessation, addressing both the physical and psychological aspects of nicotine addiction. The physical product was a circular adhesive patch, 2.5 inches in diameter and containing 30 mg of nicotine gel. Each patch was individually wrapped in a sealed, tear-resistant packet. The patch was applied to the skin, usually on the upper arm, and the nicotine was absorbed into the bloodstream to produce a steady level of nicotine that blunted the smoker's physical craving. Thirty milligrams of nicotine provided the equivalent of 20 cigarettes, without the cigarettes' damaging tar. A single patch was applied once a day every morning for two to six weeks, depending on the smoker. The average smoker was able to quit successfully (abstaining from cigarettes for a period of six months or longer) after three to four weeks.

In clinical trials, the Niconil patch alone had proven effective in helping smokers to quit. A WLI study showed that 47.5 percent of subjects using the nicotine patch abstained from smoking for a period of three months or longer versus 15 percent for subjects using a placebo patch. Among the remaining 52.5 percent who did not stop completely, there was a marked reduction in the number of cigarettes smoked. A similar study in the United States demonstrated an abstinence rate of 31.5 percent with the Niconil patch versus 14 percent for those with a placebo patch. The single most important success factor in Niconil effectiveness, however, was the smoker's motivation to quit. *Committed quitters* were the most likely to quit smoking successfully using Niconil or any other smoking cessation method.

There were some side effects associated with use of the Niconil patch, including skin irritation, sleep disturbances, and nausea. Skin irritation was by far the most prevalent side effect, affecting 30 percent of patch users in one study. This skin irritation was not seen as a major obstacle to sales as many study participants viewed their irritated skin areas as badges of merit that indicated their commitment to quitting smoking. WLI recommended placement of the patch on alternating skin areas to mitigate the problem. Future reformulations of the nicotine gel in the patch were expected to eliminate the problem entirely.

Niconil had been developed in 1985 by two scientists at Trinity College in Dublin working with Elan Corporation, an Irish pharmaceutical company specializing in transdermal drug delivery systems. Elan had entered into a joint venture with WLI to market other Elan transdermal products: Dilzem, and Theolan, a respiratory medication. In 1987, Elan agreed to add Niconil to the joint venture. Warner-Lambert planned to market the product worldwide through its subsidiaries, with Elan earning a royalty on cost of goods sold.[3]

Ireland was the first country to approve the Niconil patch. In late 1989, the Irish National Drugs Advisory Board authorized national distribution of Niconil, but stipulated that it could be sold by prescription only. This meant that Niconil, as a prescription product, could not be advertised directly to the Irish consumer.

HEALTH CARE IN IRELAND

Ireland's General Medical Service (GMS) provided health care to all Irish citizens. Sixty-four percent of the population received free hospital care through the GMS, but were required to pay for doctor's visits, which averaged £15 each, and for drugs, which were priced lower in Ireland than the average in the European Economic Community. The remaining 36 percent of the population qualified as either low-income or chronic-condition patients and received free health care through the GMS. For these patients, hospital care, doctor's visits, and many drugs were obtained without fee or co-payment. Drugs paid for by the GMS were classified as reimbursable; approximately 70 percent of all drugs were reimbursable in 1989. Niconil had not qualified as a reimbursable drug; though WLI was lobbying to change its status, the immediate outlook was not hopeful.[4]

SUPPORT PROGRAM

While the patch addressed the physical craving for nicotine, Dixon and his team had decided to develop a supplementary support program to address the smoker's psychological addiction. The support program included several components in a neatly packaged box which aimed to ease the smoker's personal and social dependence on cigarettes. A booklet explained how to change behavior and contained tips on quitting. Bound into the booklet was a personal contract on which the smoker could list his or her reasons for quitting and plans for celebrating successful abstinence. There was a diary that enabled the smoker to record patterns of smoking behavior prior to quitting and that offered inspirational suggestions for each day of the program. Finally, an audiotape included instruction in four relaxation methods that the smoker could practice in place of cigarette smoking. The relaxation exercises were narrated by Professor Anthony Clare, a well-known Irish psychiatrist who hosted a regular television program on the BBC. The tape also contained an emergency help section to assist the individual in overcoming sudden episodes of craving. A special toll-free telephone number to WLI served as a hot line to address customer questions and problems. Sample pages from the Niconil support program are presented as Exhibit 2.

While studies had not yet measured the impact of the support program on abstinence rates, it was believed that combined use of the support program and the patch could only

---

[3]A royalty of 3 percent on cost of goods sold was typical for such joint ventures.

[4]None of the products in the smoking cessation aid market was reimbursable through the GMS. Reimbursable items excluded prescriptions for simple drugs, such as mild painkillers and cough and cold remedies.

EXHIBIT 2   Sample Pages from Niconil Support Program

The first step

Fill in the contract in your own words. Write down all the reasons that are most important to you for beating the smoking habit.

Then write down how your life will be better and more enjoyable without the smoking habit.

Finally, write down how you will reward yourself for your courage and hard work. You will deserve something very special.

Choose the day

Decide when to stop and put a ring round that date on your calendar.

Try to find a time when you are not going to be under pressure for a few days. The start of a holiday is good for two reasons. You will not have the stress of work and you will be free to change your routine.

Countdown

1. In the days leading up to your stop date see if you can get your partner or a friend to stop smoking along with you.

2. Ask a local charity to sponsor you or join a non-smoking group. Having other people to talk to who have kicked the habit can be a lifeline when your willpower gets shaky. They will know and understand what you are going through. Your doctor will be able to tell you what groups are running in your area.

3. The evening before your stop date, throw away **all** your cigarettes and get rid of your lighters and ashtrays. You will not need them again.

4. Read over your smoker's diary entries. Know your habit.
   - What are the most dangerous times?
   - Where are the most dangerous places?
   - What are the most dangerous situations?
   - Who do I usually smoke with?

C O N T R A C T

1. I, ...
   **HAVE STOPPED SMOKING BECAUSE
   I WANT:**

2. **MY LIFE WILL BE BETTER WHEN I AM FREE
   OF SMOKING BECAUSE:**

3. **AFTER BEATING SMOKING FOR A MONTH
   I WILL CELEBRATE BY:**

SIGNED:

DATE:

COUNT DOWN TO D-DAY						DAY 1
Cigarette	Time of day?	Where were you?	Who were you with?	What were you doing?	How did you feel?	
1						
2						
3						
4						
5						

WEEK ONE   *THE WINNER'S DIARY*

DAY

1. Today is the greatest challenge. If you succeed today, tomorrow will be easier. You can do it.

2. Well done. The first 24 hours are over. Your lungs have had their first real rest for years.

3. Remember: smoking is for losers. If you find yourself getting tense, use your relaxation tape.

4. Read your contract again. See how much better life is getting now that you are freeing yourself from this unpleasant addiction.

5. Your body says "thank you". It's feeling fitter already.

6. Don't forget to distract yourself at key cigarette times.

7. Well done. You're through your first week. Give yourself a treat. Go out for a meal or buy yourself something you've always wanted.

increase Niconil's success. It had proven necessary to package the Niconil support program separately from the patch to speed approval of the patch by the Irish National Drug Board. A combined package would have required approval of the complete program, including the audiotape, which would have prolonged the process significantly. If separate, the support program could be sold without a prescription and advertised directly to the consumer. Development of the support program had cost £3,000. WLI planned an initial production run of 10,000 units at a variable cost of £3.50 per unit.

The support program could serve a variety of purposes. Several WLI executives felt that the support program should be sold separately from the nicotine patches. They considered the support program a stand-alone product that could realize substantial revenues on its own, as well as generating sales of the Niconil patches. Supporting this position, a pricing study completed in 1989 found that the highest mean price volunteered for a 14-day supply of the patches and the support program combined was £27.50, and for the patches alone, £22.00. The highest mean price for the support program alone was £8.50, suggesting a relatively high perceived utility of this component among potential consumers. There was a risk, however, that consumers might purchase the Niconil support program either instead of the patches, or as an accompaniment to other smoking cessation products, thus limiting sales of the Niconil patches.

Another group of executives saw the support program as a value-added point of difference that could stimulate Niconil patch sales. This group favored wide distribution of the support programs, free of charge, to potential Niconil customers. A third group of WLI executives argued that the support program was an integral component of the Niconil product which would enhance the total package by addressing the psychological aspects of nicotine addiction and improve the product's success rate, thereby increasing its sales potential. As such, these executives believed that the support program should be passed on only to those purchasing Niconil patches, at no additional cost.

Two options, not necessarily mutually exclusive, were under consideration for the distribution of the support programs. One option was to distribute them through doctors prescribing Niconil. A doctor could present the program to the patient during the office visit as he or she issued the Niconil prescription, reinforcing the counseling role of the doctor in the Niconil treatment. Supplying the doctors with support programs could also serve to promote Niconil in the medical community. A second option was to distribute the support programs through the pharmacies, where customers could receive the support programs when they purchased the Niconil patches. A disadvantage of this option was that a customer might receive additional support programs each time he or she purchased another package of Niconil. However, these duplicates might be passed on to other potential consumers and thus become an informal advertising vehicle for Niconil.

PRICING

Because all potential Niconil customers would pay for the product personally, pricing was a critical component of the Niconil marketing strategy. Management debated how many patches to include in a single package and at what price to sell each package. In test trials, the average smoker succeeded in quitting with Niconil in three to four weeks (i.e., 21 to 28 patches); others needed as long as six weeks.[5]

As Niconil was essentially a tobacco substitute, cigarettes provided a logical model for considering various packaging and pricing options. The average Irish smoker purchased a pack of cigarettes daily, often when buying the morning newspaper. Fewer than 5 percent of all cigarettes were sold in cartons.[6] Because the Irish smoker rarely purchased a multi-week cigarette supply at once, he or she was thought likely to compare the cost of cigarette purchases with the cost of a multi-week supply of Niconil. WLI thus favored packaging just a 7-day supply of patches in each unit. However, Warner-Lambert subsidiaries in continental Europe, where carton purchases were more popular, wanted to include a six-week supply of patches in each package if and when they launched Niconil. Managers at Warner-Lambert's international division wanted to standardize packaging as much as possible across its subsidiaries and suggested, as a compromise, a 14-day supply per package.

Following the cigarette model, two pricing schemes had been proposed. The first proposal was to price Niconil on a par with cigarettes. The average Irish smoker smoked 16.5 cigarettes per day and the expected retail price in 1990 for a pack of cigarettes was £2.25. WLI's variable cost of goods for a 14-day supply of Niconil was £12.00.[7] Pharmacies generally added a 50 percent retail markup to the price at which they purchased the product from WLI. A value-added tax of 25 percent of the retail price was included in the proposed price to the consumer of £32.00 for a 14-day supply. In addition, the consumer paid a £1.00 dispensing fee per prescription.

Under the second pricing proposal, Niconil would be priced at a premium to cigarettes. Proponents argued that if the Niconil program were successful, it would be a permanent replacement for cigarettes and its cost would be far outweighed by the money saved on cigarettes. The proposed price to the consumer under this option was £60.00 for a 14-day supply.

COMPETITION

Few products would compete directly with Niconil in the smoking cessation market in Ireland. Two small-niche products were Accudrop and Nicobrevin, both available without a prescription. Accudrop was a nasal spray that smokers applied to the cigarette filter to trap tar and nicotine, resulting in cleaner smoke. Anticipated 1990 manufacturer sales for Accudrop were £5,000. Nicobrevin, a product from the U.K., was a time-release capsule that eased smoking withdrawal symptoms. Anticipated 1990 manufacturer's sales for Nicobrevin were £75,000.

---

[5]Smokers were advised not to use the patch on a regular basis beyond three months. If still unsuccessful in quitting, they could resume use of the patch after stopping for at least a month.

[6]A carton of cigarettes contained 10 individual packs of cigarettes; each pack contained 20 cigarettes.

[7]This cost of goods included Elan's royalty.

The most significant competitive product was Nicorette, the only nicotine-replacement product currently available. Marketed in Ireland by Lundbeck, Nicorette was a chewing gum that released nicotine into the body as the smoker chewed the gum. Because chewing gum in public was not socially acceptable among Irish adults, the product had never achieved strong sales, especially given that its efficacy relied on steady, intensive chewing. A second sales deterrent had been the association of Nicorette with side effects such as mouth cancer and irritation of the linings of the mouth and stomach.

Nicorette was sold in 10-day supplies, available in two dosages: 2 mg and 4 mg. Smokers would chew the 2 mg Nicorette initially, and switch to the 4 mg gum after two weeks if needed. In a 1982 study, 47 percent of Nicorette users quit smoking versus 21 percent for placebo users. A long-term follow-up study in 1989, however, indicated that only 10 percent more Nicorette patients had ceased smoking compared to placebo users. The average daily treatment cost to Nicorette customers was £0.65 per day for the 2 mg gum and £1.00 per day for the 4 mg gum. Nicorette, like Niconil, was available at pharmacies by prescription only, so advertising had been limited to medical journals. Anticipated 1990 manufacturer sales of Nicorette were £170,000; however, the brand had not been advertised in three years.

FORECASTING

Although Nicorette was not considered a successful product, WLI was confident that Niconil, with its less-intrusive nicotine delivery system and fewer side effects, would capture a dominant position in the smoking cessation market and ultimately increase the demand for smoking cessation products. Precise sales expectations for Niconil were difficult to formulate, however, and two different methods had been suggested.

The first method assumed that the percentage of smokers in the adult population (30 percent in 1990) would drop by one percentage point per year through 1994. An estimated 10 percent of smokers attempted to quit smoking each year, and 10 percent of that number purchased some type of smoking cessation product. WLI believed that Niconil could capture half of these committed quitters in the first year, selling therefore to 5 percent of those who tried to give up smoking in 1990. Further, they hoped to increase this share by 1 percent per year, up to 9 percent in 1994. Having estimated the number of customers who would purchase an initial two-week supply of Niconil, WLI managers then had to calculate the total number of units purchased. Based on experience in test trials, WLI anticipated that 60 percent of first-time Niconil customers would purchase a second two-week supply. Of that number, 20 percent would purchase a third two-week supply. About 75 percent of smokers completed the program within six weeks.

A more aggressive forecast could be based on WLI's 1989 survey of the 30 percent of respondents who were smokers; 54 percent indicated that they would like to give up smoking, and 30 percent expressed interest in the nicotine patch. More relevant, 17 percent of smokers indicated that they were likely to go to the doctor and pay for such a patch, though a specific purchase price was not included in the question. A rule of thumb in interpreting likelihood-of-purchase data was to divide this percentage by three to achieve a more likely estimate of actual purchasers. Once the number of Niconil customers was calculated, the 100/60/20 percent model used above could then be applied to compute the total expected unit sales.

PRODUCTION

Under the terms of the joint venture with Elan and using current manufacturing technology, production capacity would be 1,000 units (of 14-day-supply packages) per month in the first quarter of 1990, ramping up to 2,000 units per month by year end. WLI had the option to purchase a new, more efficient machine that could produce 14,000 units per month and reduce WLI's variable cost on each unit by 10 percent. In addition, if WLI purchased the new machine and Niconil was launched in continental Europe, WLI could export some of its production to the European subsidiaries, further expanding its role as a supplier to Warner-Lambert Europe. WLI would earn a margin of £2.00 per unit on Niconil that it sold through this channel.[8] Estimated annual unit sales, assuming a launch of Niconil throughout Western Europe, are listed in Table C. Warner-Lambert management aimed to recoup any capital investments within five years; the Niconil machine would cost £1.2 million and could be on-line within nine months.

MARKETING PRESCRIPTION PRODUCTS

Prescription products included all pharmaceutical items deemed by the Irish government to require the professional expertise of the medical community to guide consumer usage.[9] Before a customer could purchase a prescription product, he or she first had to visit a doctor and obtain a written prescription which specified that product. The customer could then take the written prescription to one of Ireland's 1,132 pharmacies and purchase the product.

The prescription nature of Niconil thus created marketing challenges. A potential Niconil customer first had to make an appointment with a doctor for an office visit to

TABLE C	Estimated Unit Sales of Niconil in Western Europe
Year 1	100,000 units
Year 2	125,000 units
Year 3	150,000 units
Year 4	175,000 units
Year 5	200,000 units

---

[8]Warner-Lambert's European subsidiaries were likely to consider purchasing this new machine themselves as well.

[9]Drugs and other pharmaceutical products that did not require a written prescription from a doctor were called *over-the-counter* or OTC drugs.

obtain the necessary prescription. Next, the doctor had to agree to prescribe Niconil to help the patient quit smoking. Only then could the customer go to the pharmacy and purchase Niconil. This two-step purchase process required WLI to address two separate audiences in marketing Niconil: the Irish smokers who would eventually use Niconil, and the Irish doctors who first had to prescribe it to patients.

Niconil's potential customers were the 10 percent of Irish smokers who attempted to give up smoking each year (2 percent of the total Irish population). Market research had shown that those most likely to purchase Niconil were aged 35–44 and in either white-collar or skilled occupations (18 percent of Irish smokers). Smokers under the age of 35 tended to see themselves a "bullet proof"; because most were not yet experiencing the negative health effects of smoking, it was difficult to persuade them to quit. Upper-income, better-educated smokers found less tolerance for smoking among their peers and thus felt greater pressure to quit. Research had also indicated that women were 25 percent more likely to try Niconil as they tended to be more concerned with their health and thus more often visited the doctors from whom they could learn about Niconil and obtain the necessary prescription.

The most likely prescribers of Niconil would be the 2,000 General Practitioners (GPs) in Ireland. The average GP saw 15 patients per day, and eight out of ten general office visits resulted in the GPs writing prescriptions for patients. Although 10 percent of Irish doctors smoked, virtually all recognized the dangers of smoking and rarely smoked in front of patients. A *Modern Medicine* survey of 780 Irish GPs indicated that 63 percent formally gathered smoking data from their patients. GPs acknowledged the health risk that smoking posed to patient health, but they were usually reluctant to pressure a patient to quit unless the smoker was highly motivated. Unsolicited pressure to quit could meet with patient resistance and result, in some cases, in a doctor losing a patient and the associated revenues from patient visits. Smoking cessation was not currently a lucrative treatment area for GPs. Most would spend no longer than 15 minutes discussing smoking with their patients. To the few patients who asked for advice on how to quit smoking, 92 percent of GPs would offer "firm, clear-cut advice." Fewer than 15 percent would recommend formal counseling, drug therapy, or other assistance. GPs were not enthusiastic about Nicorette due to poor results and the incidence of side effects.

WLI was confident that Niconil would find an enthusiastic audience among Irish GPs. As a complete program with both physical and psychological components, Niconil offered a unique solution. In addition, the doctor would assume a significant counseling role in the Niconil treatment. It was anticipated that the GP would initially prescribe a 14-day supply of Niconil to the patient. At the end of the two-week period, the patient would hopefully return to the doctor for counseling and an additional prescription, if needed.

MARKETING COMMUNICATIONS

WLI intended to position Niconil as *a complete system that was a more acceptable alternative to existing nicotine replacement therapy for the purpose of smoking cessation.* Niconil would be the only smoking cessation product to address both the physical dimension of nicotine addiction through the patch, and the psychological dimension through

EXHIBIT 3	Niconil First Year Marketing Budget (£000)	
Advertising		
Ad creation	£	4
Media advertising		28
Total advertising		32
Promotion		
Development of support programs		3
Production of support programs		35
Training/promotional materials		44
Direct mailing to GPs		2
Total promotion		84
Public Relations		
Launch symposium		5
Roundtable meeting		2
Press release/materials		1
Total public relations		8
Market research		3
Sales force allocation		23
Product management allocation		50
Total budget		£200

the support program. Compared to Nicorette gum, Niconil offered a more acceptable delivery system (Niconil's transdermal system vs. Nicorette's oral system) and fewer, less severe side effects. WLI planned to promote these aspects of the product through a comprehensive marketing program. The Niconil launch marketing budget, detailed in Exhibit 3, followed the Warner-Lambert standard for new drug launches. Several WLI executives felt that this standard was inadequate for the more consumer-oriented Niconil, and pressed for increased communications spending.

ADVERTISING

Because Irish regulations prohibited the advertising of prescription products directly to the consumer, Niconil advertising was limited to media targeting the professional medical community. Three major publications targeted this audience: *Irish Medical Times, Irish Medical News,* and *Modern Medicine.* WLI planned to advertise moderately in the first year to raise awareness of Niconil in the medical community. After that it was hoped that the initial momentum could be maintained through strong public relations efforts and personal testimony to the product's efficacy. Exhibit 4 summarizes the proposed 1990 media advertising schedule for Niconil.

WLI's advertising agency had designed a distinctive logo for Niconil that would be used on all packaging, and on collateral materials such as "No Smoking" placards. These would feature the Niconil logo and be distributed to doctors' offices, hospitals, and pharmacies to promote the product. Ideally, the logo would become sufficiently well-

EXHIBIT 4 1990 Niconil Media Advertising Schedule

Publication	Frequency	Circulation	Cost/1,000	Placements
Irish Medical Times	Weekly	5,200	£154	13
Irish Medical News	Weekly	5,100	137	11
Modern Medicine	Monthly	3,700	176	5

organized that it could be used eventually on a stand-alone basis to represent Niconil to the end consumer without the brand name. This would allow some flexibility in circumventing Irish advertising restrictions to reach the end consumer. Sample logos and packaging are illustrated in Exhibit 5. The agency had also developed four concepts for a Niconil advertisement, which are summarized in Exhibit 6A-D.

DIRECT MAIL

A direct mail campaign to Ireland's 2,000 GPs was planned in conjunction with the Niconil product announcement. Two weeks prior to launch, an introductory letter would be mailed with a color photo of the product, a reply card offering a support program, and additional product information. The support programs would be mailed in response to the reply cards, arriving just prior to the launch. A response rate of at least 50 percent was anticipated based on past direct mail campaigns.

PUBLIC RELATIONS

The formal Niconil product announcement was scheduled to occur in Dublin at a professional event that WLI had dubbed the "Smoking Cessation Institute Symposium." The symposium would be chaired by Professor Anthony Clare, the narrator of the Niconil audio-tape; Professor Hickey, an expert in preventive cardiology; and Professors Masterson and J. Kelly from Elan Corporation. Open to members of the medical profession and media, the event was intended to focus attention on the dangers of smoking and to highlight Niconil as a ground-breaking product designed to address this health hazard.

WLI had sought endorsements from both the Irish Cancer Society and the Irish Heart Foundation, two national health organizations that actively advocated smoking cessation. Because both non-profit institutions relied on donations for financing and were concerned that a specific product endorsement would jeopardize their tax-exempt status, they refused to endorse Niconil directly. Representatives from each institution had, however, stated their intention to attend the launch symposium.

In advance of the symposium, a press release and supporting materials would be distributed to the media. Emphasis would be placed on the role that Niconil would play in disease prevention. It would also be noted that Niconil had been developed and manufactured locally and had the potential for worldwide sales. Other planned public relations activities included a round-table dinner for prominent opinion leaders in the

EXHIBIT 5   Sample Niconil Logo and Packaging

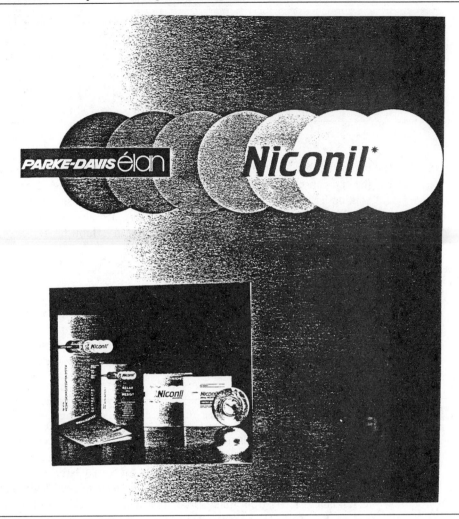

EXHIBIT 6A Niconil Advertising Concept

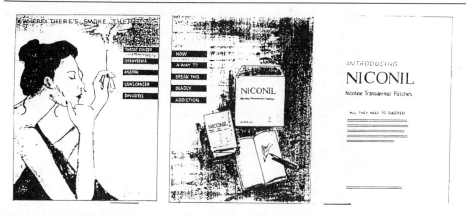

medical community. Publicity in the media was planned to coincide with key times for commitment to change such as New Year's and Lent.[10]

SALES STRATEGY

WLI Ireland had a sales force of 16 representatives, whose average annual salary, bonus, and benefits amounted to £25,000 in 1988. They focused their selling efforts on 1,600 Irish GPs who were most accessible geographically and most amenable to pharmaceutical

[10]Lent was an annual penitential period during spring of the Roman Catholic religious calendar that was still observed by many of the 95 percent of the Irish who were Roman Catholic.

EXHIBIT 6B   Niconil Advertising Concept

sales visits. The sales staff was divided into three selling teams of four to six representatives. Each team sold separate product lines to the same 1,600 GPs. The team that would
represent Niconil was already selling three other drugs from Elan Corporation that were
marketed by WLI as part of their joint venture. These four salespeople would add Niconil
to their existing product lines. Sales training on Niconil would take place one month prior
to the product launch.

EXHIBIT 6C   Niconil Advertising Concept

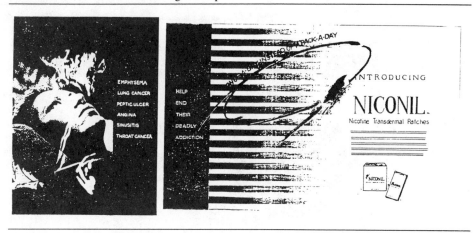

The pharmaceutical salesperson's challenge was to maintain the attention of each GP long enough to discuss each item in his or her product line. Because Niconil was expected to be of great interest to GPs, the salespeople were keen to present Niconil first during the sales visit, followed by the less exciting products. Normally, a new product would receive this up-front positioning. However, Dixon argued that Niconil should be presented last during the sales call to maximize the time that a salesperson spent with each GP and

EXHIBIT 6D   Niconil Advertising Concept

to prevent the sales time devoted to the other three Elan products from being cannibalized by Niconil. Based on revenue projections for all four products, salespeople would be instructed to spend no more than 15 percent of their sales call time on Niconil. On average, each WLI salesperson called on six to seven doctors per day. The goal was for each sales team to call on the 1,600 targeted GPs once every three months. In the case of Niconil, all sixteen sales people would present the new brand during their calls for six weeks after launch.

CRITICAL DECISIONS

With just three months to go before the launch of Niconil, Dixon felt he had to comply with the international division's suggestion to include a 14-day supply of patches in each Niconil package, but he debated whether to price the product on a par with or at a premium to cigarettes. Equally important, he had to decide which sales forecast was more accurate so that he could plan production capacity. And finally, he needed to make decisions on the communications program: which advertising concept would be the most effective, what other efforts could be made to enhance product acceptance, and whether the current budget was adequate to support Warner-Lambert's first national launch of such an innovative product.

Case 1–2

Stainmaster*

After a house and a car, carpeting is among the most expensive purchases people will ever make. Yet it is surely one of the most undermarketed products in America. While consumers spend $15 billion a year to carpet their homes, textile fiber companies normally invest only about $5 million for consumer advertising, and the ads tend to be, well, run of the mill . . .

But this year in a major turnabout, the fiber industry believes it has something worth crowing about and is putting far more money and creative effort into peddling carpet than ever before.

The Wall Street Journal, July 9, 1987

By mid-1988, Stainmaster[1] carpeting certified by Du Pont had indeed effected "a major turnabout" in the industry and in Du Pont's carpet-fiber business. The company next had to consider how best to secure this marketing-advantage foothold. Three questions were paramount: (1) what would be the best way to use the three different brands—Du Pont, Antron[2], and Stainmaster; (2) how would the increasing focus of competitors on their own stain-resistant products affect Du Pont's advertising, promotion, and distribution strategies; and (3) could a premium price and quality position be defended or should the Stainmaster name be used for lower-price/quality carpet?

DU PONT

E. I. du Pont de Nemours and Company, founded in 1802, and headquartered in Wilmington, Delaware, was, in the mid-1980s, a $30+ billion world chemical giant—the largest fiber producer in the world and a major nylon producer. The company was organized into product-line segments: Agricultural and Industrial Chemicals, Biomedical Products, Coal, Fibers, Industrial and Consumer Products, Petroleum Exploration and Production, Petroleum Refining, Marketing and Transportation, and Polymer Products. Du Pont spent $966 million on R&D in 1983.

Du Pont's fiber segment consisted of high-volume (commodity-type) fibers sold to the textile and other industries for processing into consumer and industrial goods—apparel and home fabrics, industrial applications, and carpets—and a broadly diversified mix of

---

This case was written by Bette Collins with the assistance of James D. Culley, Marketing Research Associate, External Affairs Department of E. I. du Pont de Nemours, and Professor Paul W. Farris. Copyright © 1989 by the Darden Graduate Business School Foundation, Charlottesville, Virginia.

[1]Stainmaster is a registered certification mark of the Du Pont Company.

[2]Antron is a registered trademark of the Du Pont Company.

specialty fibers used in high strength composite materials, protective apparel, packaging, and active sportswear. The Fiber Department's 1984 sales of $4.1 billion provided after-tax operating income of $319 million (total company, $1.7 billion). The nylon carpet-fiber portion of this business was an important one for Du Pont.

INDUSTRY STRUCTURE AND BACKGROUND ON CARPET FIBER

The U.S. carpet industry consisted of fiber producers (large chemical companies) who supplied nylon, polyester, and olefin; carpet mills, who provided the carpets; and retailers. In the United States, there were 10–12 major fiber producers. Major competitors of Du Pont's in this industry were Monsanto, BASF, Amoco, and Allied-Signal.

Among the 200–300 carpet mills in the U.S. industry, consolidation had been the trend during the 1980s as the mills attempted to achieve the benefits of integrated production using high-priced advances in technology. Some mills extruded their own fibers (primarily olefin). In 1987, the top 20 mills controlled 77 percent of the market. The largest—Shaw, Burlington, and Fieldcrest—had shares of 14.3, 7.5, and 5.1 percent, respectively.

About half of residential carpeting was sold in roll form to retailers, and about half in cut form (cut goods) when requested by retailers, usually within a few days. Retailers sometimes asked consumers to pay 50 percent of the price with the order, but usually paid the mill within 30–60 days after delivery.

The market consisted of Residential (60 percent), Commercial (25 percent), Auto and Aircraft (10 percent), and other (5 percent). Some 63 percent of residential floor-covering sales were made through retail outlets. About 12 percent was sold to apartment owners, and 25 percent to builders. Of the 20,000–30,000 retailers in the United States in the mid-1980s, the great majority were single-outlet operations: approximately 44 percent of retail carpet sales were through retailers with under $1 million in annual sales, another 32 percent had sales of $1–$5 million, and only 24 percent (about 150 retailers) were larger.

By far the manmade material most used in carpets was nylon, discovered by Du Pont in 1938 and introduced to the public at the 1939 World's Fair. Du Pont's nylon fiber constituted one-third of the U.S. carpet market, led by the Antron brand. Du Pont also made polyester and introduced olefin fibers to the carpet market in 1988.

The first nylon carpet fibers were round and bright in lustre. They wore well but showed the effects of soiling quickly. Carpets with second-generation nylon fibers were the first to use soil-hiding fibers using a trilobal cross-section shape to scatter or disperse light. The new shape also added bulk and resiliency to fibers. Carpets of third-generation nylon helped eliminate static problems in carpets by incorporating conductive filaments into the yarn bundles. Carpets made of fourth-generation nylon fibers were chemically modified with fluorocarbons to reduce surface energy and give the fiber anti-stick properties to resist dry soils and, if they were not given time to soak in, some resistance to certain liquid stains.

Since the late 1950s, as the improved fibers were introduced and carpet mills upgraded their products for construction and fashion, carpeting had been increasing its share of the U.S. domestic floor covering market. By 1983, carpeting represented about 70 percent of floor coverings; 80 percent of carpets were nylon, with polyester, olefin, and other fibers comprising the remaining 20 percent. Nylon for carpets came in two forms: nylon staple which was chopped up into short segments like cotton, and bulked continuous filament yarn (BCF). Nylon staple was 25–40 cents per pound less expensive than BCF nylon, but the latter gave a bulkier appearance than the staple and involved fewer steps in manufacturing. Thus, the choice of the best nylon depended on the style involved among other things. Compared to polyester and olefin, nylon had better wear characteristics and could be tufted and left undyed, allowing the mill to keep inventory in the undyed form and dye it as needed. Polyester and olefin were more difficult to dye and therefore inherently more stain resistant.

The U.S. carpet market grew at a 12 percent compound annual growth rate (CAGR) during the 1960s and a 7 percent CAGR in the 1970s. From 1979 until the launch of Stainmaster in 1986, growth had slowed dramatically, and was forecast to average only 1 percent per year throughout the 1980s and 1990s.

Jolted by the 1979 oil crisis, the world economy and the carpet industry hit bottom in 1981–1982 and began only a slow recovery. The industry's problems were compounded by overcapacity created during 1974–83 because plants were brought on stream despite the 1973–74 recession. Industry volume declined 30 percent in the 1980–81 recession. By 1983, it still had not reached the 1979 peak.

Carpet for the home had become a replacement product. Dupont's Flooring Systems Division conducted marketing research that indicated carpeting was failing to compete successfully for discretionary consumer expenditures against products such as consumer electronics, primarily because of less effective marketing.

A continuing problem in the industry was the lack of appeal of retail outlets:

> Most American carpet manufacturers are beginning to produce more stylish carpets, but more retailers are still selling carpets the way they did 25 years ago. If some substantive changes aren't made at that level, all the efforts of both the fiber producers and the carpet manufacturers won't last beyond the final advertising expenditure. What consumer's going to buy the talk about fashion and quality if she has to go into a place that looks like a warehouse to make her purchase?[3]

Declining retail margins were part of the cause. Average retail carpet prices per square yard were $12.50 in 1950, $7.75 in 1977, and $13.21 in 1982.

CONSUMER RESEARCH

Studies indicated that, in 1984, consumers visited an average of 3.6 stores before making a purchase (in 1985, 2.9), although some stores were visited five and six times before a consumer bought carpet. Only 16 percent of consumers took a month or less to decide which carpet to buy, and 27 percent needed a year or more to make up their minds. The size of order at one time varied from under 15 square yards (12 percent) to over 100 (14 percent), with an average of 50 square yards. Factors that attracted a buyer to a particular store were dominated by "bought there before" (36 percent), "store reputation" (36 percent), "recommendation" (35 percent), and "generally low prices" (32 percent), followed by "sales price" (28 percent) and store location (28 percent). The large majority

---

[3]Frank O'Neill, "The Fifth Generation," *Carpet & Rug*, October 1986, p.16.

of consumers concentrated their store visits and buying in carpet specialty stores and discount outlets (see Exhibit 1), and 60–64 percent bought carpet "on sale." The reasons for carpet purchases were: to redecorate/change, 45 percent; replace worn carpet, 26 percent; overall soiling, 16 percent; and localized stains, 13 percent.

In 1985–86, most buyers of residential carpet bought for more than one room or area at a time. Women made or influenced 85 percent of all carpet purchases. A breakdown of carpet purchases by family stages is given in Exhibit 2.

One market research report cited the following qualities, in order, as important to customers in choosing a carpet: (1) retains good looks, (2) is properly installed, (3) resists stains, (4) comes in the right color, and (5) "inexpensive." A second report indicated factors of importance in selecting wall-to-wall carpets as: color, 25 percent; surface appearance, 21 percent; durability, 14 percent; texture/style, 9 percent; soil resistance/durability, 9 percent; reputation of manufacturer, 7 percent; and fiber type, 5 percent. Length of delivery time, salesperson's recommendation, warranty, and type of backing were each important to 2–4 percent.

EXHIBIT 1 Outlet Shopped/Outlet Where Purchased: Residential, Wall-to-Wall Carpet

	Outlet Visited in Looking for Carpet*	Outlet Where Carpet was Purchased
Carpet specialty store	76%	53%
Discount carpet store	35	12
Chain store	37	5
Department store	18	4
Furniture store	15	6
Other	45	20

*Figures add to more than 100 percent because multiple outlets were visited.

Source: Du Pont Flooring Systems.

EXHIBIT 2 Wall-to-Wall Carpet Purchases by Family Life-Cycle Stage (based on square yards purchased)

Young single; one member under age 35	3.9%
Middle single; one member age 35–65	8.0
Older single; one member over 65	2.1
Young couple; age of head under 45; no children present	6.5
Working older couple; age of head 45 or older; no children present	15.3
Retired older couple; age of head 45 or older; no children present	9.5
Young parent; age of head under 45; youngest child under age 6	19.0
Middle parent; age of head under 45; youngest child over age 6	14.1
Older parent; age of head 45 or older; child present	19.3
Roommates; unmarried	2.4

Source: Du Pont Flooring Systems.

A CHANGE IN STRATEGY

In 1985, Tom McAndrews, Division director, named Bruce Koepcke to chair a long-range strategic planning committee to determine a new direction for the business. Committee members came from marketing, sales, R&D, marketing research, and manufacturing, and were joined by a financial analyst and outside marketing consultants. Basic options they evaluated against the current program were (1) move the lower-cost carpeting, (2) develop new products, (3) establish a retail-driven marketing approach, and (4) develop a stronger consumer franchise.

The committee recommended an integrated program with a low- to medium-cost position, a strong consumer advertising program, and extensive retail merchandising and cooperative advertising. The idea was to Market Du Pont products at every level in the distribution chain.

Prior to the development of Stainmaster, Du Pont carried out a test of the benefits to be obtained from additional expenditures on the sales force and advertising. The task force tested the effects of consumer advertising, a doubled sales force, and the power of both of these together, against a control market. The advertising copy used for the test emphasized the long history and quality of Du Pont carpet fibers. The advertising level tested was the equivalent of a national expenditure of $30 million. The four cells of the test each comprised three "areas of dominant influence" (media markets).

Each cell was evaluated on the basis of retail sales by store, consumer awareness, and retail attitudes. The results indicated that each major variable—consumer advertising and sales-force size—added 2 percent to Du Pont's market share. For the "both" cell, the increase was over 4 percent.

THE STAINMASTER CARPET PROCESS

A key discovery during the 1983 marketing tests was the identification of soil and stain resistance as one of the most important benefits that consumers sought in carpeting. For several years, Du Pont and the rest of the industry had been using fluorocarbon finishes and soil-hiding fiber cross-section (hollow filaments, fibers with low surface areas) in nylon carpets to provide this benefit in part. Most of the solutions, however, dealt only with soiling. Although trade and consumer advertising sometimes claimed that carpets were soil and stain resistant, true stain resistance had not yet been achieved. Food, wine, and other water-based staining materials would be repelled for a few seconds or minutes by the fluorocarbon coating but, with time, would break through and permanently stain the nylon fibers. Numerous attempts had failed to solve this basic problem with nylon. (Polyester and olefin, the other two synthetic fibers used in carpets, did not have a water-based staining problem, but they had other major deficiencies. For example, olefin was susceptible to oil-based stains, and neither polyester nor olefin held up well in high-traffic areas such as on stairs, in hallways, or by doorways.)[4]

---

[4]Hot liquids, such as coffee, would eventually reduce the effectiveness of the stain-resistant chemicals, but further research improved the stain resistance to the point that hot coffee could be included in the warranty.

The Technology. In the early 1980s, Armand Zinnato, a research chemist at Du Pont, had been working on the development of a nylon fiber dyeable at room temperature. Concerned that carpets made from such fibers would be prone to staining, Zinnato hypothesized that once the fiber was dyed, there had to be a way either to tie up the remaining dye sites or at least retard dye uptake to improve stain resistance. On a "bootleg" basis, he started exploring the application of various known, dye-resist materials to nylon carpets.

By January 1985, Zinnato had confirmed that certain dye-resist agents previously used to improve wash-fastness would also impart stain-resistance to the extent that in some samples it was nearly impossible to stain the resulting product. In March 1985, he reviewed his work with his management, who immediately recognized its potential value and asked him to pursue it on an assigned basis.

Since these dye-resist agents had previously been applied to nylon carpets under essentially the same conditions, Du Pont did not believe it was possible to obtain broad patent protection for stain-resistant carpets.

ORGANIZING TO LAUNCH THE PRODUCT

In June 1985, Chris Riley, a Flooring Systems Division strategist, became aware of Zinnato's technology. He became very excited about its stain-resistance potential and brought the product concept to his marketing peers and management. Divisional management recognized that this discovery would provide a timely opportunity to tie into the consumer marketing program that was then entering its final stages of development.

By late summer 1985, division management had established an ad hoc steering committee chaired by Bill Spencer, marketing director, with membership that included Bob Axtell, product manager, and J. F. Hesselberth, technical director. They decided to take this technology from the Fibers Department to the Du Pont Chemicals and Pigments Department to mask the purchase of the stain-resistant chemicals and keep the knowledge about Du Pont's activities from competitors. Another advantage in using the C&P Department was its experience with stain- and soil-resistant chemicals. The chemicals used were available from several sources.

Bruce Koepcke, the long-range strategist for the Flooring Systems Division, was picked to manage a team of marketing representatives from Fibers and the External Affairs Department (the corporate staff department that managed all Du Pont advertising) and formulate an aggressive consumer-marketing program. Koepcke's proposal was presented to departmental management in late 1985. His proposal contended that a strong consumer marketing approach had the potential to overcome the lack of a strong patent position. Shortly thereafter, Koepcke was appointed the end-use manager responsible for introducing and implementing Stainmaster in the retail and consumer marketplace. The new business manager for Residential Carpet, Bob Axtell, assumed responsibility for selecting, selling, and managing the mill licensees who would be the producers of the ultimate product. He obtained strict promises of secrecy from cooperating mills, and mill trials for implementing the Stainmaster process began in January 1986.

In early spring of 1986, the industry trade press noted that Monsanto was working on a carpet with improved stain resistance. Tom McAndrews asked Bruce Koepcke to launch the Stainmaster program by early September--four months before the winter carpet markets (trade show).

The launch team for Stainmaster set a series of dates for key events necessary for the product's smooth introduction:

Mill management presentations	May/June 1986
Product development	July–September 1986
Mill sales meetings	August 1986
Trade press conference	September 1, 1986
Consumer press conference	September 25, 1986
Consumer-advertising beginning	October 23, 1986

The first carpets were certified just before the introduction of Stainmaster in September 1986. In addition to the chemical, Stainmaster certification also required that certain twist levels be met, as well as minimum weights, densities, and pile heights. Thus durability and performance were added to stain resistance. The higher (tighter) the twist in carpet tufts, the longer the carpet would maintain its "like-new" appearance; the twists in Stainmaster certified carpets were heat-set (much like in hair curling). Weight and density were important to reduce crushing even further. Fibers in Stainmaster certified carpet were also treated to resist dry soil and static. The intent was to provide a comfortable feel, durability, and a longer "new look."

Pricing of Stainmaster recognized that mills would eventually be able to obtain similar chemicals from other suppliers. To reduce any tendency for mills to apply less than recommended amounts, the stain-resistant chemicals were automatically (and at no extra charge) shipped with the premium fibers. The chemicals cost Du Pont only a few cents per pound of treated fiber. Mills that signed license agreements with DuPont to manufacture Stainmaster carpets were periodically required to submit samples in different shades and styles for certification checks to Du Pont's lab in Dalton, Georgia. Du Pont contracts also specified that the lab could go directly to the mills and retail stores to obtain samples for spot checking to assure compliance with Du Pont's quality standards for Stainmaster carpet.

Trade Program.   At the launch, Du Pont limited Stainmaster to two major distributors and 1,500 retailers. A training program for the sales forces included audiovisual presentations and personal presentations by Du Pont people. Fifty field representatives were sent out to cover major markets.

Support at the retail level was intensive, with Du Pont supplying posters, banners, labels, and tags. "We had more merchandising tools than dealers dreamed possible," said Gary Johnston, marketing communications supervisor in the Flooring Systems Division. A key feature was the demonstration unit that allowed customers to dip a toothbrush-like "swizzlestick," with one treated and one untreated group of tufts, into various stains and go through the simple stain-removal process to see for themselves how Stainmaster worked (see Exhibit 3). As the campaign moved into 1987, other promotional material was added.

EXHIBIT 3 Store Demonstration Unit and Swizzlesticks

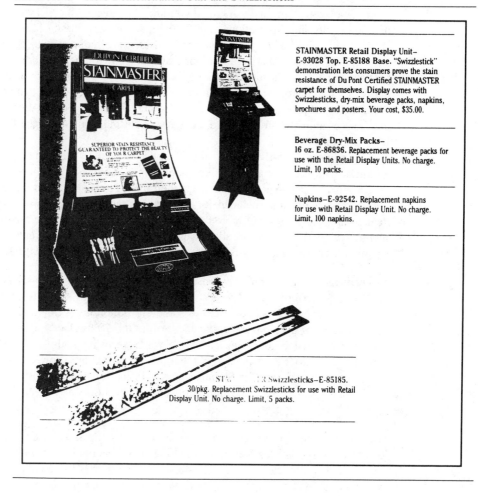

STAINMASTER Retail Display Unit–
E-93028 Top. E-85188 Base. "Swizzlestick" demonstration lets consumers prove the stain resistance of Du Pont Certified STAINMASTER carpet for themselves. Display comes with Swizzlesticks, dry-mix beverage packs, napkins, brochures and posters. Your cost, $35.00.

Beverage Dry-Mix Packs–
16 oz. E-86836. Replacement beverage packs for use with the Retail Display Units. No charge. Limit, 10 packs.

Napkins–E-92542. Replacement napkins for use with Retail Display Unit. No charge. Limit, 100 napkins.

STAINMASTER Swizzlesticks–E-85185. 30/pkg. Replacement Swizzlesticks for use with Retail Display Unit. No charge. Limit, 5 packs.

Dealers received a 12-page catalog describing what Du Pont had to offer in merchandising Du Pont Certified Stainmaster carpet, as well as the company's Antron nylon and Dacron polyester[5] products. Other literature available to the dealers included cards, brochures, cleaning instructions, and Du Pont's *Complete Book of Carpeting*. Store and product identification for dealers comprised hanging mobiles with Stainmaster logos, large canvas banners that could be hung outside showrooms, in-store wall and window posters, carpet-identification medallions, sales tags, and photo boards depicting the Stainmaster TV commercials. Promotional activities to encourage dealers to hold special events or sales to promote Stainmaster included a "Pet Parade" in Los Angeles that featured hundreds of animals—from cats to monkeys—strutting along a length of red carpet made with Stainmaster.

Among the cooperative advertising available to retailers were Stainmaster newspaper ad slicks with room to add the showroom name; Stainmaster TV tapes, which became 30-second TV spots when dealers added their names to the 8-second tag; 30-second radio commercials with time included for the dealer's tag (see Exhibit 4). Any retail carpet dealer purchasing a total of more than 5,000 square yards of Stainmaster carpet in a six-month period accrued co-op advertising dollars for Du Pont Stainmaster carpet. This program used mill and distributor data to calculate the square yardage sold by retailers.

Advertising.   The Stainmaster consumer advertising campaign focused on quality, style, fashion, and performance. The TV campaign opened with ad spots on 8 of the top 10 prime-time programs and consisted of some 1.7 billion gross impressions by the end of 1987. The newspaper coverage extended to the top 70 markets, 30 more than Du Pont had ever covered before. See Exhibit 5 for advertising budgets of Du Pont and its competitors. Two TV spots used in the initial campaign are shown in Exhibit 6.

One of Du Pont's ads for Stainmaster was in the top 10 best-noted TV commercials for the first half of 1987, and the introductory spot, "Landing," won a Clio award that year for advertising creativity.

Warranty.   Du Pont's "repair or replace" warranty for Stainmaster consisted of a full five-year stain-resistance warranty (covering most common household food and beverages), a five-year wear-resistance warranty (no more than 10 percent wear in any area, except stairs), and a lifetime anti-static warranty. The duration of the warranty came out of product testing.

Toll-Free Number.   For Stainmaster carpet dealers and buyers, Du Pont introduced a toll-free 800 number tended by operators trained in carpet-stain treatments and backed up by a sophisticated computer system for dealer ordering of sales material and recording of warranties.

Initially, the vast majority of the calls were from dealers requesting sales aids, point-of-purchase materials, extra warranty cards, swizzlesticks for in-store displays, and product information. Mills called for extra swizzlesticks, training tapes, or information literature. Later, more calls were placed by consumers.

---

[5]Antron and Dacron are Du Pont trademarks.

EXHIBIT 4   Dealer Advertising Materials

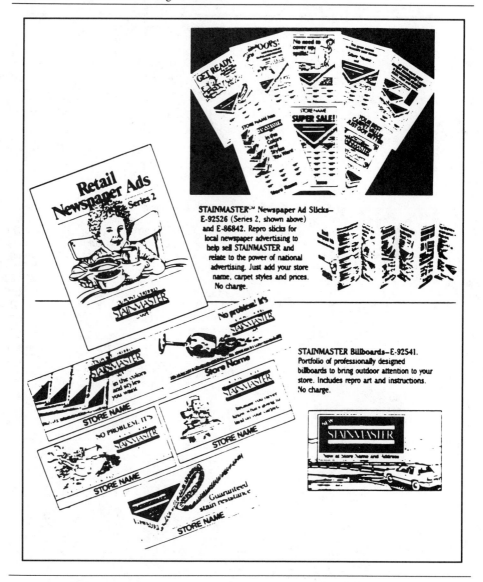

STAINMASTER™ Newspaper Ad Slicks—
E-92526 (Series 2, shown above)
and E-86842. Repro slicks for
local newspaper advertising to
help sell STAINMASTER and
relate to the power of national
advertising. Just add your store
name, carpet styles and prices.
No charge.

STAINMASTER Billboards—E-92541.
Portfolio of professionally designed
billboards to bring outdoor attention to your
store. Includes repro art and instructions.
No charge.

EXHIBIT 5   Major Fiber Producers' Advertising Expenditures, Fourth Quarter 1986—Third Quarter 1988
(estimates in thousands)

A. Cumulative Expenditures, Eight Quarters

	BAR* Network TV	BAR Spot TV	LNA† Magazines	BAR Cable TV Networks	BAR Network Ratio	LNA Outdoor	LNA Newspaper Supplements	Seven-Media Total
DuPont	$54,957.0	$1,399.9	$8,902.4	$417.4	$ 0.0	$16.8	$693.0	$66,387.0
Allied	11,788.6	501.1	1,614.1	229.7	0.0	10.7	0.0	14,144.2
Monsanto	13,584.4	597.1	3,793.6	592.5	1,078.5	0.0	0.0	19,647.1
3M	0.0	1,300.2	0.0	0.0	0.0	0.0	0.0	1,300.2
Amoco	0.0	0.0	0.0	0.0	0.0	0.0	0.0	0.0
TOTAL	$80,331.5	$3,798.3	$14,310.1	$1,239.6	$1,078.5	$27.5	$693.0	$101,478.5

B. Seven-Media Totals, Quarter by Quarter

	Fourth Quarter 1986	First Quarter 1987	Second Quarter 1987	Third Quarter 1987	Fourth Quarter 1987	First Quarter 1988	Second Quarter 1988	Third Quarter 1988
DuPont	$13,815.6	$8,394.7	$8,197.6	$3,668.1	$7,906.5	$8,994.9	$12,286.4	$3,123.2
Allied	306.2	1,054.8	3,400.8	693.2	3,328.8	2,469.4	2,761.7	129.3
Monsanto	223.5	848.8	1,461.4	1,673.1	4,366.0	2,621.7	2,991.0	5,461.6
3M	0.0	0.0	0.0	511.8	710.3	72.7	5.4	0.0
Amoco	0.0	0.0	0.0	0.0	0.0	0.0	0.0	0.0
TOTAL	$14,345.3	$10,298.3	$13,059.8	$6,546.2	$16,311.6	$14,158.7	$18,044.5	$8,714.1

C. Co-op and Trade Ads Spending by Year
(estimates in millions)

	Co-Op 1986	Trade 1986
DuPont	$11.7	$2.0
Monsanto	0.7	0
Allied	10.2	1.5
3M	.0	.0
Amoco	.0	.5

	Co-Op 1987	Trade 1987
DuPont	$13.1	$2.0
Monsanto	10.8	0
Allied	18.0	1.5
3M	.0	.5
Amoco	.0	.5

	Co-Op 1988	Trade 1988
DuPont	$14.5	$2.0
Monsanto	12.0	0
Allied	20.0	1.5
3M	.0	.0
Amoco	.0	.5

*Broadcast Advertisers Reports.
†Leading National Advertisers.

Source: *BAR/LNA* data supplied by Du Pont.

EXHIBIT 6   National Television Ads—"Landing"

BBDO

Batten, Barton, Durstine & Osborn, Inc.

| Client: DU PONT CARPET FIBERS | | Time: 30 SECONDS |
| Product: STAINMASTER | Title: "LANDING" | Comml. No.: DDTC 6023 |

CONTROL TOWER: Flight 124 fly
runway heading to

3,000. Right turn to two-seven-zero. You
are cleared for take-off.

AVO: Introducing Du Pont

certified Stainmaster carpet.

Stainmaster gives you

a revolutionary new level of protection

against stains and spills

that's better than any other carpet you
can buy today.

Because you never know . . .

STARTER: Gentlemen, start your
engines.

AVO: New Stainmaster.

AVO: From Du Pont Carpet Fibers.

EXHIBIT 6 *(concluded)*

BBDO

Batten, Barton, Durstine & Osborn, Inc.

Client: DUPONT

Product: STAINMASTER

Title: "SNAG REVISED"

Time: 30 SECONDS

Comml No.: DDTC 8083

(SFX: MUSIC REMOTE CONTROL
TRUCK)
ANNCR V.O.

you d prot in...
happening now.

but what about the traffic around your
home.

and what about those

unexpected little spills

WOMAN: What?

That's why Du Pont created Certified
Stainmaster carpet.

to survive stains and traffic

and help keep its new look.

Remember, it's not a Stainmaster carpet

if it doesn't say Du Pont.

Calls from consumers basically fit three categories: those wanting product information, those asking where to buy carpets of Stainmaster, and consumers with questions on performance and cleanability. After verifying the latter's purchase and warranty coverage, operators would talk the caller through the cleaning process. The method of stain removal varied as to length and number of steps by the type of stain and length of time it had lain untended.

Operator training required them to have tested Stainmaster carpets personally. If an operator could not correct the problem, he or she would take the customer's number and have one of the Du Pont scientists call back the next day. If all these approaches failed, Du Pont would send a local professional cleaner to the resident. As a last resort, Du Pont replaced the carpet.

RESULTS OF THE STAINMASTER CARPET PROGRAM

Initially, the thought was that Stainmaster would be only one of several carpet products in the Du Pont residential carpet line. The Du Pont Antron brand name was well established and known by both the trade and consumers. Hours after the first TV advertising for Stainmaster broke, however, the company realized that the new product would be a giant success. Du Pont's mill partners began calling their division contacts asking Du Pont to slow the program down, to deliver more product and to approve their new carpet styles. Retailers began putting pressure on their Du Pont contacts to get them more samples and to ask Du Pont to press the carpet mills to ship orders faster. Du Pont permitted mills to use the Stainmaster mark if the carpet met all standards with regard to face weights, levels of fiber twist, resistance to stain, soil, and static electricity, and was constructed of Du Pont premium residential nylon fibers. These branded products cost carpet mills 20–25 percent more per pound than commodity. Du Pont bore the cost of installing application equipment at mills, running the certification and quality control programs, and the national marketing of the Stainmaster brand.

At first, most retailers introduced Stainmaster at an average installed retail price of $18.00–$20.00 per square yard. Just a few months after its launch, Du Pont management dropped prices for residential carpet fibers going into the Stainmaster program by 15 percent, even though the fibers were in short supply and demand was strong. The price decrease was motivated by Tom McAndrew's desire to ensure the success of Stainmaster in the wake of competitive reactions. He recalled that Allied's Anso IV brand had used improved soil resistance to gain market share, and he wanted to make the most of a competitive advantage that was possibly temporary in nature. Dropping the price created an even greater shortage and encouraged carpet mills to quickly adopt the Stainmaster program. Within a few months, Shaw offered a Stainmaster carpet at $7.00 per yard. (See Exhibit 7 for a breakdown of typical carpet manufacturing costs.) The company also increased expenditures for advertising to put pressure on the carpet mills to convert styles to the Stainmaster program and to keep pressure on retailers to devote additional floor space to the carpets.

Du Pont's Stainmaster carpet campaign was widely credited for the exceptionally good year the industry had in 1986, even though it and competing products were on the market only 3–4 months of the year. Investment analysts at Wheat First Securities, a firm that

EXHIBIT 7   Functional Analysis—Carpet Mills
(38 oz., staple, 3.0/2 broadloom carpet)

Mill selling price fob plant		$7.90
Pre-tax profit		0.72
Manufacturing		
Inspection & shipping	$0.13	
Performance	0.03	
Dyeing	0.19	
Tufting	0.16	
Manufacturing services	0.06	
		0.57
Other costs		
Quality	0.08	
Claims & allowances	0.07	
Shipping & distribution	0.05	
Obsolescence	0.04	
		0.24
Raw materials		
Face yarn cost	4.63	
Packing	0.03	
Primary backing	0.19	
Latex	0.18	
Dye chemicals	0.10	
Antisoil	0.05	
Secondary backing	0.18	
		5.36
Sales & general administration		
Style & design	0.03	
Selling & marketing	0.07	
Data processing	0.08	
Commission field management	0.28	
Bad debts	0.02	
Customer service	0.08	
Advertising	0.04	
General administrative	0.13	
Finance & interest	0.11	
Sample cost	0.15	
Profit sharing	0.02	
		1.01

specialized in researching the textile fiber industry, estimated that 78 percent of the new styles introduced at winter shows were Stainmaster; 14 percent were Monsanto's Wear-Dated Gold label with StainBlocker, and 8% were Allied-Signal's stain-resistant Anso V Worry-Free. As of 1988, approximately 60 percent of carpet sold at retail had enhanced stain resistance, and the figure was expected to rise further. Almost 100 percent of Du Pont shipments to the residential carpet market was stain-resistant fibers. Although initially the number of carpet mills who were certified for the Stainmaster process was limited, by 1988 all major mills offered Stainmaster styles as well. The average retailer dealt with these three or four major mills, and therefore it was normal to find several fiber brands from each mill on the typical retail floor. Du Pont thought that Stainmaster styles had a larger share of retail floor space than any other brand.

Du Pont's consumer research indicated that, by the end of 1986, Stainmaster was far surpassing its competitors in brand awareness. An ASI Marketing Research, Inc. study in February 1987 reported the following figures for carpet brand-name awareness (aided plus unaided recall, base size of 400 respondents): Stainmaster 79 percent, Wear-Dated with StainBlocker 29 percent, and Anso V Worry-Free 27 percent. Du Pont estimated that, by April 1987, 87 million household decision-makers recognized the introductory ad, "Landing," and could recall the Du Pont Stainmaster name.

The industry continued euphoric through 1987-88. *Flooring* reported in its April 1988 issue that "78 percent of all retailers surveyed reported growth rates averaging better than 17 percent over 1986. Not bad, considering margins held at an overall average of 33 percent--with some 4 percent of retailers reporting margins as high as 60 percent. The *average* gross sales of all dealers reporting topped $1.3 million."[6] By late 1988, Du Pont figures indicated that carpet had captured almost 75 percent (square yards) of finished flooring shipments, up from 1983's 70 percent.

Polyester and olefin products had begun to gain a foothold in the market partly because of the capacity limitations of the nylon producers during 1986–88. Polyester and olefin were strong competitors also because they were cheaper fibers to make and were more resistant to common food stains than ordinary, untreated nylon.

The economy continued strong, which clearly helped the industry, but retailers attributed the bulk of their growth to the new stain-resistant products. Retail margins benefitted because the growth was in the high-end products; 59 percent of retailers surveyed reported getting premium prices for stain resistance. A study conducted by the Du Pont Residential Carpet Marketing Research Group showed that the average price per yard of carpet went from $14.62 during January–June 1986 to $16.07 during the same period in 1987.

Of dealers who advertised carpet in 1987, 68 percent said they almost always mentioned stain resistance, and another 24 percent sometimes mentioned it. Of those that reported an increase in sales in 1987, 38 percent overall indicated they spent more for advertising in 1987 than in 1986. Half of the respondents said their outlays remained about the same from 1986 to 1987, but, in general, their expenditures tended to be above the overall reported average of 4.29 percent of gross sales.

Carpet Mills. Although mill sales were up in 1987, some industry analysts noted that profits were not.

> Part of the reason for a decline in profits was that the new stain-resistant products which helped drive industry sales were expensive to produce. . . . Carpet producers had to overcome the usual hurdles involved in applying new manufacturing techniques. . . . Another hindrance was the added expense of providing retail outlets with a whole new line of samples and other marketing pieces.[7]

---

[6]Robert Blumel, "Retailers Outrun No-Growth Nightmare," *Flooring,* April 1988, p. 28 ff.

[7]David Aron and Alfred Dockery, "Carpets Roll Ahead," *America's Textiles International,* October 1988.

In the second year of stain resistance, however, several mills turned this situation around. Horizon Industries, for example, after getting through the start-up period, reported record sales for 1987 to $256 million, and doubled earnings, from $1.7 to nearly $3.5 million.

Du Pont.   Du Pont had solidified its position as the world's leading producer and marketer of carpet fibers. More importantly, perhaps, it had shifted its fiber business's emphasis from commodities to high-performance branded products (see Exhibit 8).

Du Pont expected demand for Stainmaster to remain strong. Research in the first quarter of 1988 indicated Stainmaster was outcompeting three major competitors for dealer/consumer interest and consumer brand awareness by a wide margin (see Exhibit 9).

At the time Stainmaster was introduced, all the major nylon producers were at or near capacity. By late 1988, Du Pont had raised capacity limits of existing equipment but had not made any significant plant-expansion plans. In 1987, the Fiber Division received 17 percent of the corporate capital expenditures. In the corporate magazine of September/ October 1988, Du Pont announced a new three-year program for Stainmaster, which it stated was the top-selling carpet in the retail market with a 30 percent market share.

Market shares of individual fiber producers were not known, but estimates of fiber-making capacity, by firm, were provided by Cliff Neeley, an industry analyst:

| Company | Capacity in Millions of Pounds | | | |
	Nylon BCF	Nylon Staple	Polyester	Olefin
Du Pont	600	250		
Monsanto	75	385		
Allied	150	225		
BASF	202	112	42	
Other nylon	57	30		
Amoco				140
Other poly			180	
Hercules				40
Total	1084	1002	222	180

THE COMPETITION

The announcement of Stainmaster in September 1986 was followed in the same month by Allied-Signal's announcement of stain-resistant Anso V nylon fiber and Monsanto's introduction of the Wear-Date stain-resistant nylon fiber.

Allied-Signal.   The Anso-V Worry-Free carpet of Allied-Signal (1987 corporate sales of $11,116 million) had replaced a semi-stain-resistant Anso IV product. Anso V used a new chemical, applied after dying in the mill, that Allied said "dramatically" improved stain resistance. It was backed by a "full five-year stain-resistance warranty" (from retailer newspaper ad, Fall 1988).

EXHIBIT 8   Stainmaster Shipments through Mid-1988

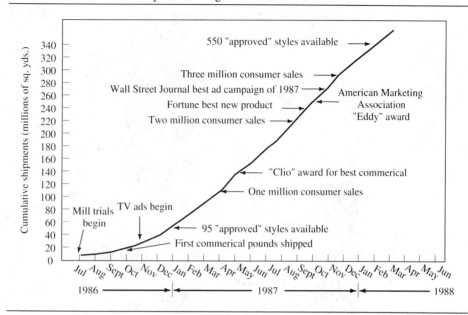

Source: DuPont Flooring Systems.

EXHIBIT 9   Stainmaster Acceptance/Awareness

	Du Pont Stainmaster	Monsanto Wear-Dated	Allied-Signal Anso V	Amoco Genesis
Stain-resist carpets shown/ discussed at retail	89%	59%	68%	54%
Total fiber brand awareness				
(by company)	95%	21%	66%	NA
(by brand)	69%	59%	31%	54%
Nylon-fiber purchases: square yards of residential wall-to-wall carpet (by company)*	43%	20%	21%	NA

*"Other" was 16 percent; 25 percent of the 5,800 purchasers surveyed were unable to name the fiber brand purchased.

Allied's advertising combined a celebrity endorser with special effects. Comedian Don Rickles literally became the carpet, and people spilled chocolate ice cream and red wine next to his face, which appeared to be woven into the carpet. Exhibit 10 is a reproduction of a later retailer's newspaper ad featuring Worry-Free.

EXHIBIT 10   Competitor Advertising

**Buy
Worry Free
Carpet From
Salem M.
Eways and
Get This
to Cover
Your Walls**

**GOOD FOR
TWO FREE
GALLONS OF
PRATT &
LAMBERT PAINT.**

**Buy 50 square yards of Worry Free Carpet from
the professionals at Salem M. Eways, and 2 gallons of
Pratt & Lambert paint are yours free.**

*Come in to Salem M. Eways between now and May ", and you'll receive this coupon
when you purchase 50 square yards or more of Worry Free carpet. Mail the coupon along
with your carpet receipt to the address on the coupon. In a week or less you'll receive
a voucher good for two free gallons of Pratt & Lambert Accolade, the world's finest paint.*

*Like Worry Free carpet, Pratt & Lambert Accolade is stain-resistant, soil-resistant and
can survive for many years without showing signs of wear. Which makes it the paint
that could also be described as worry-free.*

*So it should come as no surprise that two gallons of
Accolade have a value of over $50. But you don't have
to worry about that.*

*Because when you buy Worry Free carpet from the pro-
fessionals at Salem M. Eways, the paint's free.*

Salem M. Eways, your floor covering professionals.

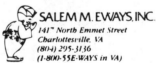

ANSO ℣
worryfree
FROM ALLIED FIBERS

**It's more than just stain resistant,
it's totally worry free.**

SALEM M. EWAYS, INC.
*141⁷ North Emmet Street
Charlottesville, VA
(804) 295-3136
(1-800-55E-WAYS in VA)*

Monsanto.   This competitor (1987 corporate sales $7.7 billion) had conducted a large promotion campaign during 1986, which included retailer training, point-of-purchase displays, and a multi-media advertising campaign focusing on the solution to the major causes of carpet stains. Monsanto, for its first stain-resistant brand commercials, showed a little boy named Jeff and his faithful cocker spaniel Spot. Unlike its competitors, Monsanto ran the ad only on cable TV and skipped the more expensive broadcast TV channels. It scheduled about 45 cable spots a week for 1987, supplemented by heavy magazine and radio advertising. Then in late 1987, Monsanto announced that Wear-Dated carpets would now have the stain-resistance, StainBlocker, locked into the fiber before shipping. Monsanto said in mid-1988 that "consumer surveys show that 92 to 95 percent prefer stain resistance that is locked-in to that which is added on at the mill."[8]

Monsanto previewed Wear-Dated with locked-in StainBlocker as part of its TV sponsorship of the Summer 1988 Olympics, and had announced in August 1988 that a new TV ad campaign was in the works for December. Monsanto was preparing new logos and point-of-purchase materials. The company also was publicizing its StainBlocker carpet by sending California's Carpet Cleaner of the Year around the country to speak to the media.

The company reported that 58 percent of retailers rated Wear-Dated as the best of the stain-resistant carpets, and that Monsanto outranked the other chemical firms in dealer support.

BASF.   A late entrant in the competition was BASF, the result of a merger in December 1985 of Badische (West Germany) and American Enka (Holland). BASF (1987 total North American corporate sales $4.4 billion) announced a branded stain-resistant fiber, Zeftron, in 1987. A Zeftron fiber had previously been successfully sold to the commercial market; the stain resistance was obtained after dyeing by application of Scotchgard, a product of 3M (1987 sales $9,429 million).

BASF did not market residential Zeftron to the consumer—only to mills. This scaled-down marketing was to allow BASF to price Zeftron lower than other branded products. The company explained, "We found that neither the retailer or the consumer perceived a difference between an unbranded product priced at, for example, $12, and a branded product at $15, but if the branded product was $13 or $14, that made a difference. Then it had a perceived advantage."[9] The only consumer advertising BASF planned was in *Good Housekeeping,* including the magazine's seal of approval. BASF trade advertising in mid-1988 was featuring double pages with the slogan: "With Zeftron nylon, the memories linger. . . . The stains don't."

Amoco.   In 1988, Amoco (1987 corporate revenues $22.4 billion) joined the competition with its Genesis brand stain-resistant olefin fiber in Permacolor carpets. Genesis used Scotchgard and carried a limited five-year warranty against stains and fading. Advertising for Genesis contained the following copy in mid-1988:

---

[8]*Floor Covering Weekly,* September 12, 1988, p. 1.
[9]"The Fifth Generation," p. 16.

The stain resistance revolution.

The introduction of stain-resistant nylon carpets was heralded as "breakthrough" and "revolutionary". But there is one small rub—these stain-resistant carpets stain. So much for the revolution.

The revolution really begins.

GENESIS Carpet certified by Amoco.

It is the right name to mark the most innovative period in carpet history. It offers an alternative fiber better equipped to meet the problems of stains and fading . . . with the ultimate stain and fade resistance. The 100% BCF olefin yarn in new GENESIS Carpet, enhanced with Scotchgard Protector, resists stains other leading stain-resistant carpets can't. And GENESIS Carpet resists fading from sunlight, ozone—even harsh chemicals like acne medicine and bleach.

THE FUTURE

After some dire forebodings just following the stock market plummet of October 19, 1987, predictions by late 1988 for the carpet industry's future were cautiously optimistic. After years of increasing, the average number of years consumers reported their previous carpet was in use showed a drop in 1988.

The Economist Intelligence Unit 1988 (*World Trade and Production Trends*) predicted world fiber demand to grow 2.4 percent a year to reach 44 million tons by 1995, and noted that a return to branding by Western fiber producers and reduced costs would be particularly beneficial. A compilation of forecasts for the GNP in 1989 was 2.3 percent growth.

America's Textiles International in August 1988 focused on short-term forecasts: "A healthy economy and a favorable outlook for incomes and spending promise to keep U.S. fiber, textile and apparel production high. However, relatively brief bouts of slack demand and inventory adjustment may appear."

Standard & Poor's *Industry Surveys* (September 8, 1988) and others noted that consolidation among mills would probably continue as part of continuing efforts to improve productively and efficient operations. Short-term S&P industry forecasts were "modest growth expected to continue in 1989."

Floor Covering Weekly in September 1988 predicted 2.1 percent growth in the carpet industry because of replacement in residences, noting that 99 percent of residences already had carpeting. The magazine forecasted continued cyclicality, low barriers to entry, and mill consolidation, but also forecasted shorter product life cycles, technological developments, rising exports (with the dollar down), and falling imports. Keys to success were predicted to be styling, marketing, and establishing distribution. A possible new growth area was said to be carpet tiles.

Case 1–3

Maison Bouygues*

In November 1990, M. Jean Gallet, Maison Bouygues' vice president of marketing, reviewed his marketing budget for 1991. As France's largest builder of single-family homes, Maison Bouygues (MB) had not escaped the effect of an ongoing economic slump. MB's home sales to date in 1990 were 20 percent below forecast. Further, the company was projecting a 15–20 percent drop in total new home sales in France in 1991.

Reviewing the marketing budget (Exhibit 1) led Gallet to consider the sales and marketing strategy that MB had employed in recent years. To stimulate demand, MB used direct marketing to a much greater extent than any of its competitors. Gallet wondered if this strategy was still appropriate during a recession. In a recent management meeting, discussion about the 1991 marketing budget had become quite heated. Claude Figneron, MB's vice president of sales had stated, "We must boost marketing spending during the recession to maintain our 1990 sales level. . . . That will also position us for the inevitable post-recession boom." Marie Suchet, MB's vice president of finance, had completely disagreed. She believed that marketing, like other departments, had to cut its costs during the recession.

Thus, Gallet had to determine whether to recommend increased, decreased, or constant total marketing spending during the economic downturn which had resulted in unemployment over 10 percent and home mortgage interest rates of 15 percent and more. Further, he had to consider whether MB's marketing funds should be allocated differently during tough times.

THE FRENCH HOME CONSTRUCTION INDUSTRY

The home construction industry was one of the largest and most visible industries in France. Total spending on new homes in 1989 approximated FF90 billion.[1]

The home construction industry was greatly affected by the number of households and by population mobility. Between 1982 and 1990, the number of households in France had increased from 20 million to 22 million. In 1990, the majority (55 percent) of these households occupied homes, while the balance (45 percent) lived in apartments.

---

*Doctoral Candidate Greg Conley prepared this case under the supervision of Professor John A. Quelch as the basis for class discussion rather than to illustrate either effective or ineffective handling of an administrative situation. Certain data have been disguised. Copyright © 1991 by the President and Fellows of Harvard College. Harvard Business School case 9–592–059.

[1]$1.00 U.S. was equivalent to 5.5 French francs (FF).

EXHIBIT 1 Maison Bouygues Marketing and Sales Department Budgets
(actual 1989, estimated 1990, and proposed 1991)

Category	Budget (in 1,000 FF)		
	1989	1990*	1991
Salesperson-months†	2,922	2,903	3,134
New home sales objective (in units)	3,653	3,472	3,650
Medium			
Marketing Department Budget:			
Television advertising (national)	10,000	0	5,000
Radio advertising (national)	0	6,000	0
Agency fees	1,911	2,565	2,842
Catalogs	3,509	4,708	3,129
Merchandising: point of sale	1,396	1,489	1,122
Market research	55	0	48
Total Marketing Department Budget	16,871	14,762	12,141
Sales Department Budget:			
Local advertising:			
Local newspapers	1,453	1,261	1,007
Free circulation newspapers	4,281	4,399	3,926
Regional magazines	979	535	484
National magazines (regional editions)	9,662	9,690	9,523
Technical fees	112	170	172
Direct mail:			
Bulk (not stamped)	6,462	5,506	5,424
Stamped	1,430	1,268	796
Telephone listings: *Yellow Pages*	250	363	293
Promotion:			
New home exhibitions:			
Cocktail parties in new homes	575	874	948
Shopping mall booths/trade shows	5,200	5,625	4,852
Sales promotions:			
Sales incentives	795	941	688
Hosts/hostesses in exhibition homes	620	696	782
Commercial:			
Trade shows	967	956	1,063
Referrals: finders' fees	202	249	437
Reserves and contingencies	0	0	449
Total Sales Department Budget	32,988	32,533	30,844
Grand Total (Marketing and Sales)	49,859	47,295	42,985

*Estimate based on actual spending for January through October and estimated spending for November and December.

†One salesperson-month equals one salesperson working for one month.

TABLE A   Single-Family Home Sales in France
(in units)

	1979	1989
Homes sold	320,000	275,000
New homes sold	290,000	185,000
Pre-owned homes sold	30,000	90,000

Note: New homes sold includes both individual homes (140,000 in 1989) and homes in housing developments (45,000 in 1989). Condominium sales are not included.

Three-quarters of the households living in homes were owners, and one-quarter were renters. Table A summarizes single-family home sales for 1979 and 1989.

Population mobility in France increased during the 1970s and 1980s. The days of the extended family living in close proximity to each other were fading as offspring often moved to distant cities when they grew older. Thus, it became increasingly common for pre-owned homes to go on the market rather than be occupied by the next generation of the same family. Many of these pre-owned homes had been built during the building boom of 1960–1980. (Since the Second World War, six million new homes had been built.)

Political developments also affected the housing market during the 1980s. The French government gradually reduced funding for mortgage assistance programs throughout the decade. A 1986 law enabled the remaining government aid to be used for either new or pre-owned homes; before 1986, government aid could be used only for new homes. Hence, it became harder for lower- and middle-income households to purchase new homes. In 1983, 70 percent of MB home buyers benefitted from government aid, yet by 1989, only 30 percent of MB home buyers qualified for such aid.

Changes were also occurring in the types of homes people were buying. The average size of new homes sold increased steadily during the 1980s. In 1986, only 24 percent of new homes sold were larger than 120 square meters. By 1989, this percentage had risen to 38 percent.

There were also marked regional differences in the French home market. Growth rates and architectural styles varied greatly. For example, new home sales in Auvergne-Limousin were 52 percent lower in 1990 than in 1982, while in Alsace, sales were 5 percent higher. Further, in some areas there were deficits of homes, while in others, there were surpluses.

MAISON BOUYGUES

MB, the largest builder of single-family homes in France, was a subsidiary of the Bouygues Group, a company founded in 1952 by Francis Bouygues to bid on industrial and construction projects in greater Paris. The Bouygues Group went public in 1970, but the

Bouygues family maintained control. In 1979, the MB subsidiary was created to address the growing new-home market.

Initially, MB focused on building small, basic homes for middle- and lower-income households. During the mid-1980s, the company shifted its focus to the higher end of the single-family housing market. During the same period, MB's main competitors were targeting the lower end of the new-home market. MB managed the design and marketing of new homes, and subcontracted all aspects of construction. MB had an in-house quality control department which selected the subcontractors and inspected homes under construction.

In 1990, MB's sales were FF1.4 billion, compared with total sales for the Bouygues Group of FF60 billion. In the Bouygues Group 1989 annual report, chairman and CEO Martin Bouygues declared:

> In the field of catalog homes, Maison Bouygues confirmed its number-one position as the largest builder of single-family homes in France by delivering some 3,200 units during the year. This remarkable performance was achieved despite a shrinking market caused by tighter consumer credit, renewed interest in city accommodations, and strong and highly fragmented competition. To meet this challenge, Maison Bouygues modified its product offering and put the emphasis on top-range products and services.

The Bouygues Group's values were stated in its annual report:

- The workforce: our most precious resource.
- The customer: our reason for being.
- Youth: the future of the company.
- Quality: the root of satisfaction.
- Technical innovation: the foundation of our Number 1 rating.
- Creativity: the wellspring of major projects.
- Training: the means to broaden our skills.
- Promotion: based on merit.
- Challenge: the driving force behind progress.
- Company spirit: the basis of our dynamism.

COMPETITORS

Maison Bouygues' principal competitors changed significantly during the 1980s. Several national companies went out of business because of poor cost control and the decline in new home sales. Gallet commented, "Paradoxically, we find it more difficult to organize our marketing effort when there are few obvious national competitors." Exhibit 2 reports sales levels for the top four new-home builders in France.

Although MB did not build homes in housing developments, it competed in the small, medium, and large new-home markets. The nature of competition differed depending on the size of the home. In the small-home market, MB's primary competition was another national home builder, Maison Phenix. In the market for medium and large homes, MB's main competitors were typically smaller regional and local builders who often offered customized homes. Competing against these smaller builders was challenging; many had cost structures which were 10–15 percent less than MB's, allowing them to offer low

EXHIBIT 2   New Homes Sales by Four Largest French Home Builders: 1979–1989

	New Home Sales (in units)		
	1979	*1984*	*1989*
Maison Bouygues	founded	4,000	3,200
Maison Phenix	15,000	7,500	1,800
Maison Familiale	8,000	3,000	1,200
Bruno Petit	3,000	2,800	600

Source: Company records.

EXHIBIT 3   Number of New Homes Built by Size of Builder (1989)

	Number of Homes Built in 1989				
	1–20	*21–50*	*51–100*	*101+*	*Total*
Number of builders	5,150	500	110	69	5,829
New homes built	40,850	19,500	7,100	23,550	91,000
% of new homes built	45%	21%	8%	26%	100%

Note: To be read, 5,150 "referenced" builders built between one and twenty homes in 1989. In 1989, 91,000 new homes were built by these referenced builders who had exhibition homes, one or more salespersons or, at least, a listing in the telephone *Yellow Pages*. About 49,000 other new homes were built by unlisted "one-man shops" or by homeowners themselves.

Source: Company records.

prices. Further, some small builders did not have a clear understanding of their costs, which also led to low price quotes. Many small builders were going out of business at the end of the 1980s as the economic recession made it more difficult for them to secure project financing from banks.

Barriers to entry in the home building industry were low. The market was fragmented and included thousands of builders, as shown in Exhibit 3. It was not uncommon for salespersons to leave existing builders to start their own companies. An entrepreneur could subcontract the building of a home, then pay subcontractors 90 days after the work was completed. However, a new law taking effect in 1991 would require that builders pay subcontractors within 30 days of completion of contracted work. This law was expected to cause financial difficulties for many small builders.

CUSTOMERS

Most new-home buyers did not want to design their homes totally from scratch. Instead, 85 percent of buyers were happy to choose from a range of model homes, then customize the home to their wishes. Almost all new homes were bought by couples and, typically, both spouses had equal influence in the home-buying decision. Moreover, most couples

EXHIBIT 4 1990 New Home Buyer Usage and Attitude Survey*

4A. Buyer Characteristics

- Habits of buyers of newly built homes included the following:
  — Do not visit cinema, theater, and restaurants frequently.
  — Avid television watchers. Average: three hours/day.
  — Value spending time with friends.
  — Frequently read newspapers and television magazines.
- The average monthly household income of MB buyers was FF15,300, the same as for all buyers in the sample.
- 24 percent of the sample had owned their previous residence; 66 percent had previously lived in a house as opposed to an apartment.

*The sample comprised 520 couples throughout France between the ages of 25 and 40 who had purchased a newly built home within the past six months. The sample was balanced such that roughly 25 percent of respondents had bought their homes from each of the following four sources: MB, multiregional builder, regional/local builders, and craftsmen. Data was collected through a one-hour interview with each couple.

4B. New Home Characteristics

	1987	1990
Average home size (in m²)*	106	126
Average home price (not including land)	FF387,000	FF480,000
Average land site price	FF189,000	FF240,000
Homes with two or more bathrooms	22%	44%
Homes with two or more stories	47%	62%
Traditional design	43%	24%

*Square meters

4C. Maison Bouygues versus Other Suppliers: New Home Characteristics (1990)

	MB Buyers	Multi-Regional	Regional or Local	Craftsmen
Average home price (in FF1,000)	448	435	497	533
Average land price (in FF1,000)	228	230	254	249
Average size (in m²)	111	114	132	140
Homes with two or more bathrooms	39%	29%	47%	54%
Homes with two or more stories	59%	51%	62%	66%
Average monthly salary of buyer (in FF)	15,300	14,200	16,000	15,500

4D. Land Plot Procurement

	MB Buyers	Multi-Regional	Regional or Local	Craftsmen
Plot suggested by builder	75%	58%	46%	10%
Plot procured independently by buyer	25%	42%	54%	90%

4E. Information Search

- 36 percent of MB home buyers, compared with 17 percent of non-MB home buyers, reported receiving information about new homes via mail.
- 62 percent of all buyers reported that their initial contact with their builder was either at an exhibition or over the phone.
- Only 3.5 percent of MB buyers, compared with 10 percent of non-MB buyers, reported that they were referred to MB by a friend or associate.

EXHIBIT 4   *(continued)*

4E. Information Search (continued)

- Among non-MB buyers, 28 percent had seen an MB catalog; 27 percent had visited an MB home; and 24 percent had met with an MB salesperson.
- 66 percent of MB buyers developed their first financing plan with MB.
- 66 percent of Craftsmen home buyers developed their first financing plan with a bank.

4F. Selling Process

- 10 percent of non-MB buyers in the sample had received an MB home price quote.
- 33 percent of all buyers considered no alternative price quotes to that of the builder they bought from. 36 percent considered one alternative price quote. 31 percent considered two or more.
- Average time from initial contact to closing the sale was 9.5 weeks for non-MB buyers and 7.5 weeks for MB buyers.

4G. Buyer Motivations

- The most frequently stated reason for buying a new home:
  "To acquire a home where we can feel comfortable—a place that we will own, not rent."
- The second most frequently stated reason for buying a new home:
  "A home which we can pass on to our children."
- Warranties expected by buyers (in order of frequency of mentions):
  1. Proper construction warranty.
  2. Building delay warranty.
  3. Builder bankruptcy warranty.

4H. Maison Bouygues' After-sale Service

- 28 percent of MB buyers were dissatisfied with after-sale service, compared with 18 percent of all buyers.

4I. Maison Bouygues Brand Image: 1987 versus 1990*

	1987	1990
All new-home buyers	6.3	5.7
MB new-home buyers	8.0	5.7
Multiregional buyers	6.1	6.1
Regional/local buyers	6.0	5.2
Craftsmen buyers	n/a	5.6

*10 = high, 1 = low

4J. Customers' Builder Selection Criteria

Stated as Most Important Criterion	Total Sample (%)	MB Buyers (%)	Multi-Regional (%)	Regional or Local (%)	Craftsmen (%)
Low price	9	6	10	10	10
Quality of builder	30	23	29	29	38
Floor plan	9	7	9	10	11
Most space	8	8	6	10	7
Maximum warranties	20	35	24	16	6
Competent salesperson	13	10	11	13	17
Other*	11	11	11	12	11

*Includes "Best Equipped Home" (2% for MB) and "Best Land Plot" (7% for MB).

EXHIBIT 4   *(concluded)*

4K. Market Segmentation

	Wealthy Savers	Wealthy Spenders	Autonomous Independents	New Anxious	New Responsible
Percent of sample	24%	16%	19%	25%	16%
MB Presence Index*	123	44	53	138	123
Buyer characteristics:					
Able to make large down payment	X	X	—	—	—
Often beneficiaries of family money	—	—	X	—	—
Comfortable using debt/credit	—	X	—	—	—
Do not have much money	—	—	—	X	—
Often owned previous home	X	—	—	—	—
Often former renters	—	—	X	—	—
Often renters who want to stop renting	—	—	—	X	—
High social level	—	—	X	—	—
Qualified hard workers	—	—	—	X	—
Hard workers	—	—	—	—	X
Intermediate professionals	—	—	—	—	X
Younger	—	—	—	—	X
Prefer to buy land site from builder	X	—	—	—	—
Use builder for land site selection	—	—	—	X	—
Very dependent on builder	—	X	—	—	—
Need to be reassured and assisted during buying process	—	—	—	X	—
Want input on design	—	—	X	—	—
Develop financial plan with builder	—	—	—	X	—
Shoppers; compare builders	—	—	—	—	X
Value oriented	—	—	X	—	X
Demanding on warranties, price, and quality	—	—	—	X	—
Sensitive to warranties	—	—	—	—	X
Want to leave property to children	—	—	—	X	X
Average size of new home (m²)	135	143	136	109	112
Average salary (FF)	18,100	19,700	16,600	12,700	14,000
Average age	36	36	33	33	33

*MB Presence Index = (% of MB unit sales from segment)/(% of total industry sales from segment). The higher the index, the greater MB's presence in that segment.

EXHIBIT 5   Unaided and Aided Brand Awareness: Major Builders (1984–1989)

Unaided Awareness
Question: "What are the names of the individual home builders that you know?"

Builder	Nov. 84	Dec. 85	Dec. 86	Dec. 87	Dec. 88	Dec. 89
Maison Phenix	39%	37%	34%	33%	31%	28%
Maison Bouygues	20%	24%	32%	50%	48%	49%
Bruno Petit	15%	11%	13%	22%	12%	11%
Maison Familiale	9%	8%	9%	8%	7%	6%

Aided Awareness
Question: "On this list (of major builders), what names of individual home bulders do you recognize?"

Builder	Nov. 84	Dec. 85	Dec. 86	Dec. 87	Dec. 88	Dec. 89
Maison Phenix	85%	84%	87%	88%	85%	88%
Maison Bouygues	58%	61%	71%	84%	85%	84%
Bruno Petit	47%	44%	49%	59%	56%	49%
Maison Familiale	50%	34%	39%	35%	43%	30%

Source: Company records.

were not greatly influenced by advice from family or friends. In France, 80 percent of households had two or fewer children, so 90 percent of new homes had four or fewer bedrooms.

MB sold homes to customers from a broad range of demographic backgrounds. To learn more about its changing customers, MB conducted an extensive customer research study every three years. Exhibit 4 reports key findings from the 1990 study. Exhibit 5 reports the results of another MB study on unaided and aided brand awareness; MB had the highest unaided brand recognition of any new home builder in all regions of France.

PRODUCT LINE

In 1986, MB had offered eight home models with unique exterior design styles in a narrow price range. By 1989, MB's product line had grown to 25 models grouped into three price/size levels. Exhibit 6 shows average sales prices and average gross margins for each level. Each home model was available in four to six different floor plans. One of MB's strengths was its ability to take a range of basic models and adapt those models to the various regional styles of architecture. In addition, MB offered numerous equipment and interior decoration options which enabled buyers to customize their homes. These options included different window shutters, garage doors, skylights, kitchen cabinets, and floor coverings. MB guaranteed a delivery date at the agreed-upon price, and all MB homes were sold with a 10-year warranty on construction and a 2-year warranty on mechanical equipment.

By 1989, MB was introducing and dropping four new home models each year. Each new model was adapted to each geographic region by a new product team that included

---

EXHIBIT 6   Maison Bouygues Product Line (1990)

Home Size	Living Area (in m²)	Number of Models	Average Price (FF)	Average Gross Margin (FF)	Percent of Sales (units)
Small	80–100	8	360,000	140,000	55%
Medium	101–145	11	448,000	162,000	35%
Large	146–200	6	650,000	200,000	10%

Note: Average prices do not include land prices and taxes.

Source: Company records.

Gallet, senior marketing and sales executives from the region, an architect, and a technical manager from headquarters. The new product development process, which typically lasted four months, was as follows:

1. For brand new product concepts, a qualitative study of the needs of the region was undertaken. Interviews were conducted with prospective buyers to learn about customer preferences.
2. Photographs of attractive houses of the region were reviewed by the new product team.
3. Drawings and small models were developed by the architect. From these, one or more models were selected to be added to the product line. No sample, full-scale homes were built before this selection occurred.
4. After a new model was selected, MB analyzed its costs and set the selling price. MB had greater experience building small homes and thus was able to estimate costs for these homes more precisely. Occasionally, a finished home was built to gather cost data; this home was then used as a combination exhibition home/MB sales office.

PRICING

Maison Bouygues' prices were non-negotiable. Prospective buyers received the same price quotes for MB homes regardless of the salesperson or region. All prices were computed using a sophisticated, in-house software package. The total price of the new home depended on the home model and on each exterior and interior equipment option selected by the customer.

SERVICES

Maison Bouygues did not offer financing to its customers. Instead, customers were responsible for securing their own home loans. However, one of France's largest banks was a large shareholder in Bouygues Group. Consequently, MB was able to facilitate customer loan applications made at this bank. This bank typically loaned money to MB customers at interest rates 1/2 percent below normal rates.

Ninety percent of new homes were purchased with bank loans. The standard down payment on a new home was 10 percent of the purchase price. However, 30–40 percent of new-home buyers bought with less than 10 percent down. Banks were able to borrow at a 1 percent lower interest rate when they used their money for new home loans.

MB did not provide the land for the home. Buyers were responsible for securing their own plots of land. However, MB did offer a free land referral service whereby each sales office maintained an updated database of plots available in its area. Approximately two-thirds of MB customers used this land referral service, while the other one-third found their own plots. This service was more important to customers at the low end of the market.

MARKETING COMMUNICATIONS

As indicated in Exhibit 1, Maison Bouygues used a variety of marketing communications techniques to raise brand awareness, to stimulate interest in buying a new home from MB, and to identify prospects. The management of marketing communications was divided between the Director of Sales and the National Marketing Manager, both of whom reported to Gallet. The Director of Sales managed all advertising relating to the regions, which included all direct marketing. The National Marketing Manager was responsible for all "image" advertising. This manager was in charge of the brand, merchandising, television and radio advertising, catalogs, market research, and public relations.

Catalogs.   MB was the only home builder in France to develop and distribute catalogs. MB, working with its advertising agency, produced two catalogs covering product line and equipment. The product line catalog contained pictures, drawings, and descriptions of all available home models. MB developed a unique product line catalog for each of its twelve regions.

The equipment catalog contained all available materials and components. For example, the catalog presented 15 types of tiles that could be used in an MB bathroom. The equipment catalog was 100 pages long and was updated every two years. This catalog cost FF1 million to develop.

Direct Marketing.   MB ran the most sophisticated direct marketing program of any home construction firm in France. While it would build anywhere in France, MB's direct marketing covered 80 percent of the country. The direct marketing program included mailings and magazine inserts which emphasized that it was possible for consumers to obtain the home of their dreams that they thought they could not afford. In addition to general information on MB and pictures of young families enjoying MB homes, the mailings invited recipients to complete a questionnaire profiling the features of their ideal home, which they could mail to MB for a no-obligation consultation. Consumers requesting information by completing a mailing or magazine insert coupon became sales prospects. MB was considering developing a television direct marketing advertisement which would include a toll-free phone number that viewers could call for information about MB. Exhibit 7 presents an MB direct mail piece. For comparison, Exhibit 8 presents a similar direct mail piece by Maison Phenix, one of MB's main competitors.

EXHIBIT 7 Sample Maison Bouygues Direct Mail Piece

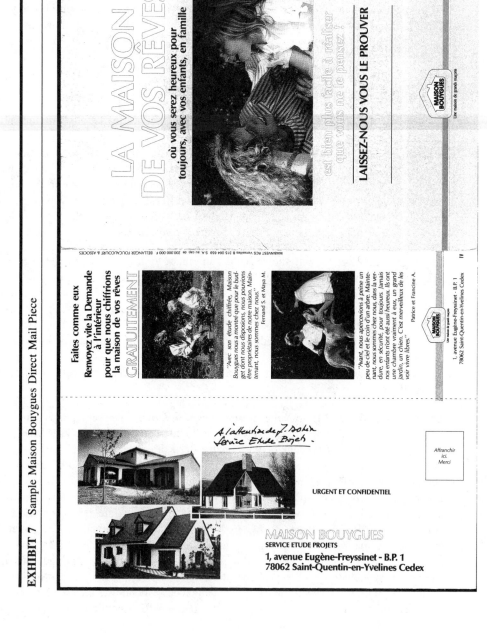

EXHIBIT 7 *(concluded)*

Dans la semaine, vous aurez :

- 1 -
VOTRE ÉTUDE CHIFFRÉE
Cette étude personnelle vous dit combien vous coûtera, chaque mois, le remboursement de votre future maison.

- 2 -
LE CATALOGUE
MAISON BOUYGUES
Sur plus de 40 pages, il vous présente beaucoup d'exemples de maisons et de plans correspondant à la région où vous souhaitez construire.

- 3 -
UN CADEAU
si vous postez cette enveloppe dans les 8 jours
LE GUIDE DES AMÉNAGEMENTS
INTÉRIEUR-EXTÉRIEUR
Des milliers d'idées en quelque 72 pages, 250 photos et 70 schémas, pour personnaliser votre future maison, à l'extérieur et à l'intérieur, du toit jusqu'aux robinets des salles de bains !

DÉTACHEZ SUIVANT LE POINTILLÉ ET SCELLEZ CETTE PATTE APRÈS AVOIR INSÉRÉ VOTRE DEMANDE D'ÉTUDE CHIFFRÉE GRATUITE.

LAISSEZ-NOUS TRADUIRE VOS RÊVES
SOUS FORME
D'ÉTUDE CHIFFRÉE GRATUITE

Une grande maison avec beaucoup d'espace pour les enfants... un beau jardin pour jardiner, jouer, respirer, manger dehors... une grande cuisine conviviale... un vaste salon pour recevoir des amis... un garage avec un coin bricolage... un sous-sol avec une salle de jeux pour les enfants... des combles aménageables pour avoir de la place en réserve...

La maison de vos rêves est bien plus facile à réaliser que vous ne le pensez. Pour le constater, renvoyez vite la Demande d'Étude Chiffrée ci-dessous. Nous chiffrerons votre grand projet, pour vous. Gratuitement et sans engagement. Dans la semaine, vous saurez comment transformer votre rêve en réalité. Facilement, économiquement.

Une maison individualisée et personnalisée à votre goût jusque dans ses moindres détails

"Le bonheur c'est si simple"

"Maison Bouygues a vraiment cherché à comprendre ce que nous aimions, ce que nous voulions et ce que nous souhaitions payer chaque mois, avant de faire cette étude chiffrée. Et c'est ainsi que nous nous sommes aperçus que notre rêve était facile à réaliser. Tout a ensuite été très vite. Le bonheur c'est si simple !"
Patrick et Muriel P.

DEMANDE D'ÉTUDE CHIFFRÉE GRATUITE DE VOTRE MAISON

LA MAISON DE VOS RÊVES
Quelle surface souhaitez-vous : .... m²
Combien de chambres souhaitez-vous : ....
Combien de salles de bains : ....
Voulez-vous une maison : ☐ de plain-pied ☐ à étage
Voulez-vous une façade : ☐ plate ☐ décalée
Aimez-vous :
☐ le style rustique   ☐ le style moderne
☐ le style classique   ☐ les poutres apparentes
Aimez-vous beaucoup recevoir des amis : ☐ oui ☐ non
Voulez-vous une cuisine : ☐ ouverte sur le séjour
☐ indépendante
Voulez-vous : ☐ un garage ☐ un sous-sol
☐ des combles aménageables
Possédez-vous un terrain : ☐ oui ☐ non

Dans quelle localité désirez-vous faire construire ? ....

VOTRE SITUATION PERSONNELLE
(Nous vous dirons les aides et prêts auxquels vous avez droit)
Êtes-vous : ☐ marié ☐ vie maritale ☐ veuf
☐ divorcé ☐ célibataire
Combien d'enfants avez-vous ? ....
Êtes-vous actuellement : ☐ propriétaire
☐ locataire de votre logement
Si vous êtes locataire,
montant mensuel de votre loyer .... F
Vous percevez : ☐ 1 salaire ☐ 2 salaires
Revenus nets mensuels de Monsieur .... F
Revenus nets mensuels de Madame .... F
Disposez-vous d'une somme de départ : ☐ oui ☐ non
Si oui, montant de cette somme : .... F
Disposez-vous d'un Plan d'Épargne Logement (P.E.L.) :
☐ oui ☐ non
Si oui, quand prend-il fin : .... Mois .... Année

VOTRE ADRESSE
Nom .... Prénom ....
Adresse ....
Code postal ☐☐☐☐☐ Ville ....
Téléphone domicile .... Téléphone bureau ....

Demande à détacher et à renvoyer dans l'enveloppe à droite sans aucun engagement ▶

EXHIBIT 8 Sample Maison Phenix Direct Mail Piece

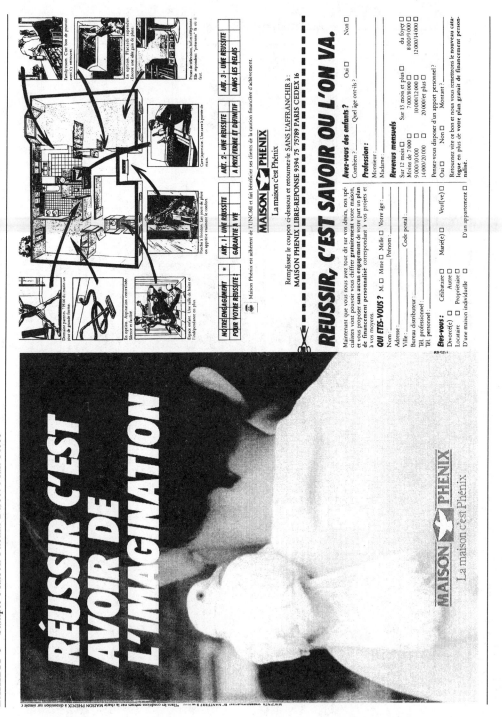

EXHIBIT 8 *(concluded)*

Advertising.   MB first used television advertising in 1987 to communicate that it was no longer just a builder of small homes but also had the skills to build larger homes. Understanding that its key competitors for larger homes were small, local builders, MB emphasized its quality control and building expertise. In 1989, MB spent FF10 million on "image" television advertising. In 1990, MB spent FF6 million on national radio to launch the new equipment catalog, and did not advertise on television. For 1991, MB planned to invest FF5 million in a recently developed "Egyptian" television advertising campaign which compared the quality and durability of MB home construction to that used in building the Pyramids. MB placed full-page print advertisements in regional newspapers, regional magazines, and regional editions of national magazines throughout France. In addition, MB was the only builder that advertised in national magazines.

Promotion.   MB also used various promotional approaches to raise brand awareness and generate sales prospects. First, MB homes were offered twice a year as grand prizes in sweepstakes and contests sponsored by French consumer goods companies and advertised on the principal television channel; MB absorbed part of the cost of the new home in return for the publicity. Second, MB sponsored cocktail parties in recently completed MB homes. New buyers were treated by MB to a party at which they could show their new home to friends and neighbors. Guests were informed that the new home had just been built by MB and were encouraged to pick up MB information packages. Third, MB appeared at all the major French home shows and maintained exhibition booths at shopping malls throughout the country. The distinctive MB orange and blue exhibition booth was a landmark outside many supermarkets. Fourth, MB sponsored sports teams to increase brand awareness. In 1989 and 1990, the company sponsored a Formula 3000 racing car which competed throughout Europe. From 1986 to 1988, MB had been the exclusive sponsor of the successful Marseille soccer team.

SALES ORGANIZATION

Headquartered in Paris, MB was organized into twelve geographic regions. In each region, MB maintained a regional sales and marketing office. Gallet was based at headquarters, yet spent a great deal of time visiting the regional offices. Gallet directed the marketing strategy, managed the marketing budget, and supervised the 12 regional marketing managers.

The vice president of sales directed the sales organization through 12 regional sales managers. Reporting to them were 65 chiefs spread across the 12 regions who were each responsible for managing a group of three to five salespersons. A chief's job was primarily managerial and was not expected to include any direct selling. A chief controlled the flow of prospects (leads) to group salespersons. Each chief received a base salary of FF11,000–16,000 per month, and earned FF2,000 for each sale above a monthly quota of three sales per sales group. The chiefs and their groups operated out of storefront offices on the high streets of the principal French towns. The MB logo (in the shape of a house) and other store insignia were standardized in MB's orange, white, and blue colors.

MB employed 250 salespersons who were expected to devote themselves entirely to selling and customer contact. Typically, each salesperson received 35 sales prospects per month, and worked to convert them into sales. Many of MB's salespersons were former insurance or car salespersons; 80 percent were aged between 25 and 35. Only 5 percent of MB salespersons actually lived in an MB home.

MB did not have a national salesperson-recruiting program. Instead, each regional office handled its own hiring. New hires travelled with an experienced salesperson for their first few weeks to learn the job. During training, MB videotaped some of a new recruit's initial sales calls. Later, the regional sales manager, chief, and trainee reviewed the tapes to identify areas for improvement. Antoinette Daveu, MB regional sales manager, noted, "One frequent failing of a new salesperson is that he or she tries to screen out prospects too quickly and scares customers away."

A salesperson's financial compensation was comprised of roughly half salary and half commission. Base salaries ranged from FF6,000 to FF8,000 per month, plus commission of about FF6,000 per unit sold. In addition, each salesperson was entitled to a company car which displayed the company name and came in white with orange and blue pin-striping. Occasionally, a regional office held a sales contest to motivate its salespersons. The prizes for these regional contests ranged from free dinners to new VCRs. MB did not sponsor any national sales contests.

Salesperson turnover averaged 120 percent per year. Of the salespersons leaving the company, approximately two-thirds resigned and one-third were asked to leave. MB's competitors experienced comparable salesperson turnover.

New salespersons who sold 45 homes during their first 24 months of employment were awarded the title of commercial engineer. Working conditions for commercial engineers and other salespersons were similar. Further, chiefs did not give special treatment to commercial engineers. However, commercial engineers earned FF10,000 per month and FF7,500 per sale. In addition, commercial engineers received higher-grade automobiles. Commercial engineer turnover averaged 25 percent. Of MB's 250 salespersons, 60 had earned the title of commercial engineer.

PROSPECTING AND THE SELLING PROCESS

In 1989, Maison Bouygues achieved one sale for every 24 prospects generated (4.2 percent). Ten years earlier, prospect yields had been significantly higher. Specifically, in 1979, MB had realized one sale for every 12 prospects (8.3 percent).

MB recorded how each prospect was generated (i.e., attended an exhibition, answered a print ad, etc.). The number of prospects generated by each communications medium and the number of sales (second signings) for 1989 and 1990 are shown in Exhibit 9. The cost per prospect and cost per second signing are presented in Exhibit 10 (calculated by dividing Exhibit 1 amounts by Exhibit 9 figures).

The home sale was basically a one-time transaction. Almost no buyers returned to MB for a "repeat purchase." Hence, the salesperson and buyer usually never saw each other again after the sale.

EXHIBIT 9 Prospects Generated and Second Signings by Communications Medium: Actual 1989, Estimated 1990, and Planned 1991

Medium	Number of Prospects			Number of Second Signings		
	1989	1990	1991	1989	1990	1991
Advertising:						
Local newspapers	1,721	1,330	878	46	30	40
Free circulation newspapers	4,573	4,689	5,345	165	113	140
Regional magazines	803	596	915	15	12	20
National magazines	35,707	36,281	32,515	920	821	860
Technical fees	0	0	0	0	0	0
Direct mail:						
Bulk (not stamped)	8,583	9,851	10,609	267	265	280
Stamped	3,175	3,312	1,910	71	85	85
Subtotal	54,562	56,059	52,172	1,484	1,326	1,425
Promotion:						
New home exhibitions:						
Cocktail parties in new homes	719	1,164	1,803	38	73	38
Shopping mall booths/trade shows	13,709	12,178	10,284	343	278	370
Commercial:						
Referrals: finders' fees	3,132	2,388	3,398	515	402	440
Subtotal	17,560	15,730	15,485	896	753	848
Unsolicited	20,029	21,235	21,851	1,273	1,393	1,540
Total	92,151	93,024	89,508	3,653	3,472	3,813

Note: Commercial trade shows contribute to unsolicited prospects and unsolicited second signings.

EXHIBIT 10 Cost per Prospect and Cost per Second Signing by Communications Medium: Actual 1989, Estimated 1990, and Planned 1991

Medium	Number per Prospect (in FF)			Number per Second Signing (in FF)		
	1989	1990	1991	1989	1990	1991
Advertising:						
Local newspapers	844	948	1,147	31,587	42,033	25,175
Free circulation newspapers	936	938	735	25,945	38,929	28,043
Regional magazines	1,219	898	529	65,267	44,583	24,200
National magazines	271	267	293	10,502	11,803	11,073
Direct mail:						
Bulk (not stamped)	753	559	511	24,202	20,777	19,371
Stamped	450	383	417	20,141	14,918	9,365
Promotion:						
New home exhibitions:						
Cocktail parties in new homes	800	751	526	15,321	11,973	24,947
Shopping mall booths/trade shows	379	462	472	15,160	20,234	13,114
Commercial:						
Referrals: finders' fees	64	104	129	392	619	993

The standard selling process at MB was as follows:

1. A salesperson received a sales prospect from the group chief.
2. The salesperson then called and set up an initial meeting with the prospect at the prospect's home. The initial meeting was scheduled when both heads of the household were available.
3. The salesperson mailed the product line catalog to the prospect to arrive before the initial meeting.
4. Initial meeting. The salesperson presented MB's capabilities and discussed the prospect's wants and needs. The salesperson gave the equipment catalog to the prospect and explained various equipment and material options. By the end of the initial meeting a specific project was discussed with the goal of setting up a second meeting at a land site, preferably within 48 hours.
5. Second meeting. At a specific site, the prospect "walked" the land and the salesperson suggested homes that would fit the site. It was important to review the land site as all price quotes were "site-specific." That is, the cost of the same model home varied by land site due to varying excavation costs.
6. Third/fourth meetings. Third and fourth meetings were held, if necessary, to discuss alternatives in detail. Salespersons were not encouraged to hold more than four meetings with a prospect. Additional meetings were held only at the prospect's request.
7. First signing. The first signing represented intent to purchase. At the first signing, MB and the prospect agreed on home model, equipment options, land site, and price.
8. Second signing. The second signing was the legal sale. Some "first signers" did not make it to the second signing due to permit problems, financing problems, or second thoughts.

MB tracked the percentage of prospects that advanced to each stage of the selling process, as shown in Table B. In other words, 70 out of 100 prospects attended an initial meeting, 30 out of 100 prospects attended a second meeting, etc.

The average time from the initial meeting to the first signing was nine weeks, and from the first signing to the second signing four weeks. After the second signing, MB applied for the necessary building permits and typically began construction six months later. Historically, 19 percent of second signings were canceled during this intervening

TABLE B Maison Bouygues' 1989 Prospect Yields by Stage of Selling Process

	Percent of Prospects Advancing to Stage
1. Prospect	100.0%
2. Initial meeting	70.0
3. Second meeting	30.0
4. Further meetings	10.0
5. First signing	6.0
6. Second signing	4.2

period. Once construction began, it took MB about six months to complete the new home.

CONCLUSION

Gallet remained concerned about the total marketing budget and its allocation among different marketing programs for the coming year. He was scheduled to present his 1991 marketing budget to MB's president in two weeks.

Case 1–4

Ontario Hydro (A)*

Our goal is to provide good energy value while caring for the environment, involving the public in planning for the future and being an open and accessible corporation.

—Ontario Hydro Annual Report 1989

In January 1989, the Coordinating Committee of Ontario Hydro's new 25-year plan, "Providing the Balance Of Power," met Friday morning, as usual. This time, however, instead of discussing the 25-year plan itself, they met to review the proposed plan for the accompanying communications program. The committee wanted a final evaluation of the program before committing to its execution.

COMPANY BACKGROUND

Ontario Hydro was created in 1906 by a special statute of the Province of Ontario to provide the people of Ontario with reasonably priced and reliable electricity. Under the Power Corporation Act, it was Ontario Hydro's responsibility to generate, supply and deliver electricity at cost throughout Ontario. Ontario Hydro also produced and sold steam and hot water as primary products. It did so through the operation of 81 hydro-electric, fossil-fuel, and nuclear generating stations and an extensive transmission and distribution system across the province. These assets, in addition to construction in progress and other current and noncurrent assets, were valued at $36,277 million in 1989.

---

*Research Associate Elisa Morton Palter prepared this case under the supervision of Professor John A. Quelch as the basis for class discussion rather than to illustrate either effective or ineffective handling of an administrative situation. Copyright © 1992 by the President and Fellows of Harvard College. Harvard Business School case N9–593–019.

EXHIBIT 1   Ontario Hydro Customer Mix, Electricity Usage and Revenue Stream: 1985–1989

	1985	*1986*	*1987*	*1988*	*1989*
Total number of customers (thousands)					
Residential	2,712	2,781	2,868	2,958	3,041
Farm	107	106	106	106	105
Commercial/industrial	354	365	377	392	404
Average annual use (in kilowatt-hours per customer)					
Residential	10,618	10,909	11,019	11,588	12,000
Farm	22,618	23,004	23,547	24,975	24,762
Commercial/industrial	213,673	216,666	220,834	224,705	228,000
Average revenue (in cents per kilowatt-hour)					
Residential	5.42	5.63	5.98	6.22	6.44
Farm	5.74	6.00	6.48	6.67	7.05
Commercial/industrial	4.03	4.20	4.40	4.62	4.87
All customers	4.44	4.63	4.87	5.10	5.35
Total revenue (in thousands)					
Residential	156,074	170,803	188,983	213,205	235,008
Farm	13,892	14,631	16,174	17,531	18,330
Commercial/industrial	304,830	333,149	366,319	406,950	701,923
Total	474,796	518,583	571,476	637,686	955,261

Ontario Hydro served 3.55 million customers on both a direct and an indirect basis. A summary of customer segments and annual usage is presented in Exhibit 1. Ontario Hydro sold wholesale electric power to 315 municipal utilities, which then sold this power to customers in each municipal service area. On a more direct basis, Ontario Hydro serviced more than 100 large industrial customers and 915,027 small business, residential, and farm customers in rural and remote areas. Net income from 1989 activities totalled $699 million on revenues of $6,346 million, an increase of 11.7 percent and 9.2 percent respectively over 1988.

FORECASTING DEMAND

In order to meet customer needs, Ontario Hydro managers spent considerable time trying to forecast future demand. Forecasting was done annually and the results were fed into both the annual business plan (with a five-year timeframe) and the yearly budgeting plan. The forecasts were vital because the facilities needed to generate new electricity supply took years to plan and build and were extremely expensive. While Ontario Hydro had done its best to revise and update these forecasts based on the best information available every year, some employees became concerned that Ontario Hydro's median annual demand growth forecast for the 1980s was only 3 percent when actual annual growth during the 1980s proved to be closer to 5 percent, peaking at 6.5 percent in 1988. Exhibit 1 shows the growth of Ontario Hydro's customer base, their demand for electricity, and revenue generated for the years 1985–89.

Forecasters predicted that demand in 2014 could range from 44.7 gigawatts (GW) (upper forecast) to 33.5 GW (lower forecast), with a median demand level of 39.8 GW.[1] The median level would represent twice the 1989 demand and about 20 times the demand in 1945. This increased demand, combined with the expectation that 25 percent of Ontario Hydro's existing facilities would be retired due to age by the year 2014, suggested a shortfall of 15.0 GW to 26.2 GW of electricity (median of 21.3 GW) by 2014. (See Exhibit 2.) This large shortfall worried many Ontario Hydro executives, particularly since there had been no re-evaluation of supply since 1977 (when the last nuclear facility had been approved), and led them to call for a longer-term, more comprehensive plan.

EARLY RESEARCH INITIATIVES

A 25-year planning cycle was considered necessary to ensure enough time to phase in short-, medium-, and long-term additions to the existing system. Preliminary efforts on the 25-year plan began in 1984, with the Demand/Supply Options Study (DSOS). In this study, Ontario Hydro talked to opinion leaders across the province about important energy-related issues. Ontario Hydro chose to use opinion leaders (such as business and community leaders) instead of members of the general public because opinion leaders were deemed to be more interested in the planning process and knowledgeable about the issues.

Opinion leaders across the province and in 13 regional communities were identified, and 102 of these were invited to participate in presentations, meetings, and workshops

---

EXHIBIT 2   Actual and Projected Electricity Demand

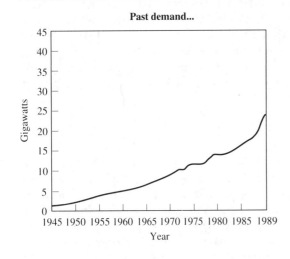

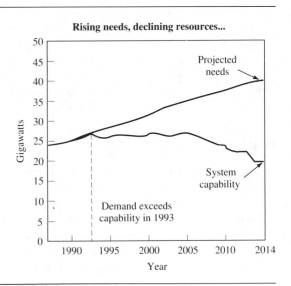

---

[1] A gigawatt (GW) is a billion watts.

At these meetings, the DSOS and the planning and consultation processes were described. Supply and demand options and general planning issues were also reviewed. Participants were asked to comment verbally or, if they preferred, in writing. Fifty-six opinion leaders chose to participate, and of these, 38 offered written submissions. (The other 46 declined due to lack of interest or time.) In general, there was agreement among participants on what issues were important, but disagreement on how to address them. For example, most participants wanted an adequate and reliable supply of electricity, but some wanted to build additional generating facilities while others preferred to emphasize demand management by implementing conservation and energy efficiency plans.

Opinion leaders also had varying views about the consultation process. For the most part, they appreciated being consulted. As one respondent said:

> We are pleased that Ontario Hydro has undertaken a process of consultation at this early stage of the planning process. . . . We are encouraged by your efforts and take them to be an expression of the Corporation's desire to open the planning process to influences that have hitherto not been present.

However, those who had praised the idea also had some concerns. Some felt they were given insufficient time to prepare for participation. Others questioned the assumptions which had been built into the program, and wondered why these had not been open for discussion.

> We have had difficulty making assessments of Hydro's specific proposals because we found that we were constantly questioning many assumptions made in the conceptual stages of these plans. . . . We discovered that many conceptual-stage assumptions fundamental to the directions of Hydro's future plans had been presented as given to be accepted without question.

One participant concluded that the consultation process, while theoretically valuable, was an exercise that was of little practical use:

> Examining the pros and cons of the various options has now reached the stage of being an academic exercise. After almost nine years since the last supply addition was committed, Ontario has now lost most of its flexibility in planning to meet load growth at levels at or higher than Hydro's most probable forecast. [The participant] believes that Hydro must now move ahead as quickly as possible on a range of options if the "unthinkable" and "unpardonable" are not to become a highly probable reality.[2]

While some of the responses were critical of Ontario Hydro, most offered valuable and constructive replies on Ontario Hydro's queries.

SYSTEMS PLANNING

The input from participants was transformed into qualitative criteria to be considered by the systems planning staff. Systems planning at Ontario Hydro had traditionally focused on technical solutions. Now the staff would also incorporate nontechnical criteria into the decision-making process.

---

[2]*Meeting Future Energy Needs: Provincial Organization Consultation Program Summary Report*, Vol. II, *Summary of Submissions*, April 1986, p. 32.

The interaction between the systems planners and the external community was unprecedented. While the process was more standard at a project level, it had never happened before at a plan level. There were many alternative factors and trade-offs to be considered once a spectrum of external values was introduced. The system planners acknowledged that the external input had enabled them to avoid being trapped in a too-narrowly-defined plan. By the end of 1986, a consensus had emerged to develop not only this plan, but a number of alternatives as well, with public review an important component. The systems planners agreed that such involvement would help them avoid the insular, narrow focus that sometimes occurred when companies were out of touch with their customers.

Concurrent with the opinion leader sessions, Ontario Hydro also conducted regional consultation meetings. Invitations were sent to over 300 people known to have interests in agriculture, business, the environment, women's issues, labor, social welfare, and other public affairs. The purpose of the regional meetings was to obtain public input on how Ontario Hydro could best meet the electricity needs of the province from the mid-1990s until the next century. Ontario Hydro interviewers asked participants a variety of questions about priorities, preferences, roles and mandates. Reliability of the electricity supply was generally cited as the most important issue. Regional leaders wanted to know that "every time I flick a switch, a light will come on." Low cost was also mentioned often. Here again, some participants were concerned about the sincerity of Ontario Hydro's consultation efforts. One participant commented that "Hydro tends to preplan its course—then sell it to the public (very effectively, too!)."

The results of both of these studies were presented in April 1986 to the Select Committee on Energy of the Ontario Legislature, which was conducting hearings into the DSOS. The studies, along with the final report of the Select Committee, helped shape a draft Demand and Supply Planning (DSP) strategy.

The draft DSP strategy was not actually a plan, but rather a set of principles, priorities, and guidelines to be used in the development and updating of demand/supply plans. Planning criteria were also defined in the draft strategy. A final strategy was developed only after the draft was reviewed by 12 government ministries, the Electricity Planning Technical Advisory Panel (appointed by the Ministry of Energy), and a second Select Committee on Energy of the Ontario Legislature (established February 1988).

The final DSP strategy, completed in March 1989, was the culmination of a five-year planning process which had involved the study and testing of options, input from the public, and several provincial government, technical and Select Committee reviews.

THE DEMAND/SUPPLY PLAN

The strategy called for a plan which balanced supply and demand management. It was clear that before people would support a decision to build a major new generating station, they wanted Ontario Hydro to explore in depth a range of alternatives such as conservation (demand management), energy efficiency, and the parallel co-generation of electricity by private producers. The DSP gave high priority to reducing demand by: 1) increasing the efficiency of the utilization of electricity, and 2) shifting the load away from peak periods of demand. This plan was expected to achieve 25 percent of the additional requirement estimated in the forecast. Other aspects of the plan included the maintenance, refurbishment, and upgrading of existing facilities, the encouragement of nonutility generators (i.e., electrical generation owned and operated by electricity producers other than Ontario Hydro), and continued development of hydraulic resources. However, the combination of these efforts was still expected to be 12 GW short of the median load forecast, and 15.7 GW short of the upper load forecast.

To meet this shortfall, the systems planning department analyzed 14 supply options. The main options were: purchases of electricity from neighboring utilities (such as Manitoba Hydro or Hydro Quebec), generation by fossil fuels, and CANDU nuclear generation. The 14 supply options were packaged into numerous demand/supply plans, and from those, Ontario Hydro selected three demand/supply plans which best met its planning criteria (cost, safety, reliability, diversity, and the environment). The preferred plan featured a combination of demand management, nuclear generation, gas-fueled units to meet peak load demands, in addition to existing fossil, nuclear, and hydraulic generation.

PUBLIC INVOLVEMENT

Once the technical solutions were determined, the question of public involvement had to be answered. Should the plan and/or all possible plans be presented to the public "for their information?" Should there be an opportunity for additional feedback? Should there be consultation with the public, or should the public be considered an equal partner in the planning process? While most managers involved in the demand/supply planning process agreed that public involvement was important, there were two views of public involvement within Ontario Hydro. Some managers felt that key publics had been involved through the entire process and that there had been opportunities for input not only under the auspices of Ontario Hydro, but also through representations to the Provincial government's Select and Technical Advisory committees.

On the other hand, some public affairs professionals felt that the public should be involved as much as possible in all the key stages of the planning process. They were concerned that the public might not have had sufficient opportunity to be involved in key decisions already taken, and felt that, even at this late date, additional input regarding alternative plans would be valuable. They recognized that the public was consulted during the early phases of the planning process, but argued that it was only informed after Ontario Hydro had decided on a preferred plan. They felt that several interest groups (the environmentalists and Aboriginals, in particular) had not received sufficient opportunities to provide input. The staff was worried that a lack of consultation with a wide range of Ontario publics would result in a plan that was created from assumptions which were tested too narrowly on the Ontario public. One such assumption was that customers would prefer to build additional supply rather than pay a premium for more efficient use of the existing supply.

ENVIRONMENTAL ASSESSMENT BOARD

Ontario Hydro had to seek approval under the Ontario Environmental Assessment Act for the siting and construction of major generating and transmission facilities. Ontario Hydro decided to submit the entire DSP to the Environmental Assessment Board (EAB) for review. The EAB was an independent body appointed by the Ontario provincial government. Ontario Hydro saw the EAB review as the first step in a two-phase plan. The utility hoped that the overall plan, or some variation, would be approved, including the rationales and requirements for the various plan components. Subsequently, environmental assessments would be made for specific sites and facilities, including public hearings if necessary, carried out by the EAB. A satisfactory conclusion of the first phase would facilitate the approval process for the site-specific facilities. Ontario Hydro's lawyers recommended as much specificity in the plan as possible in order to obtain strong and legally binding approvals. The lawyers suggested that the plan identify some "candidate" sites to show that the plan was feasible. Previously, no comprehensive multisite plan had been submitted to the EAB. Rather, Ontario Hydro usually submitted individual power generation projects for approval. However, in this case, management believed that Ontario Hydro would be better served by getting a general approval of need and the choice of technologies to meet that need before trying to obtain approval for specific sites.

While some Ontario Hydro staff recommended "cherry picking" (i.e., picking and choosing a single nuclear power plant project) in order to speed the process and allow Ontario Hydro to push the plan through, the prevailing opinion was that the public would not support that approach. The environmentalists in particular wanted to know the details and the scope of the plan, and their growing influence tipped the balance in favor of an approach that would likely add at least two to three years to the approval process.

It was important that Ontario Hydro emphasize environmental considerations in its plan because the importance of the environment had grown during the 1980s. Consumers ranked the environment much higher on their list of priorities at the end of the decade than in the middle of it. But time pressure was working against the inclusion of environmental issues in the plan. Ontario Hydro had promised the Ontario provincial government that the plan would be ready in 1989. There was concern that revisions would delay the approval and start of new supply construction to meet growing demand, which the original plan schedule set as early as 1992.

To address environmental concerns, Ontario Hydro decided to create a separate document which was exclusively dedicated to presenting all the environmental issues that had been identified. As an interested public, environmental groups would also have ample opportunity to make presentations about the plan at the EAB hearings.

COMMUNICATIONS ACTIVITIES

Once the decision was made that the EAB would be the forum to review the plan, Ontario Hydro needed to make the public aware of it. The EAB process was another opportunity for public comment. Within Ontario Hydro, there was considerable discussion about the nature of the document. Some managers wanted the document to be technically oriented to preserve the integrity of the analysis. Others felt that the document should be accessible without being patronizing so that anyone interested in the plan could read and comprehend it.

Those managers favoring a technical document believed that few people would actually read it, so it was not necessary to make it broadly understood. Robert Franklin (president and CEO) accommodated the two schools of thought by asking that both technical people and communicators work together on a range of documents for a variety of target audiences, including the general public, interest groups, and knowledgeable experts.

Franklin approved research at every stage of the communications effort so that testing could be done on everything from the concept and the language to the charts and graphs. Even the title was tested; a determination was made that *Providing the Balance of Power: Ontario Hydro's Plan to Serve Customers' Electricity Needs* portrayed both Hydro's desire to be customer-oriented and the consumers' desire to balance supply and demand components.

Broadening the accessibility of the document paid off. Research in 1989 found that 8 in 10 of those Ontario voters interviewed were at least somewhat interested in the plan, with particular interest in the environmental impact of the plan (97 percent very or somewhat interested), the technology proposed (95 percent very or somewhat interested), and the impact of the plan on rates (93 percent very or somewhat interested). Exhibit 3 summarizes the research findings in more detail.

Not only was the public interested in learning about the plan, they were also interested in having an opportunity to express their views about the plan. They felt it was very important that Ontario Hydro seriously consider their views, although only a minority believed that Ontario Hydro would in fact do so. This was a serious concern for Ontario Hydro which had to be addressed in its communications program. While Ontario Hydro's image was generally positive, there was still some concern that Ontario Hydro was just "going through the motions" in asking for public involvement. One response to this research was a strong emphasis in communications on the process of approval, informing citizens about the many ways in which they would get involved. This contrasted sharply with the earlier notion that the document should focus on the plan itself. One of the earliest process details communicated was that, under the recently-proclaimed Intervenor Funding Project Act, funds would be provided by Ontario Hydro to petitioners who required resources in order to participate in the public EAB hearings.

Research highlighted another issue: in spite of Ontario Hydro's highly credible image, most Ontarians did not believe that Ontario Hydro needed to build so many new reactors over the next 25 years to meet demand requirements. In fact, fewer than half of Ontarians interviewed perceived the existence of a supply problem. Fully 52 percent believed that Ontario had either more electrical generating capacity than required, or the correct amount. This perception was influenced by the fact that Ontario Hydro had four new nuclear reactors supposedly coming on line in 1990 at the Darlington facility. Even though consumers did not think Ontario would run short of energy, they thought it was extremely important that such a situation not occur. The perception was that, if shortages did occur, they would be caused by population growth and/or inefficient use/waste of energy.

Conservation was supported by over 50 percent of interviewees as a solution. In fact, 7 in 10 believed that effective conservation could be at least moderately effective in reducing demand. Three in 10 believed conservation could delay the construction of new supply facilities for 5 years, 24 percent anticipated that construction could be delayed 6 to 10 years, and 17 percent thought the delay could be greater than 10 years.

Research conducted in December 1988 highlighted an important fact, however. Consumers did not truly comprehend the amount that they would have to cut back in order

---

EXHIBIT 3   Selected Findings of Consumer Research Conducted Before
Release of Plan

A. How interested are you in learning about Hydro's plan?

Very interested	37%
Somewhat interested	46
A little interested	13
Not at all interested	5

Interest did not differ across regions or other segments.

*B. How interested are you in having an opportunity to make your
views on Hydro's plan known before a final decision is made on
it?*

Very interested	32%
Somewhat interested	43
A little interested	16
Not at all interested	9

C. How important is it that Hydro seriously consider your opinion?

Very important	41%
Somewhat important	36
A little important	15
Not at all important	8

*D. How likely is it that Hydro will seriously consider your opinion of
the plan?*

Very likely	7%
Somewhat likely	29
A little likely	30
Not likely at all	34

E. Ontario currently has . . .

More electrical generating capacity than it needs	17%
Less capacity than it needs	42
About the right amount	35
Don't know	5

*F. Perceived causes of any electricity shortage within the next 10 years
(respondents could check more than one item)*

Population growth	28%
Waste by consumers/unwise use	26
Poor planning by Hydro	16
Exports of electricity	15
Economic growth	10
Existing plants wearing out	8
More consumer appliances/gadgets	8
Problem with nuclear plants operating reliably	7
Not enough generating stations	6

EXHIBIT 3   (*concluded*)

Waste by industry/unwise use	6
Weather/storms	5

G. Perceived ways to avoid electricity shortages within the next 10 years (respondents could check more than one item)

Tell people and industry to conserve/use less	51%
Build new generating stations	26
Educate people on how to conserve	13
More research on alternative power sources	10
Eliminate exports of electricity	7
Better long-term planning	6
Offer people and industry incentives to use less	6

H. Action taken by people to reduce the amount of electricity they use in their homes can be _____ in delaying the building of a new generating station

Very effective	31%
Moderately effective	41
A little effective	21
Not effective at all	7

I. Hydro should concentrate its efforts on . . .

Persuading individuals and businesses to use less electricity	68%
Building a new generating station	14
Both equally	16

J. If Hydro makes a great deal of effort to persuade individuals and businesses to use less electricity, would this make you . . .

More aware of need	75%
Less aware of need	4
Neither more nor less aware	20

---

to postpone the building of a new generating station. When informed that the required reduction in use would have to be equal to the electricity used by a small town of 10,000 people, and that this reduction would have to be achieved each month for the next 12 years, fewer respondents saw demand management as a realistic option. Other respondents were persuaded that this option was infeasible under the assumption that the average consumer limited his/her demand management to "conservation without inconvenience." If inconvenience was necessary, consumers wanted to be compensated for it.

As mentioned earlier, most felt that it was wrong to begin building new generating facilities before the demand management option had been pursued fully, and almost 70 percent felt that the populace had the ability to enforce such a policy by withholding approval. Most of those interviewed did not believe that Ontario Hydro was trying as hard as it could to promote conservation.[3]

THE PLAN DOCUMENT

Given the above research, plan document writers knew that an explanation of the need for new generating facilities had to be built around two themes: need caused by growth (population growth, economic growth, and growth in numbers of household appliances) and need caused by waste and the inefficient use of electricity. Fully 72 percent of Ontarians agreed that Ontario Hydro's efforts to persuade people to conserve energy would make them more aware of the need for additional generating capacity in the province. A similar number pointed out that Ontario Hydro would not promote conservation unless it was worried about running out of electricity. An additional theme—the need to replace stations that would eventually wear out—also had to be communicated.

The document was written accordingly, with an emphasis on explaining why new facilities were needed. Also featured prominently was a description of the approval process that Ontario Hydro was undergoing and the role that the ordinary citizen could play in that process.

The document was reader-friendly and attractive: the communications team had managed to present the analyses assembled by the systems planners in a manner which was accessible without being patronizing.

All indications were that the document would accomplish Ontario Hydro's objective of informing the public. The document also promised to create a planning identity that would set the stage for a range of documents and enable Ontario Hydro to spin off future pamphlets, videos, and advertisements. Norm Simon, VP of Corporate Relations, called the process "an opportunity to create a document of the company's history and its future." It was vital that this opportunity be used to reinforce the idea that Hydro was "forging a partnership with the people of Ontario."

SUPPLEMENTARY COMMUNICATIONS

The communications effort was divided into prelaunch, launch and postlaunch programs.

Prelaunch.   In the prelaunch period, Ontario Hydro tried to respond to the results of the research. Programs were designed to create an increased awareness of need and an anticipation of the release of the plan. For example, in the summer and fall of 1989, Ontario Hydro introduced a series of print and radio advertisements around the theme "We don't want you to worry; we do want you to think." The ads explained that while Ontario Hydro was not going to run out of electricity immediately, current levels of supply were not going to be sufficient to meet estimated future demand. Ads focused on

---

[3]In 1989, Ontario Hydro in fact offered residential and business customers a variety of energy conservation programs, including: low-cost loans to motivate the installation of energy-efficient lighting, motors, and appliances; toll-free energy information telephone numbers; and energy efficiency audits of homes and places of business. The 1989 budget for these incentives and programs was $9 million, 11 percent of the marketing budget in that year.

the ways in which customers could attempt to reduce future demand through improving energy efficiency. (Research had previously determined that customers responded more positively to the term "energy efficiency" than to "conservation"; they interpreted the former as using the same level of energy more efficiently and the latter as using less energy.) The ads were used to introduce the concepts of demand management and need.

Launch.   The launch date of December 19, 1989, was preceded by a seminar for about 150 Ontario Hydro staff involved in communications across the province. The seminar familiarized them with the components of both the plan and the accompanying communications effort. Six hundred senior managers were also briefed. Staff were advised to emphasize the following messages in communications with the public:

1. Demand was going up and some generators were to be retired. Hydro needed a plan to deal with this and had to make decisions soon in order to prevent shortages from occurring.
2. The plan was part of an ongoing process to meet customer needs.
3. The plan balanced public concerns about reliability, cost, and the environment.
4. The plan emphasized better use of electricity by both Ontario Hydro and its customers.
5. New supply was to come from a balanced mix of sources.

Senior managers, once informed, were to brief Ontario Hydro's 26,000 employees. Ontario Hydro wanted to ensure that employees at every level would be equipped to respond. Each employee also received a complete information package.

Postlaunch.   Ontario Hydro did not disclose or discuss the specifics of its plan as it was developed, or at any time prior to its launch. It would, therefore, be addressing its campaign to a completely uninformed audience. Ontario Hydro knew that in order to acquaint the interested parties with sufficient knowledge to participate in the process (set to begin in the Spring of 1990), it would have to launch an impactful and highly informative campaign immediately. Additional research was conducted in July 1989 and again in December 1989 to determine more specifically the nature of the required program, the target market, and the message. (Relevant results are presented in Exhibit 4.) One important finding was that people seemed to become increasingly supportive of the DSP plan as they were exposed to additional information. As a consequence, the communications team decided to convey the specific details and rationale for the plan, and chose to do so through a variety of communications vehicles. Traditional media included advertising for the plan, budgeted at $625,000 for 1990, and copies of the plan, budgeted at $1.8 million. Three versions of the plan brochure were contemplated: a six-page summary (300,000 copies); a 52-page overview (250,000 copies); and a full environmental impact analysis (8,000 copies). In addition, the communications team planned to supplement these traditional media with the following six approaches:

1. Government relations.
2. Information centers.
3. Bill inserts and newspaper coupons.
4. An 800 number.
5. Speeches.
6. Public relations/media activity.

EXHIBIT 4 Communications Program Content Research: December 1989

A. Likelihood of action/event convincing you that Ontario will experience energy shortages within the next 10 years

	Index: Max. = 100
More frequent power failures or blackouts	82
Hydro forcing you to cut back on the amount of electricity you use in peak periods	80
News stories that Hydro was forcing some companies to cut back on the amount of electricity used	69
Hydro encouraging you to cut back on electricity used	68
Hydro encouraging you to buy energy-efficient appliances/lighting and heating equipment	68
News stories that Hydro was encouraging some companies to cut back on the amount of electricity used	65
Television ads from Hydro warning of forthcoming electricity shortages	64
Reading about forthcoming electricity shortages in an insert to your Hydro bill	62
More frequent newspaper stories about forthcoming electricity shortages	58
Television news stories about forthcoming electricity shortages	57
Speeches by public figures in Ontario about forthcoming electricity shortages	51

B. Likelihood of doing each of the following:

	Percent of Respondents			
	Very Likely	*Somewhat Likely*	*A Little Likely*	*Not Likely At All*
Read a brochure delivered to your home which highlights the key elements of the plan	80%	15%	3%	2%
Call a toll-free number to obtain more information about the plan	38	31	13	18
Call a toll-free number to voice your opinion about the plan	40	31	11	18
Answer a questionnaire attached to a brochure which summarizes the plan	64	24	6	6
Visit an information center in a shopping mall to obtain additional information about the plan	33	29	14	24
Attend a meeting in your community concerning the plan (sponsored by Hydro)	32	27	16	25
Attend a meeting in your community concerning the plan (sponsored by someone other than Hydro)	21	27	17	35

EXHIBIT 4   (*concluded*)

C. Technology preferred most, given selected information

	No Additional Information	Emissions From Coal-/Gas-Generating Deplete Ozone Layer	No Permanent Waste Disposal Facilities for Used Fuel from Nuclear Reactors
Nuclear	26%	48%	38%
Coal	29%	22%	23%
Natural gas and coal	41%	25%	33%
Don't know	1%	5%	6%

Government Relations.   One of the first groups to be briefed was the Ontario government. Ontario Hydro made presentations to relevant government representatives in the latter part of 1989, immediately following the launch period. Ontario Hydro chose to inform the government on all aspects of the plan, the legal implications, and the approval process through a combination of one-on-one and small-group meetings and a series of seminars. Follow-up packages and information sessions were to be available to any requiring supplementary details.

Information Centers.   Information centers were planned to run from January to April 1990. The mobile centers would operate throughout the province; five centers would be open at any given time (two would be bilingual). Centers would be set up for two to four days per community in town halls or community meeting places. Information packages including invitations to visit the centers would be sent out in advance to mailing lists of municipal utility employees, local elected/appointed officials, media, interest groups, and opinion leaders. These groups were to be assigned specific times, with whatever time remained, if any, to be allotted to the general public.

An additional mailing list was also compiled; it included nongovernmental organizations, senior members of government departments, major utility customers and leading members of the utility industry, general public communications facilities (libraries, Chambers of Commerce), and financial and investment institutions. These people would also be sent information packages and would be invited to attend a center at their convenience. A total of 18,000 mailings was planned.

Ads were scheduled to run in local papers the week before the center moved in, reminding people of its objective and the details of its stay. (See Exhibit 5 for sample advertisement.) It was expected that tens of thousands of consumers would visit the centers for about one hour per visit.

The centers would each be staffed by three to five people, with at least one plan expert on site at all times. Ontario Hydro had already planned a three-day training session so that all staff would have extensive knowledge of plan details. Guests could visit a series of 10 stations set up in the center to provide information on various aspects of the plan.

EXHIBIT 5 Information Center Advertisement

Ontario Hydro would like to share its thoughts on tomorrow's electricity needs

And we invite you to give us yours.

Over the years Ontario's appetite for electricity has been steadily growing. Within the next ten years, we face the very real possibility that demand may outstrip our available supply.

That's why Ontario Hydro has introduced "Providing The Balance of Power" a proposal that looks at how we can make the best possible use of all our existing resources, examines the possibilities of purchasing electricity from our neighbours, discusses the need for new generation and suggests why wise energy use at home, in fac-

tories and in the office is essential. It sets out the issues that will affect all our energy futures in the years ahead.

You're invited to discuss Providing the Balance of Power at the Ontario Hydro Information Centre.

We need your views— we need your feedback.

Staff at the Information Centre are there, not only to explain the proposal, but more importantly to listen to your ideas

and views on the future and record your suggestions.

You will receive a questionnaire which can be filled out at the Information Centre, or, if you'd prefer, mailed from home later on. And you'll also receive a copy of a comprehensive

52 page book that explains the proposal.

Your feedback is an important part of the process in meeting tomorrow's energy needs.

1-800-263-9000

At the conclusion of the visit, guests would be asked to fill out a questionnaire. They would also be given some summary information to take home.

Bill Inserts and Newspaper Coupons.   Preliminary research showed that the more people knew about the plan, the more likely they were to support it. As a result, Ontario Hydro had to get information out to as many people as possible. It planned to send out bill inserts and place print ads which contained a mail-in coupon (see Exhibits 6 and 7). Those who returned the coupon would be sent either a summary information pamphlet or the complete document (according to their request).

Ontario Hydro pursued the mail-in coupon as a way of avoiding the appearance of advocacy advertising. It was concerned that the government would disapprove of ads which advocated the plan too strongly. The mail-in coupon, on the other hand, just offered people a chance to obtain a detailed and balanced summary of the options.

800 Number.   Ontario Hydro planned to set up an 800 number the day the plan was launched. The number was to be prominently featured in all advertising and all other communications with the public. It would be staffed by trained Ontario Hydro representatives who were not only to answer questions, but were also to send out information to anyone who requested it.

Speeches.   Ontario Hydro planned to have senior company executives, including its president/CEO, available to organizations requiring or requesting speakers. Ontario Hydro had determined that its president was considered to be a credible and trustworthy public figure and planned to have him speak at every possible opportunity.

Public Relations/Media Activity.   The approval process would be lengthy, and Ontario Hydro realized that it would be difficult to continue finding "news" which could keep the campaign fresh and exciting. One of its goals was to use public relations opportunities to keep the issue in the public eye. Ontario Hydro hoped to get representatives invited onto local television and radio station talk shows to discuss the plan, and believed that it would also obtain some publicity when the media visited the information centers. Ontario Hydro also expected to have opportunities to promote the funding application process, though it did not promote its funding of groups as an example of public participation in the DSP. Still, the availability of funding for interest groups enhanced the image of public accessibility to, and involvement in, Ontario Hydro plans. Preliminary applications for funding totalled at least $50 million; an independent funding panel subsequently allocated over $23 million to more than thirty applicants.

CONCLUSION

The Coordinating Committee thought that the communications mix was satisfactory and intended to approve the plan. However, some concerns were raised. One member was afraid that some interest groups were not sufficiently targeted, while another was concerned that Ontario Hydro had armed and targeted every interest group except one which would

EXHIBIT 6   Proposed Print Advertisement

Wringing every last drop of electricity from the resources we already have still won't see us through the next ten years and beyond.

That's why we have a proposal that needs your input and feedback.

Electricity—worth thinking about

People seldom think about where electricity comes from or where it goes. It simply arrives by wire and is there at the end of the plug. It drives motors, powers communications and feeds appliances—and—with few exceptions it's dependable, reliable and always there.

However, there are times when it's important to consider where electricity comes from. This is such a time.

Will there be enough for our families and their children?

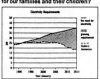

Ontario's appetite for electricity continues to grow. The chart above shows the difference between what we'll need and what's available.

The top line shows electricity growth to the year 2014, the lower line represents our current ability to meet demand. As you can see there's a gap between supply and demand that begins in a few years and grows. As early as 1993 (where the lines first cross) demand begins to outstrip reliable supply.

In another 25 years, we're going to need anywhere from 50% more to double the electricity we use today.

Putting the squeeze on Water Power

At one time people believed that falling water could give them all the electricity they'd ever need. They were mistaken. Today, falling water supplies only about 1/3 of our needs. The major rivers have already been used, but there are still some smaller sites that may yet be developed.

The Hydro proposal would develop remaining economic and accessible water power—this will give us about 10% of what's needed in the decade to come.

Buying electricity from others

We expect that private industry will begin generating more of its own electricity in the future. When this happens, Ontario Hydro will buy what they don't need. In addition, we can buy from independent power developers and from neighbouring utilities.

Doing so will meet about another 15%.

Asking everybody else to put the squeeze on electricity

Ontario Hydro is firmly committed to the idea of efficient wise use of electricity and the elimination of waste. Programs are already under way to help industry become more efficient in manufacturing and processes. Business is being encouraged to look at savings—and—there are plans underway to encourage the use of off-peak power.

Wise and efficient electricity use will wring out another 25%.

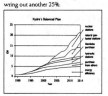

Where will we get the rest?

There are a number of options. Nuclear generation for its ability to meet day-to-day demand and its low operating costs. Gasfired generating plants, since they're relatively easy and inexpensive to build and cause little pollution. And, some gas units could also be con-

verted to use emerging technologies that turn coal into gas.

We will also be looking at alternate energy options, but, unless there are some breakthroughs in technology, nuclear and gas will make up the difference we need.

Protecting the Environment

There's a lot more to supplying electricity than reliability and cost. There's the need to balance technology with nature—and—share the public concern for the environment.

That's why the proposal is designed to wring the maximum from a combination of energy savings, utility purchases, co-generation, and the efficient production of electricity and steam, before looking at what will be needed by way of additional, traditional generating stations.

Now your input is needed.

Call or send for the 52 page book, "Providing The Balance of Power". It expands and explains the options and choices that are available.

To obtain a copy, call toll-free. At the same time, we'd like to hear of any suggestions you may have formed from reading this advertisement.

Or, if you prefer, mail in the coupon below. At the same time, you might like to ask for a speaker for your organization—somebody to explain the issues and hear your views.

We've also planned for Information Centres in most localities across Ontario. The 1-800 operator can advise where and when an information centre will be in your locality.

CLIP THIS COUPON

☐ Send me—A copy of the proposal overview—"Providing the Balance of Power"
☐ Call me about arranging a speaker for my organization/group
☐ Send me—Information on wise energy use in my home
☐ Send me—Information about Information Centres in my community

Name (Mr/Mrs/Ms first) _____ (Last) _____

Address _____ Street/Number _____ Apt _____

Town/City _____ Postal Code _____

Telephone _____

Return to Providing the Balance of Power, P.O. Box 3000, Concord, Ontario L4K 4J6

1-800-263-9000

EXHIBIT 7   Proposed Print Advertisement

PLANNING ONTARIO'S FUTURE ELECTRICITY NEEDS

Ontario Hydro's plans to meet Ontario's Future Electricity Needs...

THE PLAN

Ontario Hydro has a plan to meet Ontario's growing demand for electricity for the next 25 years.

The plans are contained in the booklet—"Providing the Balance of Power". It details why Ontario's need for electricity keeps growing and may even double by the year 2014. It fully explains how Hydro proposes to balance customer needs with existing and new resources. And, recommends a mix of options for successfully managing the demand and increasing the supply to meet expectations in the years ahead.

Inside the "Balance of Power" Overview book you will learn:
How energy efficiency at home and at work forms a vital part of the proposed plan, since more efficient use can contribute about 25% of what we'll need in the future.

•

Why Hydro is making plans to recondition and refurbish existing generating stations—making them more efficient to operate.

•

Why buying electricity from private generating sources and other utilities is part of the plan and will help meet future needs.

•

The role additional hydraulic (water power) sources will be asked to play in Ontario's electrical future.

•

Why major new generating stations will be needed.

•

How the plan strikes a balance between the use of modern technology and the need to protect our shared environment.

•

To obtain a copy of the planning booklet— "Providing the Balance of Power", simply call our toll-free customer service line, or mail the coupon shown at the bottom right. We are open from 8:00 a.m. to 5:00 p.m.

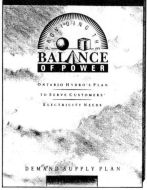

ONTARIO HYDRO'S PLAN
TO SERVE CUSTOMERS'
ELECTRICITY NEEDS

DEMAND SUPPLY PLAN

A 52-page book fully explains Hydro's plans for proposals for meeting Ontario's future electricity needs from now to the year 2014.

THE HEARING

The Ontario Government has established a panel of the Environmental Assessment Board, chaired by the Honourable Willard Z. Estey to review Hydro's proposed plan.

On April 4, 1990 a preliminary hearing will be held to deal with preliminary and procedural matters. The main hearing will begin later in 1990.

The approval requested in Hydro's application relates only to the requirement and rationale for additional facilities. For more information on the plan, or to obtain a copy of the notice for the public hearing, you may use the write-in coupon below.

Please use this coupon to order the material your require:

☐ Send me a copy of the 52 page booklet, "The Balance of Power Overview"
☐ Send me a copy of the Hearing Notice.
☐ I'm an energy saver. Please send me your Home Energy Savings Pack.

Name: (Mr/Mrs/Ms) First _____ Last _____

Street No. _____ Street _____ Apt. No. _____

Town/City: _____ Postal Code _____

Telephone: Area Code (___) Number _____

You may order any of the above directly by using the no-cost, toll-free customer service number. Simply dial. 1-800-263-9000.

Return to: The Balance of Power, P.O. Box 3000, Concord, Ontario L4K 4J6

1-800-263-9000

---

support Ontario Hydro. On the whole, however, the Committee was exceptionally pleased with the 25-year plan, *Providing the Balance of Power,* and with every aspect of the support components.

Case 1–5

British Airways*

On Sunday, April 10, 1983, a six-minute commercial for British Airways (BA) was aired in the middle of a weekend talk show. The commercial included a statement by Lord King, BA's chairman, and highlighted BA's achievements during the previous two years. The commercial also included the inaugural showing of a 90-second advertisement known as Manhattan Landing. This advertisement and three others formed the basis of an unprecedented £31 million advertising campaign designed to promote BA's brand name and corporate image worldwide.[1]

BRITISH AIRWAYS

By many criteria, BA was the largest international airline in the world. In 1982–83, BA carried 11.7 million passengers on 130,728 international departures, well ahead of Air France which carried 9.6 million international passengers. In terms of international passenger miles, BA's 37 billion a year comfortably surpassed Pan Am. BA flew to 89 cities in 62 countries outside the United Kingdom (U.K.) during 1982–83. Forty-two percent of BA sales were made in the U.K., 25 percent in the rest of Europe, and 33 percent in the rest of the world.

BA was a state-owned enterprise, formed as a result of the 1972 merger of British European Airways and British Overseas Airways Corporation. The economics of scale in the work force which many expected from the merger were slow to materialize. Partly as a result, BA continued to record annual losses throughout the 1970s. BA's financial performance was aggravated by increases in the price of fuel oil stemming from the 1973–74 energy crisis. In addition, greater price competition, especially on transatlantic routes, resulted from the deregulation of international air fares. An example of this trend was the advent of the low-price, no-frills Laker Airways Skytrain service on the lucrative transatlantic route in 1979.

---

*Professor John A. Quelch prepared this case as the basis for class discussion rather than to illustrate either effective or ineffective handling of an administrative situation. Copyright © 1984 by the President and Fellows of Harvard College. Harvard Business School case 9–585–014.

[1]BA's fiscal year ran from April 1 to March 30. At the time of the case, £1 was equivalent to about $1.50 U.S.

The election of a Conservative government in the U.K. in 1979 prompted a change in approach towards the management of BA. The new administration was determined to reduce the losses which almost all state enterprises showed each year and, in many cases, to restore these enterprises to private ownership. A new chairman, Sir John (later Lord) King, was appointed to head BA in 1980. He initiated programs to improve BA's products and services along with a hiring freeze and an early retirement program to reduce the size of the work force. By March 1983, BA's work force had been reduced to 37,500 people from 59,000 just three years earlier. In addition, BA showed a profit in 1982–83 for the first time in 10 years, compared to a £500 million loss in 1981–82 (see Exhibit 1).

EXHIBIT 1 British Airways: Income Statement, April 1, 1982–March 31, 1983

Sales Revenues	*(Million £)*
Passengers on scheduled services	£1,771
Passengers on charter services	86
Freight	151
Mail	36
Ground arrangements for package tours	100
	£2,144
Expenses	
Staff	£ 593
Aircraft	101
Engineering	107
Operations	863
Marketing	205
Accommodation, ground transport and administration	159
Recoveries	(158)
Ground arrangements for package tours	102
	£1,972
Operating surplus	£ 172
Operating surplus from nonairline acitivities*	18
Other income†	20
	£ 210
Cost of capital borrowings and tax	− 149
Profits before extraordinary items	£ 51
Profit on sale of subsidiaries	26
Profit	£ 77

*Including BA helicopters; BAAC, and IAC.
†Investments in other companies, interest earned on cash deposits, surplus from disposal of assets.

Industry observers believed that BA would have to sustain this improved performance if stock was to be offered to private investors by the end of 1984. So the programs of product and service improvement continued, together with further labor cutbacks. Recently introduced Boeing 757s were added to the fleet in 1983, a quality control division was established, and the U.K. Super Shuttle was introduced.[2]

The turnaround in performance was recognized when BA received the 1983 Airline of the Year award, based on a survey of business travelers. However, although costs were reduced and the quality of service improved, BA's public image remained weak. Along with other nationalized industries, BA continued to share a reputation for inefficiency and incompetence. Accordingly, Lord King stated that one of his main objectives was "to make the airline proud again."

ADVERTISING DURING THE 1970s

During the 1970s, BA country managers had revenue responsibility for BA's marketing and operations in their individual markets. The advertising agencies with which they dealt were appointed by BA headquarters. Foote, Cone & Belding (FCB) had held the BA account in the U.K. since 1947, and as a result, many country managers outside the U.K. also used FCB subsidiaries or affiliates.

In 1978, British Airways appointed FCB as its worldwide agency, meaning that all country managers *had to* deal with the FCB subsidiaries or affiliates in their countries. The purpose was to achieve a more favorable commission rate from FCB, rather than to increase centralized control of advertising content around the world. Indeed, in the United States, where the BA account moved from Campbell Ewald to FCB, the BA advertising theme built around Robert Morley and the slogan, "We'll take good care of you," was retained intact since it had only recently been launched (see Exhibit 2). Although the Morley campaign was considered a success, building as it did on Britain's favorable reputation in the United States for old-fashioned hospitality, the campaign nevertheless caused problems for BA executives in the United States. In the words of one, "It over-promised on customer service; every time something went wrong, my phone would ring off the hook."

Prior to the appointment of FCB as the worldwide agency, BA country managers were not required to submit their proposed advertising copy to headquarters for approval. There were certain loosely defined guidelines governing the presentation of the BA logo, but beyond that, local country managers and their agencies were free to determine their own advertising copy. Major advertising campaign concepts did, however, require headquarters approval. Following the appointment of FCB as the worldwide agency, this procedure changed. Each December, BA country managers would submit to headquarters requests for advertising funds for the following fiscal year as part of the annual planning process.

---

[2]Four shuttles operated between London and Manchester, Glasgow, Edinburgh, and Belfast. Tickets could be purchased in advance or on board, and flights typically left every hour during the day.

EXHIBIT 2   Robert Morley Campaign Magazine Advertisement

"We're up in the air
before most airlines
even wake up!"

We <u>can</u> beat the experience

British Airways beats Pan Am's experience five times a day. After all, we have more business seats to London than Pan Am and TWA combined.

You'd like a 10 a.m. flight? Of course we have it...we've had it for years. And British Airways offers something really special on it. First Class and Super Club® passengers receive a voucher worth £20 (about $33) for dinner in any one of four exclusive restaurants. Tourist passengers receive a voucher for a choice of one of five evenings of cabaret entertainment with dinner.*

British Airways has the very first flight out daily (9:30 a.m. Concorde). So we're up in the air before most airlines even wake up. We also have the last daily flight out (10:00 p.m.) and three

flights in between. And British Airways Super Club seats are by far the world's widest business-class seats.

Need we go on? We could mention our free helicopter service,** or our preferred hotel and car rental rates for business travelers, or our longstanding commitment to our 10 a.m. flight. And you'll be pleased to note that your flight miles between the U.S. and London will count as credit toward the A Advantage® travel award plan.

So you see, British Airways has no trouble beating the experience. It's experience like ours that makes us the world's favourite airline. That's why British Airways flies more people to more countries than anyone else. See your travel agent or corporate travel department.

*Offer valid April 15-October 31, 1983 and subject to government approval. For full fare USA originating passengers only. See vouchers for details.
**Helicopter service free for Concorde, First Class and Super Club passengers.

DEPARTURE	AIRCRAFT	FREQUENCY
9:30AM	Concorde	Daily
10:00AM	TriStar/747	Daily
1:45PM	Concorde	Daily
7:00PM	747	Daily
10:00PM	747	Daily

British airways
The World's Favourite Airline™

Once the commercial director at headquarters had allocated these funds, each country manager would then brief the local FCB agency or affiliate, and develop the advertising copy for the coming year. Country managers in the larger markets would submit their advertising copy to the commercial director in London more as a courtesy, while the smaller countries were required to submit their proposed copy for approval. Headquarters required changes in about five percent of cases, typically on the grounds that the advertising overstated claims or was inconsistent with the image BA wished to project.

Whatever the intent, the result of this process was inconsistent advertising from one country to another. First, campaigns varied across markets. The Robert Morley campaign was only considered suitable for the United States. And a recently developed U.K. campaign in which a flight attendant emphasized the patriotism of flying the national flag carrier could likewise not be extended to other countries. Second, commercials and advertising copy promoting the same service or concept were developed in different markets. There were limited procedures within BA and the agency for ensuring that the best ideas developed in one market were transferred to other markets. Finally, the quality of FCB's subsidiaries and affiliates varied significantly from one country to another, aggravating the problem of inconsistency.

BA advertising during this period, like the advertising for most other major airlines, tried to persuade consumers to choose BA on the basis of product feature advantages. Rather than attempting to build the corporate image, BA advertising emphasized superiority and differentiation in scheduling, punctuality, equipment, pricing, seating, catering, and/or in-flight entertainment. Advertising typically focused on particular products such as the air shuttle, BA tour packages, route schedules, and classes of service (such as Club[3]). The impact on sales of many of these product-specific and tactical advertising efforts could be directly measured. In addition, the commercial director responsible for BA advertising worldwide insisted that a price appear in all advertisements in all media. Frequently, BA advertisements compared the prices of BA services to those of competitors. The commercial director's insistence on including price information in each advertisement frequently caused problems. For example, in the United States, the APEX fare[4] to London from New York differed from that from Boston or Chicago, so different commercials had to be aired in each city.

The 1982–83 advertising budget of £19 million was allocated almost entirely to advertising of a tactical or promotional nature. Only the patriotic "Looking Up" campaign in the U.K. made any effort to develop BA's corporate image. About 65 percent of the 1982–83 budget was allocated by the commercial director to the International Services Division (ISD), about 30 percent to the European Services Division (ESD), and about 5 percent to the Gatwick Division, which handled BA air tours, package holidays, and cargo business in the U.K.[5] BA advertising expenditures during 1982–83 for 14 representative countries are listed in Exhibit 3, together with other comparative market information.

---

[3]The BA equivalent of Business Class.

[4]Advance purchase excursion fare.

[5]The geographical coverage of the ISD and ESD mirrored that of the old BOAC and BEA.

EXHIBIT 3   Comparative Data for 14 Markets

	Percent of BA 1982–83 Worldwide Passenger Revenues	1982–83 Advertising Expenditures (£1,000)	Principal BA Competitors	BA's Market Share Versus Principal Competitor	Percent Business/ Percent Pleasure BA Passengers
United Kingdom	42%	6,223	British Caledonian* Pan American	Similar	42/58
United States	14	5,773	Pan American TWA	Lower	26/74
Germany	5	228	Lufthansa British Caledonian	Lower	50/50
Australia	3	967	Qantas Singapore Airlines	Similar	6/94
France	3	325	Air France British Caledonian	Lower	52/48
Japan	3	393	Japan Airlines Cathay Pacific Airways	Lower	30/70
Gulf States	2	134	Gulf Air Kuwait Airlines	Lower	12/88
Canada	2	991	Air Canada Wardair	Lower	11/89
South Africa	2	331	South African Airways TAP (Air Portugal)	Lower	15/85
Italy	2	145	Alitalia Dan Air	Lower	50/50
New Zealand	1	125	Air New Zealand Singapore Airlines	Similar	3/97
Egypt	.5	53	Egyptair Air France	Similar	26/74
Zimbabwe	.4	41	Air Zimbabwe KLM	Higher	8/92
Trinidad	.3	77	BWIA	Higher	7/93

*These are BA's principal competitors on international routes. BA's main competitors on domestic United Kingdom routes were British Midland Airways and Dan Air.

SAATCHI & SAATCHI APPOINTED

In October 1982, the Saatchi & Saatchi (S&S) advertising agency was asked by Lord King to explore the possibility of developing an advertising campaign which would bolster BA's image and which could be used on a worldwide basis. S&S was one of the first agencies to espouse the concept of global brands. In newspaper advertisements such as that shown in Exhibit 4, S&S argued that demographic and cultural trends, and, therefore, the basic factors underlying consumer tastes and preferences, were converging. In ad-

EXHIBIT 4 Saatchi & Saatchi Newspaper Advertisement

THE OPPORTUNITY FOR WORLD BRANDS.

Nowadays, life for branded goods manufacturers is not as straightforward as it once was.

Many years ago manufacturers first recognised that advertising could provide a key foundation for their business growth.

They realised that while their customer was the retailer, the actual 'consumer' was the public; that advertising could enable them to build a solid position in their market by building the goodwill of their real customer – the 'consumer.'

They also saw that if they, the manufacturers, did something to move their goods from retailers' shelves as quickly as they arrived on them, trade would be brisk and everyone would be satisfied.

Thus the manufacturer became the advertiser of 'branded' products, the retailer became the purveyor of 'brands' and advertising became a conspicuous feature of the age.

This happy cycle produced 'brands' of startling endurance and longevity, as the table below shows.

US BRAND LEADER	
1923	CURRENT POSITION
SWIFT PREMIUM, BACON	NO. 1
EASTMAN-KODAK, CAMERAS	NO. 1
WRIGLEY, CHEWING GUM	NO. 1
NABISCO, BISCUITS	NO. 1
EVEREADY, BATTERY	NO. 1
GOLD MEDAL, FLOUR	NO. 1
LIFE SAVERS, MINT CANDIES	NO. 1
SHERWIN-WILLIAMS, PAINT	NO. 1
GILLETTE, RAZORS	NO. 1
SINGER, SEWING MACHINES	NO. 1
COCA-COLA, SOFT DRINKS	NO. 1
CAMPBELL'S, SOUP	NO. 1
IVORY, SOAP	NO. 1
	SOURCE: ADVERTISING AGE

Brand Character

Nowadays, when probed deeply, consumers describe the products they call brands in terms that we would normally expect to be used to describe people. They tell us that brands can be warm or friendly; cold or modern; old-fashioned; romantic; practical; sophisticated; stylish and so on.

They talk about a brand's persona, its image and its reputation – and this 'aura' or 'ethos' is what characterizes a brand.

It follows that all brands, like all people, have a 'personality' of one kind or another. But like the strongest individuals, the strongest brands have more than mere personality – they have 'character' – more depth, more integrity, they stand out from the crowd.

Note the importance that one major marketer attaches to this concept.

"My acid test on the issue is whether a housewife intending to buy Heinz Tomato Ketchup in a store, finding it to be out of stock, will walk out of the store to buy it elsewhere or switch to an alternative product."
A. J. F. O'REILLY,
PRESIDENT & CEO, H. J. HEINZ

This explains why the best marketers try to develop powerful brand characters. They make them less vulnerable in the market-place. They help a higher quality product to be perceived as such by consumers.

Today, the establishment of such strong and enduring brands is rather more difficult.

☐ Static populations mean static markets which means increased competition for market share.
☐ Product quality is converging, with increasing technological parity among major marketers.
☐ The influence of the retailer and retailers' own store brands is growing in many parts of the world.
☐ Marketing expenses are growing, as manufacturers respond to the ever-higher cost of reaching the consumer.

All in all, the pressures on manufacturers' brands are immense.

Superior Product Quality

Serious marketers know that in the face of these pressures the success of their brands can only rest on superior product quality.

They know that as the consumer views more products as commodities, it becomes harder to

establish a meaningful point of difference for their products. They know that clever marketing and promotion of cosmetic differences cannot paper over this.

They know that the longevity of their brands is helped by good marketing, but is founded on superior product performance and this in turn is founded on their ability to produce a *higher quality product at a lower cost.*

Which is why market leaders' priorities are now focusing on a common objective which was not among their priorities in previous decades – to work diligently to be the *low-cost producer* in their market.

Low costs provide the means to achieve that happiest of all situations – higher product quality ... fewer price increases ... and more advertising.

Low costs are the priority as a sound base for all the other steps needed to build growth.

Thus, the competitive intensity of maturing packaged goods markets around the world has brought to the fore the economic logic of world brands – *the opportunity for international economies of scale as the basis of long-term strategic security.*

Today, the most thoughtful companies are adopting a new approach to international marketing.

These companies are moving through the five basic stages in the life of a multinational corporation as seen in the chart below.

And as they pass through stages 4 and 5 the need for pan-regional and world marketing is emerging at the heart of their business strategy.

"The globalization of markets is at hand. With that, the multinational commercial world nears its end, and so does the multinational corporation.

The global corporation operates as if the entire world (or major regions of it) were a single entity; it sells the same things in the same way everywhere.

Corporations geared to this new reality can derive enormous competitive advantages from the economies of scale they develop – in production as well as marketing, distribution and management.

Corporations geared to this new reality can derive scale economies that still live in the dim linqering of old assumptions about how the world works."
FROM A NEW ERA OF THE GLOBAL MARKET, BY PROFESSOR T. LEVITT, HARVARD BUSINESS SCHOOL

A New Approach

After the vicissitudes of the 1950s and 1960s, more companies are now reaching the status of having acquired 'critical mass' in various regions of the world. They are now starting to turn from primary concern about 'return on acquisition investment' and 'overhead recovery' towards getting to grips with long-term franchise building across each world region.

At the same time the progressive harmonization of 'headquarters' and 'local' management culture and style, evolving from more frequent two-way movement of personnel, is enhancing the likelihood of successful adoption and execution of pan-regional business strategies.

And meanwhile in Europe, management's strategic thinking is beginning to broaden to match the dimensions of the Common Market as legislative harmonization focuses attention on pan-European issues.

International Growth Priority

Companies have passed through the bygone age when many of them treated 'Overseas Division' as the poor cousin of the organisation, struggling to compete in foreign markets with strongly established indigenous competitors.

The international divisions of many companies are now beginning to 'come of age' and receive their rightful allocation of corporate resource, if only for the practical reason that corporate earnings growth in many multinationals is today often provided by non-domestic markets.

Business System Economics

The strategic value of pan-regional branding lies in the scale economies it affords across the company's business system – to help make the company the low-cost producer.

Where the economies arise will vary by product category, and may include research and development, materials purchasing, manufacturing, distribution and advertising.

The optimum business system for a European beer, for example, is markedly different in that for chewing gum, but the principle is the same. Secure, franchise-protected volumes at the regional scale can allow a company to *build a price/cost/value structure which will eventually put it out of reach of competition.*

All these factors set the conceptual framework within which a truly pan-regional brand can exist in the years ahead. The international need is the starting point. Research will be conducted to look for market similarities between countries, not to seek out differences. Similarities will be the new fuel for growth.

The creative process will still be as vital as ever; marketers in each location will still be dependent on the intuitive creative judgement of locally based creative management, but this effort will be marshalled to a single-minded overall advertising strategy.

Marketing Learning Curve

There is then a real marketing learning curve that allows the progressive refinement of a success formula, as the pan-regional brands broaden their experience country by country.

The best creative brains are given an opportunity to develop advertising for an entire region of the world, and not simply for one market – to find a real advertising idea so *deep in its appeal* that it can transcend national borders previously thought inviolate.

Consumer Convergence

In the past, the successes in world branding have been few, and have been achieved by virtue of the sheer will and far-sighted commitment of managements who stayed consistently with a long-term vision for the business. Procter & Gamble is a company in this category that comes to mind.

In the future, the only winners in cross-country branding will be companies who have seen that social developments are making redundant the old idea that differences between nations are decisive in framing marketing strategy.

The most advanced manufacturers are recognising that there are probably more social similarities between Midtown Manhattan and the Bronx, two sectors of the same city, than between Midtown Manhattan and the 7th Arrondissement of Paris. This means that when a manufacturer contemplates expansion of his business, consumer similarities in demography and habits rather than geographic proximity will increasingly affect his decisions.

Demographic Convergence

Trends of vast significance to consumer marketing, such as ageing populations, falling birth rates, and increased female employment are common to large segments of the modern industrial world.

Consumer convergence in demography, habits and culture is increasingly leading manufacturers to a consumer-driven rather than a geography-driven view of their marketing territory.

Decline of the Nuclear Family

Some of the most telling developments spring from the same source – the decline of the nuclear family. Observers have attributed this to various causes – the rapid pace of technological development; higher labour productivity which reduces hours of work; and other more metaphysical notions such as the emergence of a 'liberal' philosophy, which increasingly recognizes that a woman's role can exist outside the home.

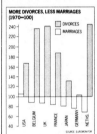

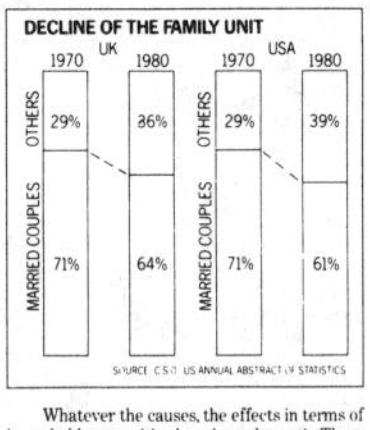

DECLINE OF THE FAMILY UNIT

Whatever the causes, the effects in terms of household composition have been dramatic. There are now less children per household, and a declining proportion of households which conform to the two-adult-two-children pattern.

The result is the erosion of the traditonal family unit and its clarity of role and relationship. The effects have been illustrated by the decline of formal meal-taking and the corresponding increase in the sales of 'instant' and 'convenience' foods. The multinational expansion of fast-food franchises like McDonalds is another manifestation of the same trend.

Changing Role of Women

The table below shows the change in the role of women in the working population over the past decade. The fact that the majority of women in most modern societies now have a job requires a major adjustment to current ideas on communicating with a consumer group that no longer conforms to the home-centred stereotype of yesteryear.

MORE WORKING WOMEN

	% CHANGE 1970–1979	
	WORKING POPULATION	WORKING WOMEN
USA	+ 24.4	+ 37.6
BELGIUM	+ 8.3	+ 24.7
NETHERLANDS	+ 10.1	+ 24.6
ITALY	+ 8.1	+ 22.8
FRANCE	+ 7.7	+ 17.3
UK	+ 4.5	+ 15.1
GERMANY	– 1.6	+ 3.5
		SOURCE: EUROSTAT

Associated with this change, there has been a well documented trend to lower marriage rates and higher divorce rates. This trend has led one group of social scientists to invent the phrase "serial monogamy" to describe what they forecast to be the nature of relationships in the 1980s and beyond. They suggest that there will be an increasing tendency for couples to live together for a number of years, then to change their partners and set up home afresh, changing again after a few years, and so on. This discontinuity in formal relationships, especially where children are involved and re-marriages occur, will have profound effects on family relationships.

MORE DIVORCES, LESS MARRIAGES (1970=100)

Static Populations

Population growth is now almost zero in the western world. All modern industrial countries are forecast to produce population growth of much less than 1% per annum over the next 20 years. It is hardly surprising that within this static population, the age structure is undergoing a transformation. The over 65s are a growing group relative to the 25–65s, and that group is growing relative to the fourteen and unders.

STATIC POPULATIONS

	% GROWTH PER ANNUM	
	1960–70	1980–2000 ESTIMATE
AUSTRALIA	2.0	0.8
CANADA	1.8	0.8
USA	1.3	0.7
SPAIN	1.1	0.7
JAPAN	1.0	0.6
FRANCE	1.0	0.4
ITALY	0.8	0.3
UK	0.5	0.2
GERMANY	0.9	0.1
		SOURCE: WORLD DEVELOPMENT REPORT

EXHIBIT 4   *(concluded)*

Higher Living Standards

In most western countries, improvements in the material standard of life have resulted in a growing demand for consumer durables and for more leisure. This is reinforced by shorter working weeks that accompany technological progress and productivity growth.

The entry of women into the labour market itself creates a demand for consumer durables to ease the strain of 'keeping house'.

HIGHER LIVING STANDARDS

	GROWTH IN REAL PERSONAL CONSUMPTION 1970–82
USA	+ 42%
UK	+ 26%
FRANCE	+ 60%
GERMANY	+ 34%
JAPAN	+ 65%

SOURCE: HENLEY CENTRE

Cultural Convergence

At the same time as demography is converging, television and motion pictures are creating elements of shared culture. And this cultural convergence is facilitating the establishment of multinational brand characters. The worldwide proliferation of the Marlboro brand would not have been possible without TV and motion picture education about the virile rugged character of the American West and the American cowboy – helped by increasing colour TV penetration in all countries.

Observers believe that cultural convergence will proceed at an accelerated rate through the next decade – particularly with the deployment of L-SAT high-power TV satellites throughout Europe.

EUROPE'S NEW SUPER STATIONS

These developments will reduce cultural barriers as countries exchange their media output through satellite networks – for the first time allowing viewers freer access to international television without the barrier of language.

Marketing Timetables

Analysis of all these demographic, cultural, and media trends is allowing manufacturers to define market expansion timetables. Essentially, marketers will be tracking trends which indicate when a region is ready for attack via programmes they have tested elsewhere.

For example, current changes in European laundry practices were foreshadowed by similar trends in the US during the late '60s and early '70s. Thus a US manufacturer of low-suds detergent would examine the growth in the penetration of front-loading washing machines in the UK to assess the ripening potential for his own product.

MARKET EXPANSION TIMETABLES
% OF HOUSEHOLDS OWNING FRONT LOADING WASHING MACHINES

SOURCE: COMPANY RESEARCH

Consider also Europe's soap powder manufacturers. Driven by improved washing machine technology and the increased popularity of relatively fragile synthetic and coloured fabrics, European laundry habits have converged. Every major nation now washes a majority of its wash loads in under 60°C water. This has created a common need for a product which performs well under these circumstances.

The result has been the marketing of single brands with a common brand name, product formulation, and positioning across the whole of Europe.

In the future, the only winners in cross-country branding will be companies who do a lot of things right and synthesise their efforts effectively around three golden rules:

1. To market clearly differentiated products that either drive, or capitalize on, real convergences in consumer habits and tastes.

2. To create a dedicated management value system that mirrors the vision of a pan-regional branded business.

3. To monitor their brands' character on a consistent, continuous, comparable basis across geography and over time.

The opportunity for world brands is there to be siezed but only for those companies with the long-term determination to meet these stringent requirements.

Here are two other examples of the global approach in action – for British Airways and Procter & Gamble's Pampers. The Pampers brand was introduced in the US in the late 1960s. Pampers created the disposable diaper market by providing a product that was more convenient and more absorbent than cloth diapers at a price consumers were willing to pay. Pampers is now Procter & Gamble's largest brand and is sold on a similar strategy almost all over the world. If the Pampers business was a separate company, it would rank in the top one-third of the 'Fortune 500' list.

Does a global advertising campaign have to be bland? Not according to the South China Morning Post which described B.A.'s new worldwide campaign as *"unique and imaginative";* or the Sydney Morning Herald – *"a radical departure from the usual formula";* or Newsweek – *"a tour de force";* or the Wall Street Journal – *the most ambitious attempt so far... to use a new world campaign";* or the London Sunday Times – *"a flash of inspiration."*

The Agency is now working on a similar exercise on Silk Cut for American Brands/Gallaher – a Company whose marketing was recently described by the Financial Times as *"an object lesson for its competitors on the rewards of brand discipline."*

65 OFFICES IN 38 COUNTRIES.

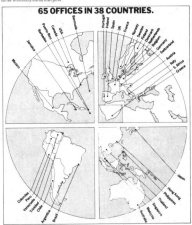

THE UK AGENCY WORKS WITH 6 OF BRITAIN'S TOP 10 ADVERTISERS.

THE US AGENCY HANDLES MORE No. 1 BRANDS THAN ANY OTHER AGENCY IN AMERICA.

THE INTERNATIONAL NETWORK WORKS WITH 44 OF THE WORLD'S TOP 200 ADVERTISERS.

Impact on Agency Structure

What are the implications of these trends for the advertising industry?

Business service companies, such as agencies, benefit from the increasing complexity of problems in their areas of expertise. Knowledge has value, and there is a greater 'value-added' during periods of turmoil and change in the business environment.

Most observers believe that the trend to pan-regional or global marketing will have a marked impact on the structure of advertising agencies... because world brands require world agencies.

A HANDFUL OF WORLDWIDE AGENCY NETWORKS WILL HANDLE THE BULK OF $125 bn WORLD ADVERTISING EXPENDITURE FOR MAJOR MULTINATIONALS.

Many expect to see the advertising industry moving in the same direction as accounting, banking, financial services, etc. – a polarization between worldwide networks servicing global corporations, and strong local firms handling domestic clients in their own country.

SOME OF THE AGENCY'S CLIENTS IN 3 OR MORE COUNTRIES

ALLIED LYONS	IBM
AMERICAN BRANDS	JOHNSON & JOHNSON
AMERICAN MOTORS	NABISCO BRANDS
AVIS	NESTLÉ
BLACK & DECKER	PEPSICO
BRITISH AIRWAYS	PROCTER & GAMBLE
BSN GERVAIS DANONE	PLAYTEX
CADBURY SCHWEPPES	ROWNTREE MACKINTOSH
CHESEBROUGH-POND'S	TIMEX
DU PONT	UNITED BISCUITS

This is pleasant for the business prospects of those agencies who can serve this global requirement, but leaves open one important question – whether this trend will result in *better* advertising? On this question opinions differ.

Some agency managers are fond of saying that they would rather operate a solid, disciplined international network than run the best creative agency in the world.

Meanwhile, others declare that they would rather have high creative standards than succumb to the arthritis of international management structures.

Both these viewpoints ignore the possibility of combining discipline and creativity in one international organisation. This is because it is hard to do.

IN 1982, OUR UK AGENCY WON MORE TOP UK ADVERTISING AWARDS THAN ALL THE OTHER MAJOR MULTINATIONAL AGENCIES PUT TOGETHER.

SOURCE: GOLD AND SILVER AWARDS IN THE CAMPAIGN PRESS AWARDS, D&AD AND BRITISH TELEVISION ADVERTISING AWARDS

The Company has always aimed to create the *our type of agency which has somehow eluded the grasp of those few men and women who have tried to achieve it –* a large agency, certainly, with all the stability that gives to employees, and all the back-up that provides for clients – but one which at the same time also succeeds in being progressive, youthful and innovative in approach.

The fact that this combination has so rarely been achieved in our industry increases the sense of purpose with which we continue to pursue it as our goal.

This has been the fundamental spur to our growth over the years.

HIGH CREATIVITY ACROSS A DISCIPLINED WORLD NETWORK. THE COMPANY'S CONSISTENT STRATEGIC GOAL.

Last month Saatchi & Saatchi Company PLC, the parent company of the worldwide agency network, announced its results for the year ended September 30th 1983. It was the Company's 13th successive year of profit growth. In the year pre-tax profits rose by 103%, earnings per share by 40%, dividends per share by 45%.

Over the last five years the Company has shown a compound average growth of 43% in pre-tax profits, 33% for earnings per share, and 37% for dividends per share.

If you would like a copy of the Chairman's Statement on these results please write to the Company Secretary, Saatchi & Saatchi Company PLC, at 80 Charlotte Street, London W1A 1AQ, or 625 Madison Avenue, New York, New York 10022.

SAATCHI & SAATCHI COMPTON WORLDWIDE.

dition, S&S noted a growing spillover of media across national borders, fueled by the development of satellite television. Given these trends and the increasing level of international travel, S&S viewed the concept of global brands employing the same advertising themes worldwide as increasingly plausible.

Following its appointment, S&S set up a Central Policy Unit (CPU) to plan and coordinate work on the worldwide BA account. This unit included a director aided by specialists in research, planning, and budgeting. Over a two-month period, the CPU developed into a complete account team, one section of which handled advertising in the U.K. and Europe, while the second handled advertising in the rest of the world. The account team included a creative group and a senior media director with international experience.

After winning the BA account, S&S had to resign its business with British Caledonian, Britain's principal private airline. This business amounted to £3.5 million in media billings in 1982. Three S&S offices in other countries had to resign competitive airline accounts. Of the 62 countries in which BA had country managers, S&S had wholly-owned agencies in 20 and partly-owned agencies in 17. In the remaining countries, S&S retained a local agency, in some cases an FCB affiliate, to continue to handle the BA account. S&S did not permit its overseas affiliates to collect commissions on locally placed media billings as compensation for working on the local BA account; rather, each affiliate received a fee or share of the commission for the services it performed from S&S headquarters in London. S&S billed BA headquarters for all of its services worldwide, except in the case of markets such as India where legal restrictions inhibited currency transactions of this nature.

The relationship between S&S affiliates and headquarters was closer than it had been when FCB handled the BA account. A BA country manager would work with the local S&S agency to develop an advertising copy proposal which would be submitted to BA headquarters in London on a standard briefing form. The BA headquarters advertising manager would then decide whether to approach the S&S account team in London to develop a finished advertisement to be sent back to the BA country manager. Under this system, neither BA country managers nor their local agencies were involved in the design of advertising copy except in terms of working requests, stating objectives, and suggesting content. According to S&S executives, the frequency with which certain types of advertisement were requested meant that it might, in the future, be possible to develop standard "ad mats." BA country managers and their local agencies would simply fill in the relevant destination and fare information of these ad mats, and would not have to submit them to London for approval.

The system described above varied somewhat from one country to another. BA country managers and their local agencies in the five most important long haul markets (United States, Canada, Australia, South Africa and Japan) had slightly more autonomy than their counterparts in less important markets. Although all advertising had to be approved in London prior to use, finished copy could be developed in the local market by the local agency in conjunction with the BA country manager.

An early example of how commercials might be developed for use in more than one country under the S&S approach occurred at the end of 1982. The U.S. country manager developed an advertising proposal for the "Inbound" line of package tours from the United

States to the U.K. Members of the U.S. agency creative team and BA executives from New York came to London to develop proposed scripts for the commercials. These were then approved by the U.S. country manager, but the commercials were shot in the U.K. so that British scenery could be included. These same commercials were subsequently used in South Africa and the Caribbean with different voiceovers; these countries' budgets could not be stretched to fund their independent production of television commercials of this quality.

Meanwhile, organization changes occurred at BA. Following the appointment of Colin Marshall as managing director in February 1983, the three divisions were replaced by eight geographic market centers which handled BA's basic passenger business and three additional business units handling cargo, air charter services, and package tours. These 11 profit centers reported to Marshall through Jim Harris, marketing director.[6] Harris also supervised a central marketing services staff involved with strategic planning, advertising, market analysis, and market research. An advertising manager who reported to the general manager for marketing services was responsible for agency relations and for the review and implementation of advertising by BA country managers. One of his assistants handled relations with the U.K. and European country managers; a second handled relations with the remaining country managers.

Under this new organization, BA country managers submitted their annual marketing plans, including proposed advertising and promotion budgets, to the appropriate market center manager in London. The country managers were informed in 1983 that their future budget proposals would have to provide detailed objectives and research support. In particular, country managers would have to forecast how their overall sales and profits would be impacted by particular advertising and promotion programs. The total advertising budget would be allocated among the country managers according to the quality of the proposals and according to which markets were designated for maintenance or development spending levels.

If a country manager required additional advertising funds during the fiscal year or wished to offer special consumer price deals and travel agency commissions above the norm applicable to the countries in that market center, the country manager could apply to the market center manager in London. The marketing director held a reserve fund to deal with such contingencies. He also reserved the right to reallocate funds designated for one market to another during the fiscal year if, for example, foreign currency fluctuations altered the attractiveness of one market versus another as a holiday destination.

DEVELOPMENT OF THE CONCEPT CAMPAIGN

The S&S creative team was charged with developing an advertising campaign which would restore BA's image and prestige, and not necessarily by focusing on specific BA products, services, and price promotions. The agency described the qualities of the ideal advertising concept for the campaign: "It had to be simple and single-minded, dramatic

---

[6]The marketing director performed the tasks previously undertaken by the commercial director. The latter title was no longer used.

and break new ground, instantly understood throughout the world, visual rather than verbal, long-lasting, likable, and confident." S&S executives believed that the type of product-feature-based advertising used by BA and traditional in the airline industry could not satisfy these objectives. First, an airline competitor could easily match any product-based claim BA might make. Second, such advertising only impacted that portion of the target market who viewed the benefit on which superiority was claimed (e.g., seat width) to be particularly important. The agency believed that only a brand concept campaign could focus consumers on the permanent and essential characteristics of BA which transcended changes in product, competitive activity, and other market variables.

The agency established five objectives for the worldwide BA concept campaign:

- To project BA as the worldwide leader in air travel.
- To establish BA as the world's most successful airline.
- To demonstrate the superiority of BA products.
- To add value in the eyes of passengers across the whole range of BA products.
- To develop a distinctive, contemporary, and fashionable style for the airline.

The account team had the benefit of consumer research which S&S had conducted in July 1982 with business and pleasure travelers in the U.K., United States, France, Germany, and Hong Kong to better understand attitudes towards, and preferences for, particular airlines. Based on these data, S&S executives concluded that consumers perceived most major airlines as similar on a wide array of dimensions. To the extent differences existed, BA was viewed as a large, experienced airline using modern equipment. However, BA was rated poorly on friendliness, in-flight service, value for money, and punctuality. In addition, BA's image varied widely among markets; it was good in the U.S., neutral in Germany, but weak in France and Hong Kong. The name of the airline and the lack of a strong image meant that consumer perceptions of its characteristics were often a reflection of their perceptions of Britain as a country.[7] BA was often the carrier of second choice after a consumer's national flag airline, particularly among consumers taking a vacation trip to the U.K.

By November 1982, BA had developed in rough form a series of 11 television commercials around the theme "The world's favorite airline." The lead commercial of the concept campaign, known as "Manhattan Landing,"[8] was to be 90 seconds long, with no voiceover during the first 40 seconds and with a total of only 35 words of announcer copy. It would show the island of Manhattan rotating slowly through the sky across the Atlantic to London, accompanied after 70 seconds by the statement that "every year, we fly more people across the Atlantic than the entire population of Manhattan."[9] Ten other

---

[7]In addition, some BA executives believed that BA was perceived more favorably in countries that had previously been served by BOAC than those previously served by BEA.

[8]The Manhattan Landing commercial was originally conceived as a corporate advertisement to be shown exclusively in the U.K. to support BA's privatization effort. When it became clear that the offering of BA stock to the public would be delayed until at least the end of 1984, it was decided to include it in the worldwide concept campaign.

[9]BA flew 1.5 million passengers across the Atlantic to the U.K. in 1982–83, more than Pan Am and TWA combined. The population of Manhattan was 1.4 million.

commercials known as the "preference" series showed individuals (from an Ingrid Bergman look-alike in Casablanca to members of a U.S. football team) receiving airline tickets and being disappointed to find that they were not booked on BA. International celebrities such as Peter O'Toole, Osmar Sharif, and Joan Collins were shown at the end of each commercial checking in for a BA flight. The announcer copy for all the preference commercials was identical. Storyboards for Manhattan Landing and one of the preference commercials are presented as Exhibits 5 and 6. The intention was to air these commercials in all BA markets worldwide, with changes only in the voiceovers.

In November, the BA board of directors approved production of Manhattan Landing and three of the preference commercials. Production costs for these four commercials were estimated at £1 million.[10] S&S executives were asked to have the finished commercials ready for launch by April 1983, a very tight schedule given the complexity of the executions.

While the commercials were being produced, members of the S&S account team and BA headquarters advertising executives traveled to each BA market. Their purpose was to introduce and explain the worldwide concept campaign at meetings attended by each BA country manager and his or her staff along with representatives of the local BA advertising agency. These visits occurred during January and February 1983, and involved the presentation of storyboards rather than finished commercials.

REACTIONS TO THE CONCEPT CAMPAIGN

Reactions varied. The concept campaign was well received in the United States, although the BA country manager was concerned about its dissimilarity from the existing Robert Morley campaign, which emphasized traditional British values. In India, there was some question as to whether Manhattan would hold any significance for the local audience. In other countries, including former British colonies, the claim "the world's favorite airline" was met with reactions such as "you must be joking!" The claim seemed to lack credibility, particularly in those markets where BA was in a relatively weak share position versus the national flag carrier. In other markets, such as France and Kuwait, only the state-owned airline was allowed to advertise on television, so the BA concept commercials could only be used in cinema advertising.

Questions about the proposed campaign were also raised by S&S affiliates. Since the parent agency had built its reputation on the importance of developing clear-cut positioning concepts, the proposed commercials seemed inconsistent with the philosophy of the agency. Even though the preference commercials were each planned to be 60-seconds long, some agency executives argued that they were too cluttered and tried to achieve too many objectives.

In particular, the 90-second Manhattan Landing commercial was greeted by some with amazement. One agency executive commented: "The net impact of three 30-second commercials would surely be greater?" The South African agency requested a 60-second version of the commercial because the South African Broadcasting Company would not

---

[10]Recent BA television commercials had cost about £75,000 to produce.

EXHIBIT 5   Manhattan Landing Storyboard

EXHIBIT 6   Casablanca Preference Campaign Storyboard

sell a 90-second piece of commercial time. S&S management had to decide whether to accommodate this request.

Other BA country managers were concerned that the concept campaign would reduce the funds available for local tactical advertising presenting fare and schedule information specific to their particular markets. One BA manager, after seeing the proposed campaign, commented, "Where are the smiling girls, the free cocktails, and the planes taking off into the sunset?" Another asked, "Will this campaign sell seats?" The BA proposal to spend half of the worldwide 1983–84 advertising budget of £26 million on the concept campaign meant that the amount available for local tactical advertising would fall from £19 million to £12 million. Preliminary BA concept and tactical advertising budgets for 14 representative countries are presented in Exhibit 7. Partly in response to the country managers' concerns, the total budget was raised to £31 million in April when BA's 1982–83 operating results were known. Forty percent of the new budget was allocated to the worldwide concept campaign, and 60 percent to tactical local market advertising.

Some country managers complained that their control over advertising would be reduced and that a corporate advertising expenditure in which they had no say would be charged against their profits. BA headquarters executives responded that while the country managers were required in 1983–84 to spend 40 percent of their budgets on the concept campaign, they were free to determine the media allocation of concept campaign expenditures in their markets and the weight of exposures given to each of the four executions. They were also free to spend more than 40 percent of their budgets on the concept campaign if they wished.

EXHIBIT 7 BA Concept and Tactical Advertising Budgets: Initial 1983–84 Plan (£000)

	Concept Campaign			Tactical Campaigns	Row Total
	April– September	October– March	Total		
United Kingdom	4,700	1,200	5,900	3,200	9,100
United States	2,600	750	3,350	2,450	5,800
Germany	450	450	900	607	1,507
Australia	500	100	600	350	950
France	150	200	350	269	619
Japan/Korea	200	70	270	400	670
Gulf States	0	35	35	190	225
Canada	900	200	1,100	400	1,500
South Africa	300	75	375	250	625
Italy	150	100	250	225	475
New Zealand	100	0	100	100	200
Egypt	50	0	50	30	80
Zimbabwe	32	0	32	25	57
Trinidad	18	0	18	27	45
Other	NA	NA	860	3,220*	4,080
Total	10,150	3,180	14,190	11,743	25,933

*Includes contingency fund.

Despite such concessions, the Japanese country manager remained adamantly opposed to adopting the concept campaign. On the London-Tokyo route, Japan Air Lines held a 60 percent market share compared to BA's 40 percent. Of the traffic on the route, 80 percent originated in Japan, and 80 percent of those on board BA flights were tourists on package tours. The Japanese country manager rejected the concept campaign as inappropriate. He presented market research evidence showing that his main challenge was selling Britain as a destination rather than developing consumer preference for BA.

THE APRIL 10 LAUNCH

Some S&S executives had hoped that BA would commit almost all of its 1983–84 advertising budget to the concept campaign. However, local marketing requirements highlighted by the country managers necessitated the continuation of tactical advertising, albeit at a reduced rate. The logo and slogan from the concept campaign were, however, to be incorporated in BA tactical advertising, and the requirement that tactical creative copy be developed by S&S in London ensured that this would be the case.

Despite all the reservations they had encountered, BA and S&S executives in London felt that they had sold the campaign effectively to most of the BA country managers. Thus, an invitation was mailed by Lord King to all BA employees in the U.K. to view the introductory television commercial on April 10. Videocassette copies of this six-minute commercial were mailed to BA offices around the world. BA country managers invited representatives of the travel industry to attend preview parties timed to coincide with the launch of the new concept campaign in their respective countries.

The campaign was launched in the U.K. on April 10 as planned and, within two weeks, was being aired in 20 countries. For two reasons, few country managers adopted a "wait and see" attitude. First, the marketing of package tours for the summer season had already started (in the Northern Hemisphere). Second, many country managers had exhausted their 1982–83 advertising budgets by the end of January, with the result that consumers had not been exposed to any BA advertising for several months.

THE CONCEPT CAMPAIGN IN THE UNITED STATES

The United States was one of the countries in which the concept campaign was launched on April 10. The BA country manager welcomed the campaign since consumer research indicated that BA's size was not recognized by most consumers in a country where, for many, bigger meant better. When asked to name the airline that carried the most passengers to the U.K., more respondents cited Pan Am and TWA than BA. The results of the survey, conducted in New York and Los Angeles in March 1983, also showed:

• Unaided awareness of BA as a leading international carrier was 41 percent in New York (Pan Am 85 percent; TWA 74 percent) and 33 percent in Los Angeles (Pan Am 76 percent; TWA 74 percent).

• Unaided recall of BA advertising was 21 percent in New York and 17 percent in Los Angeles.

- BA was mentioned as one of the three largest airlines in the world by 15 percent of New York respondents and 13 percent in Los Angeles.
- BA was mentioned as one of the three best international carriers by 11 percent of New York respondents and 9 percent in Los Angeles.

The BA country manager viewed the concept campaign as a means of addressing some of these deficiencies. Since the claim "the world's favorite airline" was well-documented, the U.S. country manager did not anticipate a legal challenge from Eastern Airlines, which used the slogan "America's favorite way to fly."

The media plan for the concept campaign (Exhibit 8) called for a combination of spot television in BA's six key gateway cities, national network television, and commercials on Cable News Network. The Manhattan Landing commercial was scheduled to be shown four times on national network television. Management argued that this would provide BA with exposure in important markets near gateway cities and would also excite the BA sales force and the travel industry. Four exposures were deemed sufficient given the commercial's creative originality. They would reach 45 percent of the U.S. adult population an average of 1.2 times.

The budget for the concept campaign from April to June was $4 million. Nevertheless, during this period, the BA country manager expected to be outspent by Pan Am and

---

EXHIBIT 8   Media Budget and Schedule of the British Airways Concept/Brand Campaign in the United States ($ millions)

	April–June 1983		September–October 1983	
	Number of Spots	Expenditures	Number of Spots	Expenditures
Spot television (in 6 gateway markets)*	686	$2,900	175	$572
Network television†	4	1,040	—	—
Cable television	40	104	25	58
Total	730	$4,044	200	$630
	Reach	*Frequency*	*Reach*	*Frequency*
Gateway cities	86%	8.7 times	63%	3.3 times
Remainder of United States	45%	1.2 times	—	—

Audience Composition	Percent of Those Reached	Index‡
Adult men	48%	102
Adult women	52%	99
Age 25–54	73%	137
Household income $30,000+	47%	169

*New York, Washington, Boston, Miami, Chicago, and Los Angeles.

†Only the Manhattan Landing execution was shown on network television. It was targeted at the 78 percent of U.S. households not reached by the spot television advertising.

‡Each index figure represents the percentage degree to which the audience reached included more or fewer people than the U.S. population at large.

TWA in BA gateway cities. In 1982–83, Pan Am and TWA advertising expenditures for domestic and international routes combined approximated $65 million and $50 million respectively.

In addition to the concept campaign, the BA country manager had also developed a business campaign and a leisure campaign for 1983–84:

Business Campaign. Recent consumer research indicated that Pan Am and TWA were perceived as superior to BA on attributes important to business flyers. BA advertising directed at business people had not significantly improved these perceptions (BA and TWA advertisements targeting the business traveler are presented as Exhibits 9 and 10). However, the perceptions of BA among its business passengers were much more positive than those of non-BA passengers, indicating significant customer satisfaction. BA's U.S. marketing director concluded that BA had a substantial opportunity to increase its share of the transatlantic business travel market.

The following three objectives were established for the 1983–84 business advertising campaign.

1. Increase awareness of the name "Super Club" as a service comparable to (or better than) TWA's Ambassador Class and Pan Am's Clipper Class.
2. Increase the business traveler's awareness and knowledge of the features of all three BA business travel services: Concorde, First Class, and Super Club.
3. Maximize the "halo" benefits of BA's Concorde in marketing efforts directed at First Class and Super Club consumers.

The media schedule for the business campaign (Exhibit 11) emphasized national magazines and both national and local newspapers. Magazines were selected which had higher-than-average percentages of readers in BA's gateway cities. Newspapers with strong business sections were given preference.

Leisure Campaign. BA advertising targeting the leisure traveler had traditionally focussed on BA's hotel, car rental, and package tour bargains. Despite high consumer recall of these "bolt-on" features, consumer perception research indicated that BA lagged its competitors on attributes such as "good value for money" and "good deal for leisure travelers." Accordingly, BA's advertising agency suggested that these bolt-on features be subordinated to the objective of creating a general impression of value for money through advertising an airfare bargain along with BA's expertise in things British.

The objectives for the 1983 summer campaign were:

1. Capitalize on BA's reputation as a marketer of good vacation buys, reinforcing consumers' willingness to arrange their European vacations with BA.
2. Promote awareness of and demand for BA's summer transatlantic leisure-oriented fare of $549 roundtrip.

A BA summer campaign newspaper advertisement and a Pan Am advertisement targeting the leisure traveler are reproduced as Exhibits 12 and 13. BA executives were planning on developing print advertisements targeting the leisure market which would mirror the commercials in the concept campaign if it proved successful.

EXHIBIT 9 BA Business Campaign Magazine Advertisement

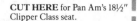

CUT HERE for Pan Am's 18½"
Clipper Class seat.

CUT HERE for TWA's 20⅞"
Ambassador Class seat.

WORLD'S WIDEST AIRLINE SEAT CUTS OTHER AIRLINES DOWN TO SIZE.

British Airways Super Club
When you're travelling on business, we offer you the widest seats in the air. We give you 24 inches between armrests — more room than TWA or Pan Am!* You'll always be next to an aisle or a window, and you have almost a foot of work space between you and the next passenger.

American Airlines AAdvantage Program
Show us your number at check-in and your flight miles on British Airways between the U.S. and London will count towards your AAdvantage travel award plan.

First Class Comfort
Lean back in luxury in our sumptuous First Class, with its sleeperseats and impeccable British service.

The Ultimate: Concorde
If you want to reach London in half the usual time, there's only one way — our Supersonic Concorde.

It's no wonder that British Airways fly more people to more countries than anyone else. After all, we're the World's Favourite Airline. Call your travel agent or corporate travel department.

British airways
The World's Favourite Airline™

*Measurements are inside armrest to inside armrest. British Airways has a few Super Club seats only 22" wide due to structural requirements. However, all Super Club seats are wider than our competitors'.

EXHIBIT 10   TWA Business Segment Magazine Advertisement

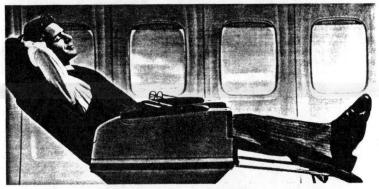

TWA.
Our First is foremost.

Only TWA has First Class Sleeper-Seats™ on every widebody.
For First Class comfort.

First and foremost, there are our First Class Sleeper-Seats.

They are available on every 747, every L-1011, and every 767, everywhere we fly in the U.S., Europe and the Middle East. So you can rest easy every time you fly TWA.

Just settle into a Sleeper-Seat, and you'll be impressed with its incredible comfort and legroom. Then settle back—the seat stretches out with you.

Royal Ambassador℠ Service.
First Class service in a class by itself.

TWA's Royal Ambassador Service is available on every transatlantic and transcontinental route we fly, as well as selected shorter domestic flights.

We offer a gourmet menu with a choice of entrees like Chateaubriand. Vintage wines from California and France. A selection of fine liqueurs and cognac. All cordially offered to you in a warm, personal manner.

We even cater to your needs before you take off. In major airports, you'll find a special First Class desk to speed you through check-in. And a special lounge for transatlantic passengers to relax in before flight time.

So call your travel agent, corporate travel department, or TWA.

Because for First Class service that's second to none, there's only one choice. TWA.

You're going to like us TWA

Source: *New York Magazine*, March 7, 1983.

EXHIBIT 11 Media Budget and Schedule of the British Airways Business Campaign in the United States ($ millions)

	December 1982–March 1983*		April–June 1983		September–October 1983	
	Number of Insertions	Expenditures	Number of Insertions	Expenditures	Number of Insertions	Expenditures
22 magazines	8	$121	30	$745	22	$674
3 newspapers†	9	563	13	371	17	276
	17	$684	43	$1,116	39	$950

Reach/Frequency: Men 25–54	Reach	Frequency	Reach	Frequency		
Gateway cities	73%	7.4 times	65%	5.4 times		
Remainder of United States	67%	6.3 times	55%	3.5 times		

Audience Composition	Percent Reach to Those Planning Foreign Travel for Business‡	Index
Adult men§	72%	147
Age 25–54	69	126
Attended/graduated college	64	197
Household income $35,000 +	55	284

*No insertions prior to February 1983.
†*The Wall Street Journal, New York Times, Los Angeles Times.*
‡Figures for December 1982 through June 1983.
§In 1982–83, about 10 percent of transatlantic business travelers were women.

The media schedule for the leisure campaign (Exhibit 14) emphasized spot television and the travel sections of local newspapers. Their late advertising deadlines meant that fare changes could be quickly communicated to consumers.

CONCLUSION

As BA and S&S executives implemented the worldwide concept campaign and the biggest advertising effort in BA history, they contemplated several issues. First, if awareness, recall, and sales data indicated that the campaign was not having the desired impact in a particular market, would BA headquarters permit the country manager to curtail the concept campaign? Second, if the campaign was successful, how long could it be sustained before becoming "tired?"

A third issue was how competitive airlines would respond to the BA concept campaign. Believing that the major carriers wished to avoid a new worldwide competitive price war, BA executives believed that they would adopt a "wait and see" attitude. However, market share losses would make retaliation inevitable, particularly in markets like the Far East where Singapore Airlines and Cathay Pacific held high market shares and were extremely price-competitive. In such a situation, should BA steadfastly continue to spend 40 percent of its advertising budget on the concept campaign, or should some of these funds be

EXHIBIT 12   BA Leisure Segment Print Advertisement

Great Britain Great Price

$549

round trip
(and only $18 a day for a hotel*)

With British Airways' fantastic fares and today's incredible dollar exchange rate, there's never been a better time to visit Britain. Plus, British Airways offers "London Hotel Bargains" including the modern, convenient Kennedy Hotel for only $18 per night (includes private bath and continental breakfast); the Regent Palace for $13 a day (without private bath but a stone's throw from Piccadilly); and "Britain Car Rental" offering a Ford Fiesta with unlimited mileage for only $17 a day. Call British Airways or your travel agent for more information on these and other great deals now!

"Good show"

British airways

Airfare valid for travel through September 14. Tickets must be purchased 21 days in advance. Minimum stay 7 days. Maximum stay 6 months. There is a weekend surcharge. Car and hotel rates valid through October 31. Petrol and tax not included with car.
*Hotel rates per person, double occupancy and include VAT and tax.

British Airways, P.O. Box 10010,
Dept. HT, Long Island City, NY 11101
Dear Mr. Morley:
Please send me the following brochures:
☐ DollarSaver™ Holidays in London
☐ Fly Drive Holidays in Britain

Name _____

Address _____

City _____

State _____ Zip _____

EXHIBIT 13 Pan Am Leisure Segment Print Advertisement

EXHIBIT 14   Media Budget and Schedule of the British Airways Leisure Campaign in the United States ($ millions)

	December 1982–March 1983		April–June 1983		September–October 1983	
	Number of Spots, Insertions	Expenditures	Number of Spots, Insertions	Expenditures	Number of Spots, Insertions	Expenditures
Spot television (10 markets)	—	—	450	$795	—	—
Local newspapers (11 markets)	3–4/market	$641	3–7/market	620	4–6/market	$550
	Reach	Frequency	Reach	Frequency	Reach	Frequency
Average market	40%	2.0 times	75%	5.0 times	47%	2.9 times

Audience Composition	Percent Reach to Those Planning a Foreign Vacation	Index
Adult men	45%	96
Adult women	55%	105
Age 25–54	60%	114
Household income $30,000+	49%	175

diverted to tactical advertising in particular local markets? The probability of such diversion of funds depended partly on the emerging profit picture during the fiscal year and partly on the level of unspent tactical advertising funds. It was, therefore, more likely to become an issue towards the end of the fiscal year.

A further related issue was the appropriate budget split between the concept campaign and tactical advertising in 1984–85. Some BA executives argued that if the concept campaign were successful, it would be possible to reduce expenditures on the campaign to a maintenance level and proportionately restore tactical advertising. They maintained that such a move would shift control of the advertising budget from S&S back to BA. But agency executives argued strongly that the concept campaign should be centrally administered from BA headquarters and that expenditures on the campaign in each country should not, unlike tactical advertising, be regarded as a route operating cost. They also argued that the concept campaign was essential to BA's long-term effectiveness and should not be sacrificed to short-term operational requirements.

Advertising, Branding, and Positioning

Case 2–1

The Black & Decker Corporation Household Products Group: Brand Transition*

In April 1984, Black & Decker Corporation (B&D) acquired the Housewares Division of General Electric Company (GE), combining the GE small-appliance product line with its own household product line to form the Household Products Group. The terms of the acquisition set the stage for a unique marketing challenge. B&D was permitted to manufacture and market appliances carrying the GE name, but only until April 1987. During the intervening three years, B&D would have to replace the GE name on all the acquired models with its own brand name.

Immediately after the acquisition, Kenneth Homa, B&D's vice president of marketing, was assigned responsibility for the brand transition. Homa had to design a marketing program to transfer the B&D name to the GE small-appliance lines without losing market share. Specifically, he had to determine the timing for the transition of the various GE product lines and the roles that advertising and promotion should play in the transition. Homa had been asked to have the proposal for the brand transition completed by June 1—only a week away. Before he began to formulate the proposal, Homa reviewed the acquisition and the challenges it presented.

THE ACQUISITION

With 1983 sales of $1,167 million, B&D was the leading worldwide manufacturer of professional and consumer hand-held power tools. Over 100 products were produced in 21 factories around the world. By the late 1970s, B&D was confronting two important problems—a slower growth rate for the power tool market worldwide, together with increasing foreign competition. At the same time, management realized that the American housewares market presented a significant opportunity. Capitalizing on its expertise in

*Research Assistant Cynthia Bates prepared this case under the supervision of Professor John A. Quelch as the basis for class discussion rather than to illustrate either effective or ineffective handling of an administrative situation. Professor Minette E. Drumwright prepared this version of the case. Proprietary data have been disguised. Copyright © 1987 by the President and Fellows of Harvard College. Harvard Business School case 9–588–015.

small-motor production[1] and cordless appliance technology, B&D introduced the Dust-buster®, a rechargeable hand-held vacuum cleaner, in 1979. The Dustbuster Vac "moved B&D from the garage into the house"; 60 percent of Dustbuster purchases were made by women. The Dustbuster's success prompted the launch of two other rechargeable products, the Spotliter™ rechargeable flashlight and the Scrub Brusher™ cordless scrubber. In 1983, these three products generated revenues of over $100 million, almost one-third of B&D's U.S. consumer product sales. Pretax profit margins on these products were estimated at a healthy 10 percent. Sales of the three products were expected to increase by 30 percent annually between 1983 and 1985.

Consumer demand for these three innovative products led B&D executives to conclude that further penetration of the housewares market could generate substantial sales and profits for the company. They resolved to develop a family of products that could address consumer needs "everywhere in the house, not just in the basement or garage." However, a significant impediment to growth was B&D's limited access to housewares buyers in the major retail chains. B&D's three housewares products, along with B&D's power tools, were sold through hardware distributors to hardware buyers and were typically stocked in the hardware sections of retail stores. B&D sought to gain access to housewares buyers through the acquisition of a competitor, the GE Housewares Division.

With 1983 sales of $500 million (GE's total sales in 1983 were $26.79 billion), GE's Housewares Division was the largest competitor in the U.S. electric housewares or small-appliance market. (GE sales of small appliances outside the United States were limited. By contrast, 40 percent of B&D's total sales were made in Europe.) GE sold almost 150 models of products in 14 categories covering food preparation, ovening, garment care, personal care, and home security. (The categories were food processors, portable mixers, electric knives, can openers, drip coffee makers, toaster ovens, toasters, electric skillets, grills and griddles, irons, hair dryers, curling brushes/irons, scales, and security alarms.) In all the appliance categories in which it competed—except food processors, hair care products, and toasters—GE ranked first or second in market share. GE's success largely resulted from continuing attention to product innovation. For example, the GE product line included the recently introduced Spacemaker™ series of premium-priced under-the-cabinet kitchen appliances. The division's 150-person sales force called on housewares buyers in all channels of distribution.

Discussions between GE and B&D culminated in an agreement, announced in February 1984, whereby B&D would acquire the GE Housewares Division for $300 million, comprising $110 million in cash, a $32 million three-year note, and 6 percent of B&D stock. In return, B&D acquired seven plants in the United States, Mexico, Brazil, and Singapore; five distribution centers; 16 service centers; and the Housewares Division's sales and management team. GE retained rights to the accounts receivable at the time of the transfer. Finally, B&D negotiated the right to continue to use the GE name on appliances in the Housewares Division product line for three years from the signing of the acquisition papers in April 1984. However, B&D could not use the GE name on any new appliances introduced after the acquisition. At a stroke, the acquisition transformed

---

[1]In 1983, B&D produced 20 million small motors, four times as many as its closest competitor.

B&D from a specialist housewares manufacturer into the dominant full-line player in the housewares market.

THE HOUSEWARES MARKET

Product Lines and Pricing

After acquiring the GE division, B&D participated in five more broad housewares categories with aggregate industry sales of $1.4 billion divided as follows:

Food preparation	$275 million
Beverage makers	$325
Ovening	$250
Garment care	$200
Personal care	$350

The housewares market was mature and fragmented. Industry growth depended primarily on the rate of household formation and the pace of new product development. About one-tenth of all small appliances in use were replaced each year. The timing of replacement purchases could be accelerated if manufacturers could persuade consumers to trade up to more highly featured, higher-priced, higher-margin models of a particular appliance.

The new B&D offered one of the broadest lines of any manufacturer, competing in 17 product groups. Market performance data for the principal product lines are summarized in Exhibit 1. In all these groups, B&D marketed multiple models that covered almost all price points and product feature configurations. For example, the B&D line included 18 different irons with suggested retail prices from $14.76 to $25.89. The range included promotional, step-up, and premium models. Proctor-Silex, B&D's closest competitor in this category, offered 12 models.

B&D's models were priced competitively within each price/feature segment but, overall, B&D's share tended to be stronger in the medium and upper rather than the lower price ranges. In the fall of 1984, the average retail price of a B&D small appliance was 16 percent higher than the average retail price of its competitors' appliances. The B&D retail price premium varied across product categories as follows:

Food preparation	8%	Cleaning (Dustbuster, Scrub Brusher)	10%
Ovening	26	Lighting (Spotliter)	6
Garment care	5	Smoke alarms	9
Personal care	16		

Some B&D executives were concerned that the price premium in certain categories left B&D vulnerable to lower-priced competition. They advocated price decreases on some models for 1985. Other executives, noting that B&D/GE housewares prices had

EXHIBIT 1   Market Performance Summary for Selected Product Lines

Product	Year	GE/B&D Unit Share	Feature Ad Share	Average Retail Price	GE/B&D Share Rank in 1984	Major Competitors	(Share and Rank)	
Food processors	1983	16%	9%	$55.00	3	Cuisinart	25%	(1)
	1984	13	7	72.00		Hamilton Beach	21	(2)
	1985*	15	8	NA		Moulinex	11	(4)
						Sunbeam	7	(5)
Mixers	1983	31	22	16.00	2	Sunbeam	28	(1)
	1984	26	20	15.40		Hamilton Beach	21	(3)
	1985*	35	16	NA				
Can openers	1983	28	25	17.65	1	Rival	30	(2)
	1984	34	23	20.52		Sunbeam	8	(3)
	1985*	30	26	NA		Hamilton Beach	6	(4)
Toasters	1983	13	16	16.63	3	Toastmaster	32	(1)
	1984	12	10	21.01		Proctor-Silex	30	(2)
	1985*	11	10	NA				
Toaster ovens	1983	56	49	45.51	1	Toastmaster	25	(2)
	1984	52	39	47.85		Proctor-Silex	8	(3)
	1985*	50	40	NA		Norelco	4	(4)
Drip coffee makers	1983	17	13	34.48	2	Mr. Coffee	19	(1)
	1984	18	15	37.63		Norelco	17	(3)
	1985*	17	16	NA		Hamilton Beach	9	(4)
						Proctor-Silex	8	(5)
Electric knives	1983	39	NA	13.54	2	Hamilton Beach	47	(1)
	1984	37	NA	17.28		Moulinex	8	(3)
	1985*	39	NA	17.65				
Irons	1983	52	39	20.44	1	Proctor-Silex	18	(2)
	1984	46	29	21.83		Sunbeam	13	(3)
	1985*	45	29	NA		Hamilton Beach	11	(4)
Hair care	1983	8	8	17.74	4	Conair	22	(1)
	1984	6	4	15.37		Clairol	12	(2)
	1985*	5	3	NA		Sassoon	8	(3)
Cordless vacuums	1983	NA	NA	NA		Douglas	8	(2)
	1984	NA	38	NA	1	Sears	8	(2)
	1985*	NA	38	25.70		Norelco	7	(4)
Lighting products	1983	65	NA	NA	1	First Alert	25	(2)
	1984	57	44	NA		Sunspot	5	(3)
	1985*	38	36	21.10		Norelco	4	(4)

Note: NA means not available.
*Figures for 1985 are estimated.

increased on average by only 10 percent between 1980 and 1984, believed that price increases were necessary to maintain margins. (The contribution margin on B&D small appliances, after variable costs, averaged 40 percent. The percentage margin was higher on premium models such as the Spacemaker products.) However, all agreed that, despite B&D's share leadership position, competitive brands did not appear to set their prices in relation to B&D's prices.

B&D's price premium in the food preparation category was largely due to the premium-priced Spacemaker line of under-the-cabinet kitchen appliances. Launched in 1982 with a can opener, the Spacemaker line was expanded in 1983 to include a toaster oven, drip coffee maker, mixer, and electric knife. The Spacemaker line attracted some first-time purchasers into these five categories but, more important, persuaded current owners to trade up. Although the Spacemaker line at first reversed GE's share erosion in these categories, lower-priced imitations soon appeared. GE's standard countertop version of the Spacemaker appliances lost share as GE's competitors slashed prices to maintain their sales volumes in countertop models. Nevertheless, Spacemaker models were expected to account for about 40 percent of B&D's 1984 unit sales in the five product categories in which they competed.

Competition

B&D's principal competitors in the housewares market were Sunbeam (a subsidiary of Allegheny International), Proctor-Silex (Westray), Hamilton Beach (Scovill), and Norelco (Philips). Few offered as broad a line as B&D, but all four competed with B&D in at least six categories. In addition, B&D had to contend with specialist competitors in each product category. For example, Cuisinart was the market share leader in food processors as was Mr. Coffee in drip coffee makers. European manufacturers, such as Krups, were increasingly penetrating and helping to expand the premium-price segment in some categories. Their higher-margin products were welcomed by department stores that sought to continue to compete with mass merchandisers in housewares. Japanese manufacturers were not a factor in the U.S. small-appliance market except for dual-voltage travel irons.

Following the acquisition announcement, B&D's housewares competitors saw the imminent demise of the strongest brand name in the housewares market (i.e., GE) as an opportunity to increase their market shares. Hence, prices on some existing models were reduced; price increases announced for 1985 were minimal, and promotion and merchandising allowances escalated. The timing of new product introductions accelerated and, in some instances, manufacturers decided to enter new product categories. Norelco and West Bend, for example, both announced that they would launch a line of irons.

Sunbeam was especially aggressive and heavily advertised two new products in the fall of 1984: the Monitor automatic shut-off iron and the Oskar compact food processor. Both were introduced at premium rather than penetration price levels. In addition, Sunbeam announced a $43 million marketing budget for 1985, including $25 million for national advertising, $10 million for cooperative advertising, and $8 million for sales promotion. The 1985 budget was more than Sunbeam had spent in the previous five years combined. Some analysts doubted that Sunbeam would follow through with this level of spending, however.

Besides GE's long-standing competitors, B&D also had to contend with imitators of its cordless vacuums and lights. Believing that the newly acquired product lines would divert B&D's management attention and resources, these imitators redoubled their efforts to capture more market share.

Distribution

Small electric appliances were distributed through various channels. Table A shows the percentages of industry dollar sales accounted for by each of seven channels.

Mass merchandisers, such as Montgomery Ward, and discount stores, such as Kmart, had gained share in recent years, mainly at the expense of department stores. Catalog showrooms, such as Service Merchandise, carried the broadest line of small appliances, whereas other channels tended to cherrypick the faster-moving items. GE had built a disproportionately strong share position with volume retailers, notably catalog showrooms and mass merchandisers. B&D was traditionally strong in hardware stores. In the fall of 1984, B&D accounts carried, on average, 30 B&D stockkeeping units (SKUs). (An SKU is an individual model or item in the product line.)

Most retailers did not view small appliances as especially profitable. Retail margins averaged 15 to 20 percent, though promotional merchandise was typically sold near cost. Hence, the space allocated to housewares by most chains remained stable, despite an increasing proliferation of new products. As a result, manufacturers were under more pressure than ever to secure shelf space through merchandising and promotion incentives.

Housewares and hardware buyers at B&D's major accounts determined twice a year which models they would specify as "basics." These selected models were carried in distribution for the following six months, usually in all the stores of a chain. Other models not specified as basics might occasionally be stocked, but only in response to temporary promotion offers.

TABLE A   Breakdown of Percent of Industry Dollar Sales by Channel

Catalog showrooms	15%
Mass merchandisers	28
Department stores	9
Drug stores	6
Hardware stores	5
Discount stores	8
Other*	29
Total	100%

*Includes sales through stamp and incentive programs, premiums, and military sales.

Basics were typically specified in January and May. Retail sales of small appliances peaked before Mother's Day and Christmas. Twenty-one percent of retail sales occurred in the first calendar quarter, 21 percent in the second, 17 percent in the third, and 41 percent in the fourth. Manufacturers and retailers scheduled their advertising and promotion efforts accordingly.

Consumer Behavior

Consumers shopping for small appliances were often characterized as having low information needs, low perceived interbrand differentiation, and high price sensitivity. A 1984 B&D survey drew the following conclusions:

- Two out of three consumers bought their last housewares appliance on sale and/or with a rebate. The highest percentages bought on sale were the countertop drip coffee makers, mixers, and can openers.
- Two out of three consumers compared the prices of different brands and checked to see which brands were on sale.
- Fewer than one out of three consumers would wait until a specific brand went on sale.
- Almost three out of four consumers were willing to switch from their current brands when they purchased replacements. However, fewer than one out of four consumers were indifferent to brand names.

A follow-up study of buying behavior for irons found that most consumers, when they needed a replacement, would not wait for a sale but would check to see if a store was having a sale. Fifty percent bought a replacement within seven days. Only 10 percent of the irons were bought as gifts. Forty-two percent of the purchasers had a specific brand in mind when they set off for the store, and 85 percent ended up buying that brand. Thirty-eight percent were attracted to a particular store by its advertisement, and most bought at the first store in which they shopped. Half of all purchasers bought their irons on sale and/or with a rebate.

PLANNING THE BRAND TRANSITION

Consumer Research

To aid transition planning, B&D surveyed 600 men and women 18 to 49 years old in four geographically representative cities during July 1984. The survey first probed consumers' awareness of 10 housewares manufacturers, their ownership of small appliances by each manufacturer, and the degree to which their overall image ratings of each manufacturer were favorable or unfavorable. These results are summarized in Exhibit 2.

Next, respondents were asked to rate each manufacturer on various attributes using a 100-point scale. Averaging all responses, the researchers identified B&D's strengths and

EXHIBIT 2   Consumer Research on Major Housewares Manufacturers

	Aided Corporate Awareness	Product Ownership	Corporate Image Ranking	
			Men	Women
General Electric	100%	91%	2	1
Black & Decker	99	67	1	2
Mr. Coffee	99	51	4	5
Conair	79	43	9	8
Hamilton Beach	93	43	5	6
Norelco	98	54	3	4
Proctor-Silex	80	28	8	7
Rival	56	19	10	10
Sunbeam	96	48	6	3
Toastmaster	92	41	7	9

weaknesses compared with its main housewares competitors (GE excluded) and then with GE (see Table B).

The survey asked respondents whether they currently perceived B&D favorably or unfavorably as a manufacturer of each of 16 products. The percentages answering "very favorably" on a four-point scale were as follows:

Smoke alarms	62%
Flashlights	60
Vacuums	48
Grills/griddles	29
Electric knives	25
Can openers	24
Scales	22
Toaster ovens	21
Irons	18
Portable mixers	17
Toasters	17
Food processors	16
Coffee makers	13
Skillets	12
Curling irons	11
Hair dryers	9

Qualitative research indicated that consumers considered B&D a suitable manufacturer of these products but were largely unaware that B&D already made them.

TABLE B   B&D's Strengths and Weaknesses

	B&D Advantage vs. Closest Competitor[a]	B&D (Dis)Advantage vs. GE
B&D Strengths		
Has high-quality workmanship	+24	+5
Makes durable products	+23	+4
Makes reliable products	+20	+1
Leader in making innovative products	+18	(7)
B&D Vulnerabilities		
Makes products that can be easily serviced	+7	(17)
Makes products most people would consider buying	+7	(12)
Makes attractive, good-looking products	+6	(8)
Makes products that are generally priced lower	+5	(9)
Makes products that are easily found	+2	(9)

[a]Other than GE.

Product Plans

Homa knew that B&D executives disagreed concerning both the timing and the manner in which the B&D name should be transferred to the GE small-appliance line. In talking with other executives, he had identified five points of view.

One group of executives argued that the name change should be executed across the entire product line as soon as possible to demonstrate B&D's commitment to the trade. At the other extreme, a second group, skeptical about the likely pulling power of the B&D brand in housewares, proposed that B&D delay the name transfer until the end of the three-year period.

A third group of executives supported a gradual transition whereby all the items in one or two product categories would be reintroduced under the B&D name in successive six-month periods. A fourth group wanted to execute the name change first on the premium quality items in several product categories to be followed later by the remaining lower-priced items in each product line. A fifth group argued that the transition schedule should be linked to a new product development program. Through such a program, the name change would be implemented in a product category only after the product line and packaging had been redesigned and/or when B&D could offer a new product with enhanced features.

As he planned the transition program, Homa also had to consider proposals for new or revised products that B&D product managers had submitted. The proposals included the following:

- The Spacemaker line of under-the-cabinet appliances, which had been acquired from GE, could be redesigned by B&D to look sturdier and more compact. The edges could be rounded for additional safety.

- B&D could develop Black Tie™, a line of "men's grooming tools," which would be priced at a 15 percent premium over the hair care line acquired from GE.
- Plans had been developed for the Stowaway line of dual-voltage travel appliances. The line would include a folding iron, hair dryer, and curling irons.
- The Handymixer cordless beater, the first extension of B&D's cordless technology into the kitchen, had been proposed.
- An automatic shut-off iron had been designed by B&D. Unlike the Sunbeam model, the B&D iron would beep to let the consumer know that it had been left on.

Communications

An effective communications plan would be integral to the brand transition. Historically, B&D and GE had implemented communications programs with fundamental differences. Specifically, GE had emphasized push programs (e.g., volume rebates, purchase

EXHIBIT 3   Advertising and Merchandising Expenditures for GE Housewares (in millions of dollars and percentage of net sales billed)

	1983		1984		1985[a]	
	Expense (millions)	Percent of Sales	Expense (millions)	Percent of Sales	Expense (millions)	Percent of Sales
Push Programs						
Purchase allowances	$17.5	3.5%	$22.5	4.5%	—	—
Volume rebates	14.0	2.8%	14.5	2.9%	$ 12.5	2.5%
Cash discounts	—	—	—	—	—	—
Subtotal	$31.5	6.3%	$37.0	7.4%	$ 12.5	2.5%
Pull Programs						
National advertising	$ 8.5	1.7%	$16.5	3.3%	$ 34.0	6.8%
Co-op advertising	26.0	5.2	25.5	5.1	32.0	6.4
Consumer rebates	13.0	2.6	9.5	1.9	15.0	3.0
Consumer promotions	1.5	0.3	1.0	0.2	0.5	0.1
Sales promotion materials	3.0	0.6	1.5	0.3	3.5	0.7
Press relations	1.0	0.2	1.0	0.2	1.0	0.2
Exhibits	1.0	0.2	1.0	0.2	1.0	0.2
Functional support expenses	1.5	0.3	1.5	0.3	2.0	0.4
Corporate promotion assessment	—	—	—	—	—	—
In-store merchandising	—	—	—	—	3.5	0.7
Subtotal	55.5	11.1	57.5	11.5	92.5	18.5
Total merchandising expenditures	$87.0	17.4%	$94.5	18.9%	$105.0	21.0%

Note: 1984 and 1985 figures continue to separate the former GE housewares line from the former B&D household products line for ease of comparison. Total 1985 B&D Household Products Group expenditures can be calculated by summing the last columns in Exhibits 3 and 4.
[a]Estimated

EXHIBIT 4   Advertising and Merchandising Expenditures for Black & Decker Household Products (in millions of dollars and percentage of net sales billed)

	1983		1984		1985[a]	
	Expense (millions)	Percent of Sales	Expense (millions)	Percent of Sales	Expense (millions)	Percent of Sales
Push Programs						
Flexible funds (off-invoice)	—	—	—	—	—	—
Retail incentive plan	—	—	—	—	$ 1.0	0.6%
Cash discounts	$ 0.9	0.9%	$ 1.2	0.9%	1.5	0.9
Subtotal	$ 0.9	0.9	$ 1.2	0.9	$ 2.5	1.5
Pull Programs						
National advertising	$ 8.9	8.9	$12.0	9.2	$18.6	11.0
Co-op advertising	2.0	2.0	3.1	2.4	7.3	4.3
Consumer rebates	—	—	2.2	1.7	11.7	6.9
Consumer promotions	—	—	—	—	—	—
Sales promotion materials	0.5	0.5	1.6	1.2	1.4	0.8
Press relations	—	—	—	—	—	—
Exhibits	—	—	0.1	0.1	0.3	0.2
Functional support expenses	—	—	0.1	0.1	0.3	0.2
Corporate promotion assessment	—	—	1.0	0.8	2.0	1.2
In-store merchandising	—	—	—	—	—	—
Subtotal	11.4	11.4	20.1	15.5	41.6	24.6
Total merchandising expenditures	$12.3	12.3%	$21.3	16.4%	$44.1	26.1%

Note: B&D household products: Dustbuster Vac, Spotliter, and Scrub Brusher.
[a]Estimated

allowances) which were aimed at the trade, while B&D had emphasized pull programs (e.g., advertising, consumer rebates) which targeted consumers. These differences are reflected in Exhibits 3 and 4, which summarize the advertising and promotion expenditures for GE and B&D before the acquisition. Homa's tentative recommendations for 1985 communications expenditures also are included in Exhibits 3 and 4.

Advertising

Increased advertising expenditures would be necessary to bolster consumer brand loyalties in the face of more aggressive competition. Homa estimated that media expenditures of $100 million would be needed for the brand transition.

The issue of how to handle the brand transition in advertising was much debated. Some executives believed that explicit references to GE in B&D's advertising were necessary to maintain market share during the transition, especially in categories where GE's brand name equity was strong. These executives wanted a transition statement such as "designed by GE, built by B&D" to be included in advertising. They also wanted hang tags on

EXHIBIT 5 Proposed 1985 Spacemaker Advertisement

(SFX: TRAFFIC)
ANNCR: (VO) One of the most densely
populated places on earth

is your kitchen counter. So crowded, the
only place to go is up.

Presenting Black & Decker Spacemaker
Appliances.

Coffeemaker,

mixer,

toaster oven,

electric knife

and can opener. The only completely
coordinated line of under-the-cabinet
appliances.

(SFX: BIRDS CHIRPING)
They return your counter

to a more natural state.

The Spacemaker line

from Black & Decker. Ideas at work.

EXHIBIT 6   Proposed 1985 Spotliter Advertisement

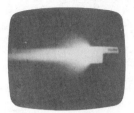

(SFX: Electronic High Tension)
ANNCR: (VO) It splits the dark with a
powerful beam.

Spotliter rechargeable light from
Black & Decker.

A light built so strong

it can survive a drop of 6 feet.

Spotliter stores all the power you need in
its own recharging base.

So on a moment's notice

it gives you light.

Light for your safety. . .and peace of
mind.

It's one utility light that does more than
just shine.

Spotliter.

One of the many lights

in the lighting series. From Black &
Decker. Ideas at work.

B&D products at the point of sale to indicate that the products had formerly been made by GE. Critics of this dual-branding approach, which included B&D's advertising agency, argued that it would confuse consumers and simply sustain the GE franchise. Exhibits 5 and 6 present television advertisements proposed by B&D's advertising agency.

Promotional Programs

Homa had to determine whether or not to maintain GE's more generous support of promotional programs. Some trade accounts already had expressed concern about potential cutbacks that B&D might implement. Competitive housewares manufacturers did all they could to cultivate this concern in an effort to secure additional basics listings and shelf space for their own products.

At the time of the acquisition, GE's promotional programs for the trade included purchase allowances, volume rebates, dating discounts, and cooperative advertising. Promotional programs for consumers focused on consumer rebates.

Purchase Allowances.   During the 1970s, GE initiated purchase allowances (PAs) on selected models against orders paid for during the first two months after Christmas and Mother's Day, the peak retail selling periods. Over time, PAs came to be offered on orders placed beyond these two-month periods. By 1983, 90 percent of shipments included an off-invoice PA.

Volume Rebates.   GE operated a volume rebate program that offered trade accounts a year-end refund of up to $4\frac{1}{2}$ percent of their net purchases during the year. Accounts qualified for various percentage rebates according to the degree to which their purchases increased over those of the previous year. There were two other features of the program. First, the rebates were computed on an account's total purchases rather than separately for each shipping point. Second, the program attempted to maintain the total number of SKUs by requiring a dealer to have incremental sales in four of six defined product categories to earn the minimum rebate.

Dating Discounts.   Dating allowed customers to pay for goods after they were shipped and received. Dating encouraged trade accounts to place early orders for goods that they did not have to pay for immediately. The seasonality of retail sales and the desire of trade accounts to avoid holding high bulk-to-value small appliances in their own ware-houses made dating programs a necessity in the small-appliance industry. Production planning and scheduling could become more efficient if a trade account placed early orders at the same time that it decided which SKUs to specify for its basics lineup.

GE Housewares Division's standard terms required full payment by the 10th of the month following an order, plus 45 days. The dating program permitted an account to place an order in May and June for shipment before September 1 and payment by December 10. A second dating program required payment by May 10 on orders placed in December and January. A schedule of early-payment allowances rewarded accounts for payment of invoices before the dating program due date. GE's purchase allowance and dating programs together permitted accounts to pay less and pay later.

Cooperative Advertising.   GE's Housewares Division had long offered trade accounts a cooperative advertising program. Accounts accrued 3 percent of their net purchases in a rolling 12-month cooperative advertising fund. (Allowances accrued more than 12 months previously that had not been spent were forfeited.) Accounts could draw on these accruals to subsidize the cost of retail advertising that featured GE products. GE paid the full cost of qualifying advertising but sometimes only partially charged accounts' accrual funds if they featured particularly profitable premium-priced products such as items in the Spacemaker line, if they ran advertisements featuring multiple GE items, or if they timed their advertising to coincide with flights of GE national advertising.

Consumer Rebates.   Initiated in the 1970s to help sell slower-moving models, consumer rebates had become endemic to the housewares category by the early 1980s. By 1983, almost all list price increases were cushioned with rebates, and three-quarters of all feature advertisements for GE housewares included references to manufacturer rebate offers. The average value of housewares manufacturers' consumer rebates escalated as each tried to outdo the other. In an effort to lead the industry toward more realistic list pricing, GE in 1983 curtailed rebates on irons and toaster ovens, two categories in which it was the market share leader. Far from following GE's lead, competitors increased their rebate offers. As a result, GE's share declined six points in both categories within six months.

Conclusion

Homa had two main concerns. How could the B&D brand name be transferred most effectively to the GE small-appliance line? What kind of communications program would facilitate the transfer?

Case 2–2

Procter & Gamble Company (A)*

In November 1981, Chris Wright, associate advertising manager of the Packaged Soap & Detergent Division (PS&D) of the Procter & Gamble Company (P&G), was evaluating how the division could increase the volume of its light-duty liquid detergents (LDLs).[1]

---

*Research Associate Alice MacDonald Court prepared this case under the direction of Professor John A. Quelch as the basis for class discussion rather than to illustrate either effective or ineffective handling of an administrative situation. Names and proprietary data have been disguised, but all essential relationships have been preserved.

Copyright © 1983 by the President and Fellows of Harvard College. Harvard Business School case 9–584–047.

[1]LDLs are defined as all mild liquid soaps and detergents designed primarily for washing dishes.

The excellent growth of Dawn dishwashing liquid since its national introduction in 1976 meant that P&G now manufactured and sold three leading LDL brands, holding a 42 percent share (by weight) of the industry's $850 million in factory sales.

Based on input from the three LDL brand managers who reported to him, as well as his own knowledge of the LDL category, Wright believed there were three major opportunities for volume growth: (1) the introduction of a new brand, (2) a product improvement on an existing brand, and/or (3) increased marketing expenditures on existing brands. In preparation for an upcoming meeting with Bruce Demill, PS&D advertising manager, Wright began evaluating the volume and profit potential of the three options.

COMPANY BACKGROUND

In 1837, William Procter and James Gamble formed a partnership in Cincinnati, Ohio, so that they could buy more efficiently the animal fats essential to the manufacture of their respective products—candles and soaps. The Procter & Gamble Company emerged from this partnership and quickly gained a reputation as a highly principled manufacturer of quality goods. As James Gamble said: "If you cannot make pure goods and full weight, go to something else that is honest, even if it is breaking stone."

In 1890 the Procter & Gamble Company was incorporated with a capital stock value of $4,500,000. This capital allowed P&G to build additional plants, buy new equipment, and develop and introduce new products. Sales volume more than doubled every 10 years following incorporation, largely as a result of new-product introductions. By 1981, P&G operated in 26 countries and sales totaled $11.4 billion, of which 70 percent were made in the United States (see Exhibit 1). P&G manufactured 90 consumer and industrial products in the United States and sold the leading brand in 14 of the 24 consumer-product categories in which the company competed (see Exhibit 2). One or more of P&G's products were used in 95 percent of U.S. homes—a penetration unequaled by any other manufacturer. P&G had historically grown both by developing products internally and by acquiring companies to which P&G's technological expertise was applied.[2]

P&G executives attributed the company's success in the marketplace to a variety of factors: (1) dedicated and talented human resources, (2) a reputation for honesty that won the trust and respect of its suppliers and customers, (3) prudent and conservative management that encouraged thorough analysis prior to decision making, (4) innovative products offering superior benefits at competitive prices, and (5) substantial marketing expertise. The following quotes from company executives and outside analysts emphasize these factors:

> *If you leave the company [P&G] its money, its buildings and its brands, but take away its people, the business will be in real jeopardy; but, if you take away the money, the buildings*

---

[2]P&G acquired the Duncan Hines Companies (prepared cake, cookie, and muffin mixes) in 1956; Charmin Paper Mills (toilet and facial tissues, paper towels, and paper napkins) in 1957; the Folger Coffee Company (ground, flaked, and instant coffee) in 1963; the Crush Companies (Crush, Sun Drop, and Hires Root Beer soft drinks) in 1980; the Ben Hill Griffin Citrus Company (concentrated fruit juices) in 1981; and Morton Norwich (pharmaceuticals) in 1982.

EXHIBIT 1   Consolidated Statement of Earnings ($ in millions except per share amounts)

	Fiscal Year Ending June 30	
	1981	1980
Income		
Net sales	$11,416	$10,772
Interest and other income	83	52
	$11,499	$10,824
Costs and expenses		
Cost of products sold	$ 7,854	$ 7,471
Marketing, administrative, and other expense	2,361	2,178
Interest expense	98	97
	$10,313	$ 9,746
Earnings from operations before income taxes	$ 1,186	$ 1,078
Income taxes	−518	−438
Net earnings from operations (before extraordinary charge)	$ 668	$ 640
Extraordinary charge: costs associated with the suspension of sale of Rely tampons (less applicable tax relief of $58)	(75)	—
Net earnings	$593	$640
Per common share		
Net earnings from operations	$8.08	$7.74
Extraordinary charge	(.91)	—
Net earnings	$7.17	$7.74
Average shares outstanding 1981—82,720,858 1980—82,659,861		
Dividends	$3.80	$3.40

Source: Company records

and the brands, but leave the people here, we will build a comparable new business in as little as a decade.

> Richard R. Deupree, Chairman of the board, P&G, 1948–1958

Our predecessors were wise enough to know that profitability and growth go hand in hand with fair treatment of employees, of customers, of consumers, and of the communities in which we operate.[3]

> Edward G. Harness, Chairman of the board, P&G, 1974–1981

---

[3]As quoted by Oscar Schisgall in *Eyes on Tomorrow* (Chicago: J.G. Ferguson Publishing, 1981). All other quotations are drawn from P&G recruitment literature.

EXHIBIT 2   Established U.S. Brands by Product Category, 1981

Consumer

| *Laundry and Cleaning* | *Food* | | *Personal Care* |

Laundry and Cleaning

All Fabric Bleach:
  Biz (1967)*

Cleaners and Cleansers:
  #1-Comet (1956)†
  Comet Liquid (1976)
  Mr. Clean (1958)
  Spic and Span (1945)
  Top Job (1963)

Detergents/Soaps:
  Bold 3 (1976)
  Cheer (1950)
  Dash (1954)
  Dreft (1933)
  Era (1972)
  Gain (1966)
  Ivory Snow (1930)
  Oxydol (1952)
  Solo (1979)
  #1-Tide (1946)

Dishwashing Detergents:
  Cascade (1955)
  Dawn (1972)
  #1-Ivory Liquid (1957)
  Joy (1949)

Fabric Softeners:
  Bounce (1972)
  #1-Downy (1960)

Food

Coffee:
  #1-Folgers (vacuum
    packed and instant,
    1963; flaked, 1977)
  Instant High Point (1975)

Oil/Shortening:
  #1-Crisco (shortening,
    1911)
  Crisco (oil, 1960)
  Fluffo (shortening, 1953)
  Puritan Oil (1976)

Orange Juice and Other
Citrus Products:
  Citrus Hill

Peanut Butter:
  #1-Jif (1956)

Potato Chips:
  Pringles (1968)

Soft Drinks:
  Crush (1980)
  Hires Root Beer (1980)
  Sun-Drop (1980)

Prepared Mixes:
  #1-Duncan Hines (cake,
    1956; brownie, 1956;
    snack cake, 1974;
    pudding recipe cake,
    1977; cookie, 1978;
    bran muffin, 1979)

Bar Soaps:
  Camay (1927)
  Coast (1974)
  #1-Ivory (1879)
  Kirk's (1930)
  Lava (1928)
  Safeguard (1963)
  Zest (1952)

Deodorants/Anti-perspirants:
  Secret (1956)
  Sure (1972)

Disposable Diapers:
  #1-Pampers (1961)
  Luvs (1976)

Disposable Incontinent
Briefs:
  Attends (1978)

Hand and Body Lotion:
  Wondra (1977)

Home Permanent:
  #1-Lilt (1949)

Personal Care

Mouthwash:
  Scope (1965)

Paper Tissue Products:
  Charmin (bathroom,
    1957)
  #1-Puffs (facial, 1960)
  White Cloud (bathroom,
    1958)

Paper Towels:
  #1-Bounty (1956)

Prescription Drugs:

Shampoos:
  Head & Shoulders (1961)
  Pert (1979)
  Prell (1946)

Toothpastes:
  #1-Crest (1955)
  Gleem (1952)

Industrial

| | *Finished Industrial Goods* | | *Unfinished Industrial Goods* |

All-purpose cleaning
  products
Floor and hard-surface
  cleaning products
Pot and pan washing
  products

Finished Industrial Goods

Cleaners
Commercial laundry
  products
Coin-vended laundry
  products
Hand-washing products

Institutional bar soaps
Coffee
Shortenings and oils
Surgical drapes and gowns

Unfinished Industrial Goods

Animal feed ingredients
Cellulose pulp
Fatty acids
Fatty alcohols
Glycerine
Methyl esters

Note: Test-market brands have been excluded.
*The date the brand became part of the P&G line is in parenthesis.
†Leading brand in the category is marked #1.

There is no potential business gain, no matter how great, which can be used to justify a dishonest act. The ends cannot justify the means because unethical means, in and of themselves, can and will destroy an organization. . . . The total dedication to integrity in every aspect of the business, and the restless, driving spirit of exploration have already been vital to the company's past and are critical to the company's future.

Owen B. Butler, Chairman of the board, P&G, 1981–

Key to Procter & Gamble's continued growth is the importance we attach to research and development . . . if anything, research and development will take on even greater importance to us in the future.

John Smale, President, P&G, 1981–

Disciplined and consistent. P&G people plan, minimize risk, and adhere to proven principles.

Ogilvy and Mather (advertising agency)

The secret, in a word, is thoroughness. P&G manages every element of its business with a painstaking precision that most organizations fail to approach.

Fortune

COMPANY ORGANIZATION

The company comprised eight major operating divisions organized by type of product: Packaged Soaps & Detergents, Bar Soap and Household Cleaning Products, Toilet Goods, Paper Products, Food Products, Coffee, Food Service and Lodging Products, and Special Products. As Exhibit 3 shows, each division had its own brand management (called advertising), and its own sales, finance, manufacturing, and product development line management groups. These groups reported directly to the division manager, typically a vice president who held overall profit and loss responsibility. The divisions used centralized corporate staff groups for advertising services,[4] distribution, and purchasing.

The advertising department was formed in 1930 when P&G initiated its brand management system. This system allowed P&G to market aggressively several brands in the same product category by assigning the marketing responsibility for each brand to a single brand manager. The manager led a brand group that included an assistant brand manager and, depending on the dollar volume and marketing complexity of the product, one or two brand assistants. This group planned, developed, and directed the total marketing effort for its brand. It was expected to manage aggressively the marketing of the brand and to know more about the brand's business than anyone else in the organization.

One of the most important responsibilities of the brand group was the development of the annual marketing plan, which established volume objectives, marketing support levels, strategies, and tactics for the coming year. This plan took approximately three months

---

[4]Advertising services included the following specialized staff departments: TV commercial production, media, copy services, art and package design, market research, field advertising, marketing systems and computer services, and promotion and marketing services.

EXHIBIT 3   Divisional Line Management Organization

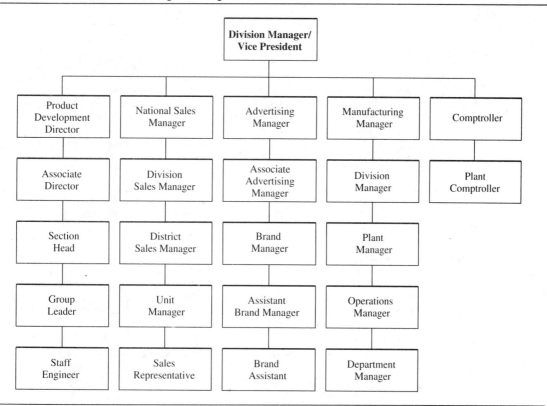

to develop. It reflected substantial analysis of previous business results by the brand group. Additionally, the brand group solicited input from 6 to 12 internal staff departments and an outside advertising agency. Then it recommended a marketing plan, which was reviewed by three levels of management: the associate advertising manager, the advertising manager, and the division general manager. Since the planning process established the marketing plans and volume expectations for the coming year, it was regarded as a key determinant of brand progress. In addition, this process offered the brand groups substantial opportunity to interact with upper management. (Details of the planning process are presented in Exhibit 4.)

Promotion was based entirely on performance, and all promotions were from within the organization. Brand managers were evaluated on their ability to build brand business and to develop their people. A brand manager who demonstrated excellent management ability was promoted to associate advertising manager (see Exhibit 3). Associate advertising managers used the skills they had developed as brand managers to guide the marketing efforts of several brands within a division, as well as to further the development of their brand managers. Associates also became involved in broader divisional and

EXHIBIT 4 Marketing Plan Development Process

Appropriate Number of Weeks Before Plan Approved	Activity or Event	Purpose
12	**Business Review** Assistant Brand Manager thoroughly reviews brand's and major competition's past 12-month shipment and share results by region, by size, and by form. Key lessons learned and indicated actions for the brand are developed by analyzing influences on brand share, including advertising copy, media weight, promotion, trade merchandising (display, co-op advertising and temporary price reduction), pricing, and distribution.	To determine what elements of the marketing mix are affecting the brand's business and to develop clear guidelines and actions to improve business results.
8	**Competitive Forecast** Brand group forecasts competitive volume and marketing expenditures for coming year, using input from Sales and advertising agency.	To allow brands to gauge level of expenditures necessary to compete effectively.
6	**Preliminary Forecast** Brand Manager forecasts brand's volume and share for the coming year, and preliminarily recommends advertising and promotion expenditures.	To allow division and P&G management to preliminarily forecast total P&G volume, expenditures, and profits for the coming year, and the brand to get preliminary agreement to volume objectives and marketing plans.
4	**Promotion Review** Brand Assistant thoroughly reviews results of past 12-month promotion plan by region, event, promoted size, and total brand. The document incorporates Sales comments, competitive brand activity, and available research to explain possible reasons for success and failure. Plan includes broadscale effort and testing activities.	To gain preliminary agreement from Advertising and Sales management to the proposed promotion plan for the coming year.
4	**Media Plan** Advertising agency develops detailed media plan, working with Brand Manager and Assistant Brand Manager. Plan includes broadscale media effort and testing activities.	To develop media plan for inclusion in budget proposal.
1	**Budget Proposal** Brand group prepares document detailing proposed volume, share, and marketing plan for coming year. Marketing plan includes detailed media and promotion plans, both broadscale effort and testing activities.	To provide a written record of the proposed plan.
0 (March)	**Budget Meeting** Brand group and advertising agency present the proposed plan to P&G management. The plan can either be approved in full, conditionally accepted provided certain issues raised in the meeting are addressed, or not approved.	To gain management input and agreement to the proposed plans.

corporate issues. For example, the associate responsible for coordinating division personnel policy would evaluate future personnel needs, coordinate recruitment efforts, ensure consistent evaluation methods, analyze training needs, develop a training budget, and work with the personnel department to implement training programs.

Each associate advertising manager reported to an advertising manager, who was responsible for the total marketing effort of all of a division's brands. The advertising manager played a significant role in the general management of the division, as he or she was responsible for approving the brand group's recommendations for volume objectives, marketing plans, and expenditures. In addition, the advertising manager had responsibility for approving each brand's advertising plans, as recommended by its brand group and its advertising agency.[5] All new advertising required the approval of the associate advertising manager and the advertising manager, while significant changes in advertising direction required division manager approval.

Historically, brands competing in the same product category were assigned to different associate advertising managers within a division to ensure maximum interbrand competition. Each of the associates promoted the interests of his or her own brand to the advertising manager, who then coordinated the most effective and efficient use of limited divisional resources. In the fall of 1981, however, the PS&D Division was reorganized; each associate advertising manager became responsible for all the brands within a single product category, as shown in Exhibit 5. This change focused authority for key decisions within category groups (e.g., LDLs) at the associate advertising manager level, thus allowing the advertising manager to spend more time on divisional issues. The brand manager promoted the interests of his or her brand, while the associate advertising manager assumed responsibility for building the business of all P&G brands in his or her category.

ADVERTISING'S RELATIONS WITH OTHER LINE DEPARTMENTS

The brand groups worked closely with the following four line departments in both the development and the implementation of their marketing plans.

Sales. P&G's consumer divisions employed 2,310 sales representatives and 574 sales managers, who serviced an estimated 40 percent of grocery, drug, and mass merchandise retail and wholesale outlets, accounting for an estimated 80 percent of all grocery and health and beauty aid sales volume.[6] The PS&D Division employed 408 sales representatives and 102 sales managers, who serviced 27 percent of grocery outlets accounting for 75 percent of grocery sales volume. The PS&D sales force did not directly service drug and mass merchandise outlets because of their modest sales potential.

---

[5]P&G retained 10 leading advertising agencies to work with the brand groups on advertising issues, of which 7 worked on the PS&D Division's products. Each LDL was handled by a separate agency. P&G's relationship with most of its agencies was long-standing, and many of the brands had been handled by the same agency since their introduction.

[6]Small convenience and corner stores accounted for most of the remaining 60 percent of retail outlets. P&G did not directly service these stores, as they accounted for only 20 percent of all commodity volume. These stores could, however, obtain P&G products through wholesalers.

EXHIBIT 5 PS&D Division Organization Chart, Fall 1981

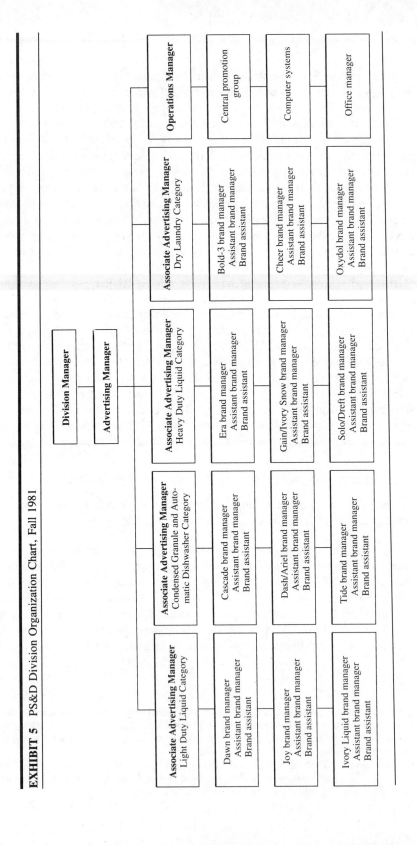

P&G sales representatives were well trained and regarded by the trade as consistently professional. Richard Penner, district sales manager, said:

> *Our sales representatives must be experts and professionals in their field. Our customers know that our sales representatives are well-trained professionals whose objective is not only to sell a good, quality product, but whose expertise can show them how to improve overall productivity; people who will bring them business-building merchandising ideas for the next feature or drive, which will reach present as well as new customers, thus increasing overall turnover and profit for the store.*

The brand groups and sales force frequently interacted. While the brand groups managed categories and brands, the sales force managed markets and accounts. As such, the sales force provided important perspective and counsel on trade and consumer promotion acceptance, stock requirements to support promotions, competitive pricing and promotion activity, and new-product activity. Each brand group worked closely with the sales force to develop the optimal sales promotion plan for its brand together with appropriate merchandising aids. An understanding of the sales function was considered so important to successful marketing planning that each brand assistant was trained as a sales representative and spent three to five months in the field sales force.

Product Development Department (PDD). Since superior product performance was key to the success of P&G products, each brand group worked closely with PDD to ensure continued improvement of its brand's quality. Fifteen professionals worked exclusively on research and development for LDLs. The PDD continually strove to upgrade product quality or explore new-product formulations. If a potential new product was developed, it was extensively tested in consumer and laboratory tests before any test marketing began.

In 1981, P&G spent $200 million on research and development. This spending supported the efforts of about 3,500 employees. Approximately 1,200 were professionally trained staff, and nearly one-third of these held doctoral degrees. P&G had six major research centers, four of which were located in the United States. The PS&D Division spent $30 million on research and development in 1981, which supported the efforts of about 500 employees.

Manufacturing Department. P&G operated 40 manufacturing plants in 24 states. The PS&D Division utilized 10 of these facilities to manufacture its products. The brand group provided the manufacturing department with detailed brand volume estimates (by month, size, and form/flavor) to facilitate efficient production, as well as five-year volume-based forecasts for capacity planning. In addition, the brand group discussed promotions requiring label or packaging changes with manufacturing to determine the most efficient production methods. Manufacturing informed brand groups about ongoing manufacturing costs and provided potential cost-saving ideas. Interaction between the advertising and manufacturing departments was particularly frequent during any new-product development process, and included discussions on manufacturing requirements, custom-packaging options for test markets, and critical paths for production.

Finance Department.   P&G's finance department was divided into three major functional areas: divisional financial/cost analysis, treasury, and taxation. Both treasury and taxation were centralized groups, while financial/cost analysis was divisionalized and reported to the division manager (see Exhibit 3). Based on volume and marketing expenditure forecasts provided by the brand groups, financial/cost analysts developed and fed back brand profit and pricing analyses as well as profit and rate-of-return forecasts on new products and promotions. This information was key in helping the brand groups to recommend action that would maximize volume and profit growth.

Advertising Services Department.   Within the department, there were nine staff groups that serviced the advertising department. These were market research, art and package design, TV commercial production, media, copy services, field advertising, marketing systems and computer services, promotion and marketing services, and advertising personnel.

P&G's extraordinary depth of staff resources was considered a key competitive advantage. For example, P&G invested an average of $20 million annually on consumer and market research,[7] 10 percent of which was spent on PS&D Division projects. PS&D market research included the following:

1. Market analysis, including bimonthly syndicated market data purchased from A.C. Nielsen Co.,[8] as well as selected data purchased from Nielsen, Selling Areas Marketing, Inc. (SAMI), and other suppliers for test markets.
2. Consumer research, including studies to:
   a. monitor how consumers used products and track consumer usage of, attitude toward, and image of P&G and competitive brands;
   b. test the performance of current products and possible product modifications under in-home usage conditions; and
   c. evaluate the advertising, packaging, promotion, and pricing of P&G brands; also, to evaluate the potential of new-product ideas, using such techniques as concept research and simulated test markets.

The major strength of P&G's consumer research was the quality of interviewing and consistent methodology among projects. This provided large data bases of comparable research over several years from which P&G could establish norms and accurately track changing consumer perceptions and habits. Only a limited amount of the research was actually conducted by P&G employees; most was conducted by outside suppliers, but was closely supervised by P&G market researchers.

LIGHT-DUTY LIQUID DETERGENTS

During the 1940s, most U.S. consumers used powdered laundry detergents to wash their dishes. Research indicated, however, that consumers found these detergents harsh on

---

[7]This $20 million was part of the $200 million the company spent on research and development.

[8]The A.C. Nielsen package that the LDL brands purchased included data on retail shelf movement and share, distribution penetration, retailer feature advertising, special displays, regular and feature prices, out-of-stocks, retail inventories, and percent of brands sold in special packs.

hands. In response to these concerns, P&G designed a mild, light-duty liquid in 1949. By 1981, the LDL industry recorded factory sales of $850 million and volume of 59 million cases.[9] The average U.S. consumer had 1.5 LDL brands at home at any one time, used 0.6 fluid ounces of product per sinkful of dishes, and washed an average of 12 sinksful each week. The average purchase cycle was three to four weeks, and an average household would use over one case of product each year. As Table A shows, the most popular sizes in the category were 32 oz. and 22 oz.

Table B suggests that increases in LDL consumption, resulting from the growing number of U.S. households,[10] were partly offset by increased penetration of automatic dishwashers (ADWs), as ADW households used one-half as much LDL as non-ADW households.[11] Based on these trends, the LDL brand groups projected category volume growth of 1 percent per year over the next five years.

LDLs could be conceptually divided on the basis of product benefit into three major segments: (1) the performance segment (35 percent of category volume) provided primarily a cleaning benefit; (2) the mildness segment (37 percent of category volume) provided primarily the benefit of being gentle to hands; and (3) the price segment (28 percent of category volume) whose primary benefit was low cost.[12]

As Exhibit 6 indicates, the performance segment had experienced the greatest growth in the past 10 years. Some LDL brand managers expected the performance segment to

TABLE A   Sizes of Dishwashing Liquid Used in Past Seven Days

	48 oz.	32 oz.	22 oz.	12 oz.
Percent of Respondents	13%	30%	42%	15%

Source: Company research.

TABLE B   U.S. LDL Market Influences

	1960	1970	1980	1990*
LDL household penetration	53%	83%	90%	92%
ADW household penetration	5%	18%	36%	44%
Total households (millions)	53	63	79	91

*Company estimates

[9]Volume is measured in P&G statistical cases, each containing 310 ounces.

[10]Household growth was a better indicator of LDL volume than population growth (research indicated LDL household consumption varied only slightly with the number of people in the household).

[11]ADW households still used LDLs for pots and pans and small cleanups.

[12]Price brands were sold to retailers for an average of $7.50 per statistical case versus $17.00 per statistical case for the premium-priced mildness and performance brands.

EXHIBIT 6   LDL Market Historic Growth Trends and Projections

Fiscal Year Ending June 30	Volume (million cases)	Percent of Category Volume		
		Mildness	Performance	Price
Actual				
1973	56.4	44%	19%	37%
1974	57.0	45	20	35
1975	56.4	44	21	35
1976	56.8	43	22	35
1977	56.1	40	28	32
1978	57.8	40	30	30
1979	57.0	39	32	29
1980	58.7	38	33	29
1981	59.0	37	35	28
Projected				
1982	59.4	37	35	28
1983	59.8	36	35	29
1984	60.1	36	35	29
1985	60.8	35	36	29
1986	61.1	35	36	29

Note: Classification and projections were based on collective brand manager judgment.

Source: Company records.

continue to grow at the expense of the mildness segment, since market research indicated that more consumers rated performance attributes (such as grease cutting and long-lasting suds) as the most important (see Exhibit 7). The price segment had been in decline, but was expected to stabilize at its current share level due to increasing consumer price sensitivity resulting from the depressed state of the economy. LDL brand managers did not expect this segment to grow because most price brands were not a good value, requiring two or three times as much volume to create the same amount of suds as a premium brand. P&G's Ivory Liquid, the market leader, used this comparison in its advertising to persuade consumers that Ivory was a better value.

The LDL market was relatively stable, with one new premium brand introduced every two and one-half years, and an average of two price brands introduced and discontinued per year. As Exhibit 8 shows, three companies sold almost 75 percent of LDLs, with P&G holding a 42 percent share[13] of the market, Colgate-Palmolive Company a 24 percent share, and Lever Brothers, the U.S. subsidiary of Unilever, a 7 percent share.[14] The remaining 27 percent of the market consisted mainly of generic and private-label brands.

---

[13]*Share of market* is defined as share of statistical case volume.

[14]In 1981, Colgate-Palmolive's U.S. sales were $5.3 billion, and Lever Brothers' U.S. sales were $2.1 billion.

EXHIBIT 7   Attribute Importance Ratings

	Percent of Respondents							
Attribute*	6	5	4	3	2	1	No Answer	Average Rating
Makes dishes shine	64%	16%	7%	6%	2%	2%	3%	5.3
Pleasant odor or perfume	40	17	11	10	7	10	5	4.2
Don't have to use much	70	13	6	5	1	2	3	5.5
Doesn't make skin rough	65	12	7	5	4	3	4	5.0
Is low-priced	50	19	10	9	3	4	5	5.0
Good for hand-washing laundry	29	14	9	11	9	23	5	3.7
Does a good job on pots and pans	75	13	4	2	1	1	4	5.6
Does not spot or streak glasses or dishes	67	15	8	3	2	2	3	5.4
Is mild to hands	68	13	5	5	3	3	3	5.2
Makes long-lasting suds	83	12	7	2	2	2	2	5.5
Cuts grease	87	6	2	1	—	1	3	5.8
Is economical to use	72	13	6	4	1	1	3	5.5
Soaks off baked-on or burnt-on food	60	17	7	5	2	4	5	5.2
Good for tough cleaning jobs	52	13	8	9	4	9	5	4.8

*Respondents were asked to rate the importance to them of LDL attributes on a 6-point scale, with 6 being "want the most" and 1 being "want the least." To be read, for example: 64 percent of respondents claimed "Makes dishes shine" as one of the attributes they wanted most in a dishwashing liquid, while 2 percent of respondents claimed this attribute as the one they wanted least.

Source: Company research.

As shown in Exhibit 9, marketing expenditures including advertising and promotion typically represented 20 percent of the sales of an established LDL brand.

Total advertising and promotion spending in the category in 1981 was $150 million, over half of which was spent by the P&G LDLs, the balance being spent primarily by Lever and Colgate-Palmolive.

Slightly over half of the marketing budgets of P&G LDLs was allocated to advertising, versus only about 40 percent for both Colgate and Lever LDLs. Colgate and Lever sold an estimated 75 percent of their LDL volume to the trade on deal, compared with about half for P&G. Both Lever and Colgate had introduced a single new brand in the past 10 years. Dermassage, introduced in 1974 by Colgate, offered a similar benefit to Ivory: mildness to hands. The brand held only a 2 percent share in 1981. Sunlight, introduced by Lever into Phoenix (test market) in 1980, offered benefits similar to Joy, as a good-cleaning, lemon-fresh LDL. The brand had achieved a 10 percent share in the test region after 12 months.

EXHIBIT 8   LDL Market Shares by Brand and Company (shares of statistical cases)

		Share of Market		
Brand	Segment	1961	1971	1981
P&G				
Joy	Performance	14.9%	12.0%	12.1%
Ivory	Mildness	17.5	14.9	15.5
Dawn	Performance	—	—	14.1
Thrill*	Mildness/performance	—	2.9	—
		32.4	29.8	41.7
Lever Brothers				
Lux	Mildness	17.3	7.3	3.1
Dove	Mildness	—	4.8	3.1
Sunlight	Performance	—	—	0.7
All others	Price	5.9	1.0	—
		23.2	13.1	6.9
Colgate-Palmolive				
Palmolive Liquid	Mildness	—	11.7	11.8
Dermassage	Mildness	—	—	3.5
All others	Price/performance	5.5	9.6	8.3
		5.5	21.3	23.6
All others LDLs	Mainly price/generics and private labels	38.9	35.8	27.8
Total LDLs		100.0%	100.0%	100.0%

*Thrill was introduced by P&G in 1969. The brand ultimately proved not to provide a needed product benefit and was discontinued in 1975 because of faltering volume.

Source: Company records.

EXHIBIT 9   Cost Structure for an Established LDL Brand

Cost of goods	51%
Distribution	7%
Selling and general administration	10%
Marketing expenditures	20%*
Profit	12%
Total	100%

*Includes advertising, trade, and consumer promotion expenditures.

Source: Company records.

PROCTER & GAMBLE'S LDL BRANDS

P&G's three brands in the LDL category (Ivory Liquid, Joy, and Dawn) together accounted for 30 percent of the dollar sales volume and profit of the PS&D Division. While each of the three brands was a different formulation that offered a distinct benefit to appeal to separate consumer needs, all were marketed similarly. All three brands were sized and priced in line with major premium-priced competition (see Table C). Price increases occurred, on average, every 18 months.

In general, brand managers spent over half of each LDL's marketing budget on advertising, of which 85–90 percent was spent on television media and commercial production, and the balance on print. Brands typically held four to six major promotion events each year, each lasting four weeks. Promotions primarily included coupons, price packs, bonus packs, and trade allowances. Consumer promotions typically accounted for at least 75 percent of promotion dollars, while trade allowances made up the balance.

P&G's LDL brands held strongly established market positions, as company research results reported in Exhibit 10 reveal. Neither Ivory Liquid nor Dawn had changed its basic product benefits or basic advertising claims since introduction. Joy, however, had undergone two basic changes. It was first introduced as a performance brand, but during the 1960s, as the mildness segment of the market began to grow, it was restaged with a mildness benefit. By the 1970s, Ivory Liquid was clearly established as the major mildness brand; as research revealed that a consumer need existed for a good cleaning brand, Joy was reformulated to provide a performance benefit and restaged.

Each brand's individual market position is discussed here:

Ivory Liquid. The product was introduced in 1957 as an excellent dishwashing liquid that provided the additional benefit of hand care. Its mildness positioning was supported by the heritage of Ivory bar soap, a patented mildness formula, and unique product aesthetics (its creamy-white color and mild scent). In 1981 it was the leading brand, with a market share of 15.5 percent. Although Ivory's share had declined slightly over the previous five years, it was expected to remain stable over the next five years. Ivory's advertising copy featured a mother/daughter comparison to demonstrate its benefit of "young-looking hands." In 1968 the brand added a value claim stressing the fact that Ivory washed more dishes per penny of product than price brands because of its

TABLE C Ivory, Dawn, and Joy Pricing

		Manufacturer's		
Size	Items per Case	Carload Case Price	Carload Item Price	Average Retail Price
48 oz.	9	$22.77	$2.53	$2.99
32 oz.	12	21.24	1.77	2.04
22 oz.	16	19.20	1.20	1.46
12 oz.	24	16.08	0.67	0.84

EXHIBIT 10 LDL User/Non-User Attribute Association (%)

| | Usual Brand* | | | | | | | | | |
| | Ivory Liquid | | Joy | | Dawn | | Palmolive | | Price Brands | |
Attribute	Yes	No	Yes	No	Yes	No	Yes	No	Yes	No
Best for mildness	89%	51%	53%	12%	41%	7%	71%	27%	13%	2%
Best overall for getting dishes clean	64	9	78	14	88	15	61	5	18	1
Best for cutting grease	41	6	49	7	96	45	35	4	16	1
Best for removing tough, cooked-on foods	47	7	55	10	88	28	41	6	19	2
Best for leaving dishes shiny	44	10	81	45	59	5	40	4	14	1
Gives the best value for your money	74	24	60	4	65	6	55	5	40	7
Makes the longest-lasting suds	79	29	60	10	67	11	50	5	12	1
Has the most pleasant fragrance	43	11	64	35	39	9	35	11	14	1

Note: Respondents were asked to indicate which one brand was best described by each attribute phrase. To be read, for example: 89 percent of respondents who claimed Ivory Liquid as their usual brand indicated that it was best for being mild to your hands; 51 percent of people who did not claim Ivory Liquid as their usual brand indicated it was best for being mild to your hands.

*A *brand user* was defined as a respondent who reported that brand as the usual brand used over the previous three-month period.

Source: Company research.

higher-sudsing formula. During 1981, Ivory allocated two-thirds of its advertising budget to the mildness message, and the remaining one-third to the value advertising copy. (Television advertising storyboards for these two campaigns are presented as Exhibits 11 and 12.) The brand was perceived by consumers as the mildest and highest-sudsing brand and had the highest ever-tried level in the category. For this reason, the principal objective of Ivory's consumer promotions was to encourage continuity of purchase rather than to stimulate trial.

Dawn. The product was introduced in 1976 as a performance brand. In two years, it rose to the No. 2 position in the LDL category, and by 1981 it held a 14.1 percent market share. Dawn captured about 70 percent of its volume from non-P&G brands, with the remaining 30 percent cannibalized equally from Ivory Liquid and Joy. Dawn's rapid growth was attributed to its unique position as the superior grease-cutting LDL in the category—a claim that was supported by its patented formula, which consumer research proved cut grease better than other formulas. The advertising claim "Dawn takes grease out of your way" was supported by a powerful product demonstration, as shown in Exhibit 13. Consumer research (reported in Exhibit 14) indicated that Dawn had the highest conversion rate of all the P&G LDL brands.[15] Dawn's promotion plan emphasized trial, with most of the budget allocated to consumer coupons. Its share was projected to increase to 16.5 percent over the next five years. It was expected to take over the leading share position from Ivory by 1985.

[15]The conversion rate was the number of people citing a brand as their usual brand divided by total triers of the brand.

EXHIBIT 11   Ivory Liquid's TV Storyboard "Mildness" Message, 1981

COMPTON ADVERTISING, INC.

625 Madison Avenue, New York, N.Y. 10022

Telephone: PLaza 4-1100

CLIENT: PROCTER & GAMBLE CO.
PRODUCT: IVORY LIQUID
TITLE: "STOKES"
COMML. # PGIL 5713   TIMING: 30 SECONDS
DATE: 10/22/80

1. (SFX: MUSIC)
ANNCR: (VO) Can you pick Jean Stokes' hands from her two daughters?

2. LISA: Mom's hands are as young-looking as ours!

3. KATHY: We sing together for charity --

4. MOM: Strictly amateur -- but your hands get noticed.

5. ANNCR: (VO) And Jean does a lot of dishes. What's her secret?

6. LISA: Ivory Liquid!
MOM: And I've told my girls how mild it is.

7. ANNCR: (VO) Lab tests show Ivory Liquid's

8. mildest of all leading brands.

9. And nothing gets dishes cleaner.

10. LISA: I'm going to stay with Ivory Liquid.

11. GROUP SINGS: Ivory Liquid.

12. ANNCR: (VO) Because young-looking hands are worth holding on to.

EXHIBIT 12   Ivory Liquid's TV Storyboard "Value" Message, 1981

COMPTON ADVERTISING, INC.
625 Madison Avenue, New York, N.Y. 10022

Telephone: PLaza 4-1100

CLIENT:	PROCTER & GAMBLE CO.
PRODUCT:	IVORY LIQUID
TITLE:	"THE KIPPERS"
COMML. #	PGIL 5573 TIMING: 30 SECONDS
DATE:	4/1/80

1. ANNCR: (VO) Is the Kippers' "bargain" brand a better buy than mild Ivory Liquid? Let's see...

2. INT: Let's test your brand against Ivory Liquid with a penny's worth of each.

3. Let's wash some dishes.

4. How are your suds? BOB: I don't have any suds now.

5. INT: How about the Ivory Liquid Mrs. Kipper? BEV: I still have a tubful.

6. INT: Let's scoop some up and compare.

7. Okay what happened? BEV: I did a lot more dishes.

8. What I thought was a bargain isn't really a bargain at all. INT: What's the bargain?

9. INT: What's the bargain? BEV: Ivory is the bargain.

10. It's gentle to my hands, and I can save money.

11. ANNCR: (VO) You don't have to give up

12. mild Ivory Liquid to save money.

EXHIBIT 13   Dawn Advertising Storyboard, 1981

B&B
BENTON & BOWLES
909 THIRD AVENUE
NEW YORK, N.Y.
(212) 758-6200

Client: **PROCTER & GAMBLE CO.**
Product: **DAWN**
Length: **45 SECONDS (PGDN 6105)**
Title: **"SLEEPOVER REV/FP"**

1. (SFX: KIDS TALKING)
   MOM: Lasagna? For breakfast? DAUGHTER: Oh, Mom! FRIEND: It's a slumber party!

2. MOM: O.K. But you <u>will</u> clean up.

3. DAUGHTER: All that grease! Yuck!!! Gross!

4. MOM: No, Dawn.

5. DAUGHTER: Ah, finished!

6. FRIEND #1: Uh-uh, forgot a glass. DAUGHTER: You forgot it. You wash it. FRIEND: After that greasy pan?

7. DAUGHTER: Try it. Dawn'll handle it.

8. FRIEND #1: The water doesn't feel greasy...and neither do my hands.

9. And this glass looks as good as the first one <u>you</u> washed.

10. ANNCR: (VO) Look. Add a half cup of grease to Dawn dishwater.

11. Dawn breaks up grease, takes it out of your way. Helps keep it away.

12. So dishes come out clean.

13. FRIEND: Dawn's great!

14. MOM: So, if lasagna's breakfast, what's dinner? DAUGHTER: Corn flakes. (GIRLS LAUGH)

15. ANNCR: (VO) Dawn takes grease

16. (SFX) out of your way.

EXHIBIT 14 Current Product Usage (percent)

	Ivory	Joy	Dawn
Usual brand	23%	13%	25%
Past 12-month trial	35%	30%	29%
Ever tried	58%	43%	54%

Note: An estimated 60–80 percent of total brand volume was consumed by usual brand users for each brand.

Source: Company research.

Joy. The product, introduced in 1949, was P&G's first LDL. Since 1970, it had been formulated to provide a performance benefit, and it was positioned in advertising to deliver "beautiful dishes that get noticed and appreciated." Joy's lemon-based formula, lemon fragrance, and yellow package supported this image. Joy's advertising (see Exhibit 15) claimed that it "cleans dishes right down to the shine and isn't that a nice reflection on you." As Exhibit 10 indicates, although Joy's image in the marketplace was good by category standards, it was not as strong as Ivory Liquid or Dawn. In addition, it had the lowest trial level of P&G's three LDLs. As a result, its promotion plan was trial-oriented, with particular emphasis on couponing. Joy's share of 12.1 percent was expected to increase by only 1 percent per year over the next five years.

Exhibit 16 reports factory shipments and market shares for each of the three brands over the previous five years, as well as the brands' estimates for the next five years. Exhibit 17 provides a demographic profile of users of each of the three P&G brands, illustrating how each brand appeals to a different consumer segment.

NEW GROWTH OPPORTUNITIES

In evaluating the opportunities for further volume growth on P&G LDLs, Wright considered the following three options:

New-Brand Introduction. The success of Dawn led Wright to wonder if another new brand with a distinctive benefit could further increase P&G's LDL volume. Based on the impact of Dawn's introduction and the current strength of P&G's LDL brands, he estimated that a well-positioned new brand could capture at least 60 percent of its share from competitive brands. However, after talking with manufacturing and PDD, he estimated that a new brand would require $20 million in capital investment to cover additional production capacity and bottle molds.[16] Further, based on input from the Dawn brand manager, he estimated that a new LDL brand would need at least $60 million for first-year introductory marketing expenditures.[17]

---

[16]This capital investment per case of estimated LDL volume was lower than the average for new P&G products, since substantial LDL manufacturing facilities already existed.

[17]This estimate was based on Dawn's 12-month introductory marketing plan. Using updated costs, a new brand would require $18 million for media support, $37 million for consumer and trade promotion support, and $5 million for miscellaneous marketing expenses.

EXHIBIT 15   Joy Advertising Storyboard, 1981

Radio TV Reports

41 East 42nd Street New York N.Y. 10017
(212) 697-5100

PRODUCT: JOY DISHWASHING LIQUID
PROGRAM: AS THE WORLD TURNS
WCBS-TV

758077
60 SEC.
1:35PM

1. MAN: Sam. MAN: Joe. It's been too long.

2. MAN: It sure has. Come on in. Honey, Sam's here. WOMAN: How do you do Captain Randall.

3. MAN: Major Randall now I hope my phone call didn't catch you two off guard. But Joe said, Sam if you're ever in town --

4. WOMAN: Well of course. And I hope you stay for dinner Major Randall. That is if you don't mind pot luck.

5. MAN: Oh, don't apologize. MAN: Sam. Make yourself at home. Honey, shouldn't we get out the good dishes?

6. WOMAN: Never mind the dishes. Ours here look fine. What about my dress? MAN: It's just fine.

7. ANNCR: When unexpected guests drop in one thing you don't have to worry about is the way your table looks when you use Joy.

8. Joy cleans every day dishes clear down to the shine. And smells fresh like lemons.

9. Keeps dishes ready for company, even if you're not.

10. MAN: Sure is nice to get home cooking.

11. And look at that shine. Looks like you were expecting company all the time.

12. ANNCR: Lemon fresh Joy cleans down to the shine.

13. And that's a nice reflection on you.

EXHIBIT 16   Shipment and Share Data for LDL Brands

	Factory shipments (millions of cases)			Market Share (Percent of LDL category)		
	Ivory	Dawn	Joy	Ivory	Dawn	Joy
Actual						
1977	9.1	6.7	6.7	16.3%	11.9%	11.9%
1978	9.0	7.3	6.7	15.5	12.7	11.6
1979	9.1	7.5	6.8	16.0	13.2	12.0
1980	9.1	8.2	6.9	15.5	14.0	11.7
1981	9.1	8.3	7.1	15.5	14.1	12.1
Estimated						
1982	9.2	8.7	7.2	15.5	14.7	12.2
1983	9.3	9.0	7.4	15.5	15.0	12.3
1984	9.3	9.3	7.5	15.5	15.5	12.4
1985	9.4	9.7	7.6	15.5	15.9	12.5
1986	9.5	10.1	7.8	15.5	16.5	12.7

Note: Projections are based on each brand manager's judgment.

Source: Company records.

Wright saw new-product potential in all three market segments. First, PDD had invented a new technology for a high-performance product. The formula, called H-80, combined suspended nonabrasive scrubbers[18] with a highly effective detergent system to provide superior cleaning compared with other LDLs when used full strength on tough, baked-on foods, and parity cleaning compared with other LDLs when diluted with water for general dishwashing. Wright believed that such a product could fulfill a clear consumer need, based on consumer research. Since market research indicated that 80 percent of U.S. households scour and scrub their dishes at least once a week, with an average household scouring four times a week, he believed that this product would be valued by a significant percentage of consumers.[19] In addition, the results of blind, in-home-use tests, reported in Exhibit 18, were positive.

Second, Wright wondered if he could capitalize on P&G's expertise in the mildness segment to introduce another mildness brand. While the segment was currently declining, he believed there might be potential for a new brand if the mildness benefit could be further differentiated—just as had been done in the performance segment. As Exhibit 19 shows, research indicated that when consumers were asked what improvement they wanted most in their current LDL, more stated "milder to hands" than any other product benefit.

Third, P&G could introduce a price brand. PDD and manufacturing had told Wright that they could produce a brand with parity performance benefits to existing price brand

---

[18]The scrubbers were made from the biodegradable shells of microscopic sea organisms.

[19]Many consumers used soap-filled scouring pads such as Purex Industries' Brillo pads and Miles Laboratories' S.O.S. pads. Retail sales of such pads approached $100 million in 1980.

EXHIBIT 17   LDL-User Demographic Profile (percent of total responding households)

	Total LDL Households	Heavy LDL Users*	Usual Brand				
			Ivory Liquid	Joy	Dawn	Palmolive	No Name/ Plain Label
ADW Usage—Past 7 Days							
Yes	36%	9%	48%	49%	51%	48%	47%
No	64	90	51	51	49	42	53
Yearly Income							
Under $15,000	32	46	28	32	35	30	36
$15,000–25,000	27	29	27	26	29	27	29
Over $25,000	41	25	45	42	36	43	35
Population Density (000/sq. mile)							
Under 50	32	39	30	33	38	28	20
50–1,999	45	40	45	44	43	46	48
2,000 and over	23	21	25	23	19	26	32
Geographic Area							
Northeast	22	26	22	23	19	24	36
North Central	28	28	26	27	31	27	31
South	33	35	34	37	35	33	16
West	17	11	18	13	15	16	17
Employment†							
Employed	48	37	48	50	49	49	55
Not employed	52	63	52	59	51	51	45
Age‡							
Under 35	33	39	31	34	38	39	35
35–50	30	25	29	31	30	30	37
51–59	16	15	17	16	15	16	12
60‡	21	30	23	19	17	24	16
Number in Family							
1–2	40	41	43	38	38	42	28
3–4	44	41	42	45	46	44	50
5+	16	18	15	17	16	14	22

Note: To be read, for example: 48 percent of respondents who claimed Ivory Liquid as their usual brand had used an automatic dishwasher in the past seven days.
*Defined as +15 sinksful per week.
†Female head of household.
‡The heavy LDL-user skew toward older respondents may be misleading. P&G management believed that, though users washed a large number of small sinkloads, they used a lesser amount of product per sinkload because they tended to live in smaller households.

Source: Company research.

competition at a cost that would allow PS&D to maintain a reasonable profit. Specifically, the percentage of sales available for marketing expenditures and profit would fall to 14 percent of sales versus the 32 percent of sales available from P&G's current LDL brands. Wright noted that P&G did not currently have an LDL entry in this fragmented segment of the market, characterized by low-share brands with little brand loyalty and substantially lower product quality than the LDL brands P&G currently marketed. He wondered if

---

EXHIBIT 18 LDL Category Assessment (4-week blind in-home-use test of H-80 in 425 households)

	H-80 with Scrubbing Instructions*	Established Competitive LDL with Scrubbing Instructions*
Attribute Ratings		
Overall	77%	71%
Cleaning	79	73
Removing baked/burnt/dried-on food	73	61
Grease removal	77	72
Amount of suds made	73	69
Mildness	55	63
Odor of product	70	68
Color of product	72	69
Favorable Comments		
Unduplicated cleaning	73	65
Cleans well	36	29
Cleans hard-to-remove food	25	15
Cuts grease	34	32
Unduplicated sudsing	49	45
Product color	6	5
Mildness	25	34
Unduplicated odor	45	40
Unduplicated cap/container	8	2
Unduplicated consistency	12	2
Like scrubbing particles/abrasives	12	—
Unfavorable Comments		
Unduplicated cleaning	4	9
Not clean well	—	1
Not clean hard-to-remove food	1	5
Not cut grease	3	8
Unduplicated sudsing	9	17
Product color	1	3
Mildness	16	14
Unduplicated odor	10	9
Unduplicated cap/container	2	2
Unduplicated consistency	12	1
Not like abrasive/gritty feel	11	1
Dishwashing Information		
Used product full strength for scrubbing	61	52
Used scrubbing implement for tough jobs	79	85

Note: To be read, for example: 77 percent of the 425 households that used H-80 rated it as 4 or above on a 5-point scale on overall performance.

*Unmarked bottles of H-80 were given to one of two representative samples of LDL users. The other sample group received unmarked bottles of an established competitive brand. Both brands were accompanied by instructions suggesting the product be diluted for general dishwashing but used full strength for tough dishwashing jobs.

Source: Company research.

EXHIBIT 19   Selected Research Data: Personal Feelings Concerning Dishwashing

	Percent of Consumers
1. What is the worst thing about doing dishes?	
The time it takes	24%
Having to do them	22
Cleaning pots and pans	15
Scrubbing/scouring	14
Cleaning greasy items	6
Hard on hands	4
2. What is the toughest dishwashing job?	
Removal of baked/burnt/fried/cooked foods	39
Removal of greasy foods	32
Cleaning of pots and pans	22
Cleaning of skillets	16
Cleaning of casseroles	7
Cleaning of dishes	3
3. What is most disappointing about your current dishwashing liquid?	
Nothing	51
Suds disappear	12
Leaves grease	8
Odor	6
Hard on hands	2
Price/expensive	4
Have to use too much	4
4. What improvement do you want the most in a dishwashing liquid?	
Milder to hands	11
Do it by magic/itself	10
Eliminate scouring or soaking	9
Cut grease	9
Soak dishes clean	9
Suds never vanish	6
Nothing/satisfied	9

Source: Company research.

P&G's marketing expertise could enable the company to capture a significant portion of the price segment with a parity product.

Product Improvement on an Existing Brand.   A product improvement on a current brand represented considerably less investment than a new brand, and Wright wondered if he would be wiser to introduce the H-80 formula as a product improvement to one of the current LDL brands. While he estimated that the capital costs associated with a product improvement would be about the same as introducing a new product ($20 million), incremental marketing expenditures over and above the existing brand budget would be only $10 million. He wondered which, if any, of his brands would benefit most from this change.

Separately, the Joy brand group was eager to restage the brand with a new "no-spot" formula. The formula, considered a technological breakthrough, caused water to "sheet" off dishes when they were air-dried, leaving fewer spots than other brands. In addition, the formula reduced Joy's cost of goods sold by about $3 million per year. The brand estimated this relaunch would cost $10 million in marketing expenses, but would require no capital investment.

Increase Marketing Expenditures on the Existing Brands. Finally, given the low-growth potential of the LDL category, Wright wondered if his overall profits might be higher if he avoided the capital investment and introductory marketing expenses of a new brand or product improvement and simply increased the marketing expenditures behind the existing brands in an effort to build volume. In particular, the brand manager for Ivory Liquid had submitted a request for an additional $4 million to support extra advertising and promotion. Half of the funds were to be used to achieve leadership media levels for Ivory by increasing its current media level from 300 GRPs[20]—which was the average level for major advertised LDL brands—to 365 GRPs. The remaining funds would be used to finance an incremental 20¢-off price-pack promotion on the 32 oz. size.

CONCLUSION

As Wright considered the various options available, he wondered about the time frame for implementation of each option. He knew that he could gain approval for increased marketing expenditures almost immediately if the plan was financially attractive—unless a test market was required, which would delay national approval by 6 to 12 months. Implementing a product improvement on an existing brand would take about a year (two years if a test market was necessary), and the introduction of a new brand would require two years plus a year in a test market before it could be expanded nationally. Could he undertake more than one option? What effect would each option have on each of the existing LDL brands? What competitive response could he expect? What were the long- and short-term profit and volume implications of each of the options?

---

[20]A GRP (gross rating point) is a measure of media delivery. Gross rating points equal the percentage of viewers reached over a specific period of time (usually four weeks) times the average number of occasions on which they are reached.

Case 2–3

Suzuki Samurai*

In June 1985, Leonard Pearlstein, president and CEO of keye/donna/pearlstein advertising agency, and his colleagues were finalizing the presentation that they would make the next day to Douglas Mazza, vice president and general manager of American Suzuki Motor Corporation (ASMC). Pearlstein's agency was competing with a half-dozen other advertising firms to represent Suzuki's new entrant into the U.S. automobile market, the Suzuki Samurai. Mazza had asked each agency the question: "How do you feel this vehicle should be positioned?" He had given keye/donna/pearlstein eight days to prepare an answer.

COMPANY BACKGROUND

Suzuki Loom Works, a privately owned loom manufacturing company, was founded in 1909 in Hamamatsu, Japan, by Michio Suzuki. In 1952, the company began manufacturing and marketing a 2-cycle, 36 cubic centimeter (cc) motorcycle, which became so popular that in 1954 the company introduced a second motorcycle and changed its name to Suzuki Motor Company, Ltd.(Suzuki).

During the late 1950s, lightweight vehicle sales boomed in Japan. Suzuki's motorcycle business grew, and in 1959 it introduced a lightweight van. The van's success encouraged Suzuki to develop lightweight cars and trucks. In 1961, it introduced its first production car, the "Suzulight," the first Japanese car with a 2-stroke engine.

In 1964, Suzuki began exporting motorcycles to the United States, where it established a wholly owned subsidiary, U.S. Suzuki Motor Company, Ltd., to serve as the exclusive importer and distributor of Suzuki motorcycles. Suzuki quickly established itself as a major brand in the U.S. motorcycle industry.

By 1965, Suzuki's product line included motorcycles, automobiles, motorized wheelchairs, outboard motors, general-purpose engines, generators, water pumps, and prefabricated houses. The company concentrated, however, on producing and marketing lightweight vehicles. Until 1979, Suzuki cars and trucks were sold only in Japan, where they were popular as economical transportation. In 1979, Suzuki automobiles were introduced into foreign markets, and by 1984 they were available in over 100 countries and Hawaii.

---

*Research Assistant Tammy Bunn Hiller prepared this case under the supervision of Professor John A. Quelch as the basis for class discussion rather than to illustrate either effective or ineffective handling of an administrative situation. Copyright © 1988 by the President and Fellows of Harvard College. Harvard Business School case 9–589–028.

In 1983, General Motors (GM) purchased 5 percent of Suzuki and helped the company develop a subcompact car for the U.S. market. The car, named the Chevrolet Sprint, was introduced on the West Coast in mid-1984 and was sold exclusively by Chevrolet dealers. The Sprint was Suzuki's first entry into the continental U.S. automobile market. The Sprint was subject to Japan's "voluntary" restraint agreement (VRA) on car shipments to the United States. The VRA, in place since 1981, limited the number of cars that each Japanese automobile manufacturer could ship to the United States in a given year. In 1984, Suzuki's total VRA quota of 17,000 cars went to GM as Sprints. GM quickly sold out of its allotment even though Sprint's distribution was limited to its West Coast dealers.

AMERICAN SUZUKI MOTOR CORPORATION (ASMC)

GM's success with Sprint showed Suzuki that a market existed for its cars in the continental United States. Suzuki, which called itself "the always something different car company," planned to introduce several unique vehicles into the U.S. market over time. Suzuki had no guarantee, however, that GM would be willing to market the vehicles. Therefore, Suzuki decided to establish its own presence in the U.S. automobile industry.

Japan's VRA quotas made it impossible for Suzuki to export any cars other than the Sprint to the United States in the foreseeable future. Consequently, in 1985, Suzuki and GM began negotiations with the Canadian government to build a plant in Ontario that could produce approximately 200,000 subcompact cars per year. Suzuki management expected the plant to be online by early 1989, and the company could then begin selling cars in the United States under its own name.

Market forces, however, made Suzuki loath to wait until 1989. In 1984, Japanese imports achieved a record of 17.7 percent share of U.S. new-car and truck sales. Based on first-quarter sales, industry experts predicted that Japanese imports would command a 19.2 percent share of the U.S. market in 1985. Total U.S. automobile sales were expected to grow by 10 percent in 1985, and this rapid growth made dealers optimistic and willing to invest money in new car lines, especially Japanese brands.

In addition, two other car companies, Hyundai Motor Company of South Korea and Zavodi Crvena Zastava (Yugo) of Yugoslavia, were expected to enter the U.S. car market in 1986. Suzuki managers believed that brand clutter might limit their success if they waited until 1989 to introduce the Suzuki name into the continental United States.

Suzuki management was convinced that the time was right to enter the continental United States and that Suzuki had the right product to do so, the SJ413. Its forerunner, the SJ410, was a mini-four-wheel-drive off-road vehicle with a 1,000 cc engine that Suzuki had introduced in 1960. By 1985, the SJ410 was sold in 102 countries and Hawaii. In 1985, Suzuki introduced the SJ413, an upgraded model that featured a 1,324 cc engine and was designed with the U.S. market specifically in mind. The SJ413 was more powerful and more comfortable than the SJ410. The upsizing of Suzuki's vehicle, combined with the downsizing of U.S. consumer automobile preferences, made the SJ413 a viable continental U.S. product.

If the SJ413 was imported without a back seat, the U.S. government classified it as a truck for customs purposes. Trucks were not subject to Japanese VRA quotas; instead, they were subject to a 25 percent tariff versus a 2.5 percent tariff on cars. The tariff was high, but Suzuki management believed that it was worth paying.

On May 10, 1985, Suzuki hired Douglas Mazza to organize and head its new subsidiary, ASMC. Mazza was charged with developing a Suzuki dealer network to begin selling the SJ413 by November 1985. He was also responsible for creating the market plan for the SJ413, which would be named the Suzuki Samurai in the United States, as it was in Canada. Suzuki planned to market two versions of the Samurai in the United States, a convertible and a hard-top.

SAMURAI DEALER NETWORK

Mazza's goal was to establish ASMC as a major car company in the United States. To achieve this goal, he believed that he had to convince prospective dealers to build separate showrooms for the Samurai. If ASMC allowed a dealer merely to display the vehicle in an existing showroom, the dealer would invest little in the Samurai, monetarily or emotionally, and probably would sell only a few Samurais each month. Low Samurai sales per dealer and lack of facility and management commitment could jeopardize Suzuki's plan to introduce other cars into the United States, starting in 1989.

Therefore, Mazza drafted a dealer agreement that required prospective Samurai dealers to build an exclusive sales facility for the Samurai. The facility had to include a showroom, sales offices, and a customer waiting and accessory display area. Service and parts could share a facility with a dealer's other car lines, but a minimum of two service stalls had to be dedicated to Suzuki and operated by Suzuki-trained mechanics. Furthermore, Suzuki dealerships had to display required signs outside the sales office and in the service stalls. A minimum of three salespeople, two service technicians, one general manager, and one general office clerk had to be dedicated to the Suzuki dealership.

The prospectus also explained that, as the product line grew, dealer requirements would expand to include a full, exclusive facility complete with attached parts and service. This upfront expansion plan was a first in the industry and was based on the belief that quick dealer profitability would be key to success—as a dealer's sales opportunities grew, so too would the financial commitment and overhead.

ASMC's planned suggested retail price for the basic Samurai was $5,995. The planned dealer invoice price was $5,095, only 7.5 percent higher than ASMC's own landed cost for the vehicle. ASMC planned to offer about 50 dealer-installed options, the sale of which would boost a dealer's average unit profit. Mazza estimated that each dealership would need to sell approximately 30 Samurais per month to cover its monthly operating costs plus the finance charges on its initial investment.

To attract good dealers, Mazza knew that he must make the opportunity match the investment requirements. He therefore planned to limit the number of Samurai dealers so that ASMC could guarantee a minimum supply of 37 units per month to each one. Thus each dealership could earn a profit every month if it sold its total allotment. Suzuki had set Mazza the goal of selling 6,000 Samurais in the first six months of U.S. distribution, but Mazza and his new management team convinced the Japanese management that the U.S. opportunity was far greater. Suzuki raised its commitment to ASMC to

10,500 vehicles for the same time period. Consequently, Mazza decided to limit his initial dealer network to no more than 47 dealers. This small network implied rolling out the Samurai in only two or three states in November 1985. Mazza chose to introduce the Samurai into California, the nation's largest automobile market, and Florida and Georgia, where Japanese import sales were higher than the U.S. average.

Before Mazza could enlist dealers, he had to decide how to position the Samurai to consumers. The position he chose would help define the vehicle's target market which, in turn, would influence ASMC's preferred dealer locations. By combining car registration data and census information, the concentration of owners of imported vehicles or owners of sports utility vehicles, for example, could be pinpointed by zip code. Dealerships could be selected with trading areas that encompassed zip codes with high concentrations of households that fell into Suzuki's target market.

SAMURAI POSITIONING

The keye/donna/pearlstein advertising agency had no experience in developing campaigns for automobiles. This appealed to Mazza, because he believed that a fresh approach was needed for his company's new product. After accepting Mazza's offer to compete for the Samurai account, Pearlstein and his associates quickly scanned automobile advertising of other manufacturers. They concluded that industry practice was to position vehicles according to their physical characteristics as, for example, subcompact cars versus compact cars versus luxury sedans. Most advertising was feature/benefit- or price-oriented. A typical ad noted that a vehicle was of a specific type and emphasized differentiating features and/or superior value for the money.

If they followed industry practice, Pearlstein's group had three options for positioning the Samurai based on its physical characteristics—as a compact sport utility vehicle, as a compact pickup truck, or as a subcompact car.

Exhibit 1 shows pictures of the Samurai. The most obvious position for the Samurai was as a sport utility vehicle. It looked like a "mini-Jeep," had 4-wheel drive capability, and was designed to drive well off-road. Such a position would be consistent with the Samurai's heritage and its positioning in the 102 countries where the SJ410 and SJ413 were sold. Foreign owners praised the Samurai's reliability, ability to go places where larger vehicles could not, and ease of repair.

The Samurai's size and price distinguished it from all other sport utility vehicles sold in the United States in 1985. The Samurai was smaller and lighter than the other vehicles, and its $5,995 suggested retail price was well below the other vehicles' $10,000 to $13,000 price range.

Pearlstein believed that if the Samurai were positioned as a sport utility vehicle, it should be advertised as a "tough little cheap Jeep." Advertising copy would show the Samurai in off-road wilderness situations, squeezing through places where bigger sport utility vehicles could not go. Ads would also emphasize that the Samurai cost only half the price of an average Jeep.

Pearlstein was unsure, however, whether a compact sport utility positioning could generate the sales volume that Mazza envisioned for the Samurai. The market for sport utility vehicles was relatively small. As Exhibit 2 shows, total 1984 compact sport utility

EXHIBIT 1   Samurai Convertible and Hardtop

EXHIBIT 2   U.S. Automobile Industry Unit Sales

Make	1984 Unit Sales	Projected 1985 Unit Sales
Compact Sport Utility Vehicles		
Suzuki SJ410 (Hawaii)	2,124	2,500
Mitsubishi Montero	2,690	2,800
Toyota 4Runner	9,181	19,300
Toyota Landcruiser	4,170	4,400
Isuzu Trooper	6,935	25,400
Total Japanese imports	25,100	54,400
Ford Bronco II	98,446	104,500
GM Chevrolet S10 Blazer/GMC S15 Jimmy	175,177	225,200
Jeep CJ/YJ series	41,627	40,100
Jeep Cherokee/Wagoneer	84,352	113,900
Total domestic	399,710	483,700
Total compact sport utility	424,810	538,100
Compact Pickup Trucks		
Mitsubishi P/U	11,102	21,900
Toyota P/U	144,675	171,500
Nissan P/U	140,864	188,700
Mazda P/U	115,303	114,600
Isuzu P/U	32,372	46,200
Total Japanese import P/U 2WD	444,316	542,900
Jeep Comanche P/U	0	3,800
Ford Ranger P/U	173,959	185,800
Chevy/GMC S10/S15 P/U	181,692	200,200
Dodge Ram 50 P/U	37,356	56,100
Total domestic P/U 2WD	393,007	445,900
Total compact P/U truck 2WD	837,323	988,800
Mitsubishi P/U 4×4	2,156	1,900
Toyota P/U 4×4	81,904	101,400
Nissan P/U 4×4	51,082	65,400
Isuzu P/U 4×4	3,537	4,900
Total Japanese import P/U 4×4	138,679	173,600
Jeep Comanche 4×4	0	4,800
Ford Ranger 4×4	48,110	56,400
Chevy/GMC S10/S15 4×4	47,409	51,200
Dodge Ram 50 P/U 4×4	12,499	12,500
Total domestic P/U 4×4	108,018	124,900
Total compact P/U truck 4×4	246,697	298,500
Total Japanese import P/U 2WD and 4×4	582,995	716,500
Total domestic P/U 2WD and 4×4	501,025	570,800
Total compact P/U 2WD and 4×4	1,084,020	1,287,300

EXHIBIT 2   *(concluded)*

Make	1984 Unit Sales	Projected 1985 Unit Sales
Subcompact Cars		
Toyota Starlet	781	0
Toyota Tercel	107,185	95,400
Toyota Corolla	156,249	173,900
Nissan Sentra	194,092	225,700
Nissan Pulsar	39,470	51,400
Mitsubishi Mirage	2,354	12,400
Honda Civic	173,561	196,800
Mazda 323/GLC	43,641	60,000
Isuzu I-Mark	4,822	13,000
Total Japanese import	722,155	828,600
Volkswagen Rabbit/Golf	85,153	71,300
Chevrolet Spectrum	1,646	51,700
Chevrolet Sprint	9,464	29,700
Dodge/Plymouth Colt	82,402	96,100
Total domestic	944,668	1,112,900
Total subcompact	1,752,248	2,016,095
Total Car and Truck		
Total Japanese car	1,846,398	2,139,500
Total Japanese truck	664,813	849,800
Total Japanese car and truck	2,511,211	2,989,300
Total industry car	10,128,318	10,888,600
Total industry truck	4,048,998	4,675,200
Total industry car and truck	14,177,316	15,563,800

Note: Sums of individual vehicle makes do not always equal totals and subtotals since only the top-selling makes are listed.

Source: R. L. Polk & Company market area report.

vehicles sales in the United States were less than 3 percent of total automobile industry sales. Mazza's goal was to build annual U.S. Samurai sales to 30,000 units within two years of the vehicle's introduction. To achieve this objective, annual Samurai sales would have to exceed the combined 1984 sales of all imported compact sport utility vehicles.

The second option, positioning the Samurai as a compact pickup truck, would tap a market that was two and one-half times the size of that for compact sport utility vehicles. Moreover, Japanese import trucks sold well in the United States, accounting for 54 percent of total 1984 compact pickup truck sales. The Samurai could be used as a truck when purchased without a back seat or when its back seat was folded up. Therefore, positioning it as a truck seemed feasible.

ASMC set the Samurai's suggested retail price at $5,995 in order to price it comparably with Japanese import compact pickup trucks, which had a high level of U.S. consumer acceptance. Therefore, in Pearlstein's view, if advertised as a truck, the Samurai's price would not be emphasized but mentioned only to indicate parity with other truck prices. Advertising copy would probably be serious, practical, male-targeted, and designed to portray the Samurai as a tough truck.

The third option, to position the Samurai as a subcompact car, would open up the largest of the three possible markets. Although the Suzuki SJ413 was not positioned as a car in Europe, a trend was developing in which professionals, especially doctors and lawyers, drove their SJ413s to their offices in the city and left their Mercedeses at home. Similarly, in the United States, especially in California, sport utility vehicles were sometimes driven in town, although none had hitherto been positioned as a car.

The Samurai boasted an average 28 miles per gallon in combined city and highway driving, was priced lower than many subcompact cars, and offered more versatility. Therefore, it could reasonably be considered by those who were shopping for an economy car. If positioned against subcompact cars, Pearlstein believed that Samurai advertising copy should emphasize the vehicle's looks. The message to consumers would be "Why buy a Toyota Tercel or a Nissan Sentra when, with the same amount of money, you can buy a much cuter vehicle, the Samurai?" However, the vehicle might not meet consumers' expectations if it was positioned as a car. Because the Samurai was built on a truck platform, its ride was stiffer and less comfortable than even the least-expensive subcompact.

MARKET RESEARCH

Pearlstein defined positioning as "the unique way we want prospects to think about a product." Before choosing a position for the Samurai, he asked Don Popielarz, director of research and planning, to conduct research in order to gain a thorough understanding of not only the attributes that prospective buyers ascribed to the Samurai versus other vehicles, but also the profile and characteristics of potential buyers. This information would help Pearlstein decide how to position the vehicle. Then his team could develop advertising copy and choose the media that would be most efficient in delivering the Samurai's message to its consumer target.

Popielarz started by reviewing the latest research available from outside sources. A demographic segmentation study conducted by J.D. Power and Associates divided new-car buyers into demographic segments based on the size/style of the car that was purchased. The "basic small-car" segment included cars such as the Chevrolet Sprint, Ford Escort, Honda Civic, Toyota Tercel, and Mazda 323. Most (54 percent) of the car purchasers in this segment were men, but only 43 percent of the principal drivers were male. The median age of the buyers was 38. The average domestic car buyer was 41, while the average imports car buyer was 36. Sixty percent of the car buyer were married; over one-third had executive/professional/technical careers, and 43 percent were college graduates. The median household size was 2.69 people, and the median household income was $34,240.

From a survey conducted by *Newsweek* for use by pickup truck and sport utility vehicle manufacturers, Popielarz learned how consumers perceived sport utility vehicles versus pickup trucks. Consumers were asked to rate 29 vehicle features of domestic and imported

EXHIBIT 3 *Newsweek* Study: Factors and the Features that Constitute Them

Factor	Feature

Everyday driving	For highway driving:
	  Acceleration/power
	  Riding comfort
	  Ease of handling
	  Quietness
	  Maneuverability in traffic
	For long-distance vacations:
	  Safety features
	  Seating comfort
	  Towing capacity

Passenger comfort	Passenger seating capacity as a family vehicle:
	  Interior roominess
	For long-distance vacations:
	  Seating comfort
	  Level of luxury
	  Riding comfort

Quality/durability	Quality of workmanship Durability/reliability Quality of materials Tough, rugged
Styling	Interior styling Exterior styling Design of instrument panel Level of luxury Ground clearance
Off-road/snow driving	Off-road capability for driving in snow Ground clearance Fun to drive Tough, rugged
Capacity	Ability to carry large items Cargo capacity Towing capacity
Gas mileage	Gas mileage/fuel economy

pickup trucks and sport utility vehicles. The features were aggregated into seven factors that were then plotted on two-dimension perceptual maps. The seven factors were everyday driving, off-road/snow driving, passenger comfort, quality/durability, styling, capacity, and gas mileage. Exhibit 3 lists the vehicle features that made up each of the seven factors. Exhibits 4 through 7 show four maps that summarize consumers' perceptions of pickup trucks versus sport utility vehicles on the seven factors.

After reviewing research from outside sources, Popielarz studied a survey that Suzuki had recently conducted in Canada, where it sold approximately 4,000 Samurais in 1984. Suzuki randomly surveyed 374 Canadian Samurai owners. The majority (75 percent) of

---

EXHIBIT 4 Perceptual Map from *Newsweek* Study: Off-Road/Snow Driving versus Everyday Driving

---

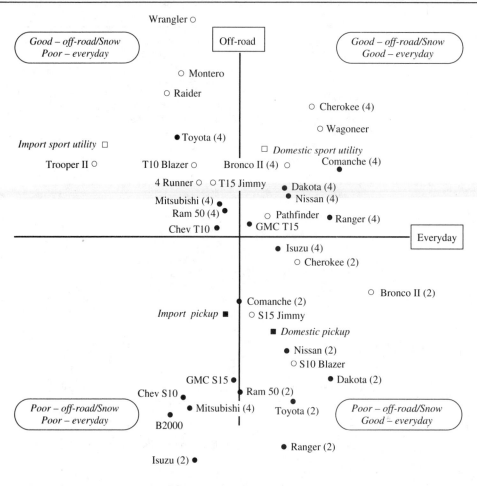

- ● Perceptions of *specific* brands/models of *pickup trucks*.
- ○ Perceptions of *specific* brands/models of *sport utility vehicles*.
- ■ Perceptions of the *category of pickup trucks*.
- □ Perceptions of the *category of sport utility vehicles*.

---

the Samurai buyers were male, and 62 percent were between the ages of 18 and 34. The average age of the buyers was 33. The most frequently mentioned occupation was a skilled tradesperson (32 percent). Only 21 percent were college graduates, and only 1 percent were currently students. Fifty-one percent of the buyers lived in two-person households, and the average household income was $43,800.

EXHIBIT 5   Perceptual Map from *Newsweek* Study: Passenger Comfort versus Styling

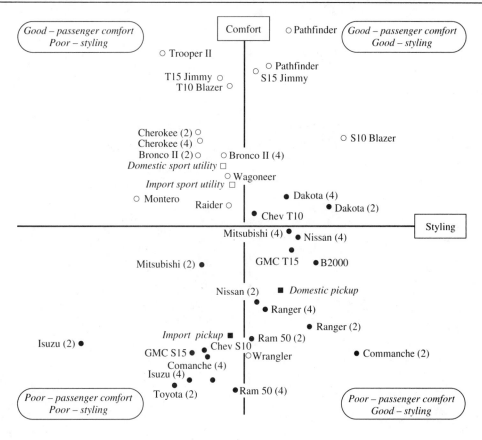

- ● Perceptions of *specific* brands/models of *pickup trucks*.
- ○ Perceptions of *specific* brands/models of *sport utility vehicles*.
- ■ Perceptions of the *category of pickup trucks*.
- □ Perceptions of the *category of sport utility vehicles*.

When asked "When you hear the name Suzuki, what do you think of?," 40 percent of the Samurai owners responded "motorcycle." Other answers included 4 × 4/4-wheel drive (23 percent), Jeep (16 percent), Japanese product/efficiency (14 percent), quality/well-made (11 percent), dependable/reliable (10 percent), versatility/work/play/goes anywhere (10 percent), small (9 percent), pleasure vehicle/fun (8 percent), my car (7 percent), and

EXHIBIT 6   Perceptual Map from *Newsweek* Study: Gas Mileage versus Everyday Driving

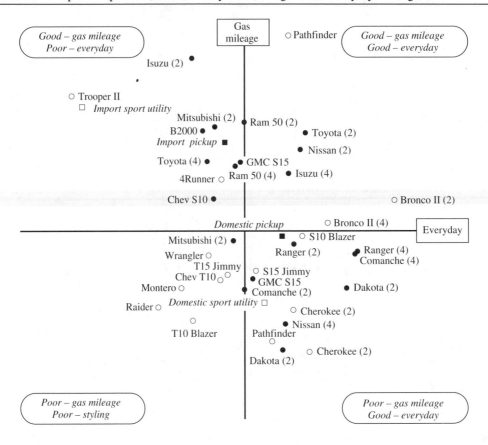

● Perceptions of *specific* brands/models of *pickup trucks.*
○ Perceptions of *specific* brands/models of *sport utility vehicles.*
■ Perceptions of the *category of pickup trucks.*
□ Perceptions of the *category of sport utility vehicles.*

economical (6 percent). When the owners were asked to describe the Samurai using only one word or phrase, the word most often mentioned was "fun." Exhibit 8 lists all the words that were volunteered by five or more owners.

As Exhibit 9 shows, design/appearance was mentioned most frequently by owners as their main reason for purchasing the Samurai. When asked "Before making your purchase, what other automobiles did you consider?," 29 percent mentioned various models of

EXHIBIT 7 Perceptual Map from *Newsweek* Study: Quality/Durability versus Passenger Comfort

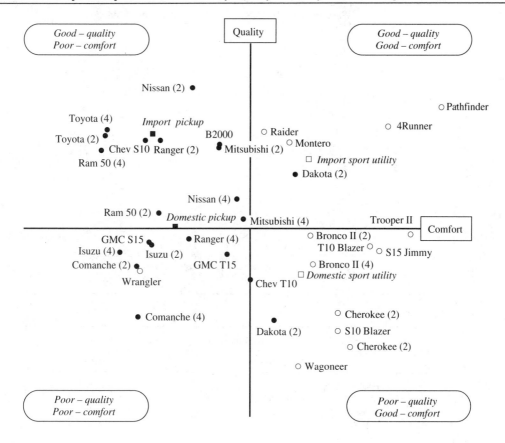

- ● Perceptions of *specific* brands/models of *pickup trucks.*
- ○ Perceptions of *specific* brands/models of *sport utility vehicles.*
- ■ Perceptions of the *category of pickup trucks.*
- □ Perceptions of the *category of sport utility vehicles.*

Jeep. Other vehicles mentioned included Ford Bronco and Ranger (24 percent), GMC Chevrolet Jimmy (7 percent), GM Chevrolet 5–10 Blazer (8 percent), Toyota 4 × 4 pickup truck and Landcruiser (12 percent), and Nissan 4 × 4 pickup truck (4 percent). No other model was mentioned by as many as 4 percent of the respondents. When asked why they selected the Samurai over their "first alternative" vehicle, the overwhelming response was economy/value (59 percent) followed by design/appearance (29 percent).

EXHIBIT 8   Canadian Samurai Buyer Survey: Suzuki Samurai One Word/Phrase Description

Word/Phrase Mentioned	Number of Mentions
Fun	41
Jeep	15
Great	13
Goes everywhere	11
Good	11
Economical	10
Practical	9
Reliable	8
All-terrain	7
Fantastic	7
Pleasure	7
Tough	7
Four-wheel drive	6
Four-by-four	5
Sporty	5
Versatile	5

Note: Samurai buyers were asked, "If you had to describe the Suzuki Samurai using only one word or phrase, what would you say about it?"

EXHIBIT 9   Canadian Samurai Buyer Survey: Reasons for Purchasing Samurai

Main Reason for Purchasing	Percent Mentioning
Design/appearance (net)	64%
4 × 4/4-wheel drive/jeep	39
Appearance/good-looking/sporty-looking	22
Convertible	19
Size/small/compact	8
Economy/value (net)	55
Economy/economical	18
Good mileage/fuel saving	18
Cost/reasonable price	18
Inexpensive/low price	10
Performance (net)	51
Traction/can go anywhere	19
All season vehicle/functional	17
Fun/fun to drive	11
Ease of driving/handling/parking	7
Reliable/service (net)	19
Dependable/reliable	13
Quality/well-made/good	7
Need for jeep/second vehicle	8
Suits my life-style/needs/I like it	5

Note: Samurai buyers were asked, "What are your main reasons for purchasing this vehicle?"

Popielarz was unsure how to interpret the data from the Canadian study, given climatic and cultural differences between the United States and Canada. Furthermore, the Samurai was positioned as a rugged utility vehicle in Canada, where it was priced higher than was planned in the United States. In Canada, the Samurai was priced similar to the least-expensive sport utility vehicles and substantially higher than both light trucks and sub-compact cars.

Fortunately, there was one continental U.S. market where Suzuki SJ410s were being sold, albeit unauthorized by Suzuki. In Florida, a "gray market" existed for Suzuki SJ410s. Since 1984, approximately 3,000 had been sold there by dealers who imported them from other Suzuki markets, including Puerto Rico, Guam, the U.S. Virgin Islands, and Panama.

Popielarz and Tim O'Mara, one of the agency's account supervisors, decided to conduct face-to-face interviews with five sales managers and sales representatives at three Florida dealerships that sold SJ410s. They asked the salespeople four questions. The first question was "Who is the buyer?" The dealers said the SJ410 buyer was young, on average between 18 and 30 years old, often single, often a first-time car buyer, and often a student. Young women seemed to like the vehicle, and many sales involved fathers buying SJ410s for their children. Additionally, there was an important secondary buyer group comprising people over 30, both single and married, who bought the Suzuki to use as a third or fourth vehicle.

The second question, "What does the buyer see as competition?," elicited a unanimous response from the dealers. There was no direct competition. Indirect competition included four-wheel drive vehicles, small cars, and convertibles. The SJ410 was less expensive than other convertibles and four-wheel drive vehicles, however, and was more "fun and (had more) style than small cars."

"Why does the buyer want this vehicle?" was the third question the dealers addressed. The "most fun for the dollars" was usually mentioned. As one sales manager stated, "I don't see too many people driving down the road in Chevettes and having a blast." Other replies included: convertible top; versatility; utility; gas mileage; durability; cute and unique; handles in rain, snow, and off-road; and great for fishing, camping, and skiing.

The final question, "How are they selling?," prompted smiles from the salespeople, who typically responded, "People were just lining up to get them. Just couldn't get enough of them in." The SJ410s sold for an average price of $8,500 at the three dealerships.

One of the dealerships, King Motors in Fort Lauderdale, routinely surveyed its automobile buyers. The dealership had surveys completed by 150 recent Suzuki SJ410 buyers, which it allowed Popielarz and O'Mara to study. The vehicle buyer filled out the questionnaire; however, in many instances, the buyer was not the ultimate driver. Information on age was incomplete, but of those who gave their age, 56 percent of the buyers were between 18 and 30; the rest were over 30. One-third of the purchasers were women.

Exhibit 10 tabulates the King Motors survey responses. The majority of buyers learned about the Suzuki through word of mouth or seeing it when driving by the dealership. Most buyers came to King Motors planning to buy the Suzuki rather than the AMC Jeep line, which was also sold there. Fewer than half of the buyers considered buying another vehicle, but when other automobiles were considered, they included both new and used Jeeps, small imported cars, and large used American convertibles.

Four-wheel drive was not the principal feature generating interest in the Suzuki. Only

---

EXHIBIT 10   King Motors' Suzuki SJ410 Buyer Survey

	Total	Total Men	Total Women
Where heard about Suzuki			
Word of mouth	41%	41%	42%
Dealer location	30	36	22
Ft. Lauderdale newspaper	20	17	24
Radio	6	5	7
Pompano Shopper	3	1	5
Came to dealer to see			
Suzuki	76	75	77
AMC Jeep	17	21	14
Encore	1	0	2
Alliance	0	0	0
Wagoneer	0	0	0
Other	5	4	7
Considered other vehicle			
Yes	40	42	37
No	60	58	63
Considered AMC Jeep first			
Yes	28	30	25
No	72	70	75
Important purchase factors			
Price	76	72	80
Convertible	62	59	66
Gas mileage	46	46	45
Four-wheel drive	40	45	32
Size of vehicle	39	37	41
Color	22	26	18
Driving and handling	20	22	16
Other	7	9	5

---

45 percent of the men and 32 percent of the women surveyed said that it was an important factor in their purchase decision. The attributes that buyers rated as most important were price and the fact that it was a convertible model.

Popielarz knew that the Florida buyers who participated in the survey might not be typical of the kinds of people who would buy the Samurai once it was introduced nationwide. He did believe, however, that the survey results gave clues about who the early adopters were likely to be.

After interviewing the Florida dealers, Popielarz and O'Mara conducted focus group interviews in California with a group of women aged 25 to 33, a group of men aged 18 to 24, and another group of men aged 25 to 35. All of the participants were actively shopping for a new vehicle that was either a sport utility vehicle, a subcompact car, or an imported pickup truck. All had visited at least one dealer showroom within the previous two months.

During the sessions, focus group members viewed pictures of both the convertible and hardtop Samurais that would be sold in the United States, pictures of a variety of people who might drive the Samurai, a five-minute videotape showing the Samurai in action, and pictures of several vehicles with which the Samurai might compete. Respondents reacted favorably to the Samurai's appearance, describing it as "cute," "neat," and "fun." The Samurai's size invoked mixed reactions. Some believed its size would add to its drivability and maneuverability; they said it looked easy to drive around town and in the country. For others, especially those with children or pets, the small size was a drawback. Also, those who planned rugged off-road use said the Samurai was too small.

Group members who needed occasional four-wheel drive capability readily accepted the Samurai as a viable alternative to other four-wheel drive vehicles. Those people who did not need the four-wheel drive feature said that it did not reduce their acceptance of the vehicle.

Some people said that the Samurai was exactly what they were looking for in a vehicle. They saw it as a symbol of their independence to do something different and their practicality to drive a versatile vehicle. Interest in the Samurai among focus group members appeared to be linked more to attitude than to age. When asked to choose potential Samurai buyers from the pictures that were shown to them, the interviewees chose the younger, more active people.

Most of the interviewees recognized the Suzuki name and associated it with motorcycles or the attributes of the Japanese manufacturers, that is, higher quality and better engineering than the domestic competition. Their price expectations were between $8,000 and $12,000, significantly higher than the planned $5,995 price tag. They were quite knowledgeable, however, about the prices of the competitive vehicles discussed. When told the Samurai's actual price, most people expressed surprise and pleasure. A few expressed suspicion about the vehicle's quality at that price.

CONCLUSIONS

Popielarz and O'Mara reviewed the market research findings with Pearlstein and Spike Bragg, the agency's exclusive vice president. They concluded that any young or young-at-heart person considering the purchase of a small car, small truck, or sport utility vehicle was a prospect for the Samurai. Suzuki should, therefore, avoid positioning the Samurai as a specific type of vehicle so as not to exclude large groups of potential buyers.

Furthermore, they reasoned that Suzuki should not "overdefine" the vehicle. The Samurai appeared to represent different things to different people. Therefore, Suzuki should try to develop a position with broad enough appeal to attract a wide range of consumers so that each person could define the Samurai in his or her own way and rationalize the purchase decision in his or her own terms. Moreover, the ad agency thought that if each consumer was allowed personally to define the Samurai, this would lead to greater congruence between the vehicle's promise and its delivery than if Suzuki tried to tell consumers what the Samurai was.

Bragg suggested that the Samurai be positioned as "the alternative to small-car boredom." He reasoned that sport utility buyers could be attracted to the Samurai just by looking at the vehicle, but that small-car buyers would need to be told that the Samurai was a fun alternative to dull automobiles. Furthermore, he believed that many purchasers of small trucks were buying them to use as cars because compact import pickup trucks were less expensive than import subcompact cars and offered more versatility. An "alternative to small-car-boredom" positioning could, therefore, attract buyers from all three vehicle segments.

Pearlstein liked Bragg's idea but expanded on it. He thought that the Samurai should be positioned as the "antidote to traditional transportation." It was important that the Samurai not be labeled as any type of vehicle. No ads should refer to it as a car, truck, or sport utility vehicle.

FINAL PREPARATIONS FOR PRESENTATION TO MAZZA

Pearlstein and his associates had to present their positioning recommendations to Mazza the following day. Although Mazza had not asked to be shown any creative execution of the position, the four men had developed copy that they believed would help to explain the "antidote-to-traditional-transportation" position that they had chosen. Exhibits 11 through 16 show examples of their proposed advertising copy.

Mazza had told Pearlstein that he planned to spend $2.5 million on advertising and promotion during the first six months after the Samurai's introduction. For 1985, estimated Jeep advertising was $40 million for the American market. Industry experts expected total 1985 car, truck, and sport utility vehicle advertising expenditures in the United States to approximate $4.25 billion. Traditionally, automobile manufacturers spent between $200 and $400 per vehicle on advertising, and up to an additional $500 per vehicle on incentives such as rebates and extended warranties.

Pearlstein and his group had to recommend how the Samurai's advertising budget should be spent. A typical automobile manufacturer spent 77 percent of its advertising dollars on television ads, 10 percent on radio commercials to add frequency to the television schedule, 10 percent on print ads, and 3 percent on highway billboards. The print ads were run in both general-interest magazines and enthusiast magazines—depending on the vehicle's positioning as a car, truck, or sport utility vehicle.

Pearlstein addressed his colleagues:

> *If we are to win the ASMC account, tomorrow we must sell our Samurai positioning strategy to Mazza. To sell it to him, we must be convinced that it is the best positioning for the Samurai. Let's now discuss the pros and cons of the "unposition" we are proposing versus the three options we originally considered. We must be able to back up our positioning recommendation with sound market research data. We must address any risks associated with our recommended positioning. Finally, we must develop a recommendation on how to spend the $2.5 million six-month advertising budget. We should discuss how our budget allocation recommendations would vary according to the positioning strategy chosen.*

EXHIBIT 11   "End of Dull" Proposed Print Ad

The end of dull. The start of Suzuki.

Introducing the Suzuki Samurai." The end of dull, point and steer, econo-box driving. The start of 4x4 versatility in a new compact size all its own, convertible or hard top. With a nifty 1.3 liter, SOHC, 4-cylinder engine, 5-speed stick, and room for four. The price? Low. The place? Where there's never a dull moment. Your Suzuki automotive dealer. See him for a Samurai test drive today.

EXHIBIT 12   "Dull Barrier" Proposed Print Ad

Stop suffering the heartbreak of econo-box boredom. Get quick relief where there's never a dull moment. Your Suzuki auto dealer.

Take one test drive in a Suzuki Samurai™ and you, too, will break the dull barrier. The Samurai handles differently than an ordinary passenger car. Avoid sharp turns and abrupt maneuvers, and always wear your seat belt. For specific details, read your owner's manual.

SUZUKI SAMURAI BREAKS

THE DULL BARRIER

(DEALER NAME)

EXHIBIT 13 "Suzuki and Driver" Proposed Print Ad

SUZUKI AND DRIVER

To a pair of calloused hands, and cowboy boots, it's a fresh workhorse. And Saturday night sidekick. To the student, it's an A+ in economics. And engineering. To commuters, an inspired excuse for driving to work the long way.

To moms, it's a happy reminder that there's life after housework. To the tennis set, it's a love match. To the surfing set, it's an irresistible bikini magnet. To us,

it's for anyone who wants more than point and steer driving.

The 1987 Suzuki Samurai™ 4×4 convertible and hard top. Our answer to all those single-minded, econo-cars guaranteed to bore you silly within 12,000 miles or 12 months, whichever comes first.

Our promise? Never a dull moment. Not with our 1.3 liter, SOHC, 4-cylinder power plant and 5-speed stick. Not to

mention its 4×4 agility, when you want to romp in the dirt with a playmate weighing barely over a ton.

Before you test drive our new Samurai, you should know that Suzuki's automotive engineering has been tested out by all kinds of drivers for over 17 years, in over 100 countries.

So, now all you have to do is call for the name of your nearest Suzuki automotive dealer. The call's on us.
1-800-447-4700.

$ SUZUKI

Please be advised that this vehicle handles differently than a conventional passenger car. Avoid sharp cornering, abrupt maneuvers and always wear your seatbelt. For specific driving information, read your owner's manual.

165

EXHIBIT 14   Copy for Proposed Television Ad

Setting:	A road leading from awesome mountains.
Atmosphere:	Dawn. Mysterious electrical storm flashes over the mountains. Something is about to happen. Something strange or wondrous.
What happens:	We see headlights approaching camera. From the dramatic music and overblown announcer, whatever's coming must be magnificent. Then the little Suzuki drives by at a casual speed. People inside wave to camera, giggle, car drives out of frame. Camera does double take, then watches car drive away.
(Dramatic music begins)	
Voice over:	"Prepare for the most extraordinary event of your lifetime . . ."
(Music builds)	
	"An event that will forever alter the course of mankind and womankind . . ."
(Music builds)	
	"The next major turning point in the history of all civilization."
(Music crescendos, then stops) (Beep, beep)	
People in the car:	"Hi!"
(Music continues)	
Voice over:	"Introducing the new Suzuki Samurai 4 × 4.
(Fades)	The beginning of the universe was dull by comparison. . . . The discovery of fire pales in significance."
(Live announcer dealer tag)	

EXHIBIT 16 Storyboard for Proposed "Amusement Park" Television Ad

EXHIBIT 16 Storyboard for Proposed "Amusement Park" Television Ad

Case 2–4

The Chevrolet Corvette*

In mid-1983, Chevrolet introduced a new, redesigned version of the Corvette. Simultaneously, the price was increased and an advertising campaign comparing Corvette to imported sports cars, primarily Porsche, was begun. Initial sales were strong, but by early 1986 sales were down 25 percent from the same period in 1985. The April 14, 1986, issue of *Autoweek* (p. 3) reported, "Corvette and Fiero production will be cut significantly this month to stem a stockpile of sports cars, which are selling slower than predicted according to General Motors. Second-shift production at the Bowling Green, Kentucky, Corvette plant will be eliminated . . ." The Corvette's advertising support appeared to have been reduced from 1983–84 levels, but special lease rates and financing plans were offered in late 1985 and early 1986.

The time was appropriate for addressing the proper strategic role for Corvette within G.M. and Chevrolet. Depending on the strategic objective selected for Corvette, the product design, distribution system, pricing, and promotion program could be in need of changes.

GENERAL MOTORS AND THE AUTOMOTIVE INDUSTRY

In 1985, it was estimated that 16 percent of private, nonagricultural workers in the U.S. were employed in the manufacture, distribution, maintenance, and commercial use of motor vehicles.[1] Some 52.8 percent of all households owned two or more cars. In households with incomes of $40,000 or more, 87 percent owned two or more cars and 43 percent owned three or more cars.[2] The net sales of G.M., Ford, Chrysler, and American Motors accounted for 3.9 percent of the 1983 Gross National Product.[3] Of the U.S. auto manufacturers, G.M. was by far the largest, dominating the 1985 new-car market with 6 of the 10 top-selling cars in the country.

---

*This case was written from public sources by Frank Conley and Nancy Trap under the supervision of Paul W. Farris, as a basis for classroom discussion rather than to illustrate either effective or ineffective handling of an administrative situation. Copyright © 1986 by the Darden Graduate Business School Foundation, Charlottesville, VA.

[1] Public Affairs Division of Motor Vehicle Manufacturers' Association of the United States, Inc., *Facts and Figures '85*.

[2] U.S. Department of Transportation, Federal Highway Administration, *Highway Statistics 1984*.

[3] Harry A. Stark, ed., *Ward's Automotive Yearbook*, 46th ed. (1984).

In recent years, the U.S. auto industry had faced major market competition from foreign manufacturers. "Voluntary" quotas slowed import penetration in 1984, but imports still accounted for 23.5 percent of total U.S.-market automobile sales.

Recent Developments at G.M.

In response to an increasingly competitive environment, G.M. had recently reorganized five former autonomous car divisions into two groups, the Oldsmobile-Buick-Cadillac group and the Chevrolet-Pontiac-G.M. group. This reorganization reflected a concern of G.M. that historic divisional distinctions between Chevrolet, Pontiac, Oldsmobile, Buick, and Cadillac had become blurred. (The problem was compounded by the fact that many of G.M.'s cars looked alike.)

Two acquisitions, Hughes Aircraft Company and Electronic Data Systems, provided access to leading-edge technologies as G.M. began to design its auto lines for the 21st century. The hope was that the aerospace technology would be adapted in automotive areas ranging from computer-integrated manufacturing to futuristic car dashboard displays. In 1986, G.M. also bought Group Lotus Cars, a British automobile engineering and production firm known for state-of-the-art automotive technology in racing cars.

New ventures for G.M. included a G.M.-Toyota joint venture that produced the new Chevrolet Nova, and the Saturn project that would produce G.M.'s first new make since the 1930s. Additionally, GM imported and marketed cars from three foreign companies.

Chevrolet

Chevrolet sold several different models of passenger cars and a line of trucks. Each model came in a variety of options and prices. In 1985, the Cavalier was the number one selling car in America, and the Celebrity and Caprice were third and seventh, respectively.

Chevrolet sales were specially subject to swings in the economy, perhaps because the cars were priced lower than other G.M. cars of the same body type. In 1983, Chevrolet Motor Division General Manager Robert Stempel commented, "The last people who stop buying new cars are rich people, and the last people out of work are rich people. That 10 percent unemployment is a helluva lot more important to me at Chevrolet than it is at a lot of upscale car companies."[4]

SEGMENTATION OF THE SPORTS CAR MARKET

Segmentation of the automobile market was complex. Individuals considered economic, status/image, comfort, and performance factors in making a purchase decision, and segments often overlapped. See Exhibit 2 for an example of a market map depicting the position of various models. Even the sports car market could be further segmented.

---

[4]McCosh, "Marketing the '83s," *Ward's Auto World*, October 1982.

TABLE 1 Chevrolet Model Line Sales

Model	1984 Units	1985 Units
Cavalier	377,446	431,031
Chevette	164,917	129,927
Camaro	202,172	199,985
Celebrity	322,198	363,619
Citation	92,174	43,667
Monte Carlo	115,930	112,585
Corvette	34,024	37,956
Other Chevrolet	258,902	280,800
Total Chevrolet	1,565,143	1,600,200
Total G.M.	4,587,508	4,607,458

EXHIBIT 1 Corvette Production Data for Selected Years

Year	Total Corvette Production (000's)	Total Chevrolet Production (000's)	Chevrolet Corvette Percent of Chevrolet	Chevrolet Percent of Domestic Production
1953	.315	1,447	.02%	24%
1958	9.3	2,367	.39%	40%
1963	21.5	2,303	.93%	30%
1968	28.3	2,148	1.31%	24%
1973	34.5	2,334	1.47%	24%
1978	46.8	2,347	1.99%	26%
1982*	25.4	1,004	2.52%	20%
1984	28.2	1,294	2.18%	19%
1985	46.3	1,626	2.85%	19%

*No 1983 Corvette model was produced.

Source: Harry A. Stark, ed., *Ward's Automotive Yearbook,* 46th ed. (1984).

Product and Price Data for Selected Sports Car Models

Model	Wheel Base (inches)	Length (inches)	Weight (pounds)	Horse-power	Price	U.S. Sales (000's)	U.S. Sales Percent of Prod.	Number of U.S. Dealers
Corvette	96.2	176.5	3,280	230	$24,891	38.0	81.0	5,050
Ferrari 308 GTBi	92.1	174.2	3,250	230	54,300	N/A	N/A	42
Mazda RX7 Turbo	95.7	168.9	2,850	182	14,145	53.8	N/A	767
Nissan 300ZX Turbo	99.2	178.7	3,255	228	17,699	67.4	N/A	1,101
Jaguar XJ SC	102.0	187.6	4,025	295	32,250	3.8	N/A	167
Porsche 944	94.5	168.9	2,900	147	21,440	16.7	N/A	317
Porsche 911	89.5	168.9	2,750	200	31,950	5.9	N/A	317
Porsche 928S	98.4	175.7	3,540	288	50,000	2.6	N/A	317

Source: *Road & Track* and *Motor Trend* magazines, 1986 issues. *Automotive News Market Data Book,* 1985, 1986.

EXHIBIT 2   Market Segmentation Map

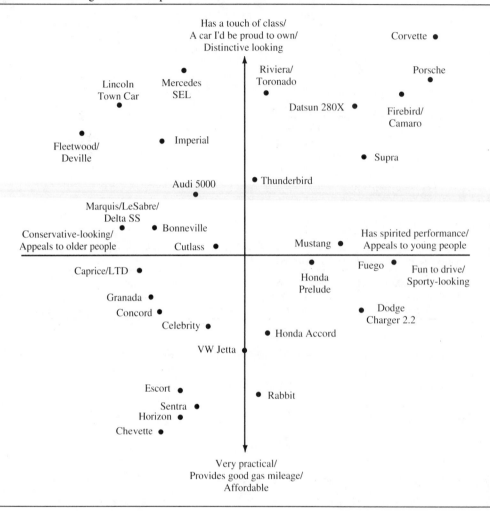

Source: Modified version of the Opinion Survey Center, Inc., using sampling of 12,000 responses as printed in "Marketing the '83's," *Ward's Auto World*, October 1982.

Economy sports cars were mass-produced and generally constructed from sub-assemblies taken from the manufacturer's parts bin and then modified and assembled to increase the overall performance of the final product. The *Grand Turismo* (GT) class of sports cars seated four people and had superior performance and handling characteristics. The *high-performance* sports cars were usually produced in relatively small numbers and often had a racing heritage. These cars generally had much higher resale values than others

---

EXHIBIT 3 New-Car Buyer Demographics, 1984

Car Make	Percent Male	Median Age (Years)	Percent Married	Medium Household Income (000's)
Chevrolet	56%	41	65%	$ 33.4
Corvette	85%	38*	59%	59.2
BMW	65%	35	58%	61.0
Jaguar	64%	44	80%	100.0+
Mercedes-Benz	68%	46	76%	87.5
Porsche	78%	36	62%	81.2

*In 1981, "median age" and "income" for Corvette owners were 33 years and $33,000, respectively.

Source: "New Car Buyer Demographics," *Automotive News*, April 1984.

---

and were looked at by some as investments.[5] (Peter Shutz, CEO Porsche, paid $8,500 for a 1976 Corvette, and three years later sold it for the same price when he moved to Europe.) High-performance sports cars also could be viewed as a subset of the *luxury-car market*. (Exhibit 3 gives demographics for buyers of selected models.)

G.M. was expected to launch its ultra-luxury two-seat convertible, the Cadillac Allante, in the beginning of 1987. The Allante, designed by Pininfarina, the Italian firm responsible for many Ferrari models, was scheduled for low-volume production and a price tag of $50,000. Industry analysts believed that G.M. was hoping the Allante would provide a "halo" effect for Cadillac, helping to update and differentiate its product image. The car had been premiered on the television series "Dallas" in Fall 1986, replacing a Mercedes Benz 450SEL that had been driven by J. R. Ewing the previous season.

HISTORY OF THE CORVETTE MODELS

1953–1955

> *Years ago this land knew cars that were fabricated out of sheer excitement. Magnificent cars that uttered flame and rolling thunder from exhaust pipes as big around as your forearm, and came towering down through the white summer dust of American roads like the Day of Judgement . . . today, they have an inheritor—the Chevrolet Corvette.*
>
> 1955 Corvette ad copy

The Corvette "dream" car was introduced to the public at the 1952 Motorama Show, and the fiberglass-bodied, two-seat convertible was the hit of the show. Chevrolet began regular production of the car in 1953, limiting the production run to 300 cars that were sold to people who qualified as "VIPs"—political figures, movie stars, business executives, and preferred customers. Unfortunately, the VIPs weren't impressed by a sports car that had pop-in plastic windows, leaked in rainstorms, had an anemic six-cylinder

---

[5]David E. Gumpert, "Porsche on Nichemanship," *Harvard Business Review*, March/April 1986.

engine with an uncivilized two-speed Powerglide automatic transmission, and was slower than a well-tuned Cadillac or Oldsmobile.[6]

1954's production run of 3,640 cars ended with a surplus of 1,500 new Corvettes. Rumors circulated that the car would be scrapped, but the Corvette's salvation occurred in two forms. First, Ford, Chevrolet's major competition, came out with the Thunderbird, a two-seat "personal" car that brought out G.M.'s competition spirit. Second, a 45-year-old German-trained enthusiast, race driver, and designer named Zora Arkus-Duntov began his 20-year association with the Corvette as its head of engineering. For 1955, the production run was 674 cars with a new V-8 engine that improved the Corvette's performance.

1956–1962

Even in Turin [Italy] no one has fuel injection! Si, e' vero'. But the really fantastic item about the new Corvette is not the fuel-injection engine, the new fourspeed gearbox, the slightshot acceleration, or the pasted-to-the-road stability. It is the fact that the Corvette, above all other high-performance sports cars in the world, is a true dual-natured vehicle. It is a genuine luxury car and a sports car, both wrapped in one sleek skin. . . .

1957 Corvette ad copy

The second generation of Corvettes received a major body change, but Chevrolet had to determine if the Corvette was to remain a sports car or forge into Ford Thunderbird territory as a "personal" luxury car. The 1956–1957 Corvettes seemed to appeal to both markets. In 1956, Corvettes took the Sports Car Club of America (SCCA) "C" Production Championship, and in 1960 four Corvettes were entered in the international Le Mans 24-Hour Endurance Race. The car was continually refined, both mechanically and stylistically. By 1962, *Motor Trend* was saying, "This is an exciting high-performance automobile with real hair on its chest—the type of car that only true enthusiasts will appreciate."

1963–1967

Corvette is America's one true sports car—has been for years. But Corvette is also two body styles. Five engines and three transmissions available. Plus enough other equipment you can order to make any kind of sports car you want. For aficionados, there's the snarly Corvette. Ordered with a 375-horsepower Ramjet, fuel-injected V8 . . . For boulevardiers, there's the plush Corvette, ordered with power brakes, steering, and windows, tinted glass. . . .

1965 Corvette ad copy

---

[6]Auto Editors of Consumers Guide, *Corvette, America's Sports Car* (New York: Beekman House, 1984).

The third-generation Corvette was derived from a G.M. styling exercise and was dubbed the Corvette "Stingray." It came in convertible and fastback coupe configurations, and had many optional features. The car was available with a variety of engines, the most powerful approaching 500 hp. Lasting only five years, this model was the most short-lived of the Corvette body styles, but its timeless styling has made it the most popular model with car collectors and enthusiasts.

1968–1979

> *Here it is. Its not really a whole lot different looking. But in 17 years we've never changed it just to change it . . . It's still a car that's built for the person who drives for the sheer excitement of it . . . No, it isn't a hard-core sports car. There are too many nice things about it. No, it isn't the smoothest-riding car you'll find. But then again it won't rattle your bones. What is it, is a new Corvette. It's refined for 1970.*

1970 Corvette ad copy

The fourth generation of the Corvette was introduced in 1968, and the "Vette" had gone through some drastic changes. Corvette production was reduced to 21,801 units in 1971 from the 1969 high of 38,762, which allowed Chevrolet Division General Manager John DeLorean to place emphasis on improving the car's slipping quality control.

The 1970s ushered in the era of government regulation. Corvette's performance steadily declined with the addition of catalytic converters and the unleaded-gasoline mandate. Its horsepower reached a low of 165 in 1975. A T-Top removable roof was introduced in 1968, offering "top down" motoring without the hassles. Subsequently, Corvette convertible models waned in popularity and were discontinued. In spite of these changes and the oil shortages and economic downturns of the 1970s, Corvette sold well. The entire 1975 Corvette production of 38,465 cars was sold out by March, and 1976 production jumped to 46,558. Because 1975 was the Corvette's 25th anniversary, it was chosen as the pace car for the Indy 500; 6,502 replicas of the pace car were made and sold at a handsome premium over the base list price of $13,653.

1980–1982

> *In this ever-changing world some things endure. A fine red wine, soft smoke on an autumn evening. A walk along the seashore. And Chevrolet Corvette. Now 26 years young. And still America's only true production sports car . . . But beyond the machinery, there is the dream—Corvette and the open road.*

1980 Corvette ad copy

In 1980, Chevrolet sent the Corvette to the fat farm so it wouldn't suffer an EPA "gas guzzler" tax. The car lost 280 lbs., and aerodynamic styling changes were added to improve fuel economy. The only engine available was a 305 cu. in. V-8, and the option of manual transmission was discontinued. All models sold were automatics. One industry observer commented that the Corvette had become a car for upwardly mobile secretaries. Even though the Corvette had lost much of its performance, it remained popular with the public and the motoring press. *Road & Track* pointed out, in its November 1982 issue, that the Corvette remained a car whose function was on par with its form: "No matter how much luxury, electric seats, remote mirrors, or teddy bear hide velour interior you pack into a Corvette, the basic honesty of the car rises above its own image."

THE "NEW" CORVETTE

Now that the skeptics have been silenced, we can get down to business. The most important piece of business concerning the new Corvette. Performance. And in tests on G.M.'s proving grounds, conducted by professional drivers, the new Corvette performs beautifully.

1984 Introductory Corvette ad copy

There was no 1983 Corvette, as production was shifted to a plant built specifically for producing the new Corvette model (it had 50 percent more production capacity than the old plant). The fifth-generation Corvette was a radical change and showcased G.M.'s latest developments in suspension, braking, and electronic engine control while still remaining true to the basic Corvette layout: front engine/rear wheel drive and fiberglass body, a two-seat, high-performance sports car.

The new Corvette had a pop-off targa roof and a 350 cu. in. V-8 engine. It featured new technology in the use of fiberglass springs and alloy castings in the suspension system, digital and LED display instrumentation, and electronically controlled fuel injection and overdrive. Its price of $23,835 represented a 73 percent increase over 1982. For 1985, improvements to the fuel-injection system increased power, and in 1986 an anti-lock braking system (ABS) and an improved anti-theft system were added. The ride was substantially softened through adjustments to the shock absorbers, and torsional steering shake was reduced with the addition of restrictors in the power steering lines. The convertible model was reintroduced in 1986, at a $4,518 premium over the base sticker price of $27,502. (See Exhibits 4 and 5 for prices and estimates of maintenance costs, respectively, for selected models.) A *New York Times* article in the July 26, 1983, issue, wondered whether the new Corvette "has not been priced out of its traditional strength, the youth-oriented market, and into one of older professionals. . . ." The article went on to say, "For G.M., the Corvette represents only a small part of the company's auto output . . . but the Corvette's real value, analysts say, is its ability to lure curious customers into showrooms."

Corvette Advertising

The advertising campaign that introduced the 1984 Corvette was lavish and technically oriented. Chevrolet ran multipage spreads in magazines touting the advanced technology and engineering that were incorporated in the newest generation of Corvettes and stressing

EXHIBIT 4   1986 Dealer's Sticker Price Information (000's)

	Corvette	Porsche 944	Porsche 944 Turbo	Porsche 928S	Datsun 300ZX Turbo
Base Car	$27.5	$24.5	$29.8	$52.0	$20.8
Average Price Paid*	23.4	24.1	N/A	N/A	N/A

*N.A.D.A Official Used Car Guide

Source: Casewriter's survey of Charlottesville, Virginia, car dealers, April 1986.

EXHIBIT 5   Maintenance-and-Repair Cost Comparison

Cost of Maintenance Parts	Average Replacement Time*	Corvette	Porsche 944T	Nissan 300ZX	Mazda RX7
Exhaust system	70,000	$413	$425	$164	$180
Engine tuneup cost		$ 90	$160	$160	$100
Clutch	N/A	$270	$892	$117	$160
Sport shocks	60,000	$360	$517	$685	$344
Factory engine	100,000	$3,900†	$5,246 (New)	$5,153 (New)	$1,000 (New)
Car warranty (months/miles)		36/36,000	24/unlimited	12/12,000	12/12,000

*Longevity of parts depends greatly on driver use and maintenance. The average vehicle was driven 10,300 miles per year.
†With multi-port fuel injection.

Source: Casewriter's survey of dealers.

its high-performance characteristics. The advertising budget was the highest in the car's history. Chevrolet spent $7,778,900 on the 1984 Corvette—compared to a previous high of $285,300 in 1977. (See Exhibit 6 for data on advertising budgets.)

The comparison campaign was launched with TV and print ads (see Exhibits 7 through 11). The cars compared to the 1985 Corvette ($26,703 price as tested) were the Lamborghini Countach, Porsche 944, Porsche 928S, Ferrari 308 GTSi, and Lotus Turbo Esprit. They ranged in price from $26,121 to $103,700, and were tested on 0–60 mph acceleration, braking from 60–0 mph, time through a slalom course, and lateral acceleration on a skid pad. The United States Auto Club (USAC) certified the testing, and the Corvette scored first in two of the tests and second and third in the remaining two tests. The scoring system that was used allotted six points for first place, five for second, etc. The Corvette was declared the overall winner in the comparison with a score of 21 points. The $103,700 Lamborghini placed second with 18 points.

EXHIBIT 6   Advertising Dollars Spent by Corvette and Competition (millions)

Car Make	1981	1982	1983	1984
Corvette	—	—	$ 7.8	$ 2.2
Jaguar XJS	—	$ 1.3	$ 3.9	$ 2.0
Nissan 280/300 ZX	$ 6.7	7.0	11.9	15.5
Nissan Total	36.3	48.9	54.7	60.1
Mazda RX7	3.1	9.7	6.1	13.1
Porsche (Total)	6.0	8.0	6.4	2.8

Source: *Leading National Advertisers.*

EXHIBIT 7   The 1986 Chevrolet Line

Chevette	An inexpensive subcompact with standard four-speed manual transmission, rack-and-pinion steering, fully reclining bucket seats, and rear hatch with fold-down rear seat. Available in two models: two-door coupe and four-door sedan. Price $5,280
Cavalier	America's best-selling compact for three years running. Standard features included front-wheel drive with rack-and-pinion steering, four-speed manual transmission, and V6 engine. Options included sunroof, choice of Delco Bose music systems, and rear luggage carrier. Thirteen models available including convertible sedan and wagon. Price: $7,600
Celebrity	America's best-selling mid-size car. Standard features were front-wheel drive with rack-and-pinion steering, V6 engine with electronic fuel injection, and cloth interior. Models included coupe, sedan, and wagon body types. Wide variety of options allowed for personally "customized" car. Price: $15,000
Camaro	America's best selling 2 + 2 sports coupe came standard with V6 multi-port fuel-injection engine, five-speed manual transmission, power steering, sports suspension, rally wheels, and rear hatch. Available options included: Delco-Bose wrap-around music system, electric rearview mirror controls, and rear-window louvers. Camaro had long received "hand-me-down" Corvette technology, and the Iroc Z28 was available with a Corvette engine option. Camaro races were becoming increasingly popular. Four models to choose from. Price $10,400
Caprice	Full-size car offered standard V6 engine with electronic fuel injection and three-speed automatic transmission, rear-drive power steering, and 20.9 cubic feet of luggage space. Model selection included Brougham and Classic series in sedan and wagon body types. Many options available for personalized customizing. Price: $11,400
Monte Carlo	Full-size rear-drive automobile with full-coil suspension, and power steering and brakes. Standard features included three-speed automatic transmission, electronically fuel-injected V6 engine, and cloth bench seat with center arm rest. Available in luxury sport and super sport models. Price: $11,700
Corvette	Performance sports car with standard features including a V8 engine with tuned-port fuel injection in a choice of four-speed manual with overdrive or four-speed automatic transmissions, vehicle anti-theft system, Bosch ABS II anti-lock brake system, corrosion-resistant fiberglass body, targa roof, air conditioning, and electronic instrument cluster. Options available included leather seats, Delco Bose stereo system, and performance handling package. Also available in convertible model. Price: $28,500

EXHIBIT 8 Comparative Advertisement

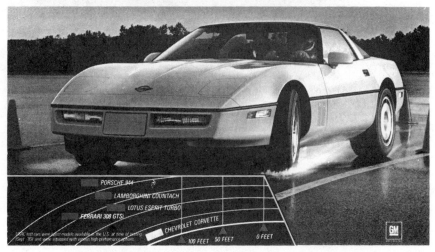

You're driving 55 MPH on a rain-slick curve. Suddenly the unexpected: You stand on the brake pedal and steer to stay in your lane. You might expect Europe's most exotic cars to handle such a crisis effortlessly. Yet for all its awesome straight-line braking ability, Ferrari 308 GTSi failed to negotiate a 150-foot radius curve at maximum braking in USAC-certified testing. Lamborghini Countach failed. Lotus Esprit Turbo failed. Porsche 944 failed. Only the 1986 Corvette demonstrated the ability to steer and stop in these conditions at the same time. Only Corvette made the turn while coming to a controlled stop. When conditions turn foul, Corvette's new computerized Bosch ABS II anti-lock braking system is designed to help improve a driver's ability to simultaneously brake and steer out of trouble.

Why does the Corvette feature the world's most advanced braking technology? Because a world-class champion should give you the edge in an emergency. **Corvette. A world-class champion.**

TODAY'S CHEVROLET Live it!

EXHIBIT 9   Corvette Advertisement

EXHIBIT 10 Excerpts from Porsche Magazine Spread—1986 Campaign

We've spent the last 23 years working on the same idea.

If there's one thing which, more than any other, characterizes Porsche's approach to building sports cars, it's our preoccupation with making every 911 demonstrably better than it was the year before.

While adhering to a styling concept so unarguably "right" that it has remained essentially unchanged since it was first introduced in 1963.

Even the 282-horsepower, 157 mph, top-of-the-line Turbo shown here, with

it's radical "whale-tail" spoiler and considerably flared rear wheel wells, is unmistakably a 911.

Today, the 911 is perhaps the most coveted high-performance sports car in the world. A 23-year beneficiary of everything we've learned in world class endurance and sprint racing.

Built, as is every Porsche, with a precision and attention to detail that's quickly

vanishing in this age of rampant robotics.

The legendary air-cooled, horizontally opposed, six-cylinder, fuel-injected engine is still hand assembled by a small team of workers, any one of whom is qualified to build the entire engine from scratch.

It's still bench tested for 45 minutes at maximum rpm. By an increasingly rare breed of technician whose gloved hand, strategically placed on a running engine, is as good a judge of quality as most of his sophisticated monitoring equipment.

At the end of the assembly line, every 911, as is every Porsche, is test driven for at least 30 kilometers on both city streets and no-speed-limit autobahns.

Everything is checked. Chassis, body, engine, transmission, suspension, brakes, paint, interior finish, everything.

Any fault they uncover, no matter how minor, is located and fixed, and the car driven again before it is released.

At Porsche, we take a great deal of pride in the fact that every new car we sell is slightly used.

911 Turbo 6-cylinder, horizontally opposed, two overhead camshafts, air-cooled rear engine with turbocharger and intercooler. 3299cc, 282 hp. Weight: 2976 lbs. Top speed: 157 mph.

We wanted to see how far we could go without changing direction.

At Porsche, nearly 30% of our employees are involved in research and development.

And having developed the 911 to a state of near perfection, many of them were more than ready for the challenge of designing a totally new car.

Professor Ferry Porsche was more than happy to oblige.

He gave them something to gladden the heart of any engineer. A clean sheet of paper. And only two requirements for the finished product.

It had to be the most technologically advanced car we had ever built.

And it had to be a Porsche.

The result, in 1978, was the 928.

A car which, to some traditionalists, broke every rule in the Porsche handbook of automotive design. But which—with it's front-mounted, liquid-cooled V-8 engine and rear-mounted transmission and differential—was as ingenious and

unexpected a solution as the 356 had been 30 years before.

Or as Professor Porsche likes to put it, "It was never my philosophy to ask where the engine should be placed, but which solution would bring the greatest gains."

After being named "Car of the Year" the minute it was introduced, the 928S has improved steadily every year since.

Today, it is one of the most sophisticated, luxurious sports cars you can buy.

But infinitely more important, it is every millimeter a "Porsche," the universally accepted synonym for performance.

The 288 horsepower, fuel-injected

V-8—with a four-valve head design adapted from our 956 endurance racer—will propel the 928S from 0 to 60 in an awesome 6.1 seconds. And to a top speed of 155 mph.

The near 50-50 weight distribution of the transaxle drive train, combined with our patented Weissach Rear Axle, contributes to the uncanny sensation that one is cornering on rails.

And it can all be brought to a quick, sure, arrow-straight stop, regardless of road conditions, by our new electronically monitored Anti-Lock Braking System.

Assuming, of course, that you ever want to stop.

928S 8-cylinder, 90 degree V, four overhead camshafts, four valves per cylinder, liquid-cooled front engine. 4957cc, 288 hp., transaxle. Weight: 3351 lbs. Top speed: 155 mph (with manual transmission).

EXHIBIT 11 Nissan Advertisement, 1986

. . . Corvette. Ferrari, Porsche, Lotus, Lamborghini. They're Europe's exotic few. And they don't let just anyone into their club. But in the case of the Chevrolet Corvette, they really didn't have a choice. In independent tests conducted by the United States Automobile Club, Corvette was the overall winner.

1985 Corvette Comparison ad copy

The comparison campaign was continued in 1986, when Corvette made the Bosch ABS II anti-braking system a standard feature on the car and then compared the braking characteristics of the Lamborghini Countach, Ferrari 308 GTSi, Porsche 944, Lotus Turbo Esprit, and Corvette on a rain-slick curve. The Corvette was the only car to demonstrate the ability simultaneously to stop and steer the curve under maximum braking conditions. Once again it was proclaimed "Corvette, A World Class Champion" against a collection of European exotic cars.

Promotion and Racing Activities

The Chevrolet Division of G.M. published *Corvette News* quarterly and sent it free to purchasers of new Corvettes for three years (thereafter $18 for three years). The 30-page, full-color, glossy magazine kept Corvette owners informed on new Corvette model developments, news of Corvettes on the race track, and do-it-yourself repairs. *Vette Magazine, Vette Vues, Corvette Fever,* and *Keep' in Track* were the titles of four independently published monthly magazines devoted exclusively to Corvette enthusiasts.

There were over 700 organized Corvette clubs in the United States and Canada and a few in Europe. These clubs were federated under the National Council of Corvette Clubs. Club activities included car shows, rallies, slalom races, drag races, and social gatherings. A separate Corvette organization was the National Corvette Restorers Society, organized for people dedicated to restoring older Corvettes to "original" condition.

John Pierce, a member of Chevrolet's Special Products Group, explained in the Summer 1985 issue of *Corvette News,* "Our policy is to develop the hardware and technology necessary to win and make sure it's properly represented in competition. We [Chevrolet] figure if we can put together a winner, then there'll be a demand for a better mousetrap." The group's efforts resulted in privately owned Corvette GTPs (Grand Touring Prototypes) participating in the IMSA (International Motor Sports Association) GT's circuit that visited 17 U.S. cities in the 1985 racing season.

For the second race of the 1986 season, the Corvette GTP car qualified for retired early due to mechanical failure. At the fourth race, Road Atlanta, the Corvette's second appearance was greeted with skepticism: "if they last . . ." (from the Ford folk); "if they live . . ." (the Porsche persons); "They can't run that fast in the race . . ." (Jaguarists).[7] The Corvette's first victory in the Road Atlanta race broke Porsche's string of 16 consecutive IMSA wins.

In another race series, Showroom Stock, Corvettes dominated. These races pit stock

---

[7]Sylvia Wilkinson, "Hand Grenades One and Two," *Autoweek,* April 14, 1986.

production cars against machines of similar performance capability. The Chevrolet Camaro was also promoted in a series of races in which professional drivers competed in modified Camaros capable of 200 MPH speeds.

In 1986, the new Corvette roadster was chosen to be the Indianapolis 500 Pace Car. Chevrolet also developed a futuristic car, the Corvette Indy, that was shown on the 1986 Automobile Show circuit. Built by Lotus, the Indy was a showcase of technology to be used in the next generation Corvette—mid-engine, four-wheel drive, and four-wheel steering.[8]

The value of racing to an automobile's image was difficult to assess. Many sports cars, including Corvette, were featured in ads for tires, auto stereo systems, other accessories, and unrelated products. For example, a Corvette was the grand prize in a toothpaste coupon sweepstakes and in numerous other promotions and contests.

Distribution

The Corvette was sold by the Chevrolet network of over 5,000 Chevrolet dealers in the United States. (Porsche, for example, had only 330 authorized dealers.) Some dealers, especially those near large population centers, were known for selling many Corvettes. However, most small dealers rarely stocked Corvettes and sold only for special orders. To help those dealers with less experience learn to sell the "new" Corvette, Chevrolet implemented a special dealer training program for 1986. Corvette mechanics also received special training.

Often the Corvette occupied a prominent place on the showroom floor, and "Register to win a Corvette" campaigns were used by Chevrolet to increase dealer traffic.

THE COMPETITION

Porsche

Porsche was a family-owned European company known for its product quality. In recent years, Porsche had introduced new models aimed at new segments. Notable successes were the 944 and 928. Standard company policy was to keep production levels just below the demand level.[9] From 1980 to 1985, Porsche sales grew 56 percent.

Schutz, CEO of Porsche, stated in the 1986 March/April issue of the *Harvard Business Review* that "Our customers are people who place high expectations on themselves. And they expect no less from the companies and people with whom they associate. . . . As a result, in positioning our company we have to strive to be what these people are as individuals. That means, among car companies, we have very high goals. And we have to pursue those goals virtually without compromise." He considered Porsche competition to come from two sectors: luxury discretionary items, such as sailboats and airplanes, and other automobile manufacturers. He believed the Porsche 944's competition included

---

[8]George Damon Levy, "Corvette Indy," *Autoweek*, January 20, 1986.
[9]Op. cit.

Corvette, Pontiac Fiero, and certain Japanese cars; the 928's competition came from Jaguars, Ferraris, Mercedes Benz large coupes, and the Cadillac Allante; that the 911 had no competition: "It drives like no other car and sounds like no other car."

In its advertising, Porsche concentrated on the thoroughness and competence of its cars. The ads appeared to be aimed at people who weren't familiar with Porsche and told a story about the company's engineers, the cars they had designed, and the constant development of Porsche cars being done on the world's most demanding racing tracks. Early in 1986, Porsche began a series of lavish magazine spreads, some as many as 12 pages each (see example in Exhibit 10). Magazines in the campaign included *Business Week, Time,* and *Newsweek.*

Shutz said Porsche supported cars in international sports car racing for three reasons: "First, it is probably the single most effective way to do our advertising and public relations. It gets us free space in the auto enthusiasts' magazines. The second factor is the contribution that it makes to our technical development . . . the most important . . . is the contribution that racing makes to our corporate culture. The racing activity is highly visible, and it has a couple of characteristics that I find extremely valuable in achieving the kind of quality we want." He added, ". . . racing is an opportunity for us to demonstrate our competence, to demonstrate the state of technology with which we're building their [the public's] automobile."[10]

Porsche's bi-monthly magazine, *Christophorus,* contained articles on Porsche race activities and recent developments, art, travel, and books. The "They Drive Porsche" section read like a "Who's Who" and carried pictures of world-class athletes, royalty, V.1.P.s, and race car drivers with their Porsches. Among those featured in the August 1985 issue were Olympic swimming champion Michael Gross, King Carl Gustaff XVI of Sweden, and a prominent West German physician. Typical advertisers in the magazine were high-quality clothing and accessory manufacturers, jewelers, and European airlines.

In August 1984, as Porsche's distribution contract with Volkswagen of America was about to expire, Peter Shutz, chief executive of Porsche AG, created a new distribution plan to abolish dealers and replace them with agents who would order the cars as they were sold. Instead of keeping inventories, the agents would be supplied by 40 company centers. Two Porsche warehouses would operate in the United States, one in Reno, Nevada, and one on the East Coast. Three weeks after the announcement of the new distribution system, Shutz abandoned it; he stayed committed only to severing Porsche's U.S. link to Volkswagen.[11]

Nissan

In recent years, Nissan's (originally Datsun) 240Z model had increased in size, weight, and price. During this time it had evolved from an "economy" sports car to something more like a GT car. A change in image resulted.

---

[10]Gumpert, "Porsche on Nichemanship."

[11]David B. Tinnin, "Porsche's Civil War with Its Dealers," *Fortune,* April 16, 1984.

> *Those in marketing who ply their trade with demographics describe the 300ZX purchaser as one who is not as concerned with ultimate performance as with the "image" of performance. To the Nissan engineers this means a suspension system whose main priority is ride comfort, not cornering power or balance. Under the hood it means a priority on smooth, docile power characteristics rather than serious horses—which might require too much driver attention, detracting from image-enhancement time. To paraphrase Nissan television advertising: "You may never need this kind of performance, but knowing it's there is awesome."*
>
> *Motor Trend*, January 1986.

Nissan advertising for the 300ZX stressed that it was the best "Z" car ever, technically advanced with a plethora of functional electronic wizardry. The ads did not mention any performance statistics or measurements for the car (see Exhibit 11).

Mazda

With the second generation of the very successful RX-7 introduced in 1986, Mazda continued to emphasize the advanced technology and engineering of its sports car model. The ads were dominated by written copy and had technical drawings of components as well as a cut-away view of the car's mechanicals. Mazda also ran ads in car-enthuasiast magazines concerning the RX-7's successful racing career. Mazda's evolution was somewhat similar to that of the Datsun (now Nissan) "Z" series. It was initially built and priced to compete in the "economy" sports car segment, but successive generations became heavier and more expensive with more "standard" options. Recent models were thought by some to resemble the Porsche 944 in appearance.

PRESS REACTIONS TO THE NEW CORVETTE

May 1983—*Motor Trend* tested the Ferrari 308 GTSi, Porsche 928S, Jaguar XJS, and the 1984 Corvette on a race track to determine the best-handling production car available in America. The Corvette was "markedly superior in every handling category and stands alone at the top of the heap . . . the Vette is now something it has never been; a world class performer." *Motor Trend* also voted the Ferrari the most sexually appealing car, and the Jaguar "one to live with day in and day out." Corvette's appeal as a "daily runner" was diluted by its harsh riding characteristics,[12] but it was the choice for "the hardest-charging backroad burner money can buy." The Porsche 928S—"by any clear-headed standard, may be the best car in the world."

November 1985—*Motor Trend* compared the improved 1986 Corvette to the just-released Porsche 944 Turbo. The Corvette was fastest from 0–70 mph; the Porsche was faster from 70–90 mph in covering the quarter mile and in top speed. The Corvette won the braking, skidpad, slalom, and road course portions of the testing. In conclusion, the testers stated, "Pressed to make a choice between these two exceptional GT's, we'd

---

[12]The ride was substantially softened in subsequent model years.

TABLE 2   1986 Performance Comparison of Selected Sports Cars

Manufacturer and Model	0–60 MPH (sec)	1/4 mile (sec)	Top Speed (MPH)	Braking 80 MPH (ft)	Slalom (MPH)	Skid-pad (G's)	Interior Noise at 70 MPH (DBA)	MPG
Corvette Coupe	5.8	14.4	154	243	58.9	.91	77	19.0
Alfa Romeo Spider	10.4	17.6	103	288	58.4	.77	93	23.8
Ferrari 308 GTBi	6.8	15.2	142	262	58.0	.81	80	16.0
Jaguar XJS HE	7.8	15.6	148	276	56.6	.73	72	13.5
Mercedes Benz 380SL	10.9	18.4	110	277	54.2	.70	74	19.0
Mazda RX7 GXL	8.5	16.5	119	267	62.0	.83	N/A	N/A
Nissan 300 ZX Turbo	7.4	15.7	133	249	62.8	.80	73	17.0
Porsche 944	8.9	16.6	123	256	62.5	.86	72	22.1
Porsche 944 Turbo	6.0	14.6	155	255	62.8	.90	72	19.4
Porsche 911 Cabriolet	5.7	14.3	130	266	59.8	.80	79	18.6
Porsche 928S	6.3	14.5	162	247	57.9	.83	71	16.3

Source: *Motor Trend's* Performance Summary.

probably opt for the Corvette. But the final choice lies in individual tastes and driving habits. There's a lot of hot rod in the Vette. A lot of flash and American brashness. The turbo Porsche is understated elegance. Quiet, confident, and subtle. Whichever approach reflects your individual driving habits and ego is the one you'll swear is the hands-down winner and the only logical choice. Just make sure you bring plenty of green stuff."

A summary of *Motor Trend* performance data is contained in Table 2. See the appendix to this case for definitions of technical terms used in the industry.

Appendix of Technical Terms

TESTS USED IN PERFORMANCE COMPARISONS

Skidpad test Measured the cornering ability of a car in a steady state. Cars that generated numbers of greater than .8 g force had a stiff suspension and harsh riding characteristics on surfaces rougher than a smooth race track.

Slalom test Measured a car's cornering ability in transient maneuvers as it wove through a course of eight pylons spaced at 100-ft. intervals.

Braking test Measured the minimal distance required to come to a full stop from a stated speed. Typically tested from 60 and 80 mph.

INNOVATIONS IN AUTOMOBILE TECHNOLOGY

Braking

Anti-lock braking system (ABS) Disc brake calipers had an electronic sensor that prevented brake lockup in panic stops. This innovation resulted in better stopping power and eliminated loss of control (skidding).

Suspension

Dynamic suspensions Being developed so that electronic sensors could detect road conditions, allowing a car's suspension components to react.

Active suspensions Sensors monitoring load-induced flex in the rear suspension to adjust the rear wheel suspension automatically.

Driver adjustable suspensions Allowed the driver to alter the stiffness of a car's shock absorbers to increase a car's handling performance or ride characteristics.

Engine

Turbocharging A method of increasing a car's horsepower output by increasing the air flow into the engine's combustion chambers.

Intercooling Creating a denser charge and increasing the horsepower of a turbocharged engine by cooling the air charge of a turbocharger.

Fuel injection A system, usually electronic, that controlled and injected fuel directly into the combustion chamber.

Twin cam   Utilized two camshafts to control a car's intake and exhaust valves allowing higher revving of an engine and increasing horsepower.

Four valves per cylinder   Increased the volumetric airflow into the combustion chambers increasing horsepower.

EPA controls   The EPA regulated the amount of pollutants engines might emit into the air through their exhaust systems. This led to much cleaner burning engines, and new cars were required to use unleaded fuel.

Electronics

Diagnostics   Sensors were placed in a car allowing mechanics to electronically monitor and diagnose a car's different systems.

Ignition   Electronic ignition systems replaced the mechanical distributor system with a rotor and points. Required less maintenance and adjustment.

Engine management systems   Controlled the different systems of an engine such as fuel mixture allowing for more efficient engines, better mileage, and less pollution.

Instrumentation   Electronics were used in digital instrumentation and engine monitoring indicators giving more precise data than the previous mechanical systems using analog instruments.

Tire and Wheels

Radial tires   Provided longer wear and less rolling resistance than bias ply tires, resulting in increased gas mileage and reduced tire replacement.

New compounds and tread designs   Developed in racing cars to improve the performance characteristics of tires: increased road adhesion, cornering, and wetroad performance.

High-speed tire   Tires were rated by their maximum safe speeds. Newly developed tires could run safely at 100 MPH.

Alloy wheels   Reduced a car's weight thus increasing gas mileage and speed.

Interior

Light fastness   Newer cars had more window space creating a greenhouse effect necessitating that manufacturers develop interior plastics and fabrics that improved fade resistance.

Music systems   Offered with four speakers, graphic equalizers, and power boosters for amplifiers. Compact disc players had recently begun to be installed in cars.

Electronic climate-control systems   Maintained the car's interior temperature within a specified range.

Ergonomics   Used to design the cars' interiors. The layout of the driver's controls were increasingly becoming user friendly, requiring less concentration by the driver.

Seating   Seats were being bolstered on the sides to add lateral support as cars became capable of achieving high g forces in turning performance. Seats came with multiple options that allowed them to be customized for the users' comfort such as power adjustable seats and heating elements for winter driving.

Cruise control   Automatically maintained the car's speed at a set level.

Seat belts and airbags   Combination lap belts and shoulder harnesses were standard in all cars. Airbags that inflated upon crash impact were offered by many manufacturers.

Message Strategy and Copy Testing

Case 3–1

Folgers 2000: The Miami University Experiment*

Doug Hall, Associate Marketing Manager for Folgers Coffee, pushed aside the stack of student surveys on his desk and reflected back on one of the first days of the just-completed Folgers 2000 experiment. He remembered standing shivering on the loading dock of Reid Hall at Miami University on a chilly February morning. It was one of the first days of Project 2000, and he had been working on this loading dock since 4 a.m., supervising and motivating a crew of students busily brewing coffee and whisking it off to dorms and classroom buildings around campus. All around him, students shouted greetings and directives to one another, coffee steamed in the twilight from specially designed coffee dispensers, and trucks pulled hastily away from the dock to dispatch the next delivery of coffee.

Now that May 1989 had arrived and the experiment was over, Hall needed to resolve some important issues before the end of the month. Current trends in the coffee industry and shifting consumer tastes in general had inspired fear and pessimism among many marketers and roasters of coffee, and he wondered whether his particular experiment at Miami University of Ohio could help determine the direction Folgers could take in the future. He knew that the results of Project 2000 might have some far-reaching implications for his brand in particular as well as for the coffee industry as a whole.

Folgers 2000 experiment gave him great hope. For the first time, the group had been actually able to increase the number of coffee drinkers. However, there were still many unresolved issues, and the research generated almost more questions than it answered. He needed to act quickly in order to translate his learnings into a viable business proposition for the brand. At stake was the future of Folgers—not to mention the coffee category as a whole.

---

*This case was prepared by Anne D. Kroemer under the supervision of Professor Paul W. Farris for purposes of class discussion only. It does not reflect either the effective of ineffective handling of an administrative situation. Copyright © 1990 by the Darden Graduate Business School Foundation, Charlottesville, Virginia.

COFFEE: ITS HISTORY

The history of coffee traces a story filled with mystery and intrigue. Coffee was enjoyed as early as 900 A.D. in Arabia, where it was consumed for its perceived medicinal properties as well as for its unusual taste. It wasn't until 1690 that the Dutch broke the Arabian monopoly of the mystical brew and smuggled some coffee plants into Holland. Soon thereafter, the Dutch shared the plants with the Europeans and helped them raise the coffee in European botanical gardens. In the early 1700s, a French army officer, fascinated with the beverage, stole a coffee plant from the Jardin des Plants and smuggled it to Martinique, where he was stationed at the time. The hardy plant survived a dramatic voyage complete with an attempted kidnapping, pirate attacks, and ferocious storms, and upon arrival in the West Indies, quickly thrived in its newfound home. Within only a few years, coffee had successfully spread to the mainland of South America.

Like the early Arabians, South American coffee producers fiercely guarded their coffee plants–the crime of attempting to abduct and export the plant was punishable by death. Brazil, finding it impossible to obtain a plant, could not cultivate coffee until a boundary dispute between two coffee-producing colonies bordering Brazil arose. When Brazil was asked for assistance, it deftly sent a young and handsome army officer to arbitrate the dispute between the colonies of Dutch and French Guyana. In the process, the officer caught the eye of the French Guyana Governor's wife. On the eve of his departure, the officer was honored with an extravagant banquet. The Governor's wife awarded him with a splendid bouquet, and hidden at the base of the flowers were stashed the coffee seedlings Brazil needed to begin cultivating coffee. Today, Brazil is one of the largest producers and exporters of coffee, producing an average of 30 million 60-kg. bags of coffee each year.

The coffee tree grows best in the tropics and subtropics as it needs at least 70 inches of rain annually to subsist. It also requires plenty of direct sunlight and complete protection from frost. A coffee plant becomes productive several years after planting; a six-year plant may yield anywhere from 1 to 12 pounds of coffee beans per year.

Once the plant blooms, a bright red "cherry" develops and ripens over a six to seven month period. The ripening is non-uniform and hence dictates hand-harvesting, a slow, labor-intensive process which has yet to be effectively mechanized. Once picked from the plant, the cherries are cured and the bean is removed, washed, and finally sorted to separate the ripe "good" beans from the unripened and damaged. The resulting "green coffee" is graded according to universal standards and is subsequently sold to processors through a variety of brokerage systems unique to each producing country.

When the coffee reaches the consuming country, it is usually blended with other varieties, roasted, and eventually packaged for sale. The most popular varieties exported include Coffee Arabica and Coffee Canephora (commonly known as robusta). Each coffee processor develops blends for what it considers optimal taste and price characteristics.

To assist exporting countries in selling coffee, many organizations have sprung up to promote orderly global trading of the commodity. The International Coffee Organization (ICO) is the most influential; over 90 percent of the coffee producers and processors are members of the ICO. Through negotiated agreements, producing countries agree to produce a quota for export, and the buying processors agree to purchase only quota coffee. The ICO oversees and enforces this system by issuing quota stickers and requiring ICO members to purchase only the coffee bags bearing these stickers.

THE COFFEE MARKET: INDUSTRY TRENDS

Over the past two decades, coffee consumption had been steadily declining. Consumption by age group was dropping across the board, and coffee drinking by young people showed the sharpest decline: in the past 20 years, coffee consumption in the 20–29 age group plummeted from 81 percent to 30 percent. The year 1962 marked the peak of coffee consumption; each American over the age of 10 consumed 3.12 cups of the brew per day according to Business Trend Analysts, Inc. By 1988, the rate had dropped off to 1.67 cups daily.

A number of influences contributed to the decline in coffee sales. One of the most important came from an unexpected and powerful outside source: the soft drink industry. According to *Beverage Industry*, in 1961 consumers drank twice as much coffee as soft drinks per capita; in 1987 it was nearly the reverse . . . twice as many soft drinks as coffee.

Particularly worrisome to coffee marketers were the sharp declines among youth since they represented tomorrow's coffee drinkers. The decline of coffee consumption was exacerbated by aggressive marketing from soft drink manufacturers, such as the Coca Cola Company's "Have a Coke in the Morning" blitz and Pepsi's introduction of the high-caffeine morning cola, Pepsi A.M. Utilizing fun, up-beat advertisements, the soft drink industry spent twice as much on advertisement as the coffee industry in 1988, luring the young baby boomers away from coffee. Even for breakfast, coffee suddenly found itself competing with soft drinks as the beverage of choice. In 1988, 20 percent of young people "regularly" and 50 percent "regularly" or "occasionally" drank a soft drink in the morning. Beyond advertising, the cola companies focused energies on pulling drinkers over from coffee to cola through convenience store "Coke in the Morning" promotion programs and through the introduction of "Breakmate," a small fountain machine specially designed to compete against the infrastructure of coffee machines located in small office and factory break rooms.

Another element contributing to coffee's decline was media reports linking caffeine with adverse health effects. Although caffeine was also found in soft drinks, chocolate, tea, and many over-the-counter medicines, coffee was the focus of most of the negative publicity. The evidence against caffeine was controversial; in 1989, most of the accusations against coffee were dropped as scientists examined studies more closely. Flaws were identified in the analysis of old studies, and new studies contradicted older studies. In fact, Dr. Sanford Miller, former Director of the Food and Drug Administration's Center for Food Safety and Applied Nutrition in Washington stated in a *People Weekly* interview in 1984 that "the caffeine debate goes on, but it's nothing to lose sleep over . . . I believe we'll still be debating its merits in the year 2090."

While the media ran multiple stories on the potential negative health effects of coffee, caffeine-containing soft drinks grew at a rapid pace. Despite the introduction of numerous "health-oriented" (i.e., juice-containing) soft drinks in the 80s, cola consumption continued to grow in both volume and share, reaching some 70 percent of the market by 1987. In response to "caffeine scares," Coca-Cola and Pepsi both introduced caffeine-free colas in 1983. However, despite significant investments supporting both brands, according to *Beverage Industry,* consumption hit a peak of only 4.9 percent of the market in 1984, declining to some 4.2 percent of the market in 1987.

EXHIBIT 1 Demographic Data for Coffee Drinkers

	Percent of Total Base Group	Whole Coffee Beans		Ground Coffee Beans		Instant or Freeze-Dried	
Total* (in 000's)		8,401		47,940		31,496	
Heavy Users†		28.7%		17.7%		21.8%	
Medium Users‡		19.6		38.9		34.1	
Light Users§		51.7		43.4		44.1	
		Regular	Decaf	Regular	Decaf	Regular	Decaf
Percent of Total Category		60.5%	39.5%	67.2%	32.8%	50.1%	49.9%
Household Income							
$50k +	17.7%	26.4%	24.0%	18.8%	19.8%	16.0%	17.7%
40–49	12.9	15.6	13.2	14.4	14.5	14.1	13.8
35–39	7.5	7.4	8.6	7.5	8.9	8.0	8.0
25–35	18.1	18.1	15.3	19.5	19.1	19.0	18.1
15–25	19.4	17.8	14.0	18.3	16.0	19.6	16.8
>15k	24.4	14.7	24.9	21.5	21.7	23.3	25.6
Geography							
Northeast	20.6%	22.5%	27.7%	23.7%	22.1%	23.5%	26.1%
Northcentral	25.1	22.8	22.9	25.8	29.6	21.3	26.4
South	35.2	29.0	30.8	32.3	32.1	32.3	31.3
West	19.1	25.7	18.6	18.2	16.2	22.9	16.2
Race							
White	87.2%	90.4%	70.8%	91.9%	89.9%	89.5%	86.7%
Black	11.1	7.2	17.9	6.8	8.8	8.2	11.5
Employment							
Full-time	42.9%	49.5%	41.2%	42.9%	32.6%	41.3%	34.1%
Part-time	8.5	11.4	8.2	8.6	9.1	8.8	8.1
No employment	48.6	39.1	50.6	48.5	58.3	49.9	57.8

*Base Group: total U.S. female homemakers, 78,526,000. (Adding totals across row does not add up to total of 78,526,000 due to cross-usage.)

†Heavy Users defined as using more than 2 lbs. of coffee beans in last 30 days or drinking more than 6 cups (ground) or 3 cups (instant) in an average day.

‡Medium Users defined as using 2 lbs. of coffee beans in last 30 days or drinking 3–6 cups (ground) or 2–3 cups (instant) in an average day.

§Light Users defined as using less than 2 lbs. of coffee beans in last 30 days or drinking less than 3 cups (ground) or 2 cups (instant) in an average day.

Source: MRI (Mediamark Research Inc.), Spring 1987.

EXHIBIT 2 Estimated Advertising Expenditures by Major Coffee Marketers (in $000)

January–September 1979

	Total	Magazines	Supplements	Network	Spot TV	Outdoor	Radio
GF	$68,794	$6,485	$3,173	$35,468	$21,233	$0	$2,436
P&G	23,292	60	0	6,903	16,329	0	0
Nestles	31,947	1,689	463	19,034	10,160	3	600
Hills Bros	4,696	99	0	338	4,260	0	0

January–September 1982

	Total	Magazines	Supplements	Network	Spot TV	Radio	Newspapers	Spot Radio
GF								
Brim	$ 18,739	$ 384	$ 228	$ 13,733	$ 4,071	$ 225	$ 98	$ 0
Int. Coffee	12,335	1,958	0	8,325	2,000	0	52	0
Maxwell House	57,223	2,773	815	31,953	13,731	2,292	1,188	4,470
Maxim	5,681	0	0	0	5,645	0	36	0
Sanka	29,821	920	218	21,414	4,592	142	655	1,880
Total	$123,798	$6,035	$ 1,261	$ 75,424	$30,040	$2,660	$2,029	$6,350
P&G								
Folgers	$ 27,651	$ 0	$ 0	$ 16,595	$10,779	$ 132	$ 145	$ 0
Highpoint	12,439	0	0	9,476	2,785	0	178	0
Total	$ 40,090	$ 0	$ 0	$ 26,071	$13,564	$ 132	$ 323	$ 0
Nestles								
Nescafe	$ 3,600	$ 0	$ 0	$ 0	$ 2,926	$ 4	$ 670	$ 0
T. Choice	21,338	34	0	17,575	2,617	0	1,113	0
Total	$ 24,938	$ 34	$ 0	$ 17,575	$ 5,542	$ 4	$1,783	$ 0
Hills Bros	$ 5,288	$ 0	$ 0	$ 0	$ 5,041	$ 0	$ 247	$ 0
MJB	2,315	91	0	273	1,666	3	282	0
Total	$ 7,602	$ 91	$ 0	$ 273	$ 6,706	$ 3	$ 529	$ 0
Grand Total	$196,428	$6,160	$ 1,261	$119,344	$55,853	$2,799	$4,663	$6,350

January–September 1985

	Total	Magazines	Network	Spot TV	Outdoor	Radio	Newspapers	Cable TV
General Foods								
Brim	$ 10,244	$ 675	$ 7,695	$ 1,331	$ 0	$ 0	$ 0	$ 543
Int. Coffee	11,234	1,804	5,870	2,849	0	0	0	711
Maxwell House	24,109	1,007	17,277	3,412	2	272	484	1,969
Sanka	11,363	346	9,564	805	0	162	91	395
Total	$ 56,950	$3,831	$40,406	$ 8,398	$ 2	$ 434	$ 575	$3,617
P&G								
Folgers	$ 31,656	$ 0	$21,112	$ 9,157	$ 0	$ 533	$ 0	$ 855
Highpoint	4,134	0	3,389	547	0	0	0	198
Total	$ 35,790	$ 0	$24,500	$ 9,704	$ 0	$ 533	$ 0	$1,053

EXHIBIT 2   *(concluded)*

January–September 1985

	Total	Magazines	Network	Spot TV	Outdoor	Radio	Newspapers	Cable TV
Nestles								
Hills Bros	$ 3,537	$1,225	$ 0	$ 3,528	$ 9	$ 0	$ 0	$ 0
Nescafe	6,080	1,034	1,247	3,442	0	0	$ 167	0
T. Choice	11,707	0	7,850	0	0	0	0	707
Total	$ 21,324	$2,259	$ 9,096	$ 6,970	$ 9	$ 0	$ 167	$ 707
Grand Total	$114,064	$6,090	$74,003	$ 25,071	$ 11	$ 967	$ 742	$5,377

Note: The estimates were gathered from what was available from public sources. The information is not complete and may not be accurate. The data should be used only for comparative purposes.

Source: Marketing and Media Decisions.

More significant than the health issues, coffee itself gained an image of being old-fashioned and out of date. This idea was strengthened by the spokespeople the giant roasters used in their advertisements: Folgers' spokeswoman Mrs. Olson and Maxwell House's Cora were both viewed as elderly busybodies. In contrast, Pepsi in the late 60s appealed directly to the youth with such advertising selling ideas as "Pepsi . . . for those who think young." This youthful focus evolved into the highly successful and award-winning "Pepsi . . . The Choice of a New Generation."

While the overall coffee market slipped, a few segments within the coffee industry showed growth. Coffee drinkers were exhibiting increased interest in gourmet, ground roast coffees. The decaffeinated ground roast segments also continued to grow, reflecting the aging of the population. In 1988, the decaffeinated segments represented almost 20 percent of all coffee consumed. Finally, specialty and flavored coffees were garnering consumers' attention. Industry experts speculated that this segment brought in people who were not coffee purists and hence attracted new drinkers.

Exhibit 1 shows demographic data for coffee drinkers. Exhibit 2 details advertising expenditures by the major coffee marketers. Exhibit 3 gives shares by company and brand. Overall trends in coffee and beverage consumption are illustrated in Exhibits 4 and 5.

ADVERTISING

Until the early 1980s, U.S. coffee marketers did little to attempt to reverse the decline of coffee consumption through advertising. Marketing efforts were targeted mostly at existing coffee drinkers in an effort to maintain market share or wrest some percentage points from other coffee roasters. Few new products were introduced. Finally, in 1982 the National Federation of Colombia Coffee Growers launched a generic advertising campaign for Colombian coffee, introducing Juan Valdez via the advertising agency DDB Needham Worldwide. In 1982, Colombian coffee sales represented 2 percent total sales; in 1988, U.S. consumers purchased 55 million pounds of Colombian coffee (5 percent

EXHIBIT 3(a)   Market Shares by Company and Brand: Ground Coffee

	1983	1984	1985	1986	1987
General Foods					
Maxwell House					
Regular	19.0%	18.6%	18.8%	18.3%	18.1%
Decaf	—	—	—	2.4	2.0
Priv. Coll.	—	—	—	—	0.2
Subtotal	19.0	18.6	18.8	20.7	20.3
Masterblend	7.5	8.0	9.0	8.4	7.6
Sanka	2.2	2.2	2.1	1.7	2.1
Yuban					
Regular	1.0	0.7	0.6	2.3	2.3
Decaf	—	—	—	0.4	0.4
Subtotal	1.0	0.7	0.6	2.7	2.7
Brim	2.7	2.6	2.6	2.4	1.8
Mellow Roast	0.5	0.4	0.3	—	—
Total	32.9	32.5	33.4	35.9	34.5
Procter & Gamble					
Folgers					
Regular	24.9	26.2	27.0	19.9	22.8
Decaf	—	—	—	2.8	3.4
Flakes	—	—	—	5.5	5.1
Total	24.9	26.2	27.0	28.2	31.3
Nestles					
Hills Bros	7.4	7.7	7.8	7.9	7.5
MJB	—	—	—	2.5	2.7
Chase & Sanborn	—	—	—	0.9	1.3
Total	7.4	7.7	7.8	11.3	11.5
Chock Full O'Nuts	5.0	5.8	5.4	4.6	5.1
Coca Cola					
Maryland Club	1.0	1.0	1.0	1.0	0.9
Butternut	1.5	1.4	1.5	1.2	1.1
Total	2.5	2.4	2.5	2.2	2.0
Subtotal	72.7	74.6	76.1	82.2	84.4
All others	27.3	25.4	23.9	17.8	15.6
Grand total	100%	100%	100%	100%	100%

Source: John C. Maxwell, Jr., "Coffee Consumption Continues to Cool Off," *Advertising Age,* 1980–1989.

of the total 1.1 billion pounds sold in 1988). DDB executives pointed out that the Juan Valdez ads apparently led to this 67 percent increase in sales of Colombian beans. A second campaign, sponsored by the ICO and costing around $24 million, featured celebrities like Jane Curtin and Kurt Vonnegut promoting coffee through a "coffee achievers" appeal.

EXHIBIT 3(b)   Market Shares by Company and Brand: Instant Coffee

	1983	*1984*	*1985*	*1986*	*1987*
General Foods					
Maxwell House					
Regular	22.5%	22.9%	23.7%	21.9%	21.5%
Decaf.	—	—	—	3.1	2.4
Subtotal	22.5	22.9	23.7	25.0	23.9
Maxim	2.6	2.4	2.3	1.6	1.5
Sanka	8.9	8.8	8.6	8.4	8.8
Freeze-dried Sanka	2.1	2.0	1.5	1.0	0.7
Yuban	0.6	0.5	0.4	0.6	0.6
Brim	3.9	2.8	2.1	1.7	1.6
Mellow Roast	0.5	0.3	—	—	—
Int.'l Coffees	1.6	1.9	2.0	2.0	2.0
Total	42.7	41.6	40.6	40.3	39.1
Procter & Gamble					
Folgers					
Regular	12.5	13.0	13.3	14.6	14.9
Decaf	—	2.0	2.6	3.5	4.0
Highpoint	2.9	2.5	1.9	1.3	1.1
Total	15.4	17.5	17.8	19.4	20.0
Nestles					
Nescafe					
Regular	6.1	5.7	5.5	7.2	7.5
Decaf	2.2	2.3	2.0	2.1	3.1
Tasters Choice					
100% Coffee	9.5	9.7	9.8	10.3	10.6
Decaf	0.3	0.2	—	—	—
TC Decaf	6.1	6.4	6.6	6.2	6.2
Sunrise	1.2	1.2	1.1	1.0	0.8
Total	25.4	25.5	25.0	26.8	28.2
Borden					
Kava	0.9	0.8	0.7	0.6	0.5
Subtotal	84.4	85.4	84.1	87.1	87.8
All other	15.6	14.6	15.9	12.9	12.2
Grand total	100%	100%	100%	100%	100%

Source: John C. Maxwell, Jr., "Coffee Consumption Continues to Cool Off," *Advertising Age.*

Separately, a Coffee House program was instituted on 56 college campuses by the Coffee Development Group (funded by the International Coffee Organization) to promote coffee. However, research studies indicated that, while the program was successful in getting those who drank coffee to "trade up" to higher-priced gourmet coffees, the program had no impact on generating new coffee users. The net result: despite significant

---

EXHIBIT 4 Consumption Trends

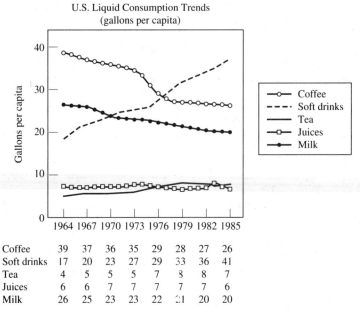

U.S. Liquid Consumption Trends
(gallons per capita)

	1964	1967	1970	1973	1976	1979	1982	1985
Coffee	39	37	36	35	29	28	27	26
Soft drinks	17	20	23	27	29	33	36	41
Tea	4	5	5	5	7	8	8	7
Juices	6	6	7	7	7	7	7	6
Milk	26	25	23	23	22	21	20	20

Source: *Beverage Industry* magazine.

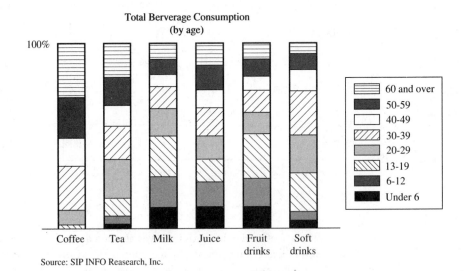

Total Berverage Consumption
(by age)

Source: SIP INFO Reasearch, Inc.

EXHIBIT 4   *(concluded)*

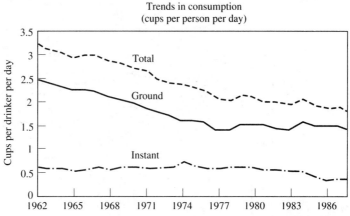

Trends in consumption
(cups per person per day)

Source: International Coffee Organization.

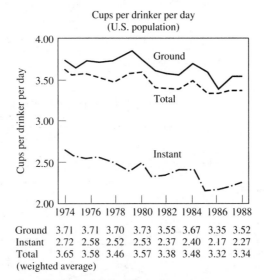

Cups per drinker per day
(U.S. population)

	1974	1976	1978	1980	1982	1984	1986	1988
Ground	3.71	3.71	3.70	3.73	3.55	3.67	3.35	3.52
Instant	2.72	2.58	2.52	2.53	2.37	2.40	2.17	2.27
Total	3.65	3.58	3.46	3.57	3.38	3.48	3.32	3.34
(weighted average)								

Source: International Coffee Organization.

EXHIBIT 5

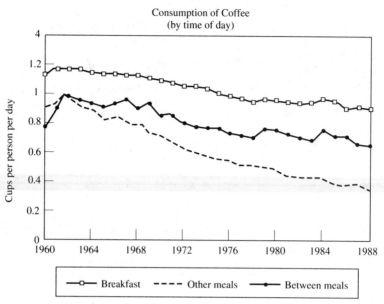

Consumption of Coffee
(by time of day)

Source: International Coffee Org.

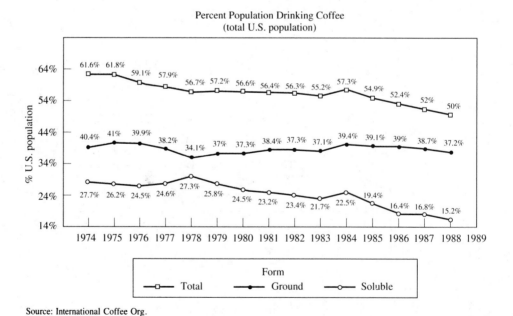

Percent Population Drinking Coffee
(total U.S. population)

Source: International Coffee Org.

EXHIBIT 5   (concluded)

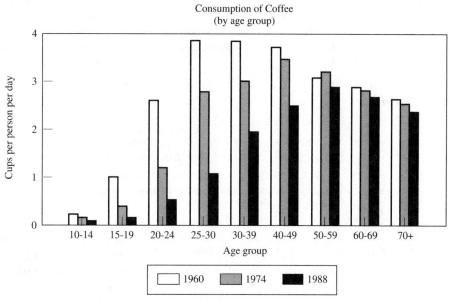

Consumption of Coffee
(by age group)

Source: International Coffee Org.

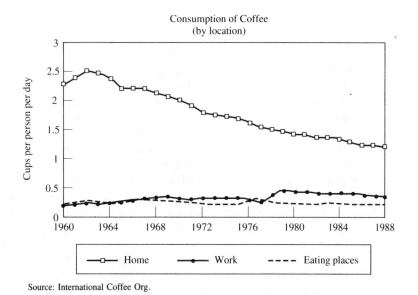

Consumption of Coffee
(by location)

Source: International Coffee Org.

investments, no sampling, promotion, or advertising effort had ever been able to convince young people to drink coffee.

The larger roasters relied mostly on TV commercials to market their brands, with advertising heaviest in the colder months. Many of the television spots appeared during daytime hours since women were still the primary purchasers of coffee. Most coffee marketers also utilized free-standing inserts and newspaper coupons to promote their products.

COMPETITION

Even with falling consumption and spotty growth prospects, the coffee business remained fiercely competitive. A handful of giant roasters dominated the industry, with smaller regional roasters scrambling to capitalize on local tastes by introducing unique regional products and focusing their marketing campaign on local preferences. The main players in both the ground and instant coffee markets were General Foods, Procter & Gamble, Nestles, and Chock Full O'Nuts.

Chock Full O'Nuts was the fourth-largest presence in the industry, with its Chock Full O'Nuts brand competing in only the ground roast category. Of the ground roast market, Chock Full O'Nuts garnered a fairly constant market share of approximately 5 percent.

The other three competitors are described in additional detail below.

General Foods

Throughout most of its history, General Foods led the industry in terms of both market share and media expenditures. As the marketer of the Maxwell House lines (ground, instant, regular, and instant decaffeinated), Master Blend, Yuban, Maxim (instant only), Mellow Roast, Sanka (decaffeinated, available in both ground and instant), and Brim (another strong player in the decaffeinated segment), General Foods had traditionally been the dominant force in the coffee industry. GF's entries into the growing flavored-coffee market, International Coffees (instant only) and Le Cafe (ground flavored coffee), also dominated this fledgling market segment. Finally, to capture sales in the specialty coffee category, General Foods introduced the Maxwell House Private Collection label in 1986, which sold at a premium price and was displayed in special cases supplied to supermarkets by the roaster. Private Collection, offered in both whole bean and ground forms, was the first nationally distributed product in the gourmet coffee category.

In 1987, for the first time, the lead held by Maxwell House was almost snatched away by Procter & Gamble's Folgers brand. At that time, General Foods fell from its historical market share of 38 percent of the $4.5 billion coffee market to nearly 34 percent. In response, GF slashed advertising expenditures by $17.5 million, concentrated on sale promotions instead, and reformulated its product to reduce costs of the beans.

In 1985, General Foods was purchased by Philip Morris for $6.7 billion, and in March of 1989, Philip Morris formed the Kraft General Foods Group to manage the food industry product lines. Industry analysts speculated that this move came in response to the disappointing year Maxwell House experienced in 1988. By the end of 1988, General Foods' share of the market had slipped further to 33 percent. Philip Morris, the world's largest consumer packaged goods company with 1988 operating revenues of almost $32 billion, restructured General Foods by closing a plant, consolidating manufacturing facilities, instituting early retirement plans, and engaging in other overhead cost reductions. The company hoped to boost Maxwell House sales in 1989 through stepped-up advertising, better quality through product reformulation, and new packaging. Additionally, new product introductions included Maxwell House Rich French Roast, a " robust European-style" blend, Maxwell House Colombian Supreme, and Maxwell House Filter Packs, pre-measured coffee packaged in a sealed filter.

Procter & Gamble

Founded in 1837 and headquartered in Cincinnati, Ohio, Procter & Gamble in 1988 marketed products in 140 countries. In the U.S. alone, P&G competed in 39 consumer-product categories and had the leading brand in 21 of these. With net sales of $20 billion in FY 1988, P&G was considered to be one of the world's premier marketers and employed over 77,000 people worldwide. P&G's largest coffee brand was Folgers Coffee, which began as a small regional brand in 1850 and was subsequently purchased by P&G in 1963. P&G took Folgers national, positioning the brand against General Foods' Maxwell House, the industry leader, in a marketing battle that still continued after two decades. By the end of 1988, P&G's Folgers' share of the ground coffee market was estimated to be 31.8 percent, as compared to all of General Foods' coffee products at 33 percent.

While General Foods had a number of coffee brands, P&G focused its efforts behind Folgers. Consequently, while General Foods' total corporate market share was slightly larger than P&G's, P&G's Folgers became the number one selling single brand of coffee in the country.

Folgers' variations included automatic drip, flaked, instant, decaffeinated, and instant decaffeinated coffee. Most of Folgers advertising consisted of spot and network television. As of 1984, Folgers' spokeswoman, Mrs. Olson, was replaced by the "best part of wakin' up is Folgers in your cup" campaign. P&G also used other advertising vehicles, such as sponsorship of a race car that appeared in southeast circuits. In recent years, P&G spent $30 million annually in advertising its Folgers line, using NW Ayer, a New York advertising firm, to promote the brand.

In 1986, P&G began test marketing individual coffee bags, representing a concept similar to that of tea bags. These coffee bags could be used in a microwave oven or simply with hot water. Called Folgers Singles, these fresh-roasted and "freeze-concentrated" single-serving bags aimed to capitalize on consumers' desire for quick, convenient products. That same year, P&G introduced Folgers Special Roast, a high-yield brand extension which competed with GF's Maxwell House Master Blend. To gain a part of the premium coffee segment, P&G introduced Folgers Gourmet Supreme in 1987 and targeted it to compete with GF's Yuban brand. Additionally, in the spring of 1988, P&G changed Folgers to a fast-roast technology. With this new technology, the beans were roasted at more intense heat, and hence more flavor could be derived from the beans. As a result, 13 ounces of the new Folgers were equivalent to 16 ounces of regular Folgers, allowing P&G to use fewer beans and offer the product at a lower price while requiring no extra marketing (packaging, labeling, and taste all remained unchanged).

Nestles

Nestle's first coffee offering was Taster's Choice, a strong player in both the decaffeinated and regular instant categories. Nestle also marketed Nescafe instant coffee, and in 1984, Nestle corrected sliding Nescafe sales with the introduction of the Custom Blended line extensions. Nestle's most recent instant coffee contender was Sunrise coffee, which Nestle introduced in the late 1970s. In the instant category, Nestle captured 33.1 percent of the market in 1988. Both Taster's Choice and Nescafe garnered an impressive consumer following in the instant coffee segment, but up until the mid-1980s, Nestle had no product entries in the ground coffee segment. To compete in the ground roast market, Nestle purchased Hills Brothers Coffee Incorporated in early 1985. Hills Brothers was the third-largest coffee roaster in the U.S. at the time, capturing 8.1 percent of the market in 1984. Later the same year, Nestle bought two other small regional brands, MJB and Chase & Sanborn, to expand its product line in the ground roast category. Additionally, line extensions were added to Hills Brothers, Nescafe, and Taster's Choice.

By 1989, Nestle launched an innovative product in England which had been test marketed in local discotheques and nightclubs. Reflecting the preferences of the young for cold, sweet beverages, this product consisted of iced coffee laced with milk and sugar. Nestles Frappe, sold in cartons, was targeted to 13 to 24-year-olds who were part of the soft drink generation. Both Procter & Gamble and General Foods were rumored to be working on a similar product.

BRAND MANAGEMENT AT P&G

P&G implemented brand management over 50 years ago to encourage personal commitment from brand managers. Organized by product type into category business units and product divisions, each division had its own brand management organization. A Brand Group usually consisted of four or five people and planned, developed, and directed the brand's marketing activities. The brand manager led the group and assigned the other members broad areas of responsibility. The company found that certain skill areas such as leadership, communication, people management and analytical/common-sense thinking were good predictors of long-term success at P&G. Brand Groups were independent units and enabled P&G to market a number of different products, many of them competitive with one another. There were several variations on the basic brand manager's job, however, as the company tried to capitalize on the strengths of individuals. Doug Hall's career with the company, and in particular the execution of the Folgers 2000 Experiment, proved an interesting example of such a variation.

Doug Hall joined P&G's brand management organization in 1981, after receiving a B.S. in chemical engineering from the University of Maine. His early brand assignments included Coast soap, Brigade toilet bowl cleaner, and Spic and Span. During his tenure of Spic and Span, he expanded Spic and Span Pine Liquid nationally, and created an award-winning promotion to celebrate the parent brand's 75th anniversary and draw consumer attention to the brand. In this anniversary promotion, consumers found "diamonds" in each bottle of Spic and Span; after taking the "diamond" to their jeweler, consumers could discern whether the item was a cubic zirconia or a genuine diamond. The promotion generated millions of dollars worth of free public relations exposure, was copied literally dozens of times by other packaged goods companies, and was placed in the PMAA "Promotion Hall of Fame" for innovative in-pack promotions. Hall served as brand manager for Safeguard bar soap, later moving on to new products brand manager for soft drinks where he invented hundreds of new beverage concepts and, perhaps more importantly, a new product invention, research, and development system.

FOLGERS 2000

In September 1988, Mark Emerson, Coffee Division manager, challenged Doug with discovering a means for getting young people to drink Folgers. Recognizing the lack of success the industry had had in attracting new users, Mark decided to utilize an autonomous venture-team approach, where a small group of enthusiastic personnel work together in a highly-focused effort creating and executing a project. Such a venture team was to handle the complete execution of the program, including purchasing, public relations, advertising, distribution, packaging, and sales.

The team was to be led by an entrepreneurial new product leader capable of pulling the group together and integrating its diverse set of skills. Doug was to assemble the best team for the job among both P&G employees and outside suppliers and would have sole responsibility for all decisions associated with the project. Mark would serve as an advisor to Doug, but would not exercise any authoritative veto power over the program. The success or failure of the project would solely be Doug's responsibility. Mark's only caveat was that the experiment was to be conducted with minimal disruption to the core business and staff in order to avoid diversion of the division's efforts away from their core focus of building Folgers business.

The mission was simple: figure out a strategic and executional program for generating new coffee users. Given the magnitude of the challenge, Hall decided that whatever they did it would be big and bold:

> *"I recognized early on that convincing young adults to drink coffee was clearly a suicide mission. In fact, the head of the International Coffee Organization's college marketing effort told me that she was no fool, she knew there was no way you can get youth to drink coffee, the best you can do is slow the decline. Given that there was such little hope, I decided to build a program so big and so audacious that if we failed there wouldn't be much option but to milk the category for profits and resign ourselves to the death of the category."*

Early in the project it became clear that if they were going to try some very bold initiatives, they would require a "small containable environment" for conducting their research. The venture team chose the campus of Miami University in Ohio as its "living laboratory." This isolated campus of 15,000 students provided an ideal environment for testing of the marketing program. It also provided an opportunity to have young people, the target market, assist the project, thus providing a great learning experience for both the Folgers 2000 team and the students. The plan involved running the program for eight weeks, split in the middle by spring break. To accelerate trial and awareness, a high-intensity executional program was developed. Hall and his team officially kicked off the Folgers 2000 Experiment on February 13, 1989, and ran the project until April 15, 1989.

THE TEAM

In November of 1988, Hall assembled his team and began Folgers 2000. As the project leader, Doug Hall identified the skills of his staff and assigned tasks and responsibilities according to each individual's talents. He had a simple interview process for identifying those corporate people and outside suppliers who were right for the team: he would explain how bad the situation was versus colas, how everything had failed to date, and give an idea of this strategy and how his team would operate. Those who rose to the challenge and answered "with a sparkle in their eye" he hired. To reinforce the attitude that they as a group would be different and would have to "invent" a solution where none had been found before, he immediately established an open and informal environment; for example, the team was to dress casually (no suits, no ties) to encourage open discussions and to encourage everyone to "get their hands dirty." In addition, the team adopted the name "Invention Team," with Doug serving as "Master Marketing Inventor" and others having similar titles.

As "Marketing Inventor" and leader of all on-campus efforts, Hall selected an Assistant Brand Manager, Eric Schulz, who managed the more than 400 Miami University students who worked for him by example. He worked along with the students, unloading trucks and brewing coffee, and learned to handle the inevitable crises with creative solutions. At one point, Schulz discovered that a truck containing the Fudge Creamers was delayed and would not be able to deliver the creamer on time for the first week of the test. After trying in vain to resolve the problem with the manufacturer, he called the president of the trucking company responsible for transporting the creamer and explained that he was the "President of the Folgers Coffee Company" and that he needed a favor. The creamer arrived at its destination within four hours.

Finally, the team included 467 Miami University students, acting as public relations and communications assistants, coffee brewers and servers, truck drivers, clean-up crew, special event organizers and assistants, etc. In employing student organizations to help implement the experiment, P&G hoped to foster a partnership between the company and the students. In selecting the students, P&G invited presentations from any of the 200 on-campus organizations, of which 15 organizations, most of them affiliated with the Greek fraternity and sorority system, actually decided to compete for the work. The organizations were subject to the same entrepreneurial start-up interview standards that Hall had applied to the P&G people and outside suppliers. The 6 organizations selected by P&G included Advertising Incorporated for creation and production of the advertising, Delta Sigma Pi for market research, Phi Mu and Alpha Phi Omega for product sampling, Shriver Center Program Board for media releases and promotions, and Gamma Phi Beta for special event marketing.

INVENTING THE MARKETING PROGRAM

The development process of Folgers 2000 consisted of several phases:

Total Background Immersion.   Here the project team absorbed all the information they could about coffee in general and Folgers in specific. This stage involved watching and listening to hours of coffee commercials, reading books about coffee, caffeine, and youth, studying various related categories (coffee makers, coffee cups, creamers, sweeteners), and drinking various brands and forms of coffee. Consumer background research in this phase included 'Candid Comments™', a system in which members of the team videotaped interviews with college students on the street, on campus, in fraternity houses, etc. at 6:00 a.m. They listened to and observed purchase and usage habits in convenience stores, school cafeterias, and fast food restaurants.

Invention.   After gathering volumes of input data on coffee, cola, youth, and Folgers, the team conducted a series of 'Eureka! Sessions' in which consumers, team members, and experts "invented" strategies and executional approaches for generating new users. 'Eureka! Sessions' were specialized creativity sessions which focused on translating the seed "facts" gathered during the Total Immersion stage into relevant yet unexpected benefits and products. To enhance the efficiency of groups, multi-dimensional creative catalysts or stimuli were provided. This was based on the belief that all ideas are feats of association or a reaction between two or more unrelated ideas. The stimuli provided at 'Eureka! Sessions' were highly varied and included visual stimuli (photos, videotape, etc.), mind mapping, trigger words, musical "moods" stimuli, projected frame-of-reference, role plays, etc.

To further stimulate ideas, the team sought to generate the most creative environment possible. Thus, 'Eureka! Sessions' were run in a "high-energy, high-fun" atmosphere. The moderators projected enthusiasm and energy, and from these sessions a wealth of new approaches to generating new coffee users was identified.

Pollster Consumer Research.   Here consumers were exposed to the wide range of strategies and approaches to increase usage among young people developed during the 'Eureka! Sessions.' Non-coffee drinkers tasted new coffee flavors, new coffee forms, new delivery systems, new image visuals, advertising selling ideas, and sampling systems. All research was done utilizing an "interactive approach" whereby the inventors themselves interviewed consumers one-on-one in their environment, i.e., in parks, fraternity houses, sports fields, and classrooms. (Research has indicated that going to the consumers in their environment led to far more candid and honest responses.)

From this phase, the key components of the Folgers 2000 strategy were identified. The Folgers 2000 program would have three key components: (1) *image change* to improve the highly negative image that coffee and correspondingly Folgers had among young adults through fun and irreverent advertising and promotions; (2) *sampling* to generate trial and retrial of Folgers coffee; and (3) *taste enhancement,* to enhance the initial taste perception of Folgers among new coffee drinkers. To accomplish the latter, a unique

Fudge Coffee creamer was invented that, when added to coffee, gave the product a smooth chocolate taste.

Image Change.   The team found that the image of coffee was clearly tarnished. Young people associated coffee with "old fashioned," "out-of-date" and "real old" . . . i.e., over 40. To change the image, very bold and dramatic steps would be required.

The objective of the Folgers 2000 advertising was to convince college students that the aroma and flavor of Folgers coffee could revitalize them. The Folgers 2000 team selected the advertising slogan "Jump Start Your Day." This unique selling idea was selected as it was felt that it could dramatically inject some "youthful irreverence and fun" into the "mature," "adult" image that coffee traditionally projected. Radio and print advertising was created expressly for the marketing experiment. Off-beat, humorous ads were created that were closely tied to the realities of college life—staying up all night studying, facing early morning statistics exams, and wrestling with deadlines for term papers. Sample print advertisements run in the student newspaper are shown in Exhibit 6.

For media, the team decided to utilize a saturation blitz approach, placing full-page ads on the back page of each issue of the student newspaper. They ran 24 radio spots a day on 97X, the very popular college radio station, and blitzed the campus with posters and flyers. Exhibit 7 shows scripts of some of the radio advertisements.

During the second half of the experiment, the team and Advertising, Inc. (a student-run advertising agency) revised the advertising strategy, focusing instead on the taste of Folgers combined with Fudge and Fudge Mint Creamers. Additionally, advertisements in the last four weeks exposed the relative disadvantages of colas: Their high sugar content (8.5 teaspoons of sugar per 12-ounce can), artificial chemicals, and relatively high cost as compared to coffee's more positive attributes (100 percent natural, no added chemicals or sugar, and inexpensive when brewed at home).

To further enhance the image of Folgers as a fun, youthful product, numerous promotional events were organized with coffee appearing as an integral part of the event. As an example, Folgers midnight movies were sponsored: those students who drank a cup of coffee, provided at the door, got in free; those who did not drink a cup had to pay $2.00. A wide variety of bright, day-glow Folgers merchandise (hats, T-Shirts, sweatshirts, coffee mugs) with bold and contemporary logos were distributed. The company purchased sponsorship to three hockey games and four basketball games in order to run its special promotions. At all sponsored games, Folgers set up coffee stands for coffee sampling, ran advertisements over the p.a. system, and conducted promotional events during the game.

Sampling.   The goal for Folgers' distribution system stipulated that lack of coffee's availability would be eliminated as an issue: coffee was to become *more* available than Coke and Pepsi throughout the duration of the experiment. This strategy replicated Coca-Cola's philosophy of always having Coke close by through machines and fountain vendors.

Twice a day, the Invention Team, through its student assistants, delivered fresh-brewed Folgers (both regular and decaffeinated) to the lobbies of all major buildings on campus. During the eight-week experiment, 700 gallons of fresh-brewed coffee (2.5 tons of liquid)

EXHIBIT 6   Sample Newspaper Advertisements

The print advertisements appeared as full-page ads on the back page of the Miami Student, the student newspaper at Miami University of Ohio.

EXHIBIT 6 *(continued)*

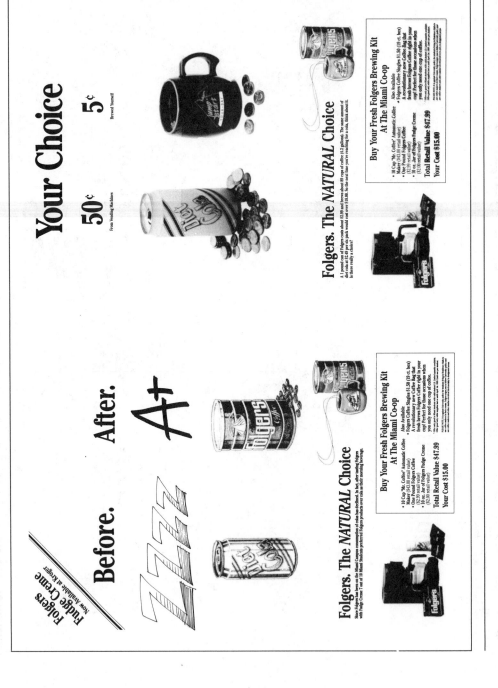

EXHIBIT 6 (*continued*)

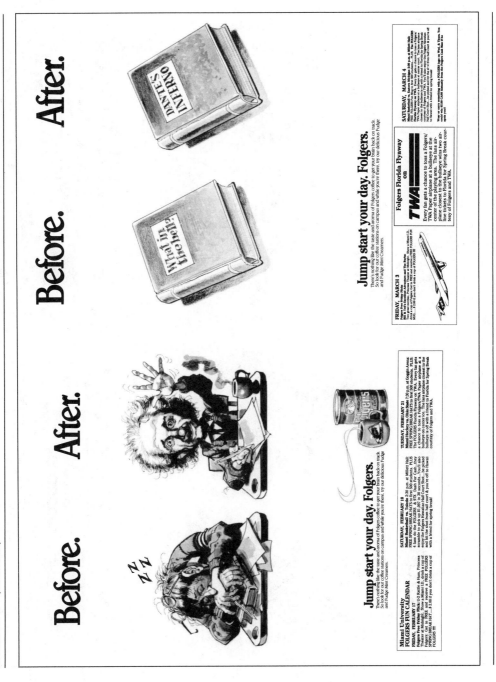

EXHIBIT 6 (continued)

EXHIBIT 6 (concluded)

Before.

After.

THANK YOU!!!

Over the past 2 months we have had the pleasure of working and living with you as we conducted our FOLGERS 2000 Research Project. This has been a very valuable learning experience for us.

Procter & Gamble and Miami University have been great partners over the years. As a result of our experience on campus, that bond is now even stronger. The research work of Delta Sigma Pi has been outstanding. The special events assistance of Gamma Phi Beta made possible the most fun and exciting promotion events we've ever had the pleasure of working on. Advertising Incorporated has written and produced advertising that rivals that of the finest Madison Avenue agencies.

However, the most incredible job of all the groups goes to the organizations who made the coffee delivering possible. Getting up at 4:30 each morning, these crews delivered coffee through rain, sleet, and snow doing an absolutely incredible job. Our deepest thanks to Phi Mu, Alpha Phi Omega and Kappa Sigma.

EXHIBIT 7 Radio Advertisements

Space Aliens

(*Sleepy student's voice; typewriter in background*)

Student:

"The possible influence of space aliens on the Magna Carta. (*Yawns.*) Okay, everything's under control. It's three A.M.; it's due out at eight A.M. 40 pages, no problem. Magna Carta, Magna Carta . . . sounds kind of French. Maybe I ought to look it up."

Announcer:

"There comes a time in every student's life when he needs a little lift. Something to get him through the impossible."

Student:

(*Typing.*) "Okay. Table of contents. (*Yawns.*) How do you spell 'contents'?"

Announcer:

"Luckily, there is one thing that can get you through. That can focus that brilliant mind of yours and make great things happen. Folgers Mountain Grown Coffee. (*Sound of coffee pouring.*) Folgers' flavor and aroma can really put your day back on track. And heaven knows, at three in the morning, anybody's day can suffer from a case of derailment . . ."

Student:

(*Typing quickly.*) "In conclusion, we can surmise from the evidence above that Christopher Columbus was actually a space alien who was blown off course in a bad storm."

Announcer:

Jump start your Day with Folgers!

Party

Announcer:

If last night sounded something like this: (*Party noises: laughter, music, excited voices, breaking glass*) then maybe your morning should sound like this: (*Sound of coffee pouring*).

Mmmmmmm. Hear that? That's the overwhelmingly delicious sound of Folgers Mountain Grown Coffee. All it takes is one whiff of Folgers' amazingly rich aroma to get your day off to an incredibly fast start.

So if you have a night like this: (*Party noises: laughter, music, excited voices, breaking glass*), have a morning like this: (*Sound of coffee pouring*). Mmmmmmm.

Jump start your Day with Folgers!

Term Paper Blues

(*Rock band playing the following jingle; male singing lead.*) oh, man.

I've got a case of the term paper blues
Don't know where to begin
I got a topic I never would choose
And it's already half past ten

Now my eyes are starting to close
I gotta get help fast
There's no way I can afford to doze
This chance could be my last

EXHIBIT 7   (*continued*)

Refrain:
Folgers, Jump Start My Day

Announcer:

If you've got a term paper to write, there's nothing like the incredible flavor and aroma of Folgers coffee to get you up for it!

Alright!
Now my typewriter's starting to hum
I think this paper will pass
Hey you know this guy's not dumb
But why did I ever take this class?

Refrain:
Folgers, Jump Start My Day
This term paper's no pain
Folgers, Jump Start My Day

Igor

SFX:

(*Lightning bolt cracks*)

Master:

Igor! Come quickly!

Igor:

What is it master?

Master:

The electrical storm failed to rouse the creature. Igor you fool! I told you not to bring me the brain of a college student: they're too hard to work with!

Igor:

Sorry master . . .

Master:

Never mind. I must think of another way to bring him back to life.

Igor:

How about cola?

Master:

Cola!?! You fool! This is a natural experiment! We can't give him any artificial chemicals! And all that SUGAR! Think Igor!

Igor:

Something with no added sugar, unlike colas, master?

Master:

Yes

Igor:

Something with no artificial sweetener or chemicals, unlike colas, master?

(*continued*)

EXHIBIT 7 *(continued)*

Master:

That's what we need

Igor:

How bout . . . Folgers . . . Folgers Coffee

Master:

YES!!!! give it to him. YES!!!!!!

Igor:

Master! He's moving!!!

Master:

He's ALIVE!!!

SFX:

(*Creature grumbling, sitting up.*)

Igor:

Master he's trying to SPEAK!

Master:

Clear his mouth!

Mocca Joe:

Mmmm—you don't have to yell, mon . . .

Master:

He talks! Say something else!!!

Mocca Joe:

You got any more Fol-jahs, mon?

Master:

It's a Natural Miracle!

Mocca Joe:

Pour the Folgers already and flip on some tunes, mon . . .

Igor:

Folgers, The Natural Choice.

Fire and Ice

(*Preacher Delivery*) Life . . . why life my friends . . . is but a series of hot and cold experiences.
Let us look . . . what does heat represent. . . . The warmth of a fire feels good (*YES*). When you're hot—you're hot . . . (*yes*)
And cold . . . what does cold stand for . . . cold feet (*yes*) . . . cold shoulders . . . cold hearts. (*yes*)
So what does this mean? . . . Heat . . . heat my friend is good . . . and cold . . . cold is the tool of the subversive.
When you wake up tomorrow . . . do you want to put your feet out on a cold floor or feel the warmth and comfort of your blanket. . . . Do you want to take an ice cold Antarctic-like shower

---

EXHIBIT 7 *(continued)*

---

or ease into a warm relaxing bathtub . . . Do you want to drink an ice cold can of cola . . . or a hot refreshing cup of All Natural Folgers Coffee . . . (*hallelujah*)

Yeah . . . What gives you that wakin' up feeling . . . the Natural flavor and Aroma . . . why, Folgers.

Announcer:

The choice has been made. Ever since Folgers has been at Miami, consumption of colas has declined. In fact, after tasting Folgers with Fudge Cream, over 7 out of 10 Miami students preferred Folgers products over colas as their morning beverage. Folgers, The Natural Choice.

Cola Cop

Cop:

Step outside with your hands up.

Student:

Yes officer—but what did I do?

Cop:

I saw you driving with an open can in your hand—that's a violation, sir, especially in the morning . . .

Student:

But officer, I was drinking a Diet Cola!

Cop:

Diet cola huh? Well then I'm arresting you for driving while drinking artificial chemicals.

Student:

What! I'm not drunk . . .

Cop:

I didn't say that—I said driving while drinking artificial chemicals . . . Boy, this is the 80s. People are drinkin' NATURAL beverages now.

Student:

But please officer—what if I promise not to drink diet cola anymore . . . I'll switch back to regular cola like when I was a kid . . .

Cop:

Regular cola! Why a can of that stuff has eight and a half teaspoons of sugar in it. You put on any more weight, boy, and you'll be mistaken for a bowling ball.

Student:

But officer . . . I promise I'll change . . . what can I do . . .
Cop:

Well I don't know . . .

Student:

Please . . . I'll start drinking natural beverages. I'll drink Folgers . . . Yeah, Folgers Coffee!

Cop:

Did you say Folgers Coffee . . .

(continued)

EXHIBIT 7   *(concluded)*

Student:

Yeah, Folgers, it's 100 percent natural and you don't need a chemist to make it . . . yeah, Folgers.

Announcer:

Folgers . . . the natural choice.

Cop:

O.K. I'll let you off this time . . . but if I ever catch you with diet cola again, I'll run you in boy . . .

Obituary

Preacher:

My dear friends, what can we say about our loved ones . . . they were so well liked, so popular, they had such attractive cans . . . But, consumption of colas is down at Miami University. It seems that people are drinking more and more Folgers Coffee. I mean, can you blame them? What with the great taste and aroma . . . It's just a shame, it had to happen like this. Once word got out that the colas had eight and a half teaspoons of sugar in every can, and once people realized that regular and diet colas were full of artificial chemicals, consumption just died . . . passed on.

Announcer:

Ever since Folgers has been at Miami, consumption of colas has declined. In fact, after tasting Folgers with Fudge Cream, over 7 out of 10 Miami students preferred Folgers products over cola as their morning beverage.

Preacher:

But my friends, we can keep the memory alive. When enjoying your cup of 100% natural Folgers, pause before your first sip . . . in honor of our departed friends.

Announcer:

Folgers, The Natural Choice.

---

were dispatched each weekday to the 80 distribution points around campus. To accomplish this feat, the group invented what a major supplier to the industrial coffee industry called "the largest daily coffee delivery system in the world." The brewing process was managed by one of the selected sororities; beginning each weekday morning at 4 a.m., five students brewed 400 gallons of coffee in four high-speed brewing machines. Each 10-gallon-capacity machine could brew 80 gallons of coffee per hour. The fresh-brewed coffee was then filled into special 5-gallon thermal-insulated containers.

Two other on-campus organizations handled the coffee delivery itself. Deliveries, made in four P&G-supplied pick-up trucks, included dispatching the coffee units to their destinations along with coffee supplies such as cups, lids, creamers, sugar, and spoons. Each truck handled one of four assigned routes, and most of the coffee reached its destination by 8:45 a.m. In each of the 80 locations around campus, sleek red Folgers dispensing stations, custom designed and manufactured by the Invention Team housed the containers, which could keep coffee hot for more than 12 hours. When the project started, crews finished the brewing and delivery process around 10 a.m.; after a few weeks of the project, the team finished by 8:30 a.m. The entire cycle described above was repeated at 4 p.m. for the afternoon shift.

To supplement delivery efforts, in week 5 the Folgers 2000 team put together a promotional kit containing a Mr. Coffee Coffeemaker, Folgers coffee, and Folgers Fudge creamer. This "Fresh Folgers Brewing Kit" was offered to students at a cost of $15.00 to help appease those students who were unhappy about Folgers ending its research and coffee sample program prior to final exam week. In addition, the kits provided a means for further researching coffee appeal and usage habits among the students. Approximately 2,000 Folgers coffee kits were sold in 20 days.

Taste Enhancement. Finally, the project team had concluded from its initial research that consumers—particularly young people—simply disliked the initial taste of coffee. Like beer and many other foods and beverages, coffee was an acquired taste. However, the students had obviously found reasons to learn to like beer, yet no reason to learn to like coffee.

To overcome this issue, the team invented two new products: Folgers Fudge and Fudge Mint Coffee Creamer. The Fudge Creamer product, a non-dairy creamer containing sweetener, cream, and natural fudge flavor, yielded a chocolate mocha-type beverage when added to coffee. The creamer, specially formulated and manufactured by the Invention Team for the project, took the bitter edge off coffee taste and appealed to the first-time drinker who preferred the sweeter taste of soft drinks. The Fudge Creamers were distributed at all sampling stations and, at the request of the local Kroger grocery store, were also made available as a retail grocery item.

RESULTS

The project team hired a professional research firm in Cincinnati to conduct daily student telephone surveys. Two Miami University faculty members also served as consultants to the project. Additionally, the school's business fraternity was retained to research student reactions to both the new products and the experiment itself. Finally, the team analyzed store sales reports to gather sales data. The results gleaned from all three sources are described below.

Overall Impact

Initial results were extremely encouraging. Students drank coffee in incredible quantities. The Folgers coffee sampling stands ran out of product rapidly. Coffee consumption among both on-campus students (who had the greatest access to the coffee stands) and off-campus students (who had to brew their own) rose at equal rates. Hall explained: "the overall excitement generated among students about coffee was amazing. To the Folgers 2000 team, it was clear that the experts had been wrong. Marketed properly, coffee could be competitive with cola soft drinks."

Impact on Coffee Consumption

During the experiment, 65 to 70 percent of students drank Folgers coffee during the first four weeks and during the second four weeks of the test. This usage level was nearly 50 percent higher than the going-in usage levels. The number of students drinking coffee regularly (defined here as consuming at least one cup per day, seven days per week) nearly doubled. At the end of the test, Folgers had an overall brand rating of 62 among students, compared to Maxwell House at 31. After the experiment, Kroger (one of the two main grocery stores used by students) reported a 400 percent increase in coffee sales, selling 40 cases of coffee per week instead of the usual 10 cases. Finally, and to many, most importantly, soft drink vending sales on campus declined by some 22 percent during the test. The Folgers team concluded that the consumer dynamic of switching from coffee to soft drinks was reversible. Marketed properly, coffee had hope of taking back some of its former volume from soft drinks.

Advertising & Promotion

The "Jump Start Your Day" advertising slogan generated extremely high awareness (95 percent) and prompted continual discussions among students. While the slogan appeared to dispel effectively coffee's traditionally stuffy image, the campaign also sparked a great deal of negative public relations and generated opposition among a small but highly vocal group of students who took the slogan literally. A series of condemning editorials and letters to the editor appeared in the student newspaper during the fourth week of the program, some of them decrying the metaphor of jump-starting the day ("like a car battery"). Others likened P&G executives to drug pushers. Copies of these editorials and samples of negative feedback from students appear in Exhibits 8 and 9. Additionally, interviews with students indicated that some found the advertisements immature and highly irreverent. Encouragingly, the advertising won a number of national advertising creativity awards for print and radio advertising.

In one dormitory, a protest arose about the "ethics" of Folgers promoting coffee to students and the 'Jump Start Your Day' advertising. The Invention Team immediately offered to withdraw the sampling station from the protest dormitory if the residents so desired. A vote was taken in the residence hall and, by the overwhelming vote of 93 percent for and 7 percent against, the sampling station was left in the residence hall.

The athletic event promotions attracted nearly 7,000 students (out of a student population of 15,000) and were extremely successful in gaining high awareness (98 percent of students were aware of them). Surveys conducted in the sports arena indicated that 50 percent of the students in attendance were there solely because of the Folgers promotions (average attendance doubled during the Folgers sponsored games). The midnight movies were also extremely successful; the theaters were filled to capacity, and many students had to be turned away.

EXHIBIT 8   Editorials & Letters to the Editor: Student Newspaper

February 24, 1989: **"THE COFFEE EPIDEMIC"**

"It's red. It's sleek-looking. It spurts dark-colored liquid. How could I resist it?

"Now, let's get something straight right now. I am not a coffee drinker, I have never been a coffee drinker, nor do I ever plan to be a coffee drinker. But I'm drinking coffee. Let me give you a little scenario here. You wake up one morning and you're really tired. Why? You don't remember. You do remember, rather suddenly and to your utmost dismay, that you have an exam today. Morning exam. That's a dangerous combination. There's only one thing you can do. You've got to jump-start your day with Folgers.

"Maybe that's a little dramatic. But it is true—and it's convenient: free coffee in the dorms, free coffee in the classroom buildings, free coffee at the movies, free movies with coffee. All right, this is getting ridiculous. There's free coffee everywhere. Heck, I think there's more coffee here from Colombia than there is—well, than anything else that might be from Colombia.

"There's no doubt—it's a coffee mecca out there. For you coffee-lovers, you've just died and gone to coffee-heaven. Even if you despise the charcoal-like liquid, you must admit, the temptation is almost too much. It's there, it's hot and liquidy, it has caffeine, and, of course, it's free. What more do you need? Now, let's take a look at those last two points. First of all, it contains caffeine. How much caffeine? Well, let's just say they're advising heart patients to drink at their own risk. Heck, I think half the campus just woke up last week. But enough with the David Letterman-like oneliners. Based on my reliable sources, this Folger's stuff they're dishing out contains about five times the amount of caffeine found in cola. You know, people do seem a little jumpy lately.

"Okay—that just about covers the caffeine issue. Let's talk about the other major incentive here: it's free. This means, of course, that it doesn't cost anything to drink it. And keep on drinking it. All you have to do is walk up to the spiffy-looking, shiny red coffee dispenser, which, I might add, represents the latest in coffee technology, and, well, dispense coffee into a little paper cup. That's right folks—coffee in a paper cup. Not to mention the plastic spoons. And then they provide you with fudge creamers (or fudge/mint creamers for those with a particular zest for mintiness). This is great. You can now drink coffee without actually having to taste it. Of course, you could always drink hot chocolate, but I guess that would kind of defeat the point.

"All right. Let's look at how this whole thing started. Some bozo up at P&G decided college students weren't drinking enough coffee. Our noble guardians of freedom up at P&G installed dispensers throughout Miami-Land, bringing coffee and democracy to all of us who have been deprived of this constitutional right. Of course, these nifty apparatuses aren't going to be here forever—our buddies up at P&G plan to remove them April 15. Let's see, finals week starts May 1. Hmmm . . .

"Well, I think that's all I can possibly say about coffee. In fact, I think that's about all anyone could possibly say about coffee. Unless, of course, you work for P&G. If you have any comments about this little column, please feel free to stop by for a cup of coffee, and we'll jump-start both our days with Folgers."

(continued)

EXHIBIT 8 *(continued)*

February 28, 1989: **"JUST BUSINESS"**

"I was most dismayed upon reading the guest column in last Friday's *Student*. The ideas set forth . . . were, simply put, irrational.

"My main disappointment in [. . . the] article lies in the accusation that the executives of Procter & Gamble are common drug dealers trying to force addiction to their drug upon us. Perhaps [the author] is not aware that a greater number of P&G employees, including executives of the highest level, are graduates of Miami. Every morning I see many students sitting in their morning classes with cans of Pepsi or Coke. These two caffeine drinks are as much a part of our generation's culture as Burger King or McDonald's and yet we don't see executives of either of these two beverage corporations being accused of pushing drugs.

"Another aspect of the Folger's campaign which must be pointed out . . . is that those P&G executives . . . are pouring many thousands of dollars into this campus. Even *The Miami Student* has received patronage in the form of full-page advertisements.

"Sure, they are offering us free coffee, and there are plenty of incentives too. But all P&G is doing is trying to increase their sales. Is there anything so wrong about that . . . ? It's all a part of good old American business.

February 28, 1989: **"JUMP START WHAT?"**

"During the past few weeks Miami students have been encouraged by Procter & Gamble to "jump start" their days with Folgers coffee. Few advertising campaigns in recent history could have raised such disconcerting imagery as this one. The metaphor, comparing to a car battery, is frightening, especially when it is suggested that one send shock waves through the former. As alarming as it is, this rather destructive metaphor is apt.

"Yet those who devised the advertising strategy did not carry through their metaphor. After a dead battery is jump started, it is still in a reduced state, just as when a tired person drinks coffee he or she does not become awake, just wired. The ads which have swamped the campus over the last few weeks have depicted coffee as a means to avoid the need to sleep or as a substitute for basic intelligence. It is not. It merely delays the need for sleep.

"When the haze of publicity is pulled away from the current events popping up all over campus, it must be recognized that coffee is essentially a drug, not a morning elixir with magic grade-improving properties. And Procter & Gamble is not a philanthropic organization with some extra hats, giving away coffee by the barrel out of the goodness of their hearts. The company is using Miami as a test market, an experiment, and the students are the guinea pigs. The firm is not only interested in how much students like coffee that tastes like hot chocolate when it is given away, but also how many will get addicted and start buying it.

"This is not necessarily evil, but it is an interesting coincidence that the experiment is slated to end shortly before finals week. Those students who are developing an immense attraction to the 80 red stands with campy writing on them would be well advised to plan ahead and start figuring a few pounds of grounds (of whatever brand) into their study snack budget.

"Besides the fact that caffeine is addictive and those creamers that so many seem to love to the point of bizarre extremes will not be in Kroger when the project is over, there is

EXHIBIT 8 *(concluded)*

another consideration which the future coffee drinkers of America should think about in this period of inclement weather. Many think that a nice hot cup of coffee will warm them up on cold mornings from the inside. Actually, caffeine lowers the core temperature of the body, reducing one's ability to resist the cold. Orange juice would do better to ward off the ailments of winter.

"In the final analysis, the Folgers/2000 campaign presents students with a choice of whether to begin drinking coffee, a habit which could become a lifelong one and could be difficult to kick. When you feel like jumpstarting your day, remember that if you cross the wires when jumpstarting a battery, the battery explodes. Think about it and make your own decision."

March 24, 1989: "BAD HABITS"

"On the campus of a university made up of students who are (for the most part) of above-average intelligence, it is an insult to them to promote the idea that a cup (or two, or three) of coffee can "jump start" one's day and have a magically positive effect on academic achievement. Promoting coffee as an antidote to the effects of mental and physical fatigue (resulting from poor health and study habits in general and especially that of the "all-nighter") shows a total lack of understanding of a college student's real needs, a primary one being to develop good, effective health and work habits now. Of course, this promotion is not meant to sell students on good habits and help them do their best work now and 10 years from now; it is meant to sell them on the idea that coffee will save one from the disastrous effects of waiting until the last night to study for an exam or feeling tired because of poor sleeping and eating habits. Most students attend college with the intention of becoming responsible, strong, and independent adults—not people who accept caffeine (or cigarettes, or alcohol, or cheating, or settling for less) as crutches or remedies for poor habits. Putting out free coffee is fine, but its role in a student's life should not be distorted the way the accompanying advertising is doing.

"One other point: if Miami approves of (and apparently encourages) providing its students with free and ample supplies of artificial stimulant in the mornings, why don't we replace the red tanks with kegs of Miller in the later afternoon? (If we can "jump start" our days in the morning, we should be able to "deaden the battery" when the day winds down.) Beer and coffee have the same capacity to alter one's behavior (in opposite directions, of course) and too much of either one, or a dependency on either one, is harmful. All right, coffee is a lot cheaper. But don't forget that its abuse (and on a college campus, that can be just as bad as alcohol abuse) seems to be perfectly okay."

New Products: The Creamers

Students responded enthusiastically to Fudge Mint Creamer; the creamers vanished rapidly from the Folgers sampling stations, and shortages of creamer were a common problem. One exasperated student wrote a letter to the editor of the student newspaper, pleading with fellow students to quit hoarding the creamer. In a taste test conducted early in the

---

EXHIBIT 9   Sampling of Negative Student Comments

"They just want to get us all addicted to coffee. I really dislike that."

"A lot of people and I are very offended by the slogan 'Jump Start Your Day.' Coffee should not be promoted as a drug. In fact, one of my friends has completely stopped drinking coffee, not only Folgers but all kinds. She will continue her boycott of coffee until the repulsive Folgers advertising campaign is over and off Miami's campus."

"The slogan 'Jump Start Your Day' is disgusting. Folgers may as well advertise chemical dependencies. I wish they'd get the hell off campus and take their drugs elsewhere."

"I think the advertising is kinda cheesy, it seems like it's advertising drugs to teenagers."

"I'm for marketing to younger people, but I think they could use a better slogan. I think Folgers' intentions could be misinterpreted. I think there's been a lot of flack that Folgers has been trying to get people addicted to caffeine. I think it's too risky. It's too vague. The slogan could apply to cola as well as coffee."

"I'd like to blow up all their stands . . . I can't believe the university is allowing them to do it."

"I used to think Folgers was a good brand, now I'm not so sure."

"I'm pretty negative towards it (the advertising) . . . it offends me . . . it doesn't represent the product . . . it represents caffeine."

"I don't know why you're bothering to keep calling (for research), nobody is taking the research seriously any more."

---

experiment, 7 out of 10 students indicated that they preferred Folgers with Fudge Creamer over cola as their morning beverage. Additionally, in paired taste testing, Folgers with Fudge Creamer was significantly more popular than General Foods Double Dutch Chocolate International Coffee. Use of the creamer depended also on the type of coffee drinker: new drinkers used the Fudge Creamer 80 percent of the time they drank coffee, while established drinkers used the creamer only 44 percent of the time. The project team concluded that the creamer was ideally suited as "training wheels" for new coffee drinkers.

CONCLUSION

As Doug Hall poured himself another cup of Folgers and turned his attention to the surveys on his desk, he contemplated the results of the experiment and wondered what conclusions he should draw from the data.

In an August 1988 editorial, *Advertising Age* called coffee marketing "one of the most momentous business challenges out there." Many coffee experts appeared to believe that the trend away from coffee could not be halted; Hall and his team had believed the experts were wrong. The Folgers 2000 experiment led them to believe that in fact it was possible to get young people to drink coffee.

However, the data and public reaction to the program raised many questions. He knew that it would be very expensive and risky to execute the Miami University program on a broader basis. The issue before him concerned translating the Miami learning into a viable business proposition for Folgers Coffee. This had many components:

• What should be done with the "Jump Start Your Day" advertising program? It had worked but it also generated some highly negative public relations. Should the campaign be kept, modified or replaced?

• How should the creamer be utilized? It clearly had had a significant impact as a sampling tool. However, the cost and time required to establish it as a new product nationally would be significant and would divert the division's highly focused attention on selling Folgers coffee.

• How should he handle investment and payout for the program? Should he utilize the same standards as with other new business investments?

• What should his target market be? Should he focus on college students only, go for the broader goal of all young adults ages 18 to 29, or pick another target entirely?

• How should he deal with the strategic and executional conflict between the way he should market towards new coffee drinkers in the youth segment and how Folgers was presently being marketed toward current coffee drinkers?

Finally, from a project management perspective, how should he manage future efforts? Many of the Folgers 2000 team members were returning to regular assignments. Should he work to keep the team intact, should he assemble a new team, or should he turn the results over to the traditional Folgers brand group and let them manage the new effort?

Case 3–2

Chevron Corporation: Corporate Image Advertising*

INTRODUCTION

The 1970s had been a tumultuous period for U.S. oil companies. The Organization of Petroleum Exporting Countries (OPEC) had united and exercised considerable pressure on world oil markets. In both 1974 and 1979, Americans suffered tenfold gasoline price spikes and endured shortages at the pump. The U.S. oil industry, already distrusted by the American public, emerged from each period with a severely tarnished image. Exhibit 1 summarizes consumer attitudes toward the U.S. oil industry between 1974 and 1990. During this time, Chevron's public opinion research captured Americans' attitudes toward the U.S. oil industry, as well as their opinions of Chevron. Favorable attitudes toward Chevron were consistently higher than those toward the industry in general; however, the company's image rose and fell with that of the industry.

Chevron withdrew all corporate advertising during 1979–81 because the public opinion environment was extremely hostile as a result of the supply and price difficulties. By late 1981, the strongly negative public opinion environment had ebbed enough that effective communications seemed possible.

In early 1982, Chevron's Public Affairs Department began systematic research to understand the factors behind Americans' attitudes toward the company, and to design a communications program to either improve attitudes, as a best-case scenario, or at least to forestall any further deterioration.

COMPANY BACKGROUND

Chevron Corporation, headquartered in San Francisco, was an integrated petroleum company. It was involved in all aspects of the energy business: exploration, production, manufacturing, transportation, marketing, and research. Chevron was the largest refiner and marketer of petroleum products in the United States. The company's origins dated to 1870, when Frederick Taylor, a wildcatter, drilled the first wells at Pico, California, just north of Los Angeles. Taylor's Pico No. 4 well became the most productive well in

---

*Professor John A. Quelch prepared this case as the basis for class discussion rather than to illustrate either effective or ineffective handling of an administrative situation. Copyright © 1991 by the President and Fellows of Harvard College. Harvard Business School case 9–591–605.

EXHIBIT 1   Attitudes toward the U.S. Oil Industry

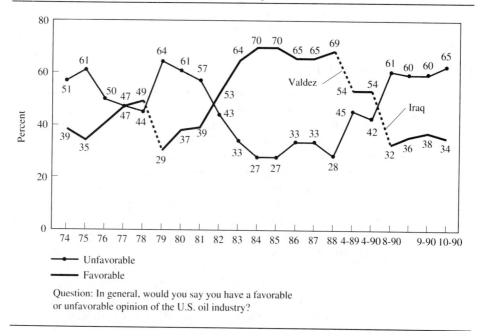

Question: In general, would you say you have a favorable
or unfavorable opinion of the U.S. oil industry?

Source: Chevron Public Opinion Monitor.

the state. Soon, his Pacific Coast Oil Company caught the eye of John D. Rockefeller and, in 1900, Rockefeller's Standard Oil Company (New Jersey) acquired the firm. Rockefeller commenced a decade of capital infusion and dramatic expansion. When the Supreme Court dissolved the Standard Oil Trust in 1911, Standard Oil (California) had oil fields, refineries, pipelines, and tankers. Since those early beginnings, the company had grown consistently, particularly in California, where the Chevron gasoline brand had long been a market leader and where the company sold about 25 percent of its products. Chevron's 1984 revenues totaled $27.8 billion; by 1989, revenues totaled $31.9 billion.

ADVERTISING HISTORY

Chevron had long been committed to advertising in support of its product marketing. Yet only in the 1970s, as a result of the energy crisis, did Chevron venture into corporate or image advertising. During the mid-1970s, Chevron's corporate campaign featured an animated dinosaur and focused on a much-needed conservation theme. In the early 1980s, J. Walter Thompson began acting as Chevron's advertising agency. It appeared that the public opinion climate had become more favorable toward Chevron, and executives believed that a new communications effort could further this progress. Together, Chevron's Public Affairs Department and the J. Walter Thompson account team began to investigate some strategic communications questions, specifically:

- Could a new corporate advertising campaign bolster favorable public attitudes toward Chevron?
- Who should be targeted for this advertising?
- What should be the key message of such communications?

OPINION RESEARCH

Lewis Winters had been appointed Chevron's manager of Public Opinion Research in the early 1970s. Winters, a Ph.D. in psychology and a specialist in advertising research, had established the Chevron Public Opinion Monitor study in 1974 to monitor overall attitudes toward the industry, Chevron, and its competitors. The Monitor also assessed public attitudes toward Chevron across a variety of "image" attributes. Exhibit 2 shows the 16 attributes that Chevron measured in the 1981-82 annual survey. Winters had a strong interest in personal values and their role in shaping public opinion. During the late 1970s, work at SRI International in Menlo Park, California, had captured his attention. A new program called "VALS" (the Values and Lifestyle Program) had been developed under the guidance of sociologist Arnold Mitchell. In Mitchell's vision, the VALS Program would be a way to "psychographically" segment the public based on their values. Values segments would help researchers to understand the underlying motivations for attitudes and behaviors of various segments of the population.

Winters believed that VALS could offer important insights for Chevron's pending corporate communications efforts. In 1983, Chevron began to apply the VALS segmentation to respondents in its Public Opinion Monitor. The results revealed important preliminary information which would ultimately guide the selection of Chevron's target

---

EXHIBIT 2   Oil Company Attributes Measured

Do you agree or disagree that Chevron:

- Contributes money to meet the health, education, and social welfare needs of the community?
- Shows concern for the public interest?
- Pays its fair share of taxes?
- Contributes money to cultural, music, or cultural arts organizations?
- Sponsors radio and television programs on PBS, the Public Broadcasting System?
- Provides good service at its stations?
- Would be a good company to work for?
- Is a good stock investment?
- Charges fair prices for its products?
- Makes too much profit?
- Makes high-quality products?
- Is seriously concerned with protecting the environment?
- Cares about how people feel about them?
- Makes public statements that are truthful?
- Is making efforts to develop alternative forms of energy?
- Is making efforts to find new sources of oil and gas, including drilling offshore?

Source: Chevron Public Opinion Monitor 1981–1982.

audience. Exhibit 3 describes the various VALS segments. Exhibit 4 reports Chevron's 1984 Public Opinion Monitor results by VALS segments. The attributes are grouped and ordered from high to low based on further data analysis discussed below.

DETERMINATION OF THE TARGET AUDIENCE AND MESSAGE

The particular VALS segment which intrigued Chevron was the Inner-Directed segment. Cross-tabulated data from the 1984 Public Opinion Monitor showed this group to be significantly more negative toward Chevron. Moreover, their ratings of Chevron across the sixteen image attributes were also lower than those of the Outer-Directed population segment. This was even more evident in Chevron's home state of California. To further understand the Inner-Directed, Winters and his staff began to explore the associations between Inner-Directeds' overall negative opinion of Chevron and their ratings of Chevron on specific company attributes. The answers to such an analysis could, it was thought, help to guide the message for the campaign. After all, the evidence of the 1970s suggested that more emphasis should be placed on improving negative attitudes than on buttressing the opinions of more favorable segments such as the Outer-Directeds.

Two types of statistical analysis proved useful in understanding the 1984 Opinion Monitor data. Factor analysis was used to discover the underlying "dimensions" in the collective response patterns of the entire sample and to simplify long attribute lists into a subset of "factors" (groups of attributes). The factor analysis performed by Chevron revealed three factors to which Winters assigned the following labels:

- Marketing/Business Conduct.
- Environmental/Social Conduct.
- Corporate Contributions.

Winters knew that multiple regression analysis could shed light on the relationship between each respondent's score on each of the three factors, and his or her opinion of Chevron. In other words, it was possible to learn which of the three factors was most associated with a favorable or unfavorable opinion of the company. Further, regression analysis could be undertaken separately for each VALS segment—perhaps, for instance, the negative attitudes toward Chevron indicated by Inner-Directeds were associated with a different factor than the more positive Outer-Directed segment? Exhibit 5 chronicles the results of the multiple regressions by VALS segment. To summarize, for the total sample, "Marketing/Business Conduct" was the most influential of the three factors. "Environmental/Social Conduct" ranked second, and "Corporate Contributions" was a distant third. However, when the same analysis was performed separately on the VALS Inner-Directed and Outer-Directed segments, Inner-Directeds placed more importance on the "Environmental/Social Conduct" factor. These data, combined with Chevron's knowledge of the high concentration of Inner-Directeds in California (28 percent of the California population versus 20 percent of the whole United States, as indicated in Exhibit 6), proved key in the selection of the advertising campaign theme and target audience for Chevron's new corporate campaign. The next step was to develop the specific commercials to improve favorable attitudes toward Chevron among the Inner-Directeds.

EXHIBIT 3 The VALS® Typology

The VALS typology, developed by the VALS Program at SRI International, is a unique and widely used segmentation tool. The typology characterizes groups within the U.S. adult population on the basis of their values, attitudes, needs, wants, beliefs, and demographics. The VALS typology is divided into three major categories, with a total of nine lifestyle types.

The Need-Drivens

The Need-Drivens are people so limited in resources, especially financial resources, that their lives are driven more by need than by choice. Their values center around survival, safety, and security. Such people tend to be distrustful and dependent, unlikely to make plans. Many live unhappy lives focused on the immediate specifics of today, with little sensitivity to the wants of others and little vision of what could be. They are furthest removed from the cultural mainstream and least aware of the events of their times.

VALS divides the Need-Driven category into two lifestyles: Survivor and Sustainer.

Survivors

Survivors are the most disadvantaged people in American society by reason of their extreme poverty, low education, old age, infirmity, and limited access to the channels of upward mobility. They are oriented to tradition, but marked by despair and unhappiness. While some may once have lived lives associated with higher levels of the VALS hierarchy, others may have been ensnared in the so-called culture of poverty.

Sustainers

Sustainers are struggling at the edge of poverty. They are better off and younger than Survivors, and many have not given up hope. They are angry, streetwise, and determined to get ahead. Many are thought to operate in the underground economy.

The Outer-Directeds

The Outer-Directeds conduct their lives in response to signals—real or fancied—from others. Consumption, activities, attitudes—all are guided by what Outer-Directeds think others may think. Psychologically, Outer-Direction is a major step forward from the Need-Driven state. The Outer-Directed perspective on life has broadened to include other people, a host of institutions, and an array of personal values and options far more complex and diverse than those available to the Need-Driven. In general, the Outer-Directeds are the most content of Americans, being well-attuned to the cultural mainstream—indeed creating much of it.

VALS has defined three Outer-Directed lifestyles: Belonger, Emulator, and Achiever.

Belongers

Belongers are the solid, comfortable, middle-class Americans that are the main stabilizers of society and the preservers and defenders of the moral status quo. Belongers tend to be conservative, conventional, nostalgic, sentimental, puritanical, and conforming. Their key drive is to fit in—to belong—and not to stand out. The Belonger's world is well-posted and well-lit, and the road is straight and narrow. Family, church, and tradition loom large. Belongers know what is right, and they adhere to the rules.

The Inner-Directeds

In contrast with the Outer-Directeds, Inner-Directeds conduct their lives primarily in accord with inner values—what is "in here" rather than what is "out there." Thus concern with inner growth is a cardinal characteristic. Inner-Directeds are self-expressive, person-centered, impassioned, individualistic, and diverse.

VALS has defined three Inner-Directed lifestyles: I-Am-Me, Experiential, and Societally Conscious.

I-Am-Me's

I-Am-Me is a short-lived stage of transition from Outer-to-Inner-Direction. Values from both stages are much in evidence. Typically, I-Am-Me's are young, fiercely individualistic, contrary, narcissistic, impulsive, and exhibitionistic. People at this stage are confused and full of emotions they do not understand; hence, they often define themselves better by their actions than by their statements. Much of their Inner-Direction shows up in great inventiveness, and in often-secret inner exploration that may later crystallize into lifelong pursuits.

234

Emulators

Emulators have aims wholly different from those of Belongers. Rather than drift with events like many Belongers, Emulators are striving to get ahead. They are trying to burst into the upper levels of the system—to make it big. The object of their emulation is the Achiever lifestyle (though many Emulators are not truly on the track to becoming Achievers). They are ambitious, upwardly mobile, status-conscious, macho, and competitive. Many see themselves as coming from the "other side of the tracks" and hence are intensely distrustful, angry, and skeptical that "the system" will give them a fair shake.

Achievers

Achievers include many leaders in business, the professions, and government. Competent, self-reliant, hard-working, and efficient. Achievers tend to be materialistic, oriented to fame and success, and comfort-loving. These are the affluent people who have created the economic system in response to the American dream. As such, they are the defenders of the economic status quo. Achievers are among the best-adjusted of Americans, being well-satisfied with their place in the system.

Experientials

At this stage of Inner-Direction, the psychological focus has widened from the intense self-centeredness of the I-Am-Me to include other people and many social and human issues. Experientials want direct experience and vigorous involvement. They are attracted to the exotic (such as Oriental religions), to the strange (such as parapsychology), and to the natural (such as organic gardening and homebaking). The most Inner-Directed of any VALS type, Experientials also are probably the most artistic, the most passionately involved with others, and the most willing to try anything once.

Societally Conscious

The Societally Conscious are mature, prosperous, and highly educated people who have extended their psychological focus beyond the self and others to the society as a whole, to the globe, or even, philosophically, to the cosmos. A sense of societal responsibility leads these people to support such causes as conservation, environmentalism, and consumerism. They tend to be innovative, active, impassioned, and knowledgeable about the world around them. The Societally Conscious seek to live lives that conserve, protect, and heal. Inner growth remains a crucial part of their lives.

EXHIBIT 4   Public Opinion Monitor Results (1984)

| | | | VALS Segments | |
| | | | Outer-Directeds | |
Do you agree or disagree that Chevron . . .	*Total* (N = 605)*	*Inner-Directeds (N = 162)*	*Achievers (N = 152)*	*Belongers (N = 202)*
Factor 1: Marketing/Business Conduct				
Makes high-quality products?	80%†	75%	84%	82%
Provides good service at its station?	69	66	67	74
Would be a good company to work for?	52	37	59	68
Is a good stock investment?	60	43	60	64
Factor 2: Environmental/Social Conduct				
Shows concern for the public's interest?	23	(4)	44	33
Pays its fair share of taxes?	10	(6)	16	24
Is seriously concerned with protecting the environment?	15	(14)	34	32
Cares about how people feel about them?	43	42	55	47
Makes public statements that are truthful?	34	19	43	38
Charges fair prices for its products?	28	27	28	36
Makes too much profit?	34	33	10	40
Factor 3: Corporate Contributions				
Contributes money to meet the health, education, and social welfare needs of the community?	22	(1)	31	29
Contributes money to cultural, music, or cultural arts organizations?	41	33	49	40
Contributes to PBS, the Public Broadcasting System?	48	44	54	46

*Results from the regionally stratified sample were adjusted to reflect the U.S. population.
†Percentages reported are "Net Agreement"—the total percent agree minus the total percent disagree.

Source: Chevron Public Opinion Monitor.

EXHIBIT 5   Unstandardized Regression Coefficients for Three Factors on Overall Favorability toward Chevron

| | Factor | | | | | *Average Favorability Rating* |
Group	*Marketing*	*Social Conduct*	*Contributions*	*Adjusted R²*	*Constant*	
"Inner-Directeds"	.16	.93	.06	.31	1.13	
(N = 90)	3.96*	3.21	3.56			4.97†
"Outer-Directeds"	.45	.39	.01	.20	2.05	
(N = 434)	4.11	3.58	3.76			5.25

*Mean value of attributes in factor on original 5-point disagree-to-agree scale.
†On 7-point scale indicating unfavorable to favorable attitude toward Chevron.

Source: Chevron Corporation.

EXHIBIT 6   Population Breakdowns by VALS Segment

	Total U.S. (percent)	California (percent)
Need-Driven		
Survivors	4%	2%
Sustainers	6	7
Outer-Directeds		
Belongers	39	26
Emulators	10	10
Achievers	21	25
Inner-Directeds		
I-Am-Me	3	5
Experiential	5	7
Societally Conscious	12	17

Source: MRI/VALS.

DEVELOPMENT OF THE "PEOPLE DO" CAMPAIGN

Based on the research findings, David Soblin, Chevron's account director at J. Walter Thompson, organized six creative teams to design potential commercials targeted at California's Inner-Directeds. After considerable refinement, six 30-second animatics (rough TV commercials) were presented to Chevron. Scripts of these animatics appear in Exhibit 7.

Chevron, like many major advertisers, had a history of testing its advertising before committing its considerable media budget to a new campaign. For the past several years, Chevron had submitted both marketing and corporate commercials to a multisponsored pretest developed by McCollum-Spielman. McCollum-Spielman advertising pretest methodology involved inviting 100 respondents into a theater-like setting, seating them in groups of 25 around television monitors, and asking them to view what they were told were excerpts from pilot television programs. Several key measures—among them attitudes toward test-sponsors and purchase behavior—were collected before the programming began. Then, as on normal television, the new programming was interspersed with several commercials, among them a Chevron test commercial.

Chevron committed to testing the animatics developed by J. Walter Thompson. For this research, respondents were prescreened to learn whether they were Inner-Directed or Outer-Directed. The tests were conducted in July–August 1984 in two California cities, since the final campaign would air only in that state, at least initially.

The McCollum-Spielman test was predicated on the assumption that advertising has three distinct functions to perform:

1. Generate awareness—the consumer should know what company or product was sponsoring the ad.
2. Communicate a message—the intended message of the ad should be understood and capable of "playback" by the viewer.

3. Motivate—the ad should have a positive influence on either product purchase disposition or attitudes toward the company.

As summarized in Exhibit 8, the six test ads reviewed via the McCollum-Spielman procedure received good measures on all three criteria. Importantly, the commercials scored well in an absolute sense against McCollum-Spielman's norms for competitive corporate advertising *and* in a relative sense as compared to previous Chevron campaigns. Among the target Inner-Directed segment, one animatic, "Water," was especially effective. It scored particularly strongly among the societally conscious subsegment of the Inner-Directeds. Consequently, the overall approach of "Water," which gave a specific example of Chevron's commitment to the environment, was determined to be the right approach. "Water" utilized a very emotional or "soft" tone to tell a story of how concern for the environment was of the utmost importance to Chevron.

The successful pretest of the "Water" animatic led ultimately to the development of a corporate advertising campaign named "People Do." In 1985, Chevron began running the first few "People Do" commercials on television, using carefully-selected media buys to ensure a large Inner-Directed audience. The commercials were shown during news programming and in magazines oriented toward Inner-Directeds. The storyboard and script for one of the first "People Do" commercials is presented in Exhibit 9.

EXHIBIT 7   Six Chevron Animatics: 1984

1. Go Softly and Gently

Video	Audio

Video

Scene of Alaskan or Yukon landscape. An owl or a hawk flies into frame. Cut to deer grazing, a stag, and a fawn. Cut to stag's head next to Chevron oil pipeline. Follow stag's head as he looks up. Reveals Chevron pipeline disappearing into landscape.

Cut to close-up on fish's eye. As he swims away we realize that we're underwater looking up at bottom of boat. Camera travels up to view two scientists in boat (still seen from just under the surface). Cut to close-up of scientist's hand holding vial of crystal-clear water.

Cut to aerial view of man walking in wilderness. He is being dwarfed by large bird's shadow. Angle to see man looking up at owl or hawk. He has Chevron logo on his jacket. Cut back to aerial view as owl (hawk) flies into camera, obscuring our view.

Focus on Chevron logo on flag being blown by stiff breeze.

Audio

Singers (children's chorus with organ-like mood music):

  Go soft and gently upon the land,
with what you build and what you plan.
Don't spite the tiny for the grand.
Go softly and gently upon the land.

Go soft and gently upon the deep
Take only that which one should reap.
And guard that which was meant to sleep
Go soft and gently upon the deep.

Go soft and gently into the sky
Leave it pure to fill the eye,
with sights that soar and dreams that fly.
Go soft and gently into the sky.

EXHIBIT 7   (*continued*)

2. Kids

Voice:

Chevron asked some very important people "Why do we need clear air?"

1st Kid:

If we had a bad atmosphere, then we'd have to move to Venus or someplace like that.

2nd Kid:

It's nice. I could, you know, fly kites, airplanes.

3rd Kid:

It's better for your body to breathe clean air.

4th Kid:

I wouldn't like bad air.

5th Kid:

Because when you breathe through their lungs they don't get, they get, they need oxygen.

Voice:

These are a few *big* reasons why Chevron works for clean air today. And a few *small* reasons why we'll be doing the same tomorrow.

6th Kid:

I like it.

3. Water

Video	*Audio*
Water pouring into something we cannot see as a shape . . . the water sparkles as it pours . . . and gradually your TV set seems to fill up with water.	The water you are looking at came from an oil refinery where it was used to help turn crude oil into gasoline. It got pretty dirty doing that.
The filling is completed and the water sits there for a moment. It looks very clean to us.	Before it goes back into the bay where it came from the traces of the work it has done have to be removed.
A stickleback fish swims into view.	Who makes sure of that? Our final inspectors . . .
Another comes in. Then a third. Then a fourth.	Oscar . . . Fred . . . Susie . . . Miranda . . . After all, they have to live in it.
Pull back to see tank in lab. Worker peers through to see that fish are doing okay.	Do people really go to all that trouble to make sure that you don't hurt the fish? Some people do.
Chevron hallmark.	

4. Friends

Voice:

Chevron asked some *very* important people "What makes a good neighbor?"

1st Kid:

A good neighbor makes a good friend.

2nd Kid:

You should really like them especially and they should really like you a lot, too.

(*continued*)

EXHIBIT 7 *(concluded)*

3rd Kid:

You buy me ice cream and stuff.

4th Kid:

It's someone to talk to, to make you feel better.

Voice:

At Chevron we think the most neighborly thing to do is to act like a friend.

5th Kid:

You mean, like, tomorrow you're going to say that (you) think that they trust in you, like to pick a flower for them.

5. Rabbit

Video	Audio
A farmer, plowing a field at sunset, discovers a nest of rabbits . . . and plows around it. Superimpose: Chevron logo.	*Song:* Tomorrow's getting closer It's almost here today Just in time to see that we Don't let the good things get away. The good things all around us Keep 'em safe for one and all For all creatures Great and small.

Voice:

The Chevron Corporation believes that industry has a responsibility to conduct itself in such a way that the future is secure for all creatures, great and small.

6. Color It

Video	Audio
Child drawing a landscape. Begin to move in on drawing. Picture begins to transform into reality. Once the landscape is real, a man walks into the picture leading the child who made the drawing by the hand. Super Chevron logo and "Let's Make it Happen."	*Music:* Color it fresh . . . Color it new . . . Color it magical . . . Color it true . . . See with the eyes of a child . . . But dream the dreams of man . . . Make your dreams come full to life by doing all you can . . .

Voice:

The Chevron Corporation believes that a future worth working for begins with a vision of the world we want our children to live in. Let's make it happen.

EXHIBIT 8 McCollum-Spielman Pretest Results

	Clutter/Awareness*		Main Idea†		Attitude‡	
	Total	Inner-Directeds	Total	Inner-Directeds	Total	Inner-Directeds
"Softly"	46%	45%	39%	46%	+18%	+16%
"Kids"	42	36	35	35	+14	+11
"Water"	37	44	29	45	+32	+36
"Friends"	34	47	24	38	+5	−9
"Color It"	39	32	20	15	+12	+1
"Rabbit"	47	45	35	35	+3	−14
Norm for 30-second corporate ads by oil companies	46		31		+16	
Range from which norm derives	(11 to 87)		(7 to 75)		(−4 to +33)	

*Clutter/Awareness: This score is the percent who mentioned seeing a Chevron commercial after one exposure to the commercial. The unaided measure is taken about 30 minutes after seeing the commercial. The Chevron commercial was embedded in a clutter of seven commercials—the other six were non-oil company commercials.

†Main idea: This score represents responses to the question "other than getting you to buy their products, what would you say were the main ideas they were trying to get across in the commercial?" Again, this was after just one exposure to the commercial in a clutter of seven commercials.

‡Attitude: This score is calculated after two exposures to the commercial when respondents are asked "did the Chevron commercial change your feelings about Chevron as a company in any way?" Those who said "yes, more unfavorably" are subtracted from those who said "yes, more favorably" to arrive at the commercial effect (attitude) score.

GAUGING COMMERCIAL EFFECTIVENESS

The artificial environment of commercial "pretest" research did not convince Chevron's management that the $5 million annual investment in the "People Do" corporate campaign was paying off. So, in order to gauge commercial effectiveness, Chevron used the "Communicus" methodology pioneered by Jack Moore. The "Communicus" approach involved benchmark interviews with "target audience" respondents in advance of the campaign, followed by natural exposure to the campaign for a designated period (usually a year) and then a reinterview of the same respondents to gauge (1) campaign awareness, (2) sponsor identification, and (3) commercial effect on either gasoline purchase, or, in the case of "People Do," favorability of attitudes toward Chevron. Generally, Chevron's senior management required a positive reading across these measures to continue campaign funding. Exhibit 10 presents data from year one of the "People Do" campaign in California, comparing consumers who were unexposed to any of the commercials to a second group who had viewed, and successfully identified Chevron as the sponsor of at least one of the commercials during the period. Here again, "People Do" met its objectives, especially among the Inner-Directed target.

Chevron produced and aired six executions of the "People Do" campaign between 1986 and 1988. All emphasized Chevron's concern for the environment and the protection of endangered species of wildlife. Chevron's 1988 tracking study found that 57 percent of respondents (65 percent of Inner-Directeds) could recall an ad from the campaign and

EXHIBIT 9   "People Do" Advertisement

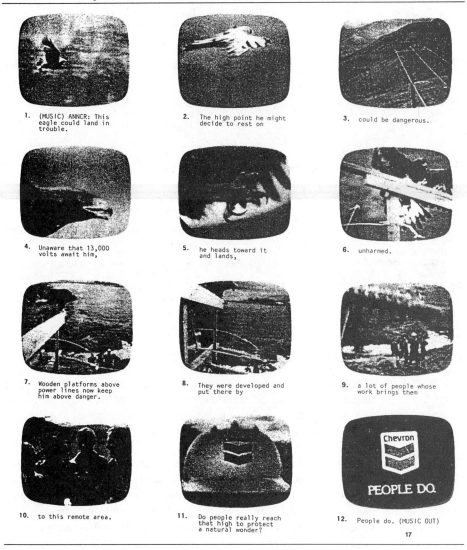

1. (MUSIC) ANNCR: This eagle could land in trouble.

2. The high point he might decide to rest on

3. could be dangerous.

4. Unaware that 13,000 volts await him,

5. he heads toward it and lands,

6. unharmed.

7. Wooden platforms above power lines now keep him above danger.

8. They were developed and put there by

9. a lot of people whose work brings them

10. to this remote area.

11. Do people really reach that high to protect a natural wonder?

12. People do. (MUSIC OUT)

17

correctly identify Chevron as the advertiser. When asked to name the oil company that exhibited the greatest environmental responsibility, 31 percent of respondents (30 percent of Inner-Directeds) mentioned Chevron; Arco was second, cited by 10 percent. Nevertheless, despite all Chevron's efforts, there remained a hard core 25 percent of Inner-Directeds who were unconvinced by the advertising even if aware of it.

EXHIBIT 10   Impact of the "People Do" Campaign

A) Proven Awareness of 1986 "People Do" Campaign

| | Net Campaign Awareness | | |
Proven Aware	Total	Inner-Directeds	Outer-Directeds
Any ads	41%	47%	41%
1–2 ads	22	15	27
3 or more ads	19	32	14

B) "People Do" Campaign Effectiveness: Attitude change toward Chevron as a company among VALS "Inner-Directeds" (California), January 1987 vs. January 1986

Attitude Change Toward Chevron (1986–1987)	Unaware of Chevron Ads (N = 47)	Aware of Chevron Ads	Advertising Effect
Favorable	+7%	+15%	+8%
Unfavorable	−3	−5	+2
Net	+10%	+20%	+10%

C) "People Do" Campaign Effectiveness: Purchase impact among total sample and VALS "Inner-Directeds" (California)

| | Advertising Awareness | | | | Advertising Effect | |
| | Unaware | | Proved Aware | | | |
Brand Bought Last Was Chevron	Total (N = 146)	Inner-Directeds (N = 47)	Total (N = 103)	Inner-Directeds (N = 41)	Total	Inner-Directeds
January 1986	24%	26%	9%	10%		
January 1987	26	21	19	27		
Net	+2%	−5%	+10%	+17%	+8%	+22%

FUTURE CHALLENGES

Chevron's polling in 1988–90 revealed important changes in public attitudes toward the environment. Specifically, environmental protection had been democratized. Polls by Chevron and major nonpartisan groups such as Gallup, Roper, and Cambridge Reports traced the phenomenal growth of the environmental movement. By 1990, over 75 percent of Americans identified themselves as environmentalists. Further, environmental attitudes were beginning to translate into changed behavior. As of September 1990, nearly 75 percent of Americans claimed to recycle paper, cans and bottles. Researchers at Chevron believed that these changes were based on shifts in personal values. It seemed that the 1980s' emphasis on personal health and safety was being projected to environmental concern. A movement that in the 1970s was largely tied to aesthetic concerns and values (green, open space, trees, restrictions on land development) appeared to be touching a much more central chord for Americans—survival of future generations.

Winters and others at Chevron questioned how the widespread concern for the environment would impact the effectiveness of the "People Do" campaign. They wondered if the target should be broadened beyond Inner-Directeds. In March 1989, the Exxon Valdez oil spill in Alaska focused public attention once again on the alleged shortcomings of the U.S. oil industry. Even though Chevron was not related to Exxon, what would that spill do to efforts by Chevron to convince the public of its environmental concern? Would the "People Do" campaign serve Chevron well should there be another fast run-up in gasoline prices, supply shortages as occurred in the 1970s, and/or a conflict in the Middle East causing severe instability in world oil markets?

Case 3–3

Ad Council's AIDS Campaign (A)*

ADVERTISING STRATEGY

In early Fall 1987, representatives from the Ad Council, The American Foundation for AIDS Research, Inc. (AmFAR), the National AIDS Network (NAN), and Scali, McCabe, Sloves, Inc. met to review progress on their AIDS campaign. The objective of the new alliance between these groups was to develop a communication strategy that would prevent or curb widespread transmission of the AIDS virus through changing current behavior of high-risk individuals by educating them in means of prevention. Their primary concern at this point was how to avoid problems an earlier campaign had encountered in gaining the cooperation of the media. In a campaign designed for New York City, Saatchi and Saatchi, one of the world's leading advertising agencies, drew heavy criticism, and the television media refused to air their advertisements. One of the biggest barriers to the Saatchi and Saatchi campaign was the mention of condoms. This was ironic, because Dr. C. Everett Koop, Surgeon General of the United States at that time, had unequivocally stated:

---

*Janet Montgomery prepared this case under the supervision of Prof. V. Kasturi Rangan as the basis for class discussion rather than to illustrate either effective or ineffective handling of an administrative situation. Copyright © 1990 by the President and Fellows of Harvard College. Harvard Business School Case 9–590–105.

> *The best protection against AIDS, barring abstinence, is the use of a condom. It's high time we started using the word "condom" when we talk about AIDS. It's a word that can mean life and death.*

Gary Verrill, the Scali, McCabe, and Sloves representative to the four-member alliance, summed up the conclusions of the team:

> *The need for a national AIDS campaign is a clear and compelling one. There is no vaccine to prevent the spread of HIV virus; there is no cure for those infected. Prevention, principally the basic modification of sexual behavior, is the only method currently at our disposal. It is clear that despite the millions of words written on the dangers of AIDS, the hundreds of hours of television time devoted to the subject, certain basic truths are not getting through. Time and time again, advertising has shown that it can effectively change fundamental attitudes and that this will, in turn, lead to fundamental behavioral modification.*

In the course of their research, the team had developed a comprehensive advertising campaign to educate people at high risk for getting or transmitting the AIDS virus. But how were they to get media acceptance for the campaign? Was the campaign appropriate in the first place?

GROUP MEMBERS AND THEIR ROLES

AmFAR. The American Foundation for AIDS Research, Inc. (AmFAR) is a private, national, not-for-profit organization dedicated to finding a cure for AIDS. It is the primary source of private funding grants for research on AIDS in the U.S. This organization has a special interest in the younger, less-prestigious researchers who might not qualify for government funding. AmFAR also serves as a source for accurate, up-to-date information about AIDS and the AIDS epidemic for the public, government officials, and the media. In addition, it seeks to identify and address unmet needs in the areas of AIDS education and prevention.

NAN. The National AIDS Network (NAN) was established to be a resource, clearing-house, advocate, and national voice for community-based AIDS education programs. NAN is aimed towards making a compassionate impact on people and serving the needs of local environments through information exchange, training, and minority program assistance. The agency has grown from representing 5 groups in 1985, to working with more than 550 community organizations nationwide in 1987.

Ad Council. The Advertising Council is a private, non-profit organization of volunteers that conducts advertising campaigns developed voluntarily by leading advertising agencies for the public good. Over the years, the Ad Council has run campaigns on subjects as diverse as child-abuse prevention, drunk-driving prevention, and Statue of Liberty restoration. The common thread of all the Ad Council's campaigns is the promotion of independent volunteer action to address social problems.

Scali, McCabe, and Sloves, Inc.   Scali, McCabe, and Sloves, Inc., which is a part of the Ogilvy group, is the 18th largest advertising agency in the world, with billings of over $850 million. Among its highly regarded campaigns are those for Perdue chickens and Volvo cars. In the past, the agency had participated in public service advertising, having helped develop campaigns for The American Diabetes Association and NAN. It was the volunteer agency for the Ad Council's new AIDS campaign.

AIDS—THE FACTS[1]

Acquired immunodeficiency syndrome (AIDS) is the final stage of a disease caused by a virus known as human immunodeficiency virus (HIV). It is not a single illness but a syndrome in which the virus attacks the immune system, destroying the body's ability to fight diseases. It destroys certain cells in the immune system and leaves the body susceptible to a host of diseases healthy people rarely get, including tuberculosis, severe diarrhea, and rare forms of pneumonia. While earlier it was felt that the disease was restricted to homosexual men, intravenous drug users, and hemophiliacs, it is now accepted that heterosexual activity involving contact with semen, blood, or vaginal fluids of an infected person can also transmit the disease. It has, however, been clearly established that AIDS cannot be transmitted through casual contact such as hugging, touching, or sharing bathroom facilities with an infected person. The virus, which appears to thrive on certain kinds of white blood cells, dies quickly when exposed to air.

AIDS has no early warning signs. Persons infected with the HIV virus may feel and appear perfectly healthy for years until, one day, the virus attacks and begins crippling the immune system and the brain. Infected persons, though physically normal for years, are capable of transmitting the virus to others, thereby increasing the threat of the disease. Some summary facts/statistics on the disease are:

- There is presently neither a cure for AIDS nor a vaccine to prevent it.
- 81,443 actual cases of AIDS have been reported in 173 countries worldwide.
- 56,212 (69 percent of total cases) have been reported in the U.S.[2]
- Between 5 and 10 million people are infected with HIV worldwide.
- Between 1.5 and 2 million are infected with HIV in the U.S.
- It is estimated that 1 in 30 people between the ages of 20 and 50 carries the HIV virus in the U.S.
- It is estimated that, worldwide, 179,000 will die of AIDS by 1991.
- By that time, the cost of health and support services for AIDS patients in the U.S. will range between $8 and $16 billion.
- According to the Surgeon General, Dr. C. Everett Koop: "With proper prevention information and motivation, as many as 12,000 to 14,000 people could be saved *just in 1991* from death by AIDS, by protecting themselves from infection."

---

[1]Material in this section is largely from *New York Against AIDS (A)*, Harvard Business School Case 9–590–036.

[2]This is based on statistics available in 1987. Updated information from the Massachusetts Department of Public Health (November 30, 1989) documents 115,158 cases reported in the U.S.

When asked, "What would you say is the most urgent health problem facing this country at the present time?," 69 percent of persons participating in a 1987 Gallup Poll responded "AIDS." However, that same Gallup Poll reported that 73 percent of 18- to 24-year-olds, 90 percent of 25- to 29-year-olds, and 95 percent of those over 30 years *did not* use condoms. The poll concluded, "people recognize the threat of AIDS, but for their own reasons they do not take preventive measures."

RESEARCH ON AWARENESS/BELIEFS ABOUT AIDS

To gain insight into target population behavior, Scali, McCabe, and Sloves led discussion groups among counselors to people at high risk for AIDS (see Exhibit 1 for a list of participating organizations). The objective of the research was to assess current awareness and attitudes of people at high risk, to determine levels of risk behavior, and to determine approaches and/or messages appropriate to each group. Important findings are summarized below.

Who Are the People These Counselors Help?

A wide cross-section of people call in for counseling or come in for tests, not just individuals at high risk (see Exhibit 2 for a breakdown on populations diagnosed with AIDS). Among them are married men, clergymen, divorcees, couples considering long-term relationships, partners of IV drug users, and people who are worried about risk behavior or sexual contacts recently as well as from the last 10 years. For a large majority of them, this reflects a reexamination of current and past behaviors. However, IV drug users rarely come to counseling centers voluntarily. Instead they must be sought out.

IV Drug Users.   Intravenous drug users, as a target group, manifest a number of communications barriers. They form a separate culture on the fringes of society, but are not united and rarely share information on AIDS (as opposed to the gay community). They are becoming increasingly aware of AIDS, but deny personal risk. As drug users don't trust hospitals, social workers, or each other, they aren't likely to pay attention to the risks. "If I got it, I got it, and I don't want to know." The discussants reported that IV drug users don't care about themselves, and think that no one cares about them. So, even if they test positive, they won't change sex or drug patterns (in fact, they may take more drugs as a means of dealing with the problem). The group with the fastest-growing infection rate, IV drug users usually request services only when symptoms appear.

Homosexual Men.   The group with the highest rate of infection, homosexual men are still at great risk from AIDS. Fortunately, this group also has the highest level of education about the disease and prevention. However, even though the gay community has for many years worked together for education, many individuals across the country are not yet using preventive measures.

EXHIBIT 1 Primary Research: Ad Council AIDS Project Discussion Group Participants
(conducted September 10, 14, and 15, 1987)

New York City Department of Health AIDS Institute
    Olga Mejia (Harlem)
    Ann Courrier (Queens)
    Debra Decarlo (Queens)
New York City Department of Health AIDS Hotline
    Jenny Gunnell, Phone Counselor
    Gail Riviera, Phone Counselor
    Don Triose, Phone Counselor
    Romeo Sanchez, Phone Counselor
New York State Narcotics and Drug Research
    Dolly Worth, NYU/NY State Narcotics and Drug Research
New York Blood Center
    Kathy Tendler, Nurse/Counselor
Gay Men's Health Crisis
    Cora Deuchman, Phone Counselor/Table Organizer
    Andy Stubbs, Phone Counselor/Table Organizer
Greenwich House
    Warren McClendon, Counselor
    Kathy Coda, Counselor
Community Health Project
    Denise Rebble, Counselor
    Mark Howard, Counselor
    Gail Spindel, Counselor
Project Return
    Essie Hall, Nurse/Counselor

Bisexual Men. Bisexual men are an easy group to reach, according to the discussants. They are well aware of the risks and are motivated by concern to protect their partners and wife/family. However, they are uncertain about how to suddenly start using condoms at home without arousing suspicion, and for this reason often decide not to broach the subject at all.

Minorities. The discussants suggested that minority men and women who came for counseling appeared to be ignorant of risk factors, and less likely to educate themselves on behavioral risks in comparison to the rest of the counsel-seeking population. Cultural/community practices and pressures often made behavior changes harder to implement. According to the research, a higher proportion of minority women (in comparison to the rest of the the population) felt that they could not be assertive enough to demand use of condoms. The research also concluded that a high proportion of minority men generally felt condom use was not part of their concept of masculinity. Denial was especially high in this group.

Heterosexually Active Women. AIDS is now one of the leading causes of death for women in their 20s. Unfortunately, women in general (and minority women in particular) are afraid to force or even bring up the subject of condoms with their partners. Most

EXHIBIT 2   The U.S. Population with AIDS: Numbers and Percentages*

	Number	Percent
Total cases as of 11/30/89	115,158	
Transmission categories (adults)	113,211	
Homosexual/bisexual male	68,567	61%
IV drug user	23,722	21
Homosexual male/IV drug user	7,923	7
Hemophilia	1,047	1
Heterosexual†	5,457	5
Transfusion/blood components	2,768	2
None of above	3,727	3
Transmission categories (<13 years)	1,947	
Parent with AIDS/at risk	1,572	81
Hemophilia	104	5
Transfusion/blood components	208	11
None of above	63	3
Breakdown by Group		
Gender		
Male	103,902	90
Female	11,256	10
Race		
Caucasian	64,618	56
Black	31,514	27‡
Hispanic	17,885	16§
Other/unknown	1,141	1
Age		
Under 13	1,947	2
13–19	447	0
20–29	23,498	20
30–39	53,174	46
40–49	24,347	21
Over 49	11,745	10

*Information for this Exhibit was taken from the Massachusetts Department of Health *AIDS Newsletter*, December 1989.

†The current number of heterosexually transmitted AIDS cases is comparable to the number of homosexually transmitted cases five years ago.

‡Afro-Americans make up only 12 percent of the population at large.

§Hispanic Americans make up only 7 percent of the population at large.

women are convinced that their partners will refuse to use condoms. Because of fears of losing their lovers or ending up alone, women are reluctant to say no to unprotected sex. As with other groups, women tend to deny their risks. A recent study in the *New England Journal of Medicine* (March 1990) shows that, although the percentage of college women using condoms has doubled in the last four years and tripled since 1975, still less than 50 percent use condoms. Fifty-two percent reported having had two to five partners; 21 percent had six or more partners. These figures on number of partners reflect little change since 1975. College women are beginning to protect themselves, but have not changed sexual behavior patterns.

Teens.   The 20–29 age group segment shows rapid growth in percentage diagnosed with AIDS. As the HIV virus has an incubation period (the time between infection and the appearance of symptoms) of up to 15 years, this group probably contracted the virus while in their teens. In a 1982 study, the National Survey of Family Growth, disclosed that 45 percent of teenagers (15–17) were sexually active. A more recent study revealed that 51 percent of 15-year-olds are sexually active. Forty percent of that group reported having had sex with three or more partners. Less than 30 percent of teens polled by Gallup in 1987 used condoms. The discussants stated that teens have a low level of understanding about prevention. In addition, peer pressure encourages drug experimentation/use.

Heterosexually Active Men.   The discussants felt that middle-class white straight males are the hardest target group to reach. These men firmly believe they won't get AIDS (denial). Most will not take responsibility for having safe sex, believing that this, like birth control, is the woman's responsibility. Straight men tend to resist condom use because they believe it interferes with sex, is not pleasurable, or simply because they don't know how to use condoms. Of those who have in the past patronized prostitutes, many still do, and generally do not use condoms. In such cases they ask the prostitute if she has AIDS; if she says no, they will have sex unprotected.

Basic Patterns—Why Behavior Hasn't Changed

The discussants believed that behavior patterns have not changed because safe sex is perceived as not spontaneous, not fun, and clumsy. Denial is a shared factor between high- and low-risk groups. "It won't happen to me" is a common expression of denial of risk factors and a rationale for not changing behavior. Many people (even those in high-risk groups) still believe that women are immune and that sex with one partner is safe. Many other myths/misperceptions persist:

"AIDS is limited to gays/drug abusers."

"I don't feel sick/look sick, so I don't have AIDS."

"He/she doesn't look sick, so he/she must not have it."

Abstinence

The discussants also agreed that "don't do it" is not an appropriate message. Although abstinence is still the most effective method of preventing the spread of AIDS, it does not seem to be an alternative most Americans are likely to choose. Abstinence from sex is not a realistic expectation (people will continue to have sex, with or without condoms). In a 1982 study, the National Survey of Family Growth showed that 86 percent of Americans between the ages of 14 and 44 are sexually active. A more recent study of women only (by the Alan Guttmacher Institute) shows that 76 percent of American women over 18 years old are sexually active. Abstinence from IV drug use is an even less acceptable message to the drug users. They will not respond to such a message; their addiction makes it physically impossible to "just say no."

PROGRAM FORMULATION

In assessing the data from these discussion groups, Scali, McCabe, and Sloves began to formulate an advertising strategy. Through their campaign on education in preventive methods, they sought to prevent or curb widespread transmission of AIDS by effecting a change in current behavior of high-risk individuals. They identified three primary target groups: 1) IV drug users and their partners, 2) homosexually active men, and 3) teens. Sub-target groups included Blacks and Hispanics (higher incidence in this group compared to the rest of the population due to higher incidence of IV drug use) and sexually-active heterosexuals (who have sex with unknown partners, with partners in high-risk group, or without prevention).

Scali, McCabe, and Sloves set up two sets of behavioral objectives. For the IV users the objectives were:

1. Use sterile works or clean works properly.
2. Do not share needles.
3. Stop using IV drugs.

For sexually at-risk target groups the objectives were:

1. Proper use of a latex condom during homosexual or heterosexual encounters.
2. Abstinence.

THE AD COUNCIL CAMPAIGN

Television

The television campaign consisted of four 30-second spots that targeted specific viewer populations (see Exhibit 3). All four featured frank, honest information:

"How I Got It" addressed the misperception that people with AIDS didn't look sick. It concluded with the narrator (a pleasant-looking woman of about 30) saying "that's how I got it," referring to unprotected sex.

"Macho," concerned with condom use, was aimed at Hispanic young men. It featured a teenager at his brother's grave, saying that his brother felt using condoms was not macho.

"Baby" and "Vilma" both asked women to consider the consequences of passing on AIDS to their unborn children. Both "Baby" and "Macho" were recorded in English and Spanish.

For the purpose of making the spots more tailored to specific viewers, Scali, McCabe, and Sloves further divided the audience by target age group: teens, young singles, and newly single (30+). This made it less likely that younger people would hear or see messages inappropriate to their level of maturity.

Ad Council made very specific program recommendations so that their message would be sure to reach target audiences. Even though Scali, McCabe, and Sloves designed the

EXHIBIT 3

HELP STOP AIDS. USE A CONDOM.

Please discontinue use:

September 30, 1989.

"HEALTHY" :30   CNAD-8130

WOMAN: You might think people with the AIDS virus look sick. But most don't. It can be years before the symptoms show up. So, if you have sex, don't take any more chances than you have to: Use a condom. Because you can get AIDS from someone who looks perfectly healthy. That's how I got it.

"MACHO" :30   CNAD-8230   (Also available in Spanish)

MAN: My brother wouldn't listen to me. I told him: "You have sex, you use condoms so you don't get AIDS." He laughed and said condoms weren't macho. My brother: He was so macho.

"BABY" :30   CNAD-8330   (Also available in Spanish)

ANNCR: (VO) This baby started life with little chance of living it. He was born with the AIDS virus. At some time in the past, one or both of his parents just weren't careful: Didn't use condoms, and caught the virus, then passed it on to him. If you don't use condoms because you're not worried about getting AIDS, try worrying about who you can give it to.

(Spot contributed to the Advertising Council by AIDSFILMS, a non-profit organization.)

"VILMA" :30   CNAD-8430

MOM: I have AIDS. And my baby has AIDS. My husband may have it, but he won't go to the doctor. In the beginning, he wouldn't even talk about it. My mother helps us, but sometimes I think she's afraid. Every night I kneel by my baby's crib and pray to be strong for him. Every night I pray that my baby won't die. ANNCR: (VO) Protect people you love. Use a condom.

A Public Service Campaign of the Advertising Council

Volunteer Coordinator: Aubrey Hawes, Vice President, Corporate Director of Advertising, Chase Manhattan Bank, N.A.

Volunteer Advertising Agency: Scali, McCabe, Sloves, Inc.

spots to be acceptable to all ages and time slots, their recommendations reflected careful thought. For the teen audiences, they suggested that "Macho" and "How I Got It" run during the early fringe and prime time; during shows like "Head of the Class," "21 Jump Street," and MTV. To reach the young singles audience, prime time and late night shows like "Moonlighting," "David Letterman," and "L.A. Law" were recommended spots for all four ads. For the newly single category, all but "Macho" were suggested for such programming in prime time and late night spots as "Dynasty," "thirtysomething," and "the Tonight Show." Such special uses of television spots as movie houses ("Macho," "How I Got It," and "Baby"), College television ("Macho," "How I Got It,"), and closed circuit television (all) were also considered.

Radio

The radio campaign also included four spots with specific messages aimed at specific audiences (See Exhibit 4 for the text of these spots):

"Under 20," with that target audience in mind, stressed the dangers of presuming that sex is safe, and made the point that symptoms could take many years to appear.

"Healthy," designed for all age groups, pointed out that the infection was not always obvious, warning the audience that appearances could indeed be deceiving.

"Reasons," aimed at the young single/newly single audience, addressed major concerns regarding condom use. Both "Healthy" and "Reasons" were recorded in English and in Spanish.

"Vilma," an actual testimonial from a mother who had an AIDS-infected baby, was targeted at women of child-bearing age.

As with the television campaign, program recommendations made it more likely that the messages intended for a specific target group reached that audience. "Under 20" and "Healthy" were especially recommended for stations or time slots that featured a Top Hits, or Urban Contemporary format. "Healthy" and "Reasons" were advised for the young single market catered to by stations or shows that carried a Classic Rock, Soft Rock, or Urban Contemporary format. Formats like News/Talk, Soft Rock, Classical and Urban Contemporary with newly single listeners also made good slots for "Reasons" and "Healthy." "Under 20," "Reasons," and "Healthy" were all promoted for college radio stations, and all were recommended for store radio networks (as in supermarkets and drug stores).

Press

The press campaign featured ads similar to those on television and radio (see Exhibits 5A–5E), all available in both English and Spanish.

"Everything," like "Under 20," provided general information about prevention and lack of early warning signs.

"You Look Like You Have AIDS" conveyed the message that appearances could be deceiving.

EXHIBIT 4   Radio Public Service Announcements

Advertising Council, Inc.

Please discontinue use: January 15, 1990.

AIDS Prevention Campaign*
On behalf of the American Foundation for AIDS Research & the National AIDS Network

"Reasons" As-recorded text :60

SFX:

(Traffic noises under initial voices)

Man:

They kinda cramp my style.

Man:

It's embarrassing to buy them.

Man:

It's just not the same, y' know.

Woman:

I'm afraid to bring it up, 'cause I'm worried my boyfriend'll get turned off.

Woman:

It can sound like you don't trust him.

Man:

I mean, they're not the most romantic things in the world, are they?

Announcer:

There are a million reasons for not using condoms, none of them as good as the reason you should. Because if you're going to have sex, a latex condom with spermicide is your best protection against the AIDS virus: a virus that's already responsible for more than 30,000 American deaths. And that number will almost double in just the next few years. Because there is no cure for AIDS. You can't walk into a store, buy some medicine, and get over it. But you can walk into a store, buy some latex condoms, and use them. After all, using a condom won't kill you; not using one, might.

Announcer:

A public service message from the American Foundation for AIDS Research, the National AIDS Network, and the Ad Council. Use condoms according to manufacturers' directions.

"Healthy"—As-recorded text :60

Man:

You look like you have AIDS. You have all the signs. You look perfectly healthy. You feel fine. And so do most of the people who have the AIDS virus. In fact, most people who are infected don't even know it. They don't look sick, they don't feel sick. It can take as long as 10 years for symptoms to start showing up. Yet, because these people *seem* healthy, they think there's no reason to be careful. So, they don't use latex condoms and spermicide, and the AIDS virus continues to spread. Don't be fooled by appearances. If you have sex, avoid unnecessary risks. Help stop AIDS, use a condom. Help stop AIDS, use a condom.

EXHIBIT 4   (*concluded*)

Announcer:

A public service message from the American Foundation for AIDS Research, the National AIDS Network, and the Ad Council. Use condoms according to manufacturers' directions.

"Under 20"—As-recorded text :60

Man:

If you're under 20, you might think you don't have much chance of getting AIDS. And with good reason. After all, how many people your age do you know who are sick with it or who died from it? Probably none. That can make you feel nice and safe. Only one problem: after someone catches the AIDS virus, it can take as long as 10 years for them to even start feeling sick from it. So, you should look at how people 20 to 25 years old are doing and, once you do that, you won't feel too safe anymore. Because that age group has the fastest-growing number of people dying from AIDS. If you're interested in seeing what the other side of 25 is like, there are a few things to keep in mind: Don't shoot up, needles can spread the AIDS virus. And, if you can't say no to sex, make sure you use a latex condom with spermicide. Because, while people under 20 can get AIDS, there's no reason you have to be one of them.

Announcer:

A public service message from the American Foundation for AIDS Research, the National AIDS Network, and the Ad Council. Use condoms according to manufacturers' directions.

*The three Spanish-language PSAs—"Motivos" :60, "Tiene Buen Aspecto" :60, and "Menos de 20" :60—are all translations of the foregoing English spots.

Another advertisement, "Using it won't kill you, not using it might," directly advocated the use of condoms.

One of the ads aimed towards women of childbearing years featured a pregnant woman, with the headline, "One of the scariest things about the AIDS virus is who you can pass it on to."

Another aimed at the same audience stated, "Any woman who wants a baby should use them," referring to condoms.

Here again, placement recommendations were tailored for different print media. Teen-slanted copy ("Everything," "You Look . . . ," "Won't Kill You") were put forth for sports and entertainment sections of newspapers, as well as teen magazines (i.e., *Tiger Beat, Right On, For Seniors Only*), with "Any woman . . . " added for magazines like *Seventeen, Teen,* and *SASSY.* The young-adult market was divided: all ads were suggested for general-audience magazines like *Time, Newsweek, Jet,* and *TV Guide*; women-target ads plus "Everything" and "You Look . . . " for *Cosmopolitan, Working Woman, Good Housekeeping,* et. al.; all not-woman-centered ads for *GQ, Playboy, Car & Driver,* etc. For the newly single category, newspapers, newsweeklies, business magazines, and science magazines were suggested. Ad Council also targeted Spanish-language magazines (all ads) to reach Hispanic audiences.

EXHIBIT 5A

EVERYTHING YOU DIDN'T WANT TO KNOW ABOUT AIDS. BUT SHOULD.

To start with, you don't have to be gay or a drug user to get it. AIDS has hit these two groups hardest because the AIDS virus hit them first, before anyone knew why or how people should protect themselves from it.

And the virus is spreading. Scientists report that about one and a half million people are already infected.

You can't tell who has it and who doesn't. Most people who have the AIDS virus don't even know it. They don't look or feel sick. It can take up to ten years for symptoms to show up. So people who seem perfectly healthy can pass the virus on to others.

HOW IS IT PASSED ON? One way is shooting up drugs with someone who's infected and sharing the needle. But most people catch the AIDS virus **THROUGH SEX.** A woman can catch it from a man. A man can catch it from a woman. A man can catch it from a man.

Obviously, the surest way to avoid the virus is to avoid sex. If you do have sex, **YOUR BEST PROTECTION IS A LATEX CONDOM** with spermicide. Use them every time, from start to finish, according to the manufacturers' directions.

You can ignore these precautions only if you and your partner have been together for at least 10 years, and both of you have been totally faithful.

Otherwise, **DON'T MAKE ANY EXCEPTIONS.**

Because the one time you do can be the one time you shouldn't have.

HELP STOP AIDS. USE A CONDOM.

 AMERICAN FOUNDATION FOR AIDS RESEARCH

 A Public Service of This Publication & The Advertising Council

 NATIONAL AIDS NETWORK

© 1988, The Ad Council.

AIDS CAMPAIGN
NEWSPAPER AD NO. AIDS-88-1377—TABLOID

EXHIBIT 5B

YOU LOOK LIKE YOU HAVE AIDS.

You have all the signs. You look perfectly healthy. You feel fine.

So do most people who are infected with the AIDS virus. In fact, they don't even know they're infected. It can take as long as ten years for someone with the virus to actually develop a full-blown case of AIDS. Even then, some people still appear healthy.

And because a lot of people with the virus think they're healthy, they aren't careful when they have sex. Neither are their partners. They don't use condoms. And the AIDS virus continues to spread.

But it doesn't have to spread to you. If you have sex, use a latex condom with spermicide. Use them every time, from start to finish, according to the manufacturers' directions.

And do it no matter how good someone looks. Because while the AIDS virus isn't something you can see, it is something you can get.

HELP STOP AIDS. USE A CONDOM.

 AMERICAN FOUNDATION FOR AIDS RESEARCH

 A Public Service of This Publication & The Advertising Council

 NATIONAL·AIDS NETWORK

© 1988, The Ad Council.

AIDS CAMPAIGN
NEWSPAPER AD NO. AIDS-88-1383—TABLOID

EXHIBIT 5C

USING IT WON'T KILL YOU.
NOT USING IT MIGHT.

Maybe you don't like using condoms. But if you're going to have sex, a latex condom with a spermicide is your best protection against the AIDS virus.

Use them every time, from start to finish, according to the manufacturers' directions. Because no one has ever been cured of AIDS. More than 40,000 Americans have already died from it.

And even if you don't like condoms, using them is definitely better than that.

HELP STOP AIDS. USE A CONDOM.

AMERICAN
FOUNDATION
FOR AIDS
RESEARCH
Photo: Jerry Friedman

Ad
Council

A Public Service of
This Publication &
The Advertising Council

NATIONAL·AIDS
NETWORK

© 1988, The Ad Council.

AIDS CAMPAIGN
NEWSPAPER AD NO. AIDS-88-1381—TABLOID

EXHIBIT 5E

ANY WOMAN WHO WANTS TO HAVE A BABY SHOULD USE THEM.

If you plan on having a child someday, you should be using latex condoms when you have sex now.

It's the best protection a sexually active woman has against the AIDS virus. A virus that has a 50-50 chance of passing from an infected mother to her child during pregnancy or birth.

And babies with AIDS rarely live to see their second birthday.

So take steps to make sure you don't get infected. Until you're ready to get pregnant, use a latex condom with spermicide. Use them every time, from start to finish, according to the manufacturers' directions.

Don't make exceptions. And don't start next week or next month.

Because no matter when you plan on having your baby, you have to start being a good mother right now.

HELP STOP AIDS. USE A CONDOM.

 AMERICAN FOUNDATION FOR AIDS RESEARCH

Photo: Jerry Friedman

 Ad Council — A Public Service of This Publication & The Advertising Council

 NATIONAL AIDS NETWORK

© 1988, The Ad Council.

AIDS CAMPAIGN
NEWSPAPER AD NO. AIDS-88-1375—TABLOID

NEW YORK AGAINST AIDS: WHAT WENT WRONG?[3]

Saatchi and Saatchi's "New York Against AIDS" campaign was aimed at preventing the spread of AIDS among heterosexuals in New York City through educational advertising. It presented a bold message on the use of condoms in prevention, summed up by the tagline "*AIDS. If you think you can't get it, you're dead wrong.*" The messages, primarily targeted towards heterosexual women, were designed to be hard-hitting and provocative. While radio and press spots gained acceptance, the three major television networks (ABC, CBS, and NBC) refused to telecast most of the commercials. They claimed the ads overemphasized sex and condoms, which would offend their viewers.

The three TV spots stressed condom use in different ways. "So Can You" portrayed a young couple kissing; the woman pushes the man away gently and hands him a condom. When he refuses to use it, the announcer says, "If he can say no, so can you." "Going out" showed an attractive young woman dressing to go out, with a James Taylor song in the background, "don't say yes," (she picks up a condom and puts it in her purse) "but please don't say no." "Mother" featured a middle-aged black woman addressing the audience directly, talking as if to her daughter, "I hate the idea of you doing things you're not ready for, but listen, if you're doing anything, you use one of these" (she holds up a condom). This advertisement was perceived as less offensive by NBC and CBS, so they agreed to run it after 11:00 pm.

Objections to those ads came from all sides. Religious leaders complained that the campaign promoted condoms and casual sex. "The ads portray an out-and-out endorsement of sexual promiscuity and mislead people into thinking that there is such a thing as safe sex." (John Woolsey, director of the Office of Christian and Family Development for the Archdiocese of New York, *UPI*, 5/12/87.) Women's groups felt the ads put the responsibility for prevention on women alone. "Put the emphasis for prevention where it belongs. On men too." (*New York Times*, 8/8/87.) Some debated the efficacy of condoms in prevention and the credibility of the threat to the heterosexual community. "The upshot is that AIDS remains primarily a homosexual disease." (*New York Post*, 10/27/87.) Though the campaign had its supporters, its vocal detractors kept up their complaints despite Saatchi and Saatchi's attempts to answer them. The exasperated social marketing consultant to the campaign remarked:

> *It is high time the media gave up its marketing orientation. It has a responsibility beyond drawing an audience and a revenue; at times it has to perform the role of proactively influencing society on social issues like AIDS. We have enough religious institutions in our country to anchor our society's conservative values, we don't need one more stumbling block to solve our problems of the future.*

DECISIONS

The four members of the alliance knew it would be impossible to please everyone as certain delicate facts could not be compromised if the message was to be effective. They wondered what to do next.

---

[3]Information contributing to this section was drawn from *New York Against AIDS (A)* and *(B)*, and Harvard Business School cases 9–590–036.

Case 3–4

USPS: The "We Deliver" Campaign (A)*

In March 1989, John Wargo, Assistant Postmaster General—Marketing, and Rod DeVar, General Manager—Creative Services Division, of the United States Postal Service (USPS), were reviewing the results of a tracking study completed the previous December under the direction of Young & Rubicam (Y&R). The study traced the effects of the recently developed "Products and Services" campaign on consumer attitudes toward USPS. That campaign consisted of two 30-second spots that aired on network television in the fall of 1988. The spots identified a variety of USPS products and services and linked them together under the "We Deliver" theme. The results indicated that the campaign improved consumer perceptions of USPS significantly, but the positive effects declined notably after the campaign ended. Wargo and DeVar wondered how well the "Products and Services" theme and music would contribute to the 1989 Express Mail advertising campaign's success.

THE MARKET

In 1988, the market for overnight-delivery service (ONDS) was $6 billion, and overnight letters represented 52 percent of 1988 overnight volume by category. The overnight market was expected to grow about 11 percent a year through 1993, down from the 20 percent annual growth rate that had characterized the previous five years. Trends in ONDS use are described in Exhibit 1, while major competitors are compared in Exhibit 2.

With a 1988 unit share of 50 percent, Federal Express (Fed Ex) was the acknowledged ONDS market leader, reporting about $3.9 billion in revenues for the fiscal year ended May 31, 1988. Although Fed Ex gained 2 market share points from 1986 to 1988, the company had been experiencing declining profit margins. Fed Ex had used volume discounts to secure a large share of business accounts. It also offered customers warehousing and inventory management in conjunction with expedited delivery of packages. In response to challenges by United Parcel Service (UPS), Fed Ex had relaxed shipment weight restrictions and had test-marketed a low-cost afternoon-delivery option for pack-

*This case was made possible through the cooperation of the United States Postal Service. It was prepared by Mark Parry, Assistant Professor of Business Administration. The author thanks Rod DeVar, General Manager—Creative Services Division, USPS, and Professor Paul W. Farris for their assistance in preparing this case. Copyright© 1989 by the Darden Graduate Business School Foundation, Charlottesville, Virginia.

EXHIBIT 1   Trends in the Overnight Delivery Service Category

Firm	Percentage of Last 100 Overnight Items Sent		OND Service Used in the Past 3 Months		Intent to Use OND Service in the Future		Total Unaided Service Awareness		Unaided Advertising Awareness	
	9/86	4/88	9/86	4/88	9/86	4/88	9/86	4/88	9/86	4/88
Federal Express	40%	37%	71%	72%	75%	79%	90%	92%	54%	54%
UPS	36	40	59	63	75	72	54	71	15	42
Regular truck	22	24	42	51	58	56				
Next-day air*	9	12	34	45	42	51				
Second-day air	4	4	19	34	28	38				
Not specified	2	†	4	4	4	7				
Express Mail	9	10	28	35	42	47	42	46	20	28
Purolator	6	5	20	16	27	25	56	37	28	11
Emery	3	2	9	9	16	16	47	26	32	11
Airborne	3	3	7	8	9	9	28	18	17	6
DHL	1	2	5	5	12	16	16	12	8	4

*When asked about ONDS use, some people responded that they used UPS regular truck service. It is unclear whether they used UPS ground service with expectations of next-day service, or whether they were confused about the question.
†Less than .5 percent.

Source: USPS documents.

EXHIBIT 2   Major Competitor Comparisons: Domestic Next-Day Delivery Market

Competitor	1987 Market Share (volume)	Share Change 1986–87	1987 Volume (million packages)	List Price (1/2 to 1-lb package)	A.M. Delivery	Electronic Tracing	Volume Discount
Federal Express	49%	+2%	165*	$11.00–$20.25†	Yes‡	Yes	Yes
UPS Next Day Air	16	+4	52	$8.50–$11.50	Yes	No	No
Express Mail	12	−2	43	$8.75–$12.00	Yes	No	No
Airborne	10	N/C	35	$8.50–$14.00	Yes	Yes	Yes
Emery/Purolator	8	−2	27	N/A	Yes	Yes	Yes
Others	5	−2	17	N/A	N/A	N/A	N/A

*Federal Express' fiscal year ended May 31; volume shown is estimated for the FY ending May 31, 1988.
†Excluded $3.00 drop-off discount.
‡Federal Express had recently begun to test an additional, lower-priced overnight service that promised next-day afternoon delivery.
Note: Prices do not reflect volume discounts that were available, except where noted.

ages weighing up to 5 pounds. To attract small businesses, Fed Ex had introduced retail kiosks and drop-off discounts. (The cost of an 8-ounce letter was $10.50, but Fed Ex offered a $3.00 discount to customers who delivered their letters to the local Federal Express retail office.) Finally, Fed Ex had expanded its overseas operations through the acquisition of Flying Tigers.

After 7 years in ONDS, UPS had 19 percent of the market; from 1986 to 1988, the company's market share had risen 4 share points. UPS offered the least-expensive overnight delivery letter, at $8.50, but did not offer discounts for volume shippers. Prior to 1982, UPS had not advertised its services; six years later, ONDS advertising had doubled from $50 million to $100 million, and UPS had the largest advertising share of any ONDS firm. To compete with Fed Ex, UPS had purchased additional planes, introduced package tracking, added guaranteed delivery and morning delivery, and expanded retail operations. USPS research indicated that the current UPS base of 870,000 customers was the focus of the shipper's ONDS marketing efforts, but some indications were that the company was seeking additional customers outside this base.

Emery-Purolator had 1987 revenues of approximately $1.2 billion; its 1988 market share of 7 percent was down 2 percent from 1986. The merger of Emery, an air service, and Purolator, a ground delivery service, had saddled the company with debt and had forced the integration of Emery's non-union operations with the union operations of Purolator.

Airborne, a small carrier that targeted large-volume corporate shippers, had 1987 total revenues of $632 million. The company had secured 11 percent of the ONDS market, primarily by offering large accounts exclusive carrier contracts featuring deep discounts. For example, Airborne had a three year contract with IBM that was estimated to be worth $30 million; industry experts believed that, to win this contract, Airborne had offered rates up to 84 percent lower than Fed Ex's list prices. The federal government had also awarded Airborne a contract that specified ONDS rates starting at $5.00 for the first pound. USPS research indicated that Airborne had increased its air-cargo capacity by 40 percent in 1987 and planned to buy another used DC-8 for its fleet.

USPS EXPRESS MAIL

From 1983 to 1987, Express Mail revenues increased from $394 million to $499 million; in fiscal year (FY) 1987 (October 1987 to September 1988), however, although the industry experienced a 20 percent growth rate, Express Mail revenues grew only 2 percent, and Express Mail share dropped from 18 to 16 percent. USPS market research attributed this slow growth rate to several factors. Many consumers did not believe Express Mail was reliable. In addition, Express Mail did not offer an overnight-letter rate or volume discounts. To stimulate growth, USPS introduced an $8.75 overnight-letter service, guaranteed morning delivery, and on-call pickup for an incremental charge of $4.00 per stop. USPS also offered several specialized Express Mail services, including drop-ship and reship service,[1] weekend/holiday delivery at no extra charge, and delivery to Post Office boxes.

---

[1]Drop-ship service permitted firms to bundle individually-addressed magazines or newsletters by destination. After receiving their bundle by Express Mail, local Post Offices unbundled the magazines or newsletters for individual delivery. Re-ship service permitted firms to direct incoming customer correspondence to local P.O. boxes. The local Post Office then bundled the correspondence and shipped it by Express Mail to a central destination specified by the firm.

Focus Group Research. Wargo and DeVar authorized Y&R to conduct focus-group interviews with current ONDS users. These interviews revealed that ONDS users typically had a carrier of choice but used one or two other services in certain situations. Federal Express users insisted on prompt, dependable consistent delivery, valued early-morning delivery, and required prompt and flexible (late) pickup service. They also required parcel tracking, were relatively unconcerned with price, and were willing to use UPS or Express Mail for less important parcels.

UPS users placed relatively less emphasis on reliability and were willing to make tradeoffs for lower cost. They appreciated the extras offered by UPS, such as the insurance of parcels for relatively higher amounts, the determination of package weight, and the acceptance of payment by check. UPS users would use Express Mail if it were more convenient (e.g., if they missed the UPS pickup). They would also use Federal Express for urgent or extremely important items.

Like UPS customers, Express Mail users were cost conscious; they placed less emphasis on reliability and were willing to make tradeoffs for lower cost. Express Mail users found the Post Office drop-off boxes convenient, and they valued ancillary services such as weekend delivery at no extra cost and delivery to P.O. boxes. Like UPS customers, Express Mail users would choose Federal Express for more important items.

Y&R executives believed that the focus-group research suggested two potential objectives for Express Mail advertising. First, an Express Mail campaign could convince current "cost-driven" users to increase their reliance on Express Mail relative to UPS and alternative low-cost services. Second, an Express Mail campaign could convince "certainty-driven" users to use Express Mail for their "less urgent" items, leading to greater confidence in Express Mail and, eventually, greater use of Express Mail for important items.

The Small and Medium Business Segment. A 1987 study USPS commissioned had revealed the following relationships between firm size and Express Mail use:

Employee Size	Percent of ONDS Category Volume	Percent of Express Mail Volume	Index
5–19	43%	52%	120
20–99	34	34	100
100+	23	13	57

Small businesses (5–19 employees) accounted for 52 percent of Express Mail volume, and medium-sized businesses accounted for an additional 34 percent. Among small businesses, Express Mail had a larger share of overnight letter volume than any of its competitors. Exhibit 3 contains further results from this study.

Although small- and medium-sized businesses accounted for 77 percent of ONDS volume, 50 percent had never tried Express Mail. Many were price sensitive but could not qualify for volume discounts from other carriers. Many also worked beyond normal business hours, so Express Mail's 365-day delivery was a relevant service feature. Y&R

EXHIBIT 3   A Demographic Profile of the ONDS User

Descriptor	Decision-Makers Index	Percent of Category Decision-Makers
Demographic		
Male	125	59%
Female	77	41
Age		
25–34	146	35
35–44	156	29
45–54	105	19
25–54	149	83
Education		
Attended college	163	30
Graduated college	234	41
Attended/graduated	198	71
Household income		
$15,000–20,000	39	4
$20,000–25,000	68	7
$25,000–30,000	76	8
$30,000–35,000	123	11
$30,000 +	182	78
Industry		
Finance	293	5
Insurance	293	4
Real estate	416	5
Business services	340	7
Legal services	344	2
Engineering & architectural services	515	2
Accounting, auditing, and bookkeeping	448	2
Proprietors	569	13

Source: USPS documents.

---

executives also believed that, among small and medium-sized businesses, Express Mail advertising could build on certain positive perceptions of USPS, because many small businesses valued the convenience of their local Post Offices and their letter carriers.

EXPRESS MAIL POSITIONING

In the spring of 1988, DeVar and Wargo met with Rich Kahn, Group Director—Young & Rubicam, and Jack Powers, Account Supervisor, in Washington, D.C. They decided that FY 1989 Express Mail advertising would have two objectives. The primary aim was to increase the perception among small- and medium-sized businesses that Express Mail Service was a reliable, fast, economical, and convenient overnight-delivery service. Four considerations prompted the decision to promote Express Mail as the superior ONDS service for this segment:

1. Express Mail offered relatively greater value to cost-conscious small- and medium-sized businesses than did carriers offering volume discounts.
2. From the perspective of these businesses, Express Mail represented a unique combination of reliability, price, and convenience that was distinct from competitors for this segment.
3. The small- and medium-sized business segment was not aggressively pursued by competitors.
4. This segment valued the ancillary services that were unique to Express Mail such as 365-day delivery and letter pickup. Moreover, USPS offered more drop-off points than any of its competitors.

A secondary objective was to inspire postal employees to take pride in Express Mail service and motivate them to increase their efficiency and professionalism.

At the recommendation of Kahn and Powers, Wargo and DeVar also decided that Express Mail advertising would be part of an umbrella campaign designed to (1) enhance public perceptions of the U.S. Postal Service, (2) increase awareness of USPS products and services, and (3) increase use of USPS products and services. For the first time, USPS would unify its marketing messages around a single theme.

EXPRESS MAIL COPY

In August 1988, Kahn and Powers returned to Washington with recommendations for an umbrella campaign built around the "We Deliver" theme. The campaign consisted of three Express Mail spots: "Jets," "Saturday," and "Drop-off," and two "Products and Services" spots. Exhibit 4 contains the lyrics from the two "Products and Services" spots. Storyboards for the three Express Mail commercials are contained in Exhibits 5, 6, and 7. Y&R designed the Express Mail commercials to communicate the following message elements:

1. Guaranteed delivery by noon between all major business markets;
2. Convenience of 19,000 Express Mail boxes and 26,000 Express Mail acceptance Post Offices;
3. Everyday, everywhere pickup by 265,000 letter carriers; and
4. Weekend and holiday delivery at no extra charge.

When Y&R conducted an animatic test of "Jets," 75 percent of the test audience reacted positively to the ad execution and only 29 percent provided negative comments (the latter percentage was below animatic-test norms). A high percentage of the audience indicated that the ad clearly communicated the message elements of service (94 percent), cost/economy (81 percent), and convenience (75 percent). A small percentage of the audience registered confusion (7 percent) and/or disbelief (5 percent). An increased interest in using Express Mail was indicated by 61 percent.

Y&R also showed finished versions of all three ads to groups of Express Mail users, prospective users, and USPS employees. Exhibit 8 contains representative reactions from

---

EXHIBIT 4 Lyrics from "Products and Services" Spots

60-Second Spot

You know we're going to be there, don't think twice,
Service is part of our name.
We're the people you rely on to get it right,
And no one else does it the same.

We're a part of your country and a part of your town,
We're the faces you see every day.
You know practice makes perfect, we've got it down,
And we're going to keep it that way.

We deliver, we deliver,
Through the rain and the sleet and the snow like we've always done.
We deliver, we deliver,
Because the eagle flies higher and surer than anyone.

We deliver, we deliver,
It's the reason to trust us,
You know that we're going to come through.
We're your Postal Service,
We deliver for you.

30-Second Spot

You know we're going to be there, don't think twice,
Service is part of our name.
We're a part of your country and a part of your town,
And no one else does it the same.

We deliver, we deliver,
It's the reason to trust us,
You know that we're going to come through.
We're your Postal Service,
We deliver for you.

---

the various test audiences. All groups reacted favorably to the messages (reliability, price, and convenience) of the three commercials. Group members liked the music and believed that the "We Deliver" theme was appropriate and memorable. Prospective users were the least receptive, however; they found the $8.75 price and the emphasis on dependability attractive, but established negative perceptions of Express Mail or USPS appeared to interfere with the advertising message elements. Prospective users did respond well to executional and strategic elements of the campaign.

In evaluating viewer reactions, Y&R concluded that the quick-paced executional format held viewer interest and, to some, symbolized the speed of Express Mail. Kahn and Powers believed that all three ads conveyed new, relevant, competitive, and actionable information about Express Mail.

EXHIBIT 5   Storyboard for "Jets"

CLIENT   U.S. POSTAL SERVICE   LENGTH   30 SECONDS
PRODUCT   EXPRESS MAIL   COMM. NO   QYPS 8853
TITLE   JETS   DATE   DECEMBER 12, 1988

V.O. Express Mail
Office

SINGERS: WE DELIVER, WE
DELIVER

V.O. A guaranteed
delivery

Air mail overnight price

$ 8.75
TOTAL CHARGES
8 oz. letter

of just $8.75

Speed

$ 8.75
TOTAL CHARGES

Convenience Price

It's a package only we can deliver

EXPRESS MAIL
We deliver.

Express Mail from your Postal
Service. SINGERS: WE DELIVER
FOR YOU. WE DELIVER FOR
YOU.   (FADE)

EXHIBIT 6   Storyboard for "Saturday"

YOUNG & RUBICAM NEW YORK

CLIENT: U.S. POSTAL SERVICE   LENGTH: 30 SECONDS
PRODUCT: EXPRESS MAIL   COMM. NO.   QYPS 8863
TITLE: "SATURDAY"   DATE: DECEMBER 12, 1988

V.O.: Express Mail from your Post Office

offers you guaranteed morning delivery

SINGERS: WE DELIVER. WE DELIVER.

V.O.: Saturday service at no extra charge

SINGERS: WE DELIVER. WE DELIVER.

V.O.: And an overnight price

of just $8.75

SINGERS: WE DELIVER. WE DELIVER.

V.O.: Speed

Convenience. Price.

It's a package only we can deliver

Express Mail from your Postal Service. SINGERS: WE DELIVER FOR YOU. WE DELIVER FOR YOU.   (FADE)

EXHIBIT 7 Storyboard for "Drop-off"

YOUNG & RUBICAM NEW YORK

CLIENT: U.S. POSTAL SERVICE
PRODUCT: EXPRESS MAIL
TITLE: "DROP-OFF"

LENGTH: 30 SECONDS
COMM. NO.: QYPS 8873
DATE: DECEMBER 12, 1988

V.O.: Express Mail from your Post Office

offers you 46,000 drop-off points

SINGERS: WE DELIVER, WE DELIVER.

V.O.: A guaranteed

morning delivery

SINGERS: WE DELIVER, WE DELIVER.

V.O.: And an overnight price of just $8.75

SINGERS: WE DELIVER, WE DELIVER.

V.O.: Speed

Convenience. Price.

It's a package only we can deliver.

Express Mail from your Postal Service. SINGERS: WE DELIVER FOR YOU, WE DELIVER FOR YOU. (FADE)

EXHIBIT 8   Comments on the "Jets," "Saturday," and "Drop-off" Commercials

---

Comments from Current Users

"It is reinforcing the current customer. It says I made a good decision because they're dependenable."

"The speed of the commerical gives you the feeling that they're fast too, the service is fast."

"I like it. Speed, convenience, price . . . exactly that we're looking for. It hit the nail on the head."

Comments from Prospects

"I like the idea of seven days a week if the $8.75 applies to the seven days. UPS and Federal Express don't deliver on Sunday, so you'll pay a lot of money for Sunday delivery."

Comments from Employees

"I wouldn't be embarrassed to tell someone I work for the Postal Service when that came on TV."

"If you were sitting in a room full of friends, that would give you a good feeling . . . Yes, we do deliver."

Source: USPS documents.

THE "PRODUCTS AND SERVICES" TRACKING STUDY

To help evaluate the impact of the "Products and Services" spot, USPS commissioned a Fall 1988 tracking study designed to

1. Measure awareness of the "Products and Services" spots;
2. Assess reactions to the spots;
3. Measure awareness of the "We Deliver" theme; and
4. Assess the impact of advertising on public perceptions of the U.S. Postal Service.

The continuous-tracking study ran from December 1988 through February 1989 and consisted of 1,916 telephone interviews with a national probability sample of respondents, and supplemental samples in specific markets. Exhibit 9 reports USPS network television advertising expenditures that were devoted to the "Products and Services" spots during the course of the tracking study. Exhibit 10 indicates relative expenditures on the "Products and Services" spots and the Express Mail spots during the same period.

Exhibits 11, 12, and 13 summarize the results of the tracking study. These results suggested the following observations to the outside research organization that conducted the study:

1. The "Products and Services" advertising increased positive feelings for the Postal Service in a number of key areas: atmosphere, quality of service, products and services, affective characteristics, and performance characteristics.
2. People who saw the advertising consistently gave the Postal Service significantly higher ratings across all measures tested than did people who did not recall seeing the advertising.

EXHIBIT 9 Media Expenditures on the Product and Services Spot: 11/88–2/89

Media	Week Start	Week-End	Dollars (000s)
NBC Sports*	12/26/88	2/20/89	$2,680
Scatter Prime†	1/2/89	1/16/89	1,000
FNN‡	1/2/89	1/23/89	20
CNN§	1/2/89	1/16/89	31
USA‖	1/2/89	1/16/89	34
CBS#	11/28/89	1/23/89	1,355
CBS–NCAA basketball	1/2/89	2/6/89	380
Total			$5,500

*NFL football, bowl games, college basketball, PGA golf.
†Unsolved Mysteries, Tattingers, Cosby Show, NBC Sunday and Monday Night Movies, Hogan Family.
‡World Business Report, Midday Market Report, Marketwrap, Wall Street Final, Money Talks, World Business Tonight.
§Headline News, Prime Rotation, Moneyweek, Your Money.
‖Murder She Wrote, Hitchcock Hour, college basketball.
#NFL football, bowl games, PGA golf.

Source: USPS documents.

EXHIBIT 10 Relative Expenditures on "Products and Services" Spots and Express Mail Spots

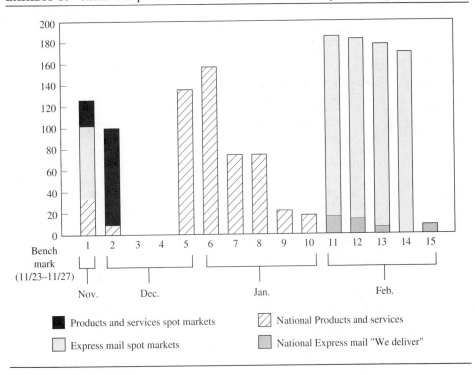

Source: USPS documents.

3. In general, recalls of the advertising and ratings of the Postal Service were highest in the markets that received the greatest concentration of advertising.

4. The continuation of the "We Deliver" theme in current Express Mail advertising appeared to be building on the equity of good feelings established by the "Products and Services" advertising because of the relative proximity of the "Products and Services" advertising.

5. The positive effects of the "Products and Services" advertising declined after the advertising ended.

The outside research organization concluded that the "Products and Services" spot performed a different function from advertising focused on a single product such as Express Mail, but did complement such advertising. Furthermore, the "We Deliver"

EXHIBIT 11   Perceptions of U.S. Postal Service Over Time

	Percentage of Respondents Who Strongly Agree			
		Waves		
	Benchmark (n = 300)	1–5 (n = 378)	6–10 (n = 374)	11–15 (n = 377)
Atmosphere and employees				
Cares about its customers	31%	38%	41%	40%
Is a pleasant place to do business	36	44	44	43
Has courteous employees	47	51	53	48
Has knowledgeable employees	40	42	46	44
Has dedicated employees	36	33	39	39
Service and Convenience				
Provides me with good service	43	49	53	52
Delivers the mail within a reasonable amount of time	47	50	51	50
Is trying to improve its service	33	35	41	39
Has convenient hours	34	40	38	35
Organization				
Is a well-run organization	33	34	36	33
Is a professional organization	43	48	51	47
Would work better if it were a privately owned business	15	13	15	15
Products and Services				
Has products and services that are reasonably priced	30	33	35	36
Provides a wide range of products and services	38	37	41	46

Source: USPS documents.

EXHIBIT 12 Comparisons between Respondents Aware of the "We Deliver" Campaign and Those Unaware of the "We Deliver" Campaign

| | Percentage of Respondents Who Strongly Agree | | | |
| | Benchmark (n = 300) | Waves 12–15 | | Difference (aware-unaware) |
		Unaware of "We Deliver" Campaign (n = 132)	Aware of "We Deliver" Campaign (n = 170)	
Atmosphere and employees				
Cares about its customers	31%	29%	45%	16%
Is a pleasant place to do business	36	35	45	10
Has courteous employees	47	39	52	13
Has knowledgeable employees	40	38	47	9
Has dedicated employees	36	31	40	9
Service and Convenience				
Provides me with good service	43	42	57	15
Delivers the mail within a reasonable amount of time	47	39	53	14
Is trying to improve its services	33	28	44	16
Has convenient hours	34	27	37	10
Organization				
Is a well-run organization	33	23	37	14
Is a professional organization	43	38	50	12
Would work better if it were a privately owned business	15	18	12	−6
Products and services				
Has products and services that are reasonably priced	30	29	40	11
Provides a wide range of products and services	38%	33%	55%	22%
Affective characteristics				
Patriotic	83%	79%	86%	7%
Caring	70	79	81	17
Warm	54	49	63	14
Impersonal	48	51	40	−11
Arrogant	30	33	24	−9
Performance characteristics				
Capable	89	87	90	3
Dependable	84	80	89	9
Efficient	76	70	76	6
Organizational characteristics				
Modern	79	73	78	5
Sophisticated	53	42	49	7
Innovative	59	54	61	7
Powerful	78	71	75	4
Bureaucratic	69	68	66	−2
Behind-the-times	19%	33%	20%	−13%

Source: USPS documents.

EXHIBIT 13 Evalutions of "Products and Services" Advertising Compared with Express Mail Advertising

	Products and Services (n = 297)	Old Express Mail Ads: Airplane/ Letter Carriers (n = 419)	New Express Mail Ads: "We Deliver" (n = 135)
Clear/understandable	93%	94%	93%
Believable	88	85	83
Personal and caring	87	85	83
I liked it	80	71	70
Left me with positive feelings about USPS	70	62	64
Thought about how important USPS is to me	60	46	50
Memorable	60	57	53
More interesting than most	48	41	42
Paid close attention	28	25	29
It's the same old thing	26	31	30
Told me something I didn't know	22	40	48
Didn't have anything to do with me or my needs	19	32	38
Made exaggerated/untrue claims	11	13	11
Irritating	7	6	6
Arrogant	7	6	7
Too complex	6	8	8

---

theme was an effective bridge between the two types of advertising as long as people could tie "We Deliver" to both types. Finally, the hard-won gains in perceptions were fragile and required reinforcement.

Y&R offered the following summary evaluation:

These tracking-study findings demonstrate a significantly positive effect of the advertising over a short span of time. It is extremely unusual to see a meaningful level of change in perceptions in this fast a time frame and given the spending levels. Past experience with tracking data for other clients further dramatizes how well advertising is working here to enhance the image of the products and services of USPS. In our judgment, these are extremely positive results and we take pride in working with The Postal Service on this campaign.

However, the ultimate success of the Express Mail Campaign would be measured in sales. Express Mail volume finished the 1989 Fiscal Year 27 percent over the 1988 volume (see Exhibit 14). This rate of growth was slightly ahead of the market and the strongest growth in more than 10 years.

EXHIBIT 14   Express Mail Next-Day Volume (fiscal 1988 and 1989 vs. SPLY)

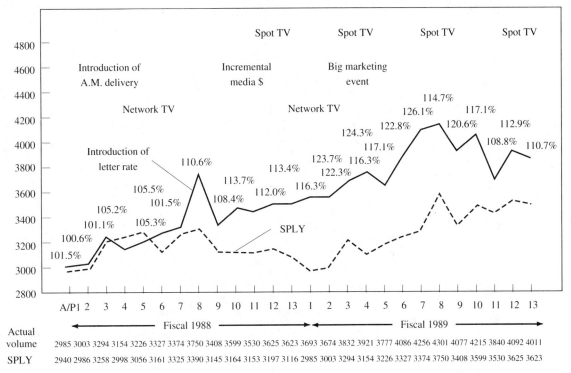

Actual
volume   2985 3003 3294 3154 3226 3327 3374 3750 3408 3599 3530 3625 3623 3693 3674 3832 3921 3777 4086 4256 4301 4077 4215 3840 4092 4011

SPLY   2940 2986 3258 2998 3056 3161 3325 3390 3145 3164 3153 3197 3116 2985 3003 3294 3154 3226 3327 3374 3750 3408 3599 3530 3625 3623

SPLY = Same period last year.

A/P = Accounting period (13/year).

PART 4

Media Strategy

Case 4–1

Becel Margarine*

Peter Zanger, product manager for Becel Margarine, had just met with the media director of the brand's advertising agency. He had received the output of the agency's media model, which constituted the agency's recommended media plan for 1975. These results of a mathematical programming analysis of media alternatives represented an attempt by the agency to maximize advertising impact under the constraints of a limited budget. Zanger would have to decide whether or not to accept the basic structure of the media plan, as well as its detailed recommendations.

COMPANY BACKGROUND AND BRAND STRATEGY

Becel was one of six brands of margarine marketed by the Union Deutsche Lebensmittelwerke, a German subsidiary of Unilever. Headquartered in Hamburg, the company manufactured and marketed a wide variety of consumer products, mostly foods or food-related items. Their Oil Milling Division also produced various vegetable oils and by-products which were sold to industrial users. Total sales of the Union in 1974 were estimated to be over DM2 billions.

The six Union margarine brands together accounted for about 50 percent of the total home margarine market. Becel's share of the market was 2 percent. It was both the newest and smallest of all the company's major brands in terms of sales and market share. Having been introduced only in 1971, however, its growth was considered more than satisfactory. It was also thought by many in the marketing department to have the most precise positioning of any Union brand in the margarine market.

Becel was a "high pufa margarine," i.e. it contained a high percentage of polyunsaturated fats relative to most other brands on the market. The first such product to be distributed through supermarkets in Germany, Becel had been developed in response to four impetuses:

1. The increasing concern, first of the medical profession and then of the public, over research linking intake of cholesterol to heart and circulatory diseases.

---

*This case was made possible through the cooperation of the Union Deutsche Lebensmittelwerke. Certain market and media data are disguised. The case was prepared by Paul W. Farris, doctoral candidate, under the supervision of HBS Professor Stephen A. Greyser, as a basis for class discussion, rather than to illustrate either effective or ineffective handling of an administrative situation. Copyright © 1975 by the President and Fellows of Harvard College. Harvard Business School case 9–576–027.

2. The growing opinion, among at least some groups, that high pufa foods could counteract cholesterol intake by lowering the cholesterol mirror.[1]
3. The increasing sales of similar products through German health food stores (Reform-Haüser).
4. The desire to market a product which would be less likely to cannibalize the Union's five other margarine brands already on the market. Many Germans still considered margarine to be an inferior product to butter, but because of Becel's high pufa content (much higher than butter), it was believed that this brand offered the Union the opportunity to increase margarine consumption in the segment of the population considered by medical authorities as "high risk" groups for heart and circulatory diseases.

Consistent with the above goals, Becel had been positioned at the top of the margarine market in terms of pufa content and other characteristics. It contained more than 50 percent polyunsaturated fatty acids; it also had added vitamins and an extremely low salt content. No preservatives were used.[2]

Both price and packaging reflected this positioning. Becel was priced at DM1.68 for 250 g, compared to an average price of DM1.05 for other brands. It was distinctively packaged in a protective carton containing a decoratively styled tub. Other brands were marketed in a tub or cube only.

Zanger had defined his target group as those consumers he thought would be most receptive (and most likely to understand) the distinctive Becel concept. Based on judgment and some research, these were consumers of butter and margarine who were:

1. Concerned about their health in general, and heart and circulatory problems in particular;
2. In older age groups;
3. In higher income groups;
4. In occupations involving more than average responsibility; and
5. Living in urban surroundings.

In addition to these consumers, he thought it was important to influence relevant opinion leaders. The latter were considered to be doctors, dieticians, nutritionists, and health spa personnel.

COMMUNICATIONS GOALS AND BUDGET

It was primarily among these consumer groups and opinion leaders that Zanger was concerned with achieving his communications goals. These were defined as encompassing three areas:

---

[1]The link between cholesterol and heart disease had not yet been conclusively proven, and was still the subject of debate among medical researchers. There was, however, substantial support from physicians concerning the desirability of increasing consumption of high-pufa foods.

[2]Becel was produced in accordance with German laws (Deutsche Diät-Verordnung) governing the manufacture of foods for consumers with special diet requirements.

1. Increasing the awareness of and concern about the "cholesterol problem" among target group members and opinion leaders, and improving consumer knowledge of the ability of high-pufa foods to lower the cholesterol mirror.
2. Developing further the "health" image of Becel.
3. Expanding the proportion of the target group using Becel.

Zanger had at his disposal DM3,000,000 to devote to his total promotional effort. This figure was the result of Zanger's negotiations with the Union's top management. It was based on his estimate of the communications expenditures necessary to achieve the brand's sales goals; the budget estimate took into account the agency's recommendations, including consideration of increasing media prices.

After subtracting DM150,000 which he believed should be used for temporary price reductions and promotions, DM2,850,000 was left for advertising. Of this amount, some DM200,000 was needed for ad production and miscellaneous expenses associated with a recipe book which was being used as a self-liquidating offer in most ads. Thus DM2,650,000 was available for the purchase of media space and time. Of this, a decision had been made in advance to spend roughly 7 percent of the total budget on professional publications directed at physicians, dieticians, nutritionists, and health spa personnel. Although Becel was considered primarily a consumer "pull" product, it was believed that advertising directed at these opinion leaders might influence them to recommend Becel to their patients and acquaintances.

MEDIA PLAN FORMULATION

After decisions had been made and approved concerning the amount of the funds to be spent for advertising media, there still remained several other media-related considerations prior to decisions on detailed media selection. The first of these was the matter of scheduling—the determination of how much of the media budget should be spent at what times during the year. In this regard, it was known that Becel sales were not subject to extreme fluctuations during the year, except for somewhat lower usage in the hot weather. Although there was increased use of margarine for cooking around holidays, Becel was not targeted specifically at this usage. However, some considerations of seasonality could not be ignored in planning the advertising schedule. Zanger wanted to distribute Becel's advertising expenditures over the year to reflect the following approximate present trend in Becel sales:

- 1st Quarter: 27 percent
- 2nd Quarter: 26 percent
- 3rd Quarter: 19 percent
- 4th Quarter: 28 percent

After considerations of timing and the already noted allowance for expenditures on professional publications, there remained a wide variety of consumer media vehicles to be considered for possible inclusion in the media plan. However, some of these could be eliminated almost immediately for various reasons.

First, whole classes of media had been eliminated for Becel because of difficulty associated with achieving a satisfactory creative translation of product claims. For this reason—the difficulty of adequately communicating the complexity of the cholesterol argument—Becel did not use radio commercials or posters and billboards. For the same reason, agency personnel considered TV only a "marginally acceptable medium" for Becel.

A second set of reasons concerned media "climate," or editorial content. More specifically, Zanger wanted to advertise in "opinion-making" vehicles with authoritative editorial content. For instance, Becel had not been advertised in such magazines as *Neue Revue*, a gossip-type magazine, because the "environment for the ad" was not considered sufficiently serious for the "health" image which Becel wanted to build.

EVALUATING RELATIVE EFFECTIVENESS

After such media classes and vehicles had been judged unsatisfactory for Becel, the task of evaluating the relative effectiveness of the remaining acceptable alternatives was begun. For this comparison procedure among media vehicles and combinations of media vehicles, the following criteria were considered important:

- *Reach*—The number of advertising exposures potentially achieved by the vehicle. This measure is not identical with circulation because a copy may be read by more than one person.
- *Audience Composition*—Description of the audience in terms of various demographic characteristics such as income, age, etc.
- *Frequency*—The average number of times an individual audience member is potentially exposed to an advertising message.
- *Overlap*—This measure is essential to the adequate evaluation of the frequency of exposures. Overlap occurs in two ways: *external* overlap, between insertions in different media vehicles (for example, some people who are readers of *Der Spiegel* are also readers of *Capital*); and *internal* overlap, between separate insertions in the same vehicle (for example, some, but not all, readers of the July issue of *Der Spiegel* are also readers of the August issue).
- *Impact*—This is an assessment of the relative qualitative advertising value of a medium or vehicle. It might be based on editorial content, format, use of color, or other variables which could affect the medium or vehicle's "effectiveness" in achieving one's advertising goals.

Weighted Exposure Value. Evaluation of any particular media vehicle is typically undertaken on the basis of cost per thousand (CPM) exposures. To do so on a total-audience basis is easy to calculate. However, it does not take into account the degree of correspondence between the specific audience composition offered by the vehicle and the specific composition of the advertiser's intended target groups. Hence, a "weighted exposure value" analysis would ordinarily be carried out to reflect both of these specific factors.

For the calculation of a media vehicle's weighted exposure value, two inputs are needed. The first is a demographic breakdown of the vehicle's audience. For most major vehicles, this information is readily available from either the publisher or from research organizations specializing in this information.

The second requirement for these calculations is the advertiser's target group weightings within the various demographic categories used to describe the relevant target groups identified for the particular brand. These weightings reflect the degree to which the advertiser regards persons within the specific demographic categories as prospective purchasers of his product. Illustrative target weightings for Becel were defined as follows:

Demographic Category	Weight
Sex	
Male	1.0
Female	1.0
Age	
0–24	0
25–34	0.8
35–49	1.2
49 and above	1.0
Income	
0–999 (DM/month)	0
1000–1749	0
1750 and above	1.0
Children	
None	1.1
1 or more	0.9
City Size	
Under 50,000	0
50,000 and over	1.0
Occupation	
Laborer	0
Supervisor or higher	1.0

These weights were based on an analysis of the brand's existing sales to subgroups within a demographic category, along with the proportion of the overall population represented by that subgroup. For Becel, these weights were derived from a combination of the product manager's judgment and the breakdown of existing sales to those categories. Weights for the various *age* groups for adults were, for instance, developed as follows:

Age Subgroups	Percent of Present Becel Sales to Subgroup	Percent of German Population in Subgroup	"Formula" Weights (1) ÷ (2)	Weights Modified by Judgment
18–24	<2%	10%	0.2	0
25–34	20	20	1.0	0.8
35–49	50	45	1.1	1.2
50–	28	25	1.1	1.0

Similar calculations were performed to determine the weights for sex, number of children, and city size. For income levels and occupation, however, the weights were designed for two purposes. The first was the standard aim—to steer the media plan toward the most likely prospects. The second was to avoid expanding Becel's communications to less-sophisticated consumers; the latter, it was thought, might misinterpret Becel's claims as being "a cure" for heart disease. (This precise targeting was considered necessary to obtain the support of medical and government authorities who were interested in raising the awareness of "the cholesterol problem" among consumers with a "high risk" of heart and circulatory disease.) For these reasons, Becel's weights for subgroups within the income level and occupation categories were assigned as either "0" or "1.0" only.

Once these factors had been determined, it was relatively easy to calculate the total weighted exposures (that is, exposures weighted by the presence of target groups in the media audience) and/or cost per thousand weighted exposures for any particular media vehicle. Exhibits 1 and 2 illustrate these calculations. Method 1 (Exhibit 1) averages the vehicle's weighted audience in the separate demographic categories to obtain an overall weighted exposure value for that vehicle. Method 2 (Exhibit 2) estimates the total weighted exposure value for the vehicle on an individual reader basis. The second method, although

EXHIBIT 1 Calculation of CPM Weighted Exposures: Method I

Vehicle X's Audience (in thousands)		Target Group Weighting	Weighted Audience	CPM Weighted Exposures*
Income (DM/month)				
0–1,000	800	0	0	$\frac{45,000}{700}$ = DM64.28
1,000–1,749	1,000	0	0	
1,750–	700	1.0	700	
	2,500		700	
Age				
0–24	800	0	0	$\frac{45,000}{2,260}$ = DM19.9
25–34	700	0.8	560	
35–49	1,000	1.2	1,200	
50–	500	1.0	500	
	2,500		2,260	
Children				
None	1,500	1.1	1,650	$\frac{45,000}{2,550}$ = DM17.64
1 or more	1,000	0.9	900	
	2,500		2,550	
Size of city				
50,000 or more	2,000	1.0	2,000	$\frac{45,000}{2,000}$ = DM22.5
Less than 50,000	500	0	0	
	2,500		2,000	
Occupation				
Laborer	1,800	0	0	$\frac{45,000}{700}$ = DM64.28
Supervisor or higher	700	1.0	700	
	2,500		700	
Average for all categories			1,640	$\frac{45,000}{1,640}$ = DM27.43

*Price of 1-page, 4-color ad = DM45,000.

EXHIBIT 1   *(concluded)*

Vehicle Y's Audience (in thousands)		Target Group Weighting	Weighted Audience	CPM Weighted Exposures*
Income (DM/month)				
0–1,000	200	0	0	$\frac{35,000}{1,000} = $ DM35.0
1,000–1,749	300	0	0	
1,750–	1,000	1.0	1,000	
	1,500		1,000	
Age				
0–24	50	0	0	$\frac{35,000}{1,490} = $ DM23.49
25–34	400	0.8	320	
35–49	600	1.2	720	
50–	450		450	
	1,500		1,490	
Children				
None	800	1.1	880	$\frac{35,000}{1,510} = $ DM24.82
1 or more	700	0.9	630	
	1,500		1,510	
Size of City				
50,000 or more	1,450	1.0	1,450	$\frac{35,000}{1,450} = $ DM24.13
Less than 50,000	50	0	0	
	1,500		1,450	
Occupation				
Laborer	300	0	0	$\frac{35,000}{1,200} = $ DM29.16
Supervisor or higher	1,200	1.0	1,200	
	1,500		1,200	
Average for all categories			1,310	$\frac{35,000}{1,310} = $ DM26.71

*Price of 1-page, 4-color ad = DM35,000.

more time-consuming, was considered by company executives to be the better since the market segment is defined as those people possessing *all* of the target-group characteristics.

Specific media vehicles may be ranked according to a number of criteria: cost, reach, audience composition, total weighted exposures, or cost per thousand weighted exposures. Depending on the criterion used and/or target-group definition, a media vehicle may appear more or less attractive for a particular advertiser. Exhibits 3 through 6 offer examples of how a number of specific media vehicles ranked differently for Becel depending on the specific criterion employed.

COMPLICATING FACTORS

Although it is possible to compare two or more media vehicles by the procedure just described, several additional factors complicate this process considerably when media *plans* or *combinations of vehicles* are compared. One of these concerns frequency and overlap. Another relates to one's views of the process of cumulative advertising effect. A third is the difficulty of analyzing and comparing many sets of media alternatives.

Frequency and Overlap Considerations. Two different media plans may yield comparable results in terms of costs and total weighted exposure values, but still differ in net reach and frequency measures. In other words, one plan may expose a *larger audience* to the advertising message *less often*, while the second plan achieves more exposures to a *smaller weighted audience*. For example:

	Net Reach	Average Number of Exposures Per Individual	Total Weighted Exposures
Plan A	250,000	4	1,000,000
Plan B	333,333	3	1,000,000

EXHIBIT 2 Calculation of CPM Weighted Exposures: Method II

Vehicle X	(DM/month) Income		Age		Children		City Size		Occupation		Net Weighting
Sample Reader 1	1,950		33		2		100,000		Lawyer		
Weighting*	1.0	×	.8	×	.9	×	1.0	×	1.0	=	.72
Sample Reader 2	1,500		39		0		500,000		Teacher		
Weighting	0	×	1.2	×	1.1	×	1.0	×	1.0	=	0
Sample Reader 3	2,000		54		0		1 million		Master mechanic		
Weighting	1.0	×	1.0	×	1.1	×	1.0	×	1.0	=	1.1

$$\left(\frac{1}{\text{Sample Fraction}}\right) \times \left(\begin{array}{c}\text{Total of individual net} \\ \text{weights in sample}\end{array}\right) = \begin{array}{c}\text{Number of weighted exposures} \\ \text{in total audience} \\ \text{(for example 650,000)}\end{array}$$

$$\text{CPM weighted exposures} = \frac{\text{DM 45,000 (cost of insertion)}}{650} = \text{DM69.23}$$

Vehicle Y	(DM/month) Income		Age		Children		City Size		Occupation		Net Weighting
Sample Reader 1	1,800		26		0		50,000		Salesman		
Weighting	1.0	×	.8	×	1.1	×	1.0	×	1.0	=	.88
Sample Reader 2	1,600		52		1		1 million		Clerk		
Weighting	0	×	1.0	×	.9	×	1.0	×	1.0	=	0
Sample Reader 3	1,900		36		4		200,000		Executive		
	1.0	×	1.2	×	.9	×	1.0	×	1.0	=	1.08

$$\left(\frac{1}{\text{Sample Fraction}}\right) \times \left(\begin{array}{c}\text{Total of individual net} \\ \text{weights in sample}\end{array}\right) = \begin{array}{c}\text{Number of weighted exposures} \\ \text{in total audience} \\ \text{(for example 942,000)}\end{array}$$

$$\text{CPM weighted exposures} = \frac{\text{DM 35,000 (cost of insertion)}}{942} = \text{DM37.15}$$

*Weights taken from "Target Group Weightings," page 284.

EXHIBIT 3   Rank Order of Vehicles According to Price of Space and Time

Vehicle	Price
*Magazines**	
Kosmos	DM5,633
Hobby	6,529
Westermann	7,768
Madame	9,224
Ratgeber	9,618
Merian	10,192
DM	11,515
Capital	15,118
Das Beste	16,830
Gong	18,886
Freundin	19,009
Frau im Spiegel	19,504
Petra	20,956
Schoner Wohnen	25,936
Der Spiegel	32,812
Eltern	34,002
Fur Sie	36,143
Quick	36,587
Bunte	38,770
BamS	41,069
Brigitte	43,988
Stern	48,988
Burda-Komb†	51,002
ADAC-Motorwelt	75,000
Hor Zu	81,282
Basis-Komb†	92,789
Television‡	
National TV spots	55,000

*Magazine price is for a full page ad.
†Komb designates the insertion of ads in a combination of two or more specific publications at a discount from placing ads in each separately.
‡Television price is for a 30-second announcement.

These differences in net reach and frequency of exposures per individual may occur because of the aforementioned internal and external overlap of readership in media vehicles.

As an illustration of these overlap effects, we might consider the following two simplified examples. Each is based on the assumption that the weighted exposure of one insertion in *Der Spiegel* is 850,000, and the weighted exposure of one insertion in *Stern* is 1,000,000.

- *Example 1*—One often uses different media vehicles in order to achieve *reach*, for instance, one insertion in *Der Spiegel*, and one insertion in *Stern*. But let us assume

---

EXHIBIT 4   Rank Order of Vehicles According
to Unweighted Reach

Vehicles	Unweighted Reach
Magazines	
Basis-Komb	16.11
Hor Zu	12.94
BAMS	8.71
Stern	8.66
Burda-Komb	7.46
ADAC-Motorwelt	6.77
Bunte	5.32
Quick	5.31
Brigitte	4.95
Der Spiegel	4.39
Das Beste	3.98
Eltern	3.42
Frau im Spiegel	3.41
Fur Sie	3.39
Schoner Wohnen	3.31
Gong	2.07
Freundin	2.01
Petra	1.59
Ratgeber	1.36
DM	1.17
Capital	1.01
Hobby	0.87
Merian	0.65
Madame	0.48
Kosmos	
Television	
National TV spots	20.00

---

that 10 percent of *Der Spiegel* readers also read *Stern*. Then our net reach is *not* 1,850,000 (850,000 + 1,000,000); instead it is (850,000 × .9) + 1,000,000, or 1,765,000. Of this number, 85,000 (10 percent of *Der Spiegel* readers) have potentially received two exposures, and the remainder one. These calculations reflect external overlap.

• *Example 2*—One often uses multiple insertions in the same media vehicle in order to achieve *frequency*, for instance, two insertions in *Der Spiegel*. But let us assume that only 70 percent of *Der Spiegel* readers for the July issue also read the August issue. Then our net reach is *not* 2 × 850,000; instead it is 850,000 + (850,000 × .3) [the .3 represents the 30 percent of new readers], or 1,105,000. Of this number, .7 × 850,000, or 595,000, have potentially been exposed to the message twice. This difference represents internal overlap.

EXHIBIT 3 Rank Order of Vehicles
According to Weighted Reach

Vehicle	Weighted Reach
Magazines	(in millions)
Basis-Komb	0.94
Hor Zu	0.93
Stern	0.84
ADAC-Motorwelt	0.79
Der Spiegel	0.70
Burda-Komb	0.46
Brigitte	0.45
Quick	0.43
Das Beste	0.40
Bunte	0.38
BamS	0.38
Schoner Wohnen	0.36
Capital	0.28
Eltern	0.27
Fur Sie	0.26
DM	0.23
Gong	0.20
Merian	0.18
Freundin	0.16
Frau im Spiegel	0.16
Petra	0.16
Madame	0.10
Ratgeber	0.09
Westermann	0.09
Kosmos	0.08
Hobby	0.07
Television	
National TV spots	0.60

It is obvious that varying degrees of internal and external overlap of media vehicles will affect the net reach and frequency measures of a particular media plan.

Different Conceptions of the Process of Cumulative Advertising Effect.   How one assesses the advertising effect of the 1st, 2nd, 3rd . . . *n*th exposure to a message thus becomes very important when evaluating media plans. Unfortunately, there is no standard method for determining such assessments of incremental effect for exposures. Some advertisers assume that the relationship is linear—that each succeeding exposure adds as much effect as the preceding one. Others believe that a "learning curve" operates; thus the effect of exposures subsequent to the first actually *in*creases up to some point (usually the 2nd or 3rd exposure), and then begins to diminish.

EXHIBIT 6   Rank Order of Vehicles According to CPM Weighted Exposures

Vehicle	CPM Weighted Exposures
Magazines	
Das Beste	DM42.08
Der Spiegel	46.87
DM	50.07
Capital	53.99
Merian	56.62
Stern	58.24
ADAC-Motorwelt	67.52
Kosmos	70.41
Schoner Wohnen	72.04
Westermann	86.31
Hor Zu	87.40
Quick	87.42
Madame	92.24
Hobby	93.27
Gong	94.43
Brigitte	97.75
Basis-Komb	98.71
Bunte	102.03
Ratgeber	107.98
BamS	108.08
Burda-Komb	110.87
Freundin	118.81
Frau im Spiegel	121.90
Eltern	126.01
Fur Sie	130.01
Petra	139.71
Television	
National TV spots*	91.66

*Unlike television in the U.S., German television had four 5-minute periods per day which were devoted solely to commercial advertisements. Thus, no "targeting" through the use of spots in specialized programming was possible.

A third view—that taken by Zanger—is that advertising has little effect on the individual consumer until a "threshold" number of exposures is reached. Thus, the task of a media schedule is to attempt to maximize the number of target-group members who will be exposed to at least the threshold number of exposures. For Becel, Zanger had selected nine exposures per quarter as the threshold level for his message with the brand's target groups. Part of the reason for this high number was that the arguments used in Becel copy were relatively complicated and thus required considerable repetition in order to achieve complete comprehension and acceptance on the part of members of the target audience.

These three conceptions of the impact of advertising can be illustrated graphically:

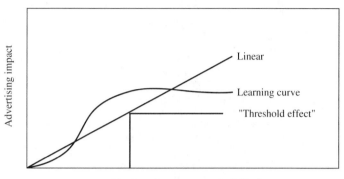

Number of exposures per individual

The development of any given media plan rests on these kinds of assumptions regarding the nature of the cumulative effect of advertising exposures. In order for a media plan to be designed in a manner consistent with the beliefs of a particular advertiser, these beliefs are expressed (implicitly or explicitly) in terms of relative weights for each exposure frequency category, that is, people potentially exposed to the advertisement 1, 2, 3, . . . n times. These relative values provide the basis for making the appropriate tradeoffs between reach and frequency in any advertising schedule.

For example, the three conceptions just described would result in relative weights as follows:

Exposure Frequency Category	Linear Conception	Learning Curve Conception	Threshold Conception
1	1.0	.4	0
2	1.0	.9	0
3	1.0	1.4	0
4	1.0	1.3	0
5	1.0	1.0	0
6	1.0	.7	0
7	1.0	.4	0
8	1.0	.1	0
9	1.0	.05	1.0

Many Alternatives to Evaluate.   The second factor that complicates our analysis is that many different media alternatives exist. Even though only a subset of these are to be considered for any one product, when one looks at the possible combinations of these, the number of feasible media plans increases enormously. It is obvious that hand calculations are not possible for more than a very few plans—especially if trade-offs on reach and frequency are going to be made.

USE OF THE AGENCY'S MEDIA MODEL

Because of these difficulties, media planners at the advertising agency employed a mathematical programming model. It attempted to maximize the impact of advertising expenditures (expressed as an objective function) within various constraints. (See the appendix for a brief explanation of these terms.)

Objective Function. The model's objective function, representing total advertisement impact, expressed this impact in terms of both reach and frequency. This was done by multiplying the weighted net reach in each frequency category by the relative weight for that particular frequency category, and then summing the results. In Becel's case, the threshold value of nine for frequency of exposures meant that the model maximized the weighted net reach in frequency categories nine and above.

An additional factor that was acceptable as input for the agency's model was a weight for the "impact" of various vehicles. As noted earlier, this "impact" factor represented evaluation of a vehicle's qualitative characteristics. In the instance of Becel, employing this factor was considered "not necessary," since vehicles which were clearly unacceptable had been totally removed from consideration beforehand.

Constraints. In the Becel situation, the specific constraints under which the objective function was to be maximized consisted of the following:

1. A limit on total advertising expenditures of DM2,650,000. (The model did, however, calculate rebates which would result after a certain number of insertions or commercials in a particular media vehicle were used, and adjusted for these.)
2. Limitations on media availability. Obviously, for a monthly magazine, only 12 insertions are possible. Also, because radio and TV commercial spots were sold by the government, and the amount of commercial time was limited, only a certain number of spots could be bought by any one company.
3. A stipulation by Zanger that consumers of each sex should receive an approximately equal number of weighted exposures.
4. Each geographic region within Germany was to receive a proportion of total advertising effort which corresponded roughly to its share of the target group. Adjustments in these proportions were often made to reflect increasing brand competition or specific marketing objectives within the regions. This particular constraint was not included in the model, but was used as a guideline by media planners to adjust the final output. Regional newspapers were primarily used to counteract any geographic imbalance in the final output.
5. Corporate policy was that no two of the firm's margarine brands should be advertised in the same issue of the same magazine or in the same "block" of TV commercials. (See footnote to Exhibit 6.)

Within the above constraints, the media model employed by the agency maximized the total advertising impact as represented by the objective function. Although computers and the use of mathematical programming had greatly expanded the number of media plans which could be evaluated or from which a "best" plan could be selected, even these two tools were not considered by the agency's media planners to be sufficient to allow them to examine *all* alternatives. Only a reasonable subset of the potential media vehicles were used as input because the processing capacity of even large computers was limited, and to examine literally all alternatives would be very expensive.

A few other print vehicles had been selected which had insufficient published data on their audiences for inclusion in the media model. Primarily these were magazines which appealed to rather select audiences, thought by Zanger and his colleagues to correspond well with the target group definition. These vehicles also accomplished a desire by Zanger to use some media which had not been included in plans of previous years, in order "to address the target audience through different channels of communication." These vehicles, together with the aforementioned professional magazines and regional newspapers, accounted for approximately 25 percent of the total media budget. Thus, for Becel, about 75 percent of DM expenditures for media were determined, at least in part, by the media model.

TIMING

Another aspect of media planning with which the computer can be of only limited help is the exact timing of insertions. This related to the so-called "wave" approach to advertising versus that of consistent spending. Essentially the "wave approach" means that advertising should be relatively heavy at the beginning of a period, and then fall off sharply to some minimum level. The theory behind this is that intensive advertising at the beginning of a period will increase awareness of the product, and that only certain reminder ads are then necessary to maintain this level of awareness for a certain time span. Then, as the "forgetting function" accelerates toward the end of the period, advertising is increased again. In contrast, some advertisers believed that optimal advertising impact was achieved by maintaining a constant level of advertising intensity.

Although Zanger tended to subscribe to the "wave approach," this was not always possible in practice. For example, Union policy against having ads for more than one of its margarine brands in a single issue of a magazine limited the precision with which timing patterns could be implemented. Other margarine product managers worried less about the general pattern of their insertions, as long as they had a sufficient number of ads around the times when the brand was likely to be used most. For example, in the case of the product manager for Sanella, a margarine positioned for the cooking segment, there was a special concern that the advertising be concentrated at holiday periods.

AGENCY RECOMMENDATIONS

Exhibits 7 and 8 are the media plan and schedule which the agency had recommended to Zanger as having the best advertising impact for Becel within the various constraints imposed. Exhibit 9 summarizes the agency's analysis of the efficiency of this schedule. After examining the proposed plan, Zanger was generally satisfied with the timing and vehicle selection which had been produced by the procedure described earlier.

EXHIBIT 7   Recommended Media Plan for 1975

Vehicle	Frequency of Publication	Number of Insertions	Cost per Insertion	Vehicle Expenditure
ADAC-Motorwelt	12/year	2	DM 75,000	DM 150,000
Architektur	2/year	2	19,000	38,000
Das Beste	12/year	12	16,700	200,400
Brigitte	24/year	8	44,000	352,000
DM	12/year	9	11,500	103,500
Kosmos	12/year	8	5,600	44,800
Madame	12/year	12	9,200	110,400
Manager	12/year	5	11,300	56,500
Der Spiegel	52/year	14	32,800	459,200
Stern	52/year	15	48,900	733,500
Total for illustrated magazines				2,250,000
Deutsche Zeitung	12/year	5	6,700	33,500
FAZ	250/year	10	9,500	95,000
Handelblatt	250/year	15	5,600	84,000
Suddeutsche Zeitung	250/year	6	8,800	52,800
Total for newspapers				265,000
Ärztliche Praxis	104/year	4	4,300	17,200
Der Deutsche Arzt	22/year	10	4,300	43,000
Deutsches Ärzteblatt	52/year	8	6,300	50,400
Medical Tribune	52/year	4	4,600	18,400
Enahrungs-Umschau	12/year	12	1,500	18,000
Baderzeitschriften	24/year	24	1,580	38,000
Total for professional and health spa magazines				185,000
Total media expenditure				

The only serious doubt he entertained concerned the number of insertions which had been allocated to *Das Beste* (*Reader's Digest*). On a CPM weighted exposure basis, this particular vehicle had been evaluated as the best advertising value (Exhibit 6). Zanger worried, however, that the page size of this magazine (5 × 7) was too small to achieve the same impact as that in *Stern* (12 × 15) or *Der Spiegel* (8 × 11). Advertisement reproduction quality for *Das Beste* was also considered rarely to be equal to that of other magazines in the media plan. He had voiced these objections in the meeting, but the agency media director asserted that even if this were true, the CPM-weighted contacts were sufficiently less than the next-best vehicle, and that *Das Beste* was still the "best buy." The Union's marketing director also favored inclusion of *Das Beste* in the media plan. Zanger was reluctant to press the matter without further thought, but still believed that too many insertions were assigned to this vehicle.

With regard to the advertising message in behalf of Becel, Zanger planned to continue the theme which Becel had been employing since its introduction. An example of a typical Becel advertisement appears as Exhibit 10A; a translation is given in Exhibit 10B.

EXHIBIT 8 Recommended Media Schedule for 1975

Week	1	2	3	4	5	6	7	8	9	10	11	12	13	14	15	16	17	18	19	20	21	22	23	24	25	26	27	28	29	30	31	32	33	34	35	36	37	38	39	40	41	42	43	44	45	46	47	48	49	50	51
ADAC-Motorwelt												•																							•																
Architektur																				•																				•											
Das Beste			•				•				•					•				•				•					•				•				•				•				•					•	
Brigitte			•								•					•								•					•				•								•				•					•	
DM			•				•									•								•					•				•								•				•					•	
Kosmos			•								•					•								•											•		•				•				•					•	
Madame				•				•				•					•								•					•			•	•				•				•			•	•				•	•
Manager				•								•										•			•												•	•													•
Der Spiegel	•				•				•			•				•				•			•			•			•	•			•				•				•	•			•					•	
Stern	•		•					•				•				•					•		•				•		•					•		•	•		•		•				•				•		•
FAZ						•								•	•		•		•		•	•			•				•	•			•				•				•				•	•		•			•
Handelblatt		•			•			•							•																•						•								•		•				
Suddeutsche Zeitung		•											•																	•							•										•				
Ärtliche Praxis					•																																										•				
Der Deutsche Arzt	•					•				•					•				•				•								•											•			•				•		
Deutsches Ärzteblatt	•				•										•					•												•					•														
Medical Tribune			•										•													•								•			•						•								
Enahrungs-Umschau	•								•				•								•					•								•					•				•					•		•	
Baderzeit-Schriften							•		•		•		•					•			•			•	•		•			•	•		•		•				•				•				•				•	
Deutsche Zeitung							•				•	•						•						•							•		•		•																

296

EXHIBIT 9 Efficiency of Recommended Media Plan

	1st Quarter		2nd Quarter		3rd Quarter		4th Quarter		Total for Year	
	Percent Reach	Cumulative Reach	Percent Reach	Cumulative Reach	Percent Reach	Cumulative Reach	Percent Reach	Cumulative Reach	Percent Reach	Cumulative Reach
Net reach as percent of target group (weighted)	79%		79%		78%		83%		88%	
Average Frequency	7.6		7.5		7.1		7.1		25.7	
Net Reach in each Exposure Frequency Category*										
1st Exposure	6.7%	79.3%	7.1%	79.3%	8.0%	77.7%	7.8%	82.6%	3.3%	87.8%
2nd Exposure	6.2	72.6	6.5	72.2	6.9	69.7	7.1	74.8	3.4	84.5
3rd Exposure	6.3	66.4	6.2	65.7	7.6	62.8	7.7	67.7	3.0	81.1
4th Exposure	6.6	60.1	6.1	59.5	8.3	55.2	8.2	60.0	2.5	78.1
5th Exposure	6.4	53.5	5.9	53.4	6.7	46.9	7.1	51.8	2.2	75.6
6th Exposure	5.2	47.1	5.0	42.5	5.3	40.2	5.7	44.7	2.1	73.4
7th Exposure	4.1	41.9	4.0	42.5	5.5	34.9	5.0	39.0	2.0	71.3
8th Exposure	3.6	37.8	3.4	38.5	4.2	29.4	4.6	34.0	1.9	69.3
9th Exposure	3.2	34.2	4.0	35.1	2.9	25.2	4.6	29.4	1.8	67.4
10th Exposure	3.3	31.0	3.2	32.1	2.9	22.3	4.5	24.8	1.8	65.6
11th Exposure	3.4	27.7	3.4	28.9	2.7	19.4	3.9	20.3	1.8	63.8
12 or more Exposures	24.3	24.3	25.5	25.5	16.7	16.7	16.4	16.4	62.0	62.0
Proportion Men/Women:										
unweighted	54/46		54/46		53/47		52/48		53/47	
weighted	49/51		49/51		48/52		49/51		48/52	

Note: The total weighted target group is approximately 2.42 million.

*To be read: In the first quarter, 6.7% of the target group had received 1 and only 1 exposure, while 79.3 percent had received at least 1 exposure; 6.2 percent had received 2 and only 2 exposures, while 72.6 percent had received at least 2 exposures, etc.

EXHIBIT 10A   Typical Becel Advertisement

Damit Sie hochkommen, ohne daß es mit Ihrem Herzen abwärtsgeht: becel.

In allen hochindustrialisierten Ländern nehmen Herz- und Kreislaufkrankheiten ständig zu.

Bei uns haben schon etwa 30% der erwachsenen Bevölkerung erhöhte Blutfettspiegel. Das begünstigt die Entstehung arteriosklerotischer Herz- und Kreislaufschäden.

Der Weg nach oben erfordert nicht nur einen klaren Kopf, sondern auch ein gesundes Herz.

Die Ursachen liegen in unserer ungesunden Lebensweise. Wir leben zu hektisch. Wir essen zu gedankenlos. Wir bewegen uns zu wenig.

Vieles können wir nicht ändern. Eines können wir: bewußter essen.

Wissenschaftler fordern gesündere Nahrungsfette.

Nahrungsfette, die reich sein müssen an mehrfach ungesättigten Fettsäuren.

Unsere Wohlstandsnahrung enthält im allgemeinen zu wenig davon.

So trägt sie dazu bei, den Blutfettspiegel hochzutreiben.

ben. Das belastet Herz und Kreislauf.

becel-Öl und becel-Margarine sind von höchstem Wert für Herz und Kreislauf.

Beide Nahrungsfette sind reich an mehrfach ungesättigten Fettsäuren. Diese senken den überhöhten Blutfettspiegel.

becel Diät-Margarine mit über 50% mehrfach ungesättigten Fettsäuren und becel Diät-

Speiseöl mit mindestens 70% tragen also wesentlich dazu bei, der Entstehung arteriosklerotischer Herz- und Kreislaufschäden entgegenzuwirken.

Die becel Diät-Margarine schmeckt gut auf Brot, Brötchen, Zwieback oder Toast.

Das geschmacksneutrale becel Diät-Speiseöl ist ideal für Salate und Rohkost. Beim Kurzbraten, Dünsten und Grillen bringt es den Geschmack der Speisen voll zur Geltung.

Zusammensetzung von becel

Zusammensetzung	Öl	Margarine
mehrfach ungesättigte Fettsäuren	mind. 70%	50–55% *)
einfach ungesättigte Fettsäuren	15–20%	20–30% *)
gesättigte Fettsäuren	10–12%	20–25% *)
Vitamin E	700 mg/l	500 mg/kg

*) bezogen auf den Fettgehalt
becel-Margarine enthält außerdem:
15.000 I.E. Vitamin A pro kg
3.500 I.E. Provitamin A pro kg
1.000 I.E. Vitamin D pro kg

Die Ernährungsfibel „Bewußter essen" mit 200 ebenso gesunden wie schmackhaften Rezepten erhalten Sie, wenn Sie DM 2,50 überweisen an:

Union Deutsche Lebensmittelwerke GmbH, becel-Beratung, Kto. 20682, Postscheckamt Hamburg.

Absender bitte deutlich schreiben.

Bewußter essen Ihrem Herzen zuliebe: becel

becel in der Lichtschutzpackung gibt es in Lebensmittelgeschäften.

EXHIBIT 10B   Translation of Copy of Advertisement

So That You Succeed Without Your Heart Failing: Becel

In all highly industrialized countries heart and circulatory disease are increasing steadily.

Already 30 percent of our adult population has high cholesterol mirrors. That promotes the incidence of arteriosclerosis and heart disease.

[Picture subtitle: The way to the top requires not only a clear head but a healthy heart as well.]

The causes lie in our unhealthy life-style. We live at a hectic pace. We eat too thoughtlessly. We get too little exercise.

Much of that we can't change. One thing we can change: be more conscioius of what we eat.

Scientists call for healthier fats in our diet. These fats must be rich in polysaturated fatty acids. Our present diet contains too little of these and thereby contributes to the raising of the cholesterol mirrors. That burdens the heart and circulatory system.

Becel oil and Becel margarine are invaluable to your heart and circulatory system.

Both are rich in polyunsaturated fatty acids. These sink the high cholesterol mirror. Becel margarine with more than 50% pufa and Becel oil with 70% pufa are valuable aids in the fight against the incidence of heart and circulatory disease.

Becel tastes good on bread, rolls, toast or crackers.

The neutral tasting Becel oil is ideal for salads. It also lets the full natural flavor of fried foods come through.

For 200 delicious and healthy recipes send DM 2.50 to Union Deutsche Lebensmittelwerke GmbH, becel-Beratung, Kto. 20682, Post-scheckamt Hamburg.

THINK ABOUT WHAT YOU EAT FOR YOUR HEART'S SAKE: BECEL

Becel Ingredients	Oil	Margarine
Polyunsaturated fatty acids	70%	50–55%
Unsaturated fatty acids	15–20%	20–30%
Saturated fatty acids	10–12%	20–25%
Vitamin E	700mg/ltr.	500mg/ltr.

Appendix

A Brief Description of Linear Programming Terms

Linear programming is one of the most frequently used tools of applied operations research. Its function deals with the optimal allocation of scarce resources among competing activities, subject to the constraints of a particular situation. These constraints may be expressed in financial, technological, marketing, or organizational terms—as long as they are stated in the form of a mathematical inequality. More generally, linear programming is a method of mathematically representing the planning of best-possible allocation of limited resources, when the model employed utilizes linear functions.

Linear programming as a technique for solving such problems was developed in 1947 by George Dantzig as an aid to the solution of military problems encountered by the U.S. Air Force. His discovery, the simplex method, together with the computational capacity of digital computers, provided the answer to a large number of previously insoluble government and business planning problems. The model can be expressed as the maximization or minimization of an objective function within the conditions imposed by a number of linear constraints. Consider the formulation of the following, highly-simplified example where an advertiser can use linear programming techniques to find a "best" combination of insertions in three different media vehicles.

If the advertiser wishes to maximize the number of unweighted exposures by purchasing ads in a monthly magazine ($v1$) and two weekly magazines ($v2$ and $v3$), the objective function may then be expressed as: Total unweighted exposure value (UEV) = a UEV + b UEV + c UEV, where a, b, and c are the number of insertions in $v1$, $v2$, and $v3$, respectively.

The advertiser might want to do this within the constraints imposed by a limited ad budget, in which case this constraint would be represented as the inequality: Total ad budget $\leq a$ (cost of insertion in $v1$) + b (cost of insertion in $v2$) + c (cost of insertion in $v3$). Because of the obvious limitation of the number of issues, both maximum and minimum numbers, the following would apply:

$$a \leq 12$$
$$b \leq 52$$
$$c \leq 52$$
$$a \geq 0$$
$$b \geq 0$$
$$c \geq 0.$$

Additional constraints might express the desire of the advertiser to employ at least three times as much of $v2$ as $v3$, which would be represented so: $b \geq 3c$.

Without the simplex method, the solution to this problem would require trial-and-error procedures.

A more complete explanation can be found in standard statistics texts.

Some of the techniques described in this case—such as those dealing with non-linear functions—are beyond the capabilities of linear programming strictly defined. They require the use of more advanced programming techniques, a description of which is not attempted here.

Case 4–2

*Media Buying at Ralston Purina**

Media buying is a complicated process of balancing advertising budgets and goals with the variety and expense of the available media vehicles. Many companies rely on their advertising agency to choose the appropriate media mix. However, marketers are under constant budget pressure, and since the media are often a large part of the marketing budget, more advertisers are becoming involved in the development of their media strategies, plans, and purchases.

MEDIA VEHICLES

The media market is an ever-changing arena. Each year, advertisers have new vehicles to choose from, including new magazines that target special audiences, as well as altogether new types of vehicles such as video jukeboxes and billboards in executive restrooms. Prices of the alternative vehicles increase at different rates, causing the price/value relationship to be constantly adjusting. In addition, the size and composition of the audience for these vehicles is constantly shifting, reflecting demographic factors, lifestyles, and fashion.

In 1985, newspapers commanded the greatest share of the advertising market through their dominant share of the local/retail advertising revenue. Television maintained a dominant share of the national advertising market, but the market continued to change. The penetration of households with cable, for example, rose from 44 to 47 percent, and videocassette recorders sold at an increasingly rapid rate, penetrating over one-third of U.S. households.

For purposes of discussion, we often separate media planning from media buying. While a complete separation is not possible or reasonable in practice, marketers are often more involved in planning and rely heavily on specialists for purchasing.

MEDIA PLANNING

Media planning begins with the marketing and financial objectives for the product or service being advertised. Given the chosen target market, its seasonality, purchasing pattern, and regional differences, the advertiser establishes a media strategy and plan to accomplish the product's stated objectives. The media-planning process has three major stages:

---

*This case was prepared by Valerie Lester under the supervision of Professor Paul W. Farris. Copyright © 1986 by The Darden Graduate Business School Foundation, Charlottesville, Virginia.

1. The evaluation and ranking of media classes, vehicles, and options. This is determined on the basis of fit with the demographics of the target audience, relative impact or influence of the media class or vehicle, and fit with the reach, frequency, and budget guidelines previously established.
2. The evaluation of various combinations of media vehicles, determined by estimating the audience overlap of different vehicles as well as their relative costs and discount schemes. Predicting audience size and interpreting sometimes-conflicting data are part of this process. There is still a major debate on how one should measure magazine audience sizes, for example, and the Nielsen "people meter" is an example of innovation and change in measuring TV audiences.
3. Determination of timing. Scheduling is planned to fit the role and the impact that the advertising is intended to have on the purchase (education, awareness, trial), while considering the product's seasonality and purchasing pattern.

Media planners must also take into consideration the environment in which the product or service is being advertised. This includes changing demographics and competitors' actions and reactions, as well as a changing media market.

MEDIA BUYING

Media buyers can distinguish themselves in at least two ways:

1. Reducing the cost of the media purchased.
2. Innovative media "package" buying.

Media buyers can often reduce prices by "gambling" that new shows will attain good ratings. Without knowing the size and composition of a vehicle audience, the price of advertising space or time means little. There is also usually a great deal of uncertainty about what the price really is. Although rate books are published with the "list price" for the various media vehicles and options, this usually represents the highest, not the average or lowest price. Advertisers who buy in large blocks of time or space receive substantial volume discounts. Rates may also be reduced by skillful buying, including bartering, exchanges, and copy splits.

Bartering refers to an exchange of goods or services for media time or space. For example, an advertiser who sponsors a television program can offer it free to individual stations. The stations receive a portion of the advertising time, and the advertiser gets a less-expensive television buy.

Exchanges occur when an advertiser buys a large block of time or space at a discount and then "exchanges" portions of that media buy with another advertiser. Copy splits are similar to exchanges, but are done on a geographic basis, allowing the advertiser to increase regional impact without paying the more expensive spot-market prices.

A media buyer may be successful at reducing costs by using any or all of these buying techniques. Often the buyer must act quickly to take advantage of "bargains."

Innovative media buying also offers advertisers more cost-efficient ways of communicating with customers. Given the ever-changing nature of the media market, there are always new media forms. For example, cable stations, videocassette recorders, and independent stations are eroding network television's mass audience and, in the process, opening up new opportunities for media buyers. Media directors indicate that clients are increasingly receptive to innovative media alternatives.

There is a growing trend toward more sophisticated methods of measuring media in order to quantify advertising's impact on product performance. There are attempts to quantify proven exposure, changes in awareness levels, geographic market and media data, and volumes of product purchased. As these measurements are developed, marketers will become more certain of the results offered by alternative media vehicles.

IN-HOUSE VERSUS OUTSIDE MEDIA BUYERS

In response to pressures for cost-effective media buying, some companies have chosen to develop in-house experts. By developing this resource, advertisers gain more control over the placement of media; they ensure that the priorities of the media buyers are in accord with company objectives.

In addition, all the media savings are passed on to the advertiser, and media buyers may be held directly accountable for their cost savings. The company also saves money by eliminating the float (usually 30 to 60 days) on the money that the agency transfers from the advertiser to the media. With more direct lines of communication and easier access to confidential information, the in-house media operation may also respond more quickly to the questions and needs of the marketing personnel.

Many advertisers continue to use advertising agencies, however, to place their media. They believe that agency buyers have greater experience than in-house staff and are in a better position to track media-buying trends. Agencies may also receive information about new media alternatives sooner than an in-house operation, and some argue that the best people are attracted to agencies. Therefore, recruiting for an in-house media operation is probably difficult, and the quality of the buyers may suffer as a result.

Ralston Purina has been one of the most successful companies at establishing its own media-buying operation, which is managed in conjunction with its in-house advertising agency, Checkerboard Advertising. The media buyers work closely with the in-house and outside advertising agencies to ensure that Ralston gets the greatest value for its advertising dollar. The following article, reprinted here with the permission of *Media Decisions*, describes that operation.

Why Ralston Gets What It Wants*

It's late January and the snow is clogging New York's streets, but William Claggett, Ralston Purina's vice president and director of marketing and advertising services, hardly notices. He has May on his mind. That's the time when the network upfront buying season gets underway, and the time when Ralston traditionally leads the pack in committing its dollars. Claggett is making his way to NBC headquarters to learn anything he can—even this early in the game—that might later give Ralston an edge over its competitors.

This early-bird syndrome is only possible because, unlike many other companies, the marketing and media functions at Ralston-Purina cooperate handsomely with each other.

*Reprinted with the permission of *Media Decisions*, Vol. 20, March 1985.

(*continued*)

Well in advance of the big buy, the two departments have adroitly meshed their needs and squared away their budgets. Ralston *knows* what it wants.

Ralston's success—its sales and earnings growth rates top the chart in the pet-food world—is largely attributable to this unstinting eye for detail. The style at Checkerboard Square is to plot out as completely as possible what courses of action are most appropriate and opportunistic for its stable of brands. While best known for pet products such as its Dog, Cat and Puppy Chows, and its Chex line of cereals, Ralston also houses fast-fooder Jack-in-the-Box, an agriculture division which sells cattle, hog, and chicken feed, and, with the acquisition of Continental Bakeries, such all-American classics as Twinkies and Wonder Bread.

Ralston spends heftily to market and advertise this lineup. Last year, it is estimated that the company shelled out more than $200 million in support of some 75 brands, with about 70 percent targeted towards network TV. These sums are not spent lightly: Ralston has a reputation for being a thorough, "totally inflexible negotiator" who knows just what it wants and what it will pay to get it, in the words of one executive who has sat across from the company as it wrangles its media buys.

Indeed, it is nearly legend that it is well-prepared Ralston who kicks off the annual upfront network TV buying season. While its buttoned-down Claggett denies any "compulsion to be first," he admits the company is never too far back.

Under Claggett's tutelage, the media budgeting and buying season is seen as a supreme challenge and a chance to test one's mettle. Unlike many of its competitors, which keep the marketing and media departments separate, though equal, Ralston gets both groups of specialists working together. Furthermore, even though Ralston has an agency roster that includes some of the largest and best, the company relies heavily on input from its own in-house agency and veteran media group.

Simply put, Ralston is a believer in the theory that the correct use of media can be the crucial key in unlocking a brand's full market potential. As a consequence, Ralston has set out to become more expert than the experts.

For example, Ralston goes through an elaborate drill in preparation for the network TV upfront buy, which usually commences around May or June. Its in-house media team—15 members strong—starts gathering intelligence on the network upfront market in January, early by most standards. It produces an analysis of market conditions in general, and forecasts pricing, with input from its agencies and in-house group. Some members of the media team even trek out to Hollywood to get an early fix on new pilots from producers and programmers. "Since we are among the first to buy every year, we don't have the luxury of waiting until *Variety* covers what they're going to do," says Claggett sarcastically.

Further into the network cycle, Ralston starts agonizing about share estimates for the networks' fall lineups, culling data from all 10 of its agencies and debating those numbers until everyone is in agreement. "I've been told on good authority that other clients don't get this deeply involved with estimating," notes Claggett, with more than a hint of pride. (See sidebar, "47 Steps to the Upfront Buy.")

"One agency may say *Crazy Like A Fox* is going to do a 22 share, another might say a 32 share, and everyone else will come in at 27–28," relates Claggett. "We then have a little debate where we can change the consensus, and many times do, depending on the reasoning behind it. But we *never* just mathematically average them all out," he says with some vehemence.

Does all this result in a better network deal for Ralston? One network observer, at least, thinks it does. "Ralston, unlike many advertisers, knows exactly what they want when they come to upfront. They say, 'Give me 26 commercials on this show and 38 on that one and how much will it cost?' Most people come in and say 'I have $10 million, I want to reach women 18–35 on Monday, Wednesday, and Friday. What do you have?' Ralston, however, picks high-rated shows and winds up buying a schedule that actually runs, which is a rarity these days. Because they are so early, they get what they want, even if they have to pay a little more for it since they're buying per-unit cost at that time." He sums up, "They're totally inflexible negotiators. They know what they want and they get it."

NBC's senior vice president of network sales, Robert Blackmore, agrees that Ralston "does an outstanding job in selecting quality shows."

Blackmore points to another Ralston advantage—its longstanding relationship (15 years) with the Paul Schulman media buying service. "One of the advantages to that setup is that Schulman can concentrate on the Ralston package—he has the time to spend on all of the nuances because he's basically concentrating on that one account," Blackmore explains.

While Ralston's attention to detail in network circles is well known, what is less understood is that all media gets put under this high-power microscope. In magazine buys, for example, Ralston's media people call on publishers and editors in New York each September to give each book its yearly report card on the previous year's performance. They also lay out Ralston's expectations for the next year. Big deal, skeptics might say—but the report card has worked for Ralston.

Claggett looks at magazine buys much like he does network TV. Unlike many advertisers which have their agencies buying magazine schedules for specific brands, Ralston buys a corporate package upfront. In addition to this upfront buy, Ralston buys magazines opportunistically. "We are able to take advantage of last-minute offers or remnant space right before magazine closings with what we call our opportunistic magazine program because this is all pre-planned in advance," he says.

"The challenge is to know as much about a product as the marketing person does," stresses Linda Pavlenko, group media director and a 13-year Ralston veteran. "It's really a team effort, and our relationship with marketing is very good," she reiterates.

And vice versa. Newly-recruited brand managers lose little time in learning the world of gross rating points (GRP's). Brand managers are required to attend a series of media seminars and are put into immediate contact with the media department. "In some companies, the media department is quite separate from the brand group, but here we discuss things back and forth," Claggett, who has spent 18 of his 53 years at Ralston, explains.

For example, at budget time in the early spring, brand managers approach media personnel to develop final marketing plans for the upcoming year. They base their requests on information that media has been feeding into the brand-management funnel throughout the year, not just during the formal budgeting process. That data accommodates the ever-changing needs of brands. When a competitor springs an unpleasant surprise, brand managers have the media data at their fingertips to retaliate. As a result, brand managers, well versed in the ways of media, have a fair idea of what media strategies they should be pursuing.

Media is equally well prepared. "It's not as though media gets involved at the point where approved budgets are coming together," explains Jack Shubert, director of advertising services for Ralston's grocery products division. "Media has been involved with marketing from the very beginning, from the 'blue skies' preplanning sessions all the way through," he emphasizes.

The In-house Advantage

This type of cooperation would not be possible without the presence of an active, in-house media department with clout. Without doubt, Ralston puts a premium on just such an entity.

(*continued*)

The best in-house media departments, in Claggett's mind, have had that kind of long-standing, side-by-side relationship with their marketing people. He admires the in-house media operations at corporate giants such as General Foods, Procter & Gamble, General Mills, Colgate, and Nabisco because they are active, smooth partnership operations.

"Somewhere in the corporation you have to be coordinating the whole activity," Claggett advises. And in his universe that translates into an in-house agency shepherding the needs of some 75 brands as well as the efforts of Ralston's 10 advertising agencies. Make no mistake about it, there is also a distinct Ralston culture that must be adhered to. To this end, Continental Baking will move its headquarters from Rye, New York, to Checkerboard Square later this year. Claggett is now working with its advertising agencies, Ted Bates and Grey, to indoctrinate the newcomers to the Ralston way of doing business.

"You'll find a lot of companies which have what they call in-house media departments, but quite frankly they spend 99 percent of their time working on network TV, negotiating, and improving the network packages," states corporate media director Don Martin, who's been with Ralston 19 years. "While our people here do that to a great extent, at the same time they might be working on 50 or so brands, and every one has been fully coordinated with a full-service agency media staff or planned in-house. Our people are coordinating plans from the very first meeting with the product managers," he adds.

Because of this hands-on approach to media, Martin believes that the in-house people are in a much better position to review, critique, and perhaps alter plans that are being prepared and presented to them by the agencies.

Not that the strong-willed Claggett means to suggest that the entire media function should be brought in-house. "It's not a goal at all, because most of the network action is done in New York," explains Claggett, recognizing that Ralston needs to rely on the resources of agencies close to the heart of Broadcast Row. Furthermore, he adds, "We feel that our system is perfect because we can tap into new media technologies at 10 different agencies and use the best of them. If we did it all ourselves, we simply could not," he concedes, his voice trailing off.

While it may not do it all, the in-house agency, in conjunction with the rest of the marketing department, sure does a lot. Checkerboard Advertising is composed of roughly 50 people, or a third of the entire marketing department. Among CA's duties are the handling of outside agency coordination work which involves coordination of agency selection and agency fee systems.

In addition to media, the department's responsibilities include TV and print advertising production, packaging development, audiovisuals for sales meetings, sales analysis, brand publicity, sales promotion, advertising research, media research, corporate market research, and even test kitchens.

Checkerboard Advertising works closely with the full agency lineup. "We involve all of our agencies in planning and in share estimates, and we select one of our agencies to work with us on every buy," Claggett explains. However, Ralston usually uses the Paul Schulman Co. to execute its media placement orders. "We have almost a partnership arrangement," says Claggett of their affiliation with Schulman, a division of one of its agencies, Gardner Advertising. In the past, Ralston has brought Wells, Rich, Greene into the act as well, and this go-round, with its CBC buys, they may involve Bates and Grey in the process, reports Claggett.

From an outsider's perspective, who does what is confusing. "We find it's more effective to do some things ourselves, and let the agencies do other things, and of course, we do some things jointly," says Claggett, trying to shed light on the subject. For example, Ralston handles all network bill/pay, all internal costing, allocation of spots, direct media buying for some brands, and spot TV pool coordination. Some areas are left to the agencies, like the bulk of the brand work, creativity, and new media and computer uses.

Ralston's media department also handles talent and residuals payments to keep costs down. Most companies leave that cleanup work to their agencies, who charge a 17.65 percent commission for the service. "I defy you to find anywhere in the universe a media department where planners or buyers are aware of how to do T&R," challenges a proud Shubert.

All in all, the in-house operation makes plenty of good business sense for the sprawling St. Louis company. Outside of better control and coordination, there's also substantial cost savings involved. "Generally speaking, our savings are somewhere between two and a half to three times the cost of running the department," confides Claggett. "In terms of eliminating the float, in terms of certain procedures we have, they by far offset the cost of the department." The operation is audited independently by a department which does not report to Claggett.

The Budgeting Process

How does Ralston make all the many pieces come together? By taking a methodical approach. At the first budgeting meeting in early spring, marketing and media sit down to go over brand marketing objectives. The turf is already very familiar to both sides, since they have already worked side-by-side on brands throughout the year.

Basics are reviewed on brand objectives. For network upfront, marketing submits its brand requirements in terms of specific target audience GRP's, weekly weights and planned budgets taken directly from respective media plans. "Our total requirements are the cumulative result of each brand's needs in each specific broadcast daypart," Martin explains. "Our responsibility in media is to then fill those requirements in the most effective way."

Meanwhile, marketing already has a pretty good idea about the total budget amount they'll need. "It's based upon the needs of the product, the stage in the life cycle, the R&D investment required, consumer information needs, competitive activity, and target audience requirements," tells Martin. Marketing must have its requests in to media so that media can be in position for the upfront network TV buy by May, or whenever the market looks like it's ready to move.

With the basics hashed out, media exits and returns only when it has a prepared plan. A frenzy of activity takes place in the media department. Life is so hectic in the media department during this time that it closes its doors to outside suppliers from March through June.

Media has bolted itself in because it is now under the gun to map out strategy for all media buys as it supervises the information streaming in from its agencies' media departments. "We're getting our act together on everything, network, TV, print, radio," ticks off Pavlenko. For example, agencies are feeding in estimates on a CPM cluster point basis (spot TV), she lists, while analysis of a cable market's subscribing base is also being done. Syndication is far from forgotten. That medium is being studied at the same time newspaper and promotional needs are being evaluated.

Pavlenko points out too that this is the period when the agencies are providing in-depth competitive spending reports of Ralston's competition. "It helps us decide how we're going to split up that money, and it's one thing we rely greatly on the agencies for," she notes.

The topper is that all of Ralston's divisions—pet foods, cereal, industrial feeds, Jack-in-the-Box, and now Continental Baking Co.—are being planned simultaneously. Some $200 million plus in expenditures are now being sliced up.

"The push and the crunch starts along as early as February and then is carried on through June or July, when the final documents are put to bed," notes Shubert. "The major push

(continued)

comes from May to June where we really get into final plans, because a lot of these documents require four or five meetings per brand. It's not just 'one media meeting, go away, bring the plan back, and you're finished,'" he sighs.

When media does finally come back to marketing with its fleshed-out media recommendations, both sides review them to make sure that all objectives are fulfilled. The media group, though, already had approved the media plans from its agencies prior to its meeting with marketing staffers. Martin says, "This is a required procedure."

If any differences of opinion between marketing and media surface from this meeting, both sides talk it out. "If we are in complete disagreement, we take it to the next higher authority," Martin outlines. The next link in the command chain would be the group marketing director. Although it has happened in the past, "It doesn't happen much now because normally you square those things away in preliminary meetings," Martin adds with relief.

After the meeting between brand managers and media, the budgets go to marketing directors who approve their individual brand budgets. The budget then gets kicked upstairs to the next layer of approval, the director of marketing for grocery products. If all goes well, the next move is up to the president of the grocery products division. From that point on, the budgets travel to a corporate budget committee and ultimately the board of directors.

With approval from the director of marketing and the president of the grocery products group, media can then determine what percentages of the budget for network TV should be spent upfront and opportunistically. While the media budget is still undergoing scrutiny from various layers of approval, the total amount of dollars for media spending has received the nod. "In effect, what we're doing is making forecasts for management of what the situation will be like in the following fiscal year," explains Claggett. "While it's more of a forecast for the coming fiscal year rather than a tight budget, we do have some parameters to deal with," he clarifies.

The forecasts come in pretty close to what is actually approved, continues Martin. "Normally the variance, from top to bottom, is in the 5 percent area, and we can live with that," he adds. "We've never really had any major problem in that area," he concludes.

"We're pretty close on the dollars, too, because we have a checkpoint, a last-minute reading of conditions right before the market opens, even the day that it's opening," Martin boasts. "This last-minute reading prevents us from making any major mistakes in terms of the total dollars that we will be committing on behalf of the company," he notes.

At Ralston, budgets are reviewed at least every quarter. "If need be, we'll do it more often," shrugs Shubert. The budgets are reviewed that often, he explains, "because things are constantly changing, and we want to have an actionable position always."

Martin concurs, adding, "Nowadays, there is no such thing as an annual plan. Anybody who thinks there is lives in the 18th century."

Although Ralston's media department seems to have all the i's dotted and the t's crossed, Claggett, the indefatigable perfectionist, says there's always room for improvement.

He would like to see more creativity in the use of media, especially cable and syndication, as the two forums are likely to take on more importance in future years. Ralston has already taken a giant step in the syndication arena with *Nashville*, which it developed from scratch. "Initially, we built that to address a problem in a certain section of the country," says Shubert. "Now it is in over 100 markets and doing very well."

Another area for improvement is personnel. One of the strong points of the media department is that many of the staff have worked together upwards of 15 years. That's one of the keys to the operation's success. But as Ralston continues to grow, the media department will also have to grow to accommodate the influx.

For companies just starting up an in-house media operation, Claggett advises finding the best professionals available. "The other ingredient is making sure they work closely with brand management," he teaches. "Sometimes, it takes years to really develop a rapport and a feeling for working with brand management groups. And when you're starting out, you have to have that," he insists.

As for adversarial relationships that sometimes develop between the media and marketing disciplines, Claggett simply won't allow that to happen. When he walks into NBC's offices, he needs everything he can get from both departments. "The two are working on the same team, working for the same company," he insists. That team is about to make its plays, and Claggett wants to enter the game knowing he can execute, and score.

Marianne Paskowski

47 Steps To The Upfront Buy

It's not by chance that Ralston Purina is yards ahead of the pack in completing its upfront TV buy each year. "While a lot of people think it's just sitting around in a fancy restaurant discussing millions of dollars," Ralston's Claggett complains, "there is a lot of detail and planning which enters into the buy." At Ralston, the process begins in January with analyses of market conditions. Claggett ticks off those 47 steps.

Preliminary Phase

1. Analyze market conditions and forecast pricing.
2. Notify brand groups and agencies of deadlines for brand needs.
3. Set efficiency goals and objectives.
4. Assemble brand requirements.
5. Estimate total corporate TV budgets by daypart.
6. Assemble overall desired package requirements.
7. Load target audience evaluative data in computer.
8. Establish qualitative evaluation criteria.

Exploratory Phase

9. Discuss new pilot scenarios with major Hollywood producers and network West Coast programmers.
10. Discuss available research and reports on new shows.
11. Examine possible fall schedules.
12. Chart past performance shares by time period, by week.
13. Communicate general requirements to each network.
14. Set timetable for negotiations.

Programming Evaluation Phase

15. Attend announcement meetings held by each network.
16. Screen all footage on new pilots.
17. Discuss future storylines on pilots with network programming people.
18. Discuss possible schedule changes.

(continued)

19. Meet with Ralston's major network agencies to develop corporate share estimates by quarter.
20. Load estimated time period shares and viewer data into computer.
21. Determine best combinations of shows through analysis of all possible or feasible packaging on an anticipated cost basis.

Offer and Bidding Phase

22. Inform networks of specific packages of shows and costs desired.
23. Receive network bids.
24. Determine last-minute schedule changes.
25. Perform computer analysis of quantitative/qualitative aspects of each plan.
26. Evaluate packages against original objectives.

Final Negotiation Phase

27. Inform networks of plan weaknesses.
28. Evaluate revised network proposals.
29. Make seasonal and scheduling adjustments in final packages desired.
30. Receive final network bids.
31. Discuss different budget level plans at each network.
32. Final evaluation and decision on total corporate package.
33. Determine contract conditions for each network.
34. Negotiate final packages at each network.

Wrap-up Phase

35. Assign shows to each brand.
36. Set up weekly rotation schedule for all brands.
37. Formalize contract specifics in order letters.
38. Advise brand groups and brand agencies of purchase details.
39. Start "opportunistic" exploration for budget amounts not committed in the upfront buy.

Re-evaluation Phase

40. Recalculate audience estimates due to schedule changes.
41. Renegotiate participations due to schedule changes.
42. Shift positions due to competitive and/or marketing considerations.
43. Negotiate make-goods.
44. Negotiate opportunistic packages.

Reporting Phase

45. Compare "goals" vs. "actual" based on A. C. Nielsen research.
46. Police purchase agreements.
47. Report actual achievements vs. goals to product management/agencies.

How Four Other Companies Play The Budget Game

While there is always a certain amount of fresh angst involved in developing annual budgets, most of the major companies adhere to a pretty tried and true approach. Oft labeled the

"Procter & Gamble method," this traditional budgeting modus operandi calls for somewhat separate and distinct roles for brand managers and media personnel. Generally, brand managers come up with the product objectives—say the goal is to increase market share by 3 percent in the Southwest—and then turn the plan over to the media group for coordinated implementation. In this instance, the media department may recommend a certain number of GRP's and suggest various exposures—regional magazines or local radio, perhaps.

At that point, the two camps get together to see if everyone agrees on the objective and solutions. When the answer is "yes," the budget is sent first to higher-level marketing executives for approval, then on to the unit's business manager, before it starts laboring its way through layers of bureaucracy for the final okay. At some companies, that go-ahead stamp is given by the president, CEO, or even the board of directors.

Not every company tackles the budgeting process in exactly the same way. Some companies, such as Ralston Purina, Campbell Soup, and Clorox, evince a corporate culture that favors well-prepared early birds. This trio already has the budgeting blueprint well underway for the upcoming year. Campbell's started planning its strategy in mid-January to meet an August deadline.

Others, such as Coca-Cola USA and Apple Computers, take their cue from their fiscal calendars. They don't even begin crunching the numbers until late spring or early summer. Coke pulls itself together in three months, tops.

"When you're selling a product which is broadly based, it's not exactly like you're cutting it as close as a gnat's eyelash," quips William Lynn, Coca-Cola's corporate media director.

And, of course, not every brand has the same needs. Some products may be seasonal in nature, necessitating a different budgeting cycle. Other brands may have their plans torn up when a competitor unveils a surprise, or the market itself undergoes an unforeseen change. (These are some of the reasons why formal quarterly budget reviews are fading away. In today's chaotic selling atmosphere, most budgets are under constant review.)

Nor does everyone speak to the same people when affixing spending levels. At many companies, marketing and media executives huddle together to hash out brand objectives and media usage. But at other companies, never the twain shall meet till late in the game. At more egalitarian marketers (at least in theory), middle management plays a much broader role. Apple Computers is a case in point.

The following are brief sketches of how four major marketers view the planning cycle.

Clorox: The Textbook Approach

This Oakland, Calif.-based consumer product specialist has a reputation for being a tough-nosed negotiator. It follows a traditional path that obviously works.

It begins the plans for its household products, which include Clorox Liquid, Softscrub, Tilex, and its newly introduced Fresh Step cat box filler, in February in order that they can be put into motion by the start of its fiscal year on July 1. Seasonal products such as charcoal, paint, and salad dressing work on a different schedule and are planned with trade/broker considerations in mind.

The nitty-gritty starts when Clorox brand managers and assistants begin pulling together marketing data from their own media departments as well as from the account servicing departments of the agencies. Needham Harper Worldwide, Young & Rubicam, Foote, Cone & Belding, and N W Ayer get involved at this early stage.

The marketing data is then presented to the advertising agency management for its review. Later, the documents, along with specific agency recommendations, are forwarded to corporate product management. Once a strategy is agreed upon for a brand, the media departments at Clorox and the agency develop concrete plans. The recipient of this outpouring is the advertising manager. Included in the plan's coverage are promotion, sales, and creative strategies. After the ad manager's okay, the budget wends its way to divisional ad managers. Later, the media budget gets wrapped into corporate budgets for the president and chairman to approve.

Clorox is not a proponent of the zero-based budgeting technique. Rather, "We test our way into making significant changes in budgets," tells Robert Bolte, director of media services at Clorox. Even with new products, the development process runs parallel to the existing formula.

Once budgets are signed off, they are rarely formally reviewed. The budget will be reopened "only if significant changes need to be made," Bolte says.

One area of change at the company has been its embrace of computers and in-house software. This technology has speeded, and made more sophisticated, formulation of the budget. Everyone, from assistant brand managers on up, is adept at using this data, notes Bolte.

Campbell Soup: Separate but Parallel

The media budgeting process has changed over the years at Campbell Soup, reports George Mahrlig, director of media services at the Camden, N.J.-based foods company. "It's much more dynamic now because we have decentralized the decision-making process to the business unit level," he says.

After the first year, for example, business unit managers from the soup division will go over these brands' basic directions with the unit's marketing managers. Media personnel are at these meetings, but are not offering input. "At this point, it's just strategic planning," describes Mahrlig. "Advertising and media will be discussed only if they are a substantial part of the brand plan, and then only directionally."

By late April or May, marketing plans have been formulated and presented to management.

The media plan has not been left out. Rather, its development is running separately yet parallel to the marketing overview. Having been in on the objectives meetings, the media group has devised its own very detailed plan. Sometime in May, the media plan is presented to the business unit manager. From that point, the chief financial officer and president of the company put their stamp of approval on the plans.

"This process has its shortcomings," concedes Mahrlig, "but it works well overall." He notes that under this method brands can start their advertising schedules even if they don't have final budgetary approval. "If there was a disagreement about strategy, it would have surfaced and been settled earlier," he points out.

Like Clorox, Campbell's has scrapped its practice of formally reviewing budgets on a quarterly basis. "The responsibility for stewarding the budget falls on the business unit, and it's really a daily, weekly, monthly, ongoing process," says Mahrlig fervently.

Coca-Cola: Getting It Together, Fast

At the soft drink king, the media budgeting process starts up around June and is finalized around August or early fourth quarter for the following year's spending. Unlike other companies, Coke gathers a slew of corporate and agency players together and pushes them into a room. Coca-Cola's brand directors and media experts sit down with their agencies' account management and media department teams. Coke's Lynn describes this set-up as a "loop," where all four entities are meeting at the same time, arguing and reconciling their views.

Soon after, marketing plans are presented and the team addresses the advertising-related portions of the brand's plans.

The media departments at Coke and its agencies then set out to translate these marketing objectives into advertising tactics. For a new product entry, Coke will do "an initial pay-out analysis on share expectations, pretty much the same way as P&G," reports Lynn. The plan goes first to the marketing director for an okay, before heading to the president for the final okay.

How often do budgets come up for review? "We try to review brand budgets quarterly, but that really depends on the brand's needs," says Lynn. "Some brands may not get reviewed at all, while others will get revised four times."

Since Coke's budgeting process is just getting going around the time the upfront TV market is convening, does the company run into problems by not having an approved and specific spending level in hand? No way, grins Lynn. He reasons that, because fourth quarter budgets are already approved and 50 percent of the upcoming buy can be cancelled, buying upfront without a firm budget represents no major obstacle. Also, networks will most likely alter a sizable chunk of the buy with second-season programming changes. "It's not a problem at all," shrugs Lynn. "You're just buying a mortgage on someone else's future, so it's not your worry."

Apple: High-tech Migration

This maverick personal computer maker thrives on creativity and individuality, so fittingly, its budget planning process is hardly traditional. Bruce Mowery, advertising, sales promotion, and public relations manager for Apple II Division (there is no counterpart for the Macintosh division as yet), says the budgeting process is dictated by the fiscal year beginning October 1.

"Around April," says the former Chiat/Day ad executive, "we begin to think of fiscal 1986—what specific TV shows or miniseries we want to appear on, and what print support there will be." This is about the time when Apple starts its business planning process, so the timing is ideal. The period also coincides with the upfront TV buys of May–June, points out Mowery.

Mowery explains that Apple's media budgeting process is "iterative" and seems to ramble on through October. Financial groups start the business plan for each division at about the time the two divisions' product managers start isolating new product introduction and pinpoint market targets for the upcoming year. Ideas for promotion and exposure are brought to Mowery's attention and he coordinates them for possible "event advertising" opportunities. "Then we migrate to the marketing director as a team and present a plan," outlines Mowery.

"There would probably be changes made, and then we'd present the plans to the general manager of the division, along with the marketing director. Marketing is very decentralized and is a team approach," he describes. "We affix a cost to each individual product manager's plan, and then figure out what is needed in advertising support. We then figure out if it's in the ballpark, and cut it if we have to," says Mowery. "It is a zero-based thing. Some items are sacrosanct (such as certain event advertising components), but you've got to build flex into it because the computer world moves so quickly," he believes.

"It is not a classic approach," he admits, "but it works for us. It is representative of middle management playing a broad role, versus a Procter & Gamble with its highly formalized structures for brand managers."

Apple does review its budgets quarterly, because, again, things move so fast in that high-tech world.

(continued)

While the media budgeting process at Apple may be fairly nontraditional and might not be as cost-effective once done, they feel they get more bang for the buck. Mathematical models and the like, Mowery continues, are useless in a budgeting process which addresses event marketing.

"CPMs are important, but you can't put a mathematical model on a 25 percent participation in a miniseries. It just doesn't apply to event marketing," he stresses.

Apple, he continues, also keeps its media budget relatively loose so that if a product does not meet expectations, or doesn't appear on time, media sums can be switched. "Because of the high technology of our products, there is always slack," Mowery sums up. "Everything is loosely tied to a product or program so we can quickly untie the knot and reallocate expenditures."

Marianne Paskowski
Pam Ellis-Simons

Case 4–3

Absolut Vodka*

You found it inserted in December 1988 issues of *LA Style* and *New York* magazines—two sheets of plastic, one clear, attached at the edges; inside them, some viscous liquid with snowdrops floating in it. You could shake it and, like an old-fashioned paperweight of a Christmas scene, snow swirled around a bottle of Absolut vodka—"Absolut Wonderland." Industry, advertisers, publishers, and news media took note. Was this (the second in Absolut's blockbuster Christmas ads) the establishment of a tradition? What next?

BACKGROUND OF ALCOHOLIC BEVERAGE INDUSTRY

The 21st Amendment, which marked the end of Prohibition in the United States, allowed each state to regulate the sale of alcoholic beverages. More than 50 years later, their sale

*This case was prepared from publicly available sources by Bette Collins, under the supervision of Professor Paul W. Farris. Copyright © 1989 by The Darden Graduate Business School Foundation, Charlottesville, Virginia.

was still highly regulated and taxed.[1] Some states had licensed private package stores, some had state-controlled stores, and the regulation of on-premise drinking laws varied considerably. A three-tiered system of distribution was, however, strictly followed: producers/importers, wholesalers, and retailer/on-premise licensees. Wholesalers were allowed to operate only within one state. All retail and on-premise licensed vendors (bars, restaurants, and clubs) were required to buy from wholesalers. Eighteen states were "control" states, meaning the state owned and operated the majority of retail outlets. In these states, bar and restaurant owners received a discount on buys but had to make all of their purchases through state stores. "Noncontrol" states required licensing but allowed competitive pricing.

Alcoholic beverages (distilled spirits, wine, and beer) were a $170 billion global market in the mid-1980s; global advertising expenditures, excluding other promotional devices such as sports sponsorships, were estimated at about $2 billion. Half of this spending was estimated to occur in the United States.[2]

Industry classification broke down the distilled-spirit group into brown goods (or whiskey) such as bourbon, blends, and Scotch, Canadian, and Irish whiskeys; white goods such as gin, vodka, rum, and tequila; and specialties—brandy, cordials, liqueurs, and premixed cocktails. By 1986, the distilled-spirits industry had been on a downward slide for some five years:

	1975		1986	
	Cases Sold* (in millions)	Share of Market	Cases Sold* (in millions)	Share of Market
Brown goods	101	53.7%	65	38.9%
White goods	65	34.6	71	42.4
Vodka	37	19.7	39	23.4
Specialties	21	11.2	32	18.8

*A case was defined as 9 liters.

One product that bucked the sliding figures throughout the rest of the distilled-spirits industry was imported vodka. Vodka was distilled from any grain material at 190 proof or above. When bottled, without aging, it was usually between 80 and 100 proof. After distillation, it was charcoal filtered to remove any flavor or aroma. In 1982, although total vodka sales were down 3.8 percent, imported vodka was up 17 percent. Big losers were domestic giants Smirnoff (sales down 8 percent in 1981, .7 percent in 1982) and Wolfschmidt (sales down 10.1 percent in 1982); big winners were import leader Stolichnaya and new-comer Absolut.

---

[1]Federal excise taxes went to $12.50 a proof/gallon (that is, higher proof beverages had higher taxes) at the producer level in 1985 from the $10.50 it had been since 1976. State taxes averaged $2.63 a proof/gallon in 1976; $3.06 in 1984. The advertising of distilled liquor on television or radio was prohibited.

[2]This and information on marketing strategies primarily from John Cavanagh and Frederick F. Clairmonte, *Alcoholic Beverages: Dimensions of Corporate Power* (New York: St. Martin's Press, 1985), pp. 129–30.

One author summarized the marketing strategies of distillers at this time as follows: (1) the targeting of women as a rising consumer group (with new brands or redefinition of old brands, which was successfully carried out by various vodka brands and by Jack Daniels); (2) capture of the youth market, although "youth" had to be redefined as states raised drinking ages from 18 to 21 in order to receive federal highway-construction monies; (3) capture of specific ethnic markets; (4) capitalizing on a trend toward lightness; and (5) focusing on superpremiums at the "summit of the income pyramid." Absolut vodka was an example of such a superpremium brand. Selected price information on vodkas is presented in Exhibit 1.

EXHIBIT 1   Selected Price Information, August 1989

A. Commonwealth of Virginia Alcoholic Beverage Control Prices (for 750-ml bottles except as noted; all prices include 20% state tax)

Vodka (Domestic)	Retail Bottle Price	Vodka (Imported)	Retail Bottle Price
Aristocrat*	$6.00	Absolut (Sweden)	$13.20
Bowman's Virginia	4.70	1.75	26.65
Fleischmann's Royal	5.00	1.00*	14.95
Gilbey's	5.40	Danzka (Denmark)	11.95
Glenmore*	6.25	Denaka (Denmark)	13.20
Gordon's	5.65	Elduris (Iceland)	12.85
Kamchatka	4.80	Finlandia (Finland)	13.30
Mr. Boston's Riva	4.80	Icy (Iceland)	13.00
Mohawk Peach (70 proof)	5.35	Luksusowa (Poland)	11.35
Nikolai	5.30	Olifant (Holland)	8.40
Odesse	5.80	Seagram's-Canada	6.80
Ostrova*	6.50	Stolichnaya (Russia)	12.85
Popov	5.05	1.75	26.00
Relsky	4.90	100*	14.95
Senator's Club	4.65	Tanqueray Sterling	
Simka Kosher	6.90	(England)	12.90
Skol	4.90		
Skyline (Virginia)	4.65		
Smirnoff #21	7.15		
#57*	9.10		
Stitzel-Weller	5.50		
Tvarscki-Cherry	9.10		
Vladimir	4.60		
Wolfschmidt	5.50		

*100 proof; proofs other than 80 or 100 noted in parentheses.

EXHIBIT 1 *(Concluded)*

B. Plain Old Pearson's (Washington, D.C.) Comparative Advertising of Vodka Specials, August 14, 1989 (1.75-liter bottles; available rebates in parentheses)

	State of Virginia	Montgomery County, Maryland	State of Pennsylvania	Everyday Prices	Extra-Special Low Prices
Absolut	$26.85	$22.99	$24.37	$19.99	—
Bowman's	10.10	9.39	—	8.99	—
Finlandia	—	22.85	24.14	18.99	$17.49
Fleischmann's	10.70	9.55	11.36	8.49	—
Gilbey's	11.40	10.85	12.08	8.99	—
Gordon's ($1.50)	12.50	11.39	13.01	8.99	—
Kamchatka	10.30	9.85	11.00	8.19	—
Popov	11.20	10.29	11.75	8.79	—
Smirnoff ($2.00)	15.70	13.89	15.85	11.29	9.99
Stolichnaya ($3.00)	26.00	22.19	24.30	19.99	—
Wolfschmidt ($2.00)	11.90	10.85	12.49	8.99	7.99

THE LAUNCH OF ABSOLUT IN THE UNITED STATES

Absolut vodka was produced and owned by the Swedish government. It was introduced in the United States in 1979 by Carillon Importers, a division of International Distillers and Vintners, Ltd. (IDV), the United States marketing subsidiary of the British alcoholic-beverage marketing firm Grand Metropolitan. Carillon sales stood at $52 million at that time, and it was the smallest of Grand Metropolitan's import/distribution subsidiaries. (Later in the decade, IDV bought Heublein, sellers of the domestic vodka brands Smirnoff and Popov and the No. 3 import brand Finlandia.)

Before the rise of Absolut as Carillon's star product, the company had focused on the orange-flavored liqueur, Grand Marnier. Grand Marnier (and later Creme de Grand Marnier) consistently grew at around 8 percent a year. Carillon also sold the imported gin Bombay.

The key to Absolut's story was Michel Roux. A Frenchman, Roux had earned a degree in hotel management and oenology (the study of wines), but has stated that more influential in his career was his stint as a paratrooper in the French army.

Roux left for the United States when he was 24. With no plans, he headed for booming Texas and worked a series of routine jobs at hotels and clubs. In 1967, he opened a French restaurant in Dallas. By the time he heard that Carillon was looking for its first salesperson, however, he had decided that both his strengths and the big money were in sales. Roux joined Carillon and, by the late 1970s, had become director of marketing.

In 1979, with U.S. vodka sales rising, the Swedish government was looking for a United States importer for Absolut. Roux recalled, "Larger distillers wanted time to mull over the project, but Carillon leapt at the chance."[3] Roux redesigned the bottle—giving it a short neck, contemporary look, and a silver and blue label—and had the label printed directly on the glass. He priced Absolut at "half again as much as domestic brands."

At the time, Stolichnaya, marketed by Monsieur Henri, had an 80-percent share of the imported-vodka market. Market research evaluations of Roux's changes were devastating:

> With its off-beat bottle and name, combined with its unlikely origins, the researchers predicted disaster. People wondered if Roux was losing his touch. Roux himself had doubts—but not for long.
>
> "We had never had market research before and we said, 'You know, we've been very successful at what we've done in the past. So why should we listen to it now?' "[4]

Roux ascribed the problem to a mismatch between market-research techniques and the Absolut marketing strategy: traditional market research asked the wrong people: the wealthy don't volunteer for tests. He decided that conventional wisdom was right that the best way to sell a luxury item was by marketing it as a status symbol, but the "status" buyer for Absolut was unconventional—the young and the hip. Roux believed they were not open to snob appeal, but they were open to wit.

The target market for Absolut has been described variously as "anyone under 35," to "the top of the pyramid," "the upper end, trend-setting, artsy crowd," to "the ferociously hip." Roux said that he used demographics when he was planning, but described the target market as "everyone 21 and older with the ability to drink. I have a whole spectrum."[5]

THE ABSOLUT ADVERTISING STRATEGY

The first advertising campaign stressed Absolut's Swedish origins. Then, a year later, Carillon's advertising firm was acquired by an agency handling Brown-Forman's competitive brands, and Carillon began searching for a separate agency to handle its Absolut account. The company looked at 94 agencies, then narrowed the field down to a small group, who were asked to do "speculative" advertising. In 1981, TBWA (which one observer had dubbed "feisty") won the account and proceeded to "break all the rules in liquor advertising."

To make sure that TBWA didn't discard any ideas, he told them to bring him what was in their garbage cans, the resting place of the "Absolut Impression" ad before its rescue. He welcomed all ideas and suggestions; a staffer's 11-year-old child was the origin for an "Absolut Magic" ad.

---

[3]This and a primary amount of information and quotations on Roux were taken from Michele B. Morse, "Absolut Truths," *Review*, December 1988.

[4]Ibid.

[5]Brian Bagot, "Neat Shot," *Marketing and Media Decisions*, March 1989.

Roux was adamant about motivating for creativity. He once took the sales staff on the Orient Express, and another time hot-air ballooning, and flew them on the SST—all because he believed that new experiences were the greatest reward one could give as a motivator and because he believed inspiration was the key ingredient of success. Gloria Steinem was the keynote speaker at a 1983 sales meeting.

Copy and Media

Wit, intrigue, and subtlety became the focus of the first TBWA Absolut ad campaign. Punning on "absolute," the ads used that superlative and usually a single other word (see Exhibit 2). Turning the weakness of an odd bottle into strength, they played with the traditional liquor ad which, for some reason, usually consisted of the bottle and a glass, or the bottle alone. Roux said, "When somebody reads an art magazine, they are reading for leisure. Their state of mind is not the same as when they're reading a weekly magazine. The brand becomes part of the enjoyment, and the ads are more conducive to the state of mind.

From the beginning, advertising outlets included not only the newsweeklies and the established glossies (*Vanity Fair*, *Rolling Stone*, *Esquire*, *Sports Illustrated*), but also off-beat magazines such as *Spy*, *Details*, *LA Style*, and *Interview*. Carillon was one of the original advertisers in *Ms.* and in *The Advocate* (a gay magazine). Roux believed that, if you got the trend-setters, the masses would follow. Ads, which generally appeared as full pages 8 to 10 times a year, were sometimes tailored to fit the magazine genre, even to the extent of asking advertising reps of magazines for ideas. The emphasis was on the medium, but the bottle was the focus, even when it took other forms. The Absolut ad used in *Vogue* in 1988 (see Exhibit 2B) pictured a silver dress, designed by David Cameron, on a woman who, in effect, became the bottle—"Absolut Cameron." TBWA noted, "The idea is to make the bottle the hero in a whimsical fashion. It's always the headliner." The ad later became part of an eight-page insert in *Vogue* of Absolut dresses created by new designers.

SPECIAL EVENTS AND PROMOTIONS

Music, art, and fashion have been consistent themes for Absolut promotion and advertising. Roux has said, "The artists and the people who buy art are the trend-setters in this world."[6]

Carillon sponsored an "Absolut Grapelli" concert at Carnegie Hall in 1988 for the violinist's 80th birthday. An "Absolut Concert" was scheduled for late 1989 at Lincoln Center's Avery Fisher Hall, to feature four modern composers conducting their own pieces. It was to end with an "Absolut Fanfare." Such special-event sponsorships generally absorbed 20 percent of the product's advertising and promotion budget.

---

[6]Andrea Adelson, "Unusual Ads Help a Foreign Vodka to the Top," *The New York Times*, November 28, 1988.

EXHIBIT 2A and 2B

EXHIBIT 2C and 2D

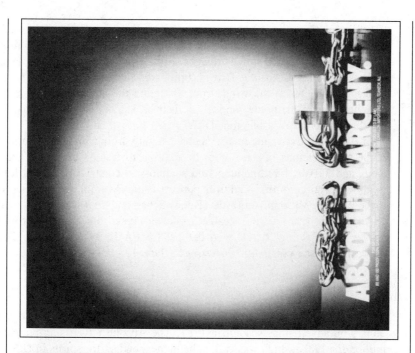

Carillon commissioned an original song by Brazilian Carlos Jobim (singer of "Bossa Nova" and "Girl from Ipanema") to run in *Rolling Stone*—"Absolut Jobim."

"Downtown" and "Uptown" images: Billboards tied to the locale, as on Rodeo Drive in Beverly Hills—"Absolut Drive"; billboards in Chicago with the letters in "Absolut Chicago" blowing in the wind; trucks roaming the streets of New York in 1988 with reproductions of the bottle, on ice, on their backs; and similar "outdoor" advertising for San Francisco and Washington, D.C.

In 1988, the advertising image changed slightly from whimsical treatments of the actual bottle to recreations of the bottle. In addition to fashion designers and photographers, Roux and TBWA hired painters and sculptors to create Absolut bottles for ads. Bottle renditions were commissioned from pop artist Andy Warhol (the drawing was later donated to the Whitney Museum) and artists Kenny Scharf and Ed Ruscha, who created an "Absolut L.A." ad. In it, the bottle became a pool of crystal blue water surrounded by a white terrace (see Exhibit 2C). It won the 1988 MPA Kelly Award for "Best in Magazine Advertising" and ran free in *Newsweek*'s June 12, 1989, issue.

BUDGETS

According to BAR/LNA, Grand Metropolitan, IDV, and Carillon spent $6.7 million dollars on advertising Absolut in 1987. The Absolut advertising budget was set at $18 million for 1988, which was called the highest budget for spirits in U.S. history, and the budget was estimated to be $22.5 to $23 million for 1989. (Carillon's fiscal year ended in October.) BAR/LNA comparative figures for January–December 1988 are given in the following table:

Class Brand	No. of Brands Combined	Dollars (000)	Percentage of Class
F330 LIQUOR			
Seagrams liquors	10	$26,380.9	11.3%
Dewars Scotch whiskeys	2	11,498.9	4.9
Johnnie Walker Scotch	3	9,481.8	4.1
Kahlua liqueurs	3	8,151.1	3.5
Absolut vodka	2	7,686.9	3.3
Bacardi rums	5	7,547.7	3.2
Puerto Rican rums	2	7,498.1	3.2
Chivas	2	7,195.4	3.1
Tanqueray	1	7,054.9	3.0
J&B Scotch whiskeys	1	6,522.9	2.8
Top ten total		$ 99,018.6	42.4%
Class total		$233,554.2	100.0%

Figures for Absolut early in the 1980s were not available; the brand was too small. But Carillon was not alone in turning to advertising to reverse declining liquor sales in the early years. When Smirnoff sales fell by 8 percent in 1981, its advertising jumped

34 percent to $9.9 million; sales were off by only .7 percent in 1982. Wolfschmidt spent $3.4 million, but its sales were down 10.1 percent. Some industry-watchers ascribed problems with Russian vodka, or even vodka associated with Russia, to the boycott of the Olympics.

Advertising Production and Costs

Carillon produced expensive ads; the "Absolut Impression" ad mentioned previously was a costly, no-print, embossed white-on-white magazine insert. But the most expensive were the Christmas specials, the first of which was in 1987 and was reported to have cost over $1 million to produce. When the ad was opened, a microchip recording played three songs, including "Santa Claus Is Coming to Town." This ad was inserted in *The New Yorker* and *New York*—"Have an Absolut Ball."

Then came Christmas 1988 and "Absolut Wonderland," also reported to have cost over $1 million to produce. Another source said the cost was $1 each, with a total of $750 thousand for two of the magazines. Carillon had been planning the ad for almost a year but was stymied by how to make the snow drift, how to keep the liquid from freezing, how to bind the edges, and how it would withstand magazine mail-handling. The company experimented with 15–20 prototypes, finally settling on a liquid composed of water, oil, and antifreeze (said to be, however, nontoxic). Rounded snowflakes were used because they didn't puncture the plastic and they drifted better than others, and the amount of snow was eventually reduced because it obscured the bottle. Copies were mailed around the country to test the ad's durability. *The Washington Post* printed the following description by Jeff Greenberg, vice-president and print-production director for TBWA:

> "The production key to this pricey undertaking," Greenberg explains, is "incredibly cheap" Asian labor. "You couldn't do it here," he says cheerily. "You couldn't pay for it."
>
> The insert required hand assembly by 300 workers, mostly teen-agers who put in 20-hour days in non-air-conditioned factories at a salary equivalent to $50 a month. "The workers are incredible—they never lift their heads up," Greenberg adds. "I'm not meaning to sound like it's slave labor."

The three-dimensional snow ad ran in *LA Style*, *New York*, and *MarketWatch*. One million were printed at around $.75 each, according to one source. "Absolut Wonderland" generated a huge amount of media coverage. Some 300 newspapers ran stories on the ad, as did 40 TV news programs.

APPROACHING 1990

The marriage of Carillon and TBWA was a boon for both partners. TBWA U.S. offices were billing $127 million mid-way through 1988, and the firm had added 12 new accounts during those 6 months alone. *The New York Times* noted the influence of the Absolut campaigns, saying it was "advertising that is so good it attracts new business to the agency." Richard Costello, president and CEO of TBWA, called Roux "the best client I ever had." Carillon sales for 1988 were $200 million.

Absolut vodka sales grew an average 22 percent a year for a decade. It became the No. 1 imported vodka in 1985 when it overtook Stolichnaya—perhaps partly as a result of a boycott of Soviet goods following the shooting down of the Korean Airlines plane in September 1983.

At the end of 1988, Absolut had something between 51 and 56 percent of the imported-vodka market in the United States, 5 percent of the total market. Its recent case sales had grown from 1.1 million in 1986 to 1.8 million in 1988. Over 2 million cases were expected to be sold in 1989. Rival Stolichnaya had 30 percent of the import market, which was 3.2 million cases (8 percent) of a total 1988 spirits market of 38 million cases. Vodka leader Smirnoff, however, was pulling in $600 million versus Absolut's $260 million.

Although total distilled-spirit volume sales were off 3.3 percent in 1988 (even imports were down 0.7 percent), *Advertising Age* noted (February 26, 1989) that "Imported vodka again outperformed all other categories and domestic vodka followed on the imports' success." Exhibit 3 gives estimated case sales and 1988 rank of top brands. Absolut had been listed 18th in 1987, 35th in 1986.

In the United States, adult drinkers made a market of 170 million people in 1988; distilled-spirit consumption per capita was 2.2 gallons a year (2.3 gallons in 1987). Vodka accounted for 24 percent of those figures. The average cost of distilled spirits was $39.90 a gallon; the average American spent $83.26 on them in 1988. Exhibit 4 presents data as of spring 1987 on vodka consumers.

By the end of the decade, brown spirits were also attempting to cash in on trends toward lower calories and lower alcohol content, or higher premiums. Seagram's Mount Royal Light boasted that its reduced calories came from a special process rather than the usual watering down. Schenley relaunched the classic Pinch Scotch with the restored wire mesh on the bottle (dropped in the 1960s because of cost) as a superpremium aged 15 years, and Schenley planned to spend $20 million advertising it over 3 years. Jack Daniels introduced a $20 bottle of Gentleman Jack.

Foreign vodkas' 22 percent growth attracted a rush of new imports. Seagram introduced a Polish vodka, Wybrowa; brands called Elduris and Denaka appeared. Elduris was Icelandic vodka going for $12–$14 a bottle. Brown-Forman spent $15 million to launch Icy (from Iceland), planning on 4.5 million cases by 1992. They opened its advertising with an ad featuring the bottle and the words, "Absolute Improvement." Carillon got a court order to stop the ad, and Roux said "there is room for people who don't try to imitate others. They have to create their own image and quality."[7] In August 1989, the Denaka vodka ad (in *Business Week*, for example) featured a woman with flowing red-brown locks leaning on a pool table by a bottle and glass. She was saying, "When I said vodka, I meant Denaka," and the caption read, "In a world of absolutes, Denaka excels."

Within vodka products at the end of the decade, one trend was toward flavors, particularly pepper. The trend appears to have started when a marketer (reportedly, Carillon) noted that restaurant managers marinated pepper corns in vodka for drinks such as Bloody Mary's, although the tradition of peppered vodka was centuries old in Europe. Many

---

[7]"What Stirs the Spirit Makers: Vodka, Vodka, Vodka," *Business Week*, June 12, 1989.

EXHIBIT 3   Liquor Industry Scoreboard*

	1988 Rank	Marketer	Sales (thousands of cases)			Five-Year Growth Rate
			1988	1987	1986	
Rum						
Bacardi	1	Bacardi	7,350	7,330	7,120	0.2%
Ron Castillo	49	Bacardi	720	720	740	−3.2
Vodka						
Smirnoff	2	Heublein	5,900	5,510	6,100	−0.7
Popov	5	Heublein	3,250	3,060	3,410	1.6
Gordon's	18	Schenley	1,650	1,610	1,650	−1.7
Kamchatka	21	Jim Beam	1,490	1,600	1,570	−3.1
Absolut	22	Carillon	1,410	1,110	900	25.1†
Skol	27	Glenmore	1,170	1,070	1,030	7.9
Gilbey's	28	Jim Beam	1,160	1,130	1,130	−2.3
Stolichnaya	38	Monsieur Henri	900	790	740	14.7
Wolfschmidt	39	Seagram ·	890	890	870	−1.4
Fleischmann's	43	Glenmore	800	850	1,000	−4.4
Barton	50	Barton Brands	660	600	610	1.0
McCormick	51	McCormick	630	590	610	13.7
Relska	58	Heublein	590	600	690	−2.8
Blended/Canadian whiskey						
Seagram's 7-Crown	3	Seagram	3,840	3,900	3,950	−4.5
Canadian Mist	4	Brown-Forman	3,370	3,410	3,560	0.0
Canadian Club	10	Hiram Walker	2,350	2,300	2,250	−1.8
Seagram's VO	11	Seagram	2,200	2,230	2,250	−5.5
Windsor Supreme	13	Jim Beam	1,900	1,920	1,990	−2.2
Black Velvet	16	Heublein	1,730	1,690	1,740	−1.9
Crown Royal	23	Seagram	1,310	1,220	1,200	5.0
Kessler	32	Seagram	1,090	1,090	1,140	−4.6
Lord Calvert	34	Seagram	1,030	1,020	1,070	−0.9
Canadian Ltd.	54	Glenmore	600	670	720	−0.8
Calvert Extra	59	Seagram	570	620	710	−8.9
Bourbon/Tennessee						
Jim Beam	6	Jim Beam	3,200	3,250	3,240	−0.3
Jack Daniel	7	Brown-Forman	3,180	3,030	2,960	0.2
Early Times	29	Brown-Forman	1,150	1,200	1,330	−4.8
Ancient Age	35	Age Internat.	960	900	930	1.9
Ten High	40	Hiram Walker	880	1,030	1,000	−4.0
Old Crow	52	Jim Beam	620	520	480	−5.6
Evan Williams	56	Heaven Hill	600	580	590	−1.7
Gin						
Seagram's	8	Seagram	3,150	2,970	2,920	3.9
Gordon's	15	Schenley	1,740	1,650	1,750	−3.9
Tanqueray	26	Schieffelin/Somerset	1,180	1,150	1,100	−4.9
Gilbey's	31	Jim Beam	1,130	1,190	1,150	−8.7
Beefeater	37	Buckingham Wile	930	950	980	−4.5
Fleischmann's	53	Glenmore	610	700	680	−2.0

(continued)

EXHIBIT 3   *(concluded)*

1988 Rank	Marketer	Sales (thousands of cases)			Five-Year Growth Rate
		1988	1987	1986	
Cordial/brandy/cocktail					
DeKuyper Cordials	9	Jim Beam	2,550	3,100	3,370	−13.0†
E&J	14	E&J Gallo	1,850	1,790	1,670	9.1
Hiram Walker	17	Hiram Walker	1,690	1,680	1,650	7.5
Kahlua	19	Maidstone	1,550	1,580	1,470	2.4
Southern Comfort	25	Brown-Forman	1,190	1,150	1,100	3.5
Christian Brothers	30	Christian Bros.	1,150	1,190	1,160	−2.2
Bailey's	36	Paddington	950	920	890	4.8
Golden Spirits	41	Seagram	850	1,350	910	−3.2†
Club Cocktails	42	Heublein	840	930	880	−2.2†
Arrow Cordials	44	Heublein	750	850	1,000	−8.6
Leroux Cordials	45	Seagram	750	810	950	−1.3
Hennessy Cognac	47	Schieffelin/Somerset	740	730	750	3.5
Courvoisier Cognac	60	W.A. Taylor	550	580	540	6.1
Scotch					
Dewar's	12	Schenley	2,100	2,070	2,160	−0.9
J&B	24	Paddington	1,260	1,320	1,300	−5.3
Johnnie Walker Red	33	Schieffelin/Smt.	1,060	1,120	1,150	−1.2
Chivas Regal	46	Seagram	740	750	750	−2.2
Cutty Sark	48	Buckingham Wile	730	760	770	−7.0
Old Smuggler	55	W.A. Taylor	600	730	750	−3.7
Scoresby	57	Glenmore	600	630	590	8.4
Tequila					
Jose Cuervo	20	Heublein	1,500	1,250	1,150	12.0

*Estimates of retail sales, rounded to nearest 10,000 mixed cases, from Jobson Beverage Alcohol Group.
†1986–88.

believed the niche would grow because of a perceived trend toward spicy foods and full-tasting drinks. The demand was said to be coming from up-scale, 25- to 50-year-old, metropolitan types. One of Carillon's competitors said, however, that the pepper-drinkers were minimum-age consumers who downed them in shot glasses at nightclubs, but that marketers didn't want to focus on this fact: "Vodka marketers don't want to admit that people are doing shots any more than the cognac marketers advertise that a lot of people drink cognac with Coke, because it's looked to be down-scale."[8]

Stolichnaya introduced Zubrowka, a musky-tasting vodka with north European buffalo grass that never caught on and was dropped; Pertsovka with pepper (in 1985); Ohkotnichya with ginger, cloves, juniper, anise, and lemon peel; and Limonnaya in 1986. Carillon's Absolut Pepper ad in 1987 showed the bottle in a jungle of peppers hanging on vines with just the brand name. The brand grew slowly to 20,000 cases by the end of 1988,

---

[8]Patricia Winters, "New Flavors Spice Up Vodka Category," *Advertising Age*, February 16, 1987.

with plans by Roux for it to grow to 500,000 by the end of 1989. Citron Absolut in early 1989 was selling 10,000 cases a month.

Adding flavors to vodka raised the long-standing issue of whether vodkas varied by taste or quality. The U.S. Bureau of Alcohol, Tobacco and Firearms had always maintained that it did not, by definition; the bureau had always objected to use of the word "taste" in advertising. Many people, however, maintained that the premium imported vodkas did, in fact, have a distinctive taste. Smirnoff tested the bureau's stance in 1989 with an ad claiming it was "So superior, you can taste it." The marketers claimed their

EXHIBIT 4   Vodkas and Media-Use Profiles (base: 172,957,000 adults; index: all adults = 100)

	A. *Vodka Consumption*		
	Percentage Of All	*Share of Users*	*Share of Volume*
Total drunk in last six months	13.8%		
Vodka Brands:			
Absolut	1.2%	6.4%	5.6%
Crown Russe	.2	.8	.6
Finlandia	.4	1.9	.6
Fleischmann's	.5	2.8	1.5
Gilbey's	1.0	5.0	5.5
Gordon's	1.3	7.1	3.6
Hiram Walker	.3	1.4	.6
Mr. Boston	.3	1.8	1.6
Nikolai	.3	1.7	1.9
Popov	1.9	10.2	19.8
Relska	.2	.9	1.2
Schenley	.2	.9	1.6
Seagram's Imported	.6	2.9	1.7
Smirnoff	6.3	33.2	30.9
Stolichnaya	1.0	5.5	3.0
Vikin Fjord	—	.2	.2
Wolfschmidt	.7	3.7	4.3
Unspecified brand @ bar/restaurant	1.8	9.5	8.5
Other	.8	4.3	7.5
Drinks or glasses in last 30 days:			
Light: none	4.4%	41.7%	1.7%
1	1.3		
Medium: 2	1.6	31.0	17.9
3	.9		
4	1.0		
5	.8		
Heavy: 6	.6	27.4	80.4
7	.3		
8	.3		
9 or more	2.7		
Men	109	114† 111†	122 118	139 83
Women	92	87 90	80 84	65 116

(continued)

EXHIBIT 4   (*continued*)

| | B. Total and Selected Brands All Vodka | | Absolut | Popov | Smirnoff | Stolichnaya | Unspecified Brand At Bar/ Restaurant |
	All Drinkers Index	Heavy Drinkers* Index	All Drinkers Index	All Drinkers Index	All Drinkers Index	All Drinkers Index	All Drinkers Index
Graduated college	140	128	182	180	116	215	171
Attended college	127	116	164	132	124	143	154
Graduated high school	95	98	75	78	102	76	82
Ages 18–24	116	122	189	138	137	135	142
Ages 25–34	109	96	152	76	117	149	116
Ages 35–44	109	77	89	88	101	125	113
Ages 45–54	105	124	64	102	106	73	71
Ages 55–64	92	108	32	128	76	58	97
Ages 65 and over	62	84	30	88	51	20	45
Household income							
$50,000 or more	137	134	179	135	126	161	121
$40,000–49,999	123	126	120	146	124	158	130
$35,000–39,999	98	109	100	72	93	124	79
$25,000–34,999	98	92	92	109	104	76	125
$15,000–24,999	80	94	48	75	83	53	77
Marketing region:							
N. England	145	161	155	111	129	171	151
Middle Atlantic	130	132	237	64	125	134	132
East Central	72	57	67	147	70	48	52
West Central	94	98	38	85	97	76	139
South East	84	82	60	74	83	69	65
South West	93	90	69	81	113	101	57
Pacific	105	110	87	150	102	140	120
Single	121	120	195	115	131	146	130
Married	97	94	75	97	94	81	90
Other	86	97	72	91	82	109	97
White	101	104	102	111	99	103	111
Black	89	63	87	17	108	59	22
Home owned	100	100	81	96	95	85	97
Daily newspapers:							
Read any	109	112					
Read one daily	104	105					
Read two or more dailies	128	135					
Sunday newspapers:							
Read any	114	110					
Read one Sunday	114	112					
Read two or more Sundays	116	97					
Heavy magazines/heavy TV	100	109					
Heavy magazines/light TV	120	104					
Light magazines/heavy TV	85	94					
Light magazines/light TV	95	93					

*More than five drinks or glasses in last 30 days.
†To be read: men are 14 percent more likely than women to be heavy users of Vodka: 11 percent more likely to drink Absolut Vodka.

EXHIBIT 4   *(concluded)*

C.   *Magazine Use of Heavy Vodka Drinkers (selected magazines only)*

	Index		Index
Barron's	56	New York Magazine	68
Byte	48	The New Yorker	110
Colonial Homes	56	PC World	194
Esquire	80	Penthouse	184
Fortune	193	Rolling Stone	106
Golf Digest	206	Runner's World	60
Guns & Ammo.	206	Scientific American	198
Health	56	Seventeen	48
Home	60	Sports Illustrated	109
Inc.	190	Travel & Leisure	270
Mother Earth News	51	True Story	43
Ms.	85	Vogue	157
Nation's Business	210	The Wall Street Journal	219
Newsweek	99	Working Woman	35

Source: Adapted from Mediamark Research, Inc.

labs had confirmed a taste difference in vodkas. The bureau ruled that it would look at the context of the word's use: that vodka has no distinctive taste but one vodka "can taste different from another vodka."[9] Carillon and TBWA planned to avoid the question altogether.

A more publicized issue facing the alcoholic-beverages industry was the question of alcohol's effects on society. In 1988, U.S. Surgeon General C. Everett Koop had called together a Workshop on Drunken Driving, the report of which was released in late 1988. The workshop called for restrictions on advertising and promotion and the raising of excise taxes that were primarily directed at the beer and wine segments. It also, however, called for higher excise taxes on liquor, a decrease in tax deductions allowable for alcohol ads, and the placement of warnings on print advertising. (Warnings on bottle labels had already been mandated by Congress.) Reaction from the alcoholic-beverage industry and broadcasters was swift, vocal, and highly critical.

The workshop and ensuing flap focused attention on a fundamental, long-standing issue of the role of advertising in consumption—its influence in general, through the advertising of adults-only products, and the influence of advertising on "abuse" versus "use." Critics of the report noted that it was based on conjecture and anecdotal evidence, and that it assumed a causal link between advertising and alcohol abuse (drunk driving) that had never been established by research. A 1987 study in the *Journal of Advertising*, for example, summarized findings as follows: "advertising has not generally been shown to *substantially* affect primary demand, relative to other influences."

---

[9]"U.S. May Let Vodka Advertisers Use 'Taste' but in a Limited Way," *Wall Street Journal*, June 28, 1989.

Nevertheless, in June 1989, Anheuser-Busch announced increased spending on its "Know when to say when" campaign. Expenditures were to be approximately $30 million a year, equivalent to its brand advertising, up from a $22 million average in recent years. Coors and Philip Morris's Miller announced similar increases to responsible-drinking programs. The Beer Institute, the industry trade group, planned to spend $2.5 million to publicize the programs already in place.

NEW DIRECTIONS

In October 1989, the holiday season and the possibility for another "blockbuster" advertising execution were drawing nearer. Recent ads had included a tag-line, "For gift delivery of Absolut Vodka (except where prohibited by law) call 1-800-243-3787," a reminder that the holiday party season would involve the giving, receiving, and consumption of spirits.

Case 4–4

*Reebok International Ltd.**

In June 1988, executives of Reebok International Ltd.'s Reebok Footwear Division (RFD) met to review the company's U.S. marketing communications program for the second half of the year. In addition to category advertising to promote specific product lines such as aerobic shoes, Reebok's vice president of advertising intended to pursue three multiproduct umbrella campaigns: television advertising during the 1988 Summer Olympics; television and print advertising with the tag line "Reeboks let U.B.U."; and print advertising to introduce Reebok's new performance feature, the Energy Return System.

In addition, Reebok executives had to review their marketing communications plan for the Human Rights Now! world concert tour. On March 29, Joe LaBonté, Reebok's president and chief operating officer, had announced that Reebok was joining Amnesty International (AI) in sponsoring this tour, which would celebrate the 40th anniversary of the United Nations' Universal Declaration of Human Rights. However, debate continued within Reebok about the merits of this sponsorship, about how aggressively Reebok

---

*Tammy Bunn Hiller prepared this case under the supervision of Professor John A. Quelch as the basis for class discussion rather than to illustrate either effective or ineffective handling of an administrative situation. Certain nonpublic data have been disguised. Copyright © 1988 by the President and Fellows of Harvard College. Harvard Business School case 9–589–027.

should publicize its association with the tour, and about how the proposed communications program for the tour related to RFD's overall marketing communications plan.

COMPANY BACKGROUND AND STRATEGY

Reebok's antecedent, J. W. Foster and Sons, was founded in England in 1895 as a manufacturer of custom track shoes that were marketed by mail worldwide. The company was renamed Reebok in 1958. In 1979, Paul Fireman bought the North American distribution rights. In 1984, he and his backers, principally Pentland Industries plc, bought the parent company.

Fireman's first imports into the United States were three styles of hand-stitched, high-priced running shoes. In 1982, convinced that interest in running would plateau and aerobics would become the next fitness craze, Fireman introduced the first aerobic/dance shoe, the Reebok Freestyle. The shoe was unique. It was made of garment leather. It was soft, supple, wrinkled at the toe, and comfortable to wear from day one. It was also more attractive than competitors' athletic shoes. Furthermore, it was the first athletic shoe specifically targeted at women.

With the introduction of aerobic shoes, Reebok began a period of phenomenal growth. Between 1982 and 1987, net sales grew from $3.5 million to $1.4 billion, and net income grew from $200,000 to $165 million. Reebok ranked first among major U.S. companies in sales growth, earnings growth, and return on equity for the years 1983 through 1987. Fireman's goal was for Reebok to become a $2 billion multinational by 1990.

Reebok's growth was accomplished through broadening of existing product lines, expansion into additional product categories, and acquisitions. Exhibit 1 presents a chronology of Reebok's new product line introductions and acquisitions. The company had five operating units: Reebok North America (which included RFD and the Reebok Apparel Division), Reebok International, Rockport, Avia, and Ellesse.

In 1987 RFD sold approximately 42.17 million pairs of shoes to its U.S. retailers. The shoes were sold to consumers for an average price of $43. RFD accounted for approximately 71 percent and 88 percent of Reebok's 1987 sales and operating profit, respectively. The division's sales and estimated operating income for 1983 through 1987 are shown in the following table:

RFD Sales and Estimated Operating Income ($ millions)

	1983	1984	1985	1986	1987
Net sales	$12.0	$64.0	$299.0	$841.0	$991.0
Cost of sales	6.8	37.9	171.0	475.0	562.0
Gross margin	$ 5.2	$26.1	$128.0	$366.0	$429.0
SG&A expense	4.0	14.0	52.0	131.0	169.0
Operating income	$ 1.2	$12.1	$ 76.0	$235.0	$260.0

In the 1980s, RFD diversified its product offerings dramatically. In 1979, the division sold three shoes. In 1988, it sold more than 300 different shoes in 10 product categories. Aerobic shoes accounted for 56 percent of the division's sales in 1984. In 1987, they constituted only 29 percent.

EXHIBIT 1   New Product Line Introductions and Acquisitions

Introductions	
Year	Product Line Introduced
1979	Reebok running shoes
1982	Reebok aerobic shoes
1983	Reebok tennis shoes
1983	Reebok fitness shoes
1984	Reebok children's athletic shoes
1985	Reebok apparel
1985	Reebok basketball shoes
1986	Reebok walking shoes
1987	Reebok volleyball/indoor court shoes
1987	Reebok sports conditioning shoes
1987	Reebok infants' and children's shoes
1987	Metaphors (women's casual comfort shoes)
1988	Reebok golf shoes
1988	Reebok cycling shoes

Acquisitions		
Date	Company Acquired	Product Line
October 1986	The Rockport Company	Casual, dress, and walking shoes
April 1987	Avia Group International, Inc.	Athletic footwear for aerobics, basketball, tennis, running, walking, fitness/sports conditioning, and volleyball
	Donner Mountain Corporation (subsidiary of Avia)	Walking and casual shoes and hiking boots
May 1987	John A. Frye Corporation	Leather boots and casual and dress shoes
June 1987	ESE Sports Ltd.	Reebok's Canadian distributor
January 1988	Ellesse USA, Inc.: exclusive rights to the Ellesse trademarks for the United States and Canada	Sportswear and athletic footwear

The division sold its shoes direct to retailers through 17 independent sales organizations. This sales force sold only Reebok-brand products and was paid on a commission basis. A staff of field service and promotion representatives, employed by Reebok, supported the sales force by traveling throughout the United States teaching retailers and consumers about the features and benefits of the division's shoes. RFD followed a limited distribution strategy. Its shoes were sold only through specialty athletic retailers, sporting goods stores, and department stores. They were not sold in low-margin mass merchandiser or discount stores.

RFD, like other major athletic shoe companies, contracted out all of its manufacturing. The shoes were made in eight countries. Most of them, 71 percent in 1987, were produced in South Korea. The division's large-volume needs, combined with labor disruptions in South Korea, caused supply problems in 1987. In late 1987, RFD added sourcing capacity in Taiwan, China, Thailand, the Philippines, and Indonesia. It also contracted to take all of the production of H.S. Corporation, a large South Korean footwear manufacturer that produced approximately 30 million pairs of shoes annually.

THE ATHLETIC FOOTWEAR INDUSTRY

Growth of the Industry

Between 1981 and 1987, the U.S. athletic footwear market more than doubled in size. Wholesale sales of branded athletic footwear neared $3.1 billion in 1987. Nonbranded footwear added another $0.4 billion. Reebok held a 32.2 percent share of branded athletic footwear in 1987, up from 3.3 percent in 1984.

The industry's dynamic growth began in the early 1980s with the running craze. The running shoe was a new product that did not replace existing lines. Compared with the sneakers of the 1970s, it was made of different materials, was more performance oriented, and was more expensive. It also became a fashion item as Americans embraced more casual, health-conscious lifestyles.

In 1983, running shoe sales declined dramatically as Americans turned to other forms of exercise. New categories such as aerobic and fitness shoes, however, continued to drive industry growth. The success of the aerobic shoe prompted many companies to develop women's shoes for traditionally male-dominated categories such as basketball. By 1987, walking shoes, targeted largely at older females, were the fastest-growing line. Industry experts expected 8 percent to 12 percent growth in the U.S. athletic footwear market in 1988.

In 1987, Reebok also held a 4.4 percent share of the $4.5 billion foreign-branded athletic shoe market. Development of foreign markets lagged three or four years behind that of the U.S. market. In 1987, the aerobics boom was just taking off in Europe, and the women's athletic shoe market was largely untapped.

The Competition

Nike, in second place, had an 18.6 percent market share, down from 31.3 percent in 1984. Founded in 1964, Nike rose to prominence in the late 1970s thanks to high-tech innovations in running shoes. In 1984, however, Nike ignored the aerobics trend, wrongly counting on its running shoes to sustain company growth. Its warehouses became over-stocked with running-shoe inventory, which Nike had to sell off through discount stores. This action tarnished Nike's reputation with the trade. From 1983 to 1985 its sales rose by only 9 percent. However, in 1985 the Air Jordan basketball shoe, named for Michael Jordan of the Chicago Bulls, generated sales of $100 million. In 1986, sales fell as quickly as they had risen when Jordan broke his foot early in the NBA season. That year Nike lost its number-one U.S. market share position to Reebok.

In 1987, Nike closed excess plant capacity, slashed overhead, and spent $23 million to promote its new Air line with a "Revolution in motion" advertising campaign that featured the Beatles' original recording of "Revolution." It also took advantage of Reebok's supply problems to revitalize its dealer relations.

Nike's expressed goal was to recapture the number-one spot from Reebok. For 1988, according to *Advertising Age* magazine, Nike was stepping up advertising spending by 36 percent to $34 million. Ten million dollars would be spent on network television for its new "Just do it" campaign, which would break in mid-August. In February 1988, Nike introduced a fashion-oriented nonathletic brand for women in an attempt to penetrate a market in which it was historically weak. The shoes, called IE, did not carry the Nike name.

Converse held an 8.1 percent share of the U.S. market in 1987, down from 11.2 percent in 1984. The Converse name was closely identified with canvas athletic shoes for children and teens, particularly for basketball. In 1988, the company introduced the Evolo line of leather athletic shoes featuring upscale Italian styling and aimed at a more fashion-conscious customer.

Adidas, the world's largest athletic shoe company, had a 5.7 percent U.S. share and a 25 percent world share in 1987. Headquartered in West Germany, Adidas lost $30 million on its U.S. sales. Its 1988 U.S. advertising budget was estimated at only $3 million.

Avia, owned by Reebok, was the fifth-largest competitor in the U.S. branded athletic shoe market. Avia emphasized design technology and targeted active athletic participants who valued performance and functionality over other product features. With 1987 sales of $157 million, its share was 4.9 percent, up from .4 percent in 1984. Avia's 1988 advertising budget of $20 million was double 1987 expenditures.

Industry experts grouped Avia with LA Gear (2.3 percent share) and Asics Tiger (2.2 percent share) as small companies with innovative products and the potential to become significant players in the market. Twenty-five other companies competed in the branded athletic shoe market. Each had found a niche for itself, but none had been able to expand beyond it.

Competition remained keen in 1988. First, higher leather costs, increased labor rates, and a weakened dollar had increased the cost of Far East production by 10 percent in 1987. Further cost hikes, which would put pressure on the margins of all competitors, were expected in 1988. Second, in order to reduce inventory markdowns, retailers were narrowing their selections to only four or five brands and one or two lines of a few other brands. Third, athletic shoe product life cycles appeared to be shortening. By 1988 the life of a new model averaged only about nine months.

CONSUMER ATTITUDES AND BEHAVIOR

Paul Fireman credited Reebok's success to an ability to stay close to the consumer. "Consumer preferences are constantly changing," he contended, "and future progress is linked to our skill in understanding the messages sent from the marketplace so we can deliver the right products."

Industry experts segmented athletic shoe consumers into serious athletes, weekend warriors who used their shoes for sports but were not zealous athletes, and casual wearers who used athletic shoes only for streetwear. The "pyramid-of-influence" model, traditionally used in marketing athletic shoes, posited that the serious athlete was a very small segment of the market but an important opinion leader for both weekend warriors and casual wearers. Casual wearers accounted for 80 percent of athletic shoe purchases, wanted both style and comfort, and were thought to select shoes based on what they saw serious athletes wearing.

The pyramid model led athletic shoe marketers to emphasize technological and performance superiority in order to appeal to serious athletes. New shoes were first introduced in exclusive sports shops and gradually expanded into wider distribution.

The validity of the pyramid-of-influence model was questioned by some Reebok executives who believed that advertising directed at the serious athlete did not reach many consumers. They pointed to the results of a June 1986 survey that indicated that friends and relatives, not athletes, were the most important influence in athletic shoe users' brand decisions. Exhibit 2 shows the sources of information that athletic shoe purchasers used to decide which brand to buy. In addition, in a world where new athletic shoe styles could be knocked off in three months, the executives questioned the appropriateness of new product introductions not directed at the mass market.

In the 1986 survey, customers were asked how important various attributes were when deciding which athletic shoes to buy. Fifty-eight percent of respondents rated comfort extremely important, followed by support/stability (43 percent), design (36 percent), quality (35 percent), price (30 percent), fashion (20 percent), and leadership (12 percent).

An October 1987, attitude and usage study indicated that 95 percent of athletic shoe owners were aware of Reebok shoes, up from 57 percent two years before. Ninety-eight percent of all teens, a segment that purchased more than three pairs of athletic shoes per year, were aware of Reebok brand. Moreover, unaided awareness of Reebok had doubled over the past two years, whereas that of Nike had dropped. Fifty-three percent of teenagers

EXHIBIT 2 Sources of Information Used by Athletic Shoe Purchasers

		Reebok	
Information Source	Total	Users	Nonusers
Friend or relative	72%	69%	74%
Coach or instructor	65	64	65
Salesperson	54	53	54
Article in magazine	50	52	48
Advertisement	45	43	47

Note: All people included in the survey had bought athletic shoes for their own use within the 12 months prior to the survey and were aware of the Reebok brand. Reebok users were people who claimed to own and wear Reebok shoes fairly regularly. Reebok nonusers were people who did not.

surveyed considered Reebok the "in" shoe, compared with 38 percent for Nike. Reebok was also rated superior to its major competitors in both quality and comfort.

The brand had high penetration. Fifty-two percent of all people surveyed and 70 percent of the teens surveyed had owned Reebok shoes. Two years before, only 18 percent of people surveyed had ever owned Reebok shoes. Reebok's current ownership was 45 percent of those surveyed, higher than for any other brand. In addition, Reebok shoes were currently worn in 61 percent of the households in which athletic shoes were purchased in 1987. The owners claimed to be loyal as well. Two out of three of those who last purchased Reebok intended to make Reebok their next purchase, a repurchase rate higher than that for any competing brand. Finally, Reebok owners were significantly more likely to buy athletic shoes at regular price than were nonowners.

The results of the attitude and usage study were positive. But a series of focus group interviews in October 1987 uncovered some disturbing qualitative information.[1] In past focus groups, when participants were asked to describe Reebok shoes, the most commonly used adjectives were *innovative, vivid, adventurous, experimental, special, vibrant,* and *new*. The October 1987 focus group members, however, used words such as *comfortable, youthful, energy, fun, diverse, clean, leader, a standard,* and *middle class*. Teens said they were still buying Reeboks, but the way they talked about them had changed. They used to brag about their Reeboks. Now some teens apologized for them. At the same time, participants insisted that Reebok was not a badge brand. In other words, wearing Reeboks did not brand one as a jock or a yuppie or any other "type." "My Reeboks" meant something different to each person.

Sharon Cohen, vice president of advertising and public relations for Reebok North America since 1984, concluded: "When Reebok was new, just being discovered, we had a cult-like following. We were fresh and exciting and had brought new dimensions to the athletic-shoe industry—style and comfort. Today we are a mass-appeal shoe, and this requires new strategic thinking. Now that everyone is wearing Reeboks, our job and the job of our advertising is to keep our brand exciting."

MARKETING COMMUNICATIONS

Before 1987

According to Cohen, Paul Fireman "always started with advertising. If he had only $100, he'd spend it on advertising." In the early years of the company, he made his own media buys. He bought astutely, making ad hoc print media purchases at low rates to make the brand ad as visible as possible even though sales were modest.

By the early 1980s, RFD's advertising program consisted of product-specific, sports-context print ads, heavy concentration in specialty periodicals targeted at serious athletes, lighter buys in related general-interest magazines, media-exposed use of the products by a select group of successful-athlete endorsers, and a great emphasis on grass-roots involvement.

---

[1]A focus group brings together 6 to 10 individuals for an open-ended discussion led by a moderator.

Reebok paid star athletes to wear the Reebok label and to participate in Reebok-sponsored promotions such as tennis clinics and autographing sessions. These athletes could also earn bonuses by winning specified tournaments/games/events or by winning specified honors within their sports, or both. In addition, lesser athletes, mostly promising youngsters, received free shoes and clothing from Reebok but were paid nothing. By supporting their training efforts in this way, Reebok increased the likelihood of signing them to endorsement contracts if they excelled later.

RFD's marketing of aerobic shoes exemplified its heavy grass-roots involvement in the sports addressed by its products. The division published aerobics newsletters, sponsored seminars and clinics, founded research on injury prevention, and created the sport's first certification program for instructors. It also offered aerobics instructors discounts on shoes and put Reebok shoes on the feet of many television aerobics instructors.

In addition, RFD communicated with its consumers through point-of-sale pieces and merchandising promotions in retail stores, outdoor advertising, radio, and, starting in 1986, television. RFD also advertised in trade publications, catalogues, and sales brochures to help its salespeople communicate better with their dealers.

As RFD's sales grew, so did its advertising, promotion, and public relations budgets. Combined, they grew from $2.7 million (4.2 percent of sales) in 1984 to $6.5 million (2.2 percent of sales) in 1985, $10 million (1.1 percent of sales) in 1986, and $34 million (3.4 percent of sales) in 1987.

In 1986, RFD began testing new approaches to advertising. It ran the advertisement shown in Exhibit 3, which featured a couple wearing Reebok shoes riding a motorcycle to brunch and was the first ad to feature an athletic shoe advertised outside of a sports context. It was followed by an 18-month-long campaign with the theme "Because life is not a spectator sport." Each print ad, an example of which is shown in Exhibit 4, emphasized the participant and the joy of the sport, not the shoe and its attributes. The ads used an unusual technique called prism color in which photographs were transformed into pastel acrylic painting. They ran in a balanced mix of 40 general-interest and specialty sport magazines.

The 1987 Program

Each year RFD developed a divisional marketing communications budget plus separate budgets for each category of sports shoe. Category managers were responsible for the decision making and management of their budgets, and Cohen was responsible for managing the divisional budget. Cohen and the category managers all reported to Frank O'Connell, the president of Reebok North America. Exhibit 5 presents the division's marketing organization in relation to the total corporation.

RFD's 1987 divisional advertising budget is outlined in Exhibit 6. In 1987 RFD advertised via print, radio, and television directed toward both the trade and consumers. Trade advertising, illustrated in Exhibit 7, emphasized that "Reebok is performance." Consumer advertising through July focused on the "Because life is not a spectator sport" campaign. In August the division began a new multi-themed campaign with different television and print ads designed for each sports category. Depending on the sport, print

EXHIBIT 3   1986 Reebok "Motorcycle" Print Ad

EXHIBIT 4   1986 Reebok "Spectator Sport" Print Ad

EXHIBIT 5 Reebok Footwear Division Marketing Organization

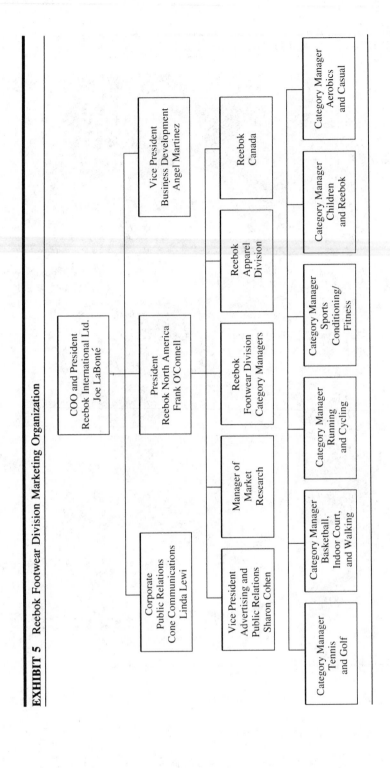

EXHIBIT 6   Reebok Footwear Division 1987 Advertising Budget ($000)

Television	
Network	$ 6,354
Spot	2,107
Cable	222
Total TV	$ 8,683
Radio Spot	$ 179
Print	
Magazines	$ 7,475
Newspapers	166
Total print	$ 7,641
Outdoor and other	$ 350
Total	$16,853

ads addressed one or more of four themes: performance, new technology, "classic" styling, and fashion. Exhibits 8 through 11 show ads for four sports categories. Five television ads each sold a different sports shoe, but all dramatically employed motion and featured "real people," not high-profile athletes. Radio was used to reinforce the television message.

The variety in RFD's 1987 advertising effort was exemplified by contrasting the second-half advertising of shoes in two sports categories, tennis and basketball. Tennis shoe advertising was targeted at 18- to 49-year-old adults. The category manager's $975,000 advertising budget was split nearly equally between television and magazines. Both the magazine and television copy evoked tennis tournaments. The television ads were shown only during the U.S. Open. The print ads ran in nine tennis magazines, including *Tennis and Racquet Quarterly,* and three general sports magazines, including *Sports Illustrated.*

Men's basketball shoe advertising was targeted at 12- to 24-year-old males. Approximately $3.2 million was spent, 60 percent on television, 24 percent on print, and the rest on radio. Ads in all media showed amateur players in action on neighborhood playground basketball courts. Television ads ran on network prime time and late night and during sports events. Magazines used were *Sports Illustrated, Boys' Life,* and *High School Sports.*

Women's basketball shoe advertising was targeted at female teens. The $960,000 women's basketball shoe budget, like that for tennis, was split evenly between television and print. Unlike the tennis ads, however, the basketball ads were fashion-oriented and did not show shoes being used in sports contexts. The television ad ran on early-fringe, weekend, and late-fringe network TV and on the MTV (music television) cable channel. The print ads ran in seven general-interest, fashion, and teen magazines, including *People, Glamour,* and *Seventeen.*

In addition to product-specific advertising, RFD sponsored a special insert in *Rolling Stone* magazine. The insert, titled "Artists of the Year 1967–1986," featured five Reebok shoe ads. These ads were one-offs, that is, they were used only once, in the *Rolling*

EXHIBIT 7 1987 Reebok Trade Advertisement

342

EXHIBIT 8   1987 Reebok Tennis Shoe Print Ad

EXHIBIT 9   1987 Reebok Basketball Shoe Print Ad

EXHIBIT 10   1987 Reebok Running Shoe Print Ad

EXHIBIT 11   1987 Reebok Aerobic Shoe Print Ad

Body developed by Kathryn Hamerski,
aerobic instructor, Minneapolis, Minnesota.
Foot support developed by Reebok.

Stone insert. Each ad featured someone giving a "Best performance in a pair of Reeboks" in a decidedly nonsports context. Exhibit 12 shows one of the ads.

Grass-roots promotions and athlete endorsements remained a large part of RFD's communications program in 1987, costing approximately $18 million. Promotional events included sponsorship of tennis tournaments for juniors and celebrities, the Reebok Teaching Pro Classic for tennis professionals, the Reebok Professional Aerobics Instructor Alliance, and the Reebok Racing Club. Shoe endorsers included basketball players Dennis Johnson, Danny Ainge, and Brad Daugherty, marathoner Steve Jones, tennis players Hana Mandlikova and Miloslav Mecir, aerobics expert Denise Austin, and the members of the U.S. National Cycling Team.

The 1988 Program

Category Advertising. The 1988 category budgets totaled approximately $22 million, $8 million of which was earmarked for category-specific print and television ads. The rest was allocated to athlete endorsements and grass-roots promotional events. The communications program for each category varied widely, as exemplified by the allocation of the 1988 budgets for tennis and basketball shown in Exhibit 13.

Almost 75 percent of the tennis category expenditures in 1988 were allocated to athlete endorsements and local and national tournament sponsorship. The objective was to maintain Reebok tennis shoes' credibility in the world of tennis. Reebok currently had a 40 percent share of the U.S. tennis shoe market, and marketed the five best-selling tennis shoes in the world. Fewer than 10 percent of Reebok tennis shoes sold, however, were used on the tennis court; the rest were used for streetwear.

Tennis shoe print advertising in 1988 was geared toward casual usage. Thirty percent of the budget was allocated to hard-core performance-oriented ads. The rest was allocated to lifestyle/fashion-oriented ads, a departure from the strict performance orientation of the past.

Reebok basketball shoes, introduced in late 1985, were the best-selling basketball shoes in the United States. The category's 1988 television and radio ads featured people talking about the greatest basketball players they had ever seen, the "legends" of the old playgrounds. Print and outdoor ads showed "real" people engaged in playground basketball. Consumer promotions were of two types. First, a court-painting program sponsored renovation of basketball courts in low-income areas. Second, 10 local basketball tournaments, such as the Gus Macker 3-on-3 tournament in Belding, Michigan, were sponsored. Players under contract to Reebok attended the events to heighten their impact.

"U.B.U." Umbrella Advertising. From the 1987 consumer research, Frank O'Connell concluded that RFD needed a new umbrella campaign to rekindle the vitality of the Reebok name while ensuring its continuity as a mainstream brand. He charged Chiat/Day with developing advertising copy that was "on the edge, far out, with a unique look that would be new not only to footwear advertising, but to the whole advertising industry." Chiat/Day recommended that the new campaign stress freedom of expression and the individuality that one could achieve wearing a pair of Reeboks, but at the same time maintain the brand's mass appeal.

EXHIBIT 12   Reebok Ad from 1987 *Rolling Stone* Magazine Insert

Best Performance in a pair of Reeboks February 12, 1982

EXHIBIT 13   1988 Tennis and Basketball Allocation of Marketing Communications Budgets

Communications Program	Basketball	Tennis
Athlete endorsements	32%	59%
Magazine ads	3	15
Television ads	37	—
Newspaper ads	4	—
Radio	5	—
Consumer promotions	8	12
Associations and clubs	—	7
Outdoor	5	—
U.S. Open sponsorship	—	7
Merchandising aids	6	—
Total	100%	100%

The result was an offbeat campaign with the tag line "Reeboks let U.B.U." The ads featured zany vignettes of people expressing their individual styles in their Reebok shoes: a three-legged man strutting in a basketball cap and raincoat, a girl dressed like a princess emerging from a subway exit wearing her crown and her Reeboks, a bevy of wood nymphs tiptoeing through a forest glade, a room full of pregnant women aerobic dancing, and a young couple rolling on the grass. Throughout the television commercials, "U.B.U." flashed on the screen in large, jagged, typewritten-style letters. In the final seconds of each ad, "Reeboks let U.B.U." appeared across the screen. The ads would be targeted at 18- to 34-year-old adults, particularly women. They would be run on prime-time and late-night shows such as "The Wonder Years," "Moonlighting," "LA Law," "thirty-something," and "Late Night with David Letterman" and on cable channels such as MTV, ESPN, and WTBS.

The proposed "U.B.U." print campaign used a revolutionary new colorization process. A marriage of photography and illustration, its finished product resembled that of colorized videos. The print ads, like the television ones, featured self-expression in Reebok shoes and used the same tag line. Exhibit 14 shows a sample print ad. The ads would run in fashion magazines such as *Esquire* and *Glamour*, entertainment magazines such as *People*, and lifestyle/special-interest magazines such as *Rolling Stone, Self,* and *New York Woman.* Insertions would begin in August issues and run at least through December. In addition, ads would appear in July editions of five athletic shoe trade magazines.

Olympics Advertising.   RFD purchased $6 million worth of television advertising time during NBC's coverage of the 1988 Summer Olympics, which spanned the last two weeks of September. Although Reebok shoes were not "Official Products of the 1988 Summer Olympics," this media purchase represented the largest concentrated spending level in the history of the athletic footwear industry and ensured the Reebok brand exclusivity in athletic footwear advertising during NBC's coverage of the Summer Games. The Olympics

EXHIBIT 14 1988 "Reeboks Let U.B.U." Print Ad

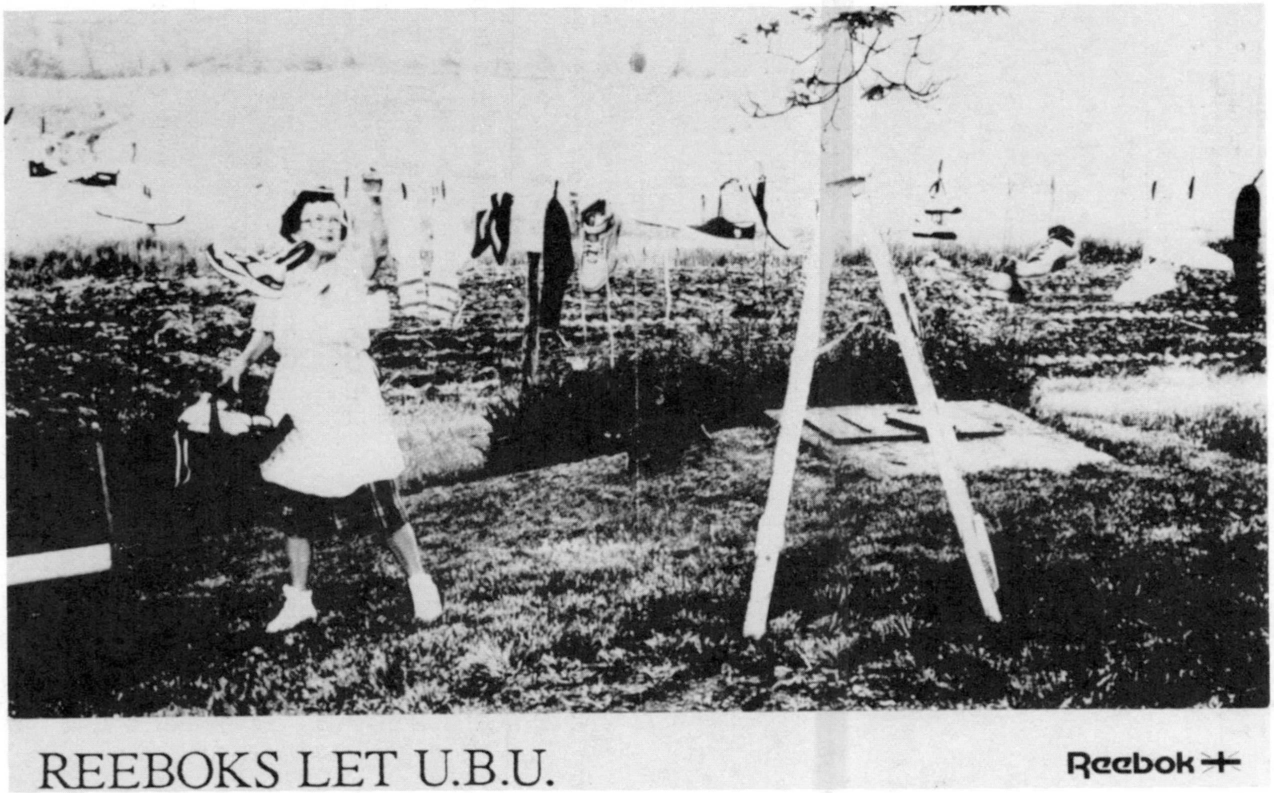

advertising was expected to excite Reebok brand dealers, many of whom believed that the principal way to sell athletic shoes was through ads associating them with sports.

The next step was to finalize copy for both the Olympics campaign and the umbrella campaign. The copy proposed by Chiat/Day for the Olympics ads featured "real" people wearing Reebok shoes frantically engaged in street or front-yard sports. Commercials began with the tag line "Summer Games, Bronx, New York" (or Baltimore, Maryland, etc.). At the end of each commercial, one person stopped his or her action and stated, "And you thought all the excitement was in Seoul."

ERS. Both the Olympics and "U.B.U." ads would be targeted at style-conscious 18- to 34-year-old adults. In order to reach active sports participants, RFD also planned to run a performance-based print campaign featuring Reebok's new Energy Return System (ERS). ERS shoes were designed to compete with Nike's Air line in the $75–$90 per pair retail price range. Compressed air—sandwiched in four brightly colored tubes visible through the sole of the shoe—cushioned the foot when it hit the ground, captured some of the energy released, and returned to it the foot for extra bounce. The proposed ERS ads would carry the slogan "The revolution is over" in response to Nike's successful 1987 "Revolution" campaign. Exhibit 15 shows a sample ad. The ads would run from June to December in sports magazines such as *Runner's World, Outside,* and *Sports Illustrated.*

RFD's divisional marketing communications budget would cover the $17 million combined cost of the "U.B.U.," Olympics, and ERS campaigns through the end of 1988. Exhibit 16 provides a breakdown of the proposed ad spending by campaign and media.

THE HUMAN RIGHTS NOW! TOUR

While O'Connell, Cohen, and Chiat/Day were developing copy for RFD's freedom-of-expression umbrella campaign, an opportunity arose to help finance a world concert tour conceived by AI. The objective of the tour, later named the Human Rights Now! world concert tour, was to support AI's worldwide effort to develop awareness of the human rights guaranteed in the United Nations Universal Declaration of Human Rights.

Chiat/Day brought the idea to Reebok and suggested that it help underwrite the tour in order to reach young people with a positive message about the company. Before proceeding, Joe LaBonté commissioned a telephone survey of 1,000 U.S. adults to determine their awareness of and attitude toward AI. Awareness was highest (60 percent) among people 18 to 34 years old. Almost half of this age group (49 percent) had a favorable attitude toward AI, and only 7 percent had an unfavorable attitude. The rest were neutral or unaware.

Joe LaBonté decided to support the Human Rights Now! world concert tour because he believed in the tour's cause and because it offered the opportunity to give something back to the young people who were responsible for the company's success. After discussions with Paul Fireman, he committed Reebok as sole underwriter of the tour. He felt that the time it would take for AI to enlist several sponsors would likely delay the concert tour until 1989. In addition, being sole corporate sponsor would give Reebok a greater voice in tour promotion decisions than if the job were shared.

EXHIBIT 15 1988 Reebok "Energy Return System" Print Ad

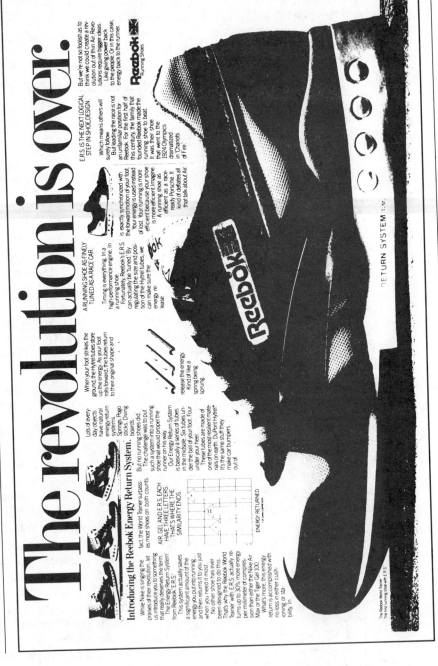

EXHIBIT 16   Reebok Footwear Division, Proposed 1988 Advertising Budget Spending by Campaign ($000)

Campaign	Television	Magazines	Outdoor	Total
"U.B.U."	$ 8,000	$1,900	$700	$10,600
Olympics	6,000	0	0	6,000
ERS	0	600	0	600
Total	$14,000	$2,500	$700	$17,200

Note: Budget excludes individual category communications budgets and Human Rights Now! tour budget. An additional $1 million in sports-specific ERS print ads would be paid for out of individual category manager budgets.

LaBonté announced Reebok's underwriting of the tour at a press conference in Los Angeles on March 29. At the same time, telegrams announcing the sponsorship were sent to all of Reebok's retailers. Soon thereafter, letters explaining Reebok's involvement with the tour and the Reebok Human Rights Award were mailed to all Reebok employees, U.S. Reebok sales agencies, and Reebok International Division distributors.

Once committed to the tour, LaBonté formed a task force consisting of himself; Linda Lewi, vice president of Cone Communications, Reebok's public relations agency; and Angel Martinez, vice president of business development, to handle the public relations and advertising surrounding Reebok's involvement with the tour. Among their most important tasks was the management of relations between Reebok and AI.

AI was a nonpartisan organization with a worldwide grass-roots network that tried to ensure respect for human rights, the release of nonviolent prisoners of conscience, fair and prompt trials for all political prisoners, and an end to torture and executions. AI was funded by 700,000 members in 150 nations. It strove to be independent and impartial. The organization did not support or oppose any government or political system and accepted no financial contributions from governments. AI's activities included letter-writing campaigns in which AI members sent letters, cards, and telegrams on behalf of individual prisoners to government officials; publicizing of human rights abuse patterns; and meetings with government representatives. Members also organized public awareness events such as vigils outside government embassies. Since its founding in 1961, AI had worked on behalf of more than 25,000 prisoners around the world. In 1987, more than 150 of the prisoners of conscience "adopted" by AI groups in the United States were released.

Human Rights Day, December 10, 1988, would mark the 40th anniversary of the Universal Declaration of Human Rights. Adopted by the General Assembly of the United Nations in 1948, the declaration, based on the twin pillars of freedom from want and freedom from fear, proclaimed fundamental and equal rights for "all people and nations." On March 3, 1988, AI launched its most ambitious campaign ever, titled Human Rights Now! Its goals were to mobilize public opinion and pressure governments to honor the declaration. In March, AI circulated copies of the declaration and petitions in support of it around the world. The combined petition would be presented to the United Nations on December 10.

In 1986, AI had sponsored an American rock music concert tour that brought AI 100,000 new members, most of whom were high school and college students. This success led AI to view music as an important vehicle to spread its message. Hence the Human Rights Now! world concert tour was conceived and scheduled to begin in September 1988. Although the venues and artists were not all finalized, AI hoped to include countries on five continents, including some with records of frequent human rights violations. Eighteen concerts were planned in 16 countries. Firm venues included Los Angeles, Philadelphia, London, and Brazil. Possibilities included Zimbabwe, the USSR, India, Thailand, Yugoslavia, Japan, Argentina, Italy, Spain, France, the Ivory Coast, Costa Rica, and Canada. The six-week tour would feature both international artists and national artists of each country in which the tour played. All artists would play for free. Sting, Peter Gabriel, Youssou N'Dour, and Tracy Chapman had committed themselves to the whole tour. Bruce Springsteen was considering joining the tour. If he did so, he would headline the event.

AI estimated that the tour would cost $22 million to produce. It expected to raise $12 million via ticket sales and broadcast rights. This left a $10 million shortfall. Therefore, for the first time in its history, AI sought corporate assistance.

In an agreement signed on April 22, Reebok made a commitment to provide $2 million seed money immediately and to finance the tour deficit to a maximum of $8 million. In addition, the nonprofit Reebok Foundation decided to fund up to $2 million.[2] The tour deficit was defined as the tour receipts received by AI from all sources other than Reebok and charitable contributions to AI minus all tour expenses.

AI had to consult with Reebok on all tour matters but had the final say on most aspects of the tour. Tour logo, name, and the design of tour merchandise required mutual approval. Reebok had certain rights to the tour name and logo as well as to photographs of the artists and audio and visual material created by AI and Reebok during the tour. Reebok could participate in the negotiation of the sale of television, radio, theatrical, and home video rights for any tour concert. The company could also create its own advertising with respect to the tour and its purposes. In addition, Reebok had the exclusive right to manufacture all tour merchandise, including clothing, posters, buttons, programs, videos, and books. The tour logo, advertising, promotional materials, and merchandise would all carry "Made possible by the Reebok Foundation" as a tag line. AI would be responsible for selling tour merchandise on the grounds of the concert on concert days. Reebok had the exclusive right to sell it through all other channels. Net profits from the sale of tour merchandise were considered tour receipts. In the unlikely event that merchandise net profits exceeded the tour deficit, the balance would be donated to AI.

To further emphasize Reebok's interest in human rights, the task force decided to establish the Reebok Human Rights Award, which was independent of AI. The $100,000 annual award, to be funded through the Reebok Foundation, would be split between two young people under 30 years of age, one male and one female. It would honor young people who, by circumstance or choice, acted against great odds to raise public awareness of and thereby help protect freedom of expression, or who suffered in their attempts to exercise their own freedom of expression.

---

[2]The Reebok Foundation was a nonprofit organization set up in 1987 to seek out grant opportunities. In its first year the foundation awarded grants to 32 organizations in the fields of education, arts/culture, human/social services, health, and religion.

In early June the task force met to finalize a marketing communications program for the tour. Lewi proposed the $5 million plan shown in Exhibit 17. This expense would be in addition to the cost of underwriting the tour. The plan consisted of pre-event, event, and postevent advertising, promotions, and public relations.

The proposed pre-event plan included the following: advertising the tour on national and spot radio; advertising on network and cable television stations via 20 public service announcements featuring celebrities talking about human rights abuses; advertising with spreads emphasizing a human rights theme in *Rolling Stone, Spin, L.A. Style, Details,* and *Interview* magazines and in the campus newspapers of the top 60 colleges and universities; speaking engagements by Reebok and AI executives before college leadership groups; interviews of AI executives and Human Rights Now! tour artists on "Good Morning America" and similar programs to explain the tour and the award; newsletters and information meetings for employees, sales agencies, and international distributors; and premiums such as T-shirts with the tour logo to be given to retail store clerks to stimulate their awareness of and excitement about the tour. The radio and magazine ads would break on August 1, followed by the television ads in mid-August and the campus newspaper ads in early September.

Tentative plans for the event communications included the following: broadcasting at least one of the concerts via network television or cable; interviews to be given by the artists and by AI and Reebok executives on "Good Morning America" and similar shows; a radio petition drive to affirm support for the Universal Declaration of Human Rights; promotions through bookstores and record stores offering free concert tickets and tour merchandise to winning consumers; employee and retailer sweepstakes with winners to be given free trips and tickets to concerts in Los Angeles or London; free tickets to be given to VIP customers in each country with a venue; hospitality suites set up at venues to entertain VIP customers; use of Reebok athletes to attend event parties and to give third-party endorsements of Reebok's underwriting of the tour; and invitations to all RFD employees to a closed-circuit viewing of one of the concerts.

The postevent plan included the following: stories released to leading newspapers, trade publications, and entertainment, lifestyle, and business magazines describing the tour's success and Reebok's charitable contribution to that success; sale of a tour documentary video and book; use of the video and book as retailer premiums; and the Reebok Human Rights Award ceremony.

The task force had to decide what changes, if any, to make to the proposed communications plan. Other Reebok executives were consulted before the meeting. Several sales managers queried, "How will this sell shoes?" They wished to explore opportunities for promotional tie-ins at the point of sale, and advocated running "U.B.U." ads during the television broadcasts of the concerts. They thought that every opportunity to exploit Reebok's association with the tour should be used to sell more shoes.

Other executives disagreed. They cited risks to Reebok from association with the tour and advised that the company keep its involvement with the tour low-key in its retail outlets. Some executives were also wary of involving Reebok's athletes in the tour communications program. They feared that any negative tour publicity could rub off on the athletes and damage their influence as opinion leaders.

At the outset of the meeting, LaBonté stated: "The Human Rights Now! concert

EXHIBIT 17   Proposed Marketing Communications Budget for Human Rights Now! Concert Tour and Reebok Human Rights Award

Marketing Unit	Proposed 1988 Budget
Advertising	
Media production	$ 50,000
Radio and campus media	1,575,000
Logo development	15,000
Merchandising brochures	25,000
Tour posters	100,000
Satellite network	375,000
Promotional materials	125,000
TV/video animated logo	15,000
Total advertising	$2,280,000
Public Relations	
Press kits	$ 6,325
Clerk program/newsletters	65,000
Media relations	215,000
Parties	30,000
Ticket purchases	187,500
Press conferences	220,000
Radio	50,000
Human Rights Award	190,000
PR fees	250,000
Human rights education/campus program	251,000
Total public relations	$1,464,825
Promotions	
Retail clerk premiums/contests	$ 200,000
Athletes program	60,000
Celebrity network TV, etc.	100,000
Internal support program	50,925
Distributors	3,000
Total promotions	$ 413,925
Merchandising	
Product for tour musicians and VIPs	$ 92,650
Staff	175,000
Other	
Contingency	250,000
Legal and accounting	260,000
Total other	$ 510,000
Total budget	$4,936,400

campaign promises to be the most exciting event this year in the athletic footwear industry. Our involvement with the tour must be perceived positively by our consumers, dealers, distributors, and employees. We must also ensure that the tour's advertising and promotion mesh with RFD's overall 1988 communications program."

Budgeting

Case 5–1

Chesebrough-Pond's Inc.: Vaseline Petroleum Jelly*

On September 2, 1977, Mary Porter was appointed product manager for Vaseline petroleum jelly (VPJ) and given three weeks to prepare the 1978 budget for the brand.[1] To project 1978 sales and profits she would have to develop a marketing plan that specified the level and nature of three types of marketing expenditures: advertising, consumer promotion, and trade promotion. Porter decided to begin by analyzing VPJ's marketing strategy over the previous five years, with particular emphasis on the nature, effectiveness, and profitability of its sales promotions.

COMPANY BACKGROUND

Vaseline petroleum jelly was the first product sold by the Chesebrough Manufacturing Company, founded by Robert Chesebrough in 1880. Chesebrough, who sold lamplighting oil, had frequently visited the oil fields of Pennsylvania, where he heard about a miraculous black jelly that formed on the rods of the oil pumps. He successfully duplicated this "rod wax" in his laboratory, lightened its color, and used a then unproven marketing technique—distribution of free samples—to introduce the product.

At the same time another entrepreneur, Theron Pond, distilled an improved kind of witch hazel from a native American shrub and sold it as a "pain-destroying and healing remedy." This product launched the Pond's Extract Company, which by the 1920s had become the leading U.S. marketer of popularly priced skin creams and cosmetics. Pond's also owed much of its early success to a marketing innovation: it was the first company to advertise with endorsements by socially prominent women.

In 1955, the two companies combined to form Chesebrough-Pond's Inc. (CPI), and Wall Street analysts hailed it "the marriage of the aristocrats." The new firm expanded through diversification. During the fiscal year which ended December 31, 1976, CPI's six divisions recorded after-tax profits of $54 million on net sales of $747 million.

---

*Research Assistant Penny Pittman Merliss prepared this case under the supervision of Professor John A. Quelch as the basis for class discussion rather than to illustrate either effective or ineffective handling of an administrative situation. Certain names and data have been disguised. Copyright © 1981 by the President and Fellows of Harvard College. Harvard Business School case 9–581–047.

[1]Vaseline, Pond's, Cutex, Q-Tips, Intensive Care, Ragu, Health-Tex, Adolph's, and Prince Matchabelli are registered trademarks of Chesebrough-Pond's Inc.

The Health and Beauty Products (HBP) Division, which accounted for 22 percent of CPI's 1977 sales, marketed VPJ. Although HBP's 1976 sales of $163 million were second only to those of the international division, HBP's five-year average growth rate of 9.3 percent was the second-lowest among CPI's divisions. The HBP Division also marketed Cutex nail care products, Pond's creams, Q-Tips cotton swabs, and Vaseline Intensive Care moisturizing products.

THE MARKET FOR PETROLEUM JELLY

Executives at HBP described petroleum jelly as "a household staple" used by over 90 percent of the population, but noted that both level and frequency of use varied substantially. A consumer survey indicated that heavy users were either women aged 45 years or older who viewed petroleum jelly as a multifunctional skin-care product or mothers who used petroleum jelly for baby care and did not consider it appropriate for their own skin care. Other results from this VPJ survey are reported in Exhibit 1.

Petroleum jelly sales to the consumer market at manufacturers' prices were estimated at $25 million in 1976, of which Vaseline petroleum jelly claimed a 90 percent share. (VPJ was also sold to institutions—hospitals, other medical facilities, and some industrial buyers. Porter was not responsible for these sales.) Direct competitors with VPJ were private label petroleum jellies, which sold primarily in 16-oz. jars at prices 30 percent below VPJ's through mass merchandisers such as K Mart. The Vaseline product did not appear to be losing share to these private labels, none of which was manufactured by CPI. It also competed in the broader skin-care market with special-purpose products, such as hand lotions and moisturizing creams.

Vaseline petroleum jelly was available in two forms, pure and carbolated; both were packaged in several sizes of jars and tubes. Carbolated VPJ was a specialized first aid product with an active ingredient. It was priced higher than pure VPJ and distributed primarily through drugstores. It was almost never featured at a discount by the trade and was not advertised separately. For several years carbolated VPJ had accounted for a stable 7 percent of VPJ dollar sales to consumers.

Exhibit 2 shows factory shipments of each size of pure VPJ from 1974 through 1977. More than half of VPJ's ounce volume was sold in the popular 3.75- and 7.50-oz. jars.

DISTRIBUTION AND PRICING

Vaseline petroleum jelly was distributed primarily through grocery, drug, and mass merchandise stores; these accounted for 85 percent of Vaseline's ounce volume. Sales through variety stores and other outlets accounted for the remainder. However, VPJ distribution varied by size among the major channels (as shown in Exhibit 3); the 15-oz jar, for example, was sold primarily through drugstores and mass merchandisers. Distribution penetration was high for the brand as a whole; in 1977 VPJ was carried in at least one size by 92 percent of grocery stores and 96 percent of drugstores.

All HBP products were sold by the same 130-person sales force. Salespeople focused on "headquarter accounts" rather than individual retail outlets. At least once a month HBP salespeople visited buyers at the head offices of food, drug, variety store, and mass

---

EXHIBIT 1 Results of VPJ Consumer Survey

During March 1977, personal interviews were conducted with 500 female heads of households who qualified as users of petroleum jelly (on the basis of having used petroleum jelly during the previous month). Sixty percent of those approached qualified.

- 90 percent of petroleum jelly purchasers last bought VPJ. When asked to name a brand of petroleum jelly, 97 percent mentioned VPJ; 23 percent recalled recently seeing or hearing VPJ advertising.
- 51 percent of heavy users were aged 18 to 34 years, and three-quarters of this group had a child under four years in their households. (Households using petroleum jelly at least once a day were considered heavy users; those using it less than twice a week were "light-using" households.)
- Heavy users made on average six purchases of petroleum jelly per year, whereas light users made on average only one purchase per year.
- 86 percent of respondents considered the size of petroleum jelly last bought their "regular" size. Heavy users were more likely than light users to purchase larger-size jars.
- 35 percent of respondents reported making their last petroleum jelly purchase in a food store, 30 percent in a drugstore, and 30 percent in a mass merchandise or discount store. Light users (46 percent) and users from households with a child under four years old (44 percent) were more likely to have made their purchases in food stores.
- 33 percent of heavy users and 46 percent of light users could not recall the price paid for the last jar of petroleum jelly they purchased.
- 70 percent of respondents agreed strongly with the statement "petroleum jelly is economical."
- 20 percent of respondents reported having more than one jar of petroleum jelly in their households.
- 86 percent of respondents stated that they kept a jar of petroleum jelly in the bathroom; 34 percent mentioned the bedroom, 6 percent mentioned the kitchen, and 2 percent mentioned the garage, basement, or workshop.
- The average quantity of petroleum jelly applied varied significantly by use from 3.1 g (sunburn) and 2.1 g (baby use) to 0.3 g (removing makeup) and 0.1 g (chapped lips). Share of total usage occasions also varied by use: 1 percent (sunburn), 4 percent (baby use), and 12 percent (chapped lips).
- The number of households using petroleum jelly was 15 percent lower in winter than summer. However, among user households, frequency of use was 25 percent higher in winter.
- For all except household uses (such as preventing rust and lubricating hinges), both the incidence and frequency of use were higher among females than males.

Source: Company records.

merchandising chains as well as buyers for wholesalers representing independent retailers in each class of trade. During 1976, chain purchases accounted for 45 percent of VPJ dollar sales to the consumer market.

Salespeople were compensated by a combination of salary and bonus based on achievement of volume quotas. Sales force management and HBP division executives negotiated quarterly volume quotas for each brand. In addition, they established a calendar of consumer and trade promotions for each brand, reflecting its need for sales force support and the number of promotion events the sales force could present to the trade at one time. Porter believed that the sales force viewed VPJ as a mature, unexciting brand which required frequent price promotions to stimulate trade interest. Salespeople often pressed for such promotions toward the end of each quarter to help achieve their quotas.

EXHIBIT 2 Pure VPJ Factory Shipments by Size, 1974–1977 (thousands of dozens)

Size (oz.)	1974	1975	1976	1977*
1.75 (jar)	1,069.5	873.6	1,012.5	849.6
	(100)†	(82)	(95)	(79)
3.75 (jar)	997.7	973.2	1,137.5	1,116.1
	(100)	(98)	(114)	(112)
7.50 (jar)	540.8	544.4	773.2	628.3
	(100)	(101)	(143)	(116)
12.00 (jar)	216.7	186.3	192.7	157.5
	(100)	(86)	(89)	(73)
15.00 (jar)	249.8	227.1	292.1	293.1
	(100)	(91)	(117)	(117)
1.00 (tube)	114.2	104.3	120.2	106.7
	(100)	(91)	(105)	(93)
3.75 (tube)	47.7	34.2	41.6	33.3
	(100)	(72)	(88)	(70)
Total	3,236.4	2,943.1	3,569.8	3,184.6
	(100)	(91)	(110)	(98)
Equivalent units‡	543.6	504.5	626.9	562.3
	(100)	(93)	(115)	(103)

*1977 sales estimated as of July 31.
†Numbers in parentheses are indices based on 1974 factory shipments by size (base = 100).
‡One equivalent unit = 360,000 oz.

Source: Company records.

EXHIBIT 3 Pure VPJ Jar Sales Volume by Outlet Type, May–June 1977 (equivalent ounce basis)

Jar Size (oz.)	Grocery	Drug	Mass Merchandiser	Total
1.75	6%	3%	0.2%	9%
3.75	18	7	2.0	28
7.50	16	8	5.0	29
12.00	8	3	2.0	13
15.00	5	11	6.0	21
Total	53%	32%	15.0%	100%

Note: To be read, "Of the 85 percent of VPJ ounce sales through the three principal channels of distribution, 6 percent were 1.75-oz. jars sold through grocery stores."

Source: Company records.

Prices for VPJ were approved by the division general manager, whose key aim was profit improvement. (Exhibit 4 lists factory and suggested retail prices as of July 1977.) The suggested prices allowed retailers who purchased direct from CPI a 40 percent margin, but actual retail prices were often 10 percent lower, particularly in grocery stores and mass merchandise outlets. In 1974, escalating petroleum costs required price increases

EXHIBIT 4 Pure VPJ Price List, July 1977

Size (oz.)	Suggested Retail Price (SRP)	SRP per Ounce	Suggested Wholesale Price (SWP)	SWP per Ounce	Manufacturer's Selling Price (MSP)	MSP per Ounce	MSP per Dozen
1.75 (jar)	$0.57	$0.33	$0.403	$0.230	$0.342	$0.195	$ 4.10
3.75 (jar)	0.79	0.21	0.558	0.149	0.473	0.126	5.68
7.50 (jar)	1.19	0.16	0.840	0.112	0.713	0.095	8.56
12.00 (jar)	1.59	0.13	1.122	0.094	0.953	0.079	11.44
15.00 (jar)	1.69	0.11	1.193	0.080	1.013	0.068	12.16
1.00 (tube)	0.69	0.69	0.487	0.487	0.413	0.413	4.96
3.75 (tube)	1.25	0.33	0.883	0.235	0.750	0.200	9.00

Note: Suggested retail prices allowed retailers a 40.0 percent margin on direct purchases from the manufacturer and a 29.4 percent margin on purchases from wholesalers. Suggested wholesale prices allowed wholesalers a 15.1 percent margin on purchases from the manufacturer.

ranging from 37 percent on the 15-oz. size to 70 percent on the 1.75-oz. size. Annual price increases between 1975 and 1977 had added a further 18 percent to manufacturer prices. Variable manufacturing costs for VPJ were expected to rise by 5 percent in 1978.

MARKETING EXPENDITURES

The three principal areas of VPJ marketing expenditures were advertising, consumer promotion, and trade promotion. Sales force expenses were treated as division overhead and not allocated among brands. The brand budgets for VPJ from 1975 through 1977 are summarized in Exhibit 5.

Advertising

The primary objective of VPJ advertising through the 1970s was to increase sales by suggesting new product uses. Earlier brand advertising had concentrated almost exclusively on baby care, but in 1972 the message began to include VPJ's versatility as a skin-care product for adults and children (see Exhibit 6). Some HBP executives believed that VPJ advertising should present product uses beyond skin care; others thought that emphasizing VPJ's usefulness as a shoe-shining aid or hinge lubricant might cause some consumers to stop using it for skin or baby care.

Bi-monthly VPJ advertising expenditures showed substantial period-to-period fluctuations (see Table 1). Porter believed these indicated a lack of sustained commitment to advertising as well as management's tendency to cut fourth-quarter advertising expenditures to meet annual profit targets.

Media selection showed greater consistency. Network television was the principal medium for VPJ advertising; print media were used primarily to announce VPJ consumer

EXHIBIT 5   VPJ Brand Budgets, 1975–1977 ($000)

	1975		1976		1977*	
Gross sales†	$17,792	(100%)	$22,491	(100%)	$22,938	(100%)
Variable manufacturing costs	8,616	(48)	10,618	(47)	10,572	(46)
Gross margin	$ 9,176	(52)	$11,873	(53)	$12,366	(54)
Advertising‡						
TV: Network	1,280		1,526		1,720	
Spot	97		586			
Print: Magazine	44		141		62	
Sunday supplement			38		45	
Newspaper					97	
Total	1,590	(9)	2,410	(11)	2,123	(9)
Consumer promotion	137	(1)	448	(2)	330	(1)
Trade promotion	1,810	(10)	2,468	(11)	2,202	(10)
Total marketing expenditures	$ 3,537	(20)	$ 5,326	(24)	$ 4,655	(20)
Profit before SG&A expenses, overhead, and taxes	$ 5,639	(32%)	$ 6,547	(29%)	$ 7,711	(34%)

*Revised budget as of July 31, 1977. By September 1977 it appeared that these estimates would closely match actual results.

†Before deductions of off-invoice and base contract allowances; includes sales of both pure and carbolated VPJ.

‡Includes production costs and public relations expenditures as well as media costs.

Source: Company records.

promotions. Both electronic and print media advertising rates rose on average 15 percent annually between 1974 and 1977.

Consumer Promotion

Historically, VPJ brand management had spent little money on consumer promotion. During 1973 only one consumer promotion (a 10-cent coupon) was run; in 1974, none occurred. In 1975, however, three events were run: a free glass jar packaged with the 7.5-oz. VPJ, a 10-cent cross-ruff coupon[2] packed in 2 million boxes of Procter & Gamble's Ivory Snow, and a 50-cent refund offer for two VPJ proofs of purchase.

1976 VPJ Events.   Consumer promotion expenditures continued to increase during 1976; that year marked four events, each coinciding with a promotion to the trade.

1. *February:* A $2 cash refund offer involving VPJ and four other HBP brands was announced in the February issues of *Family Circle* and *Ladies' Home Journal* and in full-page, four-color Sunday newspaper supplement advertisements on February 15

---

[2]A cross-ruff coupon is carried either on or inside the package of a non-competitive brand. It is used when the target markets of the sponsor and carrier brands are similar.

EXHIBIT 6 1977 VPJ 30-Second Television Commercial (titled "Year Round")

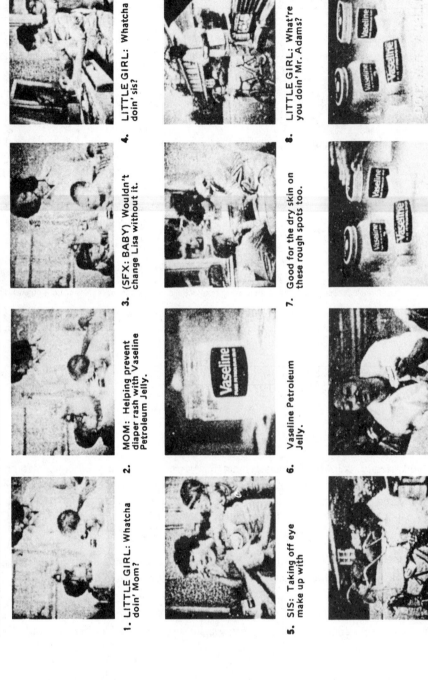

1. LITTLE GIRL: Whatcha doin' Mom?

2. MOM: Helping prevent diaper rash with Vaseline Petroleum Jelly.

3. (SFX: BABY) Wouldn't change Lisa without it.

4. LITTLE GIRL: Whatcha doin' sis?

5. SIS: Taking off eye make up with

6. Vaseline Petroleum Jelly.

7. Good for the dry skin on these rough spots too.

8. LITTLE GIRL: What're you doin' Mr. Adams?

9. MR. ADAMS: I got a little burn. I am soothing it,

10. with Vaseline Petroleum Jelly.

11. ANNCR: (VO) In all seasons, for all reasons ...

12. ...do it with Vaseline Petroleum Jelly.

TABLE 1 Index of Bimonthly Measured Media Advertising for VPJ, 1974–1977

	1974	1975	1976	1977
January–February		83	78	113
March–April		64	103	92
May–June	100	36	39	102
July–August	108	114	128	97
September–October	49	100	132	
November–December	42	11	136	

Note: (Base: May–June 1974 = 100.) Figures not adjusted for media cost inflation.

Source: Company records.

    (see Exhibit 7). Consumers could also learn of the offer at the point of purchase through four-color riser cards for end-aisle and cut-case displays, and shelf talkers including refund applications, which were shipped to retailers with each case of VPJ.[3]

2. *April:* To coincide with National Baby Week, one dollar's worth of coupons for five HBP brands used in baby care (including a 15-cent coupon for any size VPJ) were carried inside 4.65 million boxes of Kimbies disposable diapers. Coupons for Kimbies were carried by two participating HBP brands.

3. *June:* A shrink-wrapped twin pack of two 3.75-oz. jars of VPJ, with a label encouraging consumers to keep one jar in the kitchen and the other in the bathroom, was preticketed with a retail price of 99 cents. The pack also included a 50-cent refund offer for proofs of purchase from two 3.75-oz. jars. The twin pack was shipped only in cases of three dozen, to encourage the trade to feature it in special displays. (Exhibit 8 shows merchandising flyer.)

4. *September:* An eight-page "programmed learning" advertisement was run in *Reader's Digest* (October 1976) to educate consumers about skin care and the uses of VPJ, Vaseline Intensive Care lotion, and Vaseline Intensive Care bath beads. The reader could answer a "skin test" on a mailable pop-up card which doubled as an entry to the Vaseline Soft-to-Touch sweepstakes. Sweepstakes prizes, such as fur coats and cashmere sweaters, all emphasized the soft-to-touch theme. The sweepstakes was an attention-getting overlay to a $1.50 cash refund offer for a proof of purchase from each of the three participating brands. The offer was also advertised through riser cards and shelf talkers at the point of purchase (see Exhibit 9).

    The principal costs to VPJ for these events are summarized in Exhibit 10. For multiple-brand promotions, costs were allocated according to each brand's share of coupon or proof-of-purchase redemptions.

---

[3]Riser cards are attention-getting signs placed above a special display. Cut-case displays are shipping cartons that could double as store display units when cut to shape by store personnel; these allow retailers to display a product without unpacking it. Shelf talkers are small signs attached to the front of the shelf on which the product is regularly stocked.

EXHIBIT 7   1976 Newspaper and Magazine Advertisement for $2 Cash Refund Program

EXHIBIT 8   1976 Merchandising Flyer for VPJ Twin-Pack Promotion

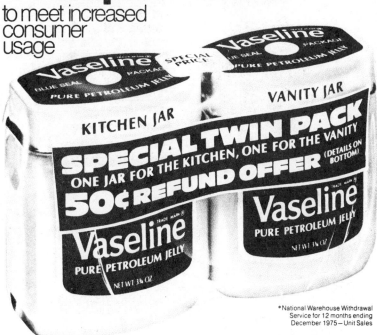

#1 selling baby item delivers multiple sales*
to meet increased consumer usage

KITCHEN JAR
VANITY JAR

SPECIAL TWIN PACK
ONE JAR FOR THE KITCHEN, ONE FOR THE VANITY
50¢ REFUND OFFER (DETAILS ON BOTTOM)

Vaseline PURE PETROLEUM JELLY
Vaseline PURE PETROLEUM JELLY

*National Warehouse Withdrawal
Service for 12 months ending
December 1975 — Unit Sales

• Sales increased 28% with multi-usage TV advertising**

**National Retail Audit Firm-Dollar Sales- 1975

EXHIBIT 8   *(concluded)*

Combine

- Aggressive pricing
- 50c Cash Refund
- Effective Cross Merchandising

for Big Profits and Fast Sell-Through

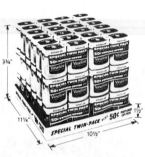

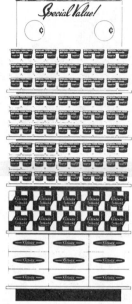

2 free with **10** off-invoice*

5% advertising allowance by separate check for a cut-price feature*

*One CPI salesman approved order only.

Product Information:

Description	Size	Code #	Sugg. Retail	Regular Cost Per Shipper	Special Cost Per Shipper	Special Cost Per Twin Pack	Shelf Pack	Case Pack
Twin Pack Display Shipper	3¾ oz.	2327-00	$1.50	$32.40	$26.99	$.749	—	3 doz. Twin Packs

Promotional Information:
Shipping Period: 6/1/76 – 6/25/76
Advertising Period: 6/1/76 – 7/23/76
Terms: 1% 30 days, net 31 days
Minimum Shipment: Regular CPI Minimums Apply
AFE #: 1-6-32-06
Display Shipper:
   Case Dimensions: 11¼ x 10½ x 9¾
   Case Cube: .682
   Case Weight: 23 lbs. per case

HEALTH & BEAUTY PRODUCTS DIVISION
Chesebrough-Pond's Inc.
GREENWICH, CONNECTICUT 06830

EXHIBIT 9 1976 Merchandising Flyer for $1.50 Cash Refund Program

A traffic builder reaching
1 out of 3 households

The biggest single
H&BA advertising event
ever run in Reader's Digest

- 18 million cash refund certificates
- 10 pages of "consumer stopping" advertising with a sweepstakes offer
- Reaching over 44 million adult readers

October issue on sale September 28

EXHIBIT 9   *(concluded)*

Merchandising for multiple sales

Riser card #2308-00
Shelf talker #2309-00

HEALTH & BEAUTY PRODUCTS DIVISION
Chesebrough-Pond's Inc.
GREENWICH, CONNECTICUT 06830

EXHIBIT 10   Costs to VPJ of 1976 Consumer Promotions

1. January: Allocated Cost to VPJ: $129,000

	Circulation (million)	Percent Response	Number of Responses	Cost per Response	Total Cost (five brands)
Sunday supplement	30.00	0.7	210,000 ⎫		⎧ $599,625
Magazines	14.50	0.2	29,000 ⎬	$2.25*	
Point-of-purchase materials	2.75	1.0	27,500 ⎭		
21,000 riser cards					27,225
60,000 shelf talkers					⎩ 15,375

2. April: Allocated Cost to VPJ: $56,620

	Circulation (million)	Redemption Rate (percent)	Number of Redemptions	Cost per Redemption	Total Cost (VPJ only)
Coupon redemption face value 15 cents*	4.65	4.0%	186,000	21.05 cents*	⎧ $39,150
Coupon artwork and printing					14,300
Package flagging and coupon insertion					⎩ 3,170

3. June: Cost to VPJ: $82,150

	Circulation (Number of twin packs)	Percent Response	Number of Responses	Cost per Response	Total Cost (VPJ only)
Refund offer	1,260,000	7.0	88,200	75 cents*	⎰ $66,150
Special packaging					⎱ 16,000

4. September: Allocated Cost to VPJ: $141,200

	Circulation (million)	% Response	Number of Responses	Cost per Response	Total Cost (three brands)
Reader's Digest	18.0	0.5	90,000 ⎫		⎧ $315,000
Point-of-purchase materials	4.5	2.0	90,000 ⎭	$1.75*	
30,000 riser cards					27,000
75,000 shelf talkers					13,000
Sweepstakes prizes, judging, handling					⎩ 54,000

*Includes face value of coupon or refund plus handling charges.

Source: Company records.

1977 VPJ Events.   Consumer promotion expenditures for VPJ were cut by one-quarter in 1977; only three promotion events were implemented.

1. *February:* A Swiss Army multipurpose knife was offered as a self-liquidating premium[4] on the labels of 7.5-oz. jars of VPJ. The knife, a $21.00 retail value bought by CPI for $10.00, was offered to consumers for $10.50 plus one VPJ front label. The 50-cent difference between purchase and selling prices covered handling. Costs of $18,000, however, were incurred for point-of-purchase display materials and 1,500 knives used as dealer loaders.[5]

2. *April:* A 25-cent coupon for large sizes of three HBP brands, including VPJ (15-oz.), was printed on packages of the 24-oz. size of Vaseline Intensive Care bath beads. To encourage multibrand displays at the point of purchase, a self-liquidating premium which doubled as a dealer loader was also offered and advertised in women's magazines. Because redemption of the on-pack coupons would be delayed until purchasers had used up the contents of the boxes, HBP managers believed an additional purchase incentive was necessary to stimulate special trade merchandising activity. Thus, in selected markets, a newspaper advertisement delivered 65 cents' worth of coupons on the three participating brands (including a 15-cent coupon toward a 15- or 12-oz. jar of VPJ). In other markets, newspaper advertising featured a $1 cash refund for proofs of purchase on two of the three brands.

3. *September:* A two-page advertisement in *Reader's Digest* (October 1977) and a similar advertisement in Sunday newspaper supplements delivered 50 cents' worth of coupons on three Vaseline brands, including a 10-cent coupon for VPJ. These advertisements, along with riser cards and shelf talkers at the point of purchase, also announced a $40,000 sweepstakes. To encourage potential entrants to find in-store Vaseline displays, the ads indicated that official entry forms and instructions were available at the point of purchase.

FUTURE CONSIDERATIONS

After reviewing the consumer promotion history, Porter wondered how much latitude she would have in planning the 1978 VPJ consumer promotions. She thought division management would again wish to include VPJ in several multiple-brand promotions. She suspected, however, that these were of most benefit to the weaker participants and that her consumer promotion dollars might be better spent on events exclusive to VPJ.

Timing the promotions was another problem. Some HBP managers believed consumer promotions should coincide with trade promotions. Others thought they should be launched between trade promotions, arguing that promotions should be spread more evenly to avoid wide demand fluctuations, which hampered efficient production and inventory control.

---

[4]A self-liquidating premium requires consumers to send cash as well as proof of purchase. The cash amount covers handling, mailing, and the cost of the premium, which is usually offered at 30% to 50% below normal retail price.

[5]A dealer loader is a sample of a premium displayed at the point of purchase until the end of the promotion, when it usually becomes the property of the store or department manager.

Porter realized that she first had to define her objectives for consumer promotion. Some HBP executives favored it to stimulate short-term sales. Others argued that indiscriminate use of premiums, coupons, and sweepstakes further increased consumer price sensitivity, and that consumer promotions were valuable only when they reinforced the brand's advertising image.

Trade Promotion

In general practice, trade promotions temporarily offered merchandise to the trade at a discount from the regular list price. Porter characterized how trade buyers usually responded to a manufacturer's limited-time trade promotion offer:

> They weigh the financial incentive of buying an above-normal quantity of the product at a discount against the financing costs associated with the additional inventory. Of course, they can minimize these costs—and make the manufacturer happy—by accelerating the product's movement off the shelves. To do this, they have to pass all or part of our incentive on to the consumer as a retail price cut. To achieve the greatest sales increases, they should feature the price cut in store advertising and set up a special in-store display.

Manufacturers used a variety of trade promotion allowances. Case allowances on products ordered during the promotion period offered either a reduction from list price on the invoice to the trade (for example, 10 percent off invoice) or free goods with a specified minimum purchase (for example, one case free with purchase of 10). Because manufacturers could not legally control retail prices, they had no assurance that case allowances would be fully or partially passed on to consumers as retail price reductions. (Many manufacturers, including CPI, sometimes permitted their trade accounts to take merchandise ordered during the promotion period in two shipments. Thus, the second shipment might arrive after the promotion and be sold at the manufacturer's regular suggested retail price.)

Additional merchandising allowances, also paid on a per-case basis, were sometimes offered. For example, a 10 percent allowance might be offered if the trade featured the product at a price discount in its consumer advertising. Or a special allowance might be offered to stores that set up end-aisle or off-shelf displays of prescribed size during the promotion period. Unlike off-invoice allowances,[6] these were paid only after the manufacturer received evidence of performance, such as an affidavit, advertising tear sheet, or display photograph.

In addition to case and merchandising allowances, manufacturers sometimes offered a *base contract* to the trade, by which any account buying a minimum quantity of the product received a percentage discount. A 5 percent base contract discount was offered on all VPJ orders over $75.

---

[6]Off-invoice and free-goods allowances are deducted from the bill sent to the trade. Merchandising allowances are paid on a "bill back" basis by separate check.

Past VPJ Events.   Given VPJ's dominance in its category, Porter was surprised to discover that over 70 percent of 1976 factory shipments were sold to the trade on promotion. The 1977 marketing plan outlined three objectives for VPJ trade promotion:

1. Stimulate cut-price feature advertising and displays, especially on larger sizes.
2. Reinforce and expand distribution of larger sizes in all trade channels.
3. Limit erosion of distribution of smaller sizes.

PORTER'S ANALYSIS

Porter summarized the terms and timing of VPJ trade promotions from late 1972 through mid-1977 (see Exhibit 11). She noted that a trade promotion had been offered on at least one size during every quarter of each year. Duration of the offers varied widely, with some lasting as long as 60 days (in contrast to most retailers, who featured brands through price advertising and special displays for one week only). With one exception, VPJ's trade promotions were national, not tailored to particular regional or city markets.[7] Porter noted that the average level of trade promotion discounts seemed to have increased over the five years. In addition, she observed that since 1973 price increases often coincided with trade promotions, complicating evaluations of their impact.

Three questions came to Porter's mind as she reviewed the VPJ trade promotion history:

1. How extensive was inventory loading during the promotional period? Trade buyers, who could often predict the timing of a brand's trade promotion offers, could deliberately let inventory run down in anticipation of a promotion, buy heavily during the promotion period, then let orders drop again. This produced peaks and valleys in the flow of factory shipments and an artificial seasonality of demand. Porter had noted a fall-off in VPJ shipments before and after most promotions. Could HBP be selling at a discount VPJ volume that the trade would buy anyway to meet normal consumer demand?
2. Just how much merchandising support was VPJ receiving at the retail level? Comparative data on the extent of feature advertising for petroleum jelly and three other product categories, reported in Exhibit 12, suggested that the trade did not view VPJ as a traffic builder. Further, most VPJ trade promotions involved case allowances. Should the proportion of performance-based allowances be increased, and, if so, could performance requirements be enforced?
3. How effective were across-the-line promotions? Traditionally, VPJ had used line promotions across all sizes to encourage retailers to stock more than one size. However, the company typically required retailers to feature only one size in a tiny "obituary" newspaper ad to take an advertising allowance on their purchases of all VPJ sizes.

---

[7]By law, different trade promotion offers could be made at the same time in different market areas, but in any given market area an equivalent offer had to be made on a proportional basis to all competing retail outlets. Major supermarket and drug chains and mass merchandisers generally preferred that manufacturers offer the same trade promotion in all market areas.

RESEARCH EVIDENCE

During 1976, VPJ factory shipments had increased 22 percent over 1975. Unit sales to consumers had risen 11 percent. During the first half of 1977, however, factory shipments and consumer sales were 11 percent and 2 percent lower than the equivalent 1976 figures. Some HBP executives suggested that heavy VPJ promotion during 1976 had overstocked the trade, the consumer, or both. To address this issue and the broader question of how much advertising, consumer promotion, and trade promotion expenditures each contributed to VPJ sales and profit performance, two research studies had been commissioned.

The first report, prepared by John Dennerlein, CPI's special projects manager, with the assistance of an independent consulting firm,[8] estimated incremental sales and contribution generated by VPJ trade promotions over a five-year period. A series of computer models estimated what the normal monthly factory shipments of each VPJ size would have been without each trade promotion, and then compared these figures with actual shipments. Similarly, the contribution from actual sales at the promotion price could be compared with the contribution normal sales would have provided at full price. The calculations of incremental unit sales and contribution took account of lost sales at full price before and after, as well as during, each promotion period.

The results of Dennerlein's investigation are presented in Exhibits 13 and 14. Exhibit 13 reports the net incremental contribution associated with each VPJ trade promotion from 1972 through June 1977, broken down by size. Dennerlein also plotted factory shipments, incremental unit sales, retail inventories, and consumer sales over time for each VPJ size. As an example, his chart for the 7.5-oz. VPJ is presented as Exhibit 14.

Dennerlein concluded that VPJ trade promotions were profitable and were "the major factor behind year-to-year changes in VPJ sales." He believed that VPJ trade promotions, especially when they coincided with consumer promotions, not only stimulated the trade to build inventories but also increased consumer sales. Dennerlein opposed any significant transfer of VPJ money from trade promotion to advertising.

A second study, conducted by the CPI market research department, measured the efficacy of VPJ advertising expenditures. It found weak correlations between quarterly VPJ advertising expenditures and factory shipments, retail inventories, and consumer sales. The researchers noted that consumer sales had declined during the first half of 1977, even though media advertising expenditures were almost 50 percent higher than during the equivalent period in 1976.

THE PROBLEM

The findings and the sales results of first-half 1977 had prompted HBP Division executives to reduce VPJ media advertising expenditures for the second half of 1977 to around $700,000, compared with $1.4 million during the same period in 1976. Porter opposed this cut. "If anything," she commented, "the 1976 promotion pumped so much VPJ into the pipeline that advertising ought to have been increased." She wanted to develop a

---

[8]SPAR (Sales Promotion Analysis Reporting), a commercial service of Pan-Eval Data Inc.

EXHIBIT 11 VPJ Trade Promotion History, 1972–1977

Date of Promotion		Sales Days Promoted	Consumer Promotion Activity	1.75 oz.	3.75 oz.
Year	Duration				
1972	9/01–10/15	29	None	5% OI staple 10% OI M/C	—
1973	1/02–2/13	31	None	5% OI staple 10% OI M/C + 5% OI on choice of one size	5% OI staple 10% OI M/C + 5% OI on choice of one size
	5/01–6/30	43	None	5% OI (SE and SW regions only)	5% OI
	9/04–11/2	46	10-cent coupon on any size VPJ	7% + 5% OI on choice of one size	7% + 5% OI on choice of one size
1974	2/01–3/15	29	None	—	—
	5/01–6/14	31	None	10% OI + 10% ad	—
	8/01–9/13	31	None	1 w/11	1 w/11
	11/01–12/13	28	None	—	10% OI
1975	1/02–2/14	31	Container pack premium with 7.50-oz. size	1 w/11	—
	3/10–4/18	32	10-cent cross-ruff coupon with P&G Ivory Snow Multibrand	—	—
	6/02–6/27	21	None	—	1 w/11 + 10% ad
	9/02–9/30	21	50-cent refund offer 2 VPJ proofs of purchase	1 w/11	—
	11/03–12/12	27	None	—	2 w/10 + 10% ad choice of one size
1976	1/05–2/27	41	$2 refund offer Multibrand	1 w/11	1 w/11
	4/05–4/30	21	15-cent cross-ruff coupon with Kimbies Multibrand	—	—
	5/14–6/25	38	50-cent refund offer for 2 VPJ proofs of pruchase		2 w/10 on twin pack + 5% ad
	8/02–9/24	43	*Reader's Digest* sweepstakes; $1.50 refund offer and sweepstakes Multibrand	1 w/11 + 5% ad	1 w/11 + 5% ad
	10/04–11/11	30	None	—	12% OI
	10/04–12/13	50	None	—	—
1977	1/03–2/25	40	Swiss Army knife self-liquidating premium	—	—
	4/04–4/29	20	25-cent coupon for 15-oz. VPJ Multibrand	—	10% OI on choice of one size + 5% ad
	5/02–5/27	21	None	—	—
	6/06–6/24	22	None	—	10% OI on twin-pack

Source: Company records.

EXHIBIT 11 (*concluded*)

7.50 oz.	12.00 oz.	15.00 oz.	Comments
5% OI staple 10% OI M/C	5% OI staple 10% OI M/C	5% OI staple 10% OI M/C	OI = off-invoice. A staple or standard case contained one dozen units. A master case (M/C) was a prepacked mix of sizes, usually including six dozen units.
5% OI staple 10% OI M/C + 5% OI on choice of one size	5% OI staple 10% OI M/C + 5% OI on choice of one size	5% OI staple 10% OI M/C + 5% OI on choice of one size	
5% OI	—	—	
7% + 5% OI on choice of one size	7% + 5% OI on choice of one size	7% + 5% OI on choice of one size	
10% OI	10%	10%	
10% OI + 10% ad	—	—	An additional 10% discount given to accounts showing evidence of feature advertising support for the brand.
1 w/11	1 w/11	1 w/11	One case provided free for every 11 ordered.
—	—	10% OI	
1 w/11	—	—	
1 w/11 or 2 w/10 on choice of one size	1 w/11 or 2 w/10 on choice of one size	1 w/11 or 2 w/10 on choice of one size	
—	—	—	
2 w/10	—	—	
—	—	2 w/10 + 10% ad choice of one size	
2 w/10	1 w/11	1 w/11	5% ad allowance for feature ad on any size.
2 w/10 on choice of one size	2 w/10 on choice of one size	2 w/10 on choice of one size	Only one order permitted during promotion period. 10% ad allowance for ads featuring all three promoted brands
2 w/10 + 5% ad	1 w/11 + 5% ad	1 w/11 + 5% ad	Bonus 5% ad allowance for ads featuring all three promoted brands. Display allowance of $3 per retail outlet for an end-aisle, off-shelf display of all three brands (minimum 15 dozen per display).
—	—	—	
—	—	15% OI	
10% OI	—	—	5% ad allowance if knife featured in advertising.
—	—	10% OI on choice of one size + 5% ad	Display allowance of $3 per retail outlet for displays of two out of three promoted brands (minimum 15 dozen per display).
2 w/10	—	—	
—	—	—	

EXHIBIT 12   Food Trade's Advertising Support for Petroleum Jelly and Other Packaged Goods

	A Ads (>3 inches)*		B Ads (1–3 inches)*		C Ads (<1 inch)*		Total		Average Number of Ads per Account per Year
	Number	Percent	Number	Percent	Number	Percent	Number	Percent	
Petroleum Jelly:									
VPJ	—	—	3	7.0%	39	93.0%	42	100%	2.63
Private label	—	—	—	—	6	100.0	6	100	0.37
Category									
Laundry detergents	109	10.1%	517	48.1%	449	41.8%	1,075	100%	67.00
Bar soaps	18	3.9	249	53.3	200	42.8	467	100	29.00
Hand lotion	2	1.2	25	14.7	143	84.1	170	100	11.00

Note: Of the 42 VPJ ads counted, 2 were for the 1.75-oz. size; 12 for the 3.75-oz. size; 20 for the 7.50-oz. size; 6 for the 12-oz. size; and 2 for the 15-oz. size.

*Ads are grouped by size in newspaper column inches. For example, a C ad would be one column wide and less than one inch long. In a large newspaper advertisement featuring many brands offered by a supermarket, a C ad (also known as an obituary ad or line mention) might consist of a single line giving the brand name and unit price. An A ad, in contrast, would usually appear in very large type and include a picture.

Source: Company records, based on 1975 Majers data for three major metropolitan markets. Majers, an independent market research firm, monitored grocery, drug, and mass merchandiser newspaper advertising support for a wide variety of products.

1978 television advertising campaign that stressed VPJ's versatility and to increase advertising expenditures at the expense of trade promotion. (Four finished commercial executions of a new television advertising campaign could be developed at an approximate cost of $200,000.) She admitted, however, that "the HBP Division's traditional orientation toward push rather than pull marketing would make this proposal tough to sell." She also expected resistance from the HBP sales force and the trade.

As she began to plan the brand budget, Porter learned that the division had scheduled several significant new product launches for the second half of 1978. Profits from established brands such as VPJ would cover the substantial marketing expenses for these introductions. Accordingly, the HBP general manager informed Porter that her 1978 VPJ budget should show a profit, after advertising and promotion expenses, at least 10 percent greater than the current 1977 estimate of $7.7 million.

EXHIBIT 13 Estimates of Trade Participation and Net Incremental Contribution (or loss) Associated with VPJ Trade Promotions, 1972–1977

Promotion Period		Sales Days Promoted	Estimated Trade Participation					Incremental Contribution (or Loss) by Size					Total Net Incremental Contribution (or loss)
Year	Duration		1.75-oz.	3.75-oz.	7.50-oz.	12.00-oz.	15.00-oz.	1.75-oz.	3.75-oz.	7.50-oz.	12.00-oz.	15.00-oz.	
1972	9/01–10/15	29	—	—	75%	55%	60%			$ 29,133	$27,246	$56,870	$113,249
1973	1/02–2/13	31	55%	65%	70	50	55	$14,522	$58,982	36,770	31,471	32,682	174,427
	5/01–6/30	43	55	70	75	—	—	14,054	21,795	61,066	—	*	96,915
	9/04–11/02	46	55	65	70	55	55	38,496	68,334	54,191	24,970	60,730	246,721
1974	2/01–3/15	29	—	—	75	55	60	—*	—*	26,204*	28,306	56,335	110,845
	5/01–6/14	31	55	—	70	—	—	11,146*	—*	24,973*	—*	—*	36,119
	8/01–9/13	31	55	65	70	55	55	(48,388)	25,881	(15,644)	43,808	24,533	30,190
	11/01–12/13	28	—	75	—	—	70	—*	8,562	—*	—*	54,615*	63,177
1975	1/02–2/14	31	55	—	75	—	—	(90,623)	—	23,148	—	—	(67,475)
	3/10–4/18	32	—	—	85	65	75	—	—	46,934	39,894	49,182	136,010
	6/02–6/27	21	—	75	—	—	—	—	(18,334)	—	—	—	(18,334)
	9/02–9/30	21	55	—	75	—	—	(13,219)	—	27,652	—	—	14,433
	11/03–12/12	27	—	75	—	—	70	—	(31,115)	—	—	29,509	(1,606)
1976	1/05–2/27	41	80	90	95	80	80	32,984*	21,921*	159,265*	50,669*	65,902	330,741
	4/05–4/30	21	—	—	90	75	80	—	—	8,939	(2,651)	15,693	28,581
	5/14–6/25	38	—	85	—	—	—	—	89,887	—	—	—	89,887
	8/02–9/24	43	70	80	85	70	75	48,863	59,310	102,004	40,103	41,278	291,558
	10/04–11/11	30	—	90	—	—	—	—	(39,570)	—	—	—	(39,570)
	10/04–12/13	50	—	—	—	—	85	—	—	—	—	26,932	26,932
1977	1/03–2/25	40	—	—	85	—	—	—*	—*	124,248*	—*	—*	124,248
	4/04–4/29	20	—	90	—	—	85	—	51,642	—	—	99,763	151,405
	5/02–5/27	21	—	—	90	—	—	—	—	11,094	—	—	11,094
	6/06–6/24	22	—	85	—	—	—	—	32,136	—	—	—	32,136
1972–77	Average	32	59%	78%	79%	62%	70%	$ 871	$26,879	$ 47,998	$ 31,535	$47,233	$ 86,160

Note: To be read: The trade promotion running from September 1 through October 15, 1972, generated a net incremental contribution of $29,133 on sales of the 7.50-oz. size, and a total net incremental contribution of $113,249.

*A list-price increase on the designated size occurred simultaneously with the promotion.

Source: SPAR research commissioned by CIP.

EXHIBIT 14   Factory Shipments, Incremental Unit Sales, Retail Inventories, and Consumer Sales for 7.5-oz. VPJ, 1972-1977

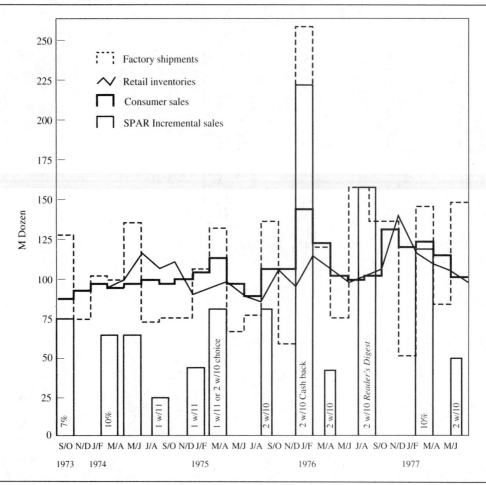

Source: Company records.

Case 5–2

*Sorrell Ridge: Slotting Allowances**

Carol Pressman, Allied Old English vice president of marketing and sales, arrived at the offices of Bromar of Southern California on June 5, 1987, expecting to close a deal. Pressman believed that California's second-largest food broker had already decided to represent the company's best-selling brand, Sorrell Ridge spreadable fruit. Sorrell Ridge sales had grown from $720,000 in 1982 to $5.9 million in 1986 as a result of the appeal to increasingly health-conscious consumers of its all-fruit products over sugared jams.

Bromar's president, vice president and five account managers listened to Pressman's proposal, then gave their response. They informed Pressman that Allied Old English would have to pay "slotting allowances in up-front cash of around $250,000" to obtain supermarket shelf space for Sorrell Ridge. Bromar also suggested Sorrell Ridge would have to distribute two million 50-cents-off coupons through free-standing inserts in Los Angeles newspapers as part of the introductory marketing program, and also launch a boysenberry conserve, a new product for Sorrell Ridge but currently fashionable in California.[1] In return, the broker committed to securing distribution for Sorrell Ridge in stores accounting for 90 percent of grocery volume within three months of the introduction.

Surprised by Bromar's requests, Pressman returned to Allied Old English's head office in Port Reading, N.J., to consult with president Fred Ross. While wanting to employ Bromar and be the first to enter the California market with an all-fruit product line ahead of their key competitors, J. M. Smucker and Polaner, Pressman and Ross felt they had to consider these options:

1. Find another broker. However, the largest broker in Southern California was already representing a competitive brand.
2. Propose a less-expensive launch program to Bromar and hope that they would still agree to represent the line.
3. Sell through grocery distributors or a middleman who would take title to the product. However, this approach would cause the retail price to be 25 percent higher.

---

*Research Associate Aimee L. Stern prepared this case under the supervision of Professor John A. Quelch as the basis for class discussion rather than to illustrate either effective or ineffective handling of an administrative situation. Proprietary data have been disguised. Copyright © 1990 by the President and Fellows of Harvard College. Harvard Business School case 9–591–011.

[1]Bromar expected a 3-4% coupon redemption rate with production, distribution and retailer and clearing house handling costs amounting to 60 cents per redemption.

COMPANY BACKGROUND

Fred Ross was heir to Allied Old English, a small family business which specialized in duck sauce and blackstrap molasses. The firm was founded by Ross's father in 1951 and distributed products primarily through health food stores. When Ross took over day-to-day operations in 1975, Allied Old English had sales of about $2.5 million, 75 percent in private label and institutional products sold to restaurants, hospitals, and schools, and 25 percent in brand names such as China Pride and Dai-Day. Realizing that sales of branded products were more profitable and dependable, he concentrated on growing his existing brands and acquiring others including Mee Tu Noodles (1977), Sorrell Ridge (1982), Hot Cha Cha (1983), and Gathering Winds (1984). He expected sales of $19 million by 1990, 93 percent of which would be from brands owned by Allied Old English.

Ross purchased the Canadian jam company Sorrell Ridge in February 1982, for $75,000. In the prior year, the company had sold 15,000 cases of honey-sweetened jam through U.S. and Canadian health food stores.

In 1982, all jams and jellies on the market were sweetened with honey, cane sugar, or corn syrup. The jams of the market leader, J.M. Smucker Co., comprised 8 percent fruit, 57 percent corn syrup and sugar, and 35 percent water from fruit and corn syrup. Ross substituted white grape juice concentrate for honey, and started promoting Sorrell Ridge as a product made entirely of fruit. Sorrell Ridge spreadable fruit consisted of 50 percent fruit and 50 percent water from fruit, and was made in the company's existing Port Reading plant. These different ingredients meant that, by 1986, Sorrell Ridge's cost of goods was six cents per pound higher than that of the established jam manufacturers.

Ross originally cooked fruit in small open kettles, brought it to a boil, then packed and cooked Sorrell Ridge in jars. The process was primitive and the product was often overcooked, resulting in loss of flavor and color. Ross invested about $800,000 in state-of-the-art manufacturing equipment that cooked the product at a consistent 130 degrees Fahrenheit and cooled it quickly, improving quality substantially.

Ross changed Sorrell Ridge's packaging to make it stand out on store shelves. Most jams were packaged in squat, round 10- to 18-ounce jars with red, purple, or orange labels. Ten- and 12-ounce jars were the best-selling sizes. Ross used tall, thin, 10-ounce jars with light green labels and matching bottle caps. Sorrell Ridge was available in 20 flavors including the best-selling strawberry, blueberry, orange marmalade, raspberry, apricot, and peach.

The commercial jam, jelly, and preserve market originally consisted of six types of fruit spreads: jams, jellies, preserves, conserves, marmalades, and fruit butters. Definitions were as follows:[2]

- *Jellies*—Made by combining strained fruit juices with sugar and cooking until the mixture reaches a clear consistency. Popular flavors: apple; crab apple; grape; black raspberry.
- *Jams*—Made of finely sliced fruits cooked with sugar until the mixture becomes slightly jellied. Popular flavors: grape; strawberry; peach; apricot.

---

[2]Source: "Jams, Jellies & Preserves Market," *Packaged Facts,* April 1986.

- *Preserves*—Made by cooking whole or cut-up fruits in a sugar syrup until clear. Popular flavors: apricot; gooseberry; peach; plum; strawberry.
- *Conserves*—Jam-like spreads made from a mixture of two or more fruits, often combined with nuts or raisins.
- *Marmalades*—Contain shreds of citrus fruits suspended in clear syrup. Popular flavors: lemon; orange; grapefruit; ginger/lime.
- *Fruit Butters*—Made from fruit pulp and sugar cooked together.

Jellies accounted for a quarter of the total volume, while jams, preserves, and conserves combined accounted for almost 70 percent.

Traditional distinctions among product types blurred over the years and the terms jams, preserves, and conserves were often used interchangeably. In 1982, Ross referred to the product line as Sorrell Ridge conserves but, when competitive all-fruit brands entered the market, he changed the product description to Sorrell Ridge spreadable fruit.

Sorrell Ridge products enjoyed an average 18-month shelf life, but lighter fruits such as peach and apricot were sensitive to heat and turned brown in the jars after six months. Sales of jams and jellies were highest in the fall and winter and lowest in the spring and summer. Sales of premium-priced gourmet items increased during the pre-Christmas shopping season.

Ross initially, in 1982, sold Sorrell Ridge through 20 percent of the 6,000 U.S. health food stores. Most of Sorrell Ridge's outlets were in the northeast. Total health food store retail sales of jams and jellies were $4.5 million in 1982. A dozen small brands, including R.W. Knudsen, Cascadia Farms, and Whole Earth, competed in the category. Two national health food distributors serviced 50 percent of health food retailers with their own brands.

Ross therefore had to sell through health food distributors. These distributors marked up each case of 12 10-ounce jars by about 25 percent, and the health food stores then retailed each jar for 40 percent more than they paid for it. In 1984, Sorrell Ridge retailed for an average of $2.59 per jar in health food stores. That year, Sorrell Ridge achieved a 60 percent market share in health food stores nationwide. Health food stores accounted for about $2.3 million of the brand's $2.8 million in wholesale sales. Ross decided that, to expand further, he had to distribute through supermarkets, which accounted for 86 percent of all retail jam and jelly sales. He approached Smucker's to explore a joint selling and distribution arrangement. However, Smucker's was not interested. Ross recalled the chairman of the company saying, "We merely want to own your niche in health food stores." Smucker executives did not believe the 100 percent fruit concept had "mass marketability."

SUPERMARKET EXPANSION

Ross first introduced Sorrell Ridge to New York-area supermarkets in 1984 because local distributors who handled the company's Chinese food line could obtain supermarket placement. The New York metropolitan area, which consisted of the five boroughs of New York City, Long Island, Westchester County, and northern New Jersey, represented about 9 percent or $60 million of national jam and jelly retail sales through supermarkets.

Ross hired Carol Pressman, a 35-year-old sales representative with a health food distributor, Island Natural Health Foods, to help with the rollout because her firm was outselling all of Sorrell Ridge's health food distributors. A working mother who had never finished college, Pressman had outstanding sales skills. She and Ross developed an aggressive presentation for New York food brokers and supermarkets. She filled an empty jam jar with sugar and a few plastic raspberries and opened her sales pitch by placing the "sugar jar" on the buyer's desks. She told them, "This is what you're buying." Pressman then explained how stocking Sorrell Ridge would help build sales in a declining category. Exhibit 1 is drawn from the merchandising flyer used in the sales presentation.

Sorrell Ridge had to use food brokers to distribute its products to supermarkets since it did not have its own sales force. Brokers worked exclusively with one manufacturer in each product category they represented. For a new principal like Sorrell Ridge, a food broker would typically help to develop the initial marketing program (including the introductory trade deal) and present it to trade buyers. In addition, the broker merchandised the brand, planned its placement on supermarket shelves, provided labor for restocking and sometimes price ticketed the product at retail. The broker also processed retail orders and sent them to the manufacturer. Food brokers typically received a 5 percent commission on the net selling price to the trade after trade allowances.

The New York market was controlled by three major supermarket chains which accounted for 42 percent of New York jam and jelly sales. Shop Rite was the largest with 180 stores, followed by Pathmark with 125, and Waldbaum with 110. In November 1984, Ross approached Shop Rite. He agreed to provide Shop Rite one free case per store per flavor as an introductory slotting allowance. The chain accepted six flavors. Starting in February 1985, Shop Rite sold 50–75 cases per week per flavor of Sorrell Ridge during its first six months on the market. In total, Ross provided New York supermarkets free goods worth $150,000 to gain distribution. One year after the introduction, Ross paid New York supermarkets additional slotting fees of two free cases per additional flavor per store to attain his minimum goal of 6–8 flavors in each store. This cost Ross an additional $50,000 in fees during 1985.

In 1984, supermarket prices for jams varied according to flavor. A 10-ounce jar of strawberry jam sold for an average of $1.39 at retail, while less heavily demanded fruits like raspberry sold at 20–30 cents more per jar. Ross suggested a single retail price of $1.99 for all flavors of Sorrell Ridge. He reduced the suggested retail selling price in 1986 to $1.79 as his sales and production volume increased. The main competitors, Smucker's and Polaner, followed his lead and also introduced line pricing, a standard price for each jar size regardless of flavor.

In March 1985, Sorrell Ridge launched a $175,000 spot television campaign in New York which ran for four weeks. The advertisement pictured sugar jam competitors and, most prominently, a fat jar of Smucker's adrift in a desert of sugar with a voiceover by actor Burl Ives. Exhibit 2 provides a storyboard of the advertisement. Smucker's sent a blistering letter to all three networks plus the Federal Trade Commission in Washington demanding that the "misleading" commercial be taken off of the air. The letter suggested that Sorrell Ridge was harmful to diabetics. Ross countered with a press conference, in July of 1985, which featured actor Tony Roberts, a board member of the Juvenile Diabetes Foundation. They handed out letters from doctors and food chemists stating that Sorrell

EXHIBIT 1   Excerpt from Merchandising Flyer

CONSERVES

Standardized Jams

(AS REQUIRED BY LAW)

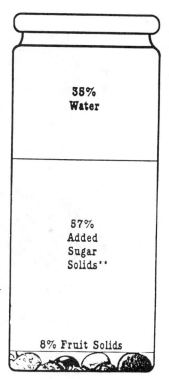

*(Fruit Solids consist of fruit and unsweetened fruit juices.)

**(May consist of one or more of the following sugar, high fructose corn syrup, corn syrup, etc.)

The fruit. And nothing but the fruit.

EXHIBIT 2   Sorrell Ridge Storyboard, 1985

ANNCR. (VO): Sorrell Ridge would like
to challenge

the giant in the jam industry.

Their preserves have mostly corn syrup,

refined sugar,

and just some fruit.

Sorrell Ridge has no corn syrup.

No refined sugar.

Just 100% fruit and fruit juice. Maybe it's
about time someone knocked the giant
down to size.

Sorrell Ridge. With 100% fruit, it has to
be better.

Ridge could be included in diabetic diets. The dispute and the associated publicity helped Ross to achieve distribution in New York supermarkets accounting for 90 percent of grocery volume by the end of 1986.

Sorrell Ridge used intensive in-store sampling to persuade consumers to try the product. Sorrell Ridge hired an independent product demonstration service to conduct the program. About 300 major stores received demos. In many supermarkets, the Sorrell Ridge line was stocked in a specialty display at the end of the fresh fruit aisle, separate from the jams and jelly section. Sorrell Ridge brokers pressed for this placement to capitalize on the all-fruit attribute of the product.

From New York, Sorrell Ridge expanded into nearby markets such as Boston, Philadelphia, and Buffalo. The brand also made minor inroads in Chicago, Denver, and Cincinnati. Ross spent most of 1986 preparing for a major new market expansion in 1987.

THE MARKET IN 1986-1987

By 1986, Sorrell Ridge factory sales had reached $5.4 million and, as indicated in Exhibit 3, accounted for over half of Allied Old English's total sales. An income statement for the Sorrell Ridge brand is shown in Exhibit 4. Sorrell Ridge's media advertising expenditures of $150,000 in 1986 compared to national spending levels of $5.3 million for J.M. Smucker, $2.1 million for Welch Foods, and $900,000 for Polaner. National retail sales and market shares for these and other competitors are reported in Exhibit 5. Market shares along with case volume and dollar sales in New York City for 1985 and 1986 are shown in Exhibit 6.

EXHIBIT 3   Sorrell Ridge Sales: 1982–87

	Sorrell Ridge Sales	*Percent of Company Sales**	*Sorrell Ridge Case Sales†*	*Number of Flavors‡*
1982	$720,000	14.4%	40,000	10/HS
1983	$1.5 million	21.4	105,000	8/HS, 8/FO
1984	$2.8 million	32.9	200,000	8/HS, 12/FO
1985	$4.8 million	50.0	360,000	15/FO
1986	$5.4 million	51.0	430,000§	20/FO
1987‖	$6.5 million	55.1	520,000	20/FO

*Percentage of total Allied Old English sales.
†A case comprised a dozen 10-ounce jars.
‡HS = honey-sweetened; FO = fruit only
§70 percent of cases were distributed through supermarkets, 30 percent through health food stores.
‖Estimated.

Source: Company records.

EXHIBIT 4   Income Statement, 1986 ($000)

Manufacturing sales	$5,356
Less expenses:	
Cost of goods	2,700
Shipping and warehousing	120
Brokers fees	206
Slotting allowances	80
Other sales promotion	300
Advertising	150
Fixed overhead	1,600
Profit before taxes	$ 200

Source: Company records.

EXHIBIT 5   Jam and Jelly Retail Sales and Market Shares: 1986

	Retail Sales (millions)	Share of Retail Sales
J.M. Smucker	$312	31%
Welch Foods	123	12
Kraft	84	8
Borden	46	5
Polaner	18	2
Private label	76	8
Other (including gourmet brands)	341	34

Source: "Jams, Jellies, and Preserves Market," *Packaged Facts,* 1986.

EXHIBIT 6   Brand Sales and Shares in the New York City Jam & Jelly Market: 1985–86

Brand	Case Sales (12 Units per Case)	Dollar Sales ($000)	Dollar Share of Category	Percentage Change	
Kraft	1985—176,263	1985—$2,899	1985—8.3%	Cases	− 13.4%
	1986—152,666	1986— 2,579	1986—7.1	Dollars	− 11.0
Sorrell Ridge	1985— 50,238	1985— 1,120	1985—3.2	Cases	+ 140.6
	1986—120,861	1986— 2,632	1986—7.3	Dollars	+ 135.0
Smucker	1985—724,087	1985—12,463	1985—35.8	Cases	− 1.5
	1986—713,115	1986—12,769	1986—35.2	Dollars	+ 2.4
Polaner	1985— 48,199	1985— 956	1985—2.7	Cases	− 42.3
	1986— 27,810	1986— 512	1986—1.4	Dollars	− 46.4
Welch Foods	1985—408,401	1985— 7,266	1985—20.8	Cases	− 2.2
	1986—399,469	1986— 6,799	1986—18.8	Dollars	− 6.4
All other	1985—764,812	1985—10,143	1985—29.1	Cases	+ 9.8
	1986—840,079	1986—10,934	1986—30.2	Dollars	+ 7.8
Total	(1985) 2,172,000	(1985) $34,847		Cases	+ 3.8%
	(1986) 2,254,000	(1986) $36,225		Dollars	+ 4.0%

Source: Company records.

Retail sales for jams and jellies in 1986 in the United States were about $800 million. Jam and jelly retail sales had declined at a compound annual rate of 3 percent between 1981 and 1985, due partly to consumer health concerns. Jams and jellies were laden with sugar, and many adults switched to low-sugar or diet spreads. Supermarkets devoted, on average, eight feet of shelf space to the jam and jelly section, which often also included peanut butter and honey. Six jar facings of Sorrell Ridge fit in one linear retail foot of shelf space. Less than one percent of total supermarket sales came from this category, yet over 100 brands competed for the limited shelf space available.

Children aged 2–17 years were above-average customers of jams and jellies. According to a product usage survey by *Progressive Grocer* magazine, 44 percent of jam and jelly consumers were single-brand users.

Higher-priced gourmet jams were gaining popularity among young urban adults. Premium-priced preserves retailed at $4.00–5.00 per jar. The leading brands were Knotts (upscale) Berry Farm line and Tiptree (Wilkin & Sons, Ltd.).

Polaner introduced its 100 percent fruit jam called All-Fruit to East Coast supermarkets in late 1985. Smucker followed with Simply Fruit in early 1987. From 1985 to 1987, domestic jam and jelly retail sales grew at a 3 percent annual rate, largely due to the introduction of all-fruit brands. Smucker only sold Simply Fruit in markets where Sorrell Ridge was a major contender because it was concerned about losing share for its sugared jams.

By the first half of 1987, all-fruit brands represented about 3–4 percent of national jam and jelly sales through grocery stores, and were expected to increase their share to 26 percent by 1992. In early 1987, Sorrell Ridge held 60 percent of retail sales in the all-fruit segment. All-fruit jams were distributed in only 40 percent of the country's supermarkets, with the majority of sales concentrated in the Northeast.

PLANNING THE SOUTHERN CALIFORNIA LAUNCH

Early in 1987, Ross and Pressman discussed which market they should enter next. Pressman was convinced that growing health consciousness made California the ideal target.

Pressman noted that the number two food broker in Southern California (which included Los Angeles, San Diego, and surrounding counties), had ceased to represent the leading regional jam manufacturer, Knotts Berry Farm, in December 1986. Knotts wanted to reduce Bromar's commissions from the standard 5 percent to 2.5 percent, but Bromar had refused. The number one food broker represented Smucker's. There were several other smaller food brokers in the market whom Pressman could also approach.

A top food broker was an asset when trying to acquire supermarket distribution. Bromar handled large-volume accounts including Starkist Tuna, Campbell Soup Co.'s Prego spaghetti sauce line, and Arrowhead Water, the number one regional brand of bottled water. It had a staff of 400 people including 25 account executives, 325 merchandising and field managers, and 50 administrative workers. As a result, Bromar could provide complete and frequent coverage of grocery stores in the market. Each Bromar customer was assigned an account executive who managed the product line and worked with supermarket chain buyers, merchandisers, and store managers to customize merchandising and marketing plans for each store.

In addition to brokers, there were six distributors in Southern California that sold supermarkets low-turnover items which were not sufficiently important or profitable for supermarkets to stock in their own warehouses. These included gourmet foods, pantyhose, and women's hair goods. Distributors took a 25 percent margin. California supermarkets expected to earn at least a 20 percent retail margin whether they bought from a distributor or direct from a manufacturer. By 1987, they expected slotting fees as well as the standard off-invoice allowance of 15 percent on their initial orders.

Pressman resolved to introduce Sorrell Ridge to Southern California supermarkets in the summer of 1987, and to enter Northern California early in 1988. "It was very important to me that I convince a broker to take us on," Pressman said, "I wanted every rollout that I did to be successful. We did not have the resources to make mistakes, and did not have the budget cushion for failure."

In 1986, 1,793,000 cases of jams and jellies were sold in Southern California, a decline of 21 percent from 1981. Exhibit 7 shows 1986 market shares by brand and by flavor in Southern California. Exhibit 8 provides price information on selected items.

The Southern California grocery retail sector was concentrated, with six chains accounting for 82 percent of grocery volume. One of the six, Certified Grocer, was a wholesale cooperative servicing 2,000 small independently owned and operated grocery stores. The sizes and strategies of the six chains are summarized in Exhibit 9.

For reasons of ethics and legality, Pressman wanted to approach all six buyers with the same opening deal. However, if those chains that depended more heavily on a strong price appeal to attract their consumers pressed for more generous terms, she would have to rethink this objective. She anticipated first-year sales of 90,000 cases, of which half would be sold under the terms of the initial orders. The price per case was set at $17.16 before allowances, 31 cents higher than in the Northeast, to offset partially freight and warehousing costs of 75 cents per case. Shipping costs to California reduced Sorrell Ridge's margin by 50 cents per case.

Pressman had heard that Smucker and Polaner also planned to introduce their all-fruit products in Los Angeles in the summer of 1987. Smucker's line included 6 flavors, and Polaner's 12. Both manufacturers expected to secure additional shelf space at the expense of private labels and weaker brands, rather than through substitution for the slower-moving items in their existing lines. Smucker's suggested retail price for a 10-ounce jar of Simply Fruit was $1.69, while Polaner planned to retail All-Fruit at $1.79. Bromar's research had uncovered some details of their launch programs as reported in Exhibit 10.

EXHIBIT 7   Brands, Shares and Flavors of Jams, Jellies, and Preserves: Southern California Market, 1986

Brand	1982 Cases Sold	1986 Cases Sold	Percent Change	1986 Share of Market	Top Flavors Flavor	Percent
Smucker	394,398	415,318	+5.3%	23.2%		
Smucker Low Sugar	90,096	109,370	+21.3	6.1	Strawberry	33.0%
Private Label/Generic	489,155	367,172	−2.5	20.5%	Grape	22.9
Knotts	236,140	226,259	−4.2	12.6	Orange Marmalade	8.9
Tropical	221,706	176,244	−20.5	9.8	Boysenberry	6.7
Kerns	354,869	141,447	−60.1	7.9	Red Raspberry	6.5
Welch's	184,868	145,299	−21.3	8.1	Apricot	4.9
King Jelly	103,449	82,055	−20.6	4.6	Apricot/Pineapple	4.4
Miscellaneous (including					Blackberry	2.5
gourmet brands)	86,319	129,836	+50.4	7.2	Peach	1.7
Total	2,161,000	1,793,000	−17.0%		Plum	1.3
					Miscellaneous	7.2

Source: Bromar.

EXHIBIT 8   Prices of Selected Jams, Jellies, and Preserves in Southern California: 1986

Package Size			Factory Case Price	Factory Unit Price	Retail Price	
Number of Jars	Number of Ounces	Brand and Item			Independent Grocery Store	Supermarket Chain
12	16	Knotts red raspberry	$18.24	$1.52	$2.03	$1.98
12	16	Knotts strawberry	16.79	1.39	2.04	1.99
12	16	Knotts boysenberry	18.75	1.56	2.24	2.19
12	12	Smucker red raspberry	13.32	1.11	1.62	1.57
12	18	Smucker strawberry preserves	17.35	1.44	2.14	2.09
12	12	Smucker boysenberry preserves	13.56	1.13	1.65	1.60
12	18	Welch's grape preserves	11.63	0.97	1.31	1.26
12	32	Welch's grape preserves	13.65	1.13	1.90	1.85
12	32	Private label strawberry preserves	10.55	0.87	1.34	1.29

Source: Key Price Book/Packaged Facts, Inc.

EXHIBIT 9   Six Principal Grocery Chains in Southern California: 1987

Store Group	Percentage of Grocery Volume	Number of Stores	Marketing Approach
Vons/Pavilions/Tianguis	24%	350	Operates on a high/low pricing philosophy. All three chains target an upscale clientele. Von's doubles manufacturers coupons up to $1.00.
Lucky/Alpha Beta/Advantage	24	350	Pursues a low retail price strategy and does not offer double-value coupons.
Ralphs	14	138	Operates on a high/low philosophy. Offers to double value of manufacturer coupons. Upscale target market.
Certified Grocers	12	2,000	The largest wholesale grocer in Southern California. Debt services charges incurred by major chains help independents continue to compete on price.
Albertson's/Grocery Warehouse	8	113	Aggressive expansion in Southern California. Market share expected to grow in 1988.
Stater Brothers	7	100	Largest independent grocery chain. The company passes on 100 percent of manufacturers' promotion allowances to consumer. Everyday low prices.
Other	11	200+	

Source: Company records.

EXHIBIT 10   Introductory Trade Promotion Expenditures Proposal for All-Fruit Jams—Southern California

Company	Date of Introduction	Case Discount	One-Time Slotting Fee	Coupons	Advertising	In-Store Sampling
Sorrell Ridge	July 1987	$2.80 off $17.16 case price. Available July and August	3 free cases per flavor per store	50 cents-off 2 million FSI planned for October 11	$150,000 TV ads. Three flights over 6 months.	$30,000 to $40,000
Simply Fruit	August 1987	$2.65 off $16.94 case price. Three weeks beginning August 24	1 free case per flavor per store	25 cents-off 2 million FSI planned for mid-September	$1 million national advertising.	None announced
All-Fruit	September 1987	$1.50 off $18.93 case price. One month beginning November	Unknown	Unknown	Unknown	None announced

Note: All three brands were sold in cases of 12 10-ounce jars.

Source: Company records.

SLOTTING ALLOWANCES

For decades, grocery products manufacturers provided the trade with an introductory deal at the time of any new product launch. Typically, such deals took the form of temporary off-invoice case allowances on the trade's initial orders or, alternatively, free goods (for example, one case free with ten). Slotting allowances emerged in the early 1980s as an added administrative charge of $25–$50 per new item per store to cover the costs of entering the new item on the retailer's computer system and of making a slot available for the product in the warehouse and on the retail shelf.

Over time, these nominal charges escalated, especially in the Northeast and in refrigerated and frozen product categories where shelf space was at a premium (see Exhibit 11). Retailers justified increased slotting allowances on the grounds that the costs of the buyer's time in reviewing and accepting a new product and, subsequently, notifying individual store managers of its listing should also be covered. However, manufacturers soon argued that the slotting charges greatly exceeded the costs involved. One consultant's report estimated that only 30 percent of slotting allowances could be attributed to the costs of the services provided. Another estimated that one-third of the $19 billion grocery manufacturers would spend on trade promotion in 1988 would be accounted for by slotting allowances.

The escalation of slotting allowances reflected the increasing power of the grocery trade. As the editor of *Supermarket Business* put it: "The way I heard it, a retailer named an outlandish fee and was as surprised as anyone else when the manufacturer paid it. Once retailers realized how much manufacturers would pay, they just kept raising the

EXHIBIT 11   Promotion Expenditures and Slotting Fees by Product Category

Product Category	Advertising and Promotion Allocations	Slotting Fees (per slot)
Frozen/refrigerated foods	1987—12% advertising, 18% consumer promotion, 70% trade promotion	1982—$ 1,000 1987—$10,000 1992—$20,000*
Candy/snacks	1987—37.5% advertising, 27.5% consumer promotion, 35% trade promotion	1982—$3,000 1987—$2,800 1992—$6,000*
Prepared foods	1987—16% advertising, 24% consumer promotion, 60% trade promotion	1982—$1,000 1987—$8,000 1992—$11,000*

*Estimated.

Source: Clayton/Curtis/Cottrell, Inc. Data based on store groups averaging 50 stores per chain.

fees." Some manufacturers believed that acceding to excessive slotting allowance demands would place them in violation of the Robinson-Patman Act which required that equivalent allowances be offered to all trade accounts in any market area. Exhibit 12 summarizes the principal clauses of the act. As the vice president of sales for a leading packaged goods manufacturer stated: "Retailers are talking out of both sides of their mouths; on the one hand, they say 'Treat us all the same!' But then they turn around and say: 'You've got to give me my own special program.'"

The cost of a slot varied from one retailer to another according to criteria such as the number of stores in the chain, the aggressiveness of the retail buyer, the perceived strength and turnover rate of the new product, and the promised level of media advertising and promotion support. No retailer published a schedule of slotting charges or publicly stated what a slot bought in terms of initial order size or the length of time the slot would be maintained before the new product's sales performance was evaluated (though 60 or 90 days appeared to be the norm).

Smaller manufacturers claimed that slotting allowances constituted a barrier to entry, especially when the trade demanded them in the form of up-front cash payments rather than free goods or credits against the invoices on new product orders. Larger manufacturers with established brands and good new-product track records were better able to resist trade demands for slotting allowances and could promise to place substantial advertising support behind their new-product introductions.

For its part, the grocery trade pointed to after-tax profit margins of only one percent as one reason for their aggressive pursuit of promotional allowances, including slotting fees, from manufacturers. In addition, the grocery trade complained about the proliferation of new item introductions, from around 2,700 in 1980 to 9,000 in 1987. Some 90 percent of these new products failed and were withdrawn within a year. The trade viewed slotting allowances as one way to discourage manufacturers from launching new brands and line extensions almost indiscriminately as they tried to maximize their share of shelf space

---

EXHIBIT 12   Summary of the Clayton Act as Amended by The Robinson-Patman Act (1936), 15 U.S.C., Section 13

Section 2(a):
Prohibits discrimination of price between two or more customers in sales of commodities in interstate commerce where the effect may be substantially to lessen competition with the seller (primary line) or the favored buyer (secondary line) or customers of the latter (tertiary line).
  Contains a defense based on different costs in serving different customers. Also includes a defense based on disposal of perishable or obsolete goods.

Section 2(b):
Permits a discrimination which is otherwise unlawful if it results from a seller's good faith meeting of competitive prices.

Section 2(c):
Prohibits a seller from paying *and a buyer from receiving* a brokerage fee or allowance in a sales transaction unless services are rendered which result in cost savings to the seller. Competitive injury is not an element of this offense and neither cost justification nor meeting competition are defenses.

Section 2(d) and (e):
Prohibits sellers' discrimination among customers with respect to promotional allowances [Section 2(d)] and services [Section 2(e)]. Competitive injury is not an element of the offense; meeting competition is a defense, but cost justification is not.

Section 2(f):
Prohibits buyers from knowingly inducing and receiving unlawful *price* discrimination. Must be a seller violation of Section 2(a), including absence of defenses, and buyer must reasonably be charged with knowledge of that violation. Receipt of illegal promotional allowances and services not covered by Section 2(f).

---

in a slow-growth market characterized by an increasing percentage of in-store purchase selections by consumers.

In an effort to control slotting allowances, Campbell Soup Company proposed failure fees as an alternative. These would be paid to the trade after the launch period if a new product failed to sell at a predetermined rate. The manufacturer would buy back any unsold product and compensate the trade for the opportunity cost associated with use of the shelf space, adjusting for actual sales performance. The major grocer chains rejected this proposal.

SLOTTING ALLOWANCES AND SORRELL RIDGE

Sorrell Ridge had paid slotting allowances when it entered New York supermarkets in 1985, but the fees had risen sharply by 1987. In New York, Ross had paid a slotting charge of one free case of product per flavor per store. To break into Southern California, Bromar told Ross he would have to offer three free cases per flavor per store.

In one Midwest market, Sorrell Ridge had paid a slotting fee to a chain for placement in the produce section. A month later, the supermarket chain moved the Sorrell Ridge line from the produce section to another area of its stores. The retailer asked Ross to pay a second slotting charge for each flavor. Ross agreed because the chain controlled 60 percent of the market. "Slotting fees are a cost of doing business in supermarkets," said Ross. "We knew we had to pay them. We didn't realize the fees would become so high. If Sorrell Ridge was starting out today as a small company trying to break into the market, we wouldn't be able to afford the charges."

Case 5–3

General Electric Company: Consumer Incandescent Lighting*

In December 1982, William Frago, general manager of the Consumer Marketing and Sales Department within General Electric (GE) Company's Lamp Products Division (LPD), was preparing to meet with Gary Rogers, LPD vice president and general manager, to discuss the 1983 operating plan for GE's consumer incandescent lighting (light bulb) business. Both Frago and Rogers had recently assumed their positions.

The discussion was to review three strategic alternatives proposed by different constituencies within the LPD to deal with GE's long-term share decline. First, the marketing programs section argued for an increased advertising program and shift in trade spending from off-invoice purchase allowances to bill-back advertising performance allowances. This plan had been tested in late 1981 and had begun to be implemented in early 1982. However, increased advertising spending and some promotion events were opposed by Consumer Sales and the Incandescent Lamp Department (ILD), and were on hold pending review by Frago and Rogers. Second, the Consumer Sales force believed LPD should attempt to gain more new distribution in the rapidly expanding channels such as mass merchandisers and discount chains. Third, ILD strongly believed LPD should invest resources to improve its cost position and utilize excess capacity to manufacture private-label light bulbs. There was a strong feeling in ILD that light bulbs were a commodity and that a more favorable cost and price position was the secret to long-term success. There was a great deal of internal dissent among each of these groups as to which course of action should be pursued.

Despite improved performance in 1982, several issues were still debated by LPD executives. Some believed that the light bulb was a push product, and that increasing

*This case was prepared by Professor John A. Quelch as the basis for class discussion rather than to illustrate effective or ineffective handling of an administrative situation. Proprietary data have been disguised. Copyright © 1986 by the President and Fellows of Harvard College. Harvard Business School case 2–587–014.

national advertising expenditures at the expense of promotion allowances was risky. They argued that GE would have to narrow further its price premium over competitive light bulbs if it was to gain market share. Others argued that the current price premium could be sustained by a strong national advertising campaign to build preference for GE light bulbs. Some members of this group did not support LPD's decision to make private-label product.

THE LAMP PRODUCTS DIVISION

GE achieved a record $26.5 billion in outside sales in 1982. John F. Welch, Jr., GE's CEO, summarized his views on GE's strategic direction in a letter to shareholders in the 1982 annual report:

> Whether it's bringing new technologies and service to the marketplace or revitalizing our strong core businesses, we want GE to be a place where the bias is toward action—a high-spirited world-class enterprise that uses the resources of a large company and that moves with the agility of the youngest and smallest. The last decade has seen a dramatic shift in our business mix—from the old to the new, from relatively mature businesses to those in their high-growth stages. . . .
>
> While our shift to high technology has been significant, we have also been upgrading our core businesses. During 1982, there were strong cost improvement efforts and major plant and equipment expenditures to increase productivity and assure the competitiveness of these important traditional businesses.

In 1982, GE's businesses were grouped into product sectors. The Consumer Products Sector, which included the Lighting Business Group (LBG), accounted for 22 percent and 13 percent of GE's 1982 revenues and net earnings, down from 25 percent and 21 percent respectively in 1980. LBG's sales were 15 percent of the sector total in 1982, but LBG's return on investment had slipped 7 percent from 1979. The LBG comprised three divisions, one of which, the Lamp Products Division, was principally responsible for the manufacture and sale of lighting products to end consumers. Commercial, industrial, and OEM sales were handled by the other divisions. The LPD accounted for 48 percent and 52 percent of LBG's revenues and earnings in 1982.

The LPD manufactured and sold eight distinct product lines to consumers: consumer incandescent, consumer fluorescent. automotive, holiday, photographic, battery, wiring devices, and outdoor. Consumer incandescent products accounted for 54 percent of LPD sales in 1982. The GE consumer incandescent line included 1,300 stockkeeping units (SKUs) manufactured in six plants.

As shown in the organization chart (Exhibit 1), responsibility for the consumer incandescent business was shared between the general managers of the Incandescent Lamp Department and the Consumer Marketing and Sales Department. Product line managers in the Lamp Department were primarily responsible for cost analysis, sales forecasting, production scheduling, capacity planning, and working with Research and Development on new products. Product marketing managers in the Marketing Department were primarily responsible for developing advertising and promotion programs and exploring product improvements and line extensions. The two departments shared profit and loss responsibility for consumer incandescent lighting. Pricing strategies were discussed by both departments and approved by the LPD general manager.

EXHIBIT 1 Lamp Products Division: 1982 Organization Chart

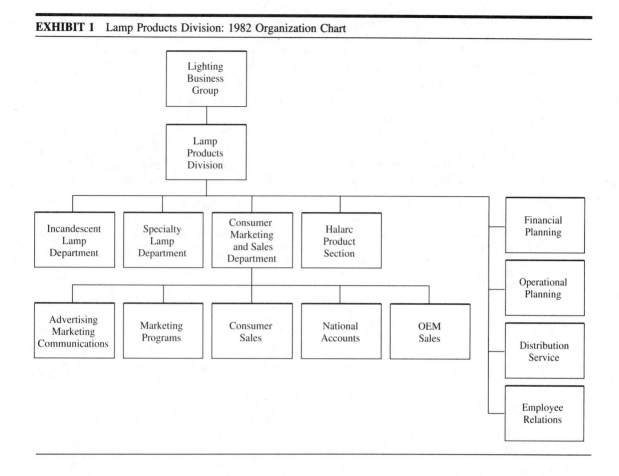

THE CONSUMER INCANDESCENT LIGHTING MARKET

Consumer incandescent lamps were invented by Thomas Edison in 1880. During the next 60 years, a series of technical improvements increased the light intensity or lumens delivered per watt. However, since 1940, no major breakthroughs occurred until 1982 when GE launched the Miser® line of energy-efficient lamps.

In 1982, manufacturers sold 1.19 billion consumer incandescent lamps in the U.S., valued at $445 million. Market demand for light bulbs was directly related to the size of the private housing stock and the size of the average housing unit. Industry sales typically correlated with the number of household light bulb sockets. During the 1970s and 1980s, sales were flat due to heightened consumer interest in energy conservation following the oil price increases of 1973 and 1979 and due to periodic decreases in housing starts. The average annual growth rate in consumer incandescent lamp unit sales was 0.4 percent between 1970 and 1980. Most recently, unit sales had declined 1 percent between 1980 and 1982. Exhibit 2 graphs industry dollar and unit sales, and GE dollar and unit market shares, since 1973. GE's dollar and unit market shares both rose 1 percent during 1982.

Consumer incandescent lamps were generally divided into five product categories: soft whites, inside frost, three-way, PAR and R, and decorative. Soft white bulbs had whitened glass that helped diffuse light and reduced harshness and glare. Inside frost bulbs, which represented an older technology than soft white, contained an inside frosting, did not diffuse light as effectively as soft white, but were lower priced and less costly to manufacture. Three-way bulbs, in conjunction with three-way lamps, allowed the user to select three different levels of brightness—such as 50, 100, and 150 watt. PAR lamps (parabolic reflectors) were for outdoor spot lighting. Reflector lamps (Rs) were primarily used as indoor flood lights. Decorative bulbs, the fastest-growing category, were used

EXHIBIT 2 Consumer Incandescent Industry Sales and GE Market Share Trends*

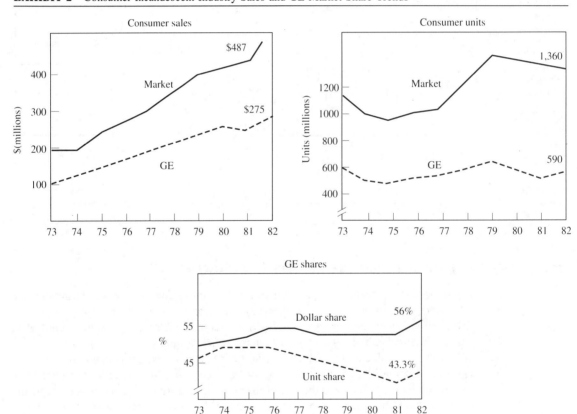

*These figures (in millions) are for all consumer
sales, branded, private label, and generic.

in chandeliers and in concealed or specialty lighting fixtures. Exhibit 3 shows each product category's share of 1982 dollar and unit sales.

DISTRIBUTION

Consumer incandescent lamps were sold through four principal channels: food stores, discount stores, hardware stores, and drug stores. A 1981 consumer survey showed that consumers were most likely to purchase incandescent bulbs in food stores, but that there were different channel patronage patterns for heavy versus light users:

Outlets for Purchase of Incandescent Bulbs in Past Two Years	Percentage by Household Use			
	Total (100%)	Low-Use (29%)	Medium-Use (44%)	High-Use* (26%)
Food Store	70%	69%	72%	69%
Discount store	52	47	52	59
Hardware store	32	26	34	38
Drug store	20	19	20	24
Department store	17	16	16	21
Home improvement center	14	9	13	21
Electric supply company	14	8	11	27
Other	6	1	7	8

*26 percent of households purchased 50 percent of consumer incandescent lamps in 1981.

Food stores were still the most important channel in 1982, though they had lost a point of share since 1980. An average food store carried 50 SKUs of light bulbs and turned its inventory six times a year. Most food stores carried a single branded line of bulbs, but many had recently added a private-label line. For many years, light bulbs had been

EXHIBIT 3 Consumer Incandescent Dollar and Unit Sales and Shares by Product Category: 1982*

	Product Category's Share of Industry $ Sales	Product Category's Share of Unit Sales	Product Category's Share of GE $ Sales
Soft white	33%	38%	43%
Inside frost	38	46	28
Three-way	9	5	13
PAR and R	13	2	10
Decorative	7	9	6

*These figures include branded, private label, and generic consumer incandescent lamp sales, both for the industry and GE. Unit sales of nonbranded GE lamps amounted to 20 million units in 1982.

an important source of profit for food stores. Compared to their average gross margin of 22 percent, food stores earned a gross margin of 56 percent on light bulbs. A 1980 GE study indicated that light bulbs alone accounted for 11 percent of the profits of one major food store chain.

Discount stores and mass merchandisers increasingly used light bulbs as traffic builders, promoting them as often as six times a year. They typically carried as many as 100 SKUs including both a branded line and private label line, but they often emphasized the latter. As many as 75 percent of the bulbs sold by some major discount chains were private label. Inventory turned six times each year. More bulbs were bought per purchase occasion in discount stores than in food stores. Discount store gross margins on light bulbs averaged 41 percent compared to the channel's overall average gross margin of 35 percent.

Hardware stores carried a broad line of lamp SKUs. They were more likely to carry new items and specialty lamps. To hold their share of lamp sales, hardware stores increasingly promoted inside frost bulbs. Their gross margin on sales of lamps averaged 45 percent compared to an overall average gross margin of 21 percent. The corresponding figures for drug stores, which typically carried one branded line of bulbs, were 45 percent and 28 percent. Exhibit 4 breaks down the 1982 sales of consumer incandescent lamps by class of trade.

Within LPD's Consumer Marketing and Sales Department, sales to the major national discount store chains, hardware co-ops, and national drug chains were handled by a national accounts group, separate from the field sales force which dealt with regional food, drug, and hardware accounts.

GE'S COMPETITIVE POSITION

GE's two main competitors in the consumer lighting business in 1982 were Westinghouse and Sylvania. Both had several decades of experience in the market and, like GE, they had invested heavily in automated assembly processes for consumer incandescent lamps. Their unit costs of production were believed to be comparable. The fourth national brand was Norelco, manufactured by the U.S. subsidiary of Philips, the $16 billion Dutch

---

EXHIBIT 4   Channel Growth Trends and Manufacturer Unit Market Share by Channel: 1982

	Food	Discount	Hardware and All Other	Drug	Total
Channel unit share	45%	25%	23%	7%	100%
Change in channel unit share (1980–1981)*	(1%)	—	1%	—	—
Industry annual unit growth rate (1980–1982)	(3%)	(1%)	5%	(2%)	(1%)
GE annual unit growth rate (1980–82)	(6%)	4%	(1%)	7%	(3%)

* ( ) Signifies negative growth rates.

electrical equipment manufacturer which dominated the consumer incandescent lamp market in Europe.

All of the major manufacturers not only sold their own brands but also contracted for private label business. GE, the last to begin private label manufacture, generated $4.0 million in consumer incandescent private-label lamp sales in 1981. Private-label unit market share was 15 percent in 1981, 17 percent in 1982. Many of the imported lamps, which accounted for 10 percent of units sold in 1982, were for private label. The largest imported brand, Action, was made in Hungary and distributed in the U.S. by Action Industries. It was often used by hardware stores as an "in and out promotional item."[1]

The competitive structure of the consumer incandescent market in 1982 had evolved over the previous decade. At the end of 1973, GE held a 46.5 percent unit share of the consumer incandescent market and sold its bulbs at a 4 percent price premium over domestic competition and a 53 percent premium over imports, which then accounted for only 3 percent of the U.S. market.

GE bulbs were distributed to retailers on consignment. In other words, GE retained ownership until they were sold. Until 1973, GE operated on the "agency" system, a form of fair trading established during the 1930s. Consignment continued after 1973, but the resale price of GE bulbs was no longer maintained.

Between 1974 and 1977, GE's price premium over domestic competition increased to 12 percent and its premium over imports to 63 percent due, in large part, to product mix changes. Moreover, a number of industry experts felt that imports of light bulbs from Eastern bloc countries were being "dumped" into the U.S. market at prices below cost. However, GE's unit share remained stable, and GE maintained its position as the single supplier of light bulbs in 78 percent of its accounts. The GE sales force concentrated on selling the trade a profitability story. Imports during these three years captured 5 percent of the market, primarily in mass merchandise discount stores. Indeed, during this period, both the discount stores and the price brands secured their footholds. As one LPD executive explained:

> We were not encouraging the trade to put any special merchandising effort behind bulbs, although the category had a lot of potential as a traffic builder, a point that the discount stores recognized. Using private labels and generics, the discount stores began promoting light bulbs aggressively as traffic builders. Those that carried branded light bulbs often did so just as a comparison to drive their private label sales.[2] As a result, the discount stores captured an increasing share of light bulb volume at the expense of the food and hardware channels where we were strong.
>
> Pretty soon, the food and hardware channels that had traditionally valued light bulbs for their good margins rather than as traffic builders started carrying private-label and generic bulbs to stay competitive with the discount stores. The food and drug chains couldn't stand the embarrassment of promoting light bulbs at higher prices than discount stores in the free-standing inserts of the Sunday newspapers. At the same time, our branded competitors, faced with volume and share losses to private labels and generics, started pressing food stores for feature advertising

---

[1] The brand was not maintained by an account in continuous distribution but was stocked temporarily on special display when an especially attractive promotional deal could be arranged.

[2] A simultaneous promotion of both a branded and a private-label line with a "compare and save" message over the private-label display was known as a promotion split.

support and offered deeper allowances to the trade to maintain their distribution. The price premium of GE bulbs over its branded competitors increased.

Between 1977 and 1979, the GE price premium grew to 19 percent over domestic competition. More discount chains began to market their own private-label bulbs. The import share of the market climbed to 8 percent. Norelco aggressively pursued food store distribution, offering substantial promotion allowances and arguing that food stores were collectively losing share to discount stores because of higher prices on G.E. bulbs. Westinghouse also was attempting to gain share by offering steeper discounts and competitive buy-outs to the trade. To new accounts, Westinghouse offered payments for the existing inventory that would be displaced, free display racks, minimal order size requirements, a progressive annual volume rebate program, and deeper-than-normal off-invoice promotional allowances on its inside frost bulbs. Westinghouse's strategy was, apparently, to use an attractive price on inside frost to gain access to an account and to earn its margin on its other consumer incandescent lines. During 1979, the trade's acquisition cost, net of trade promotion, for a Westinghouse inside frost bulb was 25 cents a unit, compared to 32 cents for a GE bulb. Many food chains appeared to pass through the Norelco and Westinghouse allowances to the consumer in the form of lower retail prices, at the same time maintaining their unit profit margins on these lines.

Between 1975 and 1979, LPD recovered from inflation with consumer incandescent price increases. LBG's return on investment peaked at an impressive 25 percent in 1979. However, two problems arose. First, as shown in Exhibit 5, GE's market share fell as its price premium over competition increased. Second, not all of GE's price increases were realized as LPD found it necessary to deal back some of the increases in additional trade promotion allowances. As one LPD executive explained:

EXHIBIT 5   Relationship between GE Unit Share and Price Premium, 1960–1981

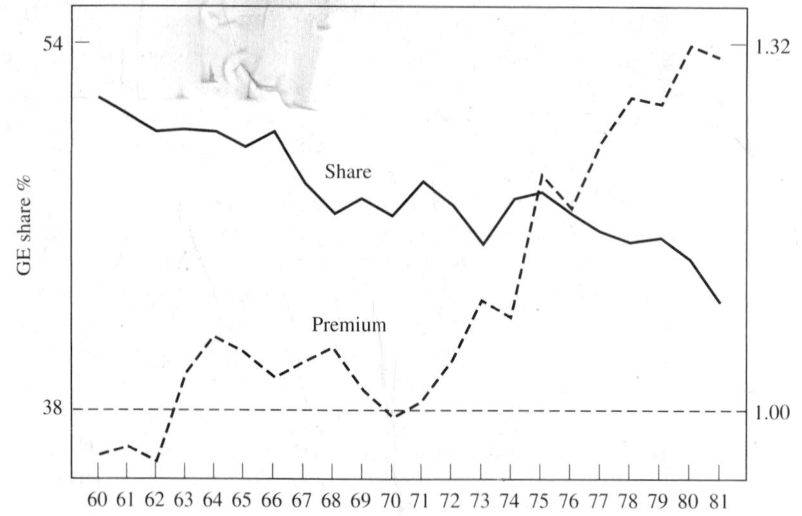

As discount store competition eroded the food chains' share of sales, they focused more on their acquisition costs. We had to devise a strategy that would let us maintain our share in our traditional channels but get a piece of the volume going through discount stores. Our first reaction was to secure distribution and offer our customers promotional packages that enabled them to lower their acquisition costs on both GE soft white and inside frost bulbs. The problem was that many of our food accounts did not pass these discounts through to the consumer. The food stores' prices on G.E. lamps remained as high as ever, and our market share continued to erode. At the same time, consumer price sensitivity was increased. I remember a March 1981 survey showing 35 percent of consumers bought light bulbs on sale. That figure was 6 percent in 1979.

The pattern continued into 1981. GE's dollar sales and unit volume in consumer incandescent lamps declined. For the first time, LPD experienced a net distribution loss of $1.5 million worth of business. In addition, the sales mix deteriorated. Inside frost sales increased at the expense of higher-margin soft white sales when LPD tried to respond to the price premium by running a strong price promotion on inside frost bulbs.

MARKET SEGMENTATION

The average consumer bought light bulbs five times each year. Some consumers bought them as needed, others kept an inventory on hand in their homes. Sixty percent of bulbs were bought for general room lighting. Other uses were reading and writing (9 percent), work aid (6 percent), decoration (7 percent), personal care (7 percent), security (5 percent), and outdoor lighting (4 percent).

As competitive pressures increased during the 1970s, LPD executives increasingly explored the segmentation of the consumer incandescent market. Their objective was to identify segments that might be interested in distinct product benefits and be willing to pay a price premium for them. To this end, five studies were conducted, four of them during 1980 and 1981:

- A 1974 study clustered respondents according to the importance they attached to different lighting benefits. However, no single advertisable benefit stood out among those appealing to consumers in each of the five segments. In addition, GE's market share was similar across the segments (Exhibit 6, p. 402).
- A 1980 Yankelovich, Skelly, and White (YSW) study identified six segments based on consumer attitudes rather than a rank ordering of lighting benefits (Exhibit 7, p. 403).
- A 1980 H.T.I. study identified six segments based on consumer rankings of different lighting benefits. GE's market share again varied only modestly from one segment to another (Exhibit 8, p. 404).
- A 1980 Opinion Research Corporation study aimed to identify the relative importance of energy efficiency, price, package shape, bulb type, and light quality. A segment of consumers especially interested in energy efficiency was identified. GE's share of this segment was relatively low (Exhibit 9, p. 405).
- A second YSW study in 1981 identified three segments based on level of involvement in lighting. Exhibits 10–12 (pp. 406–408) profile these three segments.

LPD executives were especially interested in YSW's two benefit segments. They believed that GE soft white could be positioned to appeal to the quality-of-light segment,

---

EXHIBIT 6 1974 Hale Consumer Attitude Segmentation Study

Objective: Identify consumer attitude segments and the benefits motivating each.

Methodology: 1,016 self-administered questionnaires to households representing all income levels.

Segment	Highest-Ranking Interests	Percent of Total Markets*	GE Share of Segment
1) Vision-value buyers	Reasonable price Long lasting Good value Easy to read by Eliminates eye strain	18%	50%
2) Quality-product value buyers	Economical to burn Reasonable price Long lasting	12	58
3) Quality-vision buyers	Eliminates eye strain Reasonable price Long lasting	21	58
4) Practical (price) buyers	Ready availability Glare-free light Easy to read by Good value	21	65
5) Aesthetic buyers	Wide selection Attractive bulbs/good packaging Well known manufacturer Guaranteed/pre-tested	28	58

Conclusions:
Could not identify segments where GE share was significantly higher or lower. Analysis of key interests of segments could not isolate advertisable consumer benefit.

*Percent of light bulbs purchased by consumers falling into each segment rather than percent of consumers.

---

while GE's new Miser line of energy-efficient bulbs, due to be launched in 1982, could be targeted at the utility/energy segment.

THE 1981 TEST MARKET

Based in part on the results of the market segmentation studies, LPD marketing executives decided to test the impact of an advertising and promotion program designed to pull volume through the retail channel. Believing that LPD should develop more tailored programs for different products in the line, they fixed on quality of light as the differentiating benefit to build preference for GE soft white bulbs. To address consumers interested in eye comfort and decor enhancement, a television advertisement was developed showing a painter fashioning a family portrait with the aid of GE soft white bulbs (see Exhibit 13, p. 409).

EXHIBIT 7   Yankelovich, Skelly and White, Inc., Attitude Segment Study 1980

Objective: Isolate benefit segments and describe the attitudes and motivations of each.

Methodology: 770 in-home personal interviews with consumers in households with annual income of $15,000 and above.

Segment	Description of Segment Motivations	Percent of Total Market*
1. Cost conscious	Lowest level of interest in light bulbs No reason to spend more than minimum No added value can be communicated Decide on price	12.3%
2. Convenience oriented	Want to save time and effort in changing or buying bulbs and will pay extra to achieve this Share some characteristics of cost conscious segment	12.3
3. Technology	High motivation level Always searching for a better way to do things Early adopters . . . new means better but "new" quickly becomes "not new"	5.0
4. Energy conscious	Highest motivation level Need is to save energy Socially responsible Very important to buy the very best bulb Will respond to new products	17.7
5. Undecided buyers	Low level of motivation Want to reduce risk, avoid mistakes Tend to buy leading established brands Followers, not innovators	20.2
6. Home enhancers	Seek better light to improve personal/home environment Extrinsic reasons for choice—other directed behavior Choose "quality" product to match peer group standards Brand loyal	32.5

*Note: GE share by segment not available in this study.

EXHIBIT 8   1980 H.T.I. Consumer Attitude Segmentation Study

Objective: Develop market segments based on consumer rankings of different light bulb benefits/interests.

Methodology: 1,387 self-administered mail questionnaires to consumers of all income levels.

Segment	Highest-Ranking Interests	Percent of Total Market	GE Share of Segment
1. Vision/construction of light bulb	Bulb is guaranteed Highest overall quality Bulb is attractive Is pre-tested Bulb doesn't overheat	12%	45.5%
2. Value/vision	Energy saved pays for bulb Efficient like fluorescent Economical Natural looking light Lasts as long as supposed to Good value for money	15	42.0
3. Positive attitudes	No harsh shadows Helps eliminate eye strain Glare-free light Pleasing lighted appearance Easy to read by Makes things look nice Doesn't grow dim with age Natural looking light	16	54.5
4. Reputable manufacturer	Readily available Well known manufacturer Wide selection Screws easily in and out Is pre-tested Makes things look nice Pleasing lighted appearances	18	50.2
5. Value/reliability	Reasonably priced Good value for money Lasts as long as supposed to Base doesn't twist off Durable, not easily broken Screws easily in and out Economical	19	54.8

EXHIBIT 8 *(concluded)*

Segment	Highest-Ranking Interests	Percent of Total Market	GE Share of Segment
6. No interest in lighting	Light level adjustable Durable, not easily broken Bulb is attractive	20	52.5

Conclusions:

Interpretation hampered because the items ranked included usage needs, product attributes, and general attitudes.

A key advertisable consumer benefit for each segment was hard to identify.

EXHIBIT 9 1981 O.R.C. Study

Objective: Determine the key additional benefit(s) by segment to support the basic long life position of a new line of long-lasting GE bulbs.

Methodology: 502 mall interviews with consumers of all income levels.

Segment	Highest-Ranking Interests	Percent of Total Market	GE Share of Segment
1. Energy conscious	Energy saving	16%	48.3%
2. Aesthetic	Price Package quantity	30	67.0
3. Convenience	Package quantity Bulb shape/type Price	21	63.4
4. Equal sensitivity	Equal sensitivity Price Light quality Life *Not* energy conscious	33	55.5

Conclusions:

Segments were identified among which GE's share does differ significantly.

Between October and December 1981, LPD conducted a field experiment. In four control markets, LPD continued its two current merchandising programs. These were a $1.00 on-pack rebate offer to consumers who submitted purchase proofs for three packs of four bulbs, and a cooperative advertising allowance of up to 6 percent of an account's purchases with the entire cost of advertisements paid for by LPD. In the four test markets (which accounted for 10 percent of U.S. consumer light bulb sales), 160 GRPs of advertising were aired per week at a national expenditure rate of $8 million, equivalent

---

EXHIBIT 10   Yankelovich, Skelly and White Consumer Involvement Segments*

Involved *(35% of market)*	*Uninvolved* *(10%)*	*Latent* *(55%)*

Seeking special lighting
  benefits
  Atmosphere
  Aesthetics
  Modern, unique
	Low attention to special
	  benefits
		Low attention to special
		  benefits

Highest interest in function	Lowest interest in function	High interest in function
Into lighting	*Not* into lighting	Into lighting
Needs/wants vary most on room-by-room basis	Least variation by room	Some variation by room
Price sensitive	Less price sensitive	Price sensitive
More problems in achieving end results	Fewer end-result problems	Fewer end-result problems

Satisfied with lighting effects
  in major living areas
	Not necessarily satisfied	Satisfied with lighting in
		  specific rooms

Concern with illumination
  Effectiveness
  Avoiding glare
  Interest in color
	Less concern with
	  illumination
		Concern with illumination
		  Effectiveness
		  Avoiding harshness

Greatest attention to nearly
  all bulb attributes
	Lower concern with bulb
	  attributes
		High concern with bulb
		  attributes

Highest use of lamps/ sockets/bulbs	Moderate use	Lowest use
More women	More men	More women
All ages—especially 30–64	Younger	Older
Average education	Most educated	Least educated

Most homeowners (largest
  homes)
	Fewer homeowners
	  (medium homes)
		Fewer homeowners
		  (smallest homes)

*These segments were based on respondents' importance and dissatisfaction rankings.

---

to the estimated cost of the rebate program. In addition, the trade received a three-cents-per-unit off-invoice allowance on soft white bulbs, plus an additional four- or five-cents bill-back allowance if one or two feature advertisements were run. The test program limited trade allowances to one order per feature advertisement, whereas the existing cooperative advertising program allowed the trade to accrue allowances on all its purchases. One LPD marketing executive explained the rationale for the so-called 3, 4, 5 program:

> Because consumers buy bulbs in food and drug channels for convenience, our consumer rebate offer only had impact in discount stores where consumers are more likely to purchase bulbs in volume. On the other hand, consumer advertising was thought likely to benefit sales in all channels.

EXHIBIT 11   YSW Study: Consumer Choice of Outlet for Lighting Products

Rated "Major Consideration" in Choice of Outlet for Lighting Products	Total Purchasers	Segments		
		Involved	Uninvolved	Latent
Convenience:				
Convenient location	56%	55%	48%	58%
Shop at for *other* items	41	44	39	38
Light bulbs easy to locate	33	34	19	36
Outlet Economy:				
Lower prices regularly	51	50	39	55
Frequent sales/bargains	48	50	34	50
Full-Line Outlet:				
Offers variety in bulbs— selection to choose from	33	40	19	30
Offers preferred brands	29	33	12	29
Offers best quality lighting	29	33	17	27
Offers "specialty" lighting	26	32	19	23
Offers full range of lighting products	26	30	11	25

The change in the allowance structure was designed to increase the feature advertising support given by the trade and turn the trade into a proactive marketing partner. The gap between an account's promotion acquisition cost and LPD's regular price remained at about 8 cents per soft white bulb, but now 5 cents of the discount was contingent on feature advertising support.

The highlights of the test results are summarized in Exhibit 14, p. 408. GE gained share, increased its average selling price per lamp, and narrowed the price premium over competition. In addition to sales and share data, LPD executives had the survey results from two waves of interviews conducted before and after the experiment in both test and control markets.

Both surveys included comparative questions on perceived value for money of soft white lamp brands at fixed price points for each brand and type. The GE soft white brand price was given as either 69¢, 79¢, 89¢, or 99¢ on each questionnaire on a four-way split sample basis. All competitive soft white lamps were priced at 79¢. Respondents were asked to indicate their perception of value for money (on a four-point scale) for the brands listed at the prices shown.

As the price of the GE soft white increased from cell to cell, the proportion of consumers indicating that GE soft white was a "very good value" (the top of the scale) went down and the proportion indicating the same for other soft white lamps went up.

However, the rate of loss of relative demand for GE was not matched by gains in demand by competitive brands at higher GE price points. Before exposure to the advertising (Pre), every 10¢ increase in the GE soft white price led to a loss of 8 percent of the respondent base but a gain of only 7 percent for each competitive soft white brand. After exposure to the advertising campaign (Post), competitive gains in demand were only 2–3 percent per 10¢ increment. And at parity pricing the perceived "very good

EXHIBIT 12   YSW Study: Elements of Purchase that Were Planned and Unplanned on Last Light Bulb Purchase Occasion

	Total Purchasers (percent)	Segments		
		Involved	*Uninvolved*	*Latent*
Wattage:				
Planned	84%	85%	85%	84%
Unplanned	15	13	15	15
Type of Bulb				
Planned	83	83	80	83
Unplanned	16	16	19	16
Outlet				
Planned	83	83	85	83
Unplanned	16	15	15	15
Bulb Quantity				
Planned	71	74	67	67
Unplanned	27	23	32	30
Brand Purchase				
Planned	49	55	40	48
Unplanned	48	43	57	49

YSW Study: Light Bulb Brand and Type Preferences by Segment

	Involved	*Uninvolved*	*Latent*
Segment			
Believe GE is "best for regular bulbs"	56%	47%	46%
Believe GE is "best for soft white bulbs"	46	37	37
Believe GE is "best for long life"	44	33	26
Bought a soft white bulb on last purchase occasion	53	55	41
Bought a GE bulb on last purchase occasion	57	50	43

value" rating of GE soft white increased eight percentage points (48–56 percent) while competitive brands increased three to four percentage points:

	"Very Good Value" (percent)					
	GE		*Sylvania*		*Westinghouse*	
GE Soft White Test Prices	*Pre*	*Post*	*Pre*	*Post*	*Pre*	*Post*
@69¢	61%	65%	21%	28%	25%	27%
@79¢ (competitive price point)	48	56	34	37	33	37
@89¢	41	42	38	36	39	34
@99¢	38	34	42	38	45	36
Slope	−.8	−1.1	.7	.3	.7	.2

EXHIBIT 13 Soft White Television Commercial Storyboard

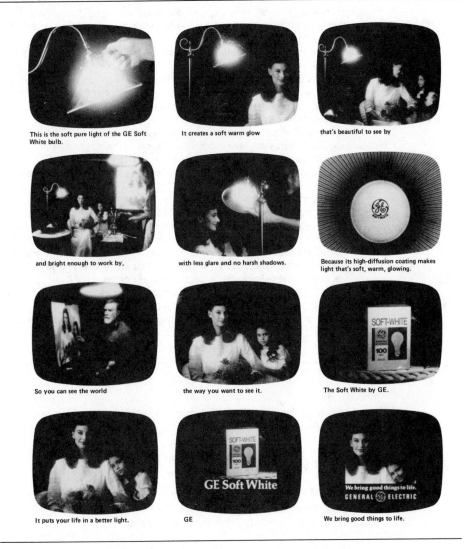

This is the soft pure light of the GE Soft White bulb.

It creates a soft warm glow

that's beautiful to see by

and bright enough to work by,

with less glare and no harsh shadows.

Because its high-diffusion coating makes light that's soft, warm, glowing.

So you can see the world

the way you want to see it.

The Soft White by GE.

It puts your life in a better light.

GE

We bring good things to life.

From these and other test data, many LPD marketing executives believed that the power of a national consumer advertising campaign had been proven. Others were more skeptical. According to one LPD sales manager:

> In my opinion, 90 percent of the share gain was due to the feature advertising prices and 10 percent due to the national advertising. The quality and share of GE's feature advertisements did improve in the food and drug channels but not in the discount chains. These price features did close the gap between our soft white and the competition. The trade recovered the lost margin

---

EXHIBIT 14   Selected Results of 1981 Test Market

- In test markets, GE soft white's unit market share increased during the experiment by 8 more points than it did in control markets. The point spread ranged from plus 23 points in drug channels to plus 1 point in food channels.
- In test markets, the unit market share of other GE bulbs increased during the experiment by 2 more points than it did in control markets. The net market share gain for all GE bulbs in test markets was plus 4 points, representing about 50 million annual unit sales.
- Partly as a result of shifting some purchasers to the higher unit margin soft white bulb from inside frost, the average manufacturer selling price of GE bulbs purchased in the test markets was 6 cents higher than in control markets.
- In test markets, 36 percent of respondents reported seeing the GE soft white advertising, and 60 percent of them were able to recall key points of the advertising unaided.
- Of those consumers who saw the GE soft white advertising:
  - 68 percent agreed that light bulbs are very or somewhat different from each other (48 percent control markets).
  - 73 percent agreed that GE soft white is different from other soft white brands (68 percent control markets). Those who valued lighting for reading and for making a room more attractive were more likely to agree that GE soft white is different.
  - 79 percent named GE as their favorite brand of light bulb (71 percent control markets).
  - 15 percent stated that they would go to another store if GE soft white bulbs were not available in their usual store (12 percent in control markets). The corresponding figures for GE inside frost bulbs were 14 percent and 9 percent.
- 72 percent of consumers choose a type of bulb (such as inside frost or soft white) first before deciding among brand alternatives within a type.
- 42 percent of respondents who reported buying GE soft white when they last purchased were not certain of the price they paid. Corresponding figures for Sylvania and Westinghouse were 31 percent and 30 percent.

---

resulting from the more frequent features by increasing prices on non-promoted GE and competitive bulbs.

THE 1982 MARKETING PROGRAM

LPD executives set out in 1982 to revitalize the consumer incandescent lighting business. Their program involved a reallocation of marketing expenditures, a new product launch and the pursuit of new distribution opportunities.

New Marketing Mix.   In 1981, LPD had spent 10 percent of its marketing funds on advertising, 9 percent on consumer rebates, 63 percent on off-invoice allowances, 5 percent on bill-back allowances for feature advertisements, and 13 percent on merchandising aids. Based on the test results, funds were shifted from off-invoice allowances and consumer rebates into national advertising, consumer coupons, and bill-back allowances. In particular:

- National advertising, principally for GE soft white bulbs, was increased by 40 percent. Some executives believed that it should have been more than doubled. However, GE's share of total category advertising was over 90 percent in 1982.

- The 3, 4, 5 program was implemented on GE soft white and 3-way bulbs, but not on inside frost. To qualify for bill-back allowances, the trade had to run feature advertisements of specified size during specified time periods which coincided with LPD's flights of national advertising.
- GE inside frost was offered at a special price once each quarter. The trade could place one order during each promotion event.
- The remaining smaller-volume consumer incandescent products were grouped together each quarter in a dealer's choice promotion. A 10 percent bill-back allowance could be earned on one order of any item after a feature advertisement was run.
- Consumer rebates were curtailed. Coupons (usually 25-cent values) were used as an alternative consumer promotion on soft white and 3-way bulbs.

New Products.   LPD planned to take its new Miser energy-efficient lamps national by the end of 1982. Miser lamps delivered 5 percent more lumens per watt than ordinary lamps. Sixty percent of in-home use testers had rated Miser lamps better than those they replaced. The Miser product group expected to sell 20 million Miser lamps by the end of 1982. A Miser product line manager commented:

> There are three advantages to new products. First, if they change consumer preferences and expectations, they can put pressure on our competitors. Second, new products broaden our line, making it easier for us to fill all the slots on a trade account's promotion calendar. Third, new products give us something worth advertising. In my view, soft white bulbs are old hat. Most of our national advertising should be put behind the Miser line.

New Distribution

LPD executives had initiated private-label sales in 1981 and had generated $4 million worth of business. In 1982, they decided to pursue more private-label business in order both to maintain their position in existing accounts and open up new accounts. The LPD national accounts manager explained the approach:

> Large trade accounts could acquire private-label bulbs at about half the price of GE bulbs. They could sell private-label bulbs at retail prices well below GE and make more money per unit. Private-label volume grew 30 percent in 1981. Given we were using only about 65 percent of our capacity for consumer incandescent bulbs, we decided in 1981 to go into private label. In order not to further commoditize the category, we decided to do this only under certain conditions. First, the customer had to be a G.E. account, and second, had to already stock or be committed to stocking private label. Finally, we decided to supply only inside frost and not soft white on a private-label basis.
>
> Early in 1982, our national accounts group solicited several discount chains, particularly those that were less price oriented. First, we'd try to persuade the account to test substituting the GE line for private label in some of its stores. Failing this, we would make both branded and private-label bulbs for them. Even chains which took on both typically moved as much volume as before without trading all of its consumers down to private label. Profits have improved for us and for the chain, so much so that, in one or two cases, we've been able to persuade trade accounts that used to carry only private label to subsequently delete the GE-made private-label product and sell only GE brand bulbs. In addition, by servicing both an account's private label and its brand

name requirements, we thought we could better help manage the account's promotion calendar. Overall, what we've discovered is that by being involved in the private-label end of the business, we've gained a more complete market perspective and we're better able to deal with the growth of private label.

1982 Results

The performance of GE's consumer incandescent lighting business in 1982 suggested that some of the initiatives which had been taken were working:

- GE consumer incandescent lamp revenues increased from $205 million in 1981 to $227 million in 1982, and operating profits increased 24 percent.
- GE's unit share of the consumer incandescent lamp market increased from 43.0 percent in 1981 to 44.5 percent in 1982, while its share of branded light bulbs rose from 45 percent to 47 percent. Sales of GE brand lamps increased from 488 million to 508 million.
- GE's average factor price per branded lamp rose from 41¢ in 1981 to 44¢ in 1982, yet GE was able to maintain its price premium at 30 percent, the 1981 level.
- In 1982, trade future advertisements for GE soft white and/or Miser bulbs increased over 1981 by 60 percent in food stores, 47 percent in drug stores, and 19 percent in discount stores.
- GE sold $6.8 million worth of private-label consumer incandescent lamps in 1982, 10 percent of all private-label units sold and a 70 percent increase over GE's 1981 private-label sales.
- GE secured $10 million worth of consumer incandescent lamp sales to new accounts.

PLANNING FOR 1983

As Frago reviewed the 1982 results and his department's marketing plans for 1983, he was primarily concerned about which overall strategy his business should pursue. He debated the relative merits of: first, a plan to increase private-label penetration, increase capacity utilization, reduce costs, and then reduce the price premium; second, a plan to secure increased distribution in emerging channels by increasing "push-oriented" off-invoice allowances; and third, a plan to reinstitute consumer advertising and merchandising performance allowances which had been cut back in mid-1982.

Price Premium.   Several LPD executives believed that GE's share of the consumer incandescent market would never increase significantly until GE's price premium was reduced. According to one:

> The way to correct the price premium is to increase promotion allowances, take a list price cut, or, at least, to take price increases less than the inflation rate. If we become more price competitive, we'll gain distribution, sell more volume, and so maintain or even increase our total margin dollars. We could also improve our margins by investing in productivity improvements to increase our machine speeds and lower unit costs.

Frago believed that the price premium should be maintained at 30 percent, but he asked for estimates of pre-tax income from the consumer incandescent business under the following three scenarios:

	Raise Premium Scenario 1	Hold Premium Scenario 2	Lower Premium Scenario 3
GE price premium in Year 7	43%	30%	25%
GE unit share in Year 7	32	45	52

The scenario analysis assumed a flat market, fixed marketing and sales expenses, steady changes in the price premium and unit share over the seven-year period, and an additional 0.5 percent annual productivity gain on increasing volume. The results of the scenario analysis, presented in Exhibit 14, seemed to support Frago's conclusion.

Promotion Allowances. Few doubted that bill-back allowances had been effective in encouraging the trade to merchandise GE bulbs more aggressively to the consumer. However, some problems were evident. According to one LPD sales manager:

> Checking performance on these allowances is an administrative nightmare and can lead to disputes with some of our most important accounts. We're rapidly overcomplicating our allowance structure. Our salespeople are too busy explaining conditions on our allowances to do any real selling. We should give the trade these allowances up front on the basis of an affidavit or letter of intent that they'll run the feature ads.

National Advertising. Several LPD marketing executives were arguing to re-institute national advertising in 1983 to support GE's soft white and Miser lines. The incremental funds were to come out of the budget for off-invoice allowances. The LPD sales force opposed this proposed shift of expenditures. Many LPD salespeople continued to be skeptical about the ability of national advertising to build the business. The following exchange took place between an LPD regional sales manager and a product marketing manager:

Sales manager:

> A light bulb is a light bulb. There's no brand differentiation. When consumers want to improve their lighting, they think of adding a lamp or a fixture rather than changing the bulb they use. What's more, demand for light bulbs is not price-elastic. Consumers don't burn them up any faster if you give them away. In short, this is a push business. Your market share depends on your share of distribution.

Product manager:

> We should be selling light, not light bulbs. We have a story to tell the consumer. Soft white stands for quality light. Miser stands for energy efficiency. There's so little light bulb advertising that a strong LPD national advertising campaign will not go unnoticed. Our share of voice will be high, so I'd expect our advertising to have impact. In addition, think what it will mean to sales force morale to be able to present a really strong national advertising campaign to the trade.

EXHIBIT 15   Pro-Forma Projections: Three Scenarios for Annual Pretax Income over Seven Years

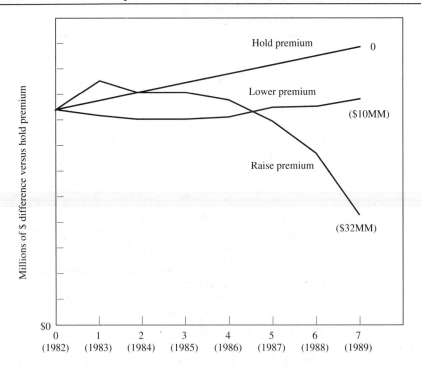

To be read: "The lower premium approach resulted in $10MM less annual pretax income than the hold premium approach."

Sales manager:

I don't agree. Heavy national advertising will make us an even more attractive traffic builder to the trade. They'll give us more advertising features and lower their retail prices further. They'll make even less money on GE bulbs than they're making now, so they'll just continue using us as a traffic builder and then emphasize private-label bulbs in their store displays because they'll make more unit margin on those than they will on GE bulbs.

Product manager:

But if we run a strong benefit-oriented national advertising program, we'll build our consumer franchise. More consumers will insist on the GE brand and be willing to pay a price premium over private label if we educate them in advertising as to why they should pay more. Our realized unit margins will improve. Yes, feature advertisements at discount prices can cause further commoditization, but only on brands which are not strongly advertised.

Sales Promotion

Case 6-1

Beecham Products U.S.A. (A)*

In October 1984, Susan Edwards, director of brand management, and Chris Weglarz, brand manager for Aqua-fresh toothpaste, were preparing for a brand group meeting on the 1985–86 media and promotion plans. Because Beecham's fiscal year began on April 1, the date of November 30, 1984, was set for completion of the plan.

Edwards noted that increased levels of media and promotion spending had been required in recent years to maintain an Aqua-fresh market share of approximately 12 percent, the level achieved in 1980, one year after the Aqua-fresh product introduction. The major factor in the rise of promotional expenditures was ever-increasing competitive spending on trade deals. Some members of the brand group questioned the level of trade promotion expenditures and argued that reallocating some trade promotion funds to consumer promotions would result in market share increases.

New information to assist in formulating the 1985–86 plan was available to the brand group. Using consumer toothpaste purchase data provided by scanner panels, the effectiveness of various promotional vehicles had been evaluated by Information Resources, Inc. (IRI).

COMPANY BACKGROUND

Thomas Beecham's study of the medicinal properties of herbs began in 1828 at the age of 8 when he started work as a shepherd to augment his family's income. By the age of 20, Beecham was selling his herbal remedies throughout England. He became firmly established in the early 1850s as a "Chemist, Druggist, and Tea Dealer." Among Beecham's accomplishments was the formulation of Beecham's Pills, a remedy for the common cold. This medicine became increasingly well-known as Beecham first distributed the pills through mail order, then developed a national marketing program. By 1859, the product was sold from Africa to Australia.

Beecham was committed to customer satisfaction through product quality. This commitment was evident in his reservations about the power of advertising:

---

*This case was prepared by Research Associate Melanie D. Spencer under the direction of Professor John A. Quelch as the basis for class discussion rather than to illustrate either effective or ineffective handling of an administrative situation. Proprietary data have been disguised. Promotion plans provided are not actual plans. Copyright © 1986 by the President and Fellows of Harvard College. Harvard Business School case 1–587–012.

It is possible, by plausible advertising, set forth in an attractive style, to temporarily arrest the attention of a certain number of readers, and induce them to purchase a particular article. But it is a more difficult matter to ensure their continued patronage. Unless the advertised article proves to be all that is claimed for it, not only do the purchasers discontinue its use, but warn others against it as a thing to be avoided.

Beecham believed in tailoring his products to the markets in which they were being sold. For example, when the company introduced Beecham's Pills in the United States, they were sweetened to appeal to American tastes. This philosophy also applied to the sales force. Beecham required that export salespersons speak the languages of their customers.

Growth continued through acquisition as well as international market expansion. Early acquisitions included Macleans, makers of a popular brand of toothpaste, and County Perfumery, which produced Brylcreem, the leading men's hairdressing in the United Kingdom. Brylcreem later spearheaded Beecham's expansion into the United States, becoming the best-selling men's hairdressing in the U.S. by 1960.

Encouraged by Brylcreem's success, Beecham made further acquisitions including S.E. Massengill (1971), a Tennessee-based producer of pharmaceuticals and feminine hygiene products, and the Calgon consumer products business (1977), which marketed well-known brands such as Cling-Free fabric softener, Sucrets sore throat lozenges, and Calgon water conditioner. The Calgon acquisition tripled the size of Beecham's U.S. consumer products business. In 1982, Beecham acquired the J. B. Williams division of Nabisco Brands, which marketed the leading U.S. iron supplement, Geritol.

By 1984, the Beecham Group, Ltd., had become a $2.5 billion consumer products and pharmaceutical company, with headquarters in the United Kingdom. Beecham Products U.S.A., the U.S. consumer packaged goods division of Beecham Group, Ltd., manufactured and marketed 17 brands, including Aqua-fresh, Massengill, Cling-Free, Calgon, Geritol, and Sucrets. The division's sales were $400 million in 1984.

Marketing within the division was organized around the classic product management system. Directors of brand management reported to the vice president of marketing. Each director of brand management was responsible for two to four brand management groups. The marketing vice president reported directly to the president of the division, making the chain of command relatively short and facilitating quick decision making.

PRODUCT CATEGORY HISTORY

Tooth powder was introduced in the U.S. in 1899. Similar in consistency to baking soda, tooth powder had to be combined with water before use, either by dipping a wet toothbrush into the powder or by forming a paste which could then be applied to the teeth. The procedure tended to be time-consuming and messy.

In 1936, three brands of toothpaste were introduced: Squibb, Colgate, and Pepsodent. The next milestone occurred in 1955, when fluoride was incorporated into toothpaste formulas to aid in tooth decay prevention. Crest, introduced by Procter & Gamble Co. in 1955, was the first toothpaste to include fluoride. The therapeutic value of brushing with a fluoride toothpaste earned Crest the first American Dental Association (ADA) seal of approval.

Brands such as Crest and Colgate, which emphasized fluoride content and cavity prevention, were targeted at families with young children. These products developed strong brand loyalty. Many children whose parents had purchased a particular product for its decay prevention continued to use the same brand as adults.

During the late 1960s and early 1970s, many new toothpaste brands were introduced, some of which emphasized cosmetic rather than therapeutic benefits. Ultra-Brite (1967), manufactured by Colgate-Palmolive, and Close-Up (1970), made by Lever Brothers, for example, focused on the whitening and breath-freshening properties of toothpaste. Advertising for these brands targeted a new audience, teenagers and young adults who were beginning to make their own purchasing decisions, and emphasized the "sex appeal" of white teeth and fresh breath. Next came Aim, introduced by Lever Brothers in 1973. Like Close-Up, Aim was a gel, but since it contained fluoride, it was positioned as a therapeutic brand.

Through the late 1970s, the toothpaste category averaged volume growth of only 2 percent per year.

THE AQUA-FRESH INTRODUCTION

Prior to introducing Aqua-fresh nationally, Beecham conducted a test market in four cities. Aqua-fresh's market share objectives ranged from 8–9 percent. The product was positioned as a cosmetic brand with advertising emphasizing breath-freshening benefits with the tag line "Oceans of Freshness." The results were disappointing, with the product achieving only a 4 percent market share during the test period.

Research in the late 1970s had shown that two-thirds of U.S. households purchased both cosmetic and therapeutic brands, with different members of the household using different brands. Beecham, therefore, repositioned the brand as Double Protection Aqua-fresh, offering both breath-freshening and cavity-prevention benefits to the consumer. To communicate visually these dual attributes, the toothpaste combined a white paste component and an aqua gel component, which gave the product a striped appearance. The toothpaste was awarded the American Dental Association (ADA) seal of approval because of its proven ability to fight cavities. Only five dentifrice brands were allowed to carry ADA seals on their cartons and in their advertising at that time: Aqua-fresh, Crest, Colgate, Aim, and Macleans. Beecham tested Aqua-fresh's new positioning in two markets in New York and Texas, with market share objectives of 10 percent and 12 percent, respectively. The achievement of their market share objectives resulted in a decision to launch Aqua-fresh nationally.

In January 1979, Beecham began a regional roll-out of Aqua-fresh in the western third of the U.S. Aqua-fresh was the first major new brand in the product category since Aim.

To stimulate trial of Aqua-fresh, Beecham undertook one of the largest sampling programs ever implemented in the industry. The weight of Aqua-fresh advertising during the introduction was also unprecedented. Mothers of teenagers were selected as the primary target market because management believed that teens, more than other consumers, faced the conflict between cosmetic and therapeutic benefits. Double Protection Aqua-fresh was believed especially appropriate for families with mothers concerned about cavity protection and with teens who insisted on a toothpaste that freshened breath. Advertising and promotion expenditures in the year following the introduction were $21.7 million and

EXHIBIT 1   Toothpaste Market Size and Competitive Brand Shares

A. C. Nielsen Retail Sales Data: 1980–1984*

	1980	1981	1982	1983	1984 (est.)
Aqua-fresh	12.9%	11.9%	11.6%	11.5%	11.4%
Crest	35.4	36.2	35.1	35.2	32.9
Colgate	17.8	18.4	22.5	22.4	23.6
Aim	10.2	9.5	9.5	9.7	9.1
Total market:					
Thousands of dozens	60,464	63,082	65,886	71,848	73,793
Retail $MM	$868	$974	$1,055	$1,130	$1,177

SAMI Warehouse Withdrawal Data: 1982–1984†

	1980	1981	1982	1983	1984 (est.)
Aqua-fresh			12.1%	12.0%	12.2%
Crest			35.2	35.8	43.1
Colgate			22.9	22.8	23.3
Aim			10.0	9.0	8.6
Total market:					
Thousands of dozen cases			39,749	42,697	41,586

*A.C. Nielsen numbers included sales of food stores, drug stores, and mass merchandisers.
†SAMI measured product withdrawals from food chain warehouses only.

$23.1 million respectively. Crest, the market leader, and Aim, the number three brand, substantially increased promotions and advertising in response to the Aqua-fresh introduction, while Colgate, the number two brand, showed little reaction.

By the end of 1979, Aqua-fresh had established a nationwide market share of 12 percent, drawn proportionately to market share from the three major competitors, Crest, Colgate, and Aim. Aqua-fresh achieved the number three share position in the category, with a higher share than Aim. Exhibit 1 shows Nielsen and SAMI[1] market share trends for the years following the Aqua-fresh introduction.

Aqua-fresh, like its major competitors, was packaged in five tube sizes: 1.4 oz., 2.7 oz., 4.6 oz., 6.4 oz., and 8.2 oz. Each size of each brand was considered an "item." The percent of Aqua-fresh's 1984 volume by size was as follows:

	Size (ounces)				
	1.4	2.7	4.6	6.4	8.2
Percent volume distribution by size	7%	13%	20%	35%	25%

[1]The A.C. Nielsen Company monitored retail sales by brand/size in a sample of retail outlets nationwide. Selling Areas Marketing Inc. (SAMI), a division of Time Inc., monitored the rate of product withdrawals from trade warehouses.

The percent of volume by item was similar for the other major brands, except that Crest and Colgate tended to sell a greater proportion of their volume in the smaller sizes. Manufacturer list prices of all the major brands were comparable.

The Aqua-fresh launch began a new era in dentifrice marketing. What historically had been a stable, predictable product category became increasingly volatile and competitive. When Aqua-fresh was introduced, 25 items accounted for 80 percent of sales volume in the category. By 1984, following introductions of several new flavors and gels by the market leaders, 40 items accounted for 80 percent of toothpaste sales volume.

PRODUCT CATEGORY DEVELOPMENT AFTER THE AQUA-FRESH INTRODUCTION

The first new product introduction after Aqua-fresh occurred in January 1981, when Procter & Gamble launched Advanced Formula Crest. Advertising implied that Advanced Formula's new fluoride gave consumers therapeutic benefits superior to those of its competitive brands. The product was presented to the trade as a one-for-one substitution for original Crest, at the same price. The number of items in the category remained the same.

In the fall of 1981, Procter & Gamble, Colgate, and Lever Brothers all introduced new flavors. Crest Gel was the third flavor of Crest toothpaste (Crest Mint had been introduced in 1955) and increased the number of Crest items from 10 to 15. Colgate Gel and Aim Mint flavors doubled the number of items for each brand from 5 to 10. The gel introductions were the result of research showing that sweeter gels appealed to a younger audience. Colgate had identified that its users were older and, therefore, developed the gel to appeal to a younger market segment. Crest already had an image as a therapeutic brand for children. In the heavy advertising and promotion war that followed these introductions, Colgate gained market share as its new gel attracted younger users. Crest, however, lost share; its new gel simply cannibalized sales of its other two formulas.

To carry the ADA seal of acceptance, toothpaste manufacturers had to have their advertising claims cleared by the ADA. During 1981, the Aqua-fresh brand attempted to clear a plaque[2] claim with the ADA. Beecham research had shown that the three most important therapeutic attributes to consumers were: "Helps prevent cavities," "Contains fluoride," and "Helps remove plaque." The research also indicated that Aqua-fresh had not yet established the reputation for therapy that Crest, Colgate, and Aim had. Despite the dual benefit positioning, Aqua-fresh users often liked the brand for its taste and breath freshening rather than for its fluoride/cavity-prevention properties. Given the results, the brand group believed the plaque claims would improve Aqua-fresh's therapeutic image. However, the claim was refused by the ADA. The ADA refused to allow any dentifrice manufacturers to make the plaque claim at that time. They later established guidelines for clinical testing that would allow manufacturers to test and clear plaque claims.

Nevertheless, with the Crest Gel, Colgate Gel, and Aim Mint introductions in the fall of 1981, the brand group felt it had to reposition Aqua-fresh to address more consumer

---

[2]Plaque is a sticky film on the teeth which can lead to gum disease and cavities if not removed.

EXHIBIT 2   Six-Month Promotion Activity for 1981–1982 Toothpaste Introductions

Crest Gel 11/81–4/82	Colgate Gel 11/81–4/82	Aim Mint 10/81–3/82	Triple Protection Aqua-fresh 1/82–6/82
$.25 mailed coupon— 12/81	$.10 FSI* coupon—11/81	$.25 FSI coupon—10/81	Trial floor stand—2/82
Trial floor stand—1/82	$.25 FSI coupon—1/82	$.15 magazine coupon—11/81	$.15 FSI coupon—2/82
$.25 on-pack coupon—3/82	Mailed samples and $.10 coupon—1/82	$.15 FSI coupon—12/81	$.12 mailed coupon—4/82
	$.25 FSI coupon—2/82	2-$.15 mailed coupon—1/82	3-$.12 BFD coupon—5/82
	$.20 mailed coupon—3/82	Trial floor stand—1/82	Trial floor stand—6/82
	1.4 oz. trial floor stand—3/82	$.15 FSI coupon—1/82	
	$.15 FSI/BFD† coupon— 4/82	$.25 FSI coupon—3/82	
	$.25 in-store coupon		

*FSI = Free Standing Insert.
†BFD = Best Food Day.

needs. Hence, in November of 1981, Beecham began shipments of new "Triple Protection Aqua-fresh" with an "even cleans stained film" claim added to the cavity-prevention and breath-freshening attributes. At that time, this was as close as the ADA would allow to a plaque claim. Consumer research had indicated that stain removal was important to consumers, and clinical research proved that Triple Protection Aqua-fresh was effective at cleaning stains. Triple Protection Aqua-fresh had three stripes, red, aqua, and white.

The new product was presented to the trade as a one-for-one substitution for the existing line. Because of the Crest Gel, Colgate Gel, and Aim Mint (15 items) introductions, Aqua-fresh's share of total shelf space declined. Nevertheless, after an initial share decline in January and February of 1982, the new formula helped Aqua-fresh regain and maintain market share at 11.5 percent, despite heavy competitive promotion and advertising support. Exhibit 2 lists the trial-generating consumer promotions fielded for each of the new brand items during their first six months.

DISTRIBUTION

Beecham Products U.S.A. employed a direct sales force which was responsible for achieving sales volume targets and implementing promotions in specific geographical regions.

Aqua-fresh was sold primarily through three channels: food stores, drugstores, and mass merchandisers. Table 1 shows Aqua-fresh and product category sales and Aqua-fresh distribution penetration by channel from 1981 to 1984 in millions of dozens.[3]

---

[3]In 1983–84, the average number of ounces of toothpaste per unit sold was 6.04 (total), 5.84 (food), 6.0 (drug), and 6.65 (mass merchandiser).

TABLE 1   Toothpaste Sales—Millions of Dozens

Aqua-fresh	1981/82	1982/83	1983/84
Food	4.8	4.8	5.2
Drug	1.6	1.6	1.8
Mass merchandiser	1.1	1.4	1.3
Total	7.5	7.8	8.3
Category	**1981/82**	**1982/83**	**1983/84**
Food	40.0	42.2	43.6
Drug	14.8	13.5	15.0
Mass merchandiser	9.0	11.7	13.7
Total	63.8	67.4	72.3

Exhibit 3 shows Beecham fiscal year 1983/84 percentage ACV distribution by size for each channel.[4]

Food stores accounted for 60 percent of category dollar sales in 1984. Historically, health and beauty aid (HBA) products had been a small part of most food stores' business; however, a trend toward larger HBA sections in food stores developed in the early 1980s as they sought to emphasize higher-margin merchandise. Food stores began to treat toothpaste as a loss leader to generate consumer traffic. As a result, food stores became more demanding regarding promotional offers from manufacturers. Most food stores tended to stock three sizes of each major brand flavor. Reflecting the number of items pressing for limited shelf space, many food stores did not carry weaker brands.

Drug stores, on the other hand, relied on HBA products as a major source of sales. For this reason, drug stores stocked most brands and sizes of toothpaste. However, they were also pressing for promotional offers to give them an edge in competing with the food stores. Drug stores considered toothpaste an important traffic builder which could lead to the sale of other higher-margin products. They, therefore, gave brands feature advertising support, maintained an average of four items per brand flavor, and realized lower margins on toothpaste than food stores, passing promotional savings through to the consumer. Drug stores accounted for 20 percent of category sales.

Mass merchandisers accounted for 20 percent of category sales volume and carried an average of four items per brand flavor. Because they typically offered the consumer an "everyday low price," trade promotions were not as important for mass merchandisers. Mass merchandisers featured toothpaste less frequently than food or drugstores, but when a feature was run, it usually generated greater percentage sales increases than a feature in either of the other two channels.

Beecham's sales force was smaller than those of the category leaders, Procter & Gamble and Colgate-Palmolive. Therefore, Aqua-fresh distribution was better in the larger chains

---

[4]An item with 70 percent ACV (all commodity volume) in grocery stores was distributed in stores that accounted for 70 percent of the sales through all grocery stores.

EXHIBIT 3   Distribution of Four Toothpaste Brands (Tubes)—1983/84

	Food—Percent ACV				
	1.4 oz.	*2.7 oz.*	*4.6 oz.*	*6.4 oz.*	*8.2 oz.*
Aqua-fresh	36.3%	80.9%	81.4%	82.8%	63.9%
Crest	38.0	83.4	85.8	87.2	71.3
Colgate	41.4	80.9	83.8	85.6	64.7
Aim	15.2	67.7	78.2	81.6	52.5

	Drug—Percent ACV				
	1.4 oz.	*2.7 oz.*	*4.6 oz.*	*6.4 oz.*	*8.2 oz.*
Aqua-fresh	67.7	71.1	84.8	80.5	59.1
Crest	83.0	73.1	89.1	93.9	68.7
Colgate	79.5	69.4	88.6	90.7	67.2
Aim	49.7	57.4	81.5	85.7	52.4

	MM—Percent of Stores				
	1.4 oz.	*2.7 oz.*	*4.6 oz.*	*6.4 oz.*	*8.2 oz.*
Aqua-fresh	53.3	69.3	80.7	97.0	82.3
Crest	44.0	73.0	74.7	99.3	96.3
Colgate	48.7	66.3	82.7	98.7	83.3
Aim	26.3	62.3	74.7	98.3	76.3

and in regions of the country where such chains were predominant. Sales to the trade in New York City, for example, were complicated by the high number of small, independent supermarkets. The sales force was also too small to devote much time to setting up displays. Therefore, the Aqua-fresh brand team relied heavily on prepacked display pieces that could be handled easily by retailers.

As competition in the toothpaste category became fiercer and item proliferation put pressure on the shelf space available to any single brand in the category, the salesperson's job became more challenging. The sales force had to handle complex Aqua-fresh promotional calendars and monitor multiple competitive trade promotions at any one time. Adding shelf space for Aqua-fresh became increasingly difficult. Sales management developed new sales pitches to defend Aqua-fresh's shelf space. For example, the organizer, shown in Exhibit 4, focused on Aqua-fresh's contribution per item compared to the contribution per item of competitive brands with broader product lines.

AQUA-FRESH MARKETING

Brand management relied on advertising, trade promotion, and consumer promotion to market Aqua-fresh. Exhibit 5 shows media and promotion spending in dollars and as a percentage of sales for Aqua-fresh and the other major brands for 1979/80 through

EXHIBIT 4 Aqua-fresh Trade Organizer

A Category that Draws the Consumer
Dentifrice Dollar Volume

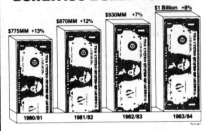

$775MM +13% 1980/81
$870MM +12% 1981/82
$930MM +7% 1982/83
$1 Billion +8% 1983/84

☐ Over last four years category has grown dramatically.
    Dollar Volume up 30% = 5.5 million cases.

☐ Aqua-fresh, Colgate, and Crest have accounted for nearly all of the category's growth.

☐ 7 of the top 10 HBA items are toothpastes— Aqua-fresh, Colgate, and Crest draw the consumer.

☐ Nearly 100% household penetration—every consumer is a potential sale.

Aqua-fresh
#1 share/SKU

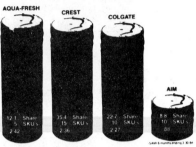

AQUA-FRESH	CREST	COLGATE	AIM
12.1 Share	35.4 Share	22.7 Share	8.8 Share
5 SKU's	15 SKU's	10 SKU's	10 SKU's
2.42	2.36	2.27	.88

(SAMI 6 months ending 3/30/84)

☐ Aqua-fresh #1 seller per SKU, outselling Crest and Colgate. Outsells Aim 3 to 1.

☐ By flavor, Aqua-fresh is vying for the #1 position with a 12.1% share.

☐ Aqua-fresh sales are about equal to Crest Regular and Colgate Regular.

Aqua-fresh
is #1 in Inventory Turns

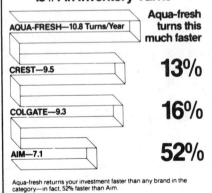

	Aqua-fresh turns this much faster
AQUA-FRESH—10.8 Turns/Year	
CREST—9.5	**13%**
COLGATE—9.3	**16%**
AIM—7.1	**52%**

Aqua-fresh returns your investment faster than any brand in the category—in fact, 52% faster than Aim.

Aqua-fresh inventory turns nearly 11 times a year—with 2% 30 terms, you sell Aqua-fresh before you pay for it!

Fast turns + unsurpassed terms = Best Profit Return—Aqua-fresh

Aqua-fresh
IS #1 IN MAKING MONEY
Annual Profit Return Per Inventory Dollar Invested

Aqua-fresh   AQUA-FRESH **$2.48**

Crest   CREST **$2.19**

Colgate   COLGATE **$2.14**

Aim   AIM **$1.63**
        Based on Average Profit Margin—Nielsen

REACT TO THE FACTS

☐ Aqua-fresh delivers more profit than Crest, Colgate and Aim.

☐ Aqua-fresh share of inventories is too lean in proportion to category shares.

☐ Aim inventories are too fat in proportion to category shares.

☐ Aqua-fresh out-of-stocks cost you money—
    Consumer delays purchase or
    Buys a brand with shorter terms of sale

SOLUTION: Carry all 5 Sizes
Make Aqua-fresh share of inventory = share of sales

EXHIBIT 4 (*concluded*)

Aqua-fresh®

#1 with your Promotion Dollars

% Increase in Movement

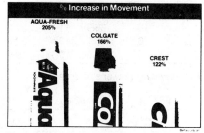

AQUA-FRESH	205%
COLGATE	166%
CREST	122%

- Aqua-fresh sells better on promotion than Crest or Colgate
- Promoting a toothpaste is a consumer draw provided the brand you use is recognized by the consumer.
- *Feature and display Aqua-fresh to get the most out of your promotion dollars.*
- It's easier and more profitable to promote Aqua-fresh

Aqua-fresh	1 SKU/size
Crest	3 SKU's/size
Colgate	2 SKU's/size
Aim	2 SKU's/size

Aqua-fresh®

Best Return Comes from Feature and Display

Based on 20% Price Reduction

	Increase in Movement	WEEKLY MOVEMENT
Price Reduction	+47%	CS
Price Reduction + Feature	+186%	CS
Price Reduction + Feature + Display	+843%	CS

Based on 30% Price Reduction

	Increase in Movement	WEEKLY MOVEMENT
Price Reduction	+85%	CS
Price Reduction + Feature	+260%	CS
Price Reduction + Feature + Display	+1.087%	CS

$ _____

Aqua-fresh®

Sells the Consumer

Advertising:
- Reaching 90% of all households
- 588 GRP's a month
- 16 commercials/week

Consumer Promotion:
- 24 million 20¢ mailed coupons week of 9/30/84

Action Plan:

_____ _____
_____ _____
_____ _____

BEECHAM PRODUCTS, Pittsburgh, PA 15230

EXHIBIT 5   Estimated Advertising and Promotion Expenditures by Brand

Category Media Spending (millions of dollars)

	1979/80		1980/81		1981/82		1982/83		1983/84		1984/85	
	$MM	Sales	$MM	Sales	$MM	Sales	$MM	Sales	$MM	Sales	$MM	Sales
Aqua-fresh	$21.7	27%	$20.7	25%	$19.5	23%	$24.5	21%	$22.9	18%	$21.6	16%
Crest	25.8	9	29.4	13	48.4	18	36.9	11	37.0	10	31.0	10
Colgate	18.1	13	17.0	15	27.7	20	26.1	12	30.0	13	28.0	12
Aim	15.7	19	15.5	25	21.3	33	17.6	19	19.5	18	18.0	20

Category Promotion Spending (millions of dollars)

	1979/80		1980/81		1981/82		1982/83		1983/84		1984/85	
	$MM	Sales	$MM	Sales	$MM	Sales	$MM	Sales	$MM	Sales	$MM	Sales
Aqua-fresh	$23.1	28%	$13.9	17%	$17.4	21%	$20.6	18%	$29.9	24%	$30.8	23%
Crest	28.1	10	31.8	14	31.1	12	36.1	11	65.1	17	55.4	14
Colgate	19.4	14	24.8	22	41.0	29	40.6	19	44.3	18	52.1	18
Aim	10.5	13	12.9	21	19.1	29	15.4	17	24.8	23	16.9	17

Aqua-fresh Promotion Spending (thousands of dollars)

	1980/81	1981/82	1982/83	1983/84	1984/85
Price pack	$ 7,278	$ 4,642	$ 9,349	$12,512	$12,829
Other trade merchandising	4,088	8,984	8,273	9,590	10,353
Trial events	2,569	3,731	3,009	7,787	7,620
Total	$13,935	$17,357	$20,631	$29,889	$30,802

1983/84. Brand management estimated that 70 percent of Aqua-fresh, Aim, and Colgate sales volume was shipped to the trade on deal; the corresponding figure for Crest was 60 percent.

Advertising

Aqua-fresh spent its advertising dollars primarily in television. Television spots focused on the brand's attributes, physically represented by the toothpaste's stripes. Exhibit 6 presents a storyboard from a typical triple-protection Aqua-fresh commercial. The major objectives of Aqua-fresh advertising were to promote awareness of the brand, communicate product benefits, and emphasize ADA approval. In 1984, brand management estimated that a 17 percent share of voice was necessary to maintain Aqua-fresh market share. They projected 1984–85 advertising expenditures of $21.6 million on sales of $134 million or 8.4 million dozens.

EXHIBIT 6   Aqua-fresh Television Advertisement

FATHER: What's this . . .

a space age toothpaste!

MOTHER: No! It's our Aqua-fresh with a brand new see-through top.
TEEN: I can see its Triple Protection Formula!
MOTHER: Only Aqua-fresh has it.

(VO): The maximum fluoride protection of the leading paste . . .

all the breath freshener of the leading gel . . .

and gentle cleaners that even remove stained film . . .

SFX: SWOOSH
concentrated in one complete toothpaste.

MOTHER: And tests prove mothers prefer Aqua-fresh to the other leading brands

ANNCR (VO): Triple Protection Aqua-fresh. A complete toothpaste.

Trade Promotions

Manufacturers often offered a trade promotion or temporary price discount on a product for a specified period of time to boost short-term sales. The allowance was often dependent on the retailer providing merchandising support (retail price cut, feature advertisement, and/or special display) for the product during the promotion period. Although increased short-term sales and consumer trial might be generated, trade promotions rarely resulted in sustained sales volume and market share increases. Manufacturers encouraged the trade to accept promoted product packed in displays or floor stands to maximize sales.

In 1980, trade promotion expenditures by packaged goods manufacturers in the United States were estimated at $6.5 billion, with health and beauty aids trade promotions alone accounting for $3.3 billion of this total.[5] Trade allowances for toothpaste since 1980 had increased in step with manufacturer price increases, keeping the dead net, the unit cost to the trade after all allowances, at roughly the same level.[6] The result was more money for retailers and escalating trade promotion expenditures by manufacturers.

Aqua-fresh trade promotions frequently included allowances with merchandising requirements. Trade promotion was considered so important to the brand that one manager characterized the marketing planning process as follows: "First we figure the trade promotion spending required to be competitive; then, we add the media cost; then, whatever is left goes for trial events." The amount of the allowance and therefore the dead net cost varied depending on the size of the item on deal, and the brand group's projections of expected competitive offers. The objective was to offer dead nets which were comparable to those of its major competitors. Proof of merchandising performance, such as an advertising tear sheet or a picture of a display, was necessary before Beecham paid a merchandising allowance.

Aggressive promotion was necessary to ensure merchandising support for the brand and to retain distribution of as many stockkeeping units (SKUs) as possible. During periods of competitive introductions of new items, promotional expenditures to the trade were critical to sustaining shelf space. The 1983/84 shares of retailer feature advertising in the toothpaste category obtained by Aqua-fresh and the other major brands by type of distribution channel are shown in Table 2.

The Crest brand was supported by regular trade promotions on key sizes plus Procter & Gamble's Cooperative Merchandising Agreement (CMA). The CMA enabled retailers to accrue a $.10–$.50 allowance per statistical case on Procter & Gamble products. A retailer could receive these allowances if it provided special merchandising support. Allowances earned on one product could be applied to the merchandising of any other product sold by Procter & Gamble's Health and Personal Care Division. The CMA helped

TABLE 2   Shares of Retailer Feature Advertising of Toothpaste

	Food	Drug/Mass Merchandiser
Aqua-fresh	14%	11%
Crest	17	17
Colgate	24	24
Aim	13	13

---

[5]Reported in Paul W. Farris and John A. Quelch, *Advertising and Promotion Management* (Radnor, Pennsylvania: Chilton Book Company, 1983).

[6]The dead net cost was the cost of an item to the retailer after all allowances had been subtracted from the manufacturer's price.

to ensure Procter & Gamble of distribution of its weaker products. A further benefit was that Procter & Gamble did not have to sell Crest consistently at a high discount to gain merchandising support for the brand. Colgate offered a similar program. Beecham did not offer a CMA. Instead, Beecham offered the trade more lucrative bonus allowances tied to specific promotions. This gave Beecham tighter control over expenditures and greater assurance of extra merchandising performance for specific events.

Consumer Promotions

Consumer promotions typically were aimed either to switch users of competitive brands to the promoted product or, secondarily, to reward current users. Aqua-fresh brand management used three types of consumer promotion: price packs, coupons, and trial sizes to generate trial of Aqua-fresh. Trial was viewed as an important objective as the brand was relatively new and consumer research showed that most consumers who tried Aqua-fresh preferred it to the other leading brands.

Price packs, with a standard price reduction (for example, "20 cents off") printed on the package, were frequently run on the 4.6-, 6.4-, and 8.2-ounce sizes of Aqua-fresh, Colgate, and Aim. Retailers were paid the amount of the price reduction and were therefore obligated to pass the reduction on to the consumer. Promotions on the 8.2-ounce size offered the advantage of taking purchasers out of the market for a longer period. In 1984, Aqua-fresh price pack values on the 8.2-ounce size were $.35, while Aim and Colgate offered $.40 and $.30 respectively. Twin packs or "buy-two-get-one-free" offers were frequently fielded on the 6.4-oz. size to take the consumer out of the market for an even longer time. Crest combined a banded pack with an on-pack premium, offering two packs banded together with free Lego building blocks to stimulate sales to families with small children. All manufacturers fielded trade promotion offers in conjunction with price packs to ensure maximum retail merchandising support.

Price packs were known to generate heavier-than-normal retail sales, especially when supported by extra merchandising effort by the trade in the form of end-aisle displays and feature advertisements. Price packs were preferred over trade promotions alone since the value of the promotion was typically passed through to the consumer in the form of a lower price rather than pocketed by the retailer. Some retailers, however, especially those that pursued an everyday low price strategy,[7] were resistant to price packs. Price packs typically required special handling. A new UPC number had to be coded into store computer systems. Trade resistance prompted Procter & Gamble to curtail Crest price pack promotions in the spring of 1983, apparently in an effort to improve the company's relations with the trade. The other manufacturers offered trade accounts off-invoice allowances as alternatives to price packs. These allowances were less attractive than price pack offers and, therefore, accounted for a small portion of promoted volume.

---

[7]"Everyday low price" retailers used their promotion allowances to offer consistently low prices on the same items from one week to the next, as opposed to advertising very low sale prices on a different set of "hot specials" each week.

While price packs permitted regular users to stock up on inventory during a price pack promotion, coupon promotions required a consumer to have a separate coupon for each unit purchased. Price packs were considered by some to detract more than coupons from a brand's image, and to make consumers less willing to purchase a product at its regular price. On the other hand, a coupon was physically separated from the package. The timing and duration of a price pack promotion were critical to its impact. If a nonuser were in the middle of a purchase cycle during the short (usually one week) period of a store's price pack promotion, the price incentive would be less likely to motivate trial and the consumer would be missed. Coupons, on the other hand, permitted the consumer to choose the timing of the purchases, but were not always effective in generating special merchandising support from retailers because of the extended period of the offer.

Aqua-fresh offered some coupons to stimulate trial. Consumer trial was particularly important to the brand as blind home-use tests had shown that consumers significantly preferred Aqua-fresh to the other major brands. Aqua-fresh coupons were distributed either through the mail, in the "Best Food Day" (BFD) sections of newspapers, or as a part of a "Free Standing Insert" (FSI) in Sunday newspapers. Research had demonstrated that direct-mail couponing generated higher redemption rates among triers; however, this method was also more expensive in terms of cost per thousand coupons distributed. Exhibit 7 shows planned coupon costs for the 1984-85 fiscal year.

A trial-size offer of 1.4-ounce tubes prepriced at $.39 was also used to stimulate brand trial. Retail inventory turnover for the trial size was high versus the normal rate. Retailers could achieve higher-than-normal margins on trial sizes. They were shipped in prepacked displays that required little special handling. Because of the high margins, the high turn, and the minimal handling requirements, retailers found this type of promotion particularly attractive. In addition, regular brand users were unlikely to purchase trial sizes because they were too small.

As the toothpaste product category became increasingly competitive, trade and consumer promotion grew in importance. As one manager said:

> Since Aqua-fresh is the third leading brand, trade promotion expenditures are important to ensure that the trade will continue to stock our product. But Aqua-fresh can't afford to escalate trade promotions to get additional merchandising support because the competition will meet the increase and we will have accomplished nothing.

MARKET RESEARCH

A market research study was conducted to measure the effect of the introduction of Triple Protection Aqua-fresh on consumer attitudes and usage. The study, conducted in February 1983, had the additional objectives of measuring the effect of the Triple Protection introduction on the brand's therapeutic image and the impact of the Crest Gel and the Colgate Gel introductions.

Brand management concluded that the introduction of Triple Protection Aqua-fresh and the competitive gels had not substantially changed the unaided awareness, past four-week usage, or retention levels of the major brands. There were, however, modest

---

EXHIBIT 7   1984–85 Aqua-fresh Coupons*

1. 20¢ free-standing insert:
Distribution (43MM × 2.25/M)	$ 98M
Printing	30
Redemption (43MM × 3.1% × 30¢)†	400
Total cost	$ 528M
Circulation	÷ 30MM
Cost per thousand delivered	$17.60

2. 20¢ BFD coupon
Distribution (45MM × $1.95/M)	$ 88M
Redemption (45MM × 2.8% × 30¢)	378
Total cost	$ 466M
Circulation	÷ 45MM
Cost per thousand delivered	$10.36

3. 20¢ Mailed Coupon
Distribution (23.9MM × $6.00/M)	$ 143M
Printing	12
20¢ Redemption (23.9MM × 5.5% × 30¢)	395
Total cost	$ 550M
Circulation	÷ 23.9MM
Cost per thousand delivered	$23.02

4. 20¢ Mailed Coupon
Distribution (30MM × $9.75/M)	$ 293M
20¢ Redemption (30MM × 8.0% × 30¢)	720
Total cost	$1,013M
Circulation	÷ 30MM
Cost per thousand delivered	$33.77

Total year: 4 coupons
Cost: $528M + $466M + $550M + 1,013M =	$2,557M
Coupons delivered: 30MM + 45MM + 23.9MM + 30MM =	128.9MM
Weighted average cost per thousand delivered	$19.84

*National coupon drops only. Some regional coupons were also fielded in defense against regional competitive activity.

†Handling each redeemed coupon, regardless of value, cost 10 cents.

---

improvements in the therapeutic image of Aqua-fresh and in the Aqua-fresh trial rate. While brand management believed that changes in advertising to emphasize Aqua-fresh's ADA seal of approval and therapeutic attributes could further improve the brand's therapeutic image, there was no agreement as to the best way to stimulate additional trial of the brand. Some managers believed that a nationwide sampling program would produce the best results, but others thought that trial sizes would be more cost effective. One manager was convinced that in-store displays were key to stimulating new trial of Aqua-fresh and advocated increased spending for trade promotions. However, none of the managers could prove that one method was more effective than another.

BEHAVIORSCAN RESEARCH

Beecham executives decided to use BehaviorScan® research from Information Resources, Inc. (IRI)[8] to evaluate the effectiveness of various types of promotion. IRI had developed a system of tracking consumer purchasing behavior for most products sold through grocery and drug stores. This system used Universal Product Code (UPC) scanners to record information on the purchases of selected panels of about 2,500 households in eight U.S. markets.

The households in the eight consumer panels were randomly selected. Each was given an I.D. card to present to the store cashier upon checkout. This I.D. card signaled the computer to record the purchase data in the file of the appropriate panel member. IRI randomly selected members of each panel to receive prizes as an incentive for continued cooperation. Because of the minimal work required of panel members, about 70 percent of consumers who were asked to be on a panel accepted, giving IRI a representative sample of consumers in each market.

IRI's eight markets were selected on the following criteria:

1. Each market had to be large enough to provide meaningful results but small enough to be manageable since IRI had to arrange to provide UPC scanners to retailers in the area.
2. Residents had to do at least 95 percent of their grocery shopping in the market area.
3. Markets in which a large proportion of all commodity volume was accounted for by a few major chains, rather than a variety of small independent stores, were preferred.
4. Each market had to be served by a newspaper with high readership so that newspaper advertising could be controlled and monitored.
5. Markets had to have cable television to permit control and monitoring of television advertising.
6. Markets had to be demographically similar to the U.S. average.
7. The boundaries of the market had to be clear, and spillover of media from adjacent markets had to be minimal.

Because of these restrictions, some critics claimed that the BehaviorScan results were not representative of purchasing patterns in the United States. They cited the size and isolation of the markets as problems for products whose strongest markets tended to be urban areas. Most BehaviorScan markets were also located in "C" counties, or counties with lower measured buying power that, consequently, had lower coupon distribution. Consequently, to test coupons in BehaviorScan markets, distribution levels to those markets had to be increased.

In addition to tracking consumer purchases, IRI also monitored consumer and trade promotion activity and in-store merchandising for each brand. This allowed IRI to report information on competitive activity. The effectiveness of different types of promotions and merchandising could also be assessed by relating this information to consumer purchasing patterns.

---

[8]See "Information Resources, Inc. (A)," Harvard Business School case 9-583-053.

By using BehaviorScan research, Aqua-fresh brand management hoped to resolve the following issues:

1. What were the relative values of trade and consumer promotions in increasing sales, market share, and consumer brand loyalty?
2. Should promotion dollars be shifted from price packs to couponing or other trial events?
3. Which consumer promotions were most effective in stimulating trial?

Given these objectives, Beecham first purchased toothpaste data from IRI's *Marketing Fact Book*. This book, compiled quarterly and annually, summarized BehaviorScan data for over 150 product categories. The book reported brand sales, market shares, volume per purchase occasion, number of purchases in a specified period, average retail prices, and the percentage of volume purchased on deal by the trade. The *Marketing Fact Book* also provided information on competitive brand purchases by households purchasing Aqua-fresh, and the percentage of volume purchased by consumers on promotion. This information is reported in Exhibit 8, while Exhibit 9 shows the *Marketing Fact Book* report on trade promotions in the toothpaste category.

IRI was commissioned by Beecham's market research department to conduct three customized studies for Aqua-fresh brand management. These measured brand loyalty, the effectiveness of different types of consumer promotions on trial and repurchase, and the effect of merchandising allowances on brand sales. Four BehaviorScan markets were included in the analysis: Pittsfield, Mass.; Marion, Ind.; Eau Claire, Wis.; and Midland, Tex.

Data used in the brand loyalty analysis were collected from February 1, 1981, to October 31, 1982. Households purchasing each of the four main toothpaste brands were divided into three groups: (1) low loyalty (the brand accounts for 40 percent or less of the household's total toothpaste consumption); (2) medium loyalty (the brand accounts for 40 percent to 70 percent of the household's total toothpaste consumption); (3) high loyalty (the brand accounts for more than 70 percent of the household's total toothpaste consumption). Detailed findings of the research are presented in Exhibit 10. Based on the results, Aqua-fresh brand management concluded:

- Aqua-fresh and Aim, the newer major brands, enjoyed less loyalty than Crest and Colgate, the older, larger-share brands.
- Households with low brand loyalty were more likely than households with high brand loyalty to purchase toothpaste on deal and/or with a coupon.
- Households with low brand loyalty tended to be "loyal" to a set of brands rather than to a single brand. They purchased whichever brand in the set was on deal at the time they were in the market.

The analysis of trial promotion effectiveness covered a mailed sample, a $.12 free-standing insert coupon (FSI), three $.12 Best Food Day (BFD) coupons (fielded and analyzed as one event), price packs, and a $.39 prepriced 1.4-ounce trial size. The study focused on trial among new users, defined as those households who had not purchased Aqua-fresh within the 24 weeks preceding each promotion, and repurchase among both

EXHIBIT 8 Competitive Sets among Buyers of Selected Products* (percent of category volume and ranking)

	Total Households		Aqua-fresh		Colgate				Crest				Aim	
					Gel		Paste		Gel		Paste			
	Rank	Percent	Rank	Percent	Rank	Percent	Rank	Percent	Rank	Percent	Rank	Percent	Rank	Percent
Crest paste	1	27.8%	2	17.5%	3	14.6%	2	16.2%	2	25.2%	1	46.8%	2	17.3%
Colgate paste	2	13.6	4	8.8	2	16.5	1	40.2	4	6.9	3	9.0	5	8.0
Crest gel	3	12.9	3	9.4	4	9.4	5	6.3	1	32.9	2	12.0	4	8.6
Aqua-fresh	4	10.0	1	29.5	5	8.4	4	6.4	3	7.9	4	7.2	3	10.7
Colgate gel	5	7.9	6	7.7	1	27.7	3	10.4	5	6.5	6	5.3	6	7.8
Aim	6	7.7	5	8.6	6	6.4	6	5.1	6	6.3	5	5.7	1	28.1

Percent of Volume Purchased via Price Deal† (index vs. total category purchases)

	Total Households		Aqua-fresh		Colgate				Crest				Aim	
					Gel		Paste		Gel		Paste			
	Deal	Index	Deal	Index	Deal	Index	Deal	Index	Deal	Index	Deal	Index	Deal	Index
Total category	26.8%	100	30.9%	100	31.1%	100	31.2%	100	28.6%	100	29.0%	100	32.8%	100
Aqua-fresh	28.3	106	28.3	92	38.6	124	40.7	130	31.3	109	32.9	113	35.5	108
Aim	26.8	100	33.2	107	36.7	118	39.0	125	28.4	99	32.0	110	26.8	82
Colgate total	28.5	106	36.8	119	28.6	92	28.1	90	31.7	111	32.1	111	39.3	120
Gel	28.6	107	37.2	120	28.6	92	26.7	86	33.6	117	32.9	113	39.4	120
Paste	28.5	106	36.5	118	28.7	92	28.5	91	29.8	104	31.6	109	39.2	120
Crest total	28.8	107	34.1	110	32.8	105	35.1	113	28.5	100	28.6	99	37.5	114
Gel	28.6	107	31.5	102	30.7	99	32.2	103	28.6	100	27.2	94	36.4	111
Paste	28.9	108	35.6	115	34.1	110	36.3	116	28.4	99	28.9	100	38.1	116

*Read as follows: In the case of the Aqua-fresh column, of those households who purchased Aqua-fresh, 17.5 percent of their annual toothpaste volume purchased was Crest paste, which ranked as the second-highest brand volume purchased. Among total households, Aqua-fresh had a 10 percent volume share.

†Price deals included store coupons, manufacturer coupons, price packs, and/or features. Read as follows: In the case of the Aqua-fresh column, of those households who purchased Aqua-fresh, 30.9 percent of their annual toothpaste volume was purchased on deal. In the case of the Aqua-fresh row, 28.3 percent of their Aqua-fresh volume was purchased on deal, 33.2 percent of their Aim volume was purchased on deal, etc.

Source: IRI *Marketing Fact Book.*

EXHIBIT 9 IRI *Marketing Fact Book* Toothpaste Results: 1984

Base Measures for Response to 10-percent Price Change

	Percent Volume Change	Rank*
Price increase	−14.5%	39
Price reduction	18.7	62
Price reduction with ad feature only	54.6	91
Price reduction with store display only	52.8	109
Price reduction with both ad and display	95.1	108
Synergy for ad and display combined†	6.4	90

Derived Measures for Response to 10-Percent Price Reduction

Difference with:	Percent Volume Change	Rank
Ad feature vs. price reduction only	35.9%	91
Store display vs. price reduction only	34.1	111
Ad display vs. price reduction only	76.4	110

Ratio Measures:	Ratio	Rank
Ad feature to price reduction only	2.92	90
Display only to price reduction only	2.82	110
Ad and display to price reduction only	5.08	104
Feature only to display only	1.03	16
Feature and display to feature only	1.74	104
Feature and display only	1.80	70

Summary of Model

	Share	
Brands Included in the Analysis‡	Minimum	Maximum
Total Aqua-fresh toothpaste	9.4	15.0
Total Colgate gel toothpaste	5.6	9.6
Total Colgate regular toothpaste	10.2	19.7
Total Ultra-Brite toothpaste	2.2	4.8
Total Aim toothpaste	6.0	10.4
Total Close-Up toothpaste	3.3	11.7
Total Check	0.8	2.1
Total Crest gel toothpaste	9.6	17.0
Total Crest Mint toothpaste	9.3	13.0
Total Crest regular toothpaste	11.0	15.8

Data Summary by Promotion Type	Percentages		Average Percent Price Reduction
	Volume	Observations	
No ad feature or display	71.0%	82.2%	6.8%
Ad feature only	10.9	7.4	12.5
Store display only	11.8	7.9	11.9
Ad feature and store display	6.4	2.5	17.7

*Indicates toothpaste's rank out of the 116 product categories reported in the *Marketing Fact Book*. For example, in the case of a 10 percent price increase, there were 38 product categories where the price increase would have resulted in less than a 14.5 percent decrease in volume.

†To measure the synergy between ad and display in combination, the "feature only" and "display only" effects were subtracted from the combination of "ad and display" (95.1 − 52.8 − 54.6 = −12.3). The price effect, 18.7, was then added back to arrive at a synergy of 6.4.

‡These brands accounted for 88.3 percent of category volume. 35,444 observations in the analysis. Average brand share was 8.9 percent.

EXHIBIT 10   Brand Loyalty in Toothpaste Category

	1983*			
	Aqua-fresh	*Colgate*	*Aim*	*Crest*
Percent of households buying brand one or more times	18.6%	25.6%	12.9%	40.8%
Share of category	11.3	21.3	7.3	39.4
Total ounces of toothpaste purchased per year per household	36.3	36.9	39.7	34.0
Total ounces of brand purchased per year per household	12.0	16.7	11.4	19.4
Brand loyalty (percent of total ounces purchased that were specific brand)	34.1	45.3	28.7	51.0
Distribution of Loyalty Among Purchasers				
Percent of brand buyers:				
Low loyalty (40% or less of category required)	57.1%	44.2%	59.1%	27.5%
Medium loyalty (40% to 70% of category required)	17.1	21.3	19.1	19.9
High loyalty (70% + of category required)	25.8	34.5	21.8	52.6
Total	100.0%	100.0%	100.0%	100.0%
Percent of brand volume:				
Low loyalty (40% or less of category required)	39.9%	23.7%	43.8%	14.6%
Medium loyalty (40% to 70% of category required)	23.7	24.7	25.6	18.1
High loyalty (70% + of category required)	36.4	51.6	30.6	67.3
Total	100.0%	100.0%	100.0%	100.0%
Percent of brand bought on deal (by each group):				
Low loyalty (40% or less of category required)	37.4%	37.0%	31.2%	33.6%
Medium loyalty (40% to 70% of category required)	30.4	33.6	20.8	32.1
High loyalty (70% + of category required)	25.4	25.0	15.7	22.5
Average	31.9%	29.9%	23.8%	25.8%

*Timing: 1983 = 11/1/82–10/30/83.

new users and current users. Exhibit 11 summarizes the results of the analysis. The major conclusions were:

- Trial size and coupon events reached a greater percentage of new users, at 60 percent and 47 percent respectively, than did price pack promotions, at 36–41 percent. For perspective, 35 percent of nonpromoted open stock purchases were made by new users. (Even with the high level of trials on open stock, brand management believed that promotions to stimulate trials were necessary for Aqua-fresh because of competitive promotions and Aqua-fresh's relatively low level of brand loyalty.)
- Price packs were the most cost-efficient trial events, generating revenues of $.13 to $.39 (depending on the size of the promoted item) per new user generated versus $.016

EXHIBIT 11   BehaviorScan Trial Promotion Effectiveness Analysis

Promotion Efficiency by Type of Promotion

	1.4-ounce Trial Size	$.12 Coupons* FSI + BFD	Price Packs		
			4.6-oz.	6.4-oz.	8.2-oz.
Average number of households purchasing	4,162M	1,867M	1,192M	2,518M	1,842M
Percent new users†	60%	47%	41%	39%	36%
Average number of new users	2,497M	877M	488M	982M	663M
Revenue from equivalent events‡	$245M	$355M	$1,212M	$997M	$1,516M
Less cost of equivalent events	$206M	$328M	$1,149M	$820M	$1,258M
Net revenues					
Total	$ 39M	$ 27M	$ 63M	$ 177M	$ 258M
Per purchase	$0.009	$0.014	$0.053	$0.070	$0.140
Per new user purchase	$0.016	$0.031	$0.129	$0.180	$0.389

Net Revenue from Aqua-fresh Coupons

	$.12 FSI	$.12 BFD	$.20 FSI	$.20 BFD	.20 Mailed
Average number of households purchasing	1,281M	2,453M	2,155M	1,296M	2,870
Percent new users	49%	46%	55%	54%	57%
Average number of new users	628M	1,128M	1,185M	700M	1,636M
Revenue from equivalent events	$ 395M	$ 315M	$ 580M	$ 622M	$1,202M
Less cost of equivalent events	$ 356M	$ 300M	$ 528M	$ 619M	$1,143M
Redemption rate	2.7%	2.4%	3.1%	2.8%	8.0%
Net revenue:					
Total (thousands of $)	$ 39M	$ 15M	$ 52M	$ 3M	$ 59M
Per purchase	$0.030	$0.006	$0.024	$0.002	$0.021
Per new user purchase	$0.062	$0.013	$0.044	$0.004	$0.036

Aqua-fresh New User Repeat Purchase§

Among New Buyers: Percent Repeat Within	$.12 FSI 10-81	$.12 BFD 5-82	1.4 oz. Trial 4-83	$.30 PP 6.4 oz. 4-83	$.15 PP 4.6 oz. 5-83	$.35 PP 8.2 oz. 5-83	$.30 PP 6.4 oz. 7-83	$.15 PP 4.6 oz. 9-83
12 weeks	13%	19%	33%	24%	15%	21%	17%	17%
24 weeks	19	43	36	29	31	30	23	25

*FSI = Free Standing Insert in newspaper; BFD = Best Food Day section of newspaper.
†New users were defined as those households who had not purchased Aqua-fresh within the 24 weeks preceding the promotion.
‡Equivalent events indicate that revenues and costs were calculated as if the same promotion had been national in scope.
§Read as follows: Among new buyers who first purchased Aqua-fresh with the $.12 FSI coupon delivered 10-81, 13 percent purchased Aqua-fresh again within 12 weeks and 19 percent within 24 weeks.

for the trial-size event and $.03 for coupons. (These values did not take account of repeat business and the strength of the revenue stream generated by a given event.)

- The 1.4-ounce trial size produced the highest level of new user repurchase within 12 weeks, and, along with the $.12 BFD coupon, generated higher levels of repurchase within 24 weeks than did the FSI coupon or the price packs. However, because the BFD coupons were fielded over a four-week period, many of the coupon repurchases might have been made with a second coupon.
- Aqua-fresh purchases tended to be limited to a single tube. Consumers did not typically make multiple purchases of Aqua-fresh when it was on promotion.

The third study by IRI analyzed the impact of price changes and retailer merchandising on the sales of Aqua-fresh, Crest, Colgate, and Aim during the 78-week period from July 26, 1982, to January 22, 1984. Findings from the research are presented in Exhibit 12. Brand management concluded the following:

EXHIBIT 12   BehaviorScan Price and Promotion Sensitivity Analysis

Increase in Total Brand Sales by Type of Promotion

	20% Price Cut	20% Price Cut + Display	20% Price Cut + Feature Ad	20% Price Cut + Display + Feature Ad
Aqua-fresh	50%	122%	113%	152%
Crest	45	91	70	122
Colgate	52	105	106	166
Aim	45	154	155	198

Effect on Sales of a Competitive 20% Price Reduction

Percent Change in Volume

20% Price Reduction	Aqua-fresh	Crest	Colgate	Aim
Aqua-fresh	—	−3%	−3%	−7%
Crest	−9%	—	−5	−18
Colgate	−5	−5	—	−6
Aim	−5	−2	−6	—

*Toothpaste Promotion Sensitivity**

	Percent of Weeks with Feature or Display	Percent of Brand Volume Moved by Feature and Display	Index of Percent Volume Moved to Percent Weeks with Feature and Display	Percent of Brand Volume Purchased by Households with Low Brand Loyalty
Aqua-fresh	10.3%	17.9%	174	30.9%
Crest	21.4	27.4	128	14.6
Colgate	12.9	20.7	160	23.7
Aim	8.2	16.8	205	43.8

EXHIBIT 12 (*concluded*)

Increase in Aqua-fresh Sales by Promotion Type†

Price Change	No Feature or Display	Price Pack Only	Display	Feature	Feature and Display
—	—	—	41%	48%	210%
−10%	24%	28%	50	59	336
−15	40	51	102	128	590
−20	47	71	186	186	843

Effect of Aqua-fresh Price Pack on Sales

	4.6 oz.	6.4 oz.	8.2 oz.
Price pack value	$0.15	$0.30	$0.35
Percent price reduction	9%	16%	15%
Sales increase from:			
"On-shelf" price cut only	18	61	45
Price pack with same price cut	20	76	75

*Read as follows: For Aqua-fresh, 17.9 percent of brand volume was sold when brand was featured or displayed. Aqua-fresh and feature or display support during 10.3 percent of the weeks measured.

†Read as follows: for a 10 percent price reduction, sales of the 6.4-oz. regular size increased 24 percent with no feature or display, 28 percent if the 10 percent reduction was delivered via a price pack, 50 percent with display support, 59 percent with feature support, and 336 percent with feature and display support.

- The degree of consumer loyalty exhibited by a brand was inversely proportional to the brand's promotion sensitivity. Aqua-fresh and Aim displayed a higher level of sensitivity to trade merchandising than Crest or Colgate.
- Given that Aqua-fresh fielded 10 promotion events annually and that an average trade account featured and/or displayed Aqua-fresh during 10.3 percent of the weeks, the average trade account appeared to be providing merchandising support for half of the promotion events.
- All types of trade merchandising increased Aqua-fresh sales, with the combination of feature advertising, special off-shelf displays, and price reductions generating tremendous increases over normal retail sales during weeks when there was no special merchandising support.
- The more generous price packs appeared to be very effective in increasing short-term sales volume for Aqua-fresh.

CONCLUSION

When the Aqua-fresh brand group met to discuss the 1985–86 media and promotion plan, there was disagreement on what actions were indicated by the BehaviorScan research. The brand manager believed the findings indicated that the combination of price packs and trade promotion should continue to be the major component of the plan. Another manager felt that the research supported couponing as the principal method of stimulating consumer trial. Still others favored sampling and argued that price packs did not reach sufficient new users and gave current users an unnecessary price break. Edwards asked each team member to review the promotion plans for 1983–84 and 1984–85 (see Exhibits 13 and 14) and develop a 1985–86 promotion spending plan for their next meeting the following week.

EXHIBIT 13   Aqua-fresh 1983–1984 National Promotion Plan*

Period	Event	Merchandising Allowance	Handling Allowance	Dead Net Unit Price	Total Cost ($000)
I	8.2 oz. 35¢ price pack† ($4.20/dozen)	$3.55	$.25	$1.40	$2,003
II	6.4 oz. 30¢ price pack ($3.60/dozen)	4.40	.25	.99	3,840
	20¢ mailed coupon	—	—	—	550
III	4.6 oz. 15¢ price pack ($1.80/dozen)	1.00	.25	.96	1,237
IV	2.7 oz. 10¢ price pack ($1.20/dozen)	.20	.25	.75	572
V	8.2 oz. 35¢ price pack ($4.20/dozen)	3.00	.25	1.43	1,894
	20¢ FSI coupon	—	—	—	528
	Mail-in umbrella premium (free with 4 proofs of purchase)	—	—	—	576
VI	2.7 oz. 10¢ price pack ($1.20/dozen)	.20	.25	.75	650
VII	6.4 oz. 30¢ price pack ($3.60/dozen)	1.00	.25	1.10	3,134
VIII	8.2 oz. 35¢ price pack ($4.20/dozen)	4.45	.25	1.35	2,186
	1.4 oz. prepriced trial size floor stand	2.70	.25	.27	1,655
IX	4.6 oz. 15¢ price pack ($1.80/dozen)	.65	.25	.99	686
	20¢ mailed coupon	—	—	—	1,092
X	6.4 oz. 30¢ price pack ($3.60/dozen)	1.05	.25	1.20	2,495

*Does not include $3,000M in consumer sampling efforts such as programs like Gift Pax, which sends samples to college students and newlyweds, $1,000M in miscellaneous trade promotion expenditures, including allowances for military sales and nontraditional channels of distribution, and $2,800M in regional defensive promotions for Aqua-fresh. These factors explain differences in total promotion costs between Exhibits 5 and 13.

†Merchandising and handling allowances are included here in the calculation of total Aqua-fresh price pack costs, but were excluded from the price pack cost data on Exhibit 5 which covered only the actual value of the price packs.

EXHIBIT 14   Aqua-fresh 1984–1985 Promotion Plan*

Period	Event	Merchandising and Handling Allowance	Dead Net Unit Price	Total Cost ($000)
I	6.4 oz. 30¢ price pack ($3.60/dozen)	$1.35	$1.10	$2,946
II	8.2 oz. 35¢ price pack ($4.20/dozen)	3.40	1.43	1,970
	20¢ FSI coupon	—		528
III	4.6 oz. 15¢ price pack ($1.80/dozen)	.90	.99	1,221
	Inflatable raft premium ($4.50 + 2 proofs)	—	—	203
IV	2.7 oz. 10¢ price pack ($1.20/dozen)	.10	.71	715
V	6.4 oz. $1.00 price pack-twin pack ($6.00/per half dozen)	.80	1.04	4,325
	20¢ mailed coupon	—	—	550
VI	1.4 oz. prepriced trial size floor stand	2.95	.26	1,103
VII	4.6 oz. 15¢ price pack ($1.80/dozen)	.90	.99	1,067
	Shower massage premium ($9.95 + 3 proofs)	—	—	94
	20¢ mailed coupon	—	—	1,013
VIII	8.2 oz. 35¢ price pack ($4.20/dozen)	4.00	1.40	2,069
IX	6.4 oz. 30¢ price pack ($3.60/dozen)	4.80	.99	4,205
	20¢ BFD coupon	—	—	466
X	2.7 oz. 10¢ price pack ($1.20/dozen)	.12	.75	630

*Does not include sampling, tests of new promotions, or promotions which were regional only.

Case 6–2

United Airlines: Price Promotion Policy*

"There are three ways to increase market share . . . price, price, and price," stated James Jackson, director of pricing for United Airlines, opening the marketing strategy session. The date was June 13, 1985, and the end of the month-long United pilots' strike appeared imminent, leaving marketing managers limited time to decide the best method for recovering traffic lost during the strike. There were differing opinions among members of the marketing staff as to what the strategy should be. One group of managers argued against any promotional activity by United on the grounds that it was sure to be matched by other carriers, leading to a new round of price and promotion fare wars. Another group was concerned that many of United's frequent flyers enrolled in its Mileage Plus Program had been forced to try American Airlines and other carriers during the strike.

The pilots' strike had forced United to cancel most flights to the majority of its flight destinations and to reduce substantially the number of aircraft servicing the others. Consequently, revenues had decreased dramatically and United's profitable business travelers had been forced to patronize other carriers. United, the largest airline in the free world, both in terms of revenues and revenue passenger miles (the sum of all miles flown on a carrier by its paying passengers), expected eventually to recover the traffic lost during the strike. However, there was concern about how long the traffic mix would remain diluted, meaning that a higher-than-normal number of passengers would be flying on discounted fares. The strike had also resulted in adverse publicity and some confusion about the airline's schedule.

COMPANY BACKGROUND

On April 6, 1926, the first private-contract air mail delivery took off for Elko, Nevada, giving birth to commercial air transportation and United Airlines, the oldest airline in the United States. Varney Air Lines was the original name of the company which soon

---

*This case was written by Research Associate Melanie D. Spencer, under the direction of Professor John A. Quelch, as the basis for class discussion rather than to illustrate either effective or ineffective handling of an administrative situation. Proprietary data have been disguised. Copyright © 1986 by the President and Fellows of Harvard College. Harvard Business School case 9–586–089.

merged with Boeing Air Transport, part of a combine that encompassed Boeing Airplane Company and Pratt & Whitney. United Airlines was created to manage the airline division of the corporation. In 1934, United became a separate entity when the combine dissolved. Capital Airlines was acquired in 1961, substantially increasing United's service area and making it the world's largest privately owned carrier. In 1969, the airline was absorbed into a holding company, UAL, Inc., whose assets also included Westin Hotels and other properties.

Throughout its history, United led the commercial airline industry in innovation. In its early years, it introduced in-flight service and dining; it was the first to initiate coast-to-coast flights, to install an automatic baggage-conveyor system, to equip its airplanes with radar, to develop a nationwide computerized reservation system for travel agents, and to fly to all 50 states. This record of innovation was partially responsible for United's strong position relative to other U.S. carriers. During the 1980s, its successful "Fly the Friendly Skies" advertising campaign, supported in 1984 by the largest advertising budget of any airline, further enhanced United's reputation for quality service. Exhibit 1 summarizes the 1984 advertising expenditures of the major carriers. United's projected advertising expenditures in 1985 were $74 million (television $49 million, radio $9 million, print $16 million).

United's emphasis on advertising appeared to be effective. It dominated the marketplace in 1984 with an 18.2 percent share of passenger traffic (measured in revenue passenger miles), its two closest rivals being American at 14 percent and Delta at 11 percent. Exhibit 2 shows United's RPMs and other operating statistics from January 1983 to May 1985.

Generally, profits in the airline industry depended on the health of the economy. With deregulation and the adverse economic conditions of the late 1970s and early 1980s, UAL, Inc., suffered heavy losses. Although the corporation made a comeback in 1983, much of its $142 million profit that year was due to tax benefits associated with losses in preceding years, and the purchase of equipment. The return of economic growth in 1984 heralded substantial performance improvement, with record operating revenues of $7 billion and $282 million in net earnings; the airline contributed $259 million.

The improvement in profitability was partially due to reorganizing of United's route

---

EXHIBIT 1   Advertising Expenditures and Financial Performance of Major Airlines (in millions)

	Advertising		1984	1984
	1984	*1983*	*Sales*	*Earnings*
UAL, Inc.*	$137	$132	$6,968	$643
American	111	89	5,354	234
Delta	67	65	3,657	260
Trans World	66	59	3,657	30
Eastern	61	71	4,364	38

*Includes Westin Hotel advertising expenditures and revenues.

Source: *Advertising Age,* September 26, 1985.

EXHIBIT 2 Monthly Statistics for United Airlines Domestic Operations

	Jan.	Feb.	Mar.	Apr.	May	June	July	Aug.	Sept.	Oct.	Nov.	Dec.	Total
Passengers (000s):													
1983	2,139	2,252	2,993	2,764	2,624	3,090	3,018	3,027	2,710	3,030	2,808	2,705	33,160
1984	2,460	2,396	3,113	2,833	3,091	3,233	3,285	3,395	2,902	3,168	2,880	3,044	35,800
1985	2,805	2,591	3,679	3,523	2,304								14,902
Revenues (000,000s)													
1983	$236	$224	$293	$294	$295	$352	$361	$369	$334	$388	$361	$338	$3,845
1984	321	316	398	354	396	411	407	417	361	389	343	347	4,462
1985	330	297	384	363	273								1,647
RPMs (000,000s)													
1983	2,152	2,231	3,050	2,747	2,596	3,068	3,068	3,067	2,652	2,923	2,654	2,622	32,830
1984	2,368	2,251	2,903	2,669	2,892	3,088	3,167	3,260	2,749	2,944	2,617	2,807	33,715
1985	2,640	2,407	3,401	3,269	2,165								13,882
Yield													
1983	11%	10%	9%	10%	11%	11%	11%	12%	12%	13%	13%	13%	
1984	13	14	13	13	13	13	12	12	13	13	13	12	
1985	12	12	11	11	11								

Notes:
Passengers = total number of domestic passengers per month of year indicated.
Revenues = total revenues in millions of dollars per month of year indicated.
RPMs = sum of per-passenger miles flown for every revenue-paying passenger per month of year indicated.
Yield = revenues/RPMs by month of year indicated.

system. The "hub and spoke" concept was developed to increase operating efficiency and to permit United to compete with low-cost carriers, such as People Express and New York Air. Chicago, Denver, and San Francisco became United's hub cities around which its route system was organized. Exhibit 3 shows a map of United's route system. These cities served as collection and distribution points for passengers whose flights originated elsewhere. For example, a passenger flying from New York to Seattle and another flying from New York to Las Vegas would both fly first to Chicago where they would board connecting flights. Close to 90 percent of United's daily flights were routed through these hubs.

Other carriers also saw improved profits. Many airlines channeled these funds into capital expenditures to add aircraft and flights. In the first several months of 1985, United's major rivals had expanded capacity at least 10 percent, while United's available seat

EXHIBIT 3 Cities Served and New Routes Added in 1984

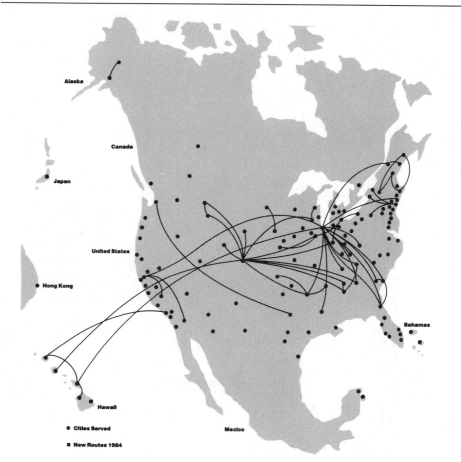

EXHIBIT 4 United Airlines Marketing Organization Chart

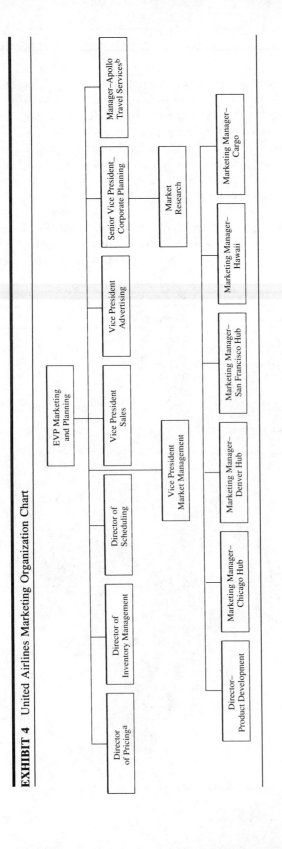

miles had increased barely 1 percent in the same period. In May of 1985, United had a fleet of approximately 320 planes.

The marketing function at United was based on the "hub and spoke" concept. As shown in Exhibit 4, marketing management was organized along geographic lines: three market managers were each responsible for the volume, scheduling, profitability, pricing, advertising, and airport facilities of a hub city; routes connecting two hub cities were allocated arbitrarily. Associate market managers, with responsibility for certain routes within a hub area, reported to each market manager. Market managers each led a team with associate managers and representatives from pricing, advertising, facilities, and scheduling departments. United tried to develop a career path that led a newly recruited MBA from an entry-level position as a pricing analyst to market management.

DEREGULATION OF THE AIRLINE INDUSTRY

Prior to 1978, the commercial airline industry was regulated by the federal government through the Civil Aeronautics Board (CAB), whose mission was to ensure that passengers were serviced fairly and cost-effectively. This was accomplished through the CAB's control of airline fares, route systems, and company mergers. In the early 1970s, the CAB believed that air fares were rising too fast and launched the Domestic Passenger Fare Investigation in an attempt to relate air fares to industry costs. The study recommended that airline service pricing be based on each flight's mileage with a proportionate allocation of average fixed costs. Some industry executives viewed the resulting fares for short-haul flights as excessive. Hence, the CAB attempted to subsidize short-haul fares by increasing prices for long-haul flights. The end result of CAB intervention, in the eyes of one observer, was "an industry with little competitive pressure and no incentive for keeping costs under control."

In 1978, the government proposed legislation to lessen gradually the control of the CAB over the airline industry, with changes culminating in the CAB's dissolution in 1985. Reactions to the proposed deregulation were mixed. Executives of many major airlines were opposed. Thomas Taylor, a Trans World Airlines vice president, stated that deregulation ignored the need for a "sound air transport system" to ensure national security and defense.[1] Delta Air Lines even filed suit against the CAB for neglecting its responsibilities. Many legislators and consumer activists, on the other hand, saw deregulation as long overdue.

Surprisingly, a major force for deregulation was the CAB chairman, Alfred Kahn. He believed that deregulation would benefit both the industry and the consumer by encouraging cost efficiency, more air travel, and lower fares. He countered criticism with humor. Departing from an awards ceremony, he remarked, "I have to go back and destroy the airline industry."[2] Many later contended that his actions accomplished just that.

Deregulation was finally approved in October 1978. Initially, the legislation gave the

---

[1]Albert R. Karr, "The Deregulator: CAB Chairman Kahn Leads Activists Spurring Competition," *The Wall Street Journal*, July 3, 1978.

[2]Ibid.

airlines more latitude in determining fares and new routes. CAB approval was no longer needed to implement minor changes to the fare structure or to add a new route. The law also provided subsidies for commuter airlines servicing small towns. The industry, however, was slow to respond to the new opportunity for flexibility in pricing. Information on competitive fares was not readily available, and individual carriers had little data on which to base price changes. Some carriers developed a computerized price list, updated daily, to remedy the situation. Pricing changes were sent to the Airline Tariff Publishing Company, which disseminated fares to all carriers for the purpose of updating their computer reservation systems. Each day, any carrier could access an industrywide price list; pricing changes made on a given day would appear in the list on the following day, allowing for pricing responses within 24 hours. Price quickly became the focal point of competitive action.

Soon after deregulation began, the industry was plagued by unforeseen problems. The worldwide oil crisis dramatically increased fuel prices. Air travel plummeted with the onset of a severe recession. The concurrent deregulation of the banking industry, combined with inflation and recession, sent interest rates soaring. The Air Traffic Controllers went on strike, substantially reducing the capacity of the nation's airports. As a consequence, many carriers, including United, suffered major financial losses in the years 1979 to 1983.

Before deregulation, regional carriers could serve only regional markets; they aided major carriers by feeding passengers to primary departure sites for longer flights on the larger airlines. In this way, the major carriers were saved the expense of maintaining extensive regional networks. After deregulation began, economic pressures led to intensified competition between carriers. Many major carriers operated nonstop flights on the more lucrative longer routes. The smaller regional companies began offering the same destinations but with one or more stops; they could provide a lower fare on long-haul destinations because of their higher load factors that resulted from many passengers flying portions of the overall route.[3] In this way, the smaller carrier could serve several destinations with a single flight, thereby lowering its relative fixed costs. Without these high fixed costs and the additional burdens of heavy debt and expensive labor agreements, regional carriers could compete aggressively on price in the long-haul markets, a situation that placed more price pressure on the established carriers. Because of the profit squeeze from lowered fares, major carriers cut schedules, eliminating many of their expensive, less heavily traveled, short-haul routes.

Entrepreneurs filled the market niches left by established carriers. The new companies they organized, such as People Express, Southwest Airlines, and New York Air, were free of heavy debt and high labor charges, and their prices reflected these lower costs. In 1978, the United States had 36 domestic carriers; by 1985 the number had increased to more than 100. To retain passengers, major airlines reacted to economy carrier competition by slashing prices, which placed profits under additional pressure.

As deregulation progressed, the major airlines' cost problems grew. Pricing pressures continued to lower revenues, yet cost-cutting measures were difficult to implement. The

---

[3]Load factor refers to the percentage of plane capacity filled.

major carriers lost money, while the new economy carriers generated substantial profits and, therefore, continued to engage in price competition. The result was the collapse of many weaker companies such as Continental Airlines and Braniff. Some companies attempted to reorganize, and, in doing so, forced renegotiation of labor agreements. The shift of power in these companies from labor to management set a precedent industrywide. As labor contracts came up for renewal, companies suffering losses decided to get tough with labor unions; they could no longer afford salaries and benefits established during regulation.

UNITED'S 1979 MACHINISTS' STRIKE

One of the first companies to feel the consequences of the labor/management struggle was United. On March 31, 1979, the International Association of Machinists began a 55-day strike at the airline after failing to reach a wage agreement. United had been under increasing pressure to lower costs as price competition increased. Labor was the single largest expense for carriers, accounting, on average, for 42 percent of costs. As one analyst stated, "Either an airline is going to control its costs, especially labor costs, or it's going to be difficult for it to compete."[4]

While United hoped the strike's outcome would cut expenses and result in long-term revenue gains, the short-term revenue losses due to the strike were substantial. Estimates placed daily lost revenue at $9.5 million on 1978 average daily revenues of approximately $11 million. Restoring full operations once the strike was over would also take at least a week. In the meantime, passengers were switching to other carriers. The strike ended with the ratification of an agreement that set wage increases of 30 percent over three years.

United began limited service immediately after the strike ended. To regain lost traffic, it announced a 50 percent-off coupon for any passenger traveling during the three weeks following the reinstatement of service. Coupons were distributed to passengers during their flights and could be redeemed against any one-way or round-trip ticket for a trip completed between July 1, 1979, and December 15, 1979. American immediately stated that it would honor United's coupons on the same terms. United's coupons therefore became transferable, and a secondary market developed for buying and selling the coupons, counteracting some of the brand loyalty objectives of the promotion. United also initiated a $108 one-way fare between New York and Los Angeles, which American and TWA matched. This route represented roughly 2 percent of United's revenues prior to the promotion.

United's executives considered the coupon program a major success. Exhibit 5 shows the increase in load factors from the end of the strike to June 17, 1979, and the distribution by class of service of passengers using the coupons. In the industry, a 65 percent load factor was considered normal, except during the summer when load factors averaged 70 percent. Of the 750,000 coupons issued, 70 percent were redeemed. People redeeming the coupons were more inclined to redeem them against first class fares.

---

[4]William M. Carley, "Squaring Off: United Airplanes Strike Reflects Industry Drive to Curb Labor Costs," *The Wall Street Journal*, May 11, 1979.

EXHIBIT 5   Results of United Airlines 1979 Coupon Promotion

Passengers and Load Factors

Date	Passengers	Load Factor
May 28	11,000	22%
May 29	27,000	36
May 30	40,000	46
May 31	51,000	42
June 1	65,000	45
June 2	50,000	37
June 3	74,000	47
June 4	91,000	48
June 5	88,000	45
June 6	96,000	57
June 7	109,000	68
June 8	110,000	69
June 9	96,000	59
June 10	115,000	65
June 11	126,000	72
June 12	121,000	69
June 13	128,000	71
June 14	140,000	79
June 15	142,000	80
June 16	128,000	75
June 17	141,000	80

Coupon Redeemers by Class of Service

Class	July	August	September	October	November
First	19%	27%	30%	35%	42%
Coach	9	14	15	19	27
Economy*	5	7	7	10	16

*Economy = any discounted fare less than full fare coach.

PRICING AND PROMOTIONS WITHIN THE AIRLINE INDUSTRY

In the consumer packaged goods industry, coupon promotions similar to United's campaign were commonplace. Consumer packaged goods companies, such as Procter & Gamble, used a variety of consumer promotions as short-term measures to increase sales or profitability. These strategies included cents-off packs, coupons, samples, refunds, premiums, and sweepstakes. The promotion's objective would be the major factor in determining which type of strategy would be most effective. For example, if the campaign's intent was to increase trials of the brand, a sample, which provided immediate value to the consumer without purchase risk, would be more appropriate than a refund, which provided delayed value.

Because of the intangible nature of service sector products, consumer promotion alternatives were not as varied as in the consumer packaged goods industry. Advertising was a challenge because few distinguishing characteristics were perceived among competitors' products. In addition, many service providers had historically operated under governmental regulation, which had rendered consumer promotion generally infeasible and unnecessary. Inexperience in planning promotions, the narrow scope of alternatives, and the ease with which pricing changes could be implemented limited airline industry use of consumer promotions, other than straight price reductions.

Two distinct market segments existed in the airline industry: the business traveler and the pleasure traveler. Exhibit 6 shows the distribution within fare type of United passengers by segment. The business traveler was considered United's "bread and butter," with an average per-passenger fare of $128 during the first half of 1985. As one United executive remarked, "We can try to be everything to everybody, but the businessman pays the bills." Demand from business travelers was relatively stable and did not react as strongly to economic downturns as the pleasure market. An airline's schedule was the main factor influencing a business traveler's purchase decision. The business market was relatively price inelastic.

To build brand loyalty, American Airlines established the first "frequent flyer" program in 1983. This promotion was primarily targeted at the business segment and permitted passengers to claim travel awards for accumulated travel mileage on American. The other major carriers implemented similar programs, each hoping its offering would induce a traveler to remain brand loyal in the face of slight inconveniences of schedule. Most business travelers, however, joined several programs, thereby limiting the promotion's effectiveness for any one airline. The airlines then tried to make their programs more attractive by signing cooperative arrangements with regional and international carriers, permitting consumers to be credited with mileage for traveling on any one of a network of carriers. What began as a one-year promotion by American Airlines quickly became a permanent part of the industry structure. By 1985, United's "Mileage Plus" program had over two million members.

Pleasure travelers were typically more price sensitive and less brand-loyal than business travelers. Price promotions were aimed principally at this segment and accounted for United's low $91 average pleasure passenger fare in the first half of 1985. Fare decreases not only motivated brand switching behavior but stimulated the overall demand for pleasure travel. Exhibit 7 shows the relative importance of factors affecting the purchase

EXHIBIT 6   United Fare Usage by Trip Purpose (January–May 1985)

Fare Types	Business	Pleasure
First	4.2%	0.8%
Coach	29.6	3.3
Unrestricted Discount	36.3	17.1
SuperSaver	1.2	4.3
EasySaver	9.8	18.1
UltraSaver	10.4	37.6
Other	8.5	18.8
Total	100.0%	100.0%

EXHIBIT 7   Relative Importance of Factors Determining Airline Choice

	Choice Factor			
Airline	Schedule Convenience	Ticket Price	Frequent Flyer Mileage Program	Airline Preference
Total	4.3	3.2	1.2	1.3
Business Passengers	5.1	1.9	1.7	1.3
Pleasure Passengers	3.5	4.6	0.6	1.3
American	4.1	2.9	1.5	1.5
Continental	4.0	4.3	0.9	0.8
Delta	4.1	2.5	1.5	1.9
Northwest	4.3	3.5	1.2	1.0
People Express	3.0	6.1	0.2	0.7
TWA	4.2	2.9	1.7	1.2
United	4.1	2.9	1.8	1.2

decisions of business versus pleasure travelers and of travelers selecting each of seven airlines.

After deregulation, consumer promotions based on fare reductions were prevalent. When an airline instituted such a promotion, it would invariably be matched immediately by competitors, possibly resulting in a fare war. As one major carrier executive explained, "Either we don't match and we lose customers, or we match and then, because our costs are so high, we lose buckets of money."[5] The first industrywide consumer promotion the airlines used was a discount fare, the Easy Saver, instituted in 1975. This fare, 30 percent off the regular coach fare, required passengers to purchase their tickets seven days in advance and to stay at their destination through one Sunday. The Easy Saver exhibited many characteristics typical of subsequent price promotions in the industry: discounts from coach fare, advance purchase requirements, and restrictions on the timing of the passenger's return. The restrictions, in large part, were imposed to prevent the business traveler from taking advantage of discount fares.

Early in January 1983, Pan Am announced a new concept in discount fares, the deep discount. For $99 one way, a passenger could go anywhere Pan Am flew so long as the travel was initiated before March 31, 1983. Fare restrictions were a seven-day advance purchase requirement, round-trip travel, and a seven-day minimum stay. TWA matched the fare systemwide, while United and American selectively met the discount in those markets where they competed with Pan Am, TWA, or other carriers that extended the fare to additional markets. United's routes from Chicago to the West Coast were especially affected.

---

[5]William M. Carley, "Rough Flying: Some Major Airlines Are Being Threatened by Low-Cost Carriers," *The Wall Street Journal,* October 12, 1983.

Pan Am's pricing change had a dramatic impact. Customers who had been ticketed at higher fares reticketed. Passengers booked on long-haul flights were especially likely to take advantage of the discount, thereby reducing carriers' revenues. The discount from regular coach fares was between 60 percent and 75 percent. Traffic was extremely heavy during the promotion, with load factors approaching 80 percent on affected routes. The principal users of the discount were pleasure travelers, who were more likely to plan travel in advance. On some flights, business travelers were unable to obtain seats or, at best, only center seats because the windows and aisles had been reserved by the advance purchase traveler. Revenues and yields suffered from a lower-than-normal percentage of seats being occupied by travelers at full coach fare. UAL, Inc.'s 1983 annual report noted: "Cutthroat pricing pushed average yield to the lowest level in three years."

In response to the adverse effect of Pan Am's promotion, American instituted a mileage-related pricing structure in the spring of 1983. American also expanded the seven-day advance purchase discount fare to all markets, but at 45 percent off the full coach price rather than the 60 percent to 75 percent previously in effect. Many competitors followed American's lead with matching price increases. United, after initially matching American, used American's pricing structure as the basis for an alternative framework that incorporated variable costs in the calculation of each fare.[6] The resulting fares were $10 to $20 above American's price levels. American and the other major carriers matched these increases.

Beginning in 1984, American expanded its schedule and route system, adding several new planes. In order to generate traffic in its new markets and compete with the economy carriers, the company established a new nonpromotional fare, the Ultra Saver. The new fare structure took effect in March, followed by a $20 across-the-board fare increase in May. While the Ultra Saver offered a deep discount of 70 percent off full coach fare, the ticket had to be purchased 30 days in advance and no more than 14 days after the reservation was made. In addition, there was a 25 percent price penalty if reservations were changed, locking consumers into their travel plans and making it difficult for other carriers to steal passengers, even with a promotion. United matched the new pricing in all markets, but disagreed with the strategy. Bernie Eilers, United's manager of system market pricing, explained: "When we go in a new city, we start with our standard fare structure, not a promotion fare. We don't want to give customers a false perception of what prices will be. We try to deemphasize pricing as much as possible. You can lose so much money so fast."

American regulated the volume of passengers taking advantage of the new fare by establishing inventory controls, selling no more than 30 percent of seats on any flight at the Ultra Saver level. United did not set as stringent controls. Up to 45 percent of each United flight could be sold at Ultra Saver fares. Load factors for each of the airlines increased; however, at United, less inventory was available for business passengers, causing revenues per passenger to decrease. In light of the increasing dilution of traffic mix, United increased its Ultra Saver fares by $20 for weekend travel (Friday, Saturday,

---

[6]Variable costs included ticketing, food, beverages, and cleaning the seating area. They averaged $15 per passenger per flight.

and Sunday). Because about half the Ultra Saver traffic consisted of pleasure travelers flying on weekends, the effective increase across the board was $10. American responded by including Mondays and Thursdays in its definition of a weekend but, instead of increasing fares, lowered the midweek level by $10. United met this move in American's markets, but filed for further increases in non-American markets. Almost 45 percent of United's total RPMs were on routes also served by American. Exhibit 8 shows the percentage of United's RPMs that each major carrier competed for during the first half of 1985.

Airline promotional activity created several fare levels. Exhibit 9 summarizes the various discount fares and the associated restrictions. Passenger distribution revenues, RPMs, and yields by fare type are shown in Exhibit 10. Because price promotions were matched by competitors, incremental revenues rarely offset the decreases in unit contribution resulting from the lower fares. This situation accounted for the seesaw strategies of various carriers. A price decrease would be implemented to increase volume; competitors would follow suit; volumes would increase slightly, but yields would decrease; a price increase would follow. The effects of the cycle of promotional pricing on industry yields are shown in Exhibit 11.

UNITED'S PILOTS' STRIKE

In early 1985, United Airlines made a further effort to curb labor costs by proposing a new wage structure for its pilots. Under the proposal, newly hired pilots would receive lower starting salaries than their predecessors. United also proposed that these new pilots

EXHIBIT 8   Percentage of United Traffic in Direct Competition with Major Carriers for First Half of 1985

Carrier	Percent of United's Total RPMs
American	43.2%
Continental	18.1
Pan Am	17.0
Northwest Orient	15.0
Frontier	14.2
Republic	7.9
Western	6.1
Delta	5.4
Eastern	5.2
PSA	4.8
Alaska	4.0
US Air	2.3
Southwest	1.1
Piedmont	0.6
Ozark	0.5
People Express	0.3

To be read (for example): American was in direct competition with United for 43.2 percent of United's RPMs.

EXHIBIT 9   Ticket Pricing Structure by Class: 1985

Class	Code	Restrictions	Maximum Load*	Price
First	F	None	100%	Coach & premium†
Coach	Y	None	100	Full coach
SuperSaver	B	None	80–90	70% of coach
EasySaver	B	7-Day advance	70	65% of coach
UltraSaver	M	14-Day advance	40	40–65% of coach
	Q	30-Day advance	30	30–40% of coach

*Maximum load was an inventory control measurement indicating the maximum percentage of seats on a plane that United is willing to sell in a particular class.
†First class premium over coach was typically 60 percent.

would not be able to reach higher salary levels as quickly as previously hired pilots. American Airlines had already implemented a similar cost-cutting wage structure. United's pilots responded by threatening to strike.

The threat of a strike adversely affected United bookings. Travel agents began to reduce the number of United reservations for fear that they would be blamed if the pilots struck and their customers' travel plans were interrupted; passengers who had ticketed in advance began to reticket on other airlines, even if this meant paying higher fares because their available inventories of discounted seats had already been sold.

On May 18, 1985, unable to reach agreement, United pilots struck. While United's wage proposals did not affect the pay of pilots currently working for the airline, job security was a major issue. The pilots were concerned that pressures to reduce labor costs would result in United favoring the new pilots. The strike's timing was no accident: to strengthen their case and encourage a quick and favorable settlement, the pilots chose to strike just before the start of the peak summer travel season, when damage to airline revenues would be highest.

The strike's effects were immediately evident. Average daily revenues dropped from $11.6 million to $3.8 million in May. Operations decreased to 14 percent of United's 1,550 daily scheduled flights. In an effort to minimize revenue loss, United maintained those flights on its more profitable routes. Using management personnel, the Chicago hub maintained 30 percent of its normal daily schedule; routes to Hawaii and Florida were eliminated completely, however. Western Airlines added extra flights to build its business on the Hawaii route. By June, United's average daily revenues had decreased from a projected level of $13.3 million to $3.3 million.

United attempted to measure the strike's effect on traveling behavior by sampling passengers on flights still in service. The findings indicated that business traffic (assumed to be all traffic except those traveling on Ultra Saver fares) had declined from 45 percent of total traffic before the strike to 24 percent of total traffic by June 1. Yields were adversely affected. Passengers holding the deeply discounted Ultra Saver fares stayed with United because of the advance purchase restrictions, and therefore represented a higher-than-normal percentage of the remaining passengers. In addition, American refused

EXHIBIT 10

Number of United Domestic Passengers by Fare Type
(thousands)

| Fare Type | 1983 | | 1984 | | 1985 | (5 mos.) |
	Number	Percent	Number	Percent	Number	Percent
First Class	879	2.7%	1,048	2.9%	399	2.5%
Coach	5,300	16.0	7,672	21.4	2,627	16.5
Discount Coach	8,975	27.1	9,395	26.2	3,942	24.8
EasySaver	3,196	9.6	5,921	16.5	1,862	11.7
SuperSaver	6,599	19.9	5,087	14.2	598	3.8
UltraSaver					4,013	25.2
Other	8,196	24.7	6,679	18.7	2,458	15.5
Total	33,145	100.0%	35,800	100.0%	15,899	100.0%

United Domestic Revenues by Fare Type
(millions)

| Fare Type | 1983 | | 1984 | | 1985 | (5 mos.) |
	Dollars	Percent	Dollars	Percent	Dollars	Percent
First Class	$ 269	7.0%	$ 325	7.3%	$ 125	7.2%
Coach	915	23.8	1,367	30.6	468	26.8
Discount Coach	944	24.5	916	20.5	387	22.2
EasySaver	366	9.5	646	14.5	187	10.7
SuperSaver	619	16.1	532	11.9	58	3.3
UltraSaver					249	14.2
Other	732	19.1	675	15.1	273	15.7
Total	$3,845	100.0%	$4,462	100.0%	$1,746	100.0%

United Domestic RPMs by Fare Type
(millions)

| Fare Type | 1983 | | 1984 | | 1985 | (5 mos.) |
	Number	Percent	Number	Percent	Number	Percent
First Class	1,070	3.3%	1,158	3.4%	433	2.9%
Coach	4,277	13.0	6,061	18.0	2,010	13.5
Discount Coach	8,678	26.4	7,269	21.6	3,121	21.0
EasySaver	3,530	10.8	6,103	18.1	1,784	12.0
SuperSaver	7,927	24.1	5,882	17.4	667	4.5
UltraSaver			4,010		26.9	
Other	7,348	22.4	7,242	21.5	2,866	19.2
Total	32,830	100.0%	33,715	100.0%	14,891	100.0%

United Domestic Yield by Fare Type

Fare Type	1983	1984	1985 (5 mos.)
First Class	25%	28%	29%
Coach	20	22	23
Discount Coach	11	12	11
EasySaver	10	10	10
SuperSaver	7	9	8
UltraSaver			6
Other	9	11	
Total Average	11%	13%	11%

EXHIBIT 11   Industry Yield for Major Airlines

	1983					1984					1985	
	1st Quarter	2nd Quarter	3rd Quarter	4th Quarter	1983 Average	1st Quarter	2nd Quarter	3rd Quarter	4th Quarter	1984 Average	1st Quarter	2nd Quarter
American	9.9	10.8	11.9	13.0	11.4	12.5	11.8	11.2	11.7	11.8	11.6	11.5
Continental	10.3	11.1	11.9	8.9	10.7	10.7	10.2	9.7	9.6	9.7	9.6	9.3
Delta	11.4	12.7	14.7	15.5	13.5	15.5	15.3	15.2	15.8	15.4	15.1	14.4
Eastern	12.1	12.7	13.1	13.0	12.7	13.6	13.5	13.4	13.9	13.5	13.9	13.0
Northwest	10.2	10.3	10.0	10.5	10.0	10.3	10.0	9.7	10.0	10.0	9.6	9.7
Pan Am	10.3	10.4	10.0	10.4	9.8	10.4	10.3	10.3	10.7	10.3	9.4	9.5
Piedmont	15.0	15.5	16.3	16.6	15.8	16.3	17.1	17.9	17.9	17.6	16.6	15.6
Republic	12.9	13.0	15.8	16.5	14.4	16.5	16.5	16.6	16.8	16.6	16.1	14.9
TWA	9.7	10.7	10.4	11.3	10.5	12.1	11.2	10.4	10.9	11.0	9.9	9.8
United	9.4	10.3	11.0	11.9	10.5	12.0	11.6	11.3	11.2	11.6	10.6	10.0
USAir	18.1	17.3	18.8	19.5	18.1	19.3	18.8	18.2	18.5	18.6	17.3	16.5
Western	9.3	10.5	11.1	11.4	10.6	11.3	11.2	11.1	10.8	11.1	11.1	11.3

Note: Yield = revenues/RPMs.

to honor the Ultra Saver fares of displaced United passengers, except on a stand-by basis, while some other carriers accepted these passengers on a reservation basis.

United sought to combat the strike's consequences by stepping up newspaper advertising in cities where it was still flying to make passengers aware of its schedule and the fact that the carrier was still operating. Two examples of Chicago newspaper advertisements are shown in Exhibit 12. Regularly scheduled advertising was discontinued, except in markets where United continued service. United estimated advertising expenditures during the strike at $1.1 million per week, with approximately $.14 million of that representing incremental expense.

STRATEGIES FOR RECOVERY

As soon as the strike was announced, United's marketing and pricing executives began thinking through strategies to speed the airline's recovery once an agreement was reached. Although many ideas were generated, nothing was decided because of the strike's uncertain length. After three weeks, when it appeared that a settlement was near, John Zeeman, United's executive vice president of marketing and planning, called a meeting of his managers to discuss the alternatives.

Zeeman conducted strategy sessions informally, allowing managers to discuss the issues and soliciting opinions on various options. The immediacy of the problem, however, required quick decisions. Bernie Eilers focused the meeting: "Getting traffic back is the primary objective, but getting the right traffic back is just as important. American has taken many of our business passengers and they'll try to match anything we do."

James Jackson, director of pricing, commented: "The business traveler is certainly important, but we must remember that the other carriers have the summer pleasure market

EXHIBIT 12   United Newspaper Advertisements in Chicago

EXHIBIT 12   (concluded)

Flying
is our job.

And we're staying
on the job.

From Chicago
we fly to all these cities.

Our schedule is reduced temporarily, but we're still serving over 50 top cities.

We'll do everything we can to fly you to business, to vacation, or back home.

We're flying with skilled United pilots, with outstanding

- *Albany*
- *Atlanta*
- *Austin*
- *Baltimore*
- *Boise*
- *Boston*
- *Buffalo/Niagara Falls*
- *Cincinnati*
- *Cleveland*
- *Columbus*
- *Dallas/Ft. Worth*
- *Dayton*
- *Denver*
- *Des Moines*
- *Detroit*
- *Hartford/Springfield*
- *Honolulu*
- *Houston*
- *Indianapolis*
- *Las Vegas*
- *Los Angeles*
- *Minneapolis/St. Paul*
- *New York (La Guardia)*

- *Newark*
- *Norfolk/Portsmouth/ Virginia Beach*
- *Oklahoma City*
- *Omaha*
- *Orlando*
- *Philadelphia*
- *Phoenix*
- *Pittsburgh*
- *Portland, OR*
- *Raleigh/Durham*
- *Rochester*
- *Salt Lake City*
- *San Diego*
- *San Francisco*
- *Seattle/Tacoma*
- *Spokane*
- *St. Louis*
- *Syracuse*
- *Tampa/St. Petersburg*
- *Tokyo*
- *Toronto*
- *Washington, D.C.*

crews and the kind of service that has made us the friendly skies.

Call your Travel Agent for schedules and reservations. Or call United at 569-3000.

You're not just flying, you're flying the friendly skies.

United

locked up with advance purchase restrictions and cancellation penalties. That alone will have a severe impact on our load factors, regardless of what we do."

To put the problem in context, Eilers presented projections of load factors (see Exhibit 13) assuming United took no special actions to accelerate a recovery of its market share. Although he expected load factors to climb to 67 percent by the end of August, for the month of July they would average only 50 percent. The pre-strike monthly forecast for 1985 and United's traffic mix before and during the strike, displayed in Exhibits 14 and 15, were also reviewed. Traffic mix trends showed increasing dilution through the middle of the strike, but a slight recovery in Coach and Super Coach traffic as the strike drew to a close. Following this presentation, the executives began brainstorming a list of possible actions. Seven key alternatives and their costs are summarized below. Costs represent rough estimates based on traffic levels from March and April rather than the lower traffic levels that would occur immediately following the end of the strike.

Agency Commission Bonus

United could lower the number of bookings required of travel agents to qualify for performance bonuses and free passes or increase their booking commissions across the board. Assuming 75 percent of fares were booked by travel agents, the monthly cost of a 1 percent commission increase would be:

First class	$225,000
Full coach	750,000
Super coach	750,000
Easy saver	260,000
Ultra saver	600,000
Other	415,000
Total	$3,000,000

Such a commission increase would encourage travel agents to favor United for booking customers' flights. Varying the commission by fare type could improve the traffic mix,

EXHIBIT 13   Projections of Load Factors Assuming No Promotion

Date	Passengers	Load Factor
	(000s)	
July 1–7	520	39.8%
8–17	600	46.0
18–24	720	55.1
25–31	803	61.5
August 1–7	850	61.9%
8–14	900	65.5
15–21	926	67.4

EXHIBIT 14 Prestrike Monthly Forecast of Industry and United Performance

	Industry RPMs*	United RPMs	Industry Revenues†	United Revenues‡	United Yield
January	16,772	2,772	$ 2,125	$ 332	12.18%
February	15,570	2,471	1,974	300	12.14
March	20,531	3,547	2,500	395	11.14
April	19,879	3,377	2,421	370	10.96
May	20,024	3,368	2,435	377	11.19
June	21,713	3,575	2,582	404	11.30
July	21,919	3,498	2,657	394	11.27
August	21,948	3,600	2,680	404	11.21
September	16,999	3,072	2,096	359	11.69
October	17,792	3,268	2,236	384	11.75
November	16,614	2,884	2,092	337	11.67
December	18,431	3,060	$ 2,284	$ 341	11.15
1985	228,192	38,442	$28,082	$4,396	11.44%

*RPMs = revenue passenger miles in millions.
†Revenues = millions of dollars.
‡RPMs and revenues of United for domestic operations only.

EXHIBIT 15 Traffic Mix Results During Strike

Ticket Type	April 1985	May			May 26– June 1	June	
		5–11	17–18	19–25		2–8	9–15
First Class	2.0%	3.1%	0.5%	1.2%	0.9%	1.1%	2.5%
Coach	20.2	16.5	6.5	6.8	5.0	5.8	11.3
Super Saver	18.7	23.5	7.9	7.9	8.0	10.0	15.4
Easy Saver	6.2	9.9	13.0	12.3	9.8	8.8	10.3
Ultra Saver	36.1	33.6	59.8	60.5	64.7	61.8	46.9
Other	16.8	13.4	12.3	11.3	11.6	12.5	13.6

as travel agents would then have an incentive to book specific fare types. This proposal could be easily matched by competitors, however, and could result in long-term increases in commission costs.

Free First-Class Upgrades

These could be offered to full-fare coach passengers and/or enrolled frequent flyers. The only additional expense would be the cost of meals and liquor for a relatively small percentage of passengers. Some managers argued that this promotion would attract additional full-fare coach passengers, primarily business people, thereby reducing dilution. Trial of first-class service could lead to regular usage by passengers not currently flying first class.

Mileage Plus Award Increase

If double mileage credit were offered to United's enrolled frequent flyers systemwide, the cost based on the average number of free trips awarded monthly at an average frequent flyer fare of $140 would be $2.4 million per month. This cost estimate, however, did not take into account redemptions of accumulated mileage redeemed for trips that would not have been taken otherwise. This promotion would reward loyal customers and perhaps attract some of those United business passengers believed to have switched to American during the strike. One manager suggested that a direct mail piece (75 cents each) might be an effective way of communicating the details of such a promotion to Mileage Plus members. The mailer and the offer could be tailored to target different segments of passengers with different levels of accumulated mileage.

Free Liquor

For all passengers this would cost approximately $1.8 million per month. Such a promotion would appeal to only a limited "segment" of the market.

Waiver of Advance Purchase Restrictions

This promotion would effectively lower fares to business travelers. If advance purchase restrictions were waived on Ultra Saver, all business passengers staying over a Saturday (37 percent of business passengers) and all Easy Saver passengers would be able to qualify for this fare. The cost would be:

Business travelers	$47 million/month
Easy savers	$10 million/month

If advance purchase restrictions were waived only on Easy Saver fares, the cost was estimated at $26 million/month. This type of promotion was seen as a way to attract business traffic back to United. For business travelers already flying with United, the effect of the promotion would be simply to lower their fares. Dilution of United's traffic mix was probable, but would be greater in the latter case. Such a promotion was unlikely to be matched by competitors because of high dilution costs.

Stand-by Fares

Such fares would help to fill capacity and attract passengers booked on later flights on other airlines. However, they would probably increase dilution by opening a new tier of lower prices and encouraging passengers to use stand-by who might have otherwise purchased tickets at a higher fare. In addition, stand-by fares could cause operational problems, including lower service quality and delayed departures.

Refund Offer

United could offer a partial refund to full-fare coach passengers, which would encourage the purchase of more high-yield full-fare tickets. A refund claim form could be distributed to be mailed in by the consumer. A mail-in requirement would result in lower costs to United than a coupon because an estimated 30 percent of qualifying consumers would fail to claim the refund. The promotion cost would depend on the percentage of the fare refunded. The cost to competitors of matching this promotion would be relatively high due to their already high load factors. As United's load progressively increased following the end of the strike, the costs of this alternative would increase.

For a promotional strategy to be effective, most United managers believed that supporting advertising would also be necessary. Extra advertising could cost $5 to $10 million per month over and above the existing advertising budget.

While all concurred that any promotion would have to be designed so that competitors would have difficulty matching it, the managers could not agree on which alternative(s) to pursue. Many believed that several of the options should be incorporated into a single promotion or sequence of promotions. There was also disagreement on the appropriate target market and on the amount and nature of advertising that should be employed to announce any promotion. With the peak summer travel season close at hand, a quick decision was essential.

Case 6–3

General Motors Acceptance Corporation (A)*

Gordon Roberts, executive vice president of General Motors Acceptance Corporation (GMAC), was reviewing the issues for discussion at a meeting scheduled three days later on July 19, 1981. At the meeting, GMAC and General Motors (GM) executives would have to decide whether temporarily to offer consumers a low interest rate on the financing of new GM cars. If they agreed to proceed, decisions would have to be made on the interest rate level, the scope and timing of the promotion, and advertising support. But the major issue promised to be how to allocate the cost savings to the consumer among the parties involved—GMAC, GM, and its dealers.

---

*This case was prepared by Professor John A. Quelch as the basis for class discussion rather than to illustrate either effective or ineffective handling of an administrative situation. Copyright © 1985 by the President and Fellows of Harvard College. Harvard Business School case 9–586–063.

COMPANY BACKGROUND

GM was the largest automobile manufacturer in the world. With 1980 sales of $58 billion, GM ranked third after Exxon and Mobil on the *Fortune* 500. However, 1980 had been a disappointing year. GM had shipped only 4.1 million passenger cars through its Chevrolet, Pontiac, Oldsmobile, Buick, and Cadillac divisions, plus 0.94 million light trucks through its Chevrolet and GMC truck divisions. These unit shipments were 17 percent fewer than in 1979. GM posted a $763 million loss for 1980.

Nevertheless during 1980, GM had held its share of U.S. car and light truck sales at 42 percent. Imports had increased their penetration of units sold by only 2 percent to 26 percent. Looking forward to the launch in May 1981 of the new J line of subcompacts (such as the Chevrolet Cavalier), designed to counter Japanese competition, GM executives entered the new year optimistically. As the 1980 GM annual report stated: "GM anticipates at least 13 million new vehicles delivered in the U.S. in 1981 compared to 11.5 million in 1980."

GM cars were distributed through 11,000 franchised dealerships in the U.S. There were 23,000 new car dealers throughout the U.S. in 1981. Some 1,600 dealerships had ceased business during the year preceding June 1981. An increasing number of GM dealers stocked more than one of the six GM makes and offered one or more non-GM makes as well.

GMAC AND AUTOMOBILE FINANCING

GMAC was established in 1919 as a wholly owned subsidiary of General Motors. By 1981, it had over 300 offices in the U.S. and 50 more overseas. GMAC's primary activities were wholesale and retail automobile financing. As such, GMAC provided substantial earnings to the parent corporation that were especially important during recession periods when sales of new vehicles were slow.

By any measure, GMAC was the largest automobile financing institution in the world. At the beginning of 1981, it held 1.6 times the dollar value of consumer automobile loans held by the 100 largest commercial bank automobile lenders in the U.S. Automobile loans outstanding at the end of the following years (in billions of dollars) were:

	1978	*1979*	*1980*
GMAC	$ 13.5	$ 17.5	$ 20.3
Ford Motor Credit Corp.	6.5	7.7	9.0
Chrysler Financial Corp.	1.7	1.5	1.7
Commercial banks	60.5	67.4	62.5
Credit unions and other	19.4	22.3	24.3
Total	$101.6	$116.4	$116.8

Credit lines of $7.4 billion were available to GMAC at the start of 1981; borrowings against these were $1 billion. The financing subsidiaries of Ford and Chrysler had to borrow more from banks and were, therefore, typically unable to beat the financing rates GMAC offered to consumers.

Wholesale financing accounted for 25 percent of GMAC's loan portfolio at December 31, 1980. GMAC financed 80 percent of all new cars acquired by GM dealers in 1980. These included non-GM cars sold through GM dealers, 10 percent of the total vehicles financed by GMAC. GMAC retained a security interest in each financed vehicle until the dealer sold it to a customer and paid off the principal and accrued interest.

Although GMAC's rates were adjusted every 15 days in response to changes in the prime rate, GMAC's rates were not nearly as volatile as the prime. In addition, each GM division subsidized its dealers for the first 90 days a vehicle was in inventory or until it was sold by paying the difference between a $4\frac{1}{4}$ percent financing charge to the dealer and whatever the GMAC financing rate happened to be at any time. As a result, GM enabled the typical dealer to stabilize his inventory carrying costs and to stock more cars than might otherwise have been the case. The GM divisions were heavily involved in determining each dealer's inventory, based on previous years' sales, the market potential of the dealer's trading area, and the dealer's capitalization. During 1980, the wholesale financed inventory turned approximately once every 76 days.

Retail financing contracts accounted for 60 percent of GMAC's loan portfolio in the United States. At the end of 1980, GMAC had over five million retail customers, between a quarter and a third of whom turned over each year. GMAC's penetration of new GM car purchases rose from 22.4 percent in January 1980 to 26.9 percent in January 1981 and 30.0 percent in June 1981. In that month, GMAC also financed 27.2 percent of GM dealers' used car sales. GMAC financed 14 percent fewer new cars and trucks and 15 percent more used at retail in 1980 than 1979. The average term of GMAC new car loans to consumers in 1980 was 42.7 months. In June 1981, this figure had risen to 43.8 months. The average principal balance financed on new cars in that month was $7,593.[1]

GMAC purchased from GM dealers retail installment obligations contracted by customers who purchased GM vehicles. The gap between the interest rate the customer paid and the interest rate at which GMAC purchased the obligation from the dealer represented the dealer's profit. In July 1981, these two rates were 17.22 percent and 15.35 percent. In that month, GMAC's marginal cost of funds was 14 percent.

After a dealer transferred a contract to GMAC, GMAC collected the payments from the consumer and repossessed the car if necessary. In 1980, collection and repossession expenses were only 0.03 percent of average receivables. Some contracts submitted by dealers might be rejected as too risky by GMAC's credit analysts, in which case the dealer might be advised to secure a larger down payment from the customer and resubmit the contract. A high percentage of GMAC's contracts were terminated early as a result of consumers selling their cars before the financing contract expired.

Exhibit 1 shows for the 14 months up to July 1981 the prime rate, the average rate paid by consumers on GMAC new car financing contracts, the average discount rate paid by GM dealers to GMAC for these contracts, and the percentage of contracts submitted that were rejected by GMAC. Salespeople in the GMAC organization did not receive bonuses based on the quality and quantity of financing contracts placed by their dealers.

GMAC advertised to both consumers and dealers. In 1980, a budget of $2,750,000 was authorized to support GMAC billboard, radio, and print advertising. That budget

---

[1]The total transaction price net of the consumer's down payment.

EXHIBIT 1 Financing GMAC Rates on New GM Cars: June 1980–July 1981

	Average Bank Prime Rate	Average GMAC Customer Rate	Average GMAC Discount Rate*	Rejections as Percent of Contracts Submitted
1980				
June	12.63%	15.46%	13.72%	22.5%
July	11.48	15.39	13.65	21.6
August	11.12	15.12	13.41	21.7
September	12.23	15.09	13.31	20.6
October	13.79	15.11	13.30	20.4
November	16.06	15.16	13.33	19.4
December	20.35	15.28	13.39	18.3
1981				
January	20.16%	15.41%	13.45%	16.5%
February	19.43	15.68	13.82	17.1
March	18.05	15.89	14.05	18.8
April	17.15	15.94	14.08	18.1
May	19.61	16.07	14.13	17.4
June	20.03	17.02	14.66	17.2
July (est.)	20.39	17.22	14.88	16.4

*A retail contract purchased by GMAC on a nonrecourse basis was discounted at a higher rate than was a comparable transaction purchased with recourse to the selling dealer. The difference was credited to the loss allowance. These average discount rates are net of the nonrecourse increments; reimbursement rates gave effect to such increments.

Source: Company records.

was reduced by $1 million in May to improve profits. In December, $2 million was allocated to a radio advertising blitz which was supplemented in January 1981 with an additional $650,000 in newspaper advertising, $300,000 of which was paid by GM. These advertisements (see Exhibit 2 for an example) emphasized the difference between GMAC's rate and the prime, but did not mention a specific interest rate. GMAC's advertising budget for the rest of 1981 was $4 million, 85 percent of which was assigned to network television.

AUTOMOBILE FINANCING BY BANKS AND CREDIT UNIONS

During the first half of 1981, about 70 percent of all new car sales through dealers were financed, either by auto finance companies, commercial banks, or credit unions. The percentage of new GM cars financed by consumers matched the industry total.

Commercial banks were involved in automobile financing in three ways. They financed dealer inventories, wrote loans directly with consumers, and purchased contracts from dealers. Because commercial banks typically used short-term funds for automobile financing, any increase in the prime rate was quickly reflected in higher automobile loan rates from the commercial banks. In addition, funding a 48-month car loan at a fixed rate was seen as increasingly risky. Not only did many commercial banks increase their

EXHIBIT 2   1981 GMAC Newspaper Advertisement

HOW TO BEAT THE BANK PRIME RATE AND GET THAT NEW GM CAR OR TRUCK YOU WANT NOW.

GMAC is in business to help you buy that new GM car or truck you want—at rates that make good sense.

In spite of the rise in the bank prime rate, the cost of financing your car or truck with GMAC hasn't rocketed up.

In fact, auto financing rates haven't changed that much from three or four years ago.

Your GM Dealer who uses GMAC has money available right now—to help you get that new GM car or truck you've had your eye on.

Check out all the 1981 models at your Chevy, Pontiac, Olds, Buick, Cadillac or GMC Truck Dealer today.

GMAC

The financing people from General Motors

CHEVROLET · PONTIAC · OLDSMOBILE · BUICK · CADILLAC · GMC TRUCKS

auto loan rates, increase their down payments, and decrease the repayment periods from 48 to 36 months during the first half of 1981, many also suspended auto financing entirely. In May 1981, the average commercial bank auto loan interest rate among the limited number of banks still offering loans was 16.04 percent. The auto finance companies took up the slack and GMAC increased its penetration.

Credit unions were increasingly involved in retail automobile financing for their members. Some 44 percent of their total loan portfolio consisted of automobile loans. They did no wholesale financing. They typically provided faster turnaround than commercial banks and often paid the dealer between $30 and $65 per signed new car contract to cover paperwork costs. Foreign auto manufacturers that did not have established financing companies in the U.S. increasingly permitted their dealers to negotiate subsidized retail auto financing rates through credit unions. Under these arrangements, the manufacturer and the dealer paid the credit union 75 percent to 100 percent of the difference between the subsidized and the market rates.

CONSUMER BEHAVIOR

In early 1981, there were some 85 million passenger cars on the road in the United States. The average American consumer was in love with his or her automobile and quite knowledgeable about cars. An Opinion Survey Center Inc. study in March 1981 classified car buyers into seven psychographic segments:[2]

1.	Practical price and value	22%
2.	A car is a car	13
3.	Engineering/I know cars	16
4.	Car of my dreams	22
5.	The driver	11
6.	First on the block	9
7.	King-size	7

According to the study, the first three segments included consumers who made logical step-by-step buying decisions but who were swayed by economic conditions. The others were "emotional" shoppers whose purchase behavior focused on styling (4), snob appeal (5), newness (6), or on trust and tradition (7).

The typical consumer attempted to negotiate price with the dealer. The bargain a consumer struck with a dealer depended on the trade-in price negotiated for a used car, the incremental dealer-installed options (such as rustproofing, stereo, security systems, and service contract) on which the dealer typically made a high margin, and the discount from the retail sticker price, largely a function of the dealer's inventory position and recent sales. Most dealers employed a financing salesperson who would arrange convenient financing for purchases through an automobile credit company or a local bank or credit union.

---

[2]Al Fleming, "Psychographics: Poking Into Buyer Personalities," *Ward's Auto World*, April 1981, p. 63.

By the middle of 1981, it was clear that uncertain economic conditions were leading many consumers to hold onto and repair their existing cars longer and to postpone replacement purchases. The used car market was also soft, indicating that consumers were not substituting replacement used cars for new cars.

Consumers were reluctant to make major purchases. The Survey Research Center of the University of Michigan tracked consumer attitudes monthly and reported the following:

- In February 1981, 69 percent of families with savings stated that now was *not* a good time to use savings to make major purchases, up from 54 percent in February 1980.
- In February 1981, 85 percent of families with access to credit stated that now was *not* a good time to use credit to make major purchases, up from 80 percent in February 1980.
- In June 1981, 35 percent of households indicated that they had postponed purchases during the previous six months due to high interest rates. The median highest interest rate that these households were willing to pay to make such purchases was 11.9 percent.

In addition, respondents were asked to cite reasons why they believed now was a good or bad time to buy automobiles. Monthly results from June 1980 through June 1981 are reported in Exhibit 3.

A survey of dealers explored the causes of buyer resistance to new car purchases. As shown in Exhibit 4, financing (availability and/or rates) was the most frequently mentioned

EXHIBIT 3 Consumer Opinions About Buying Conditions for Cars: June 1980–June 1981

	Good Time	Uncertain	Bad Time	Good Time to Buy: Reasons Why				Bad Time to Buy: Reasons Why				
				Low Prices/ Good Buys	Prices Won't Come Down	Low Interest Rates	Good Mileage	High Prices	High Interest Rates	Lack of Purchasing Power	Gas Price	Poor Selection Quality
June (1980)	37%	14%	49%	27%	9%	3%	5%	24%	22%	6%	9%	10%
July	36	14	50	25	13	4	3	27	11	9	6	13
August	42	12	46	24	12	4	7	27	11	9	5	13
September	42	14	44	20	19	4	9	31	10	6	5	11
October	45	16	39	17	17	3	12	23	14	8	4	13
November	41	15	44	17	16	3	7	28	17	7	4	10
December	33	8	59	13	12	4	5	31	29	9	5	12
January (1981)	36	13	51	18	13	5	4	33	28	7	4	9
February	39	11	50	22	12	3	4	31	27	7	8	9
March	39	11	50	30	10	2	6	34	21	10	6	9
April	42	9	49	25	19	3	4	31	22	8	5	8
May	44	7	49	23	15	4	5	33	17	6	3	10
June	33	10	57	14	12	2	5	34	28	6	2	9

To be read: Thirty-seven percent of all survey respondents in June 1980 said now was a good time to buy a car. Twenty-seven percent of *all* respondents said now was a good time to buy because of low prices and good buys. Multiple responses were permitted.

Source: Survey of Consumer Attitudes, Survey Research Center, University of Michigan.

EXHIBIT 4 Dealer Perceptions of Causes of Consumer Resistance to Buying New Cars

	Domestic Car Dealers	Import Car Dealers
Car prices	15.6%	16.8%
Financing	23.7	23.6
Trade-ins	9.7	21.5
Down payments	5.8	6.2
Gas prices	19.5	3.1
Gas availability	4.8	2.1
Inflation	5.7	8.2
Economics, politics	15.2	18.5

Source: *Ward's Auto World.*

---

barrier to purchase. Qualifying buyers for loans was a major problem. According to one dealer: "We've written 70 deals in the past month but we could only close 33 of them." Overall, 22 percent of auto financing proposals were thought to have been rejected during the first half of 1981.

THE SITUATION IN JUNE 1981

By the middle of the year, GM executives were concerned that the company's performance in 1981 might be even worse than in 1980. One divisional vice president summed up the situation as follows:

> We are looking at 1981 U.S. auto industry sales of 9.4 million units compared to 11 million units in 1980. GM shipments by the end of July this year will be 7 percent down on last year. In addition, there is a serious inventory log jam. GM passenger car inventories are at 97 days' supply compared to a normal level of 60 days, and a 42-day supply for imported cars. Even though we're now financing dealer inventories for an average of 45 days rather than the normal 15, many dealers are only taking deliveries of new cars if they have been presold.[3] To add insult to injury, in June, for the first time, the average retail price of imported cars ($8,910) exceeded that of GM cars ($8,501). We have just cancelled 5,500 units for which production material had been purchased from what remains of the 1981 model production schedule. More cancellations are likely.

Exhibit 5 presents monthly GM sales and inventory data from October 1979 through July 1981. Monthly breakdowns of car sales by body type for the first half of 1981 are shown in Exhibit 6. Similar breakdowns for GM's five passenger car divisions are presented in Exhibit 7.

Given these data, GM executives were increasingly interested in exploring additional sales promotions beyond those already planned in order to boost short-term sales. While some argued for rebates or price roll-backs on selected models, attention focused on a

---

[3]GM used to pay for 15 days' financing on every car delivered to a dealer regardless of when it was sold.

EXHIBIT 5 General Motors Sales and Inventory Data (thousands of units)

					Days Supply	
Date*	Factory Sales	Dealer Sales†	Net Field Stock‡	Gross Stock	Net Stock	Gross Stock
10/79	502	431	622	909	45	65
11/79	435	370	670	934	54	76
12/79	331	338	699	887	64	81
1/80	403	381	595	874	48	71
2/80	437	372	620	900	48	70
3/80	416	390	637	884	51	70
4/80	385	347	642	889	56	77
5/80	341	310	654	886	65	89
6/80	377	315	687	920	65	88
7/80	353	348	679	893	61	80
8/80	170	316	543	751	53	74
9/80	350	317	534	764	50	72
10/80	432	419	510	747	38	55
11/80	368	330	556	764	51	69
12/80	340	272	645	807	73	92
1/81	314	293	612	816	65	86
2/81	314	331	557	776	47	66
3/81	402	438	487	711	34	50
4/81	420	310	545	793	53	77
5/81	434	315	642	877	63	87
6/81	469	311	753	1,004	73	97
7/81 (est.)	365	304	828	1,040	84	106

*All figures are as of month-end and exclude fleet sales.
†By July 1981, dealer used car sales were expected to be 110.3 percent of those sold during the first seven months of 1980.
‡Gross stock represents all cars which have been produced but have not yet been sold by dealers. Net field stock equals gross stock less factory float, company cars, cars in transit, cars in company warehouses, and dealer demonstrator vehicles. "Normal" auto industry supply levels are 60 days (gross stock) and 45 days (net stock).

Source: Company records.

low-interest financing promotion. Informal discussions between GM and GMAC executives resulted in a tentative proposal to offer consumers 13.8 percent financing on all new 1981 GM cars as well as 1982 J cars during the entire month of August. Cars qualifying for reduced-rate financing would have to be delivered to consumers by September 23.

MANUFACTURER SALES PROMOTION

Before the early 1970s, sales promotion played a modest role in automobile marketing. Beyond occasional incentives to dealer salespeople and liquidation allowances to clear inventories at the end of each model year, there was little promotion activity. Consumer demand patterns were sufficiently predictable that minor adjustments to the production schedule could take care of any deviations from forecast.

EXHIBIT 6   General Motors Car Deliveries to Consumers by Body Type: January–July 1981

	Subcompacts	*Compacts*	*Mid-Size*	*Regular*	*High End*	*Total*
January	43,178 (74%)	62,136 (74%)	109,105 (86%)	42,456 (65%)	36,344 (79%)	293,219 (77%)
February	58,720 (93)	81,242 (99)	115,680 (99)	39,460 (58)	38,855 (86)	330,957 (89)
March	65,035 (87)	120,250 (131)	168,542 (132)	44,778 (76)	39,279 (105)	437,884 (112)
April	31,450 (67)	65,090 (77)	120,315 (98)	47,193 (105)	45,614 (134)	309,662 (89)
May	39,241 (83)	69,261 (89)	119,383 (112)	47,339 (107)	39,540 (115)	314,764 (102)
June	41,518 (87)	67,595 (91)	115,454 (103)	47,216 (100)	39,103 (117)	310,886 (99)
July (est.)	47,713 (90)	70,602 (87)	102,829 (83)	47,882 (94)	37,109 (96)	304,135 (87)
Percent financed by GMAC (Jan.– June)						
1981—	37	26	25		29	28
1980—	34	24	22		28	26

Notes: To illustrate GM's model classification system, in the Chevrolet division the Chevette and Monza models were subcompacts, the Citation and Camaro were compacts, the Malibu and Monte Carlo were mid-size, the Impala and Caprice were regular, and the Corvette was high end.

Numbers in parentheses represent 1981 deliveries as a percentage of 1980 deliveries by month and body type.

During the first half of 1981, 46.9 percent of new GM car sales were of the higher-priced lines—Buicks, Oldsmobiles, and Cadillacs—while the remainder were Pontiacs and Chevrolets. During the first half of 1980, the comparable figure was 42.6 percent.

Source: Company records.

EXHIBIT 7   General Motors Car Deliveries to Consumers by Division: January–July 1981

	Chevrolet	*Pontiac*	*Oldsmobile*	*Buick*	*Cadillac*	*Total*
January	114,255 (70%)	43,020 (73%)	67,902 (90%)	51,448 (86%)	16,594 (73%)	293,219 (77%)
February	139,323 (85)	46,845 (89)	68,140 (95)	59,505 (95)	17,144 (89)	330,957 (89)
March	187,782 (103)	59,547 (105)	93,330 (127)	79,427 (132)	17,798 (99)	437,884 (112)
April	107,696 (74)	41,454 (74)	72,610 (104)	66,706 (113)	21,200 (135)	309,666 (89)
May	109,752 (81)	51,427 (122)	76,239 (125)	59,182 (107)	18,164 (110)	314,764 (102)
June	113,320 (86)	45,136 (93)	75,709 (115)	58,352 (107)	18,369 (132)	310,886 (99)
July (est.)	120,600 (83)	48,704 (94)	65,040 (89)	51,590 (88)	18,201 (104)	304,135 (87)
Percent financed by GMAC (Jan.–June)						
1981—	32	31	23	24	23	28
1980—	29	29	21	22	21	26

Notes: Numbers in parentheses represent 1981 deliveries as a percentage of 1980 deliveries by month and division.

Source: Company records.

The oil crisis of 1973 and the incursion of Japanese imports complicated the competitive environment and made consumer demand for automobiles less predictable. At the same time, new labor contracts made short-term adjustments to the production schedule more costly and difficult to execute. A decade before the advent of flexible manufacturing systems, it took a U.S. automobile manufacturer six months to prepare for adding a second shift and three months to adjust the supply of parts to increase plant output.

Under these circumstances, the U.S. manufacturers tended to err on the side of overproduction since excess inventory could always be moved through the use of temporary sales promotions. Underproduction, on the other hand, could only lead to lost sales.

By 1981, all three major U.S. automobile manufacturers were running frequent promotions to stimulate showroom traffic and retail sales. Chrysler was especially aggressive, but Ford was the only manufacturer to have experimented with a low-interest financing program in the U.S. Between December 5, 1980, and February 7, 1981, Ford offered 12 percent financing on purchases of new Granadas, Thunderbirds, and Mustangs. Consumer sales of these three models were as follows:

	November 1980	December 1980		January 1981	
Granadas	7,656	7,416	(99%)	7,614	(107%)
Thunderbirds	6,539	7,189	(45)	6,299	(51)
Mustangs	14,216	12,639	(67)	11,490	(57)

Note: Numbers in parentheses represent percentage comparisons to sales in the same month of the previous year.

Most manufacturer promotions offered consumer rebates on new car purchases. These rebates were offered either as an absolute dollar amount ($300, for example) or as a flat percentage reduction off the retail sticker price. The rebate could be taken as a check from the manufacturer after delivery or applied to the consumer's down payment. Rebates were usually applicable to designated models ordered during the promotion period even if delivery occurred after the end of the promotion. Most rebate programs set a limit of five cars per customer to prevent fleet buyers taking advantage of them.

The cost of each rebate was typically shared by the dealer and manufacturer. This was usually stated in advertising announcing the rebate to condition consumers to expect a lower dealer discount than they otherwise would have. Occasionally, the manufacturer would absorb the dealer portion of the shared rebate cost on cars delivered, rather than just ordered, during the rebate period.

During the first quarter of 1981, Chrysler ran a variable rebate promotion called the Interest Allowance Plan. The rebate was offered to consumers who financed their new car purchases through Chrysler. The rebate varied according to the prime rate. On any day during the promotion, it was set at the number of percentage points by which the prime rate exceeded $12\frac{1}{2}$ percent. This percentage was then deducted from the retail sticker price. Halfway through the promotion, the requirement that consumers finance their cars through Chrysler to qualify was dropped. Thereafter, dealers had to contribute $200 toward each rebate.

Three other types of consumer promotions were also tried in 1981. GM offered a tie-in promotion of two free round-trip tickets on Eastern Airlines with the purchase of any new Chevrolet. To build dealer traffic, Chrysler offered cash incentives of $25–$50 for consumers who test drove specified models. Chrysler also offered a special value model preequipped with options at a lower sticker price than if the options were added separately. Chrysler gave dealers a $200 allowance on each Plymouth Horizon TC3 sold during the promotion period that did not have the special value package to ensure continuing sales of the basic model.

In addition to consumer promotions, automobile manufacturers also offered bonuses to dealers for achieving target sales levels on specified models during designated promotion periods. The unit bonus typically increased with the number of cars a dealer sold. Dealers usually allocated a portion of their bonus payments to their sales managers and floor salespeople. Sometimes, manufacturers offered an incremental "fast start" bonus to motivate salespeople to achieve their targets early in the promotion period. Manufacturers occasionally paid the bonuses to their dealers in advance on the basis of estimated sales in order to assist dealers' cash flow.

Finally, close-out allowances were also offered by all the major U.S. manufacturers on cars that had not sold off dealers' lots by the end of the model year. GM expected to pay dealers an average of $500 for each 1981 car still in stock and unsold by September 23.

THE 13.8 PERCENT RATE FINANCING PROPOSAL

Among both GM and GMAC executives, there was considerable debate about the merits of the 13.8 percent rate financing proposal and the specifics of program implementation. First, was the 13.8 percent rate sufficiently low to attract consumer attention, build dealer traffic, and sell more cars? Some executives agreed that a more attractive rate, such as 12.9 percent, would guarantee the program's success, especially if short-term interest rates unexpectedly declined.

Second, to which cars should the promotion apply? Some GM executives argued that it should be restricted to those 1981 models with the most sluggish sales and/or greatest inventory problems. Others, noting that inventory levels varied by model from one region to another, proposed that each dealer be allowed to offer the low interest rate on the models of its choice. A third group believed that this local option approach would preclude national advertising. They advocated a blockbuster promotion that would offer the low-interest rate not only on all 1981 models but also on 1982 J cars already in dealer showrooms.[4]

Third, when should the promotion be run and for how long? Some argued that it should be delayed so as not to overlap with a July promotion on GM X cars. Others cited arguments for a promotion shorter than one month. First, if the promotion proved successful, it could be extremely expensive; a two-week promotion that could be extended would be a safer approach. Second, unless a low-interest promotion could be justified as strictly temporary, GM was legally bound to offer the same interest rate to purchasers of GM cars through other financial institutions. This requirement resulted from a 1952 consent decree in which GM had agreed not to give its captive finance company, GMAC, any advantage versus other organizations engaged in consumer financing.

---

[4]GM projected sales of 32,000 J cars during August 1981 without the 13.8 percent retail financing promotion.

PROMOTION COST ALLOCATION

A fourth issue was how the cost of the promotion should be shared. On a $7,500 contract financed over 45 months at 13.8 percent rather than 17 percent, the nominal dollar savings to the consumer would be $545.[5] How should these savings be allocated among GMAC, GM, and the dealer? Several GMAC executives argued against any financial involvement. As one explained:

> The purpose of this program is to sell GM cars, not to build GMAC's business. GM should absorb the whole cost or split it with the dealers. We at GMAC will provide the financing, but we want our normal profit margin. In fact, for three reasons, we may even need to impose a surcharge. First, the program may attract more marginally qualified applicants, pushing up our long-term delinquency and loss rates.[6] Second, if the program increases financing applications too rapidly, our operations may be strained. We may have to bring people in from the field to process the extra applications. Third, if the costs are shared, we'll have to rework our accounting procedures in order to bill each GM division to make sure we collect its share of the financing subsidy.

GM executives countered that GMAC would undoubtedly gain more business as a result of the promotion. Hence, a compromise proposal was developed for discussion at the July 19 meeting that would allocate the $545 consumer savings as follows:

GM support	$254
GMAC support	87
Dealer support	204

However, both GM and GMAC executives were uncertain whether dealers would support the program. Dealers could not be directly canvassed because, if word about the program leaked, consumers might delay purchases in anticipation and a competitor might preempt the promotion. Through the first half of 1981, GM dealers nationwide averaged $300 finance income on each new GMAC contract. Most dealers were thought unlikely to back the program if their profits on financing contracts, typically 30–35 percent of their total car sale profits, were eliminated. An initial proposal was for GMAC to give each dealer $100 for each new contract written under the 13.8 percent program. However, GMAC executives discovered that, in certain states, dealers were already competing on the basis of below-market interest rates. For example, throughout the first half of 1981, dealers in Iowa averaged only $25 profit per financing contract. The $100 proposal would, therefore, overcompensate them, while dealers in other states where the average profit had exceeded $300 would find the $100 less acceptable. The compromise proposal therefore changed the GMAC subsidy to each dealer from $100 per contract to 30 percent of

---

[5] The total consumer payments at 17 percent would be $10,194, versus $9,649 at 13.8 percent and $9,903 at 15.3 percent.

[6] The delinquency rate was 2.75 percent of accounts outstanding in 1980, and losses charged against income were 0.27 percent of receivables outstanding. Higher-than-expected losses were due, in part, to the low resale value on repossessed full-size cars following the 1979 gas shortage.

the average dealer profit for financing the contracts written with GMAC during June 1981.[7]

The level of dealer support for the program was expected to vary from state to state. In Arkansas, where the state law set an interest rate ceiling of 10 percent, the program could not be made available to dealers. In Texas, aggressive lobbying by dealers had recently led to a similar interest rate ceiling being rescinded. Texas dealers averaged $570 profit per financing contract in June 1981, and were in no mood to accept a 70 percent reduction in this figure. One GMAC executive just back from Texas expressed doubt as to whether any dealer in Texas would participate in the program, as proposed, because it required that all GMAC contracts written during the promotion period had to be at the 13.8 percent rate. Dealers could opt not to participate in the program, but, if they did participate, the program currently prohibited them from offering the 13.8 percent rate on a selective basis to only those customers whom they thought required this extra incentive to make a purchase. Likewise, dealers in markets where financing rates were already a key element in interdealer competition could not selectively offer a rate below the 13.8 percent level, even if they were prepared to make up 100 percent of the difference themselves.

Some dealers were known to be more interested in obtaining assistance from GMAC on wholesale financing of their inventories rather than a retail financing program designed to move them through to the public. Other dealers had their inventories under control, were not overstocked, and were likely to resent being pressured to participate in a program designed to help other less judicious dealers. Finally, dealers with a high proportion of their business in fleet sales were likely to be, at best, indifferent since the proposed program only applied to individual consumer purchases.

ADVERTISING

A further area of debate was whether the 13.8 percent program should be nationally advertised and, if so, how aggressively and by whom. GM executives were willing to tag their national television commercials with information about the availability of the 13.8 percent program and a recommendation to consumers to check with participating local dealers for further information.[8] They were not, however, prepared to commit additional funds to advertising specifically dedicated to the 13.8 percent program.

Proponents of the promotion at GMAC had developed an advertising plan to support its introduction. In addition to the $4 million already budgeted for GMAC advertising in 1981, they proposed spending $5,370,000 during August, broken down as follows:

Network television	$1,800,000
Radio	700,000
Newspaper	2,570,000
Magazines	300,000

---

[7]Average dealer profit per financing contract in June 1981 was $291.

[8]Under the terms of the 1952 consent decree, GM could not mention GMAC by name in its advertising.

In addition, window posters, car toppers and other merchandising aids would be provided by GMAC to GM dealers. No cooperative advertising program specific to the 13.8 percent promotion was proposed. However, ad mats announcing the promotion would be provided free to dealers for incorporation into their own newspaper advertisements if they wished.

Some GMAC executives viewed this proposed expenditure as excessive, particularly if GM was not prepared to subsidize part of the advertising cost. These executives also argued that the potential consumer savings associated with the 13.8 percent rate could not be advertised in national media because interest rates varied from state to state. The following data for June 1981 for four states illustrate these differences:

	Average GMAC Consumer Rate Percent	Nominal Dollar Savings to Consumer Under 13 Percent Promotion
Nevada	19.0%	$880
New Jersey	18.0	710
Pennsylvania	16.5	460
Oregon	14.3	90

Advocates of the promotion replied that the average consumer savings could be calculated for each state, rounded down to the nearest $25, and inserted into otherwise identical newspaper and radio advertisements on a state-by-state basis. Exhibits 8 and 9 present examples of newspaper advertisements proposed by GMAC's agency. One was a general announcement of the 13.8 percent rate, the other a specific announcement of the dollar savings available to Michigan consumers.[9]

CANADIAN EVIDENCE

GMAC and GM executives were aware of two low-interest financing promotions that had been offered to Canadian consumers during 1981:

• Between January 1 and April 30, GMAC Canada offered consumers a 14.2 percent financing rate on new cars. GMAC's standard rate on January 1 was 18.2 percent. The costs were shared by GM Canada (2 percentage points), GMAC Canada (1 point), and the dealer (1 point).
• Between June 16 and July 10, GMAC Canada offered a 17.75 percent financing rate on new cars compared to its published auto loan rate of 20.75 percent. The costs of this promotion were shared between GMAC Canada (40 percent) and the dealer (60 percent).

During 1980, GMAC Canada financed 20.7 percent of cars delivered by GM dealers. As shown in Exhibit 10, GMAC doubled its penetration rate during the first seven months

---

[9]There was some concern over whether the absolute dollar savings represented by 13.8 percent financing should be presented on a net present value basis in any advertising.

EXHIBIT 8   Proposed Newspaper Advertisement for 13.8 Percent Program

GOOD NEWS FOR CAR BUYERS

GMAC LOWERS CAR FINANCING RATE TO

13.8%

ANNUAL PERCENTAGE RATE

ON AUGUST DELIVERIES OF CHEVROLETS · PONTIACS · OLDSMOBILES BUICKS · CADILLACS

This can result in a savings of hundreds of dollars to you.*

Here's the best news you've seen in months. GMAC and your participating GM dealer are now offering GMAC car financing at only 13.8%.

That's right! You can finance any new General Motors car delivered in August at just 13.8%. And this means big savings to you.

Your participating GM dealer is ready now to offer you this new 13.8% financing rate on all new GM cars, including the new Chevrolet Cavalier, Pontiac J2000 and Cimarron by Cadillac.

So see your GM dealer today and pick out that new Chevy, Pontiac, Oldsmobile, Buick or Cadillac that you've been waiting to buy.

GMAC
THE FINANCING PEOPLE FROM GENERAL MOTORS

*Actual savings will depend on the amount financed, the length of the contract and your State's automobile financing law.

EXHIBIT 9   Proposed Michigan Newspaper Advertisement for 13.8 Percent Program

GOOD NEWS FOR CAR BUYERS

GMAC LOWERS CAR FINANCING RATE TO

13.8%

ANNUAL
PERCENTAGE
RATE

ON AUGUST DELIVERIES OF
CHEVROLETS · PONTIACS · OLDSMOBILES
BUICKS · CADILLACS

This will result in an average saving of $425 in Michigan.*

Here's the best news you've seen in months. GMAC and your participating GM dealer are now offering GMAC car financing at only 13.8%.

That's right! You can finance any new General Motors car delivered in August at just 13.8%. And this means big savings to you.

Your participating GM dealer is ready now to offer you this new 13.8% financing rate on all new GM cars, including the new J-Cars.

So see your GM dealer <u>today</u> and pick out that new Chevy, Pontiac, Oldsmobile, Buick or Cadillac that you've been waiting to buy.

GMAC
THE FINANCING PEOPLE
FROM GENERAL MOTORS

*Based on GMAC financing data for June 1981 and the Michigan statutory rate ceiling applicable to automobile financing. Actual savings will depend on the amount financed and the length of the contract.

of 1981. Some executives believed that GMAC in the U.S. would be able to do even better. First, GMAC Canada's asset base was more short-term; its rates were therefore more sensitive to fluctuations in the prime rate. Second, the five largest Canadian banks advertised nationally available automobile loan rates that were highly competitive with the automobile financing companies.

ESTIMATING PROGRAM COSTS

In advance of the July 19 meeting, members of GM's Price Review Group had to finalize cost projections for the program. At a previous session, GM executives had projected an additional 40,000 new car sales during August if the 13.8 percent program were launched, resulting in total August sales of 350,000 units. Of the incremental sales, 25,000 would be from dealer stock, while 15,000 would be plus sales from GM to its dealers. At the same meeting, GMAC executives had estimated that they would finance 77,500 new GM cars during August in the absence of the program, and an additional 97,500 units (including all 40,000 incremental sales) if the program was launched. Other assumptions agreed to were as follows:

- GMAC's long-term cost of capital and its marginal cost of funds would be treated as 12 percent and 14 percent respectively.

EXHIBIT 10   GM Dealer Deliveries and Percent Financed by GMAC Canada: January 1980–July 1981

	GM Dealer Car Deliveries	Percent Financed
January 1980	30,689	21.9%
February	35,550	19.9
March	42,819	20.0
April	45,066	28.1
May	42,911	21.7
June	40,421	19.2
July	40,216	18.3
August	35,021	17.1
September	30,115	16.7
October	42,665	18.4
November	31,654	21.9
December	23,858	26.1
January 1981	27,173	35.7
February	27,994	45.2
March	40,081	44.1
April	45,280	44.8
May	34,829	47.0
June	36,272	29.5
July (est.)	27,154	42.1

Source: Company records.

- GM's average profit per car after variable cost would be treated as $2,000.
- GMAC would incur incremental administrative costs of $2 per month on each of the additional 97,500 contacts.
- By selling through 40,000 additional cars, GM would avoid obsolescence costs of $5 million on assemblies and components already purchased that could not be used to produce 1982 models.

CONCLUSION

At the July 19 meeting, Roberts, his GMAC colleagues, and GM executives would have to make a final decision on whether or not to go ahead with the promotion. If they decided in favor, details of the promotion's scope and timing would have to be finalized. In addition, a complete financial forecast and communication program would have to be developed.

The previous week, an internal memo had indicated that GM would be holding its annual price increases, to be announced in August, to below 5 percent. Ford and Chrysler were expected to do the same.

Case 6–4

*Procter & Gamble Company (B)**

It was June 1982, and Charles Garner had been brand assistant on H-80 for six months. H-80 was the code name for a new light-duty liquid detergent (LDL)[1] scheduled for introduction into test market at the end of 1982 by the Packaged Soap and Detergent Division (PS&D) of the Procter & Gamble Company (P&G). The H-80 brand group had been hard at work developing the H-80 first-year marketing plan. Under the guidance of Kate Jones, the brand manager, overall volume objectives and marketing support levels had been determined, and marketing support had been appropriately divided between

*Research Associate Alice MacDonald Court prepared this case under the direction of Professor John A. Quelch as the basis for class discussion rather than to illustrate either effective or ineffective handling of an administrative situation. Names and proprietary data have been disguised, but all essential relationships have been preserved. Copyright © 1983 by the President and Fellows of Harvard College. Harvard Business School case 9–584–048.

[1]LDLs are defined as all mild liquid soaps and detergents designed primarily for washing dishes.

introductory advertising and promotion. As brand assistant, Garner had responsibility for developing all promotion plans for H-80. His task over the next few weeks was to formulate a detailed Year 1 national sales promotion plan from which a test market plan for a limited geographical area could be derived.

COMPANY BACKGROUND

By 1981, the Procter & Gamble Company operated in 26 countries. As indicated in Exhibit 1, sales totaled $11.4 billion, of which 70 percent were made in the United States. P&G manufactured 90 consumer and industrial products in the United States, including three of the leading LDL brands: Ivory Liquid, Dawn, and Joy. It also sold the leading brands in 14 of the other 24 consumer product categories in which it competed.

The company comprised eight major operating divisions organized by type of product:

EXHIBIT 1   Consolidated Statement of Earnings ($ in millions except per-share amounts)

	Fiscal year Ending June 30	
	1981	*1980*
Income:		
Net sales	$11,416	$10,772
Interest and other income	83	52
	11,499	10,824
Costs and expenses:		
Cost of products sold	7,854	7,471
Marketing, administrative, and other		
expenses	2,361	2,178
Interest expense	98	97
	10,313	9,746
Earnings from operations before income taxes	1,186	1,078
Income taxes	518	438
Net earnings from operations (before		
extraordinary charge)	668	640
Extraordinary charge: costs associated with		
the suspension of sale of Rely tampons		
(less applicable tax relief of $58)	(75)	—
Net earnings	$593	$640
Per common share:		
Net earnings from operations	$8.08	$7.74
Extraordinary charge	(.91)	—
Net earnings	$7.17	$7.74
Average shares outstanding:		
1981—82,720,858		
1980—82,659,861		
Dividends	$3.80	$3.40

Source: Company records.

Packaged Soap and Detergents, Bar Soap and Household Cleaning Products, Toilet Goods, Paper Products, Food Products, Coffee, Food Service and Lodging Products, and Special Products. Each division had its own brand management (called advertising), as well as its own sales, finance, manufacturing, and product development line management groups. These groups reported to a division manager who had overall profit and loss responsibility. The divisions used centralized corporate staff groups for advertising services,[2] distribution, and purchasing.

The advertising department was organized on the brand management system. The responsibility for planning and directing the marketing effort for each brand was assigned to a brand group, which typically included a brand manager, an assistant brand manager, and one or two brand assistants. This group planned, developed, and directed the total marketing effort for its brand. In developing its marketing plans, the brand group worked closely with other departments within its division, with specialists in the advertising services staff groups, and with the advertising agency[3] assigned to its brand. (Exhibit 2 presents the PS&D Division advertising department's organization chart.)

LIGHT-DUTY LIQUID DETERGENTS

The LDL industry recorded factory sales of $850 million and volume of 59 million cases in 1981.[4] The average U.S. consumer had 1.5 LDL brands at home at any one time, used 0.6 fluid ounces of product per sinkful of dishes, and washed an average of 12 sinksful each week. The average purchase cycle was three to four weeks. LDL consumption increases resulting from the growing number of U.S. households[5] were partly offset by the increased penetration of automatic dishwashers (ADWs), as ADW households used one-half less LDL than non-ADW households.[6] Based on these trends, P&G executives projected category volume growth of 1 percent per year over the next five years.

The market could be conceptually divided into three major segments on the basis of product benefit. The performance segment, accounting for 35 percent of category volume, included brands providing primarily a cleaning benefit; the mildness segment (37 percent of category volume) included brands providing primarily the benefit of mildness to hands; and the price segment (28 percent of category volume) included brands whose primary benefit was low cost.[7] Three companies sold almost 75 percent of LDLs, with P&G holding a 42 percent share of the market,[8] Colgate-Palmolive Company a 24 percent

---

[2]Advertising services included the following specialized staff departments: TV commercial production, media, copy services, art and package design, market research, field advertising, market systems and computer services, promotion and marketing services, and advertising personnel.

[3]P&G retained 10 leading advertising agencies to work with the brand groups on the development and execution of advertising strategy.

[4]Volume is measured in P&G statistical cases, each containing 310 ounces.

[5]Household growth was a better indicator of LDL volume than population growth, as research indicated LDL household consumption varied only slightly with the number of people in the household.

[6]ADW households still used LDL for pots and pans and small cleanups.

[7]Price brands were sold to retailers for an average of $7.50 per statistical case versus $17.00 per statistical case for the premium-priced mildness and performance brands.

[8]*Share of market* is defined as share of statistical case volume.

EXHIBIT 2 PS&D Division Organization Chart, Fall 1981

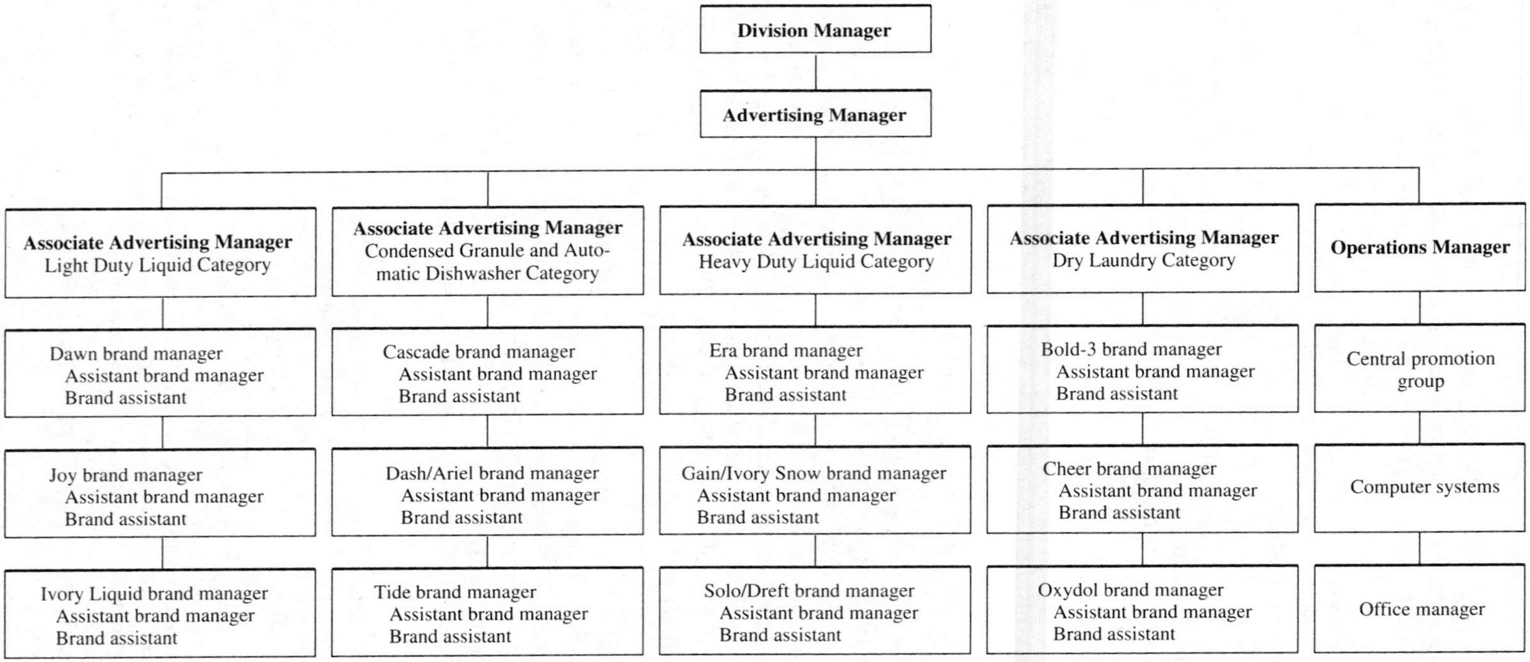

Division Manager

Advertising Manager

Associate Advertising Manager
Light Duty Liquid Category

Associate Advertising Manager
Condensed Granule and Auto-matic Dishwasher Category

Associate Advertising Manager
Heavy Duty Liquid Category

Associate Advertising Manager
Dry Laundry Category

Operations Manager

Dawn brand manager
Assistant brand manager
Brand assistant

Cascade brand manager
Assistant brand manager
Brand assistant

Era brand manager
Assistant brand manager
Brand assistant

Bold-3 brand manager
Assistant brand manager
Brand assistant

Central promotion group

Joy brand manager
Assistant brand manager
Brand assistant

Dash/Ariel brand manager
Assistant brand manager
Brand assistant

Gain/Ivory Snow brand manager
Assistant brand manager
Brand assistant

Cheer brand manager
Assistant brand manager
Brand assistant

Computer systems

Ivory Liquid brand manager
Assistant brand manager
Brand assistant

Tide brand manager
Assistant brand manager
Brand assistant

Solo/Dreft brand manager
Assistant brand manager
Brand assistant

Oxydol brand manager
Assistant brand manager
Brand assistant

Office manager

share, and Lever Brothers (the U.S. subsidiary of Unilever) a 7 percent share.[9] The remaining 27 percent of the market consisted mainly of generic and private-label brands. A higher proportion of the marketing budgets of P&G LDLs was allocated to advertising and a lower percentage to promotion than was the case for either Colgate or Lever LDLs. Colgate and Lever sold an estimated 75 percent of their LDL volume to the trade on deal compared with about half for P&G.

PROMOTION OF P&G'S ESTABLISHED LDL BRANDS

P&G's three brands in the LDL category (Joy, Ivory Liquid, and Dawn) together accounted for 30 percent of the dollar sales volume and profit of the PS&D Division. While each of the three brands was a different formulation that offered a distinct benefit to appeal to separate consumer needs, all were marketed similarly. The percentage breakdown of marketing expenditures between advertising and promotion for the three brands is indicated in Table 1.

In general, brand managers spent about half of each LDL's marketing budget in advertising, with the balance in promotion. Competitive brands allocated about 40 percent of their marketing budgets to advertising.

Ivory Liquid.   This was the leading brand in 1981 with a 15.5 percent share of the LDL category. Because Ivory had the highest trial levels in the category, the brand's primary sales promotion strategy was continuity of purchase combined with a secondary objective of stimulating trial among younger women and heavy LDL users.[10] Ivory had reduced its promotion frequency from eight 4-week events in 1972 to six events in 1982. Only 20 percent of Ivory's promotion budget was allocated to trade allowances. Despite merchandising performance requirements tied to these allowances, it was difficult to ensure that the funds were passed through to the consumer in the form of retail price cuts.

The remaining 80 percent of Ivory's promotion budget was allocated to consumer promotion. About two-thirds of Ivory's promotion events were price packs,[11] which were

TABLE 1   Advertising/Consumer Promotion/Trade Promotion Dollar Splits for P&G's LDL Brands

	1977	1978	1979	1980	1981	1982
Ivory Liquid	48/42/10	54/38/8	54/36/10	54/35/11	50/40/10	55/37/8
Dawn	NA	NA	58/31/11	51/39/10	46/42/12	51/40/9
Joy	55/36/9	51/41/8	48/42/10	55/34/11	50/39/11	60/30/10

---

[9]In 1981, U.S. sales of Colgate-Palmolive Company were $5.3 billion, and U.S. sales of Lever Brothers were $2.1 billion.

[10]Ivory Liquid's current customers tended to be both slightly older than the average and were lighter LDL users (consumers who washed eight sinksful of dishes or less per week).

[11]A price pack was defined as a specially produced retail package announcing a temporary reduction from the standard retail price—for example, "30¢ off the regular retail price." The average percent reduction to the consumer was 10%–20%.

EXHIBIT 3   Ivory Liquid's Promotion Calendars, 1981–1983

	January	February	March	April	May	June
1981	20¢-off mailed coupon *plus* $1.30 per case trade allowance	48 oz. 30¢-off price pack *plus* 22 oz. $1.30 per case trade allowance				
1982	48 oz. Harlequin Romance book on pack premium *plus* $1.30 per case trade allowance	32 oz. 20¢-off price pack			22 oz. 13¢-off price pack	32 oz. 20¢-off price pack
Proposed 1983	20¢-off BFD coupon on any size *plus* $1.80 per case trade allowance	22 oz. 20¢-off price pack		32 oz. 20¢-off price pack		32 oz. 27¢-off price pack

Notes: Coupons were redeemable on any package size.
Per-case allowances are quoted in terms of statistical cases.

intended to encourage continuity of purchase by current brand users. Such price packs accounted for 30 percent of Ivory's total yearly volume. The remaining one-third of consumer promotions were coupon offers supported by trade allowances. The brand used couponing to stimulate trial. (Exhibit 3 summarizes Ivory Liquid's 1981 and 1982 promotion plans, as well as the plans proposed for 1983.)

Dawn.   This brand was introduced nationally in 1976 as a performance brand. In two years, Dawn rose to the No. 2 position in the LDL category, and by 1981 it held a 14.1 percent market share. Dawn had captured about 70 percent of its volume from non-P&G brands, with the remaining 30 percent cannibalized equally from Ivory and Joy. Dawn's rapid growth was attributed to its unique benefit as the superior grease-cutting LDL in the category. Dawn's sales promotion strategy was trial-oriented, with two-thirds of Dawn's promotion events being trial-oriented coupon events supported by trade allowances, while the remaining one-third were price packs. (Exhibit 4 summarizes Dawn's

EXHIBIT 3 *(concluded)*

July	August	September	October	November	December
22 oz. $1.30 per case trade allowance		32 oz. 20¢-off price pack *plus* 20¢-off BFD coupon on any size		20¢-off free-standing insert coupon *plus* $1.30 per case trade allowance	
		20¢-off free-standing insert coupon *plus* $1.30 per case trade allowance			32 oz. 27¢-off price pack
22 oz. 20¢-off price pack		20¢-off free-standing insert coupon *plus* $1.80 per case trade allowance		48 oz. 40¢-off price pack	

1981, 1982, and 1983 promotion plans.) The brand manager believed that Dawn's success was due to its distinctive grease-cutting benefit. He therefore tried to design consumer promotion events that emphasized this benefit and at the same time provided an economic incentive to the consumer.

Joy. This brand ranked third in the LDL category, with a 12.1 percent market share in 1981. Its product benefit was to deliver "shiny dishes." Joy had the lowest trial level of P&G's three LDLs. To strengthen Joy's appeal, an improved "no-spot" formula was scheduled for national distribution by September 1982. The new formula caused water to "sheet" off dishes when they were air drying, leaving fewer spots than other brands. In addition, the improved formula reduced the cost of goods sold by about $3 million per year. The brand manager hoped to increase Joy's volume by 10 percent with the introduction of Joy's improved product. Marketing expenditures were to be increased modestly, with emphasis on trial-oriented consumer promotion events. Approximately half of Joy's promotions were trial-oriented couponing events (supported by trade

EXHIBIT 4   Dawn's Promotion Calendars, 1981–1983

	January	February	March	April	May	June
1981	32 oz. 20¢-off price pack		22 oz. 13¢-off price pack		32 oz. $1.30 per case trade allowance	
1982	20¢-off PCH* coupon *plus* $1.30 per case trade allowance		32 oz. 20¢-off price pack		22 oz. 13¢-off price pack	
Proposed 1983	20¢-off PCH coupon *plus* $1.80 per case trade allowance		32 oz. 27¢-off price pack		20¢-off free-standing insert coupon *plus* $1.80 per case trade allowance	

*Coupons distributed along with Publisher's Clearing House mailing.

allowances), and prepriced events.[12] The balance of events were price packs. (Exhibit 5 summarizes Joy's 1981, 1982, and 1983 promotion plans.)

The PS&D promotion planning calendar comprised thirteen 4-week promotion events. Each LDL participated in at least five events annually. While the brand groups occasionally planned regional promotion variations to facilitate testing of a new promotion idea or strengthen promotion support in a weak performance area, they usually planned national sales promotions. The groups generally avoided the simultaneous promotion of two or more of the company's LDLs whenever possible, so as not to fragment the attention of the sales force and the trade. In addition, there was concern that some trade buyers might respond by promoting only one of P&G's LDLs and ignoring the others. However, some sales managers believed that promoting all three LDLs together would lessen cannibalization among the brands by minimizing the consumer switching resulting from promotion; they argued that such line promotions would be attractive to the trade, since such promotions would include high-volume brands. The PS&D Division organized one or two divisional promotion events each year involving 3 to 10 brands, often including one or more LDLs.[13]

---

[12]A prepriced pack was defined as a specially produced retail package that had the retail price marked on the label before it was delivered to the retail store. P&G generally used prepriced packs to promote smaller LDL sizes to stimulate trial. The average percent reduction to the consumer was 30–50 percent.

[13]Such divisional promotion events typically included a sweepstakes or contest combined with cash refund offers and coupons.

EXHIBIT 4   *(concluded)*

July	August	September	October	November	December
22 oz. 13¢-off price pack		48 oz. 30¢-off price pack	32 oz. 20¢-off price pack		
48 oz. 30¢-off price pack			22 oz. 20¢-off price pack	32 oz. $1.30-off per case trade allowance	
20¢-off free-standing insert coupon *plus* $1.80 per case trade allowance			22 oz. 20¢-off price pack		20¢-off free-standing insert coupon *plus* $1.80 per case trade allowance

THE DEVELOPMENT OF H-80

H-80 was a high-performance LDL that combined suspended nonabrasive scrubbers[14] with a highly effective detergent system to provide superior cleaning compared with other LDLs when used full strength on tough, baked-on foods, and parity cleaning compared with other LDLs when diluted with water for general dishwashing. The scrubber system represented a distinctive new product benefit; it was the first major technological innovation in the category since the introduction of Ivory Liquid.[15] The H-80 formula was completely homogenous and did not require shaking.

The PS&D Division began work on this innovation in response to a 1980 Dishwashing Habits and Practices study, which revealed that 80 percent of U.S. households scour and scrub their dishes at least once a week, with an average household scouring four times a week. This research also revealed that the removal of burnt or baked-on foods was considered the toughest cleaning job by more consumers than any other dishwashing task, and that most consumers did not view their current LDL as sufficiently effective for such tough cleaning jobs. Based on this research, the advertising department concluded that a consumer need existed for a high-performance LDL.

---

[14]The scrubbers were made from the biodegradable shells of microscopic sea organisms.

[15]Ivory Liquid's formula included a detergent with a patented molecular structure that prevented the roughness and cracking that exposure to other detergents caused to human skin.

EXHIBIT 5 Joy's Promotion Calendars, 1981–1983

	January	February	March	April	May	June
1981		32 oz. 20¢-off price pack		22 oz. 13¢-off price pack		20¢-off free-standing insert coupon *plus* $1.30 per case trade allowance
1982		48 oz. two 40¢ cross-ruff* coupons distributed in 171 oz. Cheer laundry detergent *plus* 22 oz. 13¢-off price pack		32 oz. 20¢-off price pack		22 oz. 13¢-off price pack
Proposed 1983	32 oz. 27¢-off price pack	20¢-off free-standing insert coupon *plus* $1.80 per case trade allowance		22 oz. 20¢-off price pack		12 oz. 49¢ pre-priced pack

*Two coupons good on the next purchase of Joy, distributed in specially marked boxes of Cheer laundry detergent.

The product development department (PDD) began work on this project in early 1981. An H-80 brand group was established to guide the development process and test marketing of the brand. By mid-1981, the group had developed a technological breakthrough and a formula that it believed would fulfill the existing consumer need. Successful laboratory and in-home-use testing was completed by the end of 1981.

H-80 emerged from the development process as a rich, green opalescent liquid that felt slightly gritty to the touch. The liquid was thicker than that of other LDLs, and its herbal fragrance was unique within the category. The package was bright green and shaped like an arrowhead. The label carried an endorsement from the American Fine China Guild that read, "Safe for all fine china."

Based on the results of pretest market research[16] conducted to project H-80's potential market share, the brand group had recommended a market share objective of 11 percent. The pretest market research projected H-80's market share to reach 13 percent by the

---

[16]P&G used a proprietary technique for simulating test markets and predicting market shares.

EXHIBIT 5 (*concluded*)

July	August	September	October	November	December
	22 oz. 13¢-off price pack	20¢-off free-standing insert coupon *plus* $1.30 per case trade allowance		32 oz. 20¢-off price pack	
	20¢-off free-standing insert coupon *plus* $1.30 per case trade allowance		48 oz. 40¢-off price pack	20¢-off mailed coupon *plus* $1.30 per case trade allowance	
		22 oz. 20¢-off price pack		20¢-off mailed coupon *plus* $1.80 per case trade allowance	

TABLE 2 H-80 Projected Sales

Year	LDL Market Projections (million cases)	H-80 Estimated Market Share	H-80 Estimated Market Volume (million cases)	H-80 Estimated Sales* ($ millions)
1982	59.4	—	—	—
1983	59.8	7%	4.2	$ 71.4
1984	60.1	11	6.6	112.2
1985	60.8	11	6.7	113.9

*H-80 carload cost of a statistical case was $17.00 (see Table 3).

end of Year 1. However, given the aggressive competitive environment of the LDL market, the brand group had thought it prudent to set a conservative objective for H-80. (Its projection of H-80's national volume and share is indicated in Table 2.)

Planned capital investment of $20 million for H-80 was below the average for a new P&G product. The cost structure of P&G's existing LDL brands (summarized in Exhibit

6) was applicable to H-80. The brand group estimated that P&G would have to spend at least $60 million on a 12-month introductory marketing plan for H-80. While this did not meet the 36-month marketing payout objective generally sought by a new PS&D product (see Exhibit 7), the brand group believed a longer payout was justified because of the low capital investment required. However, the payout picture was further clouded because of the likelihood that some of H-80's volume would be cannibalized from the established P&G LDLs. Based on current market shares, only about 60 percent of H-80's volume would be net extra for the PS&D Division. If this occurred, it would lengthen payout for the division considerably.

P&G management was fully aware that H-80 was a risky venture. P&G's current market share of over 40 percent made cannibalization a virtual certainty and suggested a limited marketing investment to generate an attractive payout. Conversely, establishment in the increasingly competitive LDL category suggested the need for substantial marketing investment. An added element of risk was the revolutionary nature of the H-80 product, which contained a mild abrasive. Acceptance of this would require that consumers be educated and persuaded to modify current usage habits—a formidable task. Nevertheless,

---

EXHIBIT 6   Cost Structure for an Established LDL Brand (Percent)

Cost	51%
Distribution	7
Selling and general administration	10
Marketing expenditures	20*
Profit	12
Total	100%

*Includes advertising, trade, and consumer promotion expenditures.

Source: Company records.

EXHIBIT 7   H-80 Marketing Payout Schedule ($ millions)

	Year 1	Year 2	Year 3	Year 4
Revenue	$71.4	$112.2	$113.9	$113.9
Expenses:				
Marketing (20 percent of sales afer Year 1)	60.0	22.4	22.8	22.8
Cost of goods, distribution, and S&GA (68 percent of sales)	45.2	76.2	77.5	77.5
Total	$105.2	$ 98.6	$100.3	$100.3
Profit/(loss)	$ (33.8)	$ 13.6	$13.6	$13.6
Cumulative profit/(loss)	$(33.8)	$(20.2)	$(6.6)	$7.0

company management supported H-80 because it was an innovative product that met a real consumer need. The company had had outstanding successes with similar risky innovations in the past, such as Pampers, Crest, and Bounce, although other innovations had failed. P&G attempted to limit risk by test marketing new products and expanding distribution of only those that proved to have high consumer appeal in the marketplace and thus a high likelihood of success. Further, initial test market failures were frequently modified, retested successfully, and later expanded to national distribution.

The brand managers on P&G's established LDLs also expected some cannibalization, but projected that their brands' losses would be less than proportional to their market shares. As shown in Exhibit 8, Ivory Liquid and Joy expected to lose only 75 percent and 80 percent, respectively, of their proportionate losses, since their benefits would not compete directly with those of H-80.[17]

When the brand managers on Ivory, Dawn, and Joy were asked how they might change their brand marketing plans in light of the introduction of H-80, all three indicated that they would not increase their spending, but that they would formulate their promotion plans more defensively. Specifically, all three said they would plan to run strong offers designed to encourage consumers to stock up before H-80's introduction; then, following the introduction, trial-oriented couponing events would be planned to regain lost users.

Based on P&G LDL category experience, the brand group expected the following distribution by size two months after H-80's introduction: 70 percent distribution in stores representing 90 percent of total grocery volume on 48 oz., 85 percent on 32 oz., 90 percent on 22 oz., and 75 percent on 12 oz.[18] To maintain these distribution levels, Garner believed the brand had to promote all sizes of H-80 in the first year.

EXHIBIT 8 LDL Market Share Projections, 1982–1989

	Percent of LDL Market Volume						
	Without H-80			With H-80			
Year	Ivory Liquid	Dawn	Joy	Ivory Liquid	Dawn	Joy	H-80
1982	15.5%	14.7%	12.2%	15.5%	14.7%	12.2%	—
1983	15.5	15.0	12.3	14.7	14.0	11.4	7.0%
1984	15.5	15.5	12.4	14.2	13.9	11.1	11.0
1985	15.5	15.9	12.5	14.2	14.3	11.2	11.0
1986	15.5	16.5	12.7	14.2	14.9	11.4	11.0

---

[17]Proportionate loss is defined as a loss of sales proportionate to market share. For example, Ivory's 1983 share was expected to be 15.5 percent. If Ivory lost its fair share of H-80's 11 percent of the market, it would lose 15.5 percent × 11 percent = 1.7 share points.

[18]While the PS&D sales force serviced only 27 percent of grocery stores, accounting for 75 percent of grocery sales volume, additional distribution could be achieved through grocery wholesale distributors, which serviced smaller grocery stores.

P&G did not advertise a new brand until it had achieved 70 percent distribution, which the brand group expected H-80 to achieve six weeks after introduction. H-80's media plan would give the brand LDL category leadership media weights for the first six months of its introductory advertising campaign. The average media weight for the major advertised LDL brands was 300 gross rating points (GRPs)[19] every four weeks. H-80 planned 450 GRPs during weeks 6 through 18, 375 GRPs during weeks 19 through 31, and 300 GRPs during weeks 32 through 52. The Brand and Advertising Agency expected this media campaign would achieve a 65 percent consumer awareness of H-80's advertising by three months after introduction.

The H-80 advertising strategy aimed to convince consumers that H-80 was an outstanding dishwashing liquid for cleaning tough-to-remove foods from dishes. Advertising would be targeted at female heads of larger households, those aged 18 to 35. Consumer research had revealed that H-80 had the most well-defined target audience of any of the LDLs. It also suggested that H-80's target audience should be the heavy LDL user.[20]

Total cost for the 12-month media plan would be $18 million. In addition, promotion costs were expected to be $37 million, and miscellaneous marketing expenses $5 million (including point-of-sale display material and $500,000 to produce television commercials).

H-80's introductory-year advertising/promotion split would be 40 percent/60 percent—similar to the company average for a new brand. Thereafter, the brand manager's objective was to have at least 50 percent of marketing support in advertising.

H-80 would be available in four sizes and at prices equivalent to those of P&G's established LDL brands, as indicated in Table 3.

PROMOTION ISSUES FOR H-80

Reviewing Past LDL Promotions. P&G's introduction of Dawn in 1976 was considered very successful. Dawn's introductory promotion plan, outlined in Table 4 with 1982 updated costs, helped Dawn to achieve a market share equivalent to that required by H-80.

TABLE 3   H-80 Sizing and Pricing

Size	No. Items/ Actual Case	No. Items/ Statistical Case*	Manufacturer's Carload Item Price	Estimated Average Retail Price	Estimated Percent of Volume per Size†
48 oz.	9	6.5	$2.53	$2.99	10%
32 oz.	12	9.7	1.70	2.04	30
22 oz.	16	14.0	1.21	1.46	45
12 oz.	24	25.8	0.70	0.84	15

*A statistical case equals 310 ounces.
†Statistical cases.

---

[19]One gross rating point is achieved when one advertising exposure reaches 1% of the advertiser's potential audience. Gross rating points can be calculated as the product of media reach times exposure frequency.

[20]A heavy LDL user washes 12 or more sinksful of dishes per week.

With this introductory promotion program, Dawn had achieved the market share growth detailed in Table 5.

Garner realized that he would probably not be able to achieve the same results for H-80 if he simply copied the Dawn plan. When Dawn was introduced, there was little couponing in the LDL category. However, by 1982, most major LDL brands distributed coupons frequently, and (as Exhibit 9 shows) research indicated that coupons were widely used by consumers. Also, the LDL competitive environment was becoming more intense with the expansion of Sunlight by Lever Brothers in 1982. While it was still too early to tell how successful it would be with its national expansion, Sunlight had achieved an 11 percent share in the test market after only 12 months.

Sunlight's introductory promotion plan had been much more aggressive than the Dawn plan. It involved 10 promotion events, including: a $2.70/statistical case trade allowance for months 1–3 in support of a free 5-oz. sample size plus 15¢ coupons mailed to 50 percent of all households; three coupon events (one 20¢ free-standing insert coupon,[21]

TABLE 4 Dawn's Year 1 Introductory Promotion Plan

Month	Event	Cost in 1982 ($ millions)	Number of Average Weeks of Year 1 Volume per Promotion Event*
2 & 3	$2.70/statistical case trade allowance on all sizes	$ 1.8	8
	6 oz. sample mailed to 50 percent of households	30.3	—
4	22 oz./13¢-off price pack	1.2	10
6	32 oz./20¢-off price pack	1.0	10
8	48 oz./30¢-off price pack	0.3	13
10	22 oz./13¢-off price pack	1.2	10

*For example, eight weeks' worth of total Year 1 volume of all sizes would be sold with the initial trade allowance, and ten weeks' worth of total Year 1 volume on the 22-oz. size would be sold with the second event (13¢-off price pack).

TABLE 5 Dawn's Year 1 Market Share Growth

	Month						
	1–2	*3–4*	*5–6*	*7–8*	*9–10*	*11–12*	*Total Year 1*
Percent of Total Year 1 share	30%	80%	100%	120%	130%	140%	100%

---

[21]A free-standing insert coupon was a coupon and ad preprinted on heavy paper and inserted loose into a newspaper or magazine.

EXHIBIT 9   Consumer Use of Manufacturers' Coupons

Question: *How often do you use a manufacturer's coupon when you purchase a dishwashing liquid?*

	By Year			By 1981 Usage Patterns		
	1979	1980	1981	Heavy (+12 sinksful per week)	Medium (9–12 sinksful per week)	Light (1–8 sinksful per week)
Almost always	22%	25%	28%	28%	26%	24%
About half the time	17	18	18	18	19	18
Just occasionally	44	42	40	40	43	44
Never	16	14	13	13	12	13
No answer	1	1	1	1	—	1

Note: To be read, for example: In 1979, 22 percent of all respondents who had washed some dishes by hand in the past seven days claimed that they used a manufacturer's coupon almost always when they purchased a dishwashing liquid.

Source: Company research.

one 20¢ magazine coupon, and one 25¢ Best Food Day coupon)[22]; three preprice events (on 12-oz., 22-oz., and 32-oz. sizes); a 6-oz. trial size; and two trade allowance promotions (one on the 48 oz. size and one on the 22-oz. size). The cost of Sunlight's Year 1 promotion plan was estimated at $75 million on a national equivalent basis.

Minimizing Cannibalization.   Another key issue Garner faced was how to minimize H-80's cannibalization of P&G's other LDLs. As Garner examined the 1981, 1982, and 1983 promotion schedules for Ivory, Dawn, and Joy, he pondered when and how often H-80 should be promoted. He wanted to avoid the simultaneous promotion of two or more of the company's LDLs. However, given the limitation of 13 promotion periods, H-80 would have to be promoted alongside another LDL on at least some occasions.

Choosing Most-Effective Promotion Mix.   Garner also wondered what promotion mix would be most effective for the H-80 introduction. Price packs and coupons seemed to be the most commonly used promotion vehicles in the category, and recent P&G research (summarized in Table 6) indicated that these vehicles were liked and used by consumers. However, the same research also indicated that a trial size represented the best purchase incentive for a consumer who had never tried a brand (see Table 7).

Garner wondered if the less frequently used types of consumer promotion in the LDL category, such as premiums, mail-in refunds, or sweepstakes, could enable H-80 to attract the trade's attention and cut through the clutter of competitive promotions. He was particularly interested in the ability of free mail-in offers to achieve sampling of new users as reported in the independent industry research study presented in Exhibit 10.

---

[22]A Best Food Day coupon was a coupon run in a newspaper on the day that paper ran editorial material on food. This was also the edition in which most retail grocers placed their retail advertisements and hence the most advantageous day for grocers and manufacturers to run coupons.

TABLE 6 1981 Consumer Ratings and Use of Promotion Devices

	Coupons		Price Pack	Premiums		Refund/ Rebate	Trial Size	Bonus Pack	Sweepstakes
	Mfr.	Store		Pack	Mail				
Percent liking very much/fairly well	95%	85%	100%	75%	46%	74%	90%	90%	46%
Percent used past 3 months	97	87	100	51	30	56	61	74	44

Notes: These ratings were based on general consumer preferences rather than preferences within the LDL category. Index: highest-rated/used device = 100.

Source: Company research.

TABLE 7 1981 Consumer Ratings and Use of Promotion Devices (Percent)

	Coupons		Price Pack	Premiums		Refund/ Rebate	Trial Size	Bonus Pack	Sweepstakes
	Mfr.	Store		Pack	Mail				
Brand never used	46%	37%	29%	37%	17%	27%	100%	35%	13%

Index: highest-rated/used device = 100.

Independent of the types of promotion events scheduled, Garner believed—on the basis of LDL category experience—that the following percentages of incremental trial would be achieved with each subsequent promotion:

Event I—Assume all reach is incremental trial.

Event II—Assume 1/2 of reach is incremental trial.

Event III—Assume 1/4 of reach is incremental trial.

Event IV—Assume 1/4 of reach is incremental trial.

Event V—Assume 1/4 of reach is incremental trial.

Garner predicted that he would have to achieve about a 40 percent trial level to support an 11 percent share based on results of previous introductions of products with similar usage profits.

SALES PROMOTION ALTERNATIVES

Trade Allowances. Sales had advised Garner that a $2.70/statistical case trade allowance on all sizes in months 1–3 was necessary to stimulate initial stocking, in-store displays, and feature advertising by the trade. Garner also wondered whether a second trade promotion allowance event was necessary because of the competitive environment. He believed it would be most effective as a fourth event. Sales had informed him that an allowance below the current $1.80/statistical case used on the other P&G LDLs would be insufficient to generate trade support.

EXHIBIT 10　Effectiveness Ratings of Premiums and Sweepstakes by Manufacturers Who Sell through Supermarkets

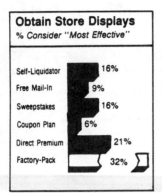

Obtain Store Displays
% Consider "Most Effective"

Self-Liquidator 16%
Free Mail-In 9%
Sweepstakes 16%
Coupon Plan 6%
Direct Premium 21%
Factory-Pack 32%

Gain Ad Readership
% Consider "Most Effective"

Self-Liquidator 8%
Free Mail-In 24%
Sweepstakes 40%
Coupon Plan 12%
Direct Premium 14%
Factory-Pack 2%

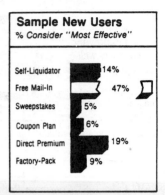

Sample New Users
% Consider "Most Effective"

Self-Liquidator 14%
Free Mail-In 47%
Sweepstakes 5%
Coupon Plan 6%
Direct Premium 19%
Factory-Pack 9%

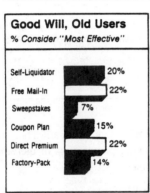

Good Will, Old Users
% Consider "Most Effective"

Self-Liquidator 20%
Free Mail-In 22%
Sweepstakes 7%
Coupon Plan 15%
Direct Premium 22%
Factory-Pack 14%

Sell-In To Dealers
% Consider "Most Effective"

Self-Liquidator 7%
Free Mail-In 8%
Sweepstakes 19%
Coupon Plan 13%
Direct Premium 31%
Factory-Pack 22%

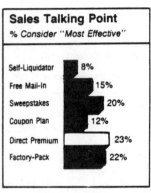

Sales Talking Point
% Consider "Most Effective"

Self-Liquidator 8%
Free Mail-In 15%
Sweepstakes 20%
Coupon Plan 12%
Direct Premium 23%
Factory-Pack 22%

Get Shelf Attention
% Consider "Most Effective"

Self-Liquidator 16%
Free Mail-In 19%
Sweepstakes 16%
Coupon Plan 4%
Direct Premium 10%
Factory-Pack 35%

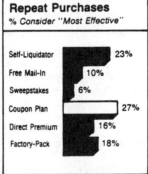

Repeat Purchases
% Consider "Most Effective"

Self-Liquidator 23%
Free Mail-In 10%
Sweepstakes 6%
Coupon Plan 27%
Direct Premium 16%
Factory-Pack 18%

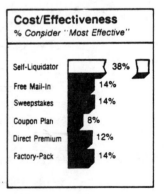

Cost/Effectiveness
% Consider "Most Effective"

Self-Liquidator 38%
Free Mail-In 14%
Sweepstakes 14%
Coupon Plan 8%
Direct Premium 12%
Factory-Pack 14%

Source: *Incentive Marketing*, December 1981.

Sampling. Sampling was considered by P&G as the most effective trial-producing promotion device. Garner considered only mailed samples, as door-to-door delivery of samples by specially recruited crews was more expensive.

Garner worked with the manufacturing department to develop mailed sample costs for various sizes, as shown in Exhibit 11. He was aware of P&G research indicating that too small a sample might not permit sufficient use to develop consumer interest in the product. He wondered which size would generate the most efficient and effective trial levels for H-80.

Couponing. Although Dawn's introductory plan had not included any couponing, Garner felt that he should consider this promotion vehicle, given its broad usage within the current LDL category and apparent appeal to consumers. He examined the costs and redemption estimates by distribution vehicle (see Exhibit 12) and by coupon value (see Exhibit 13) for five types of coupon programs:

- Coupons for H-80 alone could be mailed selectively to members of the target audience. The impact and redemption rate would be high because there would be no coupons for other brands in the mailing that might reduce consumer attention to H-80. However, this couponing method was expensive.
- Coupons for H-80 could be co-op, mailed with other product coupons. Co-op couponing had slightly less impact but was considerably less expensive since delivery costs were shared with other brands. Such co-op mailings were organized by outside agencies. Consequently, the timing of deliveries was fixed in advance, and only one LDL brand could participate in any one coupon drop. The only available delivery times open to H-80 in the test market were three months and seven months following introduction.
- Free-standing newspaper insert (FSI) coupons offered Garner more flexibility in timing. The redemption rates for FSI coupons were strong, but coupon theft and misredemption could also be high (particularly if the FSI was inserted in newsstand issues).
- Coupons distributed through the Best Food Day editions of local newspapers offered both low-cost delivery and flexibility in timing and in geographical coverage. There was, however, a greater potential for a new brand like H-80 to be lost among the many coupons run in newspapers. Also, the redemption rate was low and misredemption was high.

EXHIBIT 11 Mailed Sampling Costs per Sample Unit for H-80

Sample Size	Delivered* Cost per Unit	Percent Usage†	Percent of Consumers Who Use Sample and Repurchase
6 oz. miniature bottles	$.75	85%	50%
3 oz. miniature bottles	.53	75	40
1.5 oz miniature bottles	.41	65	35
Two .75 oz. foil packets	.31	40	30

*Includes mailing costs and manufacturing costs.
†Usage and repurchase rates vary by size.

EXHIBIT 12 Theoretical Couponing Economics (20¢-off coupon good on any size)

	Mail			Free-Standing Insert				
	Single Brand	Basic Co-Op*	Extended Co-Op†	Single Brand	Full-Page Co-op	2/5 Page Co-op	Best Food Day	Magazine (on page)
No. of coupons distributed (millions)	40	24	45	44	38	38	58	58
Distribution cost‡ ($000)	$110.00	$16.45	$14.00	$37.50	$12.05	$5.05	$9.20	$5.70
Total distribution cost	$4,400,000	$395,000	$630,000	$1,650,000	$458,000	$182,000	$478,000	$319,000
Estimated percent redemption	11.6%	11.6%	10.6%	7.6%	5.7%	5.1%	3.1%	2.6%
No. of coupons redeemed (thousands)	4,640	2,784	4,770	3,344	2,166	1,938	1,612	1,456
Total redemption costs§ ($000)	$1,322.4	$793.4	$1,357.5	$953.0	$617.3	$552.3	$459.4	$415.0
Grand total costs ($000)	$5,772.4	$1,188.2	$1,989.5	$2,603.5	$1,075.3	$744.3	$937.4	$734.0
Estimated percent misrepresentation	10%	10%	10%	25%	25%	25%	25%	10%
No. of households reached with product (thousands)	4,174	2,506	4,293	2,508	1,625	1,454	1,209	1,310
Total cases moved (thousands)	422	253	434	257	167	149	124	132
Cost per household reached	$1.37	$0.47	$0.46	$1.03	$0.66	$0.51	$0.78	$0.56
Cost per case moved	$13.56	$4.70	$4.58	$10.13	$6.44	$5.00	$7.55	$5.56

Note: This chart is based upon average redemption data. Assume a new P&G LDL brand would redeem 50 percent higher due to strong advertising, product news, and high household category penetration.

*A coupon mailing involving at least 10 noncompeting brands. Redemption rates were stable regardless of the number of brands.

†Extended coverage version of basic co-op coupon mailing.

‡Includes coupon production and preparation costs as well as cost of mailing.

§Includes trade and clearing house handling fees totaling 8.5¢ per coupon as well as amount of coupon.

EXHIBIT 13 Approximate Relationship of Redemption Rate to LDL Coupon Value

Coupon Vehicle	Coupon Value					
	20¢	*25¢*	*35¢*	*50¢*	*$1.00*	*Get One Free*
Mail						
Single Brand	100	110	125	150	200	250
Co-op	100	110	125	150	200	250
FSI Co-op	100	110	125	150	200	250
Best Food Day	100	110	125	150	200	250
Magazine	100	110	125	150	200	250
On-pack	100	110	125	150	200	NA
Cross-ruff*	100	110	125	150	200	NA

Note: Data indexed to 20¢ value.
*Advertised on pack of another brand.

- Magazine coupons also offered low delivery costs and could be targeted at specific consumer groups. However, the potential to tie in with specific retailer feature dates did not exist. In addition, the redemption rate was low.

SPECIAL PACK PROMOTIONS

Garner considered four types of special packs: trial-size packs, prepriced packs, price packs, and bonus packs. Sales had advised that special packs should not be run until at least the second half of Year 1, since the trade was reluctant to buy a special pack until a new brand was established to avoid carrying dual inventories of regular pack and special pack. However, if a new brand were introduced with a special pack, the trade would not need to carry dual inventories. (A cost comparison by value/size and vehicle is shown in Exhibit 14.)

A trial size would offer the consumer a low-risk, low-cost method of trying H-80. Because the consumer paid for the trial-size package, the cost to P&G per trial was lower than for a sampling program.

A prepriced pack would also offer the consumer a low-risk, low-cost method of trying H-80, similar to a trial size. Usually, a prepriced pack was offered on the smallest salable size, in this case the 12-oz. size.

Price packs were widely used in the LDL category. Price packs were generally regarded as an effective promotion vehicle to retain current users and encourage repeat purchasing. The trade often set up special displays of price packs that could stimulate impulse purchases. Garner wondered, however, if a price pack would be good at generating trial for H-80.

Bonus packs offered low-cost distribution of free product but were not regarded as a strong trial device since they did not reduce the financial risk of trial to the consumer who had never used the product. However, bonus packs were considered an excellent means of promoting continuity of usage and offered a strong purchase incentive to the

EXHIBIT 14   LDL Special-Pack Promotions

	Trial Size (6 ounces Product Miniature) Consumer Price per Bottle	Prepriced Size (12 ounces) Consumer Price per Bottle (savings off retail price)	Bonus Pack (32 ounce oversize) Percent of Free Product	Price Pack (cents off) Percent of Normal Retail
Value:				
High	$.19	$.39 (50%)	25% (8 oz.)	30%
Medium	.29	.49 (40)	15 (5 oz.)	20
Low	.39	.59 (30)	10 (3 oz.)	10
Cost:				
High value	36¢ per unit	Savings off retail price times number of units per statistical case plus 50¢ per statistical case manufacturing and trade handling	$6.10 per statistical case	Cents off times number of units per statistical case plus 50¢ per statistical case manufacturing and trade handling
Medium value	29¢ per unit		$5.00 per statistical case	
Low value	22¢ per unit		$4.25 per statistical case	
Amount of promoted volume sold per event	4.7 million bottles	13 weeks' business for 12 oz.	10 weeks' business for 32 oz.	10 weeks' business for 22 oz. and 32 oz.; 13 weeks' for 12 oz. and 48 oz.

Note: All three types of promotion would be accepted by stores representing 70 percent of all commodity volume (ACV).

consumer who had purchased and liked the product before. Garner wondered if a bonus pack promotion would be effective in the second half of the introductory year.

Refunds.   P&G did not usually use refund offers on a new brand because the economic benefit to the consumer was not immediately delivered and the value of the device in stimulating trial was questionable. However, Garner wondered if a high-value refund supported by point-of-purchase display material could generate significant trade and consumer interest. He also wondered if a refund requiring multiple purchases would be an effective continuity device if used in the second six months of H-80's first-year promotion plan. Garner analyzed the company's experience with refunds over the past three years (see Exhibit 15 for a refund fact sheet) and found that P&G distributed 30 percent of its refund offers through print, 27 percent through point-of-sale display material, 5 percent through in- or on-pack, and 38 percent through divisional group promotions that used a combination of all three distribution methods plus television advertising.

EXHIBIT 15   Refund Facts: Industry Experience

I. Factors that Influence Refund Response Rates

1. Method of distribution.
2. Proof-of-purchase requirements/difficulty in obtaining proofs.
3. Actual value of refund; value relative to price.
4. Length of promotion.
5. Design/appeal of offer and ad.
6. Whether store coupon used with refund offer.
7. Consumer interest in product/size of brand's consumer franchise.
8. Whether a single choice or variable offer.
9. Whether refund in cash, check, or coupon.
10. Brand's retail availability.
11. Whether offer advertised via media or trade, or publicized in refund columns and newsletters.

II. Typical Response Patterns

	Purchase Requirements		
	1 Unit Purchased (22 oz. size)	*2 Units Purchased (22 oz. size)*	*3 Units Purchased (22 oz. size)*
Refund value	$1.00	$1.00	$1.00
Consumer outlay for purchases	1.50	3.00	4.50
Percent savings on 22 oz. size	67%	33%	22%

Estimated response as percentage of offers distributed

Print	.9%	.5%	.3%
Point of sale	5.4	3.0	1.8
Direct mail	3.6	2.0	1.2
In-/on-pack other brand	8.2	4.5	2.7
In-/on-pack own brand	12.7	7.0	4.2

*III. Estimated Fulfillment Costs**

	Number Distributed (millions)			
Print	44	$530,000	$300,000	$175,000
Point of sale	3	220,000	120,000	75,000
Direct mail	25	1,200,000	670,000	400,000
In-/on-pack other brand	6	660,000	360,000	220,000
In-/on-pack own brand	6	1,020,000	560,000	335,000

*Fulfillment costs include the $1.00 refund itself plus 34¢ return for handling. In addition to the fulfillment costs, assume $70,000 to $150,000 for display material/sales aids and/or $300,000 to $500,000 for print advertising; 3¢ per unit for in-/on-pack distribution carried by own brand, no extra package cost if carried by other brand, and $16.45/per thousand for distributing direct mail offers via multibrand co-op.

Premiums. Premiums were believed useful in attracting attention at the point-of-sale and could offer excellent in-store display support, thereby stimulating impulse purchases. There were four major methods of premium distribution and types.

On-/in-pack premiums were attached to or packed in the product container and were offered free with the purchase of the promoted brand. These premiums made a strong impact on the shelf and often encouraged the trade to display the products off-shelf because of their irregular size. In-pack premiums were considered good trial-generating devices. However, the costs of extra packaging and of the premiums themselves could be significant. In addition, trade acceptance was estimated at only 30 percent to 50 percent of all commodity volume because of inventory and shelf space problems (due to irregular size) as well as the risk of pilferage.

Near-pack premiums were displayed on the shelf next to or near the promoted product. Most near-pack premiums were free with the designated purchase, but in the case of salable or price-plus near-packs the consumer was asked to pay a token sum. While near-packs offered more flexibility in the size of the premium a manufacturer could choose, they were hard to control since retailers often found it difficult to ensure that consumers made the purchases necessary to qualify to receive the premium.

A free-in-mail premium was mailed to the consumer who sent the company the purchase requirements. Such offers were easily executed but did not provide an immediate benefit to the consumer. Self-liquidating premiums were delivered through the mail, much like free mail-ins, but the consumer was required to send money as well as one or more

---

EXHIBIT 16 Objectives and Costs of LDL Premiums

Type of Premium	Marketing Objectives				
	Trial	Repeat Purchase	Obtain In-Store Displays	Increase Advertisement Readership	Copy/Product Reinforcement
Self-liquidator			●	●	●
Partial liquidator by mail		●	●	●	
Free-in-mail for multiproofs		●	●	●	●
Free-in-mail for one proof	●		●	●	●
Near-pack—in store	●		●		●
On-/in-pack—in store	●		●		●

Type of Premium	Typical Item	Offer Structure	National Cost of Promotion
Self-liquidator	Hair dryer	$9.00 plus 1 proof of purchase	$ 200,000
Partial liquidator	Hair dryer	$2.00 plus 4 proofs of purchase	400,000
Free-in-mail	Hair dryer	Free for 6 22-ounce proofs of purchase	2,200,000
Near-pack	Coupon holder	Free with one 22 ounce	950,000
On-/in-pack	Playing cards	Free with one 22 ounce	950,000

Note: Cost estimates include the premium itself, display materials, and offer fulfillment; in the case of completely or partially self-liquidating premiums, they reflect offsetting revenue from consumers.

EXHIBIT 17   P&G Group Sweepstakes Promotion

1st Prize	**2nd Prize**	**3rd Prize**

Five (5) 6-day cruises on the Flying Cloud (approximate retail value $3,200.00 per trip).*

2,000 L.L. Bean Boat and Tote™ Bags (approximate retail value $10.00).

One (1) 13-day cruise for two on the luxury schooner Fantome PLUS $5,000 cash (approximate retail value $11,300.00).*

*The First and Second Prizes include transportation to and from Freeport, Bahamas where the cruises originate.

Name _____

Address _____

_____

City _____

State _____

Zip Code _____

Telephone _____

OFFICIAL RULES—NO PURCHASE NECESSARY

1. Each entry you submit must be accompanied by one of the following:
   a. Any retail store ad dated between August 1, 1982 and September 30, 1982 which includes an ad for any one of these fine Procter & Gamble products:

Dash   Oxydol   Gain   Era   Bounty

White Cloud* or Charmin   Folger's Ground Roast or Flaked Coffee   Instant High Point   Ivory Liquid

*Available only in limited areas.
Circle the name of the product and its picture (if a picture is included in the ad) and circle the date printed on the ad.
OR
   b. A plain piece of 3″ x 5″ paper on which you have handprinted or typed the name of any one of these fine Procter & Gamble products: Dash, Oxydol, Gain, Era, Bounty, White Cloud, Charmin, Folger's Ground Roast or Flaked Coffee, Instant High Point, Ivory Liquid.

2. Mail one of the above along with an Official Entry Form or plain piece of 3″ x 5″ paper on which you have handprinted your name and address. Mail your entry to: Sail For Savings Sweepstakes, P.O. Box 4036, Blair, NE 68009.

3. Retail ads submitted must be dated between August 1, 1982-September 30, 1982. Any printed retailer ad is acceptable — newspaper ads, in-store circulars, etc. You do not

need to send the complete retail ad — only that portion which shows the participating brand and the date is necessary.

4. Enter the Sail For Savings sweepstakes as often as you wish, but each entry must be mailed separately in a hand addressed envelope no larger than 4⅛″ x 9½″ (#10 envelope). Entries must be postmarked between August 3, 1982-October 14, 1982, and received by October 22, 1982.

5. Winners will be determined in a random drawing conducted by D.L. Blair, an independent judging organization, whose decisions are final. All prizes will be awarded, limit one prize per name and address. Winners will be notified and prizes delivered by mail by approximately December 31, 1982.

6. One (1) First Prize of a 13-day cruise for two on the luxury schooner Fantome plus $5,000 cash (approximate retail value $11,300.00); five (5) Second Prizes of 6-day cruises for two on The Flying Cloud (approximate retail value $3,200.00 per trip) and 2,000 Third Prizes of L.L. Bean Boat and Tote™ Bags (approximate retail value $10.00) will be awarded. The First and Second Prize winners will also receive transportation to and from Freeport, Bahamas where the cruises originate. The cruise package includes meals while on board. All cruises awarded as First or Second Prizes must be completed by September 1, 1983; dates of departure are subject to availability.

7. This sweepstakes is open to residents of the United States, eighteen years or older at time of entry, except employees of Procter & Gamble and their advertising, judging, and promotion agencies, and the families of each. Void via participation at retail stores in Wisconsin and wherever prohibited by law. All federal, state, and local laws and regulations apply. Taxes, if any, are the sole responsibility of the prize winner. The odds of winning a prize will depend upon the number of entries received by October 22, 1982. Limit one prize per name and address. No substitution for prizes.

8. For a list of prize winners, send a separate, stamped, self-addressed envelope to: Sail For Savings Sweepstakes Winners' List, P.O. Box 4151, Blair, NE 68009.

Form No. 664-6172   528HXM

EXHIBIT 18 H-80 National Sales Promotion Plan

Event	January	February	March	April	May	June	July	August	September	October	November	December	Number of Weeks	Average Volume	Cost
Stocking Allowance: $/Physical case															
Trade Allowance: $/Statistical case															
Sampling															
6 oz.															
3 oz.															
1.5 oz.															
2 × 0.75 oz.															
Couponing															
Mail															
Single															
Co-op															
Extended															
FSI															
Single															
Full page co-op															
2/5 page co-op															
BFD															
Magazine															
Special Pack:															
Price pack															
Bonus pack															
Trial size															
Refund:															
Print															
Point of sale															
Direct mail															
In-/on-pack															
Own brand															
Other brand															
Premium:															
On-/in-pack															
Near-pack															
Free-in-mail															
Self-liquidator															
Partial liquidator															
Group Promotion															

proofs-of-purchase to cover the cost of the premium, handling, and mailing. The cost of such premiums to the consumer was between 30 percent and 50 percent lower than the regular retail price. Response rates were, however, quite modest. (Exhibit 16 presents a company fact sheet comparing typical premium costs.)

Sweepstakes/Contests. P&G was scheduled to run a group promotion four months following the introduction of H-80. Company research had revealed that smaller brands achieved good results behind group promotions because of the high distribution and display support these offers stimulated among the trade. However, Garner wondered if a new brand might get lost among P&G's established brands. (See Exhibit 17 for an example of a group promotion.) Garner estimated the cost of participating in a group FSI sweepstakes promotion would be about $50,000 and that it would achieve about a 2 percent response rate for H-80. Most brands participating in an offer of this type would also include a coupon in the FSI advertisement for the sweepstakes.

CONCLUSION

As Garner prepared to write the details of H-80's Year 1 national promotion plan in the format shown in Exhibit 18, he considered several things. How should he split his promotion dollars between trade and consumer promotions during the first year? How much of his brand should he plan to sell to the trade on deal? What promotion events should he recommend? How many times should he promote H-80 in its first year? Was the Dawn plan strong enough to work in the more competitive LDL environment H-80 faced? Would he be able to gain more leverage with the trade if he promoted H-80 with the other LDLs, or would this hurt his brand? Which potential overlaps with the other LDLs should he most try to avoid?

PART 7

Point-of-Purchase Merchandising

H.J. Heinz Co.: Plastic Bottle Ketchup (A)*

In March 1983, Barbara Johnson, product manager on Heinz ketchup, was debating whether or not to launch ketchup in a new plastic bottle and, if so, what level of support to place behind the move. The new product had been in development for three years. Johnson commented: "I have to determine if the plastic bottle is truly a 'big idea' or just another line extension."

COMPANY BACKGROUND

H. J. Heinz Company was founded in 1869 on a packaging innovation: Henry Heinz packaged horseradish in clear glass jars. In fiscal year (FY) 1983 (ending April 30), the food manufacturer recorded sales of $3.7 billion and net income of $214.3 million. During the previous 10 years, sales had grown at an average annual rate of 12.7 percent and earnings per share at 14.6 percent. In the United States, H. J. Heinz Co. consisted of five subsidiaries: Heinz USA, Star Kist Foods, Ore Ida Foods, Hubinger Co., and Weight Watchers International. Star Kist marketed tuna and pet foods (9-Lives), Ore-Ida frozen potato products, and Hubinger industrial corn sweeteners. Weight Watchers International promoted well-known weight-control programs. Heinz USA, the oldest subsidiary, employed 6,000 people and marketed such diverse products as ketchup, pickles, vinegar, baby foods, soup, ALBA dry beverage mixes, and foodservice products.

Heinz USA employed a 200-person sales force that covered the Northeastern and North Central regions. Salespeople were compensated on salary plus a bonus linked to two volume goals: a ketchup goal, and a second goal covering all other products. Heinz used brokers in the South and West.

Heinz had been selling ketchup for over a century. By FY 1983, it held a 45.6 percent share of retail ketchup volume and a 45.0 percent share of foodservice volume, making it the dominant competitor in the ketchup market. Heinz retail ketchup sales were $215 million and accounted for 30 percent of Heinz USA sales and 35 percent of profits; Heinz foodservice ketchup sales were $175 million.

---

*This case was written by Research Assistant John L. Teopaco, under the direction of Professor John A. Quelch, as a basis for class discussion rather than to illustrate either effective or ineffective handling of an administrative situation. Copyright © 1985 by the President and Fellows of Harvard College. Harvard Business School case 9–586–035.

Heinz manufactured ketchup at three plants, one of which had the world's fastest filling line for large-sized ketchup varieties. The company actively pursued technological innovations. In an early application of genetic engineering to a commercial food crop, Heinz researchers created a "super tomato" with a higher solid content and better acid balance specially suited for ketchup production.

HEINZ USA'S PRODUCT MANAGEMENT SYSTEM

Exhibit 1 shows the organizational structure of Heinz USA's product management system. Prior to 1980, the divisions were aligned with the factories; each division marketed the products made in a single plant. In 1980, the divisions were restructured to provide a greater marketing orientation. The product management organization included 40–50 professionals. Product managers were responsible for individual brands (such as Heinz ketchup), and they reported to group product managers who, in turn, reported to the general managers. Each general manager was in charge of a major product group. The Packaged Goods general managers, for example, managed more cost-sensitive, trade/push-oriented products, so the two general managers in this area were heavily involved in manufacturing cost-control projects. In contrast, the Consumer Products general managers handled more pull-oriented products.

Heinz considered its product management system lean and flexible. The number of management layers above an individual depended upon the person's level of experience. In describing the system, one Heinz manager stated: "We need people who are independent, self-starting, see what needs to get done, ask the right questions, and do not need to have their hand held through the system." Because of the organization's leanness, it was not easy to rotate managers systematically from one type of brand to another. On the other hand, the nature of assignments—particularly the products under each general manager—were often changed according to an individual's experience and development needs.

The ketchup brand group consisted of an assistant product manager, two associate product managers, and a product manager reporting to a group product manager. The group met regularly with representatives of other functions including packaging, product development, purchasing, production planning, engineering, and sales planning.

THE KETCHUP MARKET

Category Consumption. In FY 1983, U.S. retail ketchup sales were 33.8 million (equivalent) cases[1] valued at $434 million in manufacturers' selling prices. Ketchup was the 29th largest dry grocery food category in the U.S., up from 35th in 1981. During the previous three years, retail ketchup volume had increased at an average annual rate of 3 percent. Increasing consumption of ketchup was believed to reflect life-style trends favoring quick, convenient meals, such as hamburgers. In addition, ketchup consumption

---

[1]One equivalent case = 24 14-oz. bottles, or 336 ounces.

EXHIBIT 1 Heinz USA Marketing Organization

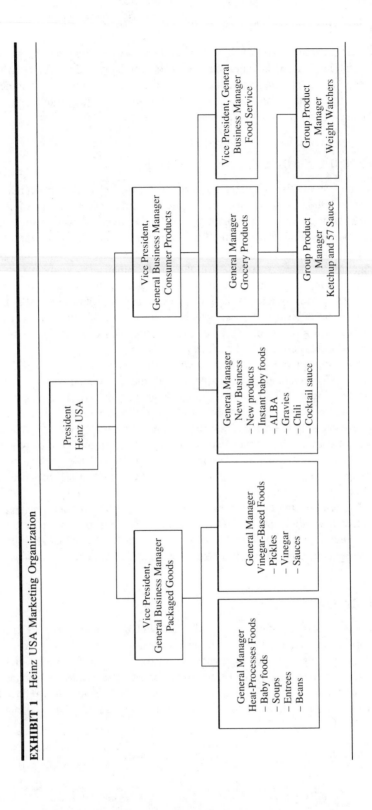

was thought to be correlated negatively with the price of beef which had fallen during each of the previous three years.

Major Competitors.   Heinz, Hunt's, and Del Monte were the three major ketchup brands. Hunt's was owned by Esmark, Inc., and Del Monte by R. J. Reynolds, Inc. Hunt's ketchup sales accounted for 3 percent of Esmark's U.S. Foods Division sales, while Del Monte ketchup sales made up 5 percent of R. J. Reynolds' Dry Grocery and Beverages Division sales. Hunt's and Del Monte employed their own sales forces to sell their products nationwide.

Heinz's 45.6 percent retail share of ketchup volume in 1983 compared to Hunt's 14.1 percent and Del Monte's 11.8 percent. Private-label, generic, and minor brands made up the remaining 28.5 percent. Heinz volume was up 23 percent over the 1979 level; it was the only major brand that had grown over the past four years. Exhibit 2 shows market shares by region for FY 1979–FY 1983. Heinz had increased its share during the previous five years, but, in FY 1983, Heinz had lost half a share point to Hunt's and private-label brands. Market shares varied by region; Heinz was strongest in the Northeast with a 60.9 percent market share, and weakest in the West and South.

Package Sizes.   In 1983, the major manufacturers sold four sizes of ketchup: 14 oz., 24 oz., 32 oz., and 44 oz. Exhibit 3 shows industry volume mix by size over the previous 20 years. In 1964, only two sizes had been available, and the 14-oz. size accounted for

EXHIBIT 2   Ketchup Brand Shares by Region

	FY 79	FY 80	FY 81	FY 82	FY 83
Northeast					
Heinz	52.9%	57.1%	59.8%	61.4%	60.9%
Hunt's	10.1	8.9	8.3	7.8	7.0
Del Monte	5.0	4.2	2.5	1.7	2.6
North Central					
Heinz	44.2	45.6	45.4	46.1	47.6
Hunt's	10.1	10.4	10.1	10.3	9.6
Del Monte	16.3	13.9	15.0	13.3	12.9
South					
Heinz	29.4	30.9	32.8	38.4	37.9
Hunt's	27.9	26.0	25.2	21.5	23.6
Del Monte	18.7	16.4	17.7	15.3	13.2
West					
Heinz	33.6	34.9	36.5	37.4	36.8
Hunt's	12.5	13.7	14.2	12.2	11.2
Del Monte	25.5	22.4	23.3	23.7	21.7
Total U.S.					
Heinz	40.1	42.0	43.4	46.1	45.6
Hunt's	16.2	15.7	15.5	13.8	14.1
Del Monte	15.4	13.3	13.9	12.5	11.8

EXHIBIT 3   Size Mix of Ketchup Category Volume

	1964	*1969*	*1974*	*1979*	*1980*	*1981*	*1982*	*1983*
14 oz.	68%	48%	33%	23%	22%	20%	19%	17%
20 oz.	32	37	24	10	6	1	—	—
24 oz.	—	—	—	5	10	13	13	11
26 oz.	—	15	20	9	3	—	—	—
32 oz.	—	—	23	49	46	50	51	55
44 oz.	—	—	—	4	13	16	17	17
Total	100%	100%	100%	100%	100%	100%	100%	100%

EXHIBIT 4   FY 1983 Volume Mix by Brand, Size, and Region

	14 oz.	*24 oz.*	*32 oz.*	*44 oz.*	*Total*
Northeast					
Heinz	20%	14%	42%	23%	100%
Hunt's	34	14	43	9	100
Del Monte	19	12	69	—	100
North Central					
Heinz	13	12	46	28	100
Hunt's	10	8	64	18	100
Del Monte	9	14	60	17	100
South					
Heinz	17	9	49	25	100
Hunt's	13	16	59	12	100
Del Monte	18	16	56	9	100
West					
Heinz	21	10	41	28	100
Hunt's	18	11	59	12	100
Del Monte	20	10	56	14	100
Total U.S.					
Heinz	18	12	45	25	100
Hunt's	16	14	57	13	100
Del Monte	13	11	63	13	100

two-thirds of the volume. By 1983, over 80 percent of ketchup sales were in sizes that had not existed 20 years earlier.

Exhibit 4 shows the volume mix by size and by region for each major ketchup brand in 1983. For the three major brands, the bulk of their business was accounted for by the 32-oz. size. This size was even more important for Hunt's and Del Monte than for Heinz.

Pricing.   Heinz was the highest-priced ketchup brand on all sizes in all regions (except for the 24-oz. size in the West, where Del Monte was priced higher by 1.7 percent). Exhibit 5 shows the major manufacturers' base selling prices and actual retail selling

EXHIBIT 5   1983 Manufacturer Base* Selling Prices and Actual Retail Prices (per bottle)

	14 ounces		24 ounces		32 oounces		44 ounces	
	Manufacturer	Retail	Manufacturer	Retail	Manufacturer	Retail	Manufacturer	Retail
Northeast								
Heinz	$.64	$.72	$1.05	$1.17	$1.34	$1.37	$1.78	$1.91
Hunt's	.61	.69	.99	1.14	1.28	1.31	1.72	1.85
Del Monte	.62	.72	1.03	1.08	1.29	1.25	NA	2.10
North Central								
Heinz	.64	.73	1.04	1.19	1.32	1.33	1.77	1.84
Hunt's	.61	.73	1.00	1.17	1.27	1.19	1.68	1.77
Del Monte	.61	.74	1.01	1.09	1.29	1.26	1.70	1.78
South								
Heinz	.64	.76	1.04	1.22	1.32	1.30	1.77	1.89
Hunt's	.64	.75	1.01	1.16	1.29	1.21	1.72	1.89
Del Monte	.62	.73	1.01	1.05	1.29	1.24	1.69	1.85
West								
Heinz	.63	.79	1.04	1.25	1.32	1.39	1.75	1.96
Hunt's	.60	.78	1.00	1.17	1.25	1.27	1.69	1.95
Del Monte	.63	.80	1.06	1.15	1.31	1.35	1.67	1.89

*Before promotional allowances.

prices by region. Except on the 14-oz. size, Heinz's retail prices were between 1 percent and 9 percent higher than Hunt's and Del Monte's. Hunt's and Del Monte's average national retail prices differed by 3 percent to 6 percent across the different sizes. As Exhibit 5 shows, the trade was taking the lowest margin on the 32-oz. size, which accounted for 55 percent of industry volume. It was believed that the trade treated the dominant 32-oz. size as a "loss leader."

Heinz had taken its last price increase in early 1982, a uniform 5 percent raise across the entire product line. Hunt's and Del Monte had followed with the same dollar per case increase. With a 40 percent manufacturer's gross margin, Heinz executives were concerned that Heinz might be priced too high. Fearing that competition could cut prices and gain market share from Heinz, Heinz management had resolved to try not to take any more price increases in the near future.

Trade Promotion.   Trade deals and allowances played a major role in ketchup marketing. A significant proportion of FY 1983 ketchup industry volume was sold on deal, as shown below:

	14 oz.	24 oz.	32 oz.	44 oz.
Percentage of size volume sold on deal	30%	40%	90%	60%
Deal rates as percent of base selling prices	9	10	15	12

Distribution.   Share of market was thought to be partially correlated with level of retail distribution. Heinz, the market leader, was in practically all food stores with at least one size (97 percent All Commodity Volume[2]), followed by Hunt's (84 percent ACV) and Del Monte (72 percent ACV). Exhibit 6 shows retail distribution during FY 1983 by brand and by size.

Heinz average sales per linear foot of grocery shelf space, $1,021 per year, were significantly higher than sales of other ketchup brands (Hunt's $539, Del Monte $619) as well as other condiments (mustard $336, salad dressing $372). In spite of this, Heinz's share of shelf space was often less than its share of sales.

Market Development.   Ketchup market development varied by region for the category and the individual brands. In terms of category volume, the South was the most important, representing 35 percent of volume, followed by the Northeast and North Central regions with 25 percent each, and the West with 15 percent. Based on a region's per capita consumption of ketchup relative to the national average, ketchup was underconsumed in the West and moderately overconsumed in the North Central and Southern regions. Exhibit 7 shows category (CDI) and brand development indices (BDI) by region. Heinz was highly developed in the Northeastern region (124 BDI) and underdeveloped in the West (71 BDI). Hunt's and Del Monte's BDIs were significantly more unbalanced. Hunt's was significantly overconsumed in the South (178 BDI) and underconsumed in the Northeast

---

EXHIBIT 6   FY 1983 Average Retail Distribution (percent ACV)

	14 oz.	24 oz.	32 oz.	44 oz.
Heinz	96%	78%	88%	80%
Hunt's	69	35	71	35
Del Monte	52	40	59	27

EXHIBIT 7   Ketchup Category and Brand Development Indices*

	National	Northeast	North Central	South	West
Category	100	94	111	109	79
Heinz	100	124	113	89	71
Hunt's	100	47	87	175	55
Del Monte	100	26	126	123	133
Annual per capital consumption of category	51 oz.	48 oz.	56 oz.	55 oz.	40 oz.

$$\text{*Index} = \frac{\text{Consumption per capita in area}}{\text{Average consumption per capita nationally}}$$

---

[2]Stores representing 97 percent of total U.S. grocery sales stocked at least one size of Heinz ketchup.

(47 BDI) and West (55 BDI). Del Monte had only a 26 BDI in the Northeast, but had over 120 in the other regions.

Advertising.   In FY 1983, ketchup category advertising totaled $18.6 million, up from $6.7 million just three years earlier. Heinz accounted for 86 percent of advertising spending. Exhibit 8 shows category spending and brand shares for FY 1980–FY 1983. Hunt's stepped up its advertising, moving from virtually no advertising in FY 1981 and FY 1982 to $2 million in FY 1983. Del Monte did the reverse, going from $2 million in FY 1981 to zero advertising in FY 1983.

Consumer Behavior.   The average U.S. household bought the equivalent of four 32-oz. bottles of ketchup per year. The most popular uses were for hamburgers, french fries, and hot dogs. Heinz market research showed that both incidence and amount of ketchup use increased in 1983: 67 percent of households (vs. 65 percent in 1981) purchased ketchup in the previous four weeks, and they used an average of 32.3 ounces per month (vs. 30.8 ounces in 1981). Other key findings from Heinz market research showed that:

- 97% of U.S. households used ketchup and 89 percent of all households used it at least once every week. However, level of use varied widely:

	Percent of Users	Percent of Consumption
Heavy users (33 oz./month or more)*	28%	54%
Medium users (17–32 oz./month)	39	34
Light users (16 oz./month or less)	33	12

*Heavy ketchup users consumed, on average, 67 ounces per month.

- Consumers used ketchup all year round. The volume consumed in the highest period, June–July, was only 14 percent higher than that consumed during the lowest period, October–January.
- Children, who made up 20 percent of the population, accounted for 30 percent of ketchup "eating occasions." Their volume per use was also greater partly due to waste in usage.

EXHIBIT 8   Ketchup Category Advertising and Advertising Shares

	FY 80	FY 81	FY 82	FY 83
Category (millions)	$6.7	$10.5	$14.4	$18.6
Heinz share (percent)	82%	82%	97%	86%
Hunt's share (percent)	3	0	1	11
Del Monte share (percent)	13	19	2	0
Private label and all other share (percent)	2	0	0	3

Exhibit 9 presents key tables from a 1983 national market survey conducted for Heinz by Market Facts. Brand loyalty for Heinz increased significantly between 1975 and 1983. Heinz was not as successful as Hunt's, however, in attracting heavy users. Most major brand purchasers selected the brand first, then the bottle size.

Exhibit 9 also reports ketchup user attitudes. Family acceptance and the "best flavor" were the most important product attributes. Heavy users were more likely to believe that ketchup brands were different, and they also paid closer attention to price.

NEW PRODUCT INTRODUCTIONS

During most of the 1970s, the ketchup industry focused on cost control rather than new product development. The 32-oz. size was the only new product, first introduced by Heinz in 1974. To streamline operations, Heinz closed four of its seven ketchup plants. Heinz enjoyed cost advantages over its competition due to quantity purchasing discounts on raw materials and lower transportation costs. After the 32 oz. introduction in 1974, Heinz new product development during the rest of the decade was focused on gravy and Weight Watchers products.

The late 1970s and early 1980s saw two major new product introductions: the 24-oz. and 44-oz. sizes. The 24-oz. size was introduced by Hunt's and Del Monte in October 1978 as a consolidation of the 20-oz. and 26-oz. sizes. Since, by that time, the 32-oz. size accounted for nearly one-half of category volume, three smaller sizes (14 oz., 20 oz., and 26 oz.) seemed excessive. Manufacturers believed that they would be unable to hold distribution for both 20-oz. and 26-oz. sizes. The 14-oz. bottle, used heavily in restaurants, was considered a "classic," so it was left in the line. Therefore, when introducing the 24-oz. size, Hunt's and Del Monte voluntarily deleted the 20-oz. and 26-oz. sizes in all regions. In January 1979, Heinz followed with its 24 oz. introduction in the South and West. Concurrently, the company also introduced a new 44-oz., keg-shaped glass bottle in the same regions.

The Heinz 32-oz. bottle, introduced in 1974, was the first ketchup container with a keg design. Heinz 44 oz. was also a keg. The keg was rounder, squatter, and shaped more like a barrel than the classic cylindrical bottle; it also had a ring or "ear" for gripping. After its simultaneous introduction with the 24-oz. size in January 1979, the 44 oz. was rolled out into the rest of the country by April 1979, taking only four months to reach 70 percent ACV. In its high BDI Northern markets, Heinz temporarily gained distribution for five sizes (the 44 oz. and the existing line). In these well-developed Heinz markets, Heinz was able to retain both the 20-oz. and 26-oz. sizes in distribution for a while. Since it was relatively easy to procure the necessary packaging materials and to adjust production lines, Hunt's and Del Monte followed with their own 44-oz. sizes about eight months later. Hunt's and Del Monte captured only about a quarter of the 44-oz. market, however.

Heinz introduced the 24-oz. size in its low BDI markets first, partly to facilitate the 44 oz. introduction in those areas. In these markets, Heinz managers believed that they had to delete the 20-oz. and 26-oz. items (and replace them with the 24 oz.) in order to make shelf space for the 44 oz. This was not thought to be the case in high BDI markets.

Although Heinz was two to three months behind Hunt's and Del Monte in the 24-oz.

EXHIBIT 9   Highlights of 1983 Market Facts Study on Ketchup Usage and Attitudes

1. Ketchup Brand Loyalty

	Percent Who Purchased Only One Brand in Past 3 Months	Brand Purchased Exclusively			
		Heinz	Hunt's	Del Monte	Private Label, Generic, All Others
1975	45%	23%	8%	8%	6%
1983	54	34	7	7	7

Percent of Respondents Who Buy This Brand Most Often, Who Bought No Other Brand in Past 3 Months

	Heinz	Hunt's	Del Monte	Private Label	Generic
1975	55%	34%	41%	42%	NA
1983	60	35	42	40	53%

2. Ketchup Brands Purchased Last by Usage Level

	Heavy Users	Medium Users	Light Users
Heinz	51%	53%	51%
Hunt's	21	18	14
Del Monte	12	14	18
Private label, generic, all other	16	15	17

3. Brand vs. Size Decision on Brand Purchased Last

	Heinz	Hunt's	Del Monte	Private Label
Selected brand first, then bottle size	88%	79%	81%	55%
Selected size first, then brand	12	21	19	45

4. Size Usage

	14 Oz.	24 Oz.	32 Oz.	44 Oz.
Purchased last	15%	13%	53%	12%
Purchased most often	15	16	52	12

5. Promotional Activity on Last Purchase

	Heinz	Hunt's	Del Monte	Private Label
Regular price	44%	46%	42%	62%
"On special," no coupon	23	30	31	28
"On special," with retailer coupon	1	1	2	—
Newspaper manufacturer coupon	22	17	18	5
Magazine/mail/on-pack coupon	9	5	6	4
On special display	18	19	21	17

(continued)

EXHIBIT 9   (*concluded*)

---

6. Importance of Ketchup Attributes

		Percent of Users Stating Attribute Is "Very Important"		
	Total	Heavy Users	Medium Users	Light Users
Whole family likes it	64%	70%	67%	57%
Best flavor	62	63	65	58
Good value for the money	56	59	58	53
Good to use on food at the table	54	60	56	48
Brand name I trust	50	50	53	47
Thick consistency	40	42	40	37

7. Attitudes Toward Ketchup

	Percent Stating That They "Definitely/Generally Agree"		
	Heavy Users	Medium Users	Light Users
Brand Differentiation:			
Some brands are much thicker than others	74%	66%	59%
There's a lot of difference between ketchup brands	59	57	51
Most brands of ketchup taste the same	15	15	11
Brand Loyalty:			
I like to stick to one brand of ketchup	59	62	58
Price/Value:			
Some brands of ketchup cost more and are worth it	47	46	46
When buying ketchup, I pay close attention to the price	57	49	45
I usually buy whatever ketchup brand is on sale	22	22	19
Packaging:			
Would pay up to 20 cents more for ketchup in a plastic bottle than I would for a glass bottle	10	8	10
I like the idea of packing it in squeeze bottles	37	33	33
The convenience of squeezable packaging for ketchup makes it worth an extra 20 cents per bottle	12	10	11

introduction in the South and West, Heinz nevertheless came to dominate this size segment. By 1983, Heinz 24 oz. had captured 5.3 percent of the ketchup market vs. Hunt's 2.0 percent and Del Monte's 1.2 percent. Exhibit 10 shows market shares by size for FY 1979–FY 1983. Heinz 24-oz. distribution built rapidly, growing from 50 percent ACV in FY 1979 to 80 percent ACV in FY 1981. Hunt's 24-oz. distribution declined from 55 percent ACV in FY 1979 to 35 percent ACV in FY 1983; Del Monte's equivalent distribution levels were 57 percent and 38 percent. Exhibit 11 shows retail distribution by size at the end of fiscal years 1979–1983.

Heinz's introduction of the 24-oz. and 44-oz. sizes was relatively easy to implement. No new capacity was required because the 44-oz. bottle could be run on the 32-oz. line, and the 24 oz. could be run on the old 20-oz. and 26-oz. lines. The sales force had no difficulty selling-in to the trade because they did not have to obtain incremental shelf space: two new items were traded for two existing items. The only additional promotional support was an introductory $1.00 per case trade allowance and a cents-off coupon promotion for each of the two new sizes in Sunday free-standing inserts (FSIs). There was no incremental advertising spending, and the advertising did not focus on the new packages. They were not considered newsworthy enough.

THE 1980s: A PERIOD OF AGGRESSIVE MARKETING

The early 1980s was a period of aggressive marketing by the major brands. During this time, Heinz concentrated its efforts in the South. Exhibit 12 shows Heinz ketchup marketing spending per case for the total United States and the South for FY 1979–FY 1983. Heinz increased total national spending per case during this period by 92 percent, and spending in the South by 147 percent. Aside from increasing advertising spending, Heinz used more competitive comparison copy. The ads featured side-by-side demonstrations of Heinz and other national brands, pointing out Heinz's thicker consistency. Exhibit 13 presents a Heinz TV commercial used in this campaign.

In 1982, Hunt's challenged the validity of this commercial in a complaint filed with the National Advertising Division (NAD) of the Council of Better Business Bureaus. Hunt's complained that the demonstrations were not related to normal use, and that the differences did not reflect true thickness. Heinz countered by arguing that resistance to separation was relevant to evaluating thickness, and they also provided blind, paired comparison test results that showed preference for Heinz over Hunt's and Del Monte. The NAD concluded that the Heinz claims were substantiated.

In 1983, Hunt's and Del Monte reformulated their ketchup to improve taste and consistency. Spices were added to improve the taste, and each company invested about $1.5 million in homogenization, a process that produced a product almost as thick as Heinz's.[3] As a result, Heinz could no longer run its comparison advertising campaign. In addition, homogenization improved Hunt's and Del Monte's variable cost per bottle.

---

[3]Homogenization processed tomatoes into very small pieces that did not coagulate, thereby producing a higher solids yield. Heinz already used this process.

EXHIBIT 10 U.S. Ketchup Market Shares by Size

| | FY 1979 | | | FY 1980 | | | FY 1981 | | | FY 1982 | | | FY 1983 | | |
	Heinz	Hunt's	Del Monte	Heinz	Hunt's	Del Monte	Heinz	Hunt's	Del Monte	Heinz	Hunt's	Del Monte	Heinz	Hunt's	Del Monte
14 oz.	8.2%	3.2%	2.8%	8.2%	3.1%	3.0%	8.8%	2.6%	2.6%	8.6%	2.5%	2.3%	8.0%	2.3%	1.4%
20 oz.	4.3	2.0	1.5	2.6	.5	.2	.1	.1	—	—	—	—	—	—	—
24 oz.	1.7	1.3	1.9	3.7	2.7	2.7	6.7	2.0	2.4	6.2	2.2	1.6	5.3	2.0	1.2
26 oz.	4.0	.8	1.5	1.4	.3	.1	—	—	—	—	—	—	—	—	—
32 oz.	19.5	8.9	6.3	15.8	7.4	6.2	17.4	8.1	6.6	19.3	7.2	6.4	20.5	8.1	6.9
44 oz.	2.4	—	—	10.3	1.7	—	10.5	2.7	1.9	12.0	2.0	1.9	11.7	1.8	1.4

EXHIBIT 11 Ketchup Retail Distribution (Percent ACV)—End of Fiscal Year

	FY 1979			FY 1980			FY 1981			FY 1982			FY 1983		
	Heinz	Hunt's	Del Monte	Heinz	Hunt's	Del Monte	Heinz	Hunt's	Del Monte	Heinz	Hunt's	Del Monte	Heinz	Hunt's	Del Monte
14 oz.	95%	70%	66%	95%	65%	62%	95%	62%	58%	95%	58%	54%	96%	79%*	51%
20 oz.	34	24	16	26	3	1	80	42	48	—	36	42	78	35	38
24 oz.	50	55	57	70	52	59	—	—	—	78	—	—	—	—	—
26 oz.	33	13	15	21	3	1	—	—	—	—	—	—	—	—	—
32 oz.	86	68	57	87	71	59	87	71	55	87	69	54	89	69	62
44 oz.	59	—	—	75	45	—	78	40	29	79	37	28	81	32	27

*Increased distribution of Hunt's 14 oz. in Fy 1983 was partly due to its introduction of a no-salt ketchup in that bottle size.

523

EXHIBIT 12 Heinz Ketchup Marketing Spending per Equivalent Case

	FY 79	FY 80	FY 81	FY 82	FY 83
Total U.S.:					
Trade promotion	$ .75	$1.20	$1.06	$1.09	$1.20
Consumer promotion	.30	.35	.22	.24	.42
Advertising	.33	.42	.55	.90	1.01
Total	$1.38	$1.97	$1.83	$2.23	$2.63
South:					
Trade promotion	$ .83	$1.25	$1.14	$1.21	$1.43
Consumer promotion	.38	.55	.53	.57	1.06
Advertising	.37	.49	.76	1.20	1.42
Total	$1.58	$2.29	$2.43	$2.98	$3.91

EXHIBIT 13 1982 Heinz Ketchup TV Commercial

LEO BURNETT COMPANY, INC. H.J. HEINZ
AS FILMED AND RECORDED (8/82)   "New Southern Plate Test/32 Oz." :30   HZHK 1330

1. PULLUP (Anncr VO): If I take some Heinz Ketchup at the start of your meal...

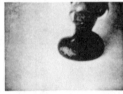
2. and put it right here...

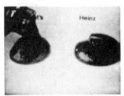
3. and put this Hunt's Ketchup right here...

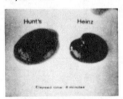
4. something amazing happens before you're half through.

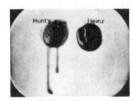
5. See the difference? We challenged the competition and they ran.

6. Heinz ketchup is thicker and Heinz is never thin on flavor.

7. Now which one would you rather have on your hamburger?

8. Heinz.

9. America's thickest, best-tasting ketchup.

As a result, Heinz lost half a point in national market share, and 1.4 points in the South, between FY 1982 and FY 1983. Heinz counterattacked with a new television advertising campaign that stressed Heinz's taste superiority and greater popularity, claiming that it was the consumer's 3–to–1 choice over any other brand. Exhibit 14 shows a commercial from this campaign. Heinz also added extra trade deals and coupon drops in the South. Overall, however, the counterattack proved to be ineffective in fighting off Hunt's offensive. In addition, Del Monte and private-label brands benefited as the two major brands competed head-to-head.

Hunt's aggressiveness, and word from packaging suppliers that plastic technology applicable to ketchup packaging was being developed, stimulated Heinz to pursue aggressively the development of a plastic bottle. Heinz had a tradition of packaging innovation—they had been first to market the 32-oz. size and the 44-oz. keg-design bottle—and wanted to be first with a plastic bottle ketchup.

EXHIBIT 14   1983 Heinz Ketchup TV Commercial

LEO BURNETT COMPANY, INC.   H.J. HEINZ CO.
AS FILMED AND RECORDED (8/83)   "RETORT II/PARITY :CC"   HZHK3780

1. WOMAN: I decided to test Heinz ketchup myself.

2. To see why more folks choose it.

3. You know what happened?

4. Heinz didn't run.

5. Then I tasted Heinz. Because, to me, that's proof.

6. One taste and I knew which ketchup I liked best.

7. (Anncr VO): Unbeatably thick, rich Heinz is America's three to one choice over any other single ketchup. Taste it for yourself.

8. WOMAN: No contest!

9. (Anncr VO): Heinz. America's favorite for thick, rich ketchup.

THE PLASTIC BOTTLE DEVELOPMENT

In describing Heinz's attitude towards new product development, Barbara Johnson noted: "We've found that the best way to be a leader is not to act like a leader, but to be hungry, always looking for new products." Heinz first started investigating plastic packaging 15 years earlier, but not until 1980 did they contact suppliers to begin developmental work. Heinz eventually signed an exclusive agreement with American Can Co. to develop a commercially feasible technology for producing the plastic for bottling ketchup. The plastic had to form a barrier such that the plastic resins could not affect the flavor of the ketchup, and oxygen could not penetrate the walls of the bottle. In addition, the plastic had to be resistant to the boiling temperature of the ketchup as it was inserted into the bottles during production.

Early in the project in 1980, only three departments at Heinz (marketing, packaging, and purchasing) were involved. Heinz did not tell suppliers of the required manufacturing equipment the full nature of the project. Heinz engineers bought parts piecemeal and made some of the equipment themselves. Company management was willing to trade slower progress for maximum secrecy. As the project showed greater viability, more Heinz departments were brought in. The project turned out to be so technically complex that management formed a task force to provide the necessary close working relationship among the various functions of purchasing, packaging, engineering, manufacturing, operations, and marketing.

Heinz's expertise with can and glass production lines was of modest value in developing a plastic line. On a glass line, for example, the weight of the bottles held them in position. Plastic bottles, however, were light and had to be secured. In addition, plastic bottles required different lubricants, a different type of glue for the labels, and special handling as they became pliable with heat. In developing a new production line, including a new bottle filling process, Heinz borrowed technology from liquid detergent manufacturers. The company spent over $2 million in three years to develop its proprietary plastic packaging process.

Heinz's prototype plastic line was a converted glass line—converted at a $1 million cost. However, the line was slower than a new line designed specifically for plastic, and higher speeds were necessary to improve profitability.

The prototype plastic bottle offered ketchup users several benefits: it was lightweight, shatterproof, squeezable for better access and portion control, and had a convenient, nonremovable flip-top cap.[4] Unlike glass bottles, however, the plastic bottle had to be refrigerated after opening.[5] The plastic flip-top cap allowed greater air inflow than the lug-style metal closure used on the glass bottle which provided a tighter seal. Refrigeration was necessary to retard the ketchup's oxidation, the chemical reaction of the ketchup with oxygen which resulted in the dark residue that formed around the seal. Although shatterproof, the plastic bottle was breakable—another potential drawback since con-

---

[4]The squeezable and flip-top cap features could be applied to smaller bottles, but not to keg-design bottles.

[5]Over 80 percent of ketchup-using households kept glass bottles in the refrigerator after opening. The plastic bottle, if introduced, would have to carry a label instruction to refrigerate upon opening.

sumers might mistakenly assume that all plastic containers were unbreakable. Refrigeration added to the problem since the plastic (polypropylene) became brittle with cooling.[6]

Heinz managers were confident that the plastic bottle delivered significant consumer benefits, but they were not sure which size(s) was right. Should they start with an existing size or create a new size for plastic? The ketchup brand group planned a consumer testing program of various package sizes, primarily 64 oz. and 28 oz. Johnson and her group started with the 64-oz. size (5 3/6″ wide × 4″ deep × 10 3/4″ tall) because plastic's shatterproof and lightweight attributes would be most beneficial in a large size. The plastic 64-oz. container offered 20 ounces more ketchup than the 44-oz. glass bottle but, when full, both packages weighed the same. In addition, the category trend was towards larger sizes, as evidenced by the success of Heinz 44-oz. ketchup.

As an alternative, the brand group originally considered a 32-oz. plastic bottle. But in order to attain a lower price point, a 28-oz. size (4 1/8″ wide × 2 1/8″ deep × 10 3/8″ tall) was pursued instead. The plastic bottle cost significantly more than a glass container of equivalent size. Exhibit 15 shows a cost comparison of the 28-oz. plastic, 32-oz. glass, and 64-oz. plastic bottles.

UNBRANDED HOME-USE TESTS

September 1981: 64-oz. Plastic and 64-oz. Glass. The first in a series of product tests of the plastic bottle used a 64-oz. size. Sixty-four-ounce plastic and glass prototypes, with no brand names, were consumer tested in two monadic (separate, single-product exposure, as opposed to paired comparison) home-use tests. The samples consisted of regular users of 44-oz. ketchup. Both products scored comparably on ketchup ratings, including overall flavor, spiciness, sweetness, consistency, pourability, and color; at least 80 percent of respondents said that both products were "about right" on each of these attributes. On overall ketchup evaluation, both products received an 82 rating (on a 100-point scale). This compared with an 83 rating that the existing 44-oz. glass package had received in a previous test.

EXHIBIT 15   Heinz Ketchup Cost Structures (per bottle)

	14-oz. Glass	24-oz. Glass	28-oz. Plastic	32-oz. Glass	44-oz. Glass	64-oz. Plastic
Ingredients	$.156	$.267	$.314	$.356	$ .496	$ .712
Bottle and case	.051	.118	.321	.219	.282	.696
Cap	.029	.029	.050	.035	.035	.063
Label	.079	.091	.044	.010	.010	.098
Labor and overhead	.027	.050	.077	.060	.083	.183
Distribution	.042	.062	.096	.098	.123	.228
Total	$.384	$.617	$.902	$.778	$1.029	$1.980

[6]One of 10 bottles, if full and dropped from counter height after refrigeration, would break.

Exhibit 16 presents results of the package ratings. On overall package evaluation, the plastic bottle received a 78 rating vs. 70 for glass. Plastic's 78 rating, however, was significantly lower than the 84 rating that 44-oz. glass had received in the earlier test.

On unpriced purchase intent, the 64-oz. plastic product scored higher than its glass counterpart on the "definitely buy" measure. However, compared to the previous test's 49 percent "definitely buy" score for 44-oz. glass, plastic's 40 percent purchase score was significantly lower. When the 64-oz. products were priced at $2.39, both received similar scores, but when both were priced at parity with 44-oz. glass on a per-ounce basis, plastic received a significantly higher purchase-intent score than 64-oz. glass. Respondents who tested the 64-oz. glass were asked their purchase interest in plastic,

EXHIBIT 16   Results of Monadic Home-Use Tests

	September 1981*		Previous Test† 44-oz. Glass (N = 394)
	64-oz. Plastic (N = 300)	64-oz. Glass (N = 540)	
Package rating‡	78	70	84
	Percent	*Percent*	*Percent*
Visual appearance			
Very attractive	12%	14%	18%
Somewhat attractive	36	41	37
Neither attractive nor unattractive	37	35	41
Somewhat unattractive	14	9	3
Very unattractive	1	1	1
Ease of handling by adults (vs. 44 oz.)			
Much easier	11	5	9
Somewhat easier	18	5	8
About the same	41	38	63
Somewhat harder	25	36	15
Much harder	3	14	3
Ease of handling by children (vs. 44 oz.)§			
Much easier	10	2	8
Somewhat easier	10	2	5
About the same	20	18	33
Somewhat harder	29	27	26
Much harder	21	37	13

*The research was designed as two monadic home-use tests—one for the 64-oz. plastic and the other for the 64-oz. glass. Qualified respondents were recruited in shopping malls if they said they bought the 44-oz. ketchup size most often. They were given one 64-oz. bottle (plastic or glass) to use in their homes for two weeks. After the usage period, telephone interviews were completed from a central research facility.

†Qualified respondents in this test bought the 32-oz. size most often.

‡100 = perfect, 90 = excellent, 80 = like very much . . . 20 = dislike very much, 10 = terrible, 0 = worst possible.

§Among households with children.

and the reverse was asked of those who tested plastic. Purchase intent was significantly higher for plastic among glass users (see Exhibit 17).

October 1982: 28-oz. Plastic. Encouraged by consumer testing results of the 64-oz. plastic bottle, the brand group decided to develop and test a squeezable, 28-oz. plastic prototype. (The 64-oz. plastic package was not designed to be squeezable: it was too bulky and did not have a flip-top cap with a narrow nozzle.) In this test, 180-day-old product was used.[7]

The ketchup in the 28-oz. squeezable bottle received an 80.2 rating compared to "Benchmark Ketchup's" 81.5 rating. "Benchmark Ketchup" was a standard formulation that Heinz management used as a control for regular testing of factory production. The 28-oz. product received uniformly high scores on overall flavor, spiciness, sweetness, pourability, and color. At least 80 percent of respondents rated the ketchup as being "about right" on these attributes.

Exhibit 18 presents results of the package ratings. On the 100-point overall rating scale, the 28-oz. package received an 84.4 rating. The bottle used in this test had a nonremovable flip-top cap. This prevented consumers from refilling the plastic bottle with ketchup from less expensive glass bottles. Aside from a removable cap's potentially adverse effect on plastic bottle sales, Heinz management was also concerned about the hygiene risk associated with consumers' refilling ketchup bottles. Since the test bottle's flip-top was nonremovable, respondents were questioned on how this feature would affect their purchase behavior. Sixty-three percent said it made no difference, while 20 percent said that they would be less likely to purchase; 25 percent said that they tried to remove the cap.

EXHIBIT 17 Purchase Intent: 64-oz. Plastic and Glass

	Unpriced		Priced @ $2.39		Same Price/Oz. as 44 Oz.		For Plastic/ Glass Testers	For Glass/ Plastic Testers
	Plastic (N = 300)	Glass (N = 540)	Plastic (N = 300)	Glass (N = 540)	Plastic (N = 300)	Glass (N = 540)	(N = 540)	(N = 300)
Definitely buy	40%	34%	24%	22%	47%	39%	27%	9%
Probably buy	44	39	53	50	34	31	47	39
Probably not buy	13	18	19	19	13	22	18	36
Definitely not buy	3	9	3	8	5	8	8	16

---

[7]The ketchup had been in the plastic bottles used in the test for 180 days. Once produced, a bottle of Heinz ketchup had a two-year life but would normally be fully consumed six months after it left the plant.

EXHIBIT 18   October 1982 Home-Use Test:* 28-oz. Plastic

	Package Ratings *(N = 200)*
Average rating†—bottle	84.4
	Percent
Difficulty with label instructions:	
Yes	3%
No	97
Trouble with cap:	
Yes, opening	4
Yes, closing	2
Yes, using	3
No trouble with cap	93
Problems with seal:	
Yes	10
No	90
Item used to break seal:	
Toothpick	7
Knife	27
Fork	16
Other	33
Try to remove cap:	
Yes	25
No	74
Effect of cap on purchase:	
More likely to purchase	17
Less likely to purchase	20
No difference	63

*Respondents who had purchased ketchup (any size) in the previous thirty days.
† 100 = perfect, 90 = excellent, 80 = like very much . . . 20 = dislike very much, 10 = terrible, 0 worst possible.

Three purchase intent scenarios were tested with the following results:

Purchase Intent: 28.-oz. Plastic (N = 200)

	Unpriced	*Priced* *@ $1.59*	*If filled* *w/Heinz*
Definitely buy	31%	20%	37%
Probably buy	52	51	43
Probably not buy	13	18	14
Definitely not buy	3	8	7

When asked to choose between a $1.59 28-oz. Heinz plastic bottle and a $1.32 Heinz 32-oz. glass bottle, 55 percent chose the latter, 40 percent the former.

Among the 83 percent of respondents who would definitely or probably buy the 28-oz. plastic bottle (unpriced), 13 percent said that they would buy the plastic bottle in addition to an existing ketchup size that they currently used, while 83 percent said that the plastic container would be used as a replacement, primarily for the 32-oz. bottle:

Size Would Replace (base-positive purchase interest, N = 164)

14 oz.	24 oz.	32 oz.	44 oz.	Other/ Don't Know
11%	10%	43%	7%	37%

When asked what they liked about the 28-oz. plastic bottle, respondents most frequently mentioned "unbreakable," "squeezable," "easy to handle," and the "flip-top cap." One-third of respondents voiced dislikes about the plastic bottle, although there was no one predominant complaint. Some of the more frequently mentioned concerns were "too large to store" and "bottom was too large." At least 85 percent of respondents stored the plastic bottle in the refrigerator after opening. Nineteen percent agreed strongly with the statement, "plastic squeeze containers are somewhat more expensive, but they're worth it."

"More Expensive, but Worth It" (base-total respondents, N = 200)

Strongly	Somewhat Agree	Neither Agree Nor Disagree	Somewhat Disagree	Strongly Disagree
19%	43%	20%	13%	5%

CONCLUSION

Barbara Johnson felt positive about the ketchup plastic bottle. The package received good scores in tests, and it would be the first lightweight, shatterproof, and, for the 28 oz., squeezable ketchup bottle. Johnson wondered, however, if consumers would perceive it as a major innovation. After all, it was still the same product—ketchup. But in addition to the marketing research results, Johnson also knew that mustard in squeezable plastic containers, which was priced higher per ounce than mustard in glass containers, now accounted for 18 percent of retail volume.

Case 7–2

*Actmedia, Inc.**

In December 1986, Bruce Failing, Jr., president and CEO of Actmedia, Inc., was reviewing issues raised by the company's rapid growth. Since Actmedia's initial public stock offering in 1983, revenues had risen from $15 million to $65 million. Failing intended to maintain a 50 percent annual growth rate throughout the 1980s through expansion and maximum utilization of resources. Between 1984 and 1986, the company's sales force had doubled, and in the first quarter of 1987 it was scheduled to double again. In the meantime, new products and channels had been added.

During its first decade, Actmedia had one product and one sales force, but in 1983 the company began introducing new products and in 1985 had divided the sales force into two groups: one for sales of the company's ad products, and another for its promotions products. With more product introductions scheduled, organization of the sales force, motivational systems, and recruitment criteria were decisions that had to be made by the start of the new year.

IN-STORE MARKETING

Actmedia was founded in 1971 to provide in-store advertising for consumer packaged goods sold in supermarkets. The company's initial product was multicolored displays, typically $8\frac{1}{2}'' \times 11''$, placed on shopping carts in supermarkets and designed to recall the graphics and slogans of the manufacturer's TV or other media advertising. By 1986, Actmedia had expanded into point-of-sale consumer promotions, and was the only national independent company with its own field service staff providing a range of marketing services in supermarkets. Actmedia was in 19 of the 20 largest grocery chains (which accounted for about 50 percent of total U.S. grocery store sales in 1986), and its services were purchased by 250 different brands from over 65 different companies, including the 20 largest packaged-goods advertisers. Five companies accounted for a third of Actmedia's revenues in 1986, a proportion in keeping with the percentage of total packaged-goods advertising attributable to these companies.

---

*Research Associate Jon E. King prepared this case under the supervision of Associate Professor Frank V. Cespedes as the basis for class discussion rather than to illustrate either effective or ineffective handling of an administrative situation. Copyright © 1987 by the President and Fellows of Harvard College. Harvard Business School case 9–588–036.

Most packaged-goods firms conducted three major types of marketing activities: advertising, consumer promotions, and trade promotions. Consumer promotions included discount coupons, premiums, sweepstakes, and samples. Trade promotions were discounts or other incentives aimed at encouraging retailers or distributors to promote a given manufacturer's product. Although philosophies differed among firms, advertising was generally used to increase customer awareness of the product, build "brand loyalty," and develop the product's image over the long term. Trade and consumer promotions were more likely to be aimed at immediately increasing sales volume or gaining new users.

During the 1970s and 1980s, new-product introductions accelerated. By 1985, food companies as a group were introducing about 30 new products weekly, twice as many as in 1980; estimates indicated that 70 percent of all grocery store products available in 1985 had come on the market since 1975. Meanwhile, supermarkets were growing larger and had opened their aisles to other items from plants to greeting cards, office supplies, and auto equipment. In 1985, the average food store was 30,000 square feet, compared to 13,000 in 1975.

Demographics, demand, and communications media were also changing. The average length of a shopping trip dropped from 28 minutes in 1975 to 21 minutes in 1985, according to trade reports. The Bureau of Labor Statistics indicated that the percentage of women working outside the home had increased from 39 percent in 1970 to 71 percent in 1985, and male involvement in purchasing decisions rose concurrently. Furthermore, studies indicated that men shopping alone were less likely to preplan the trip, make a list, check newspaper advertisements, or bring coupons to the store than women were. A 1977 survey indicated that 65 percent of every dollar spent in the supermarket resulted from in-store decision; a similar survey in 1987 indicated 81 percent. With computerized point-of-sale systems, moreover, supermarket managers had access to detailed sales information on individual items, broken down by brand, size, flavor, and color. In this environment, product life cycles were often shorter, and could be swiftly discontinued in a given chain if performance wasn't high from the start.

The three national television networks, the traditional conduits for most packaged-goods advertising, were shrinking as a percentage of television viewing, while the viewing shares for cable channels and videocassette machines were growing swiftly in the 1980s. Estimates indicated that the networks' combined share of prime-time audience fell from 91 percent in 1978 to 73 percent in 1985. Surveys also indicated a decline in the level of attention paid to TV advertisements: in 1965, 18 percent of TV viewers in phone interviews could correctly identify what brand was advertised four minutes after seeing a commercial; in 1974 that figure was 12 percent, and in 1981, 7 percent. "Zapping" from one channel to another during commercials was reportedly more frequent as 35 percent of all TV households owned remote-control devices by 1985. Moreover, daytime audiences (a traditional target for packaged-goods advertisers) had changed as more women entered the work force. The growing segments of the daytime audience were older and lower-income groups.

In response, manufacturers relied more heavily on consumer and trade promotions to establish new products or boost sales of older products. By 1986, packaged-goods companies were spending about twice as much on promotions as on advertising; 15 years earlier, that ratio had been reversed.

COMPANY BACKGROUND

In 1971, Bruce Failing, Sr., a former vice president of a food brokerage firm, founded Actmedia to provide advertising on grocery carts in upstate New York. One problem was that many others had tried unsuccessfully to develop such in-store marketing systems, leaving grocery store management with a clutter of unusable fixtures, no payoff, and residual skepticism. Yet Failing saw a large market if the chains could be convinced. He also knew that, executed properly, in-store advertising could represent income without capital investment for supermarkets, which was significant in a business that typically operated on 1 percent net margins.

With $70,000 raised from friends, Failing spent two years designing the ad frames to be attached to shopping carts. His food brokerage experience had given him broad contacts and familiarity with chain headquarters operations. By 1973, the ad frames were designed, and advertisers and chains were signed on for free tests of eight-week runs. Audits & Surveys Inc., an independent research group, then collected data to determine the impact on sales.[1] Results indicated an average sales increase of 10–12 percent for the products advertised.

Early History

Bruce Failing, Jr., joined Actmedia after graduating from Harvard Business School in 1973. In 1974, a venture capital (VC) firm and a group of private investors headed by Richard Watson (brother to Thomas Watson of IBM) agreed to provide Actmedia with $175,000. However, Failing, Jr., recalled, "The VC firm ran out of funds and folded. But Dick Watson said, 'Gentlemen don't walk out on deals,' and provided the difference out of his own pocket. That was one of many life-saving incidents in our company's history."

During this period, Failing, Jr., and two friends who had joined Actmedia, John Stevenson and Jeffrey Sturgess, approached brand managers at packaged-goods firms in order to sell the company's shopping-cart ads service. They found that budgeting processes at these firms were lengthy (with 6- to 12-month lead times the norm for marketing allocations), an obstacle for a business with high fixed costs and limited working capital. Further, brand managers were often skeptical about the concept despite test results. Failing, Jr., commented:

> Actmedia started with stores in Syracuse, New York, but it became clear that potential clients weren't interested in a service that covered only one city. We therefore started to expand, and that, in turn, increased the pressure on us to generate more sales revenue more quickly. Sometimes we were so aggressive we got thrown out.

---

[1]Since 1974, Actmedia's shopping cart ads had been tested over 380 times with independent research firms. The basic testing format was a controlled store test consisting of a number of pairs of supermarkets matched by chain, dollar volume, location, and demographics. The matching was designed to minimize variables other than Actmedia programs, such as other advertising, promotions, or pricing. Actmedia ads were then placed in half the stores, and sales results for the advertised product in controlled and noncontrolled stores were compared.

For years, we didn't fully appreciate the length of the decision-making process at the manufacturer, and all the different internal and external parties involved. As a result, we consistently overprojected sales and underprojected our losses. In addition, the oil crisis of 1974–75 hurt us badly: every dollar in additional sales was soon swallowed up in gasoline costs for our field service personnel.

Mr. Sturgess added:

By 1977 we'd had about 100 independent tests done to corroborate the sales impact of our product, and we thought clients would beat a path to our door. That misconception almost killed us: no one believed the test results. Some even took us on for test periods just to prove us wrong, and therefore didn't keep us when we were right. We eventually halved our presentation figures to 5 percent sales increases. This understatement became critical to our success later, since when actual results came back at twice the estimated levels, the brand manager became a hero to his superiors.

During this period, the company survived primarily on revenues from regional advertisers and, in Failing, Sr.'s words, "through the willingness of the grocery chains to accept consistently late payments on the spaces we leased on shopping carts: we didn't dirty their stores, and they understood they would get nothing if the company went bankrupt." In the mid-1970s, Actmedia needed more funds for expansion to additional cities, and management again approached Watson. He committed to another $300,000, but died before any documents could be signed. However, his wife decided to honor the obligation.

By 1976, Actmedia covered stores in New York City and Atlanta as well as upstate New York, and was approaching profitability. However, management decided that only national coverage would provide the reach necessary for significant sales to major package-goods firms. Actmedia raised $1.25 million from venture capital firms, but found that most potential clients had already made their 1977 budgeting decisions. As a result, sales slowed and losses doubled (see Exhibit 1 for financial information). Failing, Jr., recalled the subsequent events:

The venture capitalists were angry and pulled the plug. They fired my father and demoted me from president to a sales representative. An HBS alumnus who worked for the VC firm was brought in to fix things: he did so well that sales decreased the next year and losses tripled. By April 1978, the company was out of money.

However, we caught the venture capitalists on the fact that they had not reconstituted the board. So one Saturday we called a board meeting, fired the president and his people, and put ourselves back in charge. On Monday morning, the venture capitalists showed up in my office to put us into Chapter 11. But we hired an aggressive lawyer who ranted and raved and threatened to sue them for putting the company under. We also pointed out that we had no assets, so liquidation of the company wouldn't generate cash. They took the last $200,000 in the company's bank account and left us alone for a few years.

By 1978, we were $1 million in debt, but we kept at it for two reasons: a) we really thought it would work, and b) we were all guaranteed utter bankruptcy if it didn't. We missed three consecutive payrolls, and HBS notified me that I was the first one in my class to have my school loan go into collection. Sturgess, Stevenson, and I drove hundreds of miles on sales calls to packaged-goods firms because it was cheaper than flying, and on weekends we delivered ads to the field. My father was in almost constant negotiations with the chains and creditors, and my mother worked on convincing the field service people to stay.

EXHIBIT 1   Financial Performance ($000)

Year	Sales	Profit (Loss)
1974	$ 180	($ 476)
1975	649	(534)
1976	1,366	(196)
1977	1,913	(388)
1978	1,615	(965)
1979	2,084	(13)
1980	2,311	(253)
1981	4,740	401
1982	8,452	460
1983	14,690	1,304
1984	23,587	2,243
1985	44,014	3,694
1986	64,500	4,950

Statement of Operations ($000, except per share amounts)

	1984	1985	1986
Revenue:			
Net advertising and promotion revenue	$20,518	$38,707	$56,361
Production revenue	2,383	4,878	8,522
Testing and other revenue	685	429	529
Total	$23,586	$44,014	$65,412
Cost of sales:			
Store commissions	$ 4,749	$ 6,933	$12,119
Production costs	2,052	5,495	8,551
Testing and other costs	870	495	770
Total	$ 7,671	$12,923	$21,440
Field expenses:			
Field salaries and related costs	$ 4,113	$12,983	$15,861
Field force expenses	2,033	2,934	3,510
Other field expenses	952	3,302	4,734
Total	$ 7,098	$19,219	$24,105
Gross profit	$ 8,817	$11,872	$19,867
Selling expenses	$ 2,900	$ 3,213	$ 6,436
General and administrative expenses	2,436	4,751	6,006
Interest, dividend and sundry income	(832)	(1,586)	(1,225)
Income before income taxes	$ 4,313	$ 5,494	$ 8,650
Provision for income taxes	2,070	1,800	3,700
Net income	$ 2,243	$ 3,694	$ 4,950
Earnings per share	$.24	$.34	$.42

In 1979, Actmedia nearly broke even on sales of $2 million. But in 1980 the company tallied a loss again as Los Angeles and Chicago were added. However, with New York City, those additions proved to be, in Failing, Jr.'s words, "the magic triangle that provided us with the national presence demanded by package-foods firms. Beginning in 1980, it became somewhat easier to become part of their budget planning processes." Sales doubled in 1981, and Actmedia showed its first profit.

In 1982, management presented its forecasts to the venture capitalists who dismissed it since past forecasts had been consistently overoptimistic. Failing, Jr., noted that "We were trying to bring good news, but they had written off the investment. They said, 'If you believe those projections, why don't you buy out our share?' They had originally put in $1.25 million and asked for $3 million." The Failings borrowed money and bought the venture capitalists' 36 percent interest. In 1983, when Actmedia went public, its market value was $60 million. For much of 1986, after another public offering, the company was trading at a price/earnings multiple approaching 50, and its market value was more than $250 million. Reflecting on the company's history, Failing, Jr., remarked:

> We sold stock on the leverage built into this business, which the market recognized even if our VC friends didn't: once we had the national position, we had more selling potential with manufacturers and a base for highly profitable incremental sales revenues, since putting additional ads in the same store has low variable costs. Also, timing was important. In a sense, we were ahead of our time in the 1970s, but more people now recognize the demographic and media trends that make in-store marketing more important.
>
> "Entrepreneurship" is now a buzzword and the focus of elegant theories. However, Actmedia was not the first or last company to develop an in-store marketing program; I estimate that over 18 such firms failed before we even started. But apparently no one was willing to fail for 10 years!

Growth and New Product Development

From its founding to 1983, Actmedia had one product: ads on supermarket shopping carts. The next three years, however, saw a rapid expansion into additional products and retail outlets. In 1986, Actmedia's products (see Exhibit 2) included advertising services (shopping cart displays, Aislevision, and Shelftalk), coupon distribution (Actnow), and an in-store sampling and demonstration service (Impact). In 1986, shopping cart displays accounted for about 40 percent of company revenues, Aislevision 24 percent, Shelftalk 3.6 percent, Actnow 30 percent, and Impact for 4 percent.

Cart Ads. Actmedia's initial product, shopping cart ads, consisted of a two-sided plastic frame attached to the front of each cart in participating stores. The company's field force placed up to 12 noncompeting ads in each store, and each advertiser's ad was on a minimum of one-sixth of the shopping carts in every store. In 1986, Actmedia ad displays appeared on over 1.1 million shopping carts through more than 7,200 supermarkets operated by 220 chains. The ads, which were designed by Actmedia's customers and their ad agencies, were changed every four weeks by Actmedia's field service staff, consisting of 300 full-time and about 10,000 part-time personnel in 1986. Actmedia

EXHIBIT 2 Actmedia Product Line: 1986

Shopping Cart Ads

Ads inside every Actmedia Cart keep the product's message in front of the shopper pushing the cart; ads on the outside of every cart present a "rolling billboard" to every other shopper.

Aislevision

With the dominant presence of an AisleVision directory, the advertised brand virtually "owns the aisle" in which it is located.

Shelftalk

In 1987, a second version of the ShelfTalk program will be introduced, allowing manufacturers to place "take one" coupons on the shelf adjacent to the product being promoted.

Actnow

The Impact program allows consumers to see, in person, how a product works or what it tastes like. Free samples and coupons maintain their interest and encourage purchase.

Impact

Actnow Co-op events are supported throughout the store with product displays, the "personal selling" efforts of our in-store representatives and reminders on the shelf

offered a set calendar of four-week ad cycles, or "flights," thereby enabling advertisers to limit their participation to a minimum of four weeks. During each flight, Actmedia's field reps visited each store at least weekly to maintain and service the displays.

During 1986, Actmedia ad displays were purchased for 155 different brands manufactured by 65 different companies reaching 50 percent of U.S. households. The company's largest clients for ad displays included Procter & Gamble, General Foods, Kimberly-Clark, PepsiCo, and General Mills. Each ad was billed to clients at a rate of $.80 per thousand store transactions per month. Transactions at the check-out counter were a measure of total store traffic and therefore an index of consumers exposed to the ad. The retail chains received from Actmedia a 25 percent commission on these revenues, based on the number of monthly transactions in a given store. In general, the client's ad agency also received from Actmedia its customary 15 percent commission for advertising developed for that manufacturer.

Aislevision.   Aislevision was the company's second advertising product, introduced in 1985. This product consisted of an overhead aisle directory, a two-sided plastic-molded sign installed in a supermarket aisle, with $20'' \times 30''$ ads on each side (typically for brands in that aisle) as well as the names of product categories shelved in that aisle. Participating supermarkets typically had 12 Aislevision directories, containing 24 ads which were designed by the client and its ad agency and changed every four weeks by Actmedia field personnel. The Aislevision directories were manufactured by another company from a mold owned by Actmedia, and Actmedia's cost of producing and installing each directory was approximately $100.

Actmedia did not accept ads for directly competing products for a given Aislevision flight, but did not exclude competing ads in different products (e.g., in a given flight, one brand of shampoo could be advertised on carts and a competing brand through Aislevision displays in the same stores). Aislevision ads were priced at $.50 per thousand store transactions monthly with retailers receiving 25 percent and ad agencies 15 percent. By 1986, Aislevision was in over 7,000 stores, and 1,100 new stores were scheduled to add the product in 1987.

Shelftalk.   Shelftalk, introduced in 1986, was a $5'' \times 6\frac{1}{2}''$ two-sided display attached to the supermarket shelf in front of the product being advertised. Actmedia placed up to 60 noncompeting ads in each participating store. Like the traditional "shelftalkers" used by packaged-goods firms, the ads were designed by the client and its ad agency, and changed every four weeks by Actmedia's field personnel at the same time they changed ads for the shopping cart and Aislevision programs.

Shelftalk ads were priced at $12 per store per flight, regardless of store traffic levels, although retailers received a 25 percent commission based on monthly store transactions. In 1986, Shelftalk was used for 90 brands through more than 5,000 supermarkets.

In-Store Promotions.   "Actnow," the name of Actmedia's promotions division established in 1984, developed two sets of in-store promotions: coupon programs, and a sampling-and-demonstrations service called Impact.

Through the Actnow coupon program, booklets containing up to 20 coupons were handed directly to shoppers as they entered a supermarket. The program was supported by a prominent entrance display of all participating products and by shelf displays throughout the store. The program was typically executed in 7,000 stores over two consecutive weekends, and utilized by clients for test marketing of new products as well as promotion of existing products. In 1986, Actmedia conducted 5 national programs which distributed over 11 million coupon booklets. Manufacturers provided the samples and were charged $18 per thousand coupons and $50 per thousand samples distributed by Actmedia, while the retailer received a 25 percent commission.

Impact, started in 1985, typically involved one product, although more could participate. In this program, Impact demonstrators prepared the product for in-store trial (e.g., a cup of coffee or bowl of cereal) and distributed samples and coupons. The programs were conducted over a 2- to 3-day period in each participating store by Actmedia field personnel situated inside the store. In 1986, Actmedia conducted 57 Impact programs, distributing over 71 million coupon booklets as well as 144 million samples and solo coupons.

Over the past 12 years, Actmedia and its clients had repeatedly tested Actmedia programs through independent research firms. According to company literature, these studies indicated, on average, the following impact of various Actmedia products on the sales of client products:

- Shopping cart ads: 8.2 percent sales increase (based on 390 independent studies)
- Aislevision: 7.5 percent sales increase (based on 70 independent studies)
- Shelftalk: 4.0 percent sales increase
- Shopping carts and aislevision: 12 percent sales increase

In addition, Actmedia claimed that its Actnow coupon program generated a redemption rate twice that of standard free-standing-insert programs in magazines (9 percent redemption rate for Actnow versus an average of 4.2 percent for FSI programs in magazines or newspapers), with a corresponding effect on sales of the client's products. Further, the company believed that, on a cost-per-thousand basis (CPM, a traditional measure of advertising efficiency), its products were more efficient than many standard ad media.[2]

Actmedia's management noted that it took significant time and effort to build client interest in each new product, but that the company had accelerated its expansion into more outlets and more products for a variety of reasons, including competition and developing scale economies. Although Actmedia believed it was currently the only company with its own national field service staff providing in-store marketing services, it also believed that new product introductions were required to preempt such direct national competition. Further, there were relatively few entry barriers at the local level for many different types of in-store marketing suppliers. In addition, ad agencies and packaged-goods manufacturers themselves were potential competition. Management also saw Actmedia in indirect competition with other media, including TV, radio, magazines, and newspapers. Expansion helped to make Actmedia's services increasingly cost competitive with these media.

Another reason to introduce new products was, in Failing, Jr.'s words, "to leverage existing store relationships: since our reputation with the chains is good, we tend to encounter less resistance to placing additional products in the stores. More products also leverage the time of our field force, since a single store visit can now accomplish more

---

[2]According to Actmedia, CPM rates in 1986 were, on average, as follows: TV, $10.20; Print, $5.60; Radio, $3.60; Outdoor ads, $2.25; Actmedia Carts, $.80; Aislevision, $.50; Shelftalk, $.25.

revenue-generating tasks and since the new products generally require fewer visits and less time to change than shopping cart displays. Therefore, we have been able to move into remote locations economically."

In 1983, with its Cart program in 3,300 stores, Actmedia could advertise 12 different brands on 40,000 ad spaces during each four-week cycle. By 1986, with five programs in 13,000 stores, Actmedia had the capacity to advertise or promote 112 different products on 647,000 spaces per cycle. At capacity, Actmedia's combined programs had a revenue potential of over $500 million, according to company estimates. Further, the company was planning to expand beyond supermarkets into major chain drug stores and mass merchandisers in 1987. Commenting on the company's recent expansion, Failing, Jr., said, "We introduced new products faster than would have been ideal, but we felt it was competitively necessary. The organization would probably like to take a breather for a while, but growth is essential to our position and plans."

ORGANIZATION

Exhibit 3 indicates Actmedia's organization in 1986. The three major operating functions were: retail store relations (signing on chains and leasing space in stores); field service (executing the in-store marketing programs); and marketing and sales (selling the company's services to packaged-goods manufacturers).

Store Relations

In 1986, Actmedia leased the advertising rights to over one million shopping carts, 100,000 aisle directories, and 74,500 Shelftalk displays in 238 retail food chains such as Safeway, Kroger, A&P, Stop & Shop, and Grand Union. On average, each chain's headquarters was visited monthly by one of the company's 12 store relations staff. Leighton York, vice president for store relations, noted that "no chain has ever withdrawn from a relationship with Actmedia."

In return for a percentage of Actmedia's advertising revenue, the retailer gave Actmedia exclusive, contractual use of its shopping carts, aisle directories, and Shelftalk displays for one to five years. Other than providing traffic and sales information about its stores, supermarket chains invested no money, labor, or management time for the income they received from Actmedia.

Field Service

Betty Failing (wife of Failing, Sr.) was in charge of the field service force, which placed and maintained the ads. Field operations were divided into three zones, 11 regions, and 35 districts, each run by a district manager. In 1986, the field service force for ads included 209 full-time area service representatives (ASRs), each responsible for servicing cart ads in 25–40 stores. During the ad-change period (the first four days of each cycle), ASRs supervised approximately 6,000 part-time personnel, called "contract labor" because

EXHIBIT 3

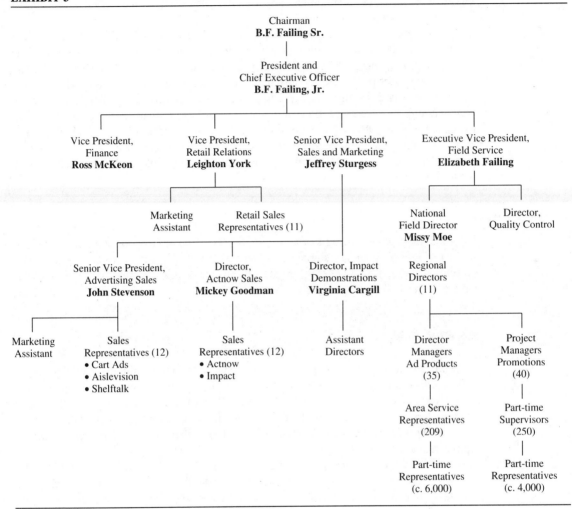

ASRs were responsible for recruiting and hiring these assistants. Similarly, Actnow project managers hired and supervised nearly 4,000 part-time personnel for promotional events. Betty Failing commented on her challenges in building the field:

I would have preferred a bigger management staff, but from the start most of Actmedia's resources had to go into sales in order to generate revenue. I had to hire people interested in other things besides maximizing salary.

We decided to build a predominantly female field force for several reasons. First, women felt natural in the supermarket environment and, second, we saw housewives as a huge, relatively untapped labor pool interested in part-time work. We offered enthusiasm, some flexibility, and a personal touch. To this day, I know every one of our full-time employees across the country, and I recognize them on birthdays or special occasions. By contrast, we really couldn't offer competitive salaries until 1984.

Most ASRs and project managers (98 percent) were women in their 20s and 30s. Salary ranged from $10,000 to $18,000, plus a car and benefits which Betty Failing valued at about $7,000. "The car and flexibility are real incentives for a family seeking to augment its income," she noted. "If a mother needs to pick up the kids from school, she can easily plan that into her schedule. Working hours are predictable, since each ASR has a specified route and the flights are at set times established here at headquarters. Also, the field managers find that the hiring of part-time personnel, and car-pooling together as they execute programs during each flight, generates a certain kind of hectic camaraderie."

Beyond supervising part-time personnel at the start of each cycle, ASRs also maintained the ads throughout the cycle. This entailed replacing ads that had been removed or damaged, as well as adding ads to carts that had been missed at the start of the cycle due to customer use or repairs at the time. ASRs also maintained detailed records on each Actmedia project in each store. During 1987, the company planned to issue hand-held computers to aid in these recordkeeping activities.

All field personnel had required uniforms of blue skirts or slacks and white blouses or shirts, with aprons and red bow ties for Actnow sample distributors. In addition, noted Betty Failing, "Our people are instructed to be meticulous in maintaining the store's appearance, because that's what store managers care about. We emphasize that, if there is a disagreement with a store manager, the customer is *always* right."

Sales and Marketing

Actmedia's 24-person sales force was divided in 1985 into Advertising Sales, under the direction of Stevenson, and a sales force for Actnow and Impact programs, under the direction of Mickey Goodman. Both groups sold Shelftalk. Salespeople were compensated on commissions which were a percentage of net sales revenues (i.e., sales minus any ad-agency fees). In 1986, the commission rate was 1 percent for Shopping Cart ads, and 2 percent for other products. Sales reps' expenses were paid by Actmedia. In 1986, compensation for sales personnel ranged from $70,000 to $210,000, with a median about $100,000. During the first year with Actmedia, a new salesperson received a guaranteed draw on commission of $100,000. Including compensation, expenses, benefits, and other relevant costs, the fully-burdened costs of fielding a salesperson were, on average, approximately $250,000 annually.

Each Actmedia product had annual sales goals, but sales reps' goals were not broken down by product. Sturgess, senior vice president for sales and marketing, noted: "The fact is, we aren't very good at setting sales targets, but we're good at meeting them. It's hard to figure which product will get the best sales when they're all new. Our sales forecasting is rule of thumb, but morale and motivation are high." Each year, Failing, Jr., established a target for company growth, which had varied between 50 percent and 70 percent annually in the past five years. Sturgess then established growth targets for each product. Then Stevenson, Goodman, and their salespeople reviewed each brand at each account, and established overall goals for each salesperson. At 100 percent of target quota, the salesperson received a 15 percent bonus, and every sale made beyond quota yielded three times the normal commission on that product.

In hiring salespeople, Actmedia looked for previous sales experience. Experience with a packaged-goods firm was considered a plus, and experience with an ad agency a "slight minus," according to one manager, "since ad people tend to have preconceived notions about our product." Sturgess commented that "we can teach someone about our product and our customers, but we can't teach them to sell. We're selling a concept, and one that still encounters lots of misunderstanding and rejections. We look for aggressive, bright, persistent people. Only one of our reps didn't make quota last year, and our best rep previously sold toys." Most salespeople were in their late 20s and early 30s, "about the same age as most brand managers," noted Stevenson.

Each salesperson was given an intensive three- to six-month training program that focused on the details of budgeting processes at packaged-goods firms, common concerns and misunderstandings about Actmedia's products, and the nature of the competitive environment facing each client's brands. Training culminated in a "final exam" role play: the trainee was instructed to prepare a 15-minute presentation about Actmedia for Failing, Jr., Stevenson, and Sturgess (who acted as brand managers and agency representatives), but when the trainee arrived, he or she was told that only five minutes could be allocated.

As well as meeting sales goals, salespeople were evaluated on "quarterly account plans, feedback about accounts, their attitude of commitment and enthusiasm," and a factor described by Stevenson as "creative lateral thinking: the ability to brainstorm new sales tactics in the heat of the moment at an account." Sturgess pointed out that, although call reports were filed, they were used by management primarily to track products sold. "Our sales-management philosophy is flexible by necessity. Our product requires our clients to change the way they do things, and they still don't have a predisposition to consider or buy it. We therefore give our salespeople the freedom and responsibility to develop accounts how they think best. John, Mickey, and I try to make calls and minimize 'face time' with the salespeople to review account planning and management, rather than relying on paperwork or systematic procedures for that communication. Of course, that ongoing, direct contact becomes harder to sustain as we grow."

SALES TASKS: ADVERTISING PRODUCTS (SHOPPING CARTS, AISLEVISION, SHELFTALK)

Actmedia's sales force called on manufacturers' product management groups and ad agencies. Salespeople utilized presentation packages customized for a product or category, and stressed that, in a cluttered media environment, Actmedia guaranteed product category exclusivity (i.e., for each category, Actmedia provided ads in each region for only one product, a feature generally unavailable in TV, radio, or print advertising). Salespeople also stressed the cost efficiency of Actmedia programs compared to alternative media. A number of clients (e.g., in 1986, PepsiCo, Procter & Gamble, and Kimberly-Clark) had purchased all of the firm's shopping cart spaces nationally for a product category for periods of time ranging from six months to one year. In 1986, about 30 percent of Actmedia's sales were from such extended-term purchases.

There were three important groups typically involved in a potential Actmedia ad sale (see Exhibit 4). The brand management group (see Exhibit 5) included the brand manager, a marketing assistant, the group product manager, and (depending on the company) perhaps the vice president of marketing. The advertising agency's account group included an account manager and an assistant as well as senior management in certain ad firms. The third group was the advertising agency's media group, which developed copy and purchased media space and usually included a media planner and media supervisors. Sturgess noted, "Informally, we subscribe to the 'two-out-of-three' theory: you need the strong support of the brand manager, and then either the group product manager or an agency executive, to close a sale for our ad products."

Brand managers who bought Actmedia, particularly in the early years, were described by Stevenson as "young Turks: aggressive and iconoclastic. Remember that most brand

---

EXHIBIT 4   Personnel Typically Contacted During Sales Process

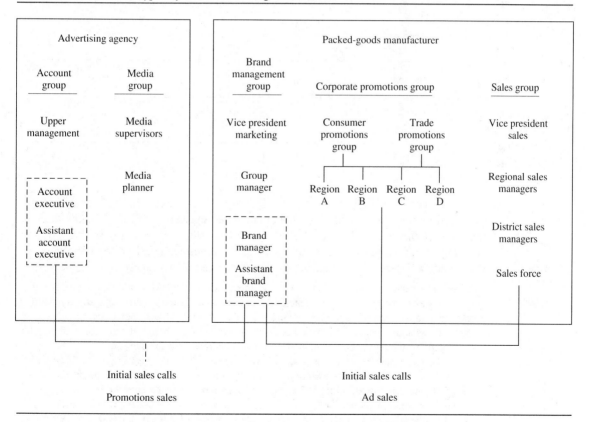

EXHIBIT 5   Brand Management at Large Consumer Packaged-Goods Company Desserts Division: Organization Chart

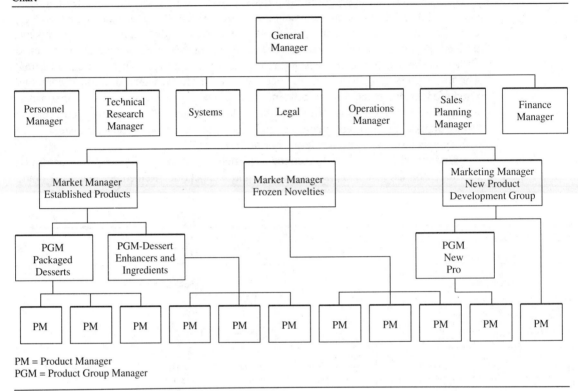

PM = Product Manager
PGM = Product Group Manager

managers stay with a given brand for only one to three years, and their goal is to get promoted as soon as possible. By definition, their superiors made their marks through media other than ours, and a perceived 'failure' usually lingers longer in the corridors of a large corporation than an in-store success." Sturgess emphasized the importance of the client's ad agency in influencing the brand's advertising strategy and channels:

In the early years we tended to ignore ad agencies because they wouldn't support us, and that was a mistake. We now give the agency a 15 percent commission even though it is atypical for an agency to be a strong supporter of Actmedia. They often have veto power over a brand's ad expenditures and, once the annual ad budget is established for a brand, it's very difficult to alter it. Therefore, our salespeople must maintain good relations with the agencies.

Despite its reputation, Madison Avenue is very conservative. For years, agencies have touted TV as the best mass medium for consumer advertising, and for a while that might have been true. But note that a multimillion dollar TV campaign requires relatively little time from agency account personnel in proportion to the 15 percent commissions generated, whereas it does take time for an agency media planner to figure out how to best spend, say, $100,000 on Actmedia. And few ad personnel know much about point-of-sale marketing.

Stevenson explained that "we typically get one big chance to make an ad presentation for a brand's annual budget, so we must match our proposed program to the brand's needs very closely. Therefore, the salesperson's first mandate is to learn everything possible about the client's ad plans, budgeting cycle, and authorization process, meaning the people involved both formally and informally in that process." Management preferred that its salespeople find a specific problem at a brand, and then present one or two Actmedia solutions, rather than presenting the range of Actmedia services, because clients were unlikely to give salespeople sufficient time or attention for the latter approach. In addition, Actmedia rarely sought more than 10 percent of a brand's ad budget. One reason, noted Stevenson, "is that we're still perceived as relatively new and therefore risky. But the ad agencies are another reason. Most agencies will concede, say, 5 percent less TV advertising in favor of Actmedia, since annual budget growth often covers that. But they'll try hard to block a sale if we usurp a large proportion of TV advertising."

Ira Lewis, an Actmedia salesman, noted that client budget allocations were often simply repeated from year to year. As a result, adding Actmedia meant cutting some other item. "Therefore," noted Lewis, "a salesperson has to know which portion of the ad budget performed poorly in the previous year, but this is often difficult due to the confidentiality of budgets. Also, brand managers are usually too busy during budgeting time to accept sales calls. In fact, many brand managers use their ad agencies as a 'front office' to screen callers during this crucial period." Lewis also noted that sales calls to those unacquainted with Actmedia often required the salesperson to educate the person about vehicles other than TV or coupons:

> Comfort with the concepts behind our products is the most important factor, and that takes time to develop. First, we point out how we resemble TV advertising, in order for them to put us into perspective. Then we show how we're different and better, or at least complementary. If we don't go through these steps, the client is not likely to recognize the special value of our point-of-sale presence, and will instead write us off as some gimmick since they were never taught about us in their training programs.

Marketing provided Actmedia salespeople with presentation cards outlining Actmedia's concepts, services, and advantages. These cards included numerical and graphic representations of each product's cost and scope. Each rep also had ad samples. Another tool was a fill-in-the-blanks card informally called "the game" (see Exhibit 6). The page listed several current national ad slogans with the brand names missing; the prospective buyer would be asked to identify the brands. Scores were consistently low, with entire product categories often missed. Lewis commented that "at this point brand managers would start listening harder because it reinforces fears of product interchangeability and demonstrates the low residual effect of TV ads. My favorite analogy is that, after months of advertising on TV, a political candidate would like to be at the polling booth on election day, but that's illegal. A brand manager, however, can be in the store through Actmedia."

SALES TASKS: PROMOTIONS PRODUCTS (ACTNOW, IMPACT)

Actmedia's ad and promotions sales forces called on many of the same clients, but coordination at the same account was only informal. Some salespeople felt close coordination was helpful, since intelligence could be shared and certain crucial decision makers

EXHIBIT 6

Actmedia fills in the blanks

1_____: "Helps hands look younger."

2 Extra-Strength_____:
   "Nothing you can buy is stronger."

3_____: "America's leading
   high nutrition cereal."

4_____: "Stops wetness better than any
   leading anti-perspirant spray."

5_____: "For your best coffee times."

6_____: "A clean so clean,
   you can feel it."

Some of the country's leading advertisers have spent
millions of dollars establishing these campaigns.
Are they getting their money's worth? If you can't fill in
the blanks in 30 seconds, they're not!

"double-teamed." But others felt this was "a waste of time," and that a joint presentation by different reps from the same company could alienate or confuse a busy brand manager.

When Actnow promotions were introduced in 1984, they did not get much sales attention. Salespeople said that promotions were new and that no explicit goals were stated. They also felt that selling the company's ad products was made more difficult by the addition of the promotions products. Goodman recalled, "Within a year, we established a dedicated sales force for Actnow, despite the fact that one reason for adding promotional services was to capitalize. on existing relationships."

Goodman also noted several differences between selling Actmedia's ad and promotional services. First, promotions were usually organized as discrete events rather than continuous policies. Consequently, clients' promotional budgets were frequently revised throughout the year, in contrast with fixed annual ad budgets. Second, "There are a limited number of companies with big promotional budgets," Goodman noted. "Consequently, word-of-mouth spread fast." Third, within these companies, more functions were involved with promotions than advertising. Goodman explained:

> Often, a coupon promotion is a means for getting more or better trade placement, so coordination with a manufacturer's sales force is very important. Their sales force may also need to coordinate our programs with their own trade promotions and, in some package-good firms, the sales vice president often oversees all in-store merchandising programs. Unfortunately, at many of these same firms, brand management and sales management rarely talk to each other. Headquarters doesn't like brand managers explicitly competing with each other for limited sales resources, and some sales vice presidents run their organizations like "black boxes" from the brand manager's point of view. But we need to coordinate Actnow with both groups.
>
> Similarly, many manufacturers have corporate staff groups for promotional activities. These groups can sometimes be a source of "not-invented-here" resistance to our programs. But even when they support our programs, they're not always the best conduit with brand managers at that company. Each brand manager wants promotions for his or her product to be unique, but the corporate promotions group is thinking in terms of scale economies and spreading costs across regions or products. Thus, brand and promotional groups often argue or simply go their own way. In fact, we're probably one of the very few promotions vendors that even speaks with brand management; most sell entirely through the promotions group.
>
> Smooth coordination and follow-up with all these internal groups is often the key to additional Actnow business at a client. By contrast, Actnow salespeople almost never speak with the ad agency.

Although cost varied depending upon the campaign, a client typically incurred the following costs for a four-week national flight of each Actmedia advertising product: Shopping Cart Ads, $320,000; Aislevision, $160,000; and Shelftalk, $60,000. Promotion products were sold as two-weekend events; the average prices for national coverage were: Actnow Couponing, $300,000; Actnow Sampling, $1,000,000; and Impact Demonstrations, $1.3 million.

ACCOUNT MANAGEMENT ISSUES

In recent years, Failing, Jr., and others had become aware of several issues that affected the company's sales efforts. One issue concerned the positioning of Actmedia as an advertising or promotions firm. Actmedia initially sold its shopping cart ads primarily on the basis of increased sales results. "Hundreds of tests corroborated our effect on product movement," noted Failing, Jr., "and we stressed this fact." In the past few years, however, management had come to feel that this meant the company's ad products were perceived as promotions, and that this, in turn, limited potential sales of those products due to evaluation criteria for advertising versus promotions at many packaged-goods firms. Promotions were typically evaluated in terms of incremental sales provided for a given level of spending. Advertising, on the other hand, was typically evaluated by the number of consumers exposed to it, a more abstract measure intended to provide an estimate of "consumer awareness" or "brand image" simulated by the ad. One Actmedia manager noted:

> No one really tests advertising. Nielsen counts the people who watch a TV program and records gross demographics, but the cost of a TV ad is based on the show's ratings, not the number of purchases resulting from an ad. For most media advertising, scope is measured and effectiveness is assumed. In our clients' budgets, moreover, media costs are essentially treated as fixed, while promotions are incremental costs measured on a per-item, return-on-sales basis.
>
> As a result, when our shopping cart, Aislevision, or Shelftalk products are perceived as promotions (because anything in-store *must* be a promotion, according to the conventional wisdom), we must do business with our accounts on a zero-based basis each year, starting from scratch and repeatedly explaining the concept behind our service. In addition, our ad products are not intended to be—nor are they priced—as promotions. They look even better, and can sell more, when they're rightly understood as in-store advertising.

During the early 1980s, Actmedia had sought to reposition itself in clients' budgeting and measurement criteria. It began pricing its products on a cost-per-thousand basis, as most ad media were priced, so clients could directly compare Actmedia costs with alternative ad media.

Another issue concerned the different selling dynamics that tended to accompany sales of each product. One manager commented:

> Cart ads reach nearly 100 percent of the consumers in a store, whereas Aislevision may reach less than 50 percent. But a big 20″ × 30″ Aislevision ad strikes some clients as more "powerful" than a smaller shopping cart ad. Nonetheless, Aislevision and cart ads are variations on the same theme compared to Shelftalk. We view Shelftalk as an ad product, but shelftalkers have a long tradition in supermarkets of being used in promotional events. So we sell Shelftalk as a crossover product through both sales forces. Finally, our products mean very different up-front costs to clients, and that also affects both the sales and account management tasks.

Some managers believed that Shelftalk, while a successful new product for Actmedia, had cannibalized a portion of Aislevision sales during 1986. "A number of brand managers see them as potentially redundant, rather than complementary, in-store vehicles," noted one manager. "They still don't make the same distinctions we do."

A third issue concerned deployment of the sales forces. Stevenson explained:

> Instead of assigning salespeople based on types of manufacturers' products, ad agencies used, or geography, we try to organize based on the individuals who do the buying at packaged-goods firms. So when we assign a salesperson to a firm, we recommend initially focusing on one or two brands. As our supporters at those brands spread to other parts of the firm, we'll try to follow them. Remember that brand managers can be rotated through several brands in less than two years. We try to keep continuity with the people who have bought us, even when they move on to other brands or other companies.

Frequency of contact is also important for us. We'll be part of a client's budget for advertising only if we get there at the right time, since brands tend to work on long cycles that are fairly rigid because of production scheduling, trade promotions, and the involvement of other functions with a given brand. If we miss a client's budgeting period, we can lose the entire year's ad business at that client. So it's important to have a supporter inside brand management to alert us to critical budgeting periods and issues.

We still sell to brands, not companies. So when we find supporters, we don't want to lose track of them. But these contacts and this deployment of the sales forces become harder to manage as we grow, add more salespeople, products, and channels, and as our champions move within and across manufacturers.

A salesperson for Actmedia added:

The rapid movement of brand management can help to spread allies, but it also tends to limit the time horizons for buying our products. Within a given brand, I must develop new relations and credibility almost annually. For example, new brand management is often unaware that previous managers for that brand have already tested Actmedia's products two or three times.

During the mid-1980s, moreover, a number of large packaged-goods firms appeared to be moving toward increasingly regionalized marketing programs. This trend appeared to be in response to scanner-generated data that revealed important regional differences formerly hidden when these data were not collected. One result of "regional marketing" was often an additional layer of marketing management at these firms in order to coordinate different regional programs, and restrictions on a brand manager's ability to develop national programs. Conversely, regional sales managers at these firms often had increased influence on the development, as well as execution, of local ad and promotional efforts. Managers at Actmedia were unsure what the implications might be for Actmedia's sales and account management practices.

CONCLUSION

Commenting in December 1986 on Actmedia, Failing, Jr., said:

Our biggest constraints are personnel. In sales, for competitive reasons, we need more people selling more spaces into more stores. Right now, however, our growing product line and new retail channels for those products are outstripping our sales and marketing capacity. We're also planning new products for 1987, some of which are similar to existing programs and some of which are new departures for us. That's why we will double the sales force during the first quarter of 1987, and perhaps add more people throughout the year.

More generally, at the rate we've grown during the past five years, management systems can easily wear thin. We still manage more by intuition than is perhaps desirable at this stage of our company's growth.

Given these changes, Failing, Jr., was considering several options for reorganizing Actmedia's sales efforts: by product, by account size or account type, and a hybrid organization combining account and product specialists.

Although Actmedia had divided its sales force into Ads and Promotions products in 1985, some managers felt the company's growth required a further subdivision of the sales force in order to ensure better product knowledge and concentration of effort by salespeople, especially for new products and new channels. Some managers believed new products would not get the attention they needed to become successful if they were sold by a full-line ad sales force, and that rapid roll-out of new products into new channels was strategically important. "Time, Inc. has a different sales force for each magazine," noted one manager, "because each provides a different audience and medium to potential advertisers, and because effective selling requires a dedicated 'champion' for each magazine. A full-line sales force would gravitate to the established magazines and neglect the others. We're evolving toward a similar situation. Our salespeople can lose touch with the dynamics of each product, and neglect new products in favor of established vehicles at established accounts."

Other managers were worried that separate sales forces would "confuse" customers, or perhaps cause salespeople to "compete" with each other for a customer's time and money. These managers believed that attention to new products and channels did not require redeployment of the sales force. "We can accomplish this objective either by changing the commission rates by product or by giving salespeople quotas for each product," suggested one manager.

Another option was to organize the sales force by account size. One proponent of this idea explained:

> Our products don't differ as much as our customers do. You can learn about Aislevision quickly, but understanding the subtleties of selling to P&G via Benton & Bowles is a long, complex, and ever-changing process. Also, because of cost considerations, some of our products seem better suited for larger companies and some for smaller companies. Focusing our salespeople by account size could allow the rep to develop insights common to the group concerning budgetary constraints, timing, brand development, product introductions, and other matters.

Other managers located the important differences in account type rather than account size. "We should organize the sales force by the nature of the product category being sold by our customers," said one manager. "The dynamics of selling in-store programs for salty-snack companies is different than those for coffee companies, and these differences are more important to our sales efforts than the differences between a big and little account."

A fourth option was what one manager described as a "hybrid" approach:

> We sell to the brand, not the corporation; so distinctions between companies are not as important as distinctions between brands. Brands from national and regional firms, big and little firms, new and established brands, can still compete for the same shopper and the same market. At the same time, our selling process requires continuity with individual companies, because our supporters in brand management move frequently.
>
> Therefore, we should have a team organization in our sales efforts: an account manager assigned by company, and Actmedia product specialists (shopping cart specialists, Aislevision specialists, etc.) assigned by the account manager to specific brands within that company. This way, we can keep continuity of contact, familiarity with a given company's budgeting processes, and still focus attention on our different products.

Other managers believed the "hybrid" approach was "an interesting idea," but "probably a pain to manage. We must keep things simple administratively; at the pace we're going, we can't afford to work in fancy structures that require a lot of coordination."

Finally, some in Actmedia believed the company should not be concerned with issues of sales organization. "We're going like crazy and still building primary demand for our in-store programs," said one manager. "So questions of reorganization are irrelevant, sap precious management time and energy, and can demotivate the sales force by making them wonder if taking time to develop business at a given account will pay off for them. Besides, all the options I've heard run the risk of turning this place into a bureaucracy. Keep things as they are now."

Another issue facing the company was recruitment criteria for new salespeople. "We're doubling our sales force soon," noted Failing, Jr., "but we haven't really clarified what kind of people we want. In recent years, we've hired about two salespeople for every one we keep, and that takes a toll in terms of expenses, opportunity costs at accounts, and management time and attention. What should we be looking for when we expand our sales efforts? Is there any common denominator or background experience that can help us make our recruitment efforts more focused and efficient? Have the selling requirements changed since John, Jeff and I *were* the sales force for Actmedia?"

Case 7–3

Coffee Brands: Direct Product Profit/Cost Exercise*

Traditionally, supermarkets and other consumer goods retailers used an item's gross margin and turnover rate as the basis for merchandising decisions. Retailers calculated the gross margin simply by subtracting the cost of the product from its selling price. The gross margin percentage (gross margin as a percentage of selling price) was used as a relative measurement of profitability to compare product categories, brands within each category, and the sizes of each brand. While the gross margin percentage was widely used as a decision-making tool by retailers, it was not a true reflection of a product's profit contribution because it did not consider the costs incurred by the retailer in getting the product from the manufacturer to the consumer. For example, one product might be far more expensive for the retailer to handle and inventory than another, yet both might have the same gross margin percentages.

*This case was prepared by Professor John A. Quelch, Research Associate Melanie D. Spencer, and Brian Cosacchi, General Foods Corporation, as the basis for class discussion rather than to illustrate either effective or ineffective handling of an administrative situation. All data are disguised. Copyright © 1986 by the President and Fellows of Harvard College. Harvard Business School case 9–587–015.

The concept of Direct Product Profit (DPP) was developed to measure product profitability more accurately. DPP was defined as the net profit contribution of a product after all trade allowances were added to gross margin and after all handling, shipping, warehousing, and other costs attributable to the product were deducted. The DPP formula assigned retailer handling and distribution costs to each individual stockkeeping unit (SKU), as opposed to lumping such costs into "overhead," thereby allowing retailers to account for variations in item costs when making merchandising decisions. Nevertheless, when the concept was conceived in the late 1960s, it had little practical application; the cost measurements required for DPP analysis were too difficult to obtain and too expensive to manipulate at that time.

By 1986, industry analysts believed that the DPP concept and its use would grow in importance as retailers refined accounting practices and improved management information systems. UPC scanning[1] and the increasing cost-effectiveness of computer applications involving large quantities of data were also expected to increase the use of DPP. Finally, in an industry such as grocery retailing characterized by thin before-tax profit margins of around 2 percent, the effective application of DPP was seen as providing a possible competitive edge.

CALCULATING DIRECT PRODUCT PROFIT

The Direct Product Profit formula had two major components, Direct Product Costs (DPCs) and Adjusted Gross Revenue. Direct Product Costs were defined as costs incurred by the retailer in moving each unit of a product from the manufacturer's shipping dock to the point at which it was purchased by a consumer. Exhibit 1 defines a variety of DPCs.

Adjusted Gross Revenue was defined as all revenue attributable to each unit of a product, including trade deals and allowances, cash discounts, backhaul monies, and forward-buy profits. Trade deals and allowances were monies associated with the temporary promotion of a product to stimulate inventory loading and additional retail merchandising support to sell the extra inventory through to the consumer. Cash discounts included discounts from the manufacturer for prompt payment of invoices. Backhaul monies were manufacturer allowances that compensated a retailer using a truck that was returning empty from a store to the retailer's warehouse to pick up product at the manufacturer's factory or warehouse, thus saving the manufacturer transportation costs. When a retailer purchased product on promotion for normal inventory rather than or in addition to the volume of product purchased for sale to the consumer at a lower-than-normal retail price, forwarded-buy profits were realized. These profits represented the difference between the manufacturer's regular price and the promotional price for the stock that the retailer sold at regular price after the promotion was over.

---

[1] Computerized scanning systems at retail checkouts could "read" bar codes (known as universal product codes, or UPCs) on product labels or packages and automatically ring up the correct price as well as record the transaction. In 1986, supermarkets accounting for 40 percent of U.S. grocery volume were equipped with UPC scanning systems.

EXHIBIT 1 Factors in the Calculation of Direct Product Profit

Factor	Explanations
Sales	Reconstructed from warehouse withdrawals or scanning data
	Adjusted for retail inventory changes
	Adjusted for retail promotions
Cost	Cost from invoice including off-invoice allowance*
Merchandising allowances	All non-off-invoice allowances*
Payment terms	Discount for early payment plus interest for days
Distribution allowances	Tax-stamping allowance†
	Backhaul allowance per case cube
	Freight allowance
Warehouse direct labor (in- and out-labor)‡	Time standard model at hourly rate per pallet, case, cube, pound§
Warehouse operating labor	Supervision assigned by direct labor (in- and out-labor)‡
	Operating expense assigned by space (warehouse space)‡
Warehouse investment cost (warehouse space)‡	Assigned by space
Transportation expense (transportation)‡	Calculated for cube volume
Warehouse inventory cost (inventory, cell = I39)‡	Based on buying model and current interest rates‖
Retail stocking labor (pricing and other labor)‡	Time standard model at hourly rate per case, cube, pound, package
Retail checkout labor (checking and bagging)‡	Time standard model at hourly rate per cube, package
Retail operating expense	Supervision assigned by direct labor (other labor)‡
	Operating expense assigned by space (selling space)‡
Retail investment cost (selling space)‡	Assigned by space
Retail inventory cost (inventory; cell = I44)	Dollars of inventory at retailer's cost $\times$ current interest rate

*Off-invoice allowances were temporary price reductions offered by manufacturers to the trade that were deducted from the manufacturers' invoices.

†A tax-stamping allowance might be paid by a cigarette manufacturer to a trade account that affixed a tax stamp to each package at its warehouse.

‡Descriptions in parentheses show Direct Product Cost components as they appear in the Direct Product Profit (DPP) model at the end of the text of this case.

§A time standard model calculated the labor cost associated with moving a unit of product in and out of the warehouse based on the product's shape and weight.

‖This model calculated the cost of financing the inventory in the warehouse, based on current interest rates.

The DPP formula reflecting these definitions is shown in Exhibit 2. This equation yielded a DPP value per stockkeeping unit. Other useful measures of DPP could be obtained, such as DPP per case or DPP per week, by performing additional calculations. The actual DPP calculation could vary slightly depending on a manager's assumptions. Occupancy costs, for example, were sometimes excluded from the equation by users who believed that such costs could not be attributed to each unit of product and would have been incurred anyway.

RETAIL APPLICATIONS

DPP had two major applications for retail management: as a method to measure and reduce handling/operational costs, and as a tool to achieve better merchandising decisions. Because real costs had to be assigned to each SKU in DPP analysis, management had to

EXHIBIT 2   Overview of DPC/DPP Calculations

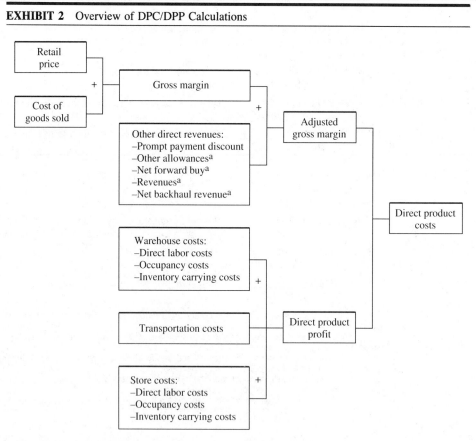

[a]If earning these revenues involves extra costs, the corresponding expenses should be included in the DPC calculation.

monitor closely these costs. If total operational costs were found to be increasing, retailers could determine which SKUs were contributing disproportionately to the increases. Once high-cost product lines were identified, programs could be developed to improve existing handling practices in each cost area.

In the case of products with a high bulk-to-value ratio, package size and shape had an especially significant impact on the product's DPCs and, thus, the profit contribution of the product as measured by DPP. Possible methods of reducing specific costs by using the information provided by the DPP formula included:

Warehouse: Develop a separate, specialized warehouse or warehouse area for handling high-cube products.[2]

Receiving: Improve equipment efficiency and develop methods of unloading large numbers of cases at once.

Put away: Determine ways to increase the number of cases moved on each pallet.[3]

Replenish: Minimize the number of required pallet moves; for example, have large floor storage areas near the pick slots.[4]

Transportation: Ship high-cube products to the stores on slip sheets or deadpile, thereby trading off equipment or labor costs at the store for transportation savings.[5]

Store: Develop methods of minimizing travel and storage time in the stocking process. Determine optimal packaging designs to reduce item stocking time.

By using DPP analysis, retailers could also tailor merchandising decisions to maximize sales of the high DPP items in general and/or in a particular product category. Merchandising and promotional considerations which could be affected by retailer DPP analyses included: pricing, product assortment and variety, new product listing decisions,[6] advertising and promotion, space allocation, and shelf and section location. Application priorities would likely vary according to each chain's overall merchandising philosophy (full service, discount price, one-stop shopping, etc.) and the competitive environment.

In 1986, use of DPP by grocery retailers varied widely. The more advanced chains used it to evaluate the relative profitability of different product categories through gross margins adjusted for DPCs and, in so doing, to optimize shelf space allocation.

MANUFACTURER IMPLICATIONS

For manufacturers, the use of DPP by retailers had significant implications. They would have to consider each trade account's DPCs in setting their policies on pricing, retail margins, and promotional allowances. In addition, they would have to work to reduce

---

[2]High-cube products were bulky items such as kitchen towels and ready-to-eat breakfast cereals.

[3]A pallet was a wooden base measuring 48″ × 40″ and 6″ high on which merchandise could be stacked for warehousing and transportation. The pallet size was standardized to facilitate movement by fork-lift trucks.

[4]A pick slot was a warehouse space in which a product was stored and from which stock was drawn.

[5]A slip sheet was a more efficient form of pallet. It measured 51″ × 43″ when its four 3″-high sides were folded down, and was only 1/2″ thick at its base. Deadpile merchandise was not stored on a pallet or slip sheet and, therefore, had to be loaded and unloaded by hand.

[6]Listing occurred when a retail buying committee decided to stock a new product.

the DPCs on their products. For example, packaging changes that increased a product's "stackability" might significantly lower the cost of stocking shelves and, therefore, increase the product's unit DPP. This increase might be reflected in the product's retail price, the number of stores in which the product was distributed, shelf space/location, and promotional support. Manufacturers that made an effort to understand DPP from the perspective of the retailer and educated their sales forces about DPP were thought likely to gain a competitive advantage.

THE DIRECT PRODUCT PROFIT COMPUTER MODEL

A Direct Product Profit computer model for seven disguised coffee brands was developed for use with this case to provide an opportunity to practice working with DPP and DPC. The model is on diskette and is intended for use with the Lotus 1-2-3 version 1A software package on an IBM or IBM-compatible personal computer.

The model is based on the coffee product category and includes DPP and DPC factors used by the retail trade in 1986. The exercise does not cover all DPC factors and data. For example, advertising costs and revenues and forward-buying profits are not included, and unit costs are averaged over all the SKUs of each brand. The variety of DPCs contained in the model does, however, provide opportunities for realistic exploration of the impact of three hypothetical promotional scenarios presented at the end of this case.

The DPP model includes six sections. Sections I-III include basic information on the seven coffee brands and the DPC values associated with each. Section IV provides an area for input of variables for a hypothetical promotional scenario. Section V provides information on the effect of the hypothetical promotion on DPP. Section VI provides comparative DPP information on the seven brands and the three hypothetical promotions presented in the exercises at the end of the case. If the hypothetical promotion affects DPCs, changes to DPCs must be entered into the appropriate area of Section III.

Several cells in the model are protected; the values within the cells cannot be changed by entering new values into the model. Some protected cells contain formulas, however, and the values within these cells may change when other cells in the worksheet are modified. Unprotected cells, on the other hand, can be modified to reflect the assumptions of hypothetical scenarios simply by entering new values into the cells. In the model, unprotected cells appear in bolder type on the screen than do protected cells. Unprotected cells in each section are noted and described in the instructions that follow. *Do not insert new rows into the model. It will impair its function.*

INSTRUCTIONS FOR LOADING THE DPP MODEL

- Load Lotus 1-2-3 Spreadsheet in Drive A and
- Place DPP Model diskette in Drive B.
- Retrieve the file DPPFILE by typing: /FR DPPFILE and pressing the "enter" key.

DESCRIPTIONS OF SECTIONS OF THE DPP MODEL

Section I

Section I provides the following information for nonpromoted weeks for each of the seven coffee brands covered in the model: the number of stockkeeping units (SKUs) carried, cubic feet of shelf space, retail price, unit cost, gross margin percentage, weekly unit volume, weekly cost to retailer of all units sold, weekly retail dollar sales, direct product profit per unit, per cubic foot, and per week, and gross margin per unit, per cubic foot, and per week. It also shows the appropriate totals and averages for the coffee category. This section of the model is located in cells A1–X14 and AA1–AF13. When the model is loaded, the screens from Section I will appear as they are shown in Exhibit 3.

The information contained in Section I is the most basic data on the seven coffee brands, showing the characteristics of each brand under normal nonpromoted circumstances. Several cells in Section I are unprotected to allow flexibility in using the model; however, these unprotected cells need not and should not be changed to complete the exercises at the end of this case. They already contain the necessary data for the exercises.

Unprotected Cells	Information in Cells
C6–C12	Number of SKUs
E6–E12	Cubic feet of shelf space
G6–G12	Retail price
I6–I12	Unit cost
M6–M12	Weekly unit sales
J1	Case pack (number of items per case)

If, in working with the model, changes are made to the unprotected cells, the other data in Section I will be calculated by pressing F9.

Section II

Section II shows a variety of Standard Direct Product Cost factors for each brand. Exhibit 4 shows Section II screens as they appear when the model is loaded. These DPC factors are presented in two sections, Warehousing DPCs and Store DPCs. Warehousing DPCs include costs incurred by the retailer before the brand reaches the store, such as: in-labor (labor used moving product from the truck to the appropriate place in the warehouse), out-labor (labor used selecting and moving product from warehouse to truck), warehouse space (allocation of warehouse costs to the warehouse space used by the product), invoice (cost of checking invoice), transportation, and inventory holding cost. Store DPCs include: pricing labor (labor to place prices on products), checking and bagging labor, other labor (primarily labor to stock shelves), selling space (allocation of store costs to the selling space used by the product), inventory holding cost, and totals. Section II is located in

EXHIBIT 3 Section I Screens

	A	B	C	D	E	F	G	H
		*			DIRECT PRODUCT PROFIT--COFFEE			
1								
2	************************		**					
3				* CU.FT.		* RETAIL		*
4	CANNED COFFEE	*	# SKU	* SHELF		* PRICE		*
5	************************		**					
6	GOLD BLEND	*	16 *	25.71	*	$2.92		*
7	MOUNTAIN TOP	*	4 *	4.92	*	$2.36		*
8	MORNING GLORY	*	9 *	10.45	*	$2.66		*
9	CABANA	*	6 *	6.17	*	$2.42		*
10	LATIN PRIDE	*	11 *	14.9	*	$2.64		*
11	PRIVATE LABEL	*	6 *	8.75	*	$2.66		*
12	RICARDO	*	4 *	10.1	*	$2.81		*
13	************************		**					
14	TOTAL COFFEE	*	56 *	81	*	$2.67		*
15	- - - - - - - - - - - - - - - - *		- - - - - - - - - - - - *	- - - - - - - - - - - - - *		- - - - - - - - - - - - - - - - - *		

	I	J	K	L	M	N	O	P	Q	R	S	T
1		24										
2	**********		**********		**********		******************		******************		*	**********
3	UNIT	*	MARGIN	*	WEEKLY	*	WEEKLY COST	*	WEEKLY SALES	*	*	PER
4	COST	*		*	UNITS	*		*			*	UNIT
5	************		************		************		******************		******************			************
6	$2.66	*	8.90%	*	651	*	$1,731.66	*	$1,900.92	*	*	$0.19
7	$2.06	*	12.71%	*	417	*	859.02	*	984.12	*	*	$0.25
8	$2.41	*	9.40%	*	280	*	674.80	*	744.80	*	*	$0.18
9	$2.06	*	14.88%	*	144	*	$296.64	*	348.48	*	*	$0.29
10	$2.44	*	7.58%	*	192	*	468.48	*	506.88	*	*	$0.10
11	$2.47	*	7.14%	*	167	*	412.49	*	444.22	*	*	$0.12
12	$2.54	*	9.61%	*	81	*	205.74	*	227.61	*	*	$0.16
13	************		************		************		******************		******************			************
14	$2.41	*	9.85%	*	1932	*	$4,648.83	*	$5,157.03	*	*	$0.18
15	- - - - - - - - - *		- - - - - - - - *		- - - - - - - - *		- - - - - - - - - - - - - *		- - - - - - - - - - - - - - - *			- - - - - - - - *

	U	V	W	X	Y	Z	AA	AB	AC	AD	AE	AF
1	DIRECT PRODUCT PROFIT								GROSS MARGIN			
2	**						**					
3	* PER		* PER		*		* PER	*	PER		*	PER
4	* CU.FT.		* WEEK		*		* UNIT	*	CU.FT.		*	WEEK
5	**						**					
6	* $4.82		* $124.02		*		* $0.26	*	$6.58		*	$169.26
7	* $20.83		* $102.50		*		* $0.30	*	$25.43		*	$125.10
8	* $4.70		* $49.14		*		* $0.25	*	$6.70		*	$70.00
9	* $6.75		* $41.63		*		* $0.36	*	$8.40		*	$51.84
10	* $1.32		* $19.68		*		* $0.20	*	$2.58		*	$38.40
11	* $2.26		* $19.76		*		* $0.19	*	$3.63		*	$31.73
12	* $1.24		* $12.57		*		* $0.27	*	$2.17		*	$21.87
13	**						**					
14	* $4.39		* $355.54		*							
15	* - - - - - - - - - - - - - *		* - - - - - - - - - - *		*							

Note: Boldface numbers designate unprotected cells.

EXHIBIT 4   Section II Screens

	A	B	C	D	E	F	G	H
16	----------------------*		----------*		------------*		----------*	
17	DIRECT PRODUCT COSTS *			*	WAREHOUSING DPC			*
18	********************************		IN		OUT		WHSE	
19	CANNED COFFEE	*	LABOR	*	LABOR	*	SPACE	*
20	********************************		**************		**************		**************	
21	GOLD BLEND	*	$0.0063	*	$0.0166	*	$0.0046	*
22	MOUNTAIN TOP	*	$0.0046	*	$0.0152	*	$0.0042	*
23	MORNING GLORY	*	$0.0079	*	$0.0165	*	$0.0038	*
24	CABANA	*	$0.0047	*	$0.0165	*	$0.0037	*
25	LATIN PRIDE	*	$0.0075	*	$0.0214	*	$0.0056	*
26	PRIVATE LABEL	*	$0.0055	*	$0.0171	*	$0.0049	*
27	RICARDO	*	$0.0106	*	$0.0274	*	$0.0067	*
28	********************************		**************		**************		**************	
29	TOTAL COFFEE	*	$0.0067	*	$0.0187	*	$0.0048	*
30	********************************		**************		**************		**************	

	I	J	K	L	M	N	O	P	Q	R	S	T
16	---------*		---------*		---------*		----------*		-----------*		*----------	
17		*		*		*			STORE		DPC	
18	INVOICE		TRANS	*	INVNTRY	*	PRICING	*			*	*	OTHER
19		*		*		*	LABOR	*	CHK & BAG	*	*	LABOR
20	**************		**************		**************		**************		**************			**************
21	$0.0005	*	$0.0063	*	$0.0013	**	$0.0016	*	$0.0086	*	*	$0.0159
22	$0.0006	*	$0.0062	*	$0.0004	**	$0.0016	*	$0.0084	*	*	$0.0146
23	$0.0007	*	$0.0061	*	$0.0025	**	$0.0016	*	$0.0082	*	*	$0.0190
24	$0.0007	*	$0.0047	*	$0.0005	**	$0.0017	*	$0.0083	*	*	$0.0206
25	$0.0008	*	$0.0071	*	$0.0033	**	$0.0017	*	$0.0082	*	*	$0.0236
26	$0.0006	*	$0.0063	*	$0.0010	**	$0.0017	*	$0.0085	*	*	$0.0168
27	$0.0010	*	$0.0095	*	$0.0005	**	$0.0017	*	$0.0084	*	*	$0.0286
28	**************		**************		******************************				**************			**************
29	$0.0007	*	$0.0066	*	$0.0014	**	$0.0017	*	$0.0084	*	*	$0.0199
30	**************		**************		******************************				**************			**************

	U	V	W	X	Y	Z	AA	AB	AC	AD	AE	AF
16	*	----------*		----------*								
17	*		*	*				DIRECT PRODUCT PROFIT TOTALS				
18	*	SELLING	*	INVTRY	*	TOTAL		TOTAL		TOTAL		*
19	*	SPACE	*		*	WAREHOUSE	*	STORE	*	DPC		*
20	*	**************		**************		******************		******************		******************		
21	*	$0.0113	*	($0.0035)*		$0.0356	*	$0.0339	*	$0.0695		*
22	*	$0.0031	*	($0.0047)*		$0.0312	*	$0.0230	*	$0.0542		*
23	*	$0.0100	*	($0.0018)*		$0.0375	*	$0.0370	*	$0.0745		*
24	*	$0.0123	*	($0.0028)*		$0.0308	*	$0.0401	*	$0.0709		*
25	*	$0.0185	*	($0.0002)*		$0.0457	*	$0.0518	*	$0.0975		*
26	*	$0.0127	*	($0.0034)*		$0.0354	*	$0.0363	*	$0.0717		*
27	*	$0.0208	*	($0.0004)*		$0.0557	*	$0.0591	*	$0.1148		*
28	*	**************		**************		******************		******************		******************		
29	*	$0.0127	*	($0.0024)*		$0.0388	*	$0.0402	*	$0.0790		*
30	*	**************		**************		******************		******************		******************		

cells A16–AE30. All of the data in this section have been protected. Entries of new values cannot be made. Changes to DPCs that would result from implementing the hypothetical promotion scenarios in the exercises at the end of this case should be made in Section III.

Section III

Section III provides product and cost data on a specific coffee brand. Section III screens are shown in Exhibit 5. The location of the section is in cells A31–E43 and G31–J46. The name of the specific coffee brand appears in cell C34. The coffee brand data appearing in Section III can be changed by holding down the "ALT" key and pressing the letter "M." A menu will appear in the upper left of the screen containing abbreviated brand names. Select a brand by moving the cursor using the right arrow, then press Enter. All data in Columns C and I will change to reflect your selection (except C42 and I45).

Unprotected Cells	Information in Cells
C34–C41	Presents cost, price, DPP, and DPC data per unit and DPP data per cubic foot for normal nonpromoted weeks. *These cells are unprotected but data should not be entered here. The model will enter data for each brand when "ALT" and "M" are pressed and a brand selection is made.*
I34–44	Standard Direct Product Costs, as defined in Section II, that can be modified to reflect the influence of hypothetical promotional scenarios.

To change the brand data, hold down the "ALT" key and press the letter "M." A menu will appear in the upper left of the screen.

To calculate Cell C42, Cell I45, and Cells E35–42, press F9.

"What Ifing" can be practiced with any DPC in Column I. (Results of changes will be seen in Section V.)

Caution: Information in Cells C34–41 and I34–44 is not protected. Care should be taken not to inadvertently enter data here.

Comment: If after bringing up the Special Brand Menu (Alt M) you wish to "Escape" without making a selection, press "CTRL" and "Break" at the same time.

Section IV

Major assumptions of hypothetical promotional offers should be entered in Section IV. This section is located in cells A43–E50. Exhibit 6 shows the screen for Section IV. Four pieces of information should be entered into the unprotected cells of this section: the type of offer (not necessary to the function of the model), the specific case allowance in dollars per case, the projected retail price during the feature period, and the anticipated

EXHIBIT 5 Section III Screen

```
                       A                  B         C        D      E      F
31 *****************************************  ***********************************
32 PROMOTION                         PRESS ALT M FOR MACRO            *
33 *****************************************  ***********************************
34 PRODUCT                           *    GOLDEN BLEND **            *
35 NORMAL RETAIL/UNIT & /CASE        *        $2.92  **    $70.08 *
36 NORMAL % MARGIN           ·       *        8.90%  **     8.90%*
37 NORMAL DPP/UNIT & /CASE           *      $0.1905  **     $4.57 *
38 NORMAL COST/UNIT & /CASE          *        $2.66  **    $63.64 *
39 NORM WKLY SALES-UNITS,CASES       *          651  **        35 *
40 NORMAL DPC/UNIT & /CASE           *      $0.0695  **     $1.67 *
41 NORMAL DPP/CU FT & PER WEEK       *        $4.82  **   $124.02 *
42 NORMAL MARGIN/UNIT & /CASE        *        $0.26  **     $6.24 *
43 *****************************************  ***********************************


       F      G        H       I      J
31 ***********************************************
32 **  DIRECT PRODUCT COST CHANGES
33 ***********************************************
34 **   IN LABOR     **    $0.0063  **
35 **   OUT LABOR    **    $0.0166  **
36 **   WHSE SPACE   **    $0.0046  **
37 **   INVOICE      **    $0.0005  **
38 **   TRANSPORT    **    $0.0063  **
39 **   INVENTORY    **    $0.0013  **
40 **   PRICING      **    $0.0016  **
41 **   CHK & BAG    **    $0.0086  **
42 **   OTHER LABOR  **    $0.0159  **
43 **   SELL SPACE   **    $0.0113  **
44 **   INVENTORY    **   ($0.0035) **
45 **   TOT. DPC     **    $0.0695  **
46 ***********************************************
```

Note: Boldface numbers designate unprotected cells.

increase in volume during the feature period shown by entering a number times normal volume (i.e., if volume were expected to increase 50 percent, the number entered would be 1.5). Cells E46–49 will calculate the assumptions on a per case basis.

Unprotected Cells	Information to be Entered
B44	Type of offer (maximum of 25 letters)
E45	Specific case allowance in dollars per case
C47	Projected retail price during the feature period
B49	Number times normal volume anticipated during the feature period

All other data in Section IV will be calculated after pressing F9.

Section V

Section V provides an area to enter additional assumptions associated with each hypothetical promotion. These assumptions include, for example, the number of weeks the manufacturer offers a brand or trade deal prior to it being featured by the retailer. The DPP results for all data entered in other sections are also calculated in this section. Exhibit 6 shows the Section V screen. It is located in cells A51–C65 and E52. The information that needs to be entered into the unprotected cells in this section is somewhat complicated. Each of the unprotected cells is described below. An example follows these descriptions.

Unprotected Cells	Information to be Entered
C56	Enter number of weeks, if any, at pre-feature DPP before the brand is featured but while the promotional deal is in effect—for example, the two weeks preceding the brand feature but included in the period of the promotional offer.
C59	Following a brand feature, there is usually a decrease in brand volume that is proportionate to the magnitude of the feature. This cell accounts for the week(s) at that post-feature volume while the brand remains on deal to the retailer. Enter the percent of normal volume (e.g., 0.5) for the week(s).
C61	Enter number of weeks, excluding the feature week(s), at post-feature volume—for example, the one week following the brand feature but included in the period of the promotional offer.

Example: A manufacturer places a brand on deal for four weeks. For the first two weeks of the promotional period, the brand continues to be sold at its normal retail price (i.e., the brand is not yet featured). In cell C56, the number "2" should be entered to represent the two weeks. The brand is featured for one week. During the fourth week while the brand can still be bought on deal from the manufacturer, retail brand volume drops to 60 percent of pre-feature volume. The number "0.6" should be entered in cell C59 to account for this post-feature volume. To represent the one week of post-feature volume after the feature week, the number "1" should be entered into cell C61.

Definitions of Calculated Values:

C52—revised DPC, as determined by changes in Section III, Column I (Cell E52 = revised DPC per case).

C53—promotion week DPP/Loss—normal margin minus revised DPC times volume for the week(s) while the brand is featured.

C54–C63—other pre-feature/reduced volume weeks.

C55—pre-feature DPP plus any trade deal times pre-feature volume.

C58—total DPP at pre-feature week volume plus deal.

C60—post-feature DPP per week.

C63—total post-feature DPP.

C64—total DPP for all weeks.

Section VI

Section VI presents a table showing DPPs per unit, per cubic foot, and per week for the seven coffee brands. This section also provides a seven-brand average DPP and space for DPP information associated with the deals presented in the exercises at the end of the case. Section VI is located in cells A81–H100. The screen for Section VI is shown in Exhibit 6. Once each DPP analysis in the exercises at the end of the case is performed and the F9 key is pressed, the resulting DPP per unit, per cubic foot, and per week will appear in cells C100, E100, and G100, respectively. These numbers can then be entered into the appropriate cells for each exercise as follows:

Exercise 1:	C95	DPP per unit for Exercise 1
	E95	DPP per cubic foot for Exercise 1
	G95	DPP per week for Exercise 1
Exercise 2:	C96	DPP per unit for Exercise 2
	E96	DPP per cubic foot for Exercise 2
	G96	DPP per week for Exercise 3
Exercise 3:	C97	DPP per unit for Exercise 2
	E97	DPP per cubic foot for Exercise 2
	G97	DPP per cubic foot for Exercise 2

When the information above is entered into the model, average DPPs for the seven coffee brands, including the deals in Exercises 1 and 2, can be calculated by pressing the F9 key. These averages will appear in cells C98, E98, and G98.

EXERCISES

The exercises in this section were designed to provide practice in using the DPP model and to show how the attractiveness of different manufacturer promotions to the trade may vary according to how the terms of the promotion impact DPCs. Three different scenarios are presented with promotional and DPC assumptions explained. The DPC assumptions are meant to represent the probable cost changes associated with each scenario and may not be all-inclusive. Each assumption should be entered into the model in the appropriate place, and the DPP should be calculated by pressing F9 once changes are made.

1. Off-invoice trade allowance of $3.00 per statistical case on Cabana brand.
   Assumptions:
   a. Trade allowance is $3.00 (cell E45 = 3).
   b. DPC: pricing up 20 percent (cell I40 = 0.0020).
            other labor up 50 percent (cell I42 = 0.0309) to deal with out-of-stocks.

EXHIBIT 6 Section IV Screen

	A	B	C	D	E	F	G	H
43	**************************		**************************				SELL SPACE	**
44	TYPE OFFER		REDUCED PRICE FEATURE			**	INVENTORY	**
45	CASE RATE	*			$0.00	**	TOT. DPC	**
46	COST UNIT/CASE	*	$2.66		$63.84	**************************		
47	RETAIL PRICE	*	$2.92		$70.08	**		
48	MARG. @ SUG.RET.	*	$0.26		$6.24	**		
49	PROMO VOL (X NORM)		651		27	**		
50	**************************		**************************					

Section V Screen

	A	B	C	D	E	F	G	H
51	***							
52	REVISED DPC	*	$0.0695	**	$1.6680	**		
53	PROMO WK DPP/LOSS	*	$124.02					
54	OTHER WKS DPP/LOSS	*	***********					
55	NORMAL+TRADE DEAL	*	$124.02					
56	TIMES WEEKS	*	2					
57	TOTAL DPP NORMAL		--------------					
58	NON FEATURE WEEKS	*	$248.03					
59	OTHER (%NORMAL)+DEAL	*	100.00%					
60	OTHER WEEKS DPP	*	$124.02					
61	TIMES WEEKS	*	1					
62	TOTAL DPP ALL		--------------					
63	OTHER WEEKS	*	$124.02					
64	TOTAL DPP ALL WEEKS	*	$496.06					
65	***							

Section VI Screen

	A	B	C	D	E	F	G	H
81	COMPARISON OF DEALS WITH CURRENT TERMS USING THREE DPP MEASURES:							
82		*			DIRECT PRODUCT PROFIT			
83	**************************		***					
84			PER	*	PER	*	PER	*
85	CANNED COFFEE	*	UNIT	*	CUBIC FT	*	WEEK	*
86	**************************		*************		*****************		***************	
87	GOLDBL	*	$0.19	*	$4.82	*	$124.02	*
88	MINTOP	*	$0.25	*	$20.83	*	$102.50	*
89	MOGLO	*	$0.18	*	$4.70	*	$49.14	*
90	CABANA	*	$0.29	*	$6.75	*	$41.63	*
91	LATIN	*	$0.10	*	$1.32	*	$19.68	*
92	PVTLBL	*	$0.12	*	$2.26	*	$19.76	*
93	RICARDO	*	$0.16	*	$1.24	*	$12.57	*
94	7 BRND AV	*	$0.18	*	$5.99	*	$52.76	*
95	DEAL #1	*	$0.00	*	$0.00	*	$0.00	*
96	DEAL #2	*	$0.00	*	$0.00	*	$0.00	*
97	DEAL #3	*	$0.00	*	$0.00	*	$0.00	*
98	AV W/DEAL 1&2		$0.11	*	$4.34	*	$29.09	*
99								
100	PROPOSED DEAL	*	$0.19	*	$4.82	*	$124.02	*

Note: Boldface numbers designate unprotected cells.

c. Retail price change to $2.29 (cell C47 = 2.29).

d. Promotional volume times normal = 3 (cell B49 = 3).

e. 2 weeks at pre-feature volume (normal retail price) (cell C56 = 2).

f. 1 post-feature week (cell C61 = 1) at 60 percent (cell C59 = 0.60) pre-feature volume.

2. Direct store-door delivery (as opposed to warehouse delivery) of pre-packed, pre-priced floor stands of Gold Blend brand.

   Assumptions:

   a. DPC: No in-labor cost (i.e., drops to 0) (cell I34).

            No out-labor cost (cell I35).

            No warehouse space cost (cell I36).

            No transportation cost (cell I38).

            No warehouse inventory cost (cell I39).

            No pricing cost (cell I40).

            Selling space up 100 percent (cell I43).

   b. No promotional offer (cell C45).

   c. Retail price change to $2.85 (cell C47).

   d. Promotional volume times normal = 1.5 (cell B49).

   e. 2 weeks at pre-feature volume (cell C56).

   f. 1 week at post-feature volume (cell C61) at 70 percent of pre-feature volume (cell C59 = .70).

3. A pallet-sized end-aisle display with prepriced product and a trade allowance of $4.00 per statistical case delivered cross-dock (i.e., displays not placed or stored in trade warehouse but moved directly across the dock to be transported to the chain's stores) for Morning Glory brand.

   Assumptions:

   a. Trade allowance is $4.00.

   b. DPC: In-labor down 25 percent.

            Out-labor down 25 percent.

            No warehouse space cost.

            No warehouse inventory cost (cell = I39).

            Pricing cost down 20 percent (prepriced package results in much lower cost; however, prepriced stock must be placed on shelves).

            Other labor down 10 percent (restocking of shelves lower than normal because of end-aisle display).

            Selling space up 150 percent (space for end-aisle display).

   c. Retail price change to $2.19 (prepriced by manufacturer).

   d. Promotional volume times normal = 10.

   e. 2 pre-feature weeks at pre-feature volume.

   f. 1 post-feature week at 40 percent pre-feature volume.

If you were a salesperson presenting these three programs to a major trade account with the DPCs and DPPs presented in the model, what arguments would you make in each case? How might you amend or improve upon the assumptions provided? What concerns would you or the trade account have in each case? How would those concerns change if the trade account used gross margin rather than DPP to evaluate each deal?

The model also contains several graphs that can be used to compare brands and the deals presented in the exercises above. These graphs can be accessed by typing:

/GNU (This stands for the Lotus commands Graph, Name, and Use.)

The graph names will appear at the top of the screen. To view a graph, select a name using the cursor and press Enter. The graph will appear on the screen.

Case 7–4

Ukrop's Valued Customer Card*

Bob and Jim Ukrop wondered what would be the next step. The Valued Customer Card program was considered a success; indeed, Ukrop's share of market grew from 25 percent to 30 percent during the card's first year of chainwide implementation. The Valued Customer Card represented 60 percent of all store transactions and just under 85 percent of total sales volume.[1] As shown in Exhibit 1, Ukrop's had the highest market share in Richmond.[2] To capitalize on the Valued Customer program, Ukrop's was in the process of implementing Citicorp's "Reward America" program, but preliminary conclusions concerning customer response were not clear.

Following a successful recapture of many customers lost to competitors' stores, Ukrop's had initiated a new-customer-acquisition program using the same techniques. This program had, however, failed to generate sufficient interest. Thus, Bob and Jim were concerned about the future of Ukrop's target-marketing efforts. At the heart of their concern was a question of marketing philosophy. As a local supermarket chain, should Ukrop's concentrate on rewarding loyal customers, or should it spend its efforts attracting new ones? Could it consistently and effectively do both?

COMPANY BACKGROUND

Ukrop's was a family-owned and -operated supermarket chain located primarily in the Richmond, Virginia, area. The chain began under Joseph Ukrop, who started with a small market in the southern end of town in 1937. Joseph Ukrop was a man committed to

*This case was prepared by Kenneth V. Smith, as a Supervised Business Study, under the supervision of Professor Paul W. Farris. Copyright © 1990 by the Darden Graduate Business School Foundation, Charlottesville, Virginia.

[1]"Valued Shopper Card Swells Ukrop's Sales," *Supermarket News,* May 15, 1989.
[2]*Media General* Survey of Supermarket Shoppers in the Richmond area, 1989.

EXHIBIT 1   Ukrop's Market-Share Information

Market share by type of grocery buyer. The following chart(s) are from the Richmond Media
General survey of local food stores. The charts compare and contrast Ukrop's share of market
with its competitors relative to household size, income, and store location.

Market Share by Household Size

	One	Two	Three	Four +
Ukrop's	32%	33%	36%	33%
Safeway	26	19	16	16
Food Lion	7	11	14	14
Farm Fresh	8	7	8	7
Others	22	23	19	22

Market Share by Household Income ($000)

	Under $20	$20–$34.9	$35–$49.9	$50–$74.9	$75 +
Ukrop's	23%	30%	38%	41%	43%
Safeway	19	17	18	20	23
Food Lion	12	12	14	13	7
Farm Fresh	10	11	6	4	6
Others	28	22	18	18	17

Market Share by Richmond Area (Number of Stores in Area)

	Central	East	South	West-Northwest
Ukrop's	25% (1)	21% (1)	39% (10)	36% (5)
Safeway	26 (3)	13 (2)	18 (6)	19 (7)
Food Lion	6 (1)	14 (1)	15 (7)	10 (4)
Farm Fresh	8 (0)	6 (1)	6 (2)	5 (2)
Others	30 (?)	35 (?)	15 (?)	20 (?)

---

making shopping at his store as pleasant an experience as possible. Word of his emphasis
on friendly service and clean stores and his commitment to quality food at competitive
prices made his store successful. Indeed, throughout the years, word-of-mouth advertising
was Ukrop's main promotion vehicle.

During 1963, a second Ukrop's store was opened—three years later Jim, the eldest
son, graduated from William and Mary and joined his father. Bob graduated from the
University of Richmond in 1969 and joined the family business after completing an MBA
program in 1972.

Ukrop's grew rapidly in terms of both stores and sales. Its pragmatic approach to
deciding whether or not to open a store consisted of making sure it had the total number
of experienced staff needed to do the job well and the customer base needed to support
the store. Ukrop's had sales in 1988 of $270 million and estimated 1989 sales of $300

million.[3] Although requests to open stores in both the Charlottesville and Hampton Roads areas had been made, Ukrop's had no desire to expand beyond Richmond:

"We have an advantage being local," says Jim Ukrop. "We live here; we have our friends here. We talk to our neighbors [and] hear what they like and what they don't like. We're able to put our arms around our business. We can do a lot of things that companies with branches can't do."[4]

However, the Ukrop name and its reputation had spread far beyond southern Virginia:

"The stores [Ukrop's] have a national reputation for excellence," said Bill Bishop, a food retailing analyst with Willard Bishop Consulting in Barrington, Ill. "The people that know them, know them as a company that runs superb food stores. I think that far and away the most important thing that Ukrop's does is to put their customer number one. A lot of people say that, but it's not done all that frequently, and they do that."[5]

Throughout the years, the Ukrop name had translated into respectable, community-conscious business practices. Ukrop's had made the commitment to: (1) donate 10 percent of operating profit to charity, and (2) not sell alcoholic beverages. During the latest three summers, Ukrop's had donated 2 percent of sales tapes turned in by group supporters to their favorite nonprofit groups, and this component of Ukrop's charitable donations had totaled more than $2 million. According to Bob Ukrop, "Giving to charity is just the way it ought be. You can't separate what's family and what's business." Ukrop's was 100 percent family owned.

It was this devotion to excellence, community, and employees that separated them from many of their competitors (see Exhibit 2 for a list of Ukrop's corporate mission). Similar to Ukrop's, Food Lion also centralized their pricing, advertising, and buying decisions and was enjoying a period of growth. However, Food Lion achieved their strong performance by operating a no-frills business which helped keep their prices low. They eliminated slow-moving non-food items such as nonprescription drugs, and their employees worked at substantially lower wages and for fewer benefits.[6] In contrast, Ukrop's insisted on variety, and invested the money not spent on promotions into their employees. Workers were encouraged to memorize the corporate values (Exhibit 3) and recite them in public, and were rewarded for doing so.

THE RETAIL FOOD INDUSTRY

As part of the $1 trillion retail industry, the retail supermarket sector was over $300 billion in 1988.[7] On the whole, supermarkets traditionally operated with margins of less than 2 percent, and net income was often less than 1 percent of sales. Data on supermarkets were categorized both in terms of sales and chain affiliation; on average, between 1984

[3]Dun and Bradstreet, February 22, 1990.

[4]*Marketing News,* Vol. 23, Issue 12, June 5, 1989, p. 6.

[5]Ibid.

[6]Mechling, Thomas, "Food Lion: Cut-Rate Prices and Cutthroat Practices," *Business and Society Review,* 72 (Winter) 1990, pp. 39–41.

[7]Remaining figures in this section are Nielsen estimates, *Progressive Grocer,* July 1989.

EXHIBIT 2   Corporate Mission

Ukrop's
Mission Statement

The mission of Ukrop's Super Markets, Inc. is to serve our customers and community more effectively than anyone else by treating our customers, associates, and suppliers as we personally would like to be treated.

To our customers, we will provide the greatest value possible by offering wide variety and excellent service, while fulfilling our customers' desire for high quality, uncompromising freshness, and low prices. We will do our best to make their food shopping experience pleasant by providing clean stores, courteous and competent associates, and a friendly, caring attitude.

For our associates, we will promote a pleasant and challenging work environment where work can be an enjoyable experience. We will give our associates an opportunity to grow and advance according to their proven abilities and demonstrated desire to improve themselves professionally. We will fairly compensate our associates for their performance and they will share in the success of the company through profit-sharing bonuses.

To our suppliers, we will do our best to provide a fair return on their investments of time and resources. We will treat suppliers fairly and honestly by striving to meet or exceed their expectations of Ukrop's.

In our community, we will be financially active, returning 10% of our profits to the community to support worthwhile activities. We will encourage our associates to become involved in making our community a better place to live and conduct business.

We believe we can best accomplish our mission and achieve profitable growth and long-term financial success by promoting an atmosphere of mutual trust, honesty, and integrity between Ukrop's and our customers, our associates, our suppliers, and our community.

EXHIBIT 3   Corporate Values

Ukrop's

CORPORATE VALUES

We can fulfill our mission by living up to these values.

SUPERIOR CUSTOMER SERVICE - The result of great execution, a caring attitude, and a sense of urgency

HONESTY AND FAIRNESS - Treating others as we personally would like to be treated

VALUE - The best combination of price and quality

SUPERIOR QUALITY AND FRESHNESS - Uncompromising in our commitment

COST CONSCIOUSNESS - Minimizing waste and vigorously pursuing productivity improvements

TEAMWORK - Where leadership and cooperation come together

ATMOSPHERE - Safe, clean, challenging, and fun

LONG TERM PROFITABILITY AND GROWTH - A measure of success which associates share through bonuses and new opportunities

HEALTH AND FITNESS - Essential for productive and creative minds

LIFE LONG LEARNING - For personal and career growth

and 1989, supermarket chain affiliations saw their share of market increase from 69.8 percent to 71.6 percent. Share of market for small nonchain stores, those under $2 million in sales, decreased from 13.1 percent in 1985 to an estimated 11.0 percent in 1989. A breakdown of performance measures by sales volume and store size is provided in Exhibits 4 and 5.

In the 1980s, food stores saw a decreasing percentage of total retail sales. Food-away-from-home sales increased in total sales from $118 billion in 1984 to $155 billion in 1988. The retail-food-sector growth during the 1980s was predominantly in prepared and fast foods.

GROWING USE OF MANUFACTURERS' AND RETAILERS' COUPONING

During the 1980s, manufacturers and retailers had an extreme love/hate affair with coupons. In 1981, some 114 billion coupons were distributed (Exhibit 6); by 1990, over 279 billion coupons were distributed. A survey of 144 executives indicated that not only had the percentage using coupons remained strong over a 5-year period, but that the gap between couponing and other forms of promotion had increased (Exhibit 7). In dollar terms, most respondents stated that they had increased their dollars committed to coupons from the prior year over the most recent period (Exhibit 8).

Coupon redemptions had not, however, grown with coupon issues. In fact, during the period of increasing coupon distribution, the number of coupons redeemed stayed relatively flat (Exhibit 6). However, due to the increasing value of coupons, consumer savings with coupons rose during this time (Exhibit 9). Couponing, for better or worse, had become an integral part of the retail food business. Free-standing inserts (FSI) pushing a varied array of grocery products were traditionally sent out through one of four vehicles: (1) the local daily newspaper, (2) magazines, (3) the Sunday newspaper, and (4) manufacturer direct mail or in-pack. During the middle to late 1980s, more and more coupons were distributed through Sunday magazines and in direct mail or in-pack, while fewer coupons were placed in daily newspapers and magazines (Exhibit 10). Redemption rates for each of these vehicles are illustrated in Exhibit 11.

Additionally, coupons were increasing at the same time as mailers and circulars were; the number of food-store ads grew between 1984 and 1988, but advertisements placed in newspapers decreased, from over 46 percent in 1984 to 23 percent in 1988.[8] In contrast, mailers and circulars sent directly from supermarkets increased both in average size (from four pages in 1984 to six pages in 1988) and relative percentage (32 percent of the total in 1984 and an increase to 45 percent of the total in 1988).

During the latter part of the 1980s, some manufacturers, hoping to get a better handle on coupon redemptions, ran a pilot test of scannable coupons. Ukrop's and Citicorp's information service group, in what had the potential to revolutionize couponing, developed a plan to blend scanner/bar-code technology and couponing: they implemented the electronic coupon.

---

[8]Ibid.

EXHIBIT 4   Supermarket Operations by Sale Volume: 1990

		$2–$4 million	$4–$6 million	$6–$8 million	$8–$10 million	$10–$12 million	$12+ million	Average
Physical store measures:								
Selling area (average	I*	9,907	13,416	17,008	20,342	22,995	32,273	14,815
square feet)	C†	14,710	18,558	20,884	24,818	24,750	34,889	25,346
Total area (average	I	12,702	17,579	22,153	27,363	28,730	42,863	19,427
square feet)	C	18,697	23,015	26,952	31,376	32,151	44,886	32,506
Items stocked	I	10,942	14,107	16,663	19,368	18,126	23,672	11,611
(SKUs)	C	9,709	12,784	15,492	16,896	17,138	23,526	17,901
Inventory value ($000)	I	$216	$296	$367	$493	$545	$820	$337
	C	282	415	480	624	630	995	646
Front-end measures:								
Percent of stores	I	43%	64%	77%	87%	88%	96%	61%
scanning	C	37	69	75	77	88	98	80
Number of weekly	I	5,447	7,530	9,119	11,039	11,710	16,946	8,147
transactions	C	6,386	8,010	9,301	11,286	12,489	18,031	12,197
Number of checkouts	I	4.1	5.4	6.2	7.4	7.8	11.2	5.7
	C	4.7	6.1	7.0	8.0	8.9	11.6	8.5
Selling area per	I	2,442	2,482	2,739	2,741	2,939	2,894	2,618
checkout (square feet)	C	3,015	3,029	2,999	3,111	2,789	3,012	2,997
Employee measures:								
Number full-time	I	12.9	18.5	25.3	31.9	33.6	49.7	21.1
employees	C	13.3	17.1	22.1	29.6	31.5	50.3	31.4
Number part-time	I	13.9	23.6	31.3	45.0	45.5	83.3	27.8
employees	C	21.5	28.5	34.7	41.0	52.5	84.3	50.6
Full-time equivalent	I	20.0	30.5	41.2	54.6	56.6	91.5	35.2
(two p.t. = f.t. equivalent)	C	24.3	31.6	39.6	50.3	58.0	92.7	56.9
Selling area per full-time	I	494	434	411	384	405	348	419
equivalent employee (sq. ft.)	C	606	581	532	492	425	376	444
Total area per full-time	I	636	572	534	505	510	464	546
equivalent employee (sq. ft.)	C	776	728	677	623	555	480	565
Full-time equivalent	I	4.9	5.7	6.6	7.4	7.3	8.2	6.2
employees per checkout	C	5.0	5.2	5.7	6.3	6.5	8.0	6.7
Store hours:								
Hours open per week	I	90	96	101	101	108	129	95
(median average)	C	100	104	108	110	130	168	114
Hours open per week	I	93	101	108	110	118	130	102
(mean average)	C	102	113	113	120	132	143	125
Percent open on	I	89%	91%	91%	97%	93%	89%	90%
Sunday	C	98	100	99	99	100	100	99
Percent open 24 hours at	I	5%	11%	15%	19%	26%	46%	13%
least one day a week	C	7	18	19	25	45	59	24
Percent open 24 hours	I	5%	10%	14%	17%	24%	40%	12%
seven days a week	C	7	14	16	19	32	51	28

*I = Independents
†C = Chains

Source: *Progressive Grocer*, 1991

EXHIBIT 5   Supermarket Operations by Store Size: 1990

Selling Area (000's of sq. ft.)		Less than 10	10–15	15–20	20–25	25–30	30–35	35+
Physical store measures:								
Selling area (average	I*	7,220	11,782	16,732	21,551	26,662	31,994	44,466
square feet)	C†	7,501	11,955	17,553	21,851	26,444	31,596	43,609
Total area (average	I	9,801	15,794	21,663	28,101	33,907	41,762	56,120
square feet)	C	11,969	16,335	23,187	28,024	33,575	39,452	55,138
Items stocked	I	9,924	13,836	15,443	18,700	20,904	21,648	26,699
(SKUs)	C	9,130	11,363	13,811	16,818	19,014	20,920	25,001
Inventory value ($000)	I	$196	$265	$357	$458	$643	$715	$969
	C	274	354	483	555	651	784	1,172
Front-end measures:								
Percent of stores	I	39%	56%	76%	77%	92%	93%	99%
scanning	C	31	51	78	78	89	93	98
Number of weekly	I	5,640	6,858	8,638	9,909	13,234	14,650	17,451
transactions	C	6,258	8,704	10,207	10,845	12,997	14,960	17,298
Number of checkouts	I	3.8	5.0	6.0	7.3	8.9	9.3	12.9
	C	4.4	5.5	7.2	7.5	9.2	9.9	12.0
Selling area per	I	1,890	2,373	2,794	2,945	3,007	3,440	3,459
checkout (square feet)	C	1,691	2,161	2,448	2,933	2,923	3,188	3,647
Employee measures:								
Number full-time	I	13.5	16.8	22.8	30.8	38.3	35.6	51.0
employees	C	14.1	18.13	24.2	26.6	31.8	38.3	50.9
Number part-time	I	14.5	20.7	29.1	41.1	54.3	66.7	89.0
employees	C	19.7	32.3	38.7	36.0	54.8	59.9	87.6
Full-time equivalent	I	20.9	27.3	37.5	51.6	65.6	69.0	95.7
(two p.t. = f.t. equivalent)	C	24.2	34.6	43.8	44.8	59.3	68.4	94.9
Selling area per full-time	I	345	430	446	417	406	464	458
equivalent employee (sq. ft.)	C	310	345	401	487	454	461	459
Total area per full-time	I	469	577	570	539	515	594	581
equivalent employee (sq. ft.)	C	495	472	533	620	563	574	577
Full-time equivalent	I	5.5	5.5	6.3	7.1	7.3	7.4	7.5
employees per checkout	C	5.5	6.3	6.1	6.0	6.4	6.9	8.0
Store hours:								
Hours open per week	I	88	93	97	104	114	119	168
(median average)	C	95	103	112	115	115	115	138
Hours open per week	I	92	97	104	109	123	130	142
(mean average)	C	97	111	122	127	126	128	138
Percent open on	I	88%	88%	94%	93%	93%	90%	95%
Sunday	C	100	99	100	100	99	97	100
Percent open 24 hours	I	6%	7%	14%	13%	32%	42%	64%
at least one day a	C	5	21	30	39	33	34	49
week								
Percent open 24 hours	I	5%	6%	14%	11%	31%	39%	54%
seven days a week	C	5	15	24	28	29	32	44

*I = Independents
†C = Chains

Source: *Progressive Grocer*, 1991.

EXHIBIT 6 Coupon Distribution and Redemption

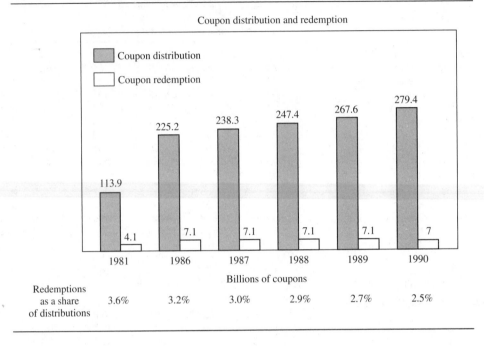

Coupon distribution and redemption

	1981	1986	1987	1988	1989	1990
Redemptions as a share of distributions	3.6%	3.2%	3.0%	2.9%	2.7%	2.5%

Billions of coupons

EXHBIT 7 Manufacturer Usage of Consumer Promotion Strategies

	Percent of Respondents				
	1985	1986	1987	1988	1989
Couponing (consumer direct)	93%	91%	96%	92%	93%
Money-back offer/cash refunds	85	85	87	85	74
Premium offers	79	58	74	68	73
Sweepstakes	77	72	66	72	70
Sampling new products	77	64	71	68	66
Cents-off promotions	78	70	69	74	64
Couponing in retailers' ad	56	45	57	63	63
Sampling established products	76	57	65	63	57
Pre-priced shippers	70	58	56	52	44
Contests	55	40	38	46	41

Source: Donnelly Marketing 12 Annual Survey of Promotional Practices.

EXHIBIT 8 Comparison of Coupon Usage: 1988 versus 1987 [based on dollars committed]

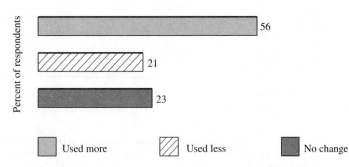

Comparison of coupon usage 1988 versus 1987
(based on dollars committed)

Source: Donnelly Marketing 12th Annual Survey of Promotional Practices.

EXHIBIT 9 Consumer Savings with Coupons

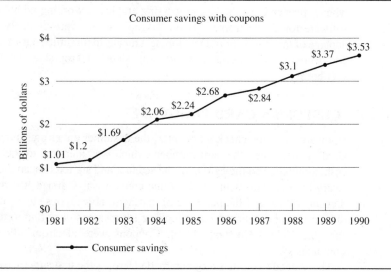

Consumer savings with coupons

Source: Progressive Grocer (10/91).

EXHIBIT 10 Grocery Coupon Distribution by Vehicle

	1984	1985	1986	1987	1988
Coupons distributed (billions)	133.5	145.5	159.4	173.9	174
Daily newspapers	40.7%	34.3%	17.4%	12.3%	9.2%
Sunday paper	42.7	49.0	67.3	73.3	77.6
Magazines	7.9	8.1	5.3	3.4	1.9
Direct mail/in-pack	8.7	8.6	10.0	11.0	11.3

Source: Manufacturer's Coupon Control Center.

EXHIBIT 11 Redemption Rates of Grocery Coupons by Vehicle

	1984	1985	1986	1987	1988
Daily newspapers	5.3%	4.7%	4.5%	4.0%	3.5%
Sunday paper	6.6	6.2	5.5	4.8	4.3
Magazines	6.7	6.3	5.7	5.4	4.9
Direct mail	8.1	7.0	6.4	5.8	4.9
In/on-pack	40.8	36.8	36.7	35.3	30.7
Instant on-pack	27.9	30.4	29.5	31.0	33.2

Source: Manufacturer's Coupon Control Center.

Ukrop's had traditionally used in-ad coupons to help build business. Consequently, when a former Ukrop's data-processing employee working with Citicorp helped develop software for an electronic coupon, Ukrop's stores were uniquely positioned to take advantage of this innovation. Developing a means to minimize out-of-date or invalid coupons and decrease coupon-handling costs appealed to Ukrop's; so the Valued Customer Card was born.

THE VALUED CUSTOMER CARD PROGRAM

Upon arrival at the checkout counter, the customer either presented the Valued Customer Card or mentioned the card number (which was identical to their phone number). The cashier then passed the card over the scanner and started to scan the customer's groceries. Every time an item with an electronic coupon was scanned, the display registered 25 or 35 cents off toward the purchase of that item; no coupons changed hands. This customer did not have to scour the paper looking for coupons nor bring to the store anything more than the Valued Customer Card. Coupons were electronically stored in the Ukrop's computer system.

The Valued Customer program made Ukrop's the first supermarket chain in the country to use electronic coupons. By 1990, over 200,000 of Ukrop's customers participated in the program.

To help defray the cost of the program, manufacturers were charged on a sliding scale, about $1,800 for each coupon they listed in the program. Indications were that manufacturers' representatives were pleased with their involvement with Ukrop's electronic couponing efforts. Dave Cottrell of Retail Services, Crozet, Virginia, asserted, "The Program [Ukrop's Valued Customer Card] moves cases better. I believe on a per-case basis, dealing with Ukrop's is now less expensive [to manufacturers] than what it used to be. To me, it's the best bargain around." [9]

Manufacturers participating in the program received exclusive coupon-category rights. For example, if there were a special on Reynolds aluminum foil wrap, then no other aluminum foil wrap coupon would be listed. Ukrop's and the manufacturer's or broker's representatives would negotiate the value and item of the electronic coupon, which would then be listed on the Ukrop's system. The value of the coupon could be determined from ad allowances, bill-backs, sales busters, or any other promotional monies available. In contrast to paper coupons, most of the cost of electronic couponing came out of the manufacturers' trade promotion budgets rather than their consumer promotion funds.

Each of Ukrop's valued customers completed an application (Exhibit 12) that requested the customer's name and address and also provided an optional section where the customer could include income, size of family, and age of primary shopper. Upon completion of the Valued Customer application (the service was free), the customer received a card; a monthly statement showed which new coupons were available for the following month, and a dollar amount stated how much money the shopper had saved to date. The Valued Customer program included both manufacturers' and in-store coupons. Ukrop's allowed its Valued Customer Card members to use paper coupons also, and if the paper coupon the customer brought was an item already listed as a special, the customer would receive the higher of the two values.

CITICORP'S INFORMATION SERVICES

Citicorp's point-of-sale information services (CPOS) group had been instrumental in making Ukrop's Valued Customer program successful. CPOS helped make the use of this highly complex and sophisticated information technology possible.

At the heart of the Valued Customer data-collection system was controller software technology developed by Citicorp and Post Software International. Each and every transaction scanned was recorded. Information was captured down to the item level. This system tracked customer purchases and was the backbone of the electronic coupon system.

Each Ukrop's store had two custom-built IBM personal computers. These PCs were linked to both the IBM POS terminal and Ukrop's scanning equipment. The customer transaction records were polled periodically by a Citicorp data-processing center.

Although Citicorp would sell controller software systems straight to a retailer, Citicorp personnel believed not many retailers would buy the technology alone. Donald Irion, a Citicorp vice president stated:

---

[9]Casewriter conversation, April 5, 1990.

EXHIBIT 12   Valued Customer Program Application

Sign up today for Ukrop's Valued Customer Program

☐ **Get a FREE Valued Customer Account and enjoy additional savings on your Ukrop's purchases.**

When you sign up for a Ukrop's Valued Customer Card, you receive a special coupon account for your family's use. Each month, we'll deposit into your account many valuable coupons from manufacturers and from our own departments. To take advantage of this wide variety of coupons, all you have to do is present your Valued Customer Card before you check out. We take care of the rest!

☐ **Save AUTOMATICALLY with your Ukrop's Valued Customer Card, without clipping or presenting coupons.**

There's nothing to clip or bring to the store! You'll automatically receive the Valued Customer savings on the products you purchased, and these savings will be printed on your register tape. You'll also receive instant savings on Ukrop's weekly in-ad coupons—also without clipping or presenting any paper coupons.

☐ **Get NEW coupons every month from Ukrop's and from manufacturers**

At the beginning of each month, Ukrop's will deposit new coupons in your Valued Customer Account. These coupons give you savings on a variety of products from all our departments—from grocery manufacturers' items to items from our deli, produce department, bakery, and meat and seafood departments. And don't forget—these coupons are in addition to the coupons featured in Ukrop's weekly newspaper ads.

☐ **Save on every shopping trip with your Ukrop's Valued Customer Card.**

Take advantage of the savings in your Valued Customer Account every time you shop by simply presenting your Valued Customer Card at the beginning of your order. All the savings available on the products you've purchased will be deducted from your total immediately.

☐ **Receive FREE Ukrop's Valued Customer News and a Valued Customer mailing each month.**

Each month, Ukrop's will mail to your home:

L Your Valued Customer shopping list, organized by category, showing all the new coupons deposited in your account for the upcoming month.

L The latest edition of Ukrop's *Valued Customer News*, containing recipes, product information, community news, and more.

L Information about upcoming promotions, changes, and improvements at Ukrop's.

Remove the temporary card and Print your name in the area indicated.

Sign Up Today! Save Today!

APPLICATION FOR FIRST-TIME ENROLLMENT IN UKROP'S VALUED CUSTOMER PROGRAM

To receive a Ukrop's Valued Customer Card and open your new Ukrop's Valued Customer Account, print the information in the blanks below. Return your completed application to any store, remove your temporary card, and start saving automatically TODAY!

Name 1.☐ Ms. 3.☐ Mrs.
2.☐ Miss 4.☐ Mr.

First   M.I.   Last   Suffix

Address

Number   Street   P.O. Box, Route, Apartment

City   State   Zip Code   Area Code   Home Telephone

If you wish to obtain an additional Ukrop's Valued Customer Card for use by another household member, please fill in the spaces below.

Additional Name

First   M.I.   Last   Suffix

By signing here, I ask that a Ukrop's Valued Customer Card be issued as I have requested. I agree to allow Ukrop's Super Markets, Inc. and their data processing suppliers to record and make use of information about the products I purchase. I would also like to receive valuable savings and special information by mail from Ukrop's Super Markets, Inc. and packaged good manufacturers.

Signature   Date

We ask for the following information to serve you better. *(These questions are optional.)*

1. Age of primary grocery shopper in your household: _____
2. Number of people in your household: _____
3. Number of children in your household: _____ their ages: _____

4. Your approximate household income:
a) ☐ Less than $25,000   c) ☐ $35,000-$49,999
b) ☐ $25,000-$34,999   d) ☐ Over $50,000

2.

It's one thing to say just because you have a computer, that computer will do everything or anything. [For example] Say your average $10 million store runs 15,000 transactions a week and there are 12 items in each market basket that goes across the register. That's 175,000 items per week, and you have thousands of households and you have to sort that data in many different ways for many different purposes. A retailer does not buy that technology to handle that kind of data storage and data manipulation needs. That requires a great deal of development effort beyond what they are capable of doing—and that's the business that Citicorp is in.[10]

In fact, Citicorp's 1989 annual report stated, "[Citicorp Information Business Division] initiatives consist of developing a point of information service that will assist packaged goods manufacturers and retailers in marketing to consumers. . . ."[11]

Part of the Ukrop's/Citicorp relationship called for CPOS to advise Ukrop's on how best to use the data. The resulting "Reward America" program was the combined effort of Citicorp, various manufacturers, and Ukrop's.

THE "REWARD AMERICA" PROGRAM

"No Coupon Clipping, No Forms, No Mailing, and No Hassles" were the claims for Citicorp's electronic couponing program, "Reward America." The program built on Ukrop's Valued Customer program and allowed consumer-goods purchasers to receive coupon discounts without the coupons. The "Reward America" program worked in the following manner:

1. Customers completed a Valued Customer "Reward America" application form, which specified that consumers list (1) name, address, and phone number, and (2) optional information about income, size and household, and age.
2. Customers shopped for participating "Reward America" brands, which would have special signs that identified them. Customers had to purchase a minimum amount of an item in order to qualify for a rebate; however, that amount did not have to be at one time. For example, if a minimum of four boxes of tissues were required to receive a rebate, the minimum could be purchased as one box per week, two boxes every other week, or four boxes in a single trip. As long as the customer purchased four boxes or more during the reward period, he or she qualified for a rebate. All purchases that qualified for the program were added to the Valued Customer's account at the register (redemptions were not cash).
3. Each month that the Valued Customer Card was used for "Reward America" purchases, the customer received in the mail a rebate certificate that gave credit toward additional purchases.

The "Reward America" program provided customers with an additional opportunity to save while purchasing specific items. The store profited because the consumers earned rebates only by purchasing items within Ukrop's. Manufacturers benefited because the program encouraged repeat purchase.

---

[10]"Ukrop's Tests Database Marketing Program," *Chain Store Executive,* September 1987, pp. 73–75.
[11]Citibank 1989 annual report, p. 24.

ELECTRONIC FUND TRANSFER (EFT)

Electronic couponing was not the only technological introduction into supermarkets during this period. Many stores were experimenting with electronic fund transfer such as debit or credit cards. Credit cards were accepted in 19 percent of all supermarkets and the number was expected to continue to grow. There were three major reasons why a store decided to introduce a credit system: (1) customer convenience—many supermarkets were expanding the number of product lines and competing directly with mass merchandisers; therefore to successfully compete they needed to accept credit; (2) faster transaction at the checkout—a credit transaction took approximately 10 seconds, comparable to cash, but considerably faster than the 90 seconds a check transaction took[12]; and (3) increased sales per customer—the average transaction amount for a credit payment was $46.00, for check $42.25, and for cash $9.09. However, there were some significant drawbacks to credit systems including: (1) an average of $20,000 per store was required for the processing equipment; and (2) bank fees—with profit margins already slim, many supermarkets could ill afford to pay the typical interchange rate. The average cost, based on a discount rate of 1.2 percent and a transaction cost of $46, for a credit card purchase was 55 cents, check 53 cents, and cash 19 cents. (Food Marketing Institute estimated that the cost of a debit card purchase was 31 cents and a food stamp purchase was 32 cents.[13])

THE TOM THUMB PROMISE CLUB[14]

CPOS had been expanding its efforts. After working with Ukrop's, CPOS helped the Tom Thumb stores in Dallas implement a program similar to Ukrop's Valued Customer Card.

Tom Thumb's Promise Club Card started as a desire to integrate electronic funds transfer (EFT) into daily operations. The card was inspired by EFT's ability to improve customer throughput and reduce bank processing fees. With a delayed-debit card, grocery customers would move through the check-out line faster, and the card's EFT capability would, after a 24-hour period, automatically deduct grocery purchases from the customer's bank account.

Customer focus groups, unfortunately, were unimpressed by Tom Thumb's delayed-debit card's capabilities. The focus group members perceived that the debit card added little value to their shopping experiences and, in essence, wondered what was in the card for them. Thus, initial Promise Club results were negative.

These negative results, and the fact that Tom Thumb's management resources had been strained from a recent leveraged buyout, almost killed the Promise Card project. Ukrop's success with buyer incentive programs, however, gave the card new life.

New strategy for the Promise Card combined marketing the successful electronic coupon

---

[12]Michael Garry, "The Credit Boom," *Progressive Grocer,* October 1991, pp. 55–60.

[13]Ibid.

[14]Blake Ives, Ruth F. Constantine, and J. Eugene, Executive Summary of *The Tom Thumb Promise Club,* Edwin L. Cox School of Management, Southern Methodist University, Dallas, Texas.

aspects found in Ukrop's Valued Customer program with the operational efficiency found in EFT. The Promise Card boasted the ability to give its holders automatic discounts from electronic coupons on grocery and consumer-goods products, as well as to transfer funds electronically from the customer's bank account.

Preliminary data from Tom Thumb's pilot project suggested that the time needed to process transactions by a Promise Club Card member was 80 seconds faster than for non-club members. Tom Thumb apparently believed, however, that the long-term payoff from the program was still to come. Essentially, Tom Thumb's management hoped that it would provide customer-profile data, thus allowing Tom Thumb to spend its advertising dollars more efficiently and "sell more groceries."[15]

UKROP'S USE OF THE VALUED CUSTOMER INFORMATION DATABASE[16]

Starting in May 1988, Ukrop's began using data gathered from the Valued Customer Card program. At this time, Ukrop's faced major competitive challenges. The first was a competitor's store opening near a Ukrop's location, and the second was a competitor opening a "superstore" in the middle of five very busy Ukrop's locations.

Ukrop's, based on data gathered from the Valued Customer Card program, was able to track those customers whose purchases dropped after the opening of the competitor's supermarket. Ukrop's then developed a plan to recover these lost customers. The plan targeted 300 customers whose Ukrop's purchases declined after the opening of the competitor's store. These customers received both a personal letter and coupons. In less than one month, 24 percent of the 300 target customers resumed their precompetition shopping patterns.

In the second challenge, where a major competitor had opened a superstore, Ukrop's identified about 3,000 customers whose purchases had decreased. Ukrop's sent half the customers both coupons and a letter inviting them back and sent the other half a letter only. This effort netted 22 percent of the "lost" customers, and no significant response difference was shown between the two groups.

Ukrop's management believed this effort demonstrated that its target-marketing efforts worked to retrieve lost customers. They therefore decided to use this experience to seek new customers.

For new-customer acquisition, Ukrop's chose areas where Ukrop's stores had a good presence but there were significant numbers of people who were not current shoppers. The program thus focused on areas where Ukrop's Valued Customer Cards were found in at least 35 percent but less than 60 percent of the target area. Management believed these areas showed a good level of Ukrop's penetration but a high potential for new-customer growth.

In order to contact these potential new customers, Ukrop's purchased a list of households

---

[15]Ibid.

[16]Adapted from Carol Beth Spivey, "Evaluating Direct-Mail Effectiveness in Building Sales and Attracting New Customers," Research Thesis, March 19, 1990.

in the target areas from Donnelly Marketing. Ukrop's then matched the Donnelly list with its Valued Customer database and eliminated matches in order to concentrate on those shoppers who did not have Valued Customer Cards.

Ukrop's used a zip code trial to test the benefits of deep-discount coupons in helping bring new customers into the store. In the trial, Ukrop's divided 7,000 households into three equal-size groups. Group 1 received a Valued Customer application form, a letter, and two discount cards entitling the shopper to 20 percent off food purchases, up to $100. Group 2 received a Valued Customer application and a letter. The letter requested these people to *pick up* two discount cards from their local Ukrop's store. Group 3 received no letters or discount cards and served as a control group.

Of the 4,667 letters and discount cards mailed, 562 were returned by the post office and 140 were redeemed by new customers during the four-week trial period (98 redemptions came from group 1; 42 came from group 2).

Analysis of the results of this mail effort revealed an initial slightly higher average purchase rate by shoppers in groups 1 and 2 when compared with control group 3. Eighteen weeks later, however, no group's shopping purchases showed any significant difference. Thus, Ukrop's management believed the incremental expense of this effort did not raise customers' purchases enough to justify its costs.

CONCLUSION

Ukrop's management now faced a new challenge. Unquestionably, the Valued Customer Card gave them better information about their customers' buying behavior: as their target marketing efforts illustrated, a Ukrop's customer could be swayed by the personal touch. However, new customers were not so easily convinced to try shopping at Ukrop's.

Ukrop's, as a niche player in the supermarket business, was still faced with how best to use its resources. For the foreseeable future, Ukrop's would continue competing against many larger supermarket chains. Management thus wanted the best use possible of the data gathered from the various information-technology options. Would EFT be a profitable strategy and if so which form of EFT would be best for Ukrop's and the customer? Should Ukrop's review its policy of stores not differentiating by price across different advertising areas? Should the new-customer-acquisition program be modified and pursued further? Would the "Reward America" program make a difference in sales? Finally, how long would electronic coupon capability continue to be a significant customer attraction unique to Ukrop's?

Agency Relations and Management

Francis, Berther & Allfreed*

Max Lewis,[1] the management supervisor of the Perque account at Francis, Berther & Allfreed (FB&A), had asked Robert Craig, Account Executive, and Tony Shorrocks, account supervisor, to meet with him that afternoon to give him an explanation of the crisis that had arisen with the account. Just before they had entered his office, however, his phone rang. Apparently he had been expecting the call, because he motioned for them to wait in the hall. Ten minutes later, Lewis' secretary waved them in. Lewis was staring out the window. When they entered, he turned to them. His face was red. "That was my good friend, Alf Lawrence, president of Hilton's Coffee Division, on the phone," he began. "And he is only a little more upset than I am."

"He feels," he continued, "that we have wasted his money producing commercials that are on the wrong strategy, when we could have avoided it. To make matters worse, we came within an eyelash of making a commercial that wasn't legal." Lewis turned toward the window again. "Finally, he threatened that he may fire FB&A if we don't have a new campaign on air by October 1, because he has promised that date to the Hilton Products Board of Directors. We've had the Perque account for 20 years, gentlemen. We are not going to lose it now. We are going to have a new campaign by October 1 or FB&A won't be the only one being fired. Is that clear?"

COMPANY ORGANIZATION

FB&A was one of the largest advertising agencies in the U.S., servicing some of the largest businesses worldwide. Throughout the 1970s, FB&A had acquired a number of advertising agencies. Though it maintained its prominence as a New York-based agency, FB&A had become a multi-office agency capable of providing an array of communications services.

Within a given office, FB&A was organized into six functional departments: account management, creative, research, media, production, and traffic (Exhibit 1). In some offices other support groups, such as a legal department, also existed. While each functional department head held responsibility for setting quality standards for his or her specialty

---

[1]All names in this case have been disguised.

*This case is based on materials prepared by John P. Foote and was written by Shauna Doyle, Research Assistant, under the direction of Assistant Professor David H. Maister, as the basis for class discussion rather than to illustrate either effective or ineffective handling of an administrative situation. Copyright © 1980 by the President and Fellows of Harvard College. Harvard Business School case 9–681–060.

EXHIBIT 1 Partial Organizational Chart of an FB&A Office

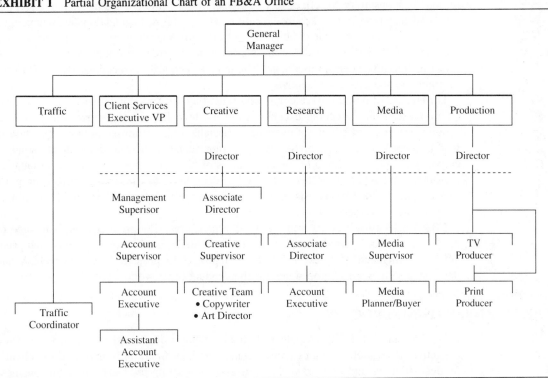

and for ensuring that work performed met these standards, FB&A employed a "product group" philosophy of organization for delivering service on individual accounts. A product group consisted of one or more representatives from every department whose work was required for a particular account. Assignment of individuals to the group was made by the department head, with members of some product groups assigned full-time, others for only a portion of their time. FB&A had a policy of rotating individuals on accounts every few years in order to ensure that no one person indirectly "owned" an account.

The actual work was executed in the various departments, and it was up to each product group member to gather together any necessary assistance as back-up in his or her department. Each member of the product group was responsible for keeping the account executive informed about changes, developments, and new information in his or her area. The account executive was responsible for feeding this information to all members of the product group to whom it was pertinent, and also for funnelling information from the client to the product group, for seeing that research findings were known to all, and for pulling together information from within the agency and outside of it.

The product group assumed a joint responsibility for the sales success of a product. Its members, meeting sometimes in small groups and occasionally as a large group, jointly sought solutions to clients' problems. The account management department held the ultimate responsibility for effectively implementing the product group system. Meetings were called and run by the account executive, who established agenda, made assignments, set due dates, and coordinated the group's efforts. Most product groups held only a small number of full meetings of the entire membership, in order to minimize the amount of unproductive time spent in meetings. The number and size of meetings were left to the discretion of the account executive.

Differences of opinion were commonly settled by "reasoned judgment" rather than by compromise or fiat. Account executives did not hold line authority over other product group members, and could not overrule a specialist (e.g., from media) on a question in that member's area of expertise. When a representative of one department failed to convince the product group of the correctness of his or her position, that representative consulted with superiors in his or her department either to confirm or correct the point of view adopted or for analysis of why it was not possible to "sell" the point of view to other members of the group.

FB&A prided itself on its informal work atmosphere. The product group's method of operation was not "formularized" since products, marketing situations, clients, and product group members' "styles" differed from project to project. However, FB&A had developed some regular procedures for the conduct of its work.

FB&A'S ADVERTISING PROCESS

In the first stage of the development of an advertising campaign (Exhibit 2), the account executive, a research account executive, and the client first jointly reviewed the client's product strengths and its market share vis-à-vis competing products. Once this business strategy analysis had been conducted, FB&A and the client were then able to define the product's marketing problems. By combining their knowledge of the customer with their knowledge of the competition, the client's needs were identified and specific advertising objectives formulated. At this stage, a "prospect profile" was also developed which addressed such concerns as prospective customers, their brand attitudes, and demographic and psychographic characteristics.

Account management, together with creative, media, and research inputs, usually developed at least three alternative strategies for clients, for which the terms of execution were explicitly stated. The strategies were then first presented to senior members of FB&A and, after the agency reached internal agreement on which one strategy to recommend, to the client for approval. After the client's approval was procured, the product group created a media work plan and a creative work plan. These planning decisions involved the selection of the appropriate medium to effectively reach the potential consumer and the creative message needed to best communicate about the product.

Once agreement was reached both internally and with the client about the strategic approaches to execution, the next stage was execution itself. From a creative viewpoint, execution included the development of "blueprints," such as storyboards for TV or the rough headlines and layouts. Once FB&A received approval from the client on the "blueprints," then the actual production began. The media execution phase was similar:

EXHIBIT 2 Development of Advertising Program

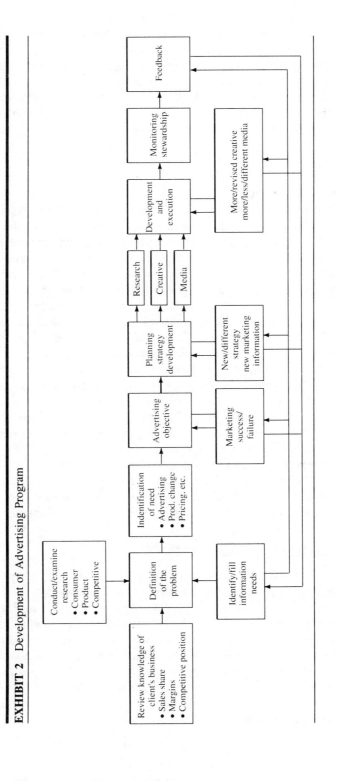

once its communications approach was approved by the client, FB&A's media department bought the client TV space, or print space was ordered.

After the execution, the advertising was monitored for its impact in terms of meeting marketing objectives, effective communication to the consumer, and for its overall technical quality. The monitoring phase provided feedback and allowed FB&A to recommend improvements to the client's advertising program. Inevitably, this led the client and FB&A back to a redefinition of the client's problems and, therefore, the need for new strategic planning.

QUALITY CONTROL

Although each department had the responsibility for seeing that the work in its area of specialization met predetermined quality standards, FB&A also had a system for evaluating the work turned out by the various Product Groups. There were three "quality control boards" at FB&A—a Strategy Review Board, a Creative Review Board, and a Media Review Board. The purpose of these boards was to assure management review of the agency's product at critical stages in its development.

When all pertinent sales, research, competitive, and other data had been analyzed, and at least three alternative strategies had been completed as the basis for creative, media, and promotional execution, the Strategy Review Board made its evaluation. Following approval from this board, the strategic work was ready for client presentation. When the creative work had been completed by the product group and approved by the management supervisor and associate creative director, it was evaluated by the Creative Review Board to determine whether it was on strategy and whether it was up to FB&A standards. The purpose of the Media Review Board was to ensure that the media execution was on strategy with the media work plan. It also acted as quality control, and made certain that all reasonable alternatives had been considered.

Independent of these quality control boards, FB&A also had in operation an *Advisory Board* which was available to product groups on short notice. This board provided independent help and advice in thinking through problems, in generating alternate solutions to these problems, and sometimes in simply contributing another perspective.

ACCOUNT MANAGEMENT DEPARTMENT

There existed four levels within the account management department at FB&A: management supervisor, account supervisor, account executive, and assistant account executive. The management supervisor was the senior line account management representative on assigned accounts. His/her areas of primary responsibility included: the supervision of important projects and the execution of the agency's policies; up-to-date knowledge of a client's business and individual product performance; negotiating with top-level client personnel when necessary; and the use of all of FB&A's resources to service an account properly. The management supervisor had overall managerial responsibility for an account, but as one FB&A supervisor commented, "I try not to get involved unless I see that things are going really badly."

The account supervisor reported to the management supervisor and had direct supervision over one or more account executives. The supervisor monitored and directed the work of the account executives in order to ensure that strategies were executed in accordance with a client's needs. The account supervisor's responsibilities also involved reporting on an account's activity to a management supervisor, and assisting the management supervisor in the long-term marketing strategy development of a client's product.

The FB&A account executive directed and coordinated the day-to-day agency efforts on behalf of the client's product. He or she maintained the on-going relationship between the client and the agency, and received client approval of proposed plans and recommendations. The account executive planned, analyzed, and evaluated the components of a marketing strategy and the agency output relevant to agreed-upon client's needs, and coordinated and managed the activities necessary to meet those needs within a prescribed time period. As one FB&A account executive put it, "The major difficulties in the day-to-day management of an account are juggling the reliance on others and checking up on everyone's activities."

The assistant account executive provided daily administrative and client service support to the account executive in order to broaden his or her knowledge base and experience in preparation for an account executive position. The assistant account executive's major responsibility was to monitor and coordinate the internal work flow, which included commercial sheets, preparation of status reports, and legal clearances. As one FB&A assistant account executive commented, "When my account executive asks me to get something done, and I can say I've done it already, I know I'm performing well."

CREATIVE SERVICES DEPARTMENT

The associate creative director primarily assessed and maintained the quality and quantity of the creative resources necessary to service each client's business, and reported to a group creative director. He or she identified creative staffing requirements for each account in consultation with the management supervisor, and maintained a liaison with account management and research. FB&A's associate creative director acted as an arbitrator on on-going problems and monitored the progress of important accounts.

The creative supervisor was responsible for developing the creative work plan on an account and for ensuring that all creative output was consistent with it through to the execution of the campaign. He or she assigned work and directed a number of creative teams (consisting of a copywriter and an art director), and monitored their creative work quality and timeliness.

RESEARCH MANAGEMENT

FB&A's associate director of account research was the senior research representative with overall responsibility for the research activity on assigned accounts. He or she had day-to-day contact with account management and frequent contact with creative management. The associate director supervised the development of research ideas, and designed research studies relevant to strategy development. As one FB&A associate director commented,

"My job is to understand the bigger issues and push for research that will be useful to the overall FB&A effort."

The research account executive, using business and research data and methods, provided direction on strategic and creative approaches for assigned accounts. He or she primarily planned and analyzed surveys and other pertinent research information, and implemented and monitored approved research studies. His or her level of client contact was limited mostly to the client's research personnel.

A NEW ASSIGNMENT

In April 1979, Robert Craig smiled to himself as he left the office of Max Lewis, management supervisor on the Perque account. "Wow!" he thought, "I've just been made the account executive on Perque, just about the most important Hilton Products account at FB&A. That's a very nice reward for doing things right."

Craig had indeed done things right since he joined FB&A three years before. During his two six-month stints as an account assistant and his two years with his own brand, he had always done what was expected of him. He'd always listened to advice from other departments and relied on them to help make decisions as to what to recommend to his client. As Max Lewis had suggested, Craig went to see Tony Shorrocks, account supervisor on Perque. Shorrocks began, "We've promised the management of the Coffee Division at Hilton Products that Perque will have a new campaign in six months. It's based on this research on usage patterns." (Exhibit 3.) "However, a lot of the groundwork has been done. We have an approved creative work plan and prospect profile." (Exhibits 4 and 5.) "Everyone believes we're on the right track. Tomorrow we have a meeting with the Perque product manager and the group product manager for decaffeinated coffees in the Coffee Division. When you hear them talk about our new strategy, you'll see that they agree, too."

Craig spent the rest of the day introducing himself to some of his new product group

---

EXHIBIT 3 Perque Consumption Patterns

	Households Purchasing Coffee		
	Caffeinated Only	Caffeinated and Decaf	Decaffeinated Only
12 months ending March 1	76%	18%	6%

	Percent of Coffee Requirements Fulfilled by Perque Among its Users		
	Caffeinated	Perque	Other Decaf
Percent of coffee consumed by Perque households that was . . .	48%	46%	5%

Source: Marketing Research Corporation of America (MRCA) Quarterly Survey of Household Purchasing Patterns for Coffee

---

EXHIBIT 4   Creative Work Plan

---

1. *Key fact:*
   Although about one-third of U.S. households use Perque, nearly half of them continue to use caffeinated coffee as well.
2. *Consumer problem the advertising must solve:*
   Dual users believe that they have sufficiently reduced their caffeine intake by using Perque only part of the time.
3. *Advertising objective:*
   To convince dual users of Perque and caffeinated coffee to use Perque exclusively.
4. *Creative strategy:*
   A. *Prospect definition:*
      Dual users of Perque and caffeinated coffee (35 +).
   B. *Principal competition:*
      The caffeinated coffee being used by prospects.
   C. *Consumer benefit:*
      Perque is the only brand of coffee you should be drinking. It is better for you and provides all the enjoyment and taste of good coffee.
   D. *Reason why:*
      Perque doesn't have the caffeine that can make you nervous and tense. Also, it's 100 percent real coffee and provides the taste satisfaction of real coffee.
5. *(If necessary) Mandatories and policy limitations:*
   None.

---

members. Ann Davis, Account Assistant, had only three months' experience, but she seemed bright and eager. Roger Bennett, Research Account Executive, explained how he and Millie Blatt in HP's research department had developed the new research summary and prospect profile Craig had received. Bennett also talked about his vacation plans. He had five weeks coming in mid-June. Craig also met Earl Okin, his counterpart in another FB&A product group specializing in industrial marketing. Okin handled a separate part of the Perque advertising account, that of promoting sales of Perque "packets" to institutions and restaurants. The separation of consumer and industrial product groups for the same brand was not unusual at FB&A. In line with many other agencies, FB&A believed that the marketing and skills in industrial marketing differed sufficiently from consumer marketing that specialist expertise was required. Even within Hilton Products, separate divisions handled the marketing of Perque to consumers and institutions. Okin commented, "We've just fielded a research study designed to identify what, if any, differences there are between in-home and restaurant consumption patterns of Perque." He agreed to send Craig a copy of the report of this study, which was due June 15th. Craig politely thanked him and left.

The next day, Craig indeed learned that the client was happy with the new strategy. "This data was really a breakthrough," noted Lou Saltzman, the product manager at Hilton Products. "Before we looked at it in depth, we had been assuming that most Perque drinkers used it almost exclusively. As a result, we had directed our advertising toward attracting new users, who were concerned about caffeine, away from caffeinated coffee." He then added, "But since we now realize that there are a lot of people who use both Perque *and* a brand of caffeinated coffee, we know there's probably more volume

---

EXHIBIT 5   Prospect Profile

Basic category designation:
Caffeine-concerned drinkers of Perque.

Category experience/usage:
Tend to drink about the same number of total cups per day as drinkers of caffeinated coffee.
   Started out as exclusive user of caffeinated coffee and continues to drink it *and* Perque.

Wants/needs regarding category:
Concerned about the amount of caffeine they take in because of impact on nerves.
Taste/flavor requirements on a par with drinkers of caffeinated coffee by compromise for
   decaffeination benefits of Perque. (May continue to use caffeinated coffee because of
   preference for its taste vs. Perque.)
Like fresh/real coffee taste and coffee that's never bitter.

Brand experience/usage:
Currently use Perque (for health reasons) and the brand(s) of caffeinated coffee which they used
   prior to trying Perque. Occasionally buy a competitive decaf (primarily Sanka, Brim, Taster's
   Choice Decaffeinated, or Nescafe-Decaffeinated) in place of Perque.

Brand Attitudes:
Do not expect, or believe, Perque to taste as good as caffeinated coffee.
Tend to perceive Perque as artificial, not real coffee.
High level of awareness of Perque's decaffeinated/health benefits. Tend to perceive Perque as
   "healthier" than competitive decafs.
Tend to associate Perque with older people who are in poor health and/or cannot tolerate
   caffeine.

Demographic characteristics:
Incidence of Perque use increased as age of household head increased (35+ represents 70
   percent of volume).
Perque households tend to be smaller (3 or fewer members), in line with older households.
Perque use tends to be slightly more in large cities/urban areas.
Education and income are about average.
Used more by women (55 percent of volume) than men.

Psychographic characteristics:
Health conscious, "hypochondriacal."
Somewhat tense, less able to relax.
More prone to dieting and vitamin/nutrition supplements than average.

---

opportunity to be gotten by increasing their use of Perque than there is by attracting new users."

Saltzman's boss, Steve Weaver, the group product manager at Hilton Products, was also enthusiastic about the new direction. "Perque has been around for a long time and has an 'old-lady' stigma to it. I think that most people who aren't using it, *won't* use it no matter what *we* do, so why should we try to attract new people? Better to let them start drinking Perque on their *own*, when they or their doctor decide that they should drink a decaf. Then we'll convince them to drink Perque exclusively. That's our safest bet for increasing volume." Craig nodded and said, "I agree. We owe a lot of credit to Bennett and Millie Blatt. They're the ones who developed the interpretation of the new data and brought it to our attention. It's great to have people like them that you can depend on for guidance."

"THIS LOOKS EASY"

Later that afternoon, Craig and Shorrocks met with Peter Fishman, the associate creative director on Perque, and Bessie Cross, the creative supervisor. Fishman assured them that, since work based on the new strategy had already begun, they would be able to review storyboards within two weeks. Craig went to his office to prepare a timetable leading up to the October air date for the new campaign, as Shorrocks had requested. Since this was only April 27th, there was plenty of time for copy development, necessary internal and client approval steps, legal clearances, and production. Craig thought to himself, "Perque's not only a good assignment, it looks like it'll be easy. All I have to do is make sure everyone else does their job on time." (The timetable, which he sent to Lou Saltzman the next day, is attached as Exhibit 6.)

Two weeks later, as promised, Fishman and Cross presented three storyboards to Shorrocks and Craig. Everyone agreed that a campaign which involved candid interviews with Perque drinkers who would talk about why *they* went from using both Perque and a caffeinated brand to exclusive use of Perque would probably be the most effective. (The "prototype" script is Exhibit 7.) It was agreed that they would present all three storyboards, but recommend production of only the candid campaign. Craig added, "The idea of producing only one campaign will make the client happy. The production budget's a little tight, and with the rising cost of TV production, we'll be heroes for keeping costs to a minimum." Getting the clients' approval wasn't difficult. Fishman's presentation was well thought out and the client agreed that the idea was a good one. By June 1, they had approvals from all levels in the Coffee Division and Hilton Products. Legal clearance at FB&A was received on June 16. Further Hilton Products provisos given in a memo from their legal department were that: (1) people interviewed could not be "led" into saying what was wanted; (2) that they now be exclusive Perque drinkers who at one time

---

EXHIBIT 6   Perque "Increased Usage" Campaign Timetable (prepared 4/27)

Week of	Activity
May 15	Internal FB&A review of storyboard(s) for new campaign(s).
May 22/29	Client approvals.
June 5	Submission of storyboard for legal clearances by Legal Department and HP Coffee Division's Claims Review Board.
June 12	Final clearances expected.
June 12	Request for production estimate.
June 26	Receipt/client approval of production estimate.
July 3	Screening for interviewees begins.
July 10	Preproduction meeting.
July 17	Shoot commercial(s).
July 31	Screen/approve rough, first edited version of commercial ("work print").
August 7	Screen/approve second, corrected print and sound track ("slop print").
August 21	Screen/approve final version of commercial ("answer print").
September 11	Ship quantity 16 mm prints of commercial to TV stations.
October 2	First air date.

EXHIBIT 7   "Prototype" Script for Candid Campaign

Announcer:

We're talking to Mrs. "X" about the reasons why she drinks Perque Decaffeinated Coffee and *only* Perque.

Mrs. "X":

I had been having trouble sleeping and I seemed to be jittery all the time.

My doctor said I drank too much coffee. I guess I was drinking quite a bit and I know caffeine can make you nervous. Well, I bought a jar of Perque like he said.

Interviewer:

Did you continue to buy your old brand?

Mrs. "X":

Yes, I wasn't sure I could give up the taste. I liked it. I figured I would use both for awhile.

Interviewer:

What then? How was the Perque?

Mrs. "X":

Oh, I was surprised at the taste. It was really good. After awhile, I didn't miss my old brand at all.

Interviewer:

And how did you feel?

Mrs. "X":

Much better. I got along with people a lot better. I guess that was because I didn't snap at everybody. Little things didn't bother me anymore. I was a lot calmer and I slept better, too.

Interviewer:

Do you buy your old brand of coffee anymore?

Mrs. "X":

Oh no. Perque's completely taken its place. Perque's the only brand I buy.

Announcer:

Perque Decaffeinated Coffee. Maybe it's the only brand *you* need, too.

---

drank both Perque and a caffeinated coffee; and (3) that candid statements could be used only if they were supported by consumer research.

As he reread the legal memo from Hilton Products the following Monday, Craig said, "Well, now there's even more consumer research." He picked up the research report on restaurant vs. in-home consumption patterns of Perque by individual consumers which Okin had sent that morning. It was about 100 pages thick and Craig had a busy schedule. "I'll send this to Bennett for his point-of-view," he thought. "He's the research expert, let him earn his keep." When his secretary reminded him that Bennett was on vacation and wouldn't be back to the office until July 17th, Craig just shrugged. "That's O.K. I doubt if a study on restaurant use of Perque means anything to us anyway. Send it to him." The estimating process also went well, although all three estimates were in excess of $40,000. The lowest bid was submitted by a production house that had experience with candid commercials, though, and Thomas had approved it without question. An interviewer who had done candid commercials for Hilton Products before and knew the legal restrictions on interviews was selected. "This has been a snap," thought Craig at the end of the well-done preproduction meeting on July 11, "everything is on schedule."

"MAYBE IT'S NOT AS EASY AS I THOUGHT"

The day after the preproduction meeting, Craig was describing the account group's role at a shoot to Ann Davis, since Davis was going to attend to add to her experience. As he finished, he added, "At a candid commercial shooting, we're kind of surrogate lawyers. It's our job to make sure that the people selected as potential 'interviewees' meet legal requirements and that the interview is conducted properly."

"I'd like to contribute something. What can I do?" asked Davis.

"Well, the production house is calling people on the phone at random to find people who are exclusive Perque drinkers," said Craig. "You could check the questionnaires being filled out on each person the production house calls. There should be about 100. This will help us make sure that we ask only the people who fit the legal criteria to come in for a 'second interview.' They're not to know a TV commercial is in the works, by the way."

"Oh, I know that," said Davis. "I know all the legal criteria."

The next morning, Davis pored over the questionnaires and selected 12 people that she felt met the legal criteria. She called the production house, gave them the names, and posted Craig on her accomplishment. Finally, as Craig had requested, she sent copies of the 12 questionnaires to the legal departments of Hilton Products and FB&A for their files.

The day of the shoot, everything was ready. The interviewer was in a small room with a hidden camera behind him. The camera was aimed at the chair in which the interviewees would sit, one-by-one. Next to the camera was a one-way mirror. Behind the mirror sat Creative Supervisor Bessie Cross, Craig, Lou Saltzman, and Davis. They could see into the room, but couldn't be seen from it. Eight people had shown up and all interviews went well. One woman, in fact, had almost made the exact statements that were in the prototype script. Her name was Pat Fisher. All agreed that shoot had been successful. "I think we got some great comments," said Saltzman, "but I'm surprised that no one talked much about the time when they were using both Perque and a caffeinated brand. I guess I expected to hear some of them talk about how inconvenient it had been. You know, buying two brands, or something like that."

"Don't worry about it, Lou," said Craig. "The shoot went well."

The next day, Saltzman's query was answered. The HP legal department called to inform him that, in their opinion, four of the eight interviewees shouldn't be used in a commercial. According to the questionnaires, it appeared that the four may have switched directly from their caffeinated brand to exclusive use of Perque. If this was so, they had never really been dual users and, therefore, didn't meet the legal criteria. Saltzman was upset when he called Craig to tell him. "Why weren't those questionnaires checked more carefully? I'm going to catch hell if we have to reshoot, and it's your fault!"

Craig finally calmed Saltzman down and suggested they set up a meeting between themselves and the legal representatives at HP and FB&A. After a few more phone calls, the meeting was set for July 27, the earliest date possible. Craig then spoke to Davis. It became apparent that she hadn't completely understood the legal restrictions. She hadn't known that the questionnaire had to *clearly* identify the person as having been a dual user at one time in order for them to be a valid interviewee. They reviewed the questionnaires of the four people in question. They were ambiguous. Despite this, Craig felt they might be able to persuade the legal department to let them use these people. He hoped they could, since these four had been the best subjects. Included among them was Fisher, the woman who had been so good.

The meeting with Hilton Products' legal department did not go well. Sheldon Baker, the Hilton Products lawyer, had discussed the situation all the way up the line. The decision was final. The four could not be used. Saltzman agreed that they should try to make the best commercial possible from one of the other four interviews. Reshooting would take too much time. Their air date was only nine weeks away. In addition, it would cost more money, and the explanations that would be demanded would be embarrassing. Craig next had to tell Bessie Cross of the decision. She was disappointed. "I've spent all my time since the shoot working on a commercial using Fisher. In fact, it's done, and I was going to show it to you today." The decision was final, however, and she agreed to start working with the four approved people the next day. She thought she could have a new commercial the following week.

"Well," thought Craig, "at least we're still on schedule. Bessie's good. She'll fix the situation."

MORE BAD NEWS

When Craig got back to his office, there was a memo from Bennett waiting for him. As he read it, the loss of the four interviews seemed to become a very small problem compared to the one the memo presented. "It appears," Bennett had written about Okin's research, "that this data completely contradicts the conclusions drawn from the household purchase data about exclusive/dual usage of Perque and caffeinated coffees. It shows that there is very little dual usage of Perque and caffeinated brands by individual consumers. Thus, it appears that although many households purchase both Perque and a brand of caffeinated coffee, the two are for different people who are exclusive users of one or the other." A chart taken from the research was attached (Exhibit 8).

The part of the memo that really hit hard was the section on "Implications." In it, Bennett pointed out that "the volume opportunity for increased usage among dual users appears to be very limited. In addition, increased usage among exclusive Perque drinkers seems impossible. Their cup consumption is already relatively high." Craig reviewed the memo with Tony Shorrocks. "This means our whole strategy could be wrong," said Shorrocks. "Does the client know about this?"

"No," replied Craig. "The research was conducted for the institutional sales product group to learn if there were any differences between in-home and restaurant consumption patterns of Perque. The Hilton Coffee Division wasn't sent a copy of the report."

"Well, I guess the proper thing to do is to request a Strategy Review Board to help us sort out the issue," said Shorrocks. "Set it up."

"But our air date is only nine weeks away," cried Craig.

EXHIBIT 8   Attachment to Roger Bennett's Memo

	Percent of Coffee Drinkers		
	Exclusive Caffeinated	Dual: Decaf/ Caffeinated	Exclusive Decaffeinated
In-home consumption	80.6%	2.3%	17.1%
	Consumption: Cups per Day		
	Exclusive Caffeinated	Dual: Decaf/ Caffeinated	Exclusive Decaffeinated
In-home consumption (Index)	3.42 (100)	3.51 (103)	3.25 (95)

Source: A Study of Individuals' Consumption Patterns of Perque In-home and Away-from-home.

"This is a critical issue," replied Shorrocks. "Our top management and that of Hilton Products both bought into the new strategy. I'm not going to change it without going through proper channels." He then added, "I guess we'd better tell Max Lewis and the client." That was that. Craig set up a Strategy Review Board for August 17 and began work on the documents the Board required.

"Incredible," muttered Steve Weaver, the Hilton Products group product manager, as Craig finished summarizing the key findings of the new research. "What does the agency recommend we do about this?"

"We've requested a Strategy Review Board for August 17, the earliest available date," replied Shorrocks. "Before we even consider a change in strategy, I want to make sure that my top management agrees. Then we'll make our recommendation."

Weaver was annoyed and it showed. "My top management expects a new campaign by October 2. That's only eight weeks from now. I want action, not a Strategy Review Board." Shorrocks tried to placate him. "They'll just have to understand. This research didn't come to our attention until just last week." It almost worked. "You have a point there," said Weaver. "But," he continued, "where the hell has this research been for the last eight weeks? The date on the report is June 15!" Shorrocks glanced at Craig who was staring at the floor. Neither knew what to say.

HOW THE HELL COULD THIS HAPPEN?

The Strategy Review Board's opinion was unanimous and concise. Perque should return to a strategy of trying to attract new users to stimulate growth. Increased usage among current users appeared to have little or no potential. Shorrocks, Craig, and the creative group recommended this to Weaver and Saltzman. They agreed and approved a new creative work plan. Craig also presented a new timetable that called for a first air date of December 1. "Lawrence won't be happy about this air date," said Weaver. Lawrence was the president of the Coffee Division and had asked Weaver and Saltzman to post him on all the details of the situation that afternoon.

"But we need the time," replied Craig. "We're starting over from scratch."

"Yeah, almost 10 weeks too late," snapped Weaver. "About equal to the delay from the first air date that Lawrence was promised."

On that unpleasant note, their meeting ended. Shorrocks and Craig headed back to FB&A as Weaver and Saltzman went to face Lawrence. Their meeting with him was reported in the opening paragraph of this case.

Later, as Craig and Shorrocks were leaving his office, Max Lewis glared at them threateningly, and muttered (loud enough for them to hear), "How the hell could this happen?" They turned around. "No, you get going. I'll deal with explanations later." As he sat at his desk, Max Lewis knew he faced some difficult decisions. He had told Craig and Shorrocks to get the new campaign going, but he did not know what that decision was going to cost FB&A. How much overtime? How much disruption, ill-will, and delays on other projects? Should he have thought about it more? He also had to decide what, if any, punitive action he should take when and if he discovered who was to blame. And what was he going to tell the Hilton Products people? Should he tell *them* what went wrong, and why? Should he "sacrifice" someone to preserve the good name of FB&A. "As management supervisor," he mused, "this is really *my* problem. What do *I* do next?"

Case 8–2

*Hill, Holliday, Connors, Cosmopoulos, Inc. Advertising (A)**

In January 1990, after years of double-digit growth, Boston-based Hill, Holliday, Connors, Cosmopoulos, Inc. Advertising, found itself confronted by one of the steepest challenges in its history.

The New England economy was in a downturn. The lagging economy affected the entire region's advertising industry, and revenues had been flat for months. As clients tightened their advertising budgets, even strong firms like Hill, Holliday began to feel

*Research Associate Cynthia Cook prepared this case under the supervision of Professor Nitin Nohria as the basis for class discussion rather than to illustrate either effective or ineffective handling of an administrative situation. Copyright © 1991 by the President and Fellows of Harvard College. Harvard Business School case 9–491–016.

the repercussions acutely. Compensating for the sagging business climate was proving difficult: since Hill, Holliday already had about 25 percent of the New England advertising market—with clients distributed across many categories—there were few sizeable new accounts it could win in the New England geographical area.

Not everything could be blamed on the economy. Over the past year, Hill, Holliday had met with limited success in its attempts to attract new business. Although the numerous uncertainties and chance events involved in the winning of new business made it hard to assess the reasons for this lack of success, it was perceived internally that the firm had suffered from the loss of "star" creative talent. There was some concern that the firm was no longer able to deliver the "breakthrough" creative advertising that had built the firm's reputation.

The agency's account executives, who were directly responsible for satisfying client needs, saw the necessity for broad change. They communicated their concerns to the agency's top management, who upon looking at the firm's financial projections for the 1991 fiscal year (beginning May 1, 1990), realized that the problem was indeed significant (Exhibit 1). Jack Connors, president/CEO and one of the two principals in the company, believed that flat revenues and increased costs would have a profound impact on the firm's profitability, and that action needed to be taken immediately.

Since the costs in an advertising business were primarily wages, with little capital investment (Exhibit 2), Connors concluded that "either everyone could take a reduction in pay, or Hill, Holliday could reduce manpower." His inclination was to seek ways to do the latter because Hill, Holliday, he felt, "had more layers of people than could possibly be efficient." Convinced that greater efficiency was necessary, Connors communicated his concerns to Felice Kincannon, managing director of the Boston office, and charged her with coming up with a proposal as quickly as possible.

THE ADVERTISING BUSINESS

History

Advertising, the attempts of a company to promote its products to potential customers, had existed as a formal industry for over a century. A feature article in *The Economist* on June 9, 1990, described the history of the advertising industry:

> The original advertising agents sold space on behalf of newspapers. N.W. Ayer's agency, which was founded in 1863, was the first to start buying space on behalf of clients. Shortly afterwards another American, James Walter Thompson, offered to design advertisements for his clients.
>
> Most of the first generation of mass-produced branded goods, such as Coca-Cola and Ivory soap, date from the same period. The new brands relied on cheap mass-manufacturing techniques to undercut local storekeepers' products. And they used advertising to appeal directly to the customer—first through newspapers, magazines, and billboards, and then through radio and television.
>
> Last year such media advertising, still known as "above-the-line" marketing, cost companies worldwide $240 billion. Add in other selling gimmicks such as packaging design and sales promotions (which are all referred to as below-the-line advertising) and the total marketing budget was $620 billion—or $120 for every person in the world.

EXHIBIT 1 Hill, Holliday Growth

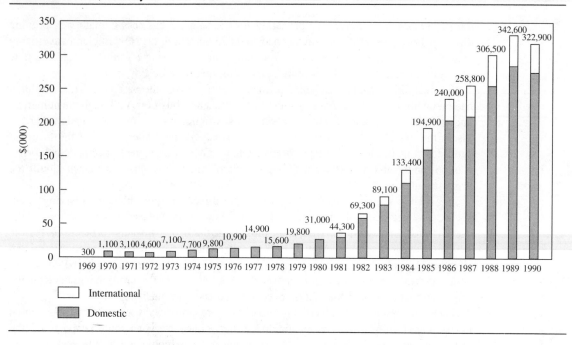

International
Domestic

Six-Year Billings Analysis—International

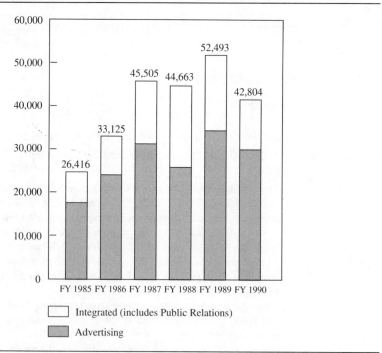

Integrated (includes Public Relations)
Advertising

Six-Year Billings Analysis—Domestic

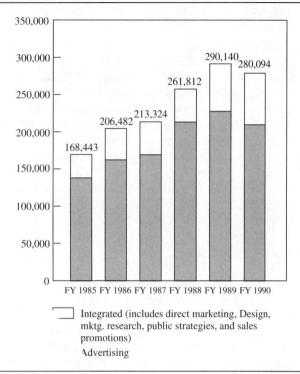

Integrated (includes direct marketing, Design, mktg. research, public strategies, and sales promotions)

Advertising

EXHIBIT 2   FY'90 Costs Worldwide (in order of magnitude)

Payroll	53.9%
Fringe benefits	11.2
Total payroll and fringe	65.1%
Office and related (rent, depreciation, etc.)	15.3
All other*	19.6
	100.0%

*Includes: non-billable client expenses, subscriptions, computer/office equipment, and office supplies.

In 1990, there were hundreds of advertising agencies in the United States, ranging from tiny two-person "shops" as firms in the industry were called—to global corporations with thousands of employees. Even the largest firms, though, were smaller businesses than their financial reports indicated. As explained in *The Economist:*

Firms measure their own size by the media-spending plus production costs ("billings") of their clients. Yet, the agencies get only a commission, traditionally 15 percent, on that expenditure.

Last year the commission revenues of the biggest western agency, Saatchi & Saatchi Advertising, were $890 million; Procter & Gamble's advertising budget alone was over $2.4 billion. The stockmarket value of the world's biggest advertising business, WPP Group, which owns J. Walter Thompson and Ogilvy & Mather, was $450 million.

The conglomerate or "mega" agencies, such as WPP Group, had numerous domestic and international offices and could offer global advertising for multinational clients. Hill, Holliday and its competitors, including Chiat/Day/Mojo, Ammirati & Puris, Weiden and Kennedy, Fallon McElligott, Scali McCabe Sloves, and Hal Riney & Partners, were smaller in size and positioned themselves as national "boutiques" that were able to produce innovative and award-winning advertising. These boutiques claimed that the very success that enabled an advertising firm to establish a global presence tended to subvert its creative edge, since agencies with more and larger clients tended to become increasingly risk averse. As competition among these "full service" agencies grew, the industry was also being shaped by firms that specialized in offering specific advertising services such as media brokerage, direct marketing, sales promotions, design, and public relations.

Agency Performance

The success of advertising agencies depended on their ability to win and retain clients. Client companies choosing an advertising agency usually invited a number of agencies to make a new business presentation. In general, potential clients gave the agencies no more than a few months to come up with a solution to meet needs that often were only vaguely specified. While companies occasionally offered a small retainer to the competing agencies, the sum rarely began to cover the cost of making the new business pitch. The stakes were high: the gain or loss of one sizable account could have a large impact on an advertising agency, and could often serve either to create or to disband an entire organization. For example, Hill, Holliday's Los Angeles office, which employed over 100 people, was set up to handle Nissan's Infiniti account. On the other hand, several international offices were closed when Wang's fortunes in the international marketplace declined.

Clients, once won, could prove at turns loyal and fickle. While only approximately 10 percent of accounts were transferred annually, companies could terminate an account at any time. Since agency performance was not concretely quantifiable, it was difficult for clients to assess the effectiveness of the relationship. Clients could enjoy and measure sales increases, but it was hard to prove that success was due to a particular advertising campaign. In the absence of more quantifiable measures, a firm's reputation was absolutely crucial. There were many highly competitive advertising award shows every year, and recognition for an agency's creative work was vital in the securing of new clients.

Companies also paid careful attention to whether an agency served any competitors, and agencies normally only worked for one company in any particular industry. When Hill, Holliday won Infiniti as a client, it resigned from the smaller Ford Dealers of New England account.

Once a company selected an advertising agency, the agency had to work continuously to develop and maintain the client relationship. Clients usually committed to 18-month affiliations, but could and did fire agencies at any time. An account executive worked to create a good relationship with the client by understanding its needs, communicating these needs to the creative staff, and helping explain the agency's product—the creative ideas—to the client. Account executives performed a balancing act between the client's desire to have advertising with which it felt comfortable and the creative department's desire to provide innovative work. It was a cliché of the business that an agency's best and most creative work was never seen by the public, as it was perceived by the client as too unusual to release. But as Jack Connors said, "There is no such thing as the right ad. There is only the one that is placed. That is the one that sells the product."

HILL, HOLLIDAY

History

Hill, Holliday was founded in 1968 by four people who left BBDO/Boston and struck out on their own (Holliday and Cosmopoulos have since left the company). The very survival of the agency was doubtful during its first months, as the partners encountered a number of unexpected and unforeseeable difficulties. For example, a telephone strike that coincided with the opening of the first office forced them to go to the bank every day, purchase rolls of dimes, and cold call potential customers from street-corner phones.

The firm grew dramatically in its first 20 years of operation. During its first decade, total billings grew from $250,000 in the first year to $15 million in the 10th. With seven years of 50 percent growth in the eighties, Hill, Holliday could claim annual billings of $300 million by the end of its second decade.

Hill, Holliday's success was traceable in part to the breakthrough creative work that the firm provided. In the 1980s, the award-winning team of creative director Don Easdon and writer Bill Heater set the tone for the rest of the agency and created advertising that was mimicked by the rest of the industry. An example of this work was the "real life, real answers" campaign produced for John Hancock Life Insurance. Later, the winning of Nissan's Infiniti account underscored the creative success of Hill, Holliday. The controversial advertising for Infiniti received much critical acclaim. The Zen-inspired scenes of nature—unusual in being the first automotive advertising that did not portray a vehicle in any way—built a unique image for the product and created an extremely high level of brand awareness. (See Exhibit 3 for examples of the firm's creative product.)

Culture

Hill, Holliday employees ascribed a large part of their firm's success to the corporate culture. Kathy Sharpless, director of the design group, summed it up as a "family culture, which starts with Jack Connors, a relatable, caring person." Connors figures prominently in employees' descriptions of the company culture. He was often described as "a charismatic leader," "a street-smart salesman," and "visionary." Felice Kincannon echoed the reactions of many when she said, "He's phenomenal! He has a very strong personality, and is very dynamic. He can talk anybody into almost anything." Employees had a sense

EXHIBIT 3

BEAUTY IS BALANCE.

In our minds, the balance of three things is essential to making a luxury car, luxurious.

Performance.

Comfort.

Styling.

No one idea is more important than the other. Each idea contributes in its way to a personal definition of luxury.

The Infiniti Q45 sedan will not disappoint a performance enthusiast.

It is also an ideal car to drive from Boston, Massachusetts to West Point, New York at peak foliage season with five adults and six suitcases.

It has a modern look. Original. The Infiniti Q45 was not styled to look like someone else's idea of a luxury car.

In a similar way, the Infiniti M30 coupe, though sportier, is both comfortable and performs well. Why?

Balance.

It's why walls that were built 200 years ago haven't fallen down and why designs that are classic in 1990 will still stand up in 2010.

If you'd like to set up a test drive, call this number: 1-800-826-6500. We'll put you in touch with the Infiniti dealer nearest you.

Thank you.

created by Nissan

```
Linda Fuller
Age:  37
Divorced; one child, age 2

Occupation  Librarian

Income
Salary                                              $20,000
Child Support                                         6,000
                                                    $26,000

Assets
Apartment Furnishings                                $6,000
Photograph Collection                                 4,000
Cash, Savings                                         4,150

Estimated Expenses
Income Tax                                           $6,400
Rent                                                  3,600
Renter's Insurance                                      150
Daycare (3 hours daily)                               2,000
Food, Clothing                                        5,000
Auto Loan and Insurance                               1,700
Miscellaneous                                         3,000
                                                    $21,850

Needs
To provide for child's education
To save money
Long-term security

Answers
John Hancock Bond Trust
John Hancock Disability Income Insurance
John Hancock Universal Life
John Hancock Cash Management Trust/Transactions Account
John Hancock Auto Insurance
```

One morning, taking her two-year-old to daycare, Linda Fuller began to think of college.

Look at John Hancock's answers to see the types of products and plans we'd suggest given her goals, her income and her obligations.

What we'd like you to see is Hancock's ability to meet real life problems with real life answers.

Contact your nearest John Hancock representative for more information or a current prospectus.

Real life, real answers.

John Hancock
Financial Services

of Hill, Holliday as being a place where only people who were "smart and nice" were rewarded. The premium placed on being "nice" was such that there were instances of valuable "smart" employees being let go when they did not meet the "nice" standard. The emphasis Connors placed on maintaining a supportive environment was expressed in his desire to make sure that "Hill, Holliday provided employees with the opportunity to take care of their lives." From 1986 to 1989, *McCall's Working Mother* cited the agency as being one of the best workplaces for women in America.

Hill, Holliday's culture was closely tied to its emphasis on promoting breakthrough creative work. The agency's emphasis on creativity led to a concern about getting bogged down with "too much organization" and "too many rules." As Dr. Jack Sansolo, the firm's president of domestic operations, declared, "we are not in a business that can be run by the numbers. We thrive on intuition. The ultimate rule in advertising is to have flexibility."

There was also an emphasis on being responsive to the needs of clients and being service-oriented. Hill, Holliday prided itself on its very high client retention rate, its ability to maintain relationships longer than was usual in the industry. The agency considered this a result of being able to work with and understand clients, instead of trying to force feed them undesired and "too-creative" advertising.

The culture of Hill, Holliday was shaped to a great extent by the kind of people it attracted. The creative departments were staffed with creative directors who had often studied art or design, and writers who had an even wider variety of backgrounds. Account executives and the managers of product groups were recruited out of undergraduate and business school. There were few MBAs. It was difficult to attract MBAs unless they had previous advertising experience and wanted to get back into the field, because there was no point in paying them significantly more than others who faced the same learning curve. The people at Hill, Holliday were young, driven, worked long hours, enjoyed public exposure, were conscious of style, and enjoyed the creative aspect of advertising. As Jack Sansolo described, "We attract very competitive people who can cope with the highs and lows which result from the constant need to prove oneself, accompanied with the imminent risk of getting fired from an account." These individuals, as was typical in this industry, often moved across firms as they tried to build their personal careers and reputations by seeking opportunities for growth.

GROWTH

Product Expansion

As Hill, Holliday grew from a local to a national firm, it moved from being an agency that provided print and media advertising materials to being a full-service communications company. Billed on a project basis, these services consisted of market research, design, direct marketing, and sales promotion. Market research helped clients with market and competitive analysis, concept testing, strategy development, product positioning, new product development, and tracking advertising success. The design department did work in such areas as corporate identity and logos, information and collateral materials, annual reports, product design and packaging, exhibits for trade shows, and point-of-sale advertising materials. Direct marketing worked with clients to enable them to reach customers by mail or other targeted media using advertising material such as brochures, catalogues, or coupons. The sales promotion department had been recently formed to meet clients' increasing needs for promotions that would build brand loyalty in light of the growing parity of most major brands. Hill, Holliday had also tried at different times to break into the public relations and public strategies areas. Management believed that these "integrated services" (also known as "integrated disciplines") served as a source of competitive advantage over the other creative boutiques, and that they enabled Hill, Holliday to match many of the services of the largest global agencies. (Exhibit 4 shows the recent growth trends of the various services provided by the firm.)

Despite the firm's expansion and diversification, however, Connors had no desire to let Hill, Holliday become a typical large advertising agency. "Hill, Holliday is a niche player," he said. "We're not and will never be a global or one-market company . . . In a world of service, this is a family business. The person whose name is on the door will greet them, feed them, and make sure their meal was satisfactory." Although Connors claimed that he did not want Hill, Holliday to become a stereotypical national firm with a "vanilla" creative product, the need for growth remained. He had to consider his and Jay Hill's investment in the company, as well as the needs of his employees. Hill, Holliday personnel had become used to an extraordinarily high level of growth, upward mobility, and a constant expansion in their responsibilities. Without growth, account managers had begun rubbing shoulders, at times uncomfortably.

New Offices

In order to win national accounts, Connors decided it was important to open an office in New York, the center of the advertising industry in the United States. An office was opened there in 1982 and was initially successful, but the managing director, who had previously worked at a much larger agency, soon began to have disagreements with the parent company in Boston. He left and took a number of accounts with him. Originally, Boston management had wanted to transplant Hill, Holliday's unique culture to New York. Frequent tampering with the New York office to achieve this meant that the office was never given a chance to be independently successful. The New York office struggled for clients, even as its existence became a matter of pride for Connors, who felt that closing it would condemn Hill, Holliday to regional stature.

To service the international Wang account, Hill, Holliday opened overseas offices in Paris, Frankfurt, Sydney, Toronto, London, and Hong Kong. The original plan was to use the Wang account as a "seed" for business in the new markets, but only the Hong Kong office achieved any measure of success. Paris, Frankfurt, Sydney, and Toronto were subsequently closed, and London remained a money-losing venture. Wang's financial troubles were a significant factor in the closing of the offices.

Most recently, Hill, Holliday had opened a Los Angeles office to service Nissan's Infiniti account. The opening of the Los Angeles office, however, drained the Boston office of some of its best talent, as several key employees from both the creative and client services areas moved to the West Coast. The migration included Don Easdon,

EXHIBIT 4

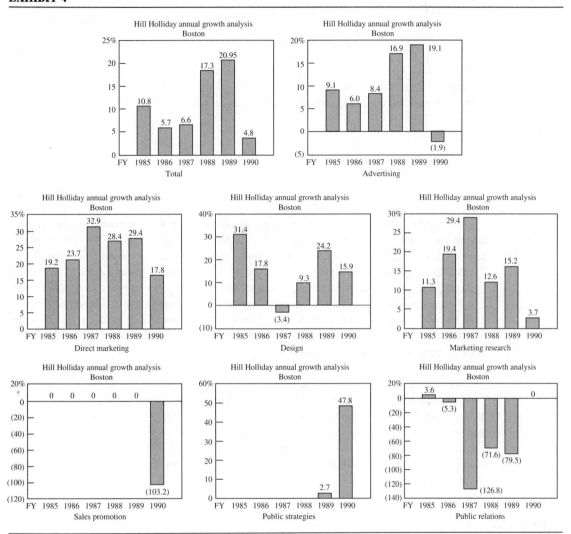

member of the Easdon/Heater creative team, who was excited about the opportunities involved in working on Hill, Holliday's largest account. Easdon's partner, however, did not want to uproot his family and leave Boston, so the creative team was broken up. Without Easdon's support and protection from administrative pressures, Heater was not happy, and quit to become an author. He continued to work with Easdon as a part-time consultant.

Hill, Holliday personnel viewed the opening of the Los Angeles office and its concomitant problems as part of the ordinary digestion process of winning a new, large account. The drain of staff and work—as the Los Angeles office grew from needing Boston office support to being able to stand alone—were unavoidable. In the Los Angeles office, there was intense pressure to retain Infiniti as a client, as that account was the mainstay of an office which would close without it. Over time, however, the Los Angeles office was able to serve Nissan successfully and won other accounts, including projects for the *Los Angeles Times* and Pacific Telephone. Having learned from the agency's experience in New York, and assisted by the distance between the two cities, Boston management avoided the temptation to meddle in the daily operations of the new office.

Creative Department

While the Los Angeles office matured, Hill, Holliday's creative staff in Boston suffered from the loss of the Easdon/Heater team. No new sizable accounts were won by the Boston office after their departure through the end of 1989. Dick Pantano was the creative director of the Boston office, and had the responsibility for checking the quality of the general advertising work presented to clients. Managing the creative department in an advertising agency was complicated; creative talent had tremendous egos and needed to be stroked and carefully nurtured. Pantano had to direct and inspire the creative staff, but also needed to produce his own work to maintain his creative reputation and credibility. In his own view, he had more creative talent than administrative expertise, so to some extent the managing of the creative staff fell to Ann Finucane, who was also in charge of account services for general advertising.

"In every creative field, advertising included," Pantano pointed out, "there are the stars, and then there is everyone else." Easdon and Heater were true advertising stars, and during their tenure in Boston they dominated the rest of the creative staff. After their departure, Pantano looked hard for replacements who would be worth the expense of up to a million dollars a year that the best creative talent could demand. Hill, Holliday management also decided to attempt to grow the firm's own talent into new stars, a lengthy process, but one that had successfully been done before—with Heater and Easdon, for example.

STRUCTURE

As Hill, Holliday grew and incorporated different services, the company was organized into different profit centers. General advertising remained the mainstay of the firm and its largest profit center. General advertising had a client services department staffed by 38 account executives and a creative department that had 26 people. Each integrated service was a separate profit center. The areas of market research, direct marketing, and design (with roughly 12, 40, and 20 full-time professionals respectively) all had their own account executives and the latter two their own creative departments. While the public strategies, public relations, and sales promotion departments had been organized as profit centers, they had since been disbanded due to their lack of success.

There were a few centralized services that were not profit centers. One of them was the media department that negotiated and monitored contracts for various media as television spots or magazine pages to place client advertisements. Most of the media department's services were employed by general advertising clients. The only integrated discipline that used them was direct marketing, and the media department charged them on the basis of the personnel who were dedicated to that work. New business development was another centralized group that was responsible for canvassing for new business and coordinating and managing new business presentations.

Each of Hill, Holliday's other offices in the U.S. and abroad was a self-sufficient entity and an independent profit center. Clients that used the full range of services offered by Hill, Holliday were often served by account executives and creative persons from a number of different disciplines. They formed what was known as a "core team" that provided all the services required by the client. Generally, the account manager responsible for general advertising had the responsibility of putting together and managing the core team.

Management Structure

Jack Connors and Jay Hill ran Hill, Holliday for 20 years, as it grew from a tiny boutique to a national firm. Connors led the account management team and set the course for the agency, while Hill and a series of creative directors managed the creative department. But Connors was an entrepreneur, not a professional manager, and as the firm continued to grow, he decided to hire a manager to make the increasingly large numbers of day-to-day operating decisions. He asked Dr. Jack Sansolo to take on this task. "Dr. Jack" (a Ph.D. in social psychology from Harvard University) had an unusual background for a manager of an advertising agency—he had run a marketing research firm in New York City before coming to Hill, Holliday to run its research department.

Dr. Jack later became president of the firm's entire U.S. operations, including the Los Angeles and New York offices, and had to pull back from making daily decisions in Boston in order to concentrate on national strategy. A management committee was put together to make decisions for the Boston office.

The management committee, which varied between six and eight members, consisted of individuals from different functional areas of the firm. The diverse viewpoints of the various members were all considered during the decision-making process. Predictably, the democracy of the system tended to impede the pace at which decisions could be made. Also, since decisions were made by committee, accountability was diffuse. Carolyn Clark, director of marketing services, claimed that "the management committee worked okay, but was blamed for a lack of vision. It became an administrative group, not a leadership group. There was no one leader, and there was constant debate." "The Jacks" (Connors and Sansolo) decided that a reorganization was required in order to eliminate the problems inherent in the management committee structure.

In September of 1989, Connors and Sansolo disbanded the management committee. They promoted Felice Kincannon to the position of managing director of the Boston office. Her duties specifically included the provision of leadership and vision for the office. Carolyn Clark was given responsibility for managing all the integrated marketing services. Ann Finucane was put in charge of client relations for general advertising, overseeing Tom Woodard and Justin Harrington who managed groups of accounts (Exhibit 5 shows the organizational chart).

EXHIBIT 5 Organization Chart (January, 1990).

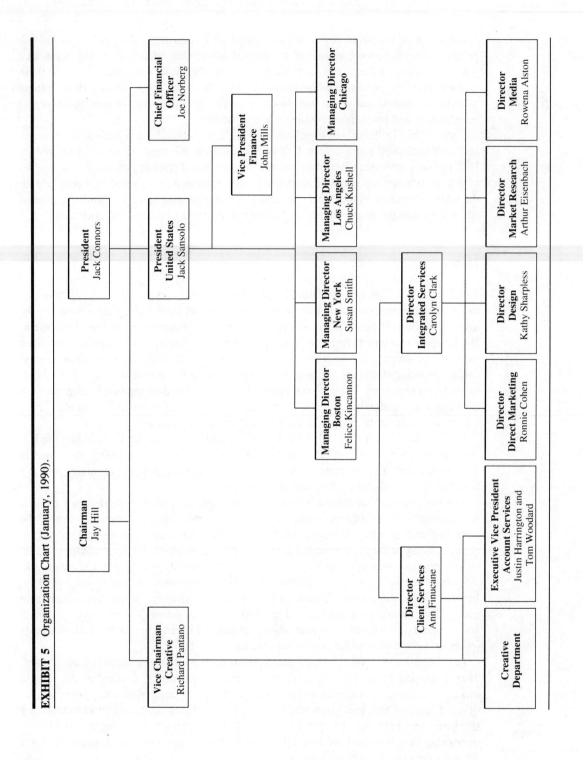

CONTROL SYSTEMS

Accounting System

Hill, Holliday had two sources of revenues, general advertising and the integrated services. Revenues consisted of both commissions on total media placements (for general advertising) and time-based fees. Costs consisted mostly of salaries and overhead. The company employed two broad approaches to allocating costs and revenues. For the general advertising part of the business, revenues and costs were measured on a client-by-client basis. Billings were measured by client and could be directly translated into revenues. Costs were allocated on the basis of the time spent by the account managers and creative staff assigned to each of the general advertising accounts. Both account managers and creative staff were required to report their time allocation by client on a weekly basis. Production costs were assigned to clients, and an additional general administrative overhead was charged as a fraction of the total staff costs. By this method, general advertising had complete profit and loss statements available on a per-client basis. For the integrated services profit centers, salaries, direct costs, and overhead were not allocated per client. These areas produced only an aggregate profit and loss statement.

Budgeting and Capital Allocation Systems

Though each profit center was required to submit a yearly budget that was reviewed quarterly, the system was not seen by the profit center managers as being very important to the way they ran their business. Dr. Jack's sentiment that the advertising business could not be run by numbers alone was widely accepted among executives. Nevertheless, profit center managers did consider it important to satisfy broadly their budgeted targets for revenues and profits.

There were few capital allocation decisions that had to be made at the level of the profit center manager. The major capital allocation decisions that had to be made for the firm as a whole were decisions regarding new business pitches. These could often cost the firm as much as $300,000, and since there was "no reward for second place," questions of allocation were taken seriously. Since allocation decisions regarding new business pitches were infrequent (4–5 per year) and did not recur on a regular basis, there was no well-defined process for arriving at them. In general, the top management of the firm would wrestle with the issues, finally arriving at a consensus view of whether they would participate in the pitch and how much they were willing to spend on it.

THE REORGANIZATION DILEMMA

Barely settled into her role as the managing director of the Boston office, Felice Kincannon now faced the challenge of responding to the charge of Connors and Sansolo to come up with a new plan of organization that would increase efficiency and cut costs. The simplest solution, in her view, "would have been to ask every department for a list of the people who could be let go. Then we would have haggled about the names on the list and finally arrived at a hard decision."

While there were precedents for this sort of response, Kincannon felt that layoffs were not necessarily the solution. Mass layoffs were not unusual in the advertising business, and Hill, Holliday itself had fired 17 employees a few years earlier. Kincannon, however, believed that the current situation was an occasion to develop more than a stopgap solution, and that it was instead an opportunity to reassess the entire organization to see if there were any genuine efficiencies to be gained. After all, one new medium-sized client could increase revenues to the point of profitability and make the layoffs unnecessary. As Jay Hill pointed out, "If we landed a $30 million [in billings] account it would solve a lot of problems." However, Kincannon could not rely on winning a new client any time soon, and costs were an immediate concern.

Her objective, therefore, was to devise a plan that allowed Hill, Holliday efficiently to satisfy three objectives: (1) to be able to provide a fully integrated communications strategy to their clients; (2) to provide improved relationship management to increasingly cost-conscious and savvy clients; and (3) to continue to be a top-quality agency that attracted the best talent in the industry to work there. To develop such a plan, she invited the former members of the management committee to join her in developing a course of action.

While all the members of this group shared the view that there were some inefficiencies in the present organization, they diverged in their assessment of its advantages and disadvantages. Much of the debate centered on the profit center structure.

Advantages of the Current Organization

One of the strongest supporters of the profit center structure was John Mills, executive vice president of finance. "In the beginning," he reminisced, "we established different profit centers when we added different functions with different skill sets. This had a number of justifications. Primarily, the integrated disciplines of market research, direct marketing, and design were distinctly different from general advertising, and people in those departments had dissimilar skills. Designing a corporate logo or a merchandise catalogue to sell products was an art unlike that involved in designing a one-page print or 30-second television advertisement intended to attract attention and create brand awareness. The creative training and expertise varied tremendously. Likewise, the talents of the account management staff were different. Account managers had to have extensive knowledge of their particular discipline." This logic, in his view, had not changed, and hence the profit center structure needed to be maintained.

The current structure allowed the various disciplines of the integrated services to maintain their own relationships with each client, separate from those of general advertising. Integrated services management felt that although this could lead to a redundancy in account management personnel, it was necessary. There was no guarantee that general advertising account managers would effectively cross-sell the value-added integrated services. Moreover, about 25 percent of the revenues of the integrated services came from clients that were not general advertising clients. It was felt that these clients could receive short shrift if not separately serviced.

A related argument for maintaining the independence of the integrated services was that account managers in general advertising and the integrated services often dealt with different contacts at any particular client firm. The corporate person who approved advertising campaigns was not necessarily the same person who approved logos, or who commissioned marketing research, or who decided on a direct mail campaign. Ed Bernard, creative director of direct marketing, said, "People make direct marketing and advertising decisions differently. Direct marketers speak a different dialect." There were few benefits to be gained by integrating the management of a particular account when individual clients might have numerous purchasing points of contact that were not directly connected. Instead, by maintaining the account executives in each integrated discipline, as Kathy Sharpless, director of design, noted, Hill, Holliday had "a lot of hooks to the client. It's easier to retain them than if there was just one key contact person who could leave."

Each integrated discipline also recruited from separate labor markets. Attaining the required expertise in each integrated discipline meant a high degree of specialization, which reduced the ability to move among departments. Certainly, account managers and creative persons in the integrated disciplines could with proper training perform the tasks of general advertising, and vice versa. In reality, however, there was limited movement among disciplines and between the disciplines and general advertising. Vic Cevoli, creative director of design, said "Creative skills in general advertising and design are not really translatable. Most creative people make that choice in school." The division of the firm along disciplinary lines allowed each area to tap into its related external labor market with ease.

Finally, the profit centers of the integrated disciplines facilitated both measurement and accountability within each department. Each discipline had to justify its existence financially. Management could easily judge what functions were financially successful, and had the latitude to add new ones with the knowledge that they could be easily measured and removed if not profitable. Management considered this an important part of the growth strategy. Jack Connors said, "We start things all the time. Most of them fail. You only need a couple of winners. And these winners have to be measurable."

Disadvantages of the Current Organization

The organization of Hill, Holliday into a collection of functionally distinct profit centers was not without its shortcomings. Perhaps of most concern was the replication of effort involved in having separate creative departments and account management teams. Each function had its own hierarchy of people who worked on a particular account. Especially during a slow economy, the costs of such redundancy seemed excessive.

This division of functions also meant that Hill, Holliday was unable to present clients with one point of contact and responsibility. Clients had to divide their approach to Hill, Holliday just as the agency divided its approach to the client.

Associated with the lack of a single locus of responsibility was the problem of internal communications. It was important for everyone working with a particular client to have an idea of the full scope of the work being done for that client, to avoid the embarrassment that might result from not being aware of all the elements of the client's program or from suggesting ideas that the client had already rejected or accepted. Yet the need to coordinate all the relevant knowledge, in Dick Pantano's view, "sometimes caused people to step on each others' toes." In an organizational structure not geared toward inter-functional communication, it was increasingly difficult to assemble and disseminate the information people needed to do their jobs.

The divided nature of the agency also meant that it was more difficult to present consistent Hill, Holliday quality. Different creative departments meant the work sent to a client ran the risk of not always being thematically unified.

Finally, when a client used only one functional area of Hill, Holliday, there was the risk that there would be insufficient cross-selling of services. Market research could not be expected to have responsibility for convincing an account to use the design department. And the design department in turn could resent the other departments for not doing a sufficiently good job of selling its services.

PROPOSED REORGANIZATION

After due consideration and much discussion with the former members of the management committee, Kincannon felt she had an initial plan for the reorganization. She decided to alter the structure of the profit centers and make "clients the basis of analysis instead of disciplines." Rather than just having profit centers organized along internal departmental lines, Kincannon planned to put together account groups, perhaps five in total, and make each one a separate profit center. Each account group would have representatives from general advertising and all of the integrated disciplines. They would also be fully staffed with creative directors and writers. Kincannon could then divide the accounts among the newly formed groups, which would be able to unite all the services performed for each client. This would remove some of the double staffing in the account services area, and would thus cut costs, meeting Connors's requirement. The basic idea, according to Ronnie Cohen, was "to organize mini-agencies by client and hold each group accountable for the performance of its client accounts."

A key factor of the proposed reorganization was that the groups would have to compete with each other for new business, in a process similar to the internal "beauty contest" creative groups traditionally held before presenting the winning idea to clients at new business pitches. This could be a divisive force at Hill, Holliday, as people fought to find a place in successful groups and as rancor was created between the competitors. Kincannon predicted that group management would have to negotiate for talented employees, arranging trades or loans if necessary. Rather than viewing the process negatively, as divisive, she thought that it would force managers to manage better and smarter, and that Hill, Holliday's friendly culture and small size would encourage people to overcome any short-term problems. "The new proposal will create tension, and good relationships will be key," she said.

The proposed reorganization also meant that the existing decision-making structure would be changed. Questions arose as to who would decide what work should be done and who should do it, how work would be charged, who would control quality, assess performance, and determine rewards, and so on. Since decision rights would be rendered unclear, they would have to be shared or negotiated across disciplines and account groups. It was difficult to say who would hold ultimate accountability in the new organization.

Accountability within integrated disciplines had given a clear responsibility to particular individuals for maintaining high product quality and excellent client service. If the disciplines became part of general account groups, accountability within the integrated disciplines would become more problematic and persons without direct experience or control of that discipline would be accountable for its successful integration into the client's overall marketing plan.

New control systems would have to be devised. Formerly, profits and losses could be assigned to each department and conceivably to each client within each department, although the latter only took place for general advertising clients. Under the proposed reorganization, each account management group as a whole and each individual client could be its own profit center. However, there would be no clear way of assessing and assigning costs for the integrated disciplines and general advertising as separate functions, because the same account management and creative personnel would perform all functions for particular clients.

The proposed reorganization threatened the integrity of the integrated disciplines, which required professionals with specialized knowledge. Ronnie Cohen, director of direct marketing, said, "We could have a big, happy, efficient relationship if we integrated, but we have to guard against losing expertise." If personnel from the integrated disciplines were divided among the account service groups, Kincannon would have to devise a method of keeping them on top of their respective fields. The plan called for retaining small departments for the integrated disciplines, with the department heads, according to Carolyn Clark, "being responsible for nurturing and integration." There were further apprehensions that if the integrated disciplines departments were completely eliminated, it would be difficult for Hill, Holliday to continue to offer cutting-edge services in these areas.

The plan also raised concerns regarding individual career paths and performance measurement. According to the plan, individuals with integrated discipline experience would be assigned to one of the account groups. Along with maintaining specialization, the functional profit center structure had allowed for career paths within each discipline. As knowledge and skill increased, people could be rewarded with increased tasks and responsibility. It was no longer clear how promotion ladders would be designed in the context of the account group structure.

If persons with integrated discipline skills were assigned to general advertising groups, performance measurement could be problematic. They would no longer be working in a department where their performance could be compared to their peers and evaluated by experts. Instead their work might be judged by non-experts who did not fully understand it. There needed to be a clear assignment of responsibility for performance assessment and measurement of individual contributions.

Some worried that the dispersal of Hill, Holliday's specialized services could lead to morale loss, as individuals with integrated discipline expertise lost the camaraderie and nurturing that came from working with people in their own fields. Kincannon understood that "advertising people have tremendous egos, and they need to be fed. Constantly."

There were other concerns regarding the proposal. It did not address the question of whether Hill, Holliday was overstaffed at the upper management level. The young, talented managers of Hill, Holliday already worked for the most prestigious Boston firm, and did not want to leave Boston's quality of life, which they considered unattainable in the city 220 miles to the southwest. Instead of letting some of them go, Kincannon could give upper management more operating duties and eliminate members of middle management. Kincannon also had to consider the effects of a young top management team on recruitment. Potential hires had to be convinced that the career ladders at Hill, Holliday were still open and that they had opportunities for growth.

Hill, Holliday employees had traditionally been rewarded with frequent promotions and salary increases. If the new proposal was adopted, they would have to adjust to a structure that would differ from that of other firms in the industry, which were for the most part organized along disciplinary lines. Titles were used as a reward, as a means of creating and recognizing status within the firm. "Jack Connors hands them out like candy," one employee said. But Hill, Holliday was not alone in having title inflation; it was endemic to the industry. Employees were concerned that if the new reorganization was adopted, it would lead to the creation of titles that were not industry standards, and that other firms would not recognize their position and level of responsibility at Hill, Holliday.

Titles were only part of a reward system that also included a monetary incentive structure. Salaries at Hill, Holliday were high for the Boston advertising market, and were essentially on par with New York. Kincannon wondered if there existed a more effective, and less expensive, way of encouraging high performance. Bonus incentives in the advertising industry were not common, and were usually received only by top managers. Kincannon had to determine if an effective incentive bonus system could be designed for people at all levels. Since there was a large luck factor in the winning of new accounts, bonus systems that were tied to new business would not necessarily reward excellent performance. Moreover, bonuses at Hill, Holliday did not always seem to be explicitly correlated with performance in the first place: employees felt that those working more closely with Connors at bonus time were often more generously rewarded. This may have been unintentional, but Kincannon still had to develop a less subjective method of measuring and rewarding performance.

Kincannon's most important task was to achieve a consensus and convince her fellow Hill, Holliday employees to accept and support the final proposal. No matter what its relative advantages and disadvantages, no plan for reorganization would succeed unless it could win the support of the firm as a whole.

Case 8–3

WPP Group and Its Acquisitions*

Martin Sorrell, CEO of London's WPP Group, supervised his firm's acquisition of New York's JWT Group, parent company of J. Walter Thompson, in 1987. Good will of $465 million was recognized on the deal, and WPP took this amount out of its shareholders' equity account, leaving the company with a negative £64 million net worth at the end of that year. But in 1988, WPP said that the brand name value of J. Walter Thompson and JWT's Hill and Knowlton public relations firm was £175 million. At the end of 1988, WPP reported shareholders' equity of positive £61 million. To outsiders, this change in value seemed impossible to explain, but the explanation could be found in a discrepancy between standard accounting procedures in the United States and the United Kingdom.

A year later, in mid-1989, Sorrell bought Ogilvy & Mather for $862 million, bringing the controversy to the forefront again. The Ogilvy & Mather brand name was also valued at £175 million. Now, even with the controversial accounting policy, WPP's balance sheet carried £600 million in long-term debt and negative stockholders' equity of £330 million. (See Exhibit 1 for WPP 1987, 1988, and 1989 financial statements.)

BACKGROUND

WPP Group plc was an enormous communications empire with revenues of nearly £1 billion in 1989. WPP's six service sectors included strategic marketing, media advertising, public relations, market research, non-media advertising, and specialist communications.

Martin Sorrell had built WPP from nothing. From 1977, after earning his MBA from the Harvard Business School, until 1986, he was chief financial officer to the leading British advertising agency Saatchi & Saatchi. But Sorrell's responsibilities there were beyond financial matters. He helped Maurice and Charles Saatchi build their small shop into an international firm touting the virtues of "global marketing" which to them meant selling a product the same way in every country.

Sorrell explained, "Maurice and Charles Saatchi used global marketing to differentiate themselves from others."[1] Eventually, Sorrell came to believe that global marketing could work for a few choice brands like Coca-Cola and Marlboro, but in reality only a small portion of an advertising agency's revenues could realistically come from such products.

---

[1]*Forbes*, July 8, 1991.

*Susan S. Harmeling prepared this case under the supervision of Professor William Bruns as the basis for class discussion rather than to illustrate either effective or ineffective handling of an administrative situation. Copyright © 1991 by the President and Fellows of Harvard College. Harvard Business School case 9–192–038.

EXHIBIT 1 Excerpts from Annual Reports of 1987, 1988, and 1989

The consolidated profit and loss accounts, end-of-year consolidated balance sheets, selected notes from the annual reports, and auditors' reports of the WPP Group plc for the years 1987, 1988, and 1989 are reproduced on the following pages.

Consolidated Profit and Loss Account* (for the year ended December 31, 1987)

	1987 (£000)	1986 (£000)	1987 ($000)	1986 ($000)
Turnover	£284,082	£23,685	$477,258	$39,791
Cost of sales	(65,160)	(17,761)	(109,469)	(29,839)
Gross profit	£218,922	£ 5,924	$367,789	$ 9,952
Other operating expenses	(197,468)	(4,502)	(331,746)	(7,563)
Operating profit	£ 21,454	£ 1,422	$ 36,043	$ 2,389
Interest receivable	3,739	530	6,282	891
Interest payable and similar charges	(11,076)	(195)	(18,608)	(328)
Profit on ordinary activities before taxation	£ 14,117	£ 1,757	$ 23,717	$ 2,952
Tax on profit on ordinary activities	(6,810)	(613)	(11,441)	(1,030)
Profit on ordinary activities after taxation	£ 7,307	£ 1,144	$ 12,276	$ 1,922
Minority interests	(222)	(75)	(373)	(126)
Profit before extraordinary items	£ 7,085	£ 1,069	$ 11,903	$ 1,796
Extraordinary items	—	32	—	54
Profit for the financial year	£ 7,085	£ 1,101	$ 11,903	$ 1,850
Dividends paid and proposed	(2,337)	(352)	(3,926)	(592)
Retained profit for the year	£ 4,748	£ 749	£ 7,977	$ 1,258
Earnings per share	32.1p	13.2p	$ 0.54	$ 0.22

*The main reporting currency of the group is the pound sterling and the accounts have been prepared on this basis. Solely for convenience, the accounts set out are also expressed in U.S. dollars using the approximate average rate for the year for the profit and loss account ($1.68 = £1), the rate in effect on December 31, 1987, for the balance sheets ($1.8785 = £1), and a combination of these for the statement of source and application of funds. This translation should not be construed as a representation that the pound sterling amounts actually represent or could be converted into U.S. dollars at the rates indicated.

So in 1986, when Sorrell left Saatchi & Saatchi, he pursued a very different strategy. He set out to acquire a number of small shops in specialty areas of marketing services. He began by purchasing a British maker of grocery baskets and used it to acquire several small marketing firms.

At that time, in early 1986, Sorrell claimed that he was "three or four years away" from making a big advertising agency purchase. But at the end of 1986, a New York analyst mentioned JWT to Sorrell. JWT, along with its affiliated public relations group Hill and Knowlton, had suffered two quarters of losses, the company's CEO and chairman had left, and major clients were putting their accounts up for review.

Meanwhile, Sorrell discovered that about 30 percent of JWT's business came from marketing services other than advertising in fast-growing sectors like public relations and

EXHIBIT 1 (*continued*)   Consolidated Balance Sheet* (as of December 31, 1987)

	1987 (£000)	1986 (£000)	1987 ($000)	1986 ($000)
Fixed assets:				
Tangible assets	£ 79,184	£ 4,801	$148,747	$ 9,019
Investments	3,464	—	6,507	—
	£ 82,648	£ 4,801	$155,254	$ 9,019
Current assets:				
Stocks and work-in-progress	37,920	1,810	$ 71,233	$ 3,400
Debtors	247,836	11,852	465,560	22,263
Assets held for resale and investments	115,273	1,040	216,540	1,954
Cash at bank and in hand	72,616	8,554	136,409	16,069
	473,645	23,256	$889,742	$43,686
Creditors: amounts falling due within one year	(454,733)	(21,510)	(854,216)	(40,407)
Net current assets	£ 18,912	£ 1,746	$ 35,526	$ 3,279
Total assets less current liabilities	101,560	6,547	190,780	12,298
Creditors: amounts falling due after more than one year	(91,333)	(2,725)	(171,568)	(5,119)
Provisions for liabilities and charges	(74,719)	(300)	(140,360)	(563)
Net assets (liabilities)	£(64,492)	$ 3,522	($121,148)	$ 6,616
Capital and reserves:				
Called-up share capital	£ 3,670	£ 1,139	$ 6,894	$ 2,139
Share premium	—	8,396	—	15,772
Merger reserve	(89,423)	(9,388)	(167,981)	(17,635)
Other reserves	13,233	646	24,858	1,213
Profit and loss accounts	6,963	2,027	13,080	3,808
Shareholders' funds	£(65,557)	£ 2,820	($123,149)	$ 5,297
Minority interests	1,065	702	2,001	1,319
Total capital employed	£(64,492)	£ 3,522	($121,148)	$ 6,616

Signed on behalf of the Board on 6th May 1988
R. E. Lerwill and M. S. Sorrell, Directors

*The main reporting currency of the group is the pound sterling and the accounts have been prepared on this basis. Solely for convenience, the accounts set out are also expressed in U.S. dollars using the approximate average rate for the year for the profit and loss account ($1.68 = £1), the rate in effect on December 31, 1987, for the balance sheets ($1.8785 = £1), and a combination of these for the statement of source and application of funds. This translation should not be construed as a representation that the pound sterling amounts actually represent or could be converted into U.S. dollars at the rates indicated.

market research. In February of 1987, Sorrell decided to acquire JWT, and with JWT's disappointing record on Wall Street, he had every reason to believe his bid would succeed. WPP quietly accumulated just under 5 percent of JWT at an average price of $31 between March and June 1987. On June 10, Sorrell surprised everyone with his $45-a-share cash bid for JWT. Five days later he raised the bid to $50.50 as rumors of rival bidders surfaced. After meeting with his advisers at First Boston Corp. on June 25, Sorrell delivered his clinching bid of $55.50. With the generous earnings multiples awarded to

EXHIBIT 1 (*continued*)   Consolidated Balance Sheet* (as of December 31, 1987)

(£000)	Freehold	Long Leasehold*	Short Leasehold*	Plant and Machinery	Fixtures and Fittings	Motor Vehicles	Total
		Land and Buildings					
Cost or valuation:†							
Beginning of year	£ 2,147	£ 88	£ 569	£1,905	£ 1,615	£ 929	£ 7,253
New subsidiaries	7,878	4,094	40,580	1,668	25,345	1,325	80,890
Additions	1,486	316	1,726	574	4,045	1,131	9,278
Disposals	(429)	(112)	(883)	(322)	(1,949)	(635)	(4,330)
Exchange adjustments	130	(155)	(5,481)	(155)	(2,985)	(103)	(8,749)
Revaluation	1,474	—	—	—	—	—	1,474
End of year (see below)	£12,686	£4,231	£36,511	£3,670	£26,071	£2,647	£85,816
Depreciation:							
Beginning of year	£ 35	£ 4	£ 93	£1,044	£ 891	£ 385	£ 2,452
Charge	190	389	1,744	728	3,287	487	6,825
Disposals	(225)	(14)	(558)	(300)	(1,158)	(390)	(2,645)
End of year	£ —	£ 379	£ 1,279	£1,472	£ 3,020	£ 482	£ 6,632
Net book value:							
December 31, 1987	£12,686	£3,852	£35,232	£2,198	£23,051	£2,165	£79,184
December 31, 1986	2,112	84	476	861	724	544	4,801

*Leased assets included above have a net book value of £322,000 (1986: £142,000).
†Basis of valuations: Plant and machinery (including fixtures and fittings) are shown at cost. Land and buildings include certain properties professionally revalued during 1987, by Messrs. James Andrew Badger (Surveyors & Valuers), on an open market, existing use basis. The historic gross cost of such land and buildings is £1,859,000 (1986: £333,000).

ad agencies in Britain, some $340 million of the $566 million purchase price came from a new stock offering and the remainder from long-term debt.

This acquisition marked the beginning of a heated debate over how to account for brand names and goodwill on the balance sheet and on income statements. After the acquisitions were completed, the two brand names together were valued at £175 million with JWT representing £150 million and Hill and Knowlton £25 million. Such substantial valuation of brand names as intangible assets had many observers questioning WPP's accounting.

Two years later, Sorrell and WPP bought Ogilvy & Mather for $862 million—26 times O&M's earnings. Sorrell rationalized the high prices he paid for both companies in the following three ways:

- The pound was strong against the dollar, making U.S. properties relative bargains.
- His stock was strong. When Sorrell bought JWT, WPP traded at about 35 times earnings, versus a multiple of about 15 for most U.S. ad companies.
- U.K. accounting rules allowed goodwill to be written off as a charge to owners' equity

EXHIBIT 1 (*continued*) Consolidated Profit and Loss Account* (for the year ended December 31, 1988)

	1988 (£000)	1987 (£000)	1988 ($000)	1987 ($000)
Turnover†	£2,251,306	£1,097,775	$4,010,702	$1,844,262
Revenue	£ 547,129	£ 284,082	$ 974,710	$ 477,258
Cost of sales	(105,313)	(65,160)	(187,615)	(109,469)
Gross profit	£ 441,816	£ 218,922	$ 787,095	$ 367,789
Other operating expenses (net)	(390,380)	(197,468)	(695,462)	(311,746)
Operating profit	£ 51,436	£ 21,454	$ 91,633	$ 36,043
Interest receivable	7,926	3,739	14,120	6,282
Interest payable and similar charges	(19,044)	(11,076)	(33,926)	(18,608)
Profit on ordinary activities before taxation	£ 40,318	£ 14,117	$ 71,827	$ 23,717
Tax on profit on ordinary activities	(18,930)	(6,810)	(33,724)	(11,441)
Profit on ordinary activities after taxation	£ 21,388	£ 7,307	$ 38,103	$ 12,276
Minority interests	(266)	(222)	(474)	(373)
Profit for the financial year	£ 21,122	£ 7,085	$ 37,629	$ 11,903
Dividends paid and proposed	(7,033)	(2,337)	(12,529)	(3,926)
Retained profit for the year	£ 14,089	£ 4,748	$ 25,100	$ 7,977
Earnings per share	55.0p	32.1p	$0.98	$0.54

*The main reporting currency of the Group is the pound sterling and the accounts have been prepared on this basis. Solely for convenience, the accounts set out are also expressed in U.S. dollars using the approximate average rate for the year for the profit and loss account (1988: $1.7815 = £1; 1987: $1.6800 = £1), the rate in effect on December 31, for the balance sheets (1988: $1.8090 = £1; 1987: $1.8785 = £1), and a combination of these for the statement of source and application of funds. This translation should not be construed as a representation that the pound sterling amounts acutally represent or could be converted into U.S. dollars at the rates indicated.

†Note on the difference between Turnover and Revenue: "Turnover comprises the gross amounts billed to clients in respect of commission based income together with the total of other fees earned. Revenue comprises commissions and fees earned in respect of turnover.

"Turnover and revenue are stated exclusive of VAT, sales taxes and trade discounts."

when purchased, rather than capitalized to be expensed as a charge against earnings in future years (as practiced according to U.S. rules).[2]

With respect to their valuing the brand names and capitalizing them, in effect reversing part of the goodwill write-off, he said, "I see no difference between valuing a brand and valuing a piece of property. Advertising agencies' names can be brands in the same way as KitKat or Polo." He was unmoved by the protests of accountants that such intangibles should not be taken into account on balance sheets. "I wanted our balance sheets to reflect a true and fair view of the value of the assets. It is unfortunate that accounting systems were designed for manufacturing companies and not for service companies."

[2]*Forbes*, July 8, 1991.

EXHIBIT 1 (*continued*) Consolidated Balance Sheet* (as of December 31, 1988)

	1988 (£000)	1987 (£000)	1988 ($000)	1987 ($000)
Fixed assets:				
Intangible assets (Note 10)	£175,000	£ —	$316,575	$ —
Tangible assets (Note 11)	86,378	79,184	156,258	148,747
Investments	4,678	3,464	8,463	6,507
	£266,056	£ 82,648	$481,296	$ 155,254
Current assets:				
Stocks and work-in-progress	£ 34,340	£ 37,920	$ 62,121	$ 71,233
Debtors	266,405	247,836	481,927	465,560
Investments and assets held for resale	13,912	115,273	25,167	216,540
Cash at bank and in hand	92,591	72,616	167,497	136,409
	£407,248	£ 473,645	$ 736,712	$ 889,742
Creditors: amounts falling due within one year	(437,079)	(454,733)	(790,676)	(854,216)
Net current assets (liabilities)	**£ (29,831)**	**£ 18,912**	**$ (53,964)**	**$ 35,526**
Total assets less current liabilities	236,225	101,560	427,332	190,780
Creditors: amounts falling due after more than one year	(140,761)	(91,333)	(254,637)	(171,568)
Provisions for liabilities and charges	(34,603)	(74,719)	(62,597)	(140,360)
Net assets (liabilities)	£ 60,861	£(64,492)	$110,098	$(121,148)
Capital and reserves:				
Called-up share capital	£ 3,973	£ 3,670	$ 7,187	$ 6,894
Merger reserve	(150,603)	(89,423)	(272,441)	(167,981)
Other reserves	185,259	13,233	335,134	24,858
Profit and loss accounts	21,052	6,963	38,083	13,080
Shareholders' funds	£ 59,681	£ (65,557)	$107,963	$(123,149)
Minority interests	1,180	1,065	2,135	2,001
Total capital employed	£ 60,861	£(64,492)	$110,098	($121,148)

Signed on behalf of the Board on 9 May 1989
R. E. Lerwill and M. S. Sorrell, Directors

*The main reporting currency of the Group is the pound sterling and the accounts have been prepared on this basis. Solely for convenience, the accounts set out are also expressed in U.S. dollars using the approximate average rate for the year for the profit and loss account (1988: $1.7815 = £1; 1987: $1.6800 = £1), the rate in effect on December 31, for the balance sheets (1988: $1.8090 = £1; 1987: $1.8785 = £1), and a combination of these for the statement of source and application of funds. This translation should not be construed as a representation that the pound sterling amounts actually represent or could be converted into U.S. dollars at the rates indicated.

EXHIBIT 1 (*continued*)   Notes to the Accounts (December 31, 1988)

Note 10—Intangible Fixed Assets

	1988 (£000)	1987 (£000)
Corporate brand names	£175,000	—

Corporate brand names represent the directors' valuation of the brand names J. Walter Thompson and Hill and Knowlton which were acquired in 1987 as part of JWT Group, Inc. These assets have been valued under the Alternative Accounting Rules of the Companies Act 1985 in accordance with the group's accounting policy for intangible fixed assets. The directors in the course of their valuation have consulted their advisers Samuel Montagu & Co. Limited.

Note 11—Tangible Fixed Assets

(a) Group

The movement in the year was as follows:

(£000)	Land and Buildings			Plant and Machinery	Fixtures and Fittings	Motor Vehicles	Total
	Freehold	Long Leasehold*	Short Leasehold*				
Cost or valuation:†							
Beginning of year	£12,686	£4,231	£36,511	£3,670	£26,071	£2,647	£ 85,816
New subsidiaries	1,099	163	507	719	1,856	441	4,785
Reclassification	—	(2,523)	2,523	—	—	—	—
Additions	2,122	325	1,776	1,493	8,244	3,055	17,015
Disposals	(5,732)	(26)	(2,022)	(1,274)	(2,188)	(990)	(12,232)
Exchange adjustments	649	494	2,117	185	1,435	52	4,932
Revaluation	3,202	—	1,350	—	—	—	4,552
End of year	£14,026	£2,664	£42,762	£4,793	£35,418	£5,205	£104,868
Depreciation:							
Beginning of year	£ —	£ 379	£ 1,279	£1,472	£ 3,020	£ 482	£ 6,632
Charge	275	154	3,896	599	5,572	1,123	11,619
Disposals	(204)	(20)	(42)	(208)	(521)	(402)	(1,397)
Exchange adjustments	40	31	677	110	760	18	1,636
End of year	£ 111	£ 544	£ 5,810	£1,973	£ 8,831	£1,221	£ 18,490
Net book value:							
December 31, 1988	£13,915	£2,120	£36,952	£2,820	£26,587	£3,984	£86,378
December 31, 1987	12,686	3,852	35,232	2,198	23,051	2,165	79,184

*Leased assets (other than leasehold property) included above have a net book value of £1,373,000 (1987: £322,000).

†Basis of valuation: Plant and machinery (including fixtures and fittings) are shown at cost. Land an buildings include certain properties professionally revalued during 1987 and 1988, by James Andrew Badger (Surveyors & Valuers), on an open market, existing use basis. The historic net book value of such land and buildings is £6,511,000 (1987: £1,859,000).

Auditor's Report

To the members of WPP Group plc:

We have audited the accounts set out on pages 63 to 84 in accordance with approved Auditing Standards.

In our opinion, the accounts, which have been prepared under the historical cost convention, as modified by the revaluation of land and buildings and corporate brand names, give a true and fair view of the state of affairs of the Company and of the Group at 31 December 1988 and of the Group profit and source and application of funds for the year then ended, and comply with the Companies Act 1985.

Arthur Andersen & Co.

London

9 May 1989

EXHIBIT 1 (*continued*) Consolidated Profit and Loss Account* (for the years ended December 31, 1989)

	1989 (£000)	1988 (£000)	1989 ($000)	1988 ($000)
Turnover†	£4,406,898	£2,251,306	$7,190,735	$4,010,702
Revenue	£1,005,453	£ 547,129	$1,640,598	$ 974,710
Gross profit	£ 843,032	£ 441,816	$1,375,575	$ 787,095
Other operating expenses (net)	(740,550)	(390,380)	(1,208,355)	(695,462)
Operating profit	£ 102,482	£ 51,436	$ 167,220	$ 91,633
Interest receivable	16,072	7,926	26,224	14,120
Interest payable and similar charges	(43,515)	(19,044)	(71,003)	(33,926)
Profit on ordinary activities before taxation	$ 75,039	$ 40,318	$ 122,441	$ 71,827
Tax on profit on ordinary activities	(34,532)	(18,930)	(56,346)	(33,724)
Profit on ordinary activities after taxation	£ 40,507	£ 21,388	$ 66,095	$ 38,103
Minority interests	(2,306)	(266)	(3,763)	(474)
Profit for the financial year	£ 38,201	£ 21,122	$ 62,332	$ 37,629
Preference dividends	(8,413)	—	(13,727)	—
Profit attributable to ordinary shareholders	£ 29,788	£ 21,122	$ 48,605	$ 37,629
Ordinary dividends	(9,913)	(7,033)	(16,175)	(12,529)
Retained profit for the year	£ 19,875	£ 14,089	$ 32,430	$ 25,100
Earnings per share:				
Basic	73.0p	54.3p	$1.19	$0.97
Fully diluted	71.2p	NA	$1.16	NA

*The main reporting currency of the Group is the pound sterling and the accounts have been prepared on this basis. Solely for convenience, the accounts set out are also expressed in U.S. dollars using the approximate average rate for the year for the profit and loss account (1989: $1.6317 = £1; 1988: $1.7815 = £1), the rate in effect on December 31 for the balance sheets (1989: $1.6125 = £1; 1988: $1.8090 = £1), and a combination of these for the statement of source and application of funds. This translation should not be construed as a representation that the pound sterling amounts actually represent, or could be converted into U.S. dollars at the rates indicated.

†Note on the difference between Turnover and Revenue: "Turnover comprises the gross amounts billed to clients in respect of commission based income together with the total of other fees earned. Revenue comprises commissions and fees earned in respect of turnover.

"Turnover and revenue are stated exclusive of VAT, sales taxes and trade discounts."

EXHIBIT 1 (*continued*)   Conslidated Balance Sheet* (as of December 31, 1989)

	1989 (£000)	1988 (£000)	1989 ($000)	1988
Fixed assets:				
Intangible assets (Note 9)	£ 350,000	£ 175,000	$ 564,375	$ 316,575
Tangible assets	156,583	86,378	252,400	156,758
Investments	19,774	4,678	31,886	8,463
	£ 526,357	£ 266,056	$ 848,751	$ 481,296
Current assets:				
Stocks and work-in-progress	£ 91,004	£ 34,340	$ 146,744	$ 62,121
Debtors	648,778	266,405	1,046,155	481,927
Investments and assets held for resale	6,759	13,912	10,899	25,167
Cash at bank and in hand	233,016	92,591	376,707	167,497
	£ 980,158	£ 407,248	$1,580,505	$ 736,712
Creditors: amounts falling due within one year	(1,149,858)	(437,079)	(1,854,146)	(790,676)
Net current assets	£ (169,700)	£ (29,831)	$ (273,641)	$ (53,964)
Total assets less current liabilities	356,657	236,225	(575,110)	427,332
Creditors: amounts falling due after more than one year	(535,618)	(140,761)	(863,684)	(254,637)
Provisions for liabilities and charges	(151,170)	(34,603)	(243,762)	(62,597)
Net (liabilities) assets	£ (330,131)	£ 60,861	$ (532,336)	$ 110,098
Capital and reserves:				
Called-up share capital	£ 25,505	£ 3,973	$ 41,127	$ 7,187
Share premium	192,721	—	310,763	—
Goodwill reserve	(797,811)	(150,603)	(1,286,470)	(272,441)
Other reserves	196,247	185,259	316,447	335,134
Profit and loss accounts	40,927	21,052	65,995	38,083
Shareholders' funds	£ (342,411)	£ (59,681)	$ (552,138)	$ 107,963
Minority interests	12,280	1,180	19,802	2,135
Total capital employed	£ (330,131)	£ 60,861	$ (532,336)	$ 110,098

Signed on behalf of the Board on 9 May 1989
R. E. Lerwill and M. S. Sorrell, Directors

   *The main reporting currency of the Group is the pound sterling and the accounts have been prepared on this basis. Solely for convenience, the accounts set out are also expressed in U.S. dollars using the approximate average rate for the year for the profit and loss account (1989: $1.6317 = £1; 1988: $1.7815 = £1), the rate in effect on December 31 for the balance sheets (1989: $1.6125 = £1; 1988: $1.8090 = £1), and a combination of these for the statement of source and application of funds. This translation should not be construed as a representation that the pound sterling amounts actually represent or could be converted into U.S. dollars at the rates indicated.

EXHIBIT 1 (*continued*)   Notes to the Accounts

Note 9—Intangible Fixed Assets

Value of Corporate Brand Names	(£000)
Beginning of year	£175,000
Additions at fair value to the group—Ogilvy & Mather	175,000
End of year	£350,000

Corporate brand names represent the directors' valuation of the brand names J. Walter Thompson and Hill and Knowlton which were valued in 1988 and Ogilvy & Mather acquired in 1989 as part of The Ogilvy Group, Inc. These assets have been valued in accordance with the group's accounting policy for intangible fixed assets and in the course of this valuation the directors have consulted their advisers, Samuel Montagu & Co. Limited.

Note 10—Tangible Fixed Assets

a) Group
The movement in the year was as follows:

(£000)	Land and Buildings		Fixtures, Fittings and Equipment	Total
	Freehold	Leasehold*		
Cost or valuation:†				
Beginning of year	£14,026	£45,426	£45,416	£104,868
New subsidiaries	3,969	24,060	30,181	58,210
Additions	139	7,108	19,112	26,359
Disposals	(851)	(1,665)	(4,134)	(6,650)
Exchange adjustments	419	4,974	5,354	10,727
Revaluation	2,445	(350)	—	2,095
End of year	£20,147	£79,553	£95,909	£195,609
Depreciation:				
Beginning of year	£ 111	£ 6,354	£12,025	£ 18,490
Charge	146	4,780	14,903	19,829
Disposals	(12)	(100)	(1,073)	(1,185)
Exchange adjustments	34	411	1,447	1,892
End of year	£ 279	£11,445	£27,302	£ 39,026
Net book value:				
December 31, 1989	£19,868	£68,108	£68,607	£156,583
December 31, 1988	13,915	39,072	33,391	c86,378

*Leasehold land and buildings comprises £3,485,000 (1988: £2,120,000) held on long leasehold and £64,623,000 (1988: £36,952,000) held on short leasehold. Leased assets (other than leasehold property) included above have a net book value of £1,812,000 (1988: £1,373,000).

†Basis of valuation: Fixtures, fittings and equipment are shown at cost. Land an buildings include certain properties professionally revalued during 1989, by Messrs. James Andrew Badger (Surveyors & Valuers), on an open market, existing use basis. Other properties are included at historic cost. The amount included in respect of revalued properties is £16,444,000 (1988: £12,314,000); the historic net book value of such land and buildings is £8,542,000 (1988: £6,511,000).

EXHIBIT 1 (*concluded*)   Notes to the Accounts

Auditor's Report

To the members of WPP Group plc:

We have audited the accounts set out on pages 41 to 63 in accordance with approved Auditing Standards.

In our opinion, the accounts give a true and fair view of state of affairs of the Company and of the Group at 31 December 1989 and of the profit and source and application of funds of the Group for the year then ended, and have been properly prepared in accordnace with the Companies Act 1985.

Arthur Andersen & Co.
London

THE GOODWILL CONTROVERSY

For the sake of debate, the issue of brands was "inextricably linked to the goodwill issue in the minds of most finance directors."[3]

> British firms used brand values primarily to boost their balance sheets; by recording brand values as intangible assets, they could magically increase their assets while drawing attention to their important brands. U.S. accounting rules didn't allow any such advantages.
>
> Brand valuations made sense for companies that were potential takeover targets, too. A company thinking that its stock was undervalued might make its brand values public in order to prompt an increase in the share price and thwart potential raiders . . .[4]

Many other companies such as Grand Metropolitan and Ranks Hovis MacDougall also put high brand values on their balance sheets.

Goodwill was treated very differently in the United States and the United Kingdom. In fact, the problem of goodwill was dealt with differently around the world. (See Exhibit 2 for chart on international goodwill procedures.) In the United States, the goodwill issue only arose when a purchaser was paying some amount in excess of the fair market value of identifiable assets of the target firm. This excess could arise, for example, because of a particularly strong brand name that was expected to be of some mutually agreed-upon value in the future. In the United States, goodwill was capitalized on the balance sheet and written off against the income statement over a maximum period of 40 years.

In the United Kingdom, goodwill was written off against shareholders' equity at the time of purchase. It was *not* charged as an expense item against income so companies in the United Kingdom did not have to burden their future earnings by charging goodwill against the income statement.

In certain firms, advertising agencies for example, where tangible assets (desks, paper, office equipment) were quite small relative to intangible assets like the good reputation of the company, intellectual property, etc., this discrepancy in accounting practices was significant indeed. For such firms in the United States, the write-off of these large

---

[3]*Financial Times*, August 3, 1989.
[4]*Wall Street Journal*, February 9, 1989.

EXHIBIT 2   Goodwill*

Country	Predominant Method	Comments
U.S.	Capitalize	Amortize to expense over useful life— not to exceed 40 years.
U.K.	Direct write-off versus reserves (i.e., retained earnings) in the year of acquisition.	Capitalization is permitted. If capitalized amortize to earnings over useful life, if determinable. If useful life is not reasonably determinable, the goodwill should not be written off. There is no stated maximum useful life restrictions.
Canada	Capitalize	Similar to U.S.
Japan	Capitalize the amount by which the purchase price exceeds the book value of net assets acquired (not Fair Value).	If capitalized, amortize to expense over useful life—not to exceed five (5) years. Expense is tax deductible.
France	Capitalize	Amortize to expense over a 5- to 20-year period.
Germany	Capitalize	Amortize to expense over a 4-year period (can be extended if justified in the circumstances). Expense is tax deductible on a straight line basis over 15 years.
Switzerland	Option to write off versus reserves in the year of acquisition or to capitalize.	Goodwill purchased as a pre-existing asset of an acquired company is capitalizable and the amortization of this goodwill is tax deductible.
Netherlands	Options: 1. Capitalize 2. Write-off to expense in the year of acquisition. 3. Write-off vs. equity in the year of acquisition.	If capitalized, amortize over 5 years (can be extended to 10 years if justified in the (2) circumstances.)
Hong Kong	Similar to the Netherlands.	If capitalized, amortize to expense *only if, and to the extent,* that value has diminished.
Australia	Capitalize	Amortize to expense over useful life— not to exceed 20 years.
Malaysia	Capitalize	Amortize to expense over useful life with no stated maximum.

Description: Goodwill arises from Business Combinations accounted for under the purchase method. It is defined as the amount by which the purchase price of the Acquired Company exceeds the fair value of the Acquired Company's net assets. Goodwill may either be capitalized by the Acquiror and amortized ratably over its Estimated Useful Life (with stated maximums) or written off in the year of acquisition. Such a direct write-off normally is directly against Shareholders' Equity (called Reserves in the United Kingdom). The amortization of Goodwill is not a tax-deductible expense except as noted above.

*Reprinted with the permission of John Fawls, CPA, Merrill Lynch Capital Markets. Copyright © 1989.

intangible assets as an expense on the income statement had a great impact on future earnings relative to firms in the United Kingdom where the entire transaction was completed at the time of purchase.

THE BRAND VALUATION PROCESS

In order to measure the value of a given brand name, it was necessary to develop a system which was both "objective and scientific." This was easier to do for consumer goods than for the "brand name" of a service firm such as an advertising agency. For consumer goods, the procedure, developed at the Henley Centre, an economic forecasting consultancy in London owned by WPP Group, worked as follows: First, the level of income arising from sales of a brand was split conceptually into two categories, those sales due to short-run marketing influences, and those sales due to loyalty to the brand. The aim of this approach was to isolate short-run marketing influences by obtaining a mathematical formula based on statistical analysis to explain the sales of the brand in the recent past.

Once brand loyalty sales had been isolated, the profit element attributed to brand loyalty could be assessed. At any point in time, however, many factors could operate in determining the total level of sales of a brand. This range of factors likely to exercise a systematic and important influence on sales included: spending power of consumers, demographics, price, competitors' price, advertising, competitors' advertising, promotion, and distribution. For each brand, a unique mathematical formula was generated, and the appraisers were allowed to choose which factors were important in a particular case. Once the formula was derived and tested, the level of brand loyalty sales could be calculated.

While this technique was proven to work well for consumer goods, there were practical problems in obtaining information on these factors, and especially in obtaining information on competitors, in the case of service firms. But even before consideration of this problem, there was a further point related to services that needed to be examined. This was the extent to which loyalty to the service depended upon the individual providing the service rather than the brand. (See Exhibit 3 for a more detailed description of these problems.)

In addition, there was a major difference in auditing standards between the United States and the United Kingdom. In the United States, an auditor, working with the firm he or she was to represent, had to follow strict guidelines, the Generally Accepted Accounting Principles (GAAP). It was the responsibility of the auditor to follow these guidelines or risk prosecution for material misstatement or fraud. (From *The New Auditor's Report* of the AICPA.)

In the United Kingdom, the overriding requirement was to give a "true and fair view" of the value of the assets of any given company. The British philosophy was that rules alone could not necessarily result in a complete measure of value. Thus, all relevant information regarding value had to be weighed and taken into account in each specific case.

This approach was difficult to define and thus gave auditors in the United Kingdom more discretion in deciding what the "true and fair" value really was for each firm. In addition, while GAAP restricted U.S. auditors from certain "liberal" practices, the "true and fair" approach allowed U.K. auditors to measure value in closer accordance with the wishes of each firm's management team.

EXHIBIT 3 Valuing the JWT Brand

In thinking along the lines of corporate versus personalized loyalty it might be useful to introduce a simple analogy. If one thinks of a football team this is clearly a case of corporate loyalty. Individual players and managers may come and go, but the fans' loyalty is predominantly with that abstract corporate notion—the "team." On the other side of the coin, one can imagine a consultant's (e.g., a doctor's) relationship with a client—a relationship based primarily upon personal factors. Should the consultant in question leave his present firm it's quite conceivable that he will take his clients with him. The question now is where along this corporate-loyalty, personal-loyalty continuum lies the world of the advertising agency.

In approaching this question the following general factors need to be considered:

A People Profession

Undoubtedly the advertising world is grounded upon a considerable degree of personal interaction. Within such an environment individual relationships and loyalties naturally flourish—even more so given the need for confidentiality and campaign consistency. The exact extent of the "personal factor" is difficult to quantify since it will vary from case to case and depend upon the influence of the person in question. There is no doubt, however, that in some cases a client's loyalty is primarily to their contact within an agency rather than with the agency itself. There have been some notable examples of this, through clients following key individuals when they leave the agency. A famous example in 1981 was a number of clients who followed Frank Lowe from Collet Dickenson Pearce to Lowe Howard-Spink. Recent examples include:

- **December 1988**—David Harrisin leaves Leo Burnett Direct and formed RSCG Direct. He takes with him the Bankers Clearing Services Consortium account which he brought to the company when he joined.
- **December 1988**—David Pasley leaves FCB Pasley Woods and takes clients with him.
- **1988**—Malcolm Gaskin leaves TBWA to form WMGO and takes the Wolverhampton and Dudley Breweries accounts with him.
- **November 1987**—John Collington joins CTMC from Hilton Consumer and takes the Answercall account with him.
- **June 1987**—Chris Davis seems set to leave AHH and industry sources suggest that if he leaves, a number of clients with whom he has worked will be prompted to review.

A Capricious Profession

Given the advertising world's dependence upon creativity, there is an inherent danger of it becoming a hostage to fads and novelty. The continual quest for innovation makes it a volatile environment and can at times dictate against a lasting client-agency relationship. This tendency was demonstrated recently upon the transferral of H.R. Owen's account to Leagas Shafron, during which their marketing manager stated that "it wasn't that we were unhappy with Connell May and Stevenson, but it was felt that the time was right for change." This type of philosophy can clearly impinge upon the loyalty of an agency's client-base.

EXHIBIT 3   (*continued*)

A Predatory Profession

The advertising world is, in a client sense, a highly acquisitive environment. *Advertising Age,* for example, found that 72 percent of its sample of company advertising directors had been approached within the previous three months by agencies trying to acquire their business. In such a competitive arena corporate (and individual) loyalty is put under a strain.

This volatility is further increased by the prevalence of new agencies; in the case of Britain an average of 20 a year (in 1981 there were 43 new agencies launched). The disruptive effect of these new players is increased by the fact that their very newness may, for the creative reasons alluded to earlier, be perceived as attractive in itself.

Agency Size (Client Base)

To set the above, the size of the agency is a very important fact. The larger the agency, the easier it is to replace important individuals with others of similar standing in the profession. Obviously in the case of JWT, its list of accounts is among the most comprehensive of all agencies on a world scale. Just as important though is the quality of the client base. Here, JWT is again impressive with names such as Kellogg, Rowntree Mackintosh, and Draft on its books. The strength of these brands is in part attributable to JWT's own guidance, and it can be said that some of their brand strength has rubbed off on to JWT itself. This will be particularly true where the relationship is longstanding. In this sense JWT again looks good with an average length of service for its present clients standing at 13 years—with many accounts going back much further, e.g., Kraft 1926, Lever 1927, and Kellogg 1938. This evidence would suggest that to a large extent, JWT transcends the erratic nature of the advertising game. Moreover this duration of client relationship would also imply that JWT's clients do not easily transfer their loyalty from the corporate body to individuals within it.

Most examples of accounts moving with individuals relate to the smaller agencies rather than to the major players in the game.

To illustrate this latter point, advertising agencies are categorized according to their age. This is most commonly expressed in the form of three separate "waves" of agencies. This corruption of Toffler's term represents a rather obtuse form of description, although it does provide a reasonably convenient way of approaching the subject.

Although exact definitions vary, the "first wave" is generally used to refer to those agencies, such as JWT, which existed prior to 1970. Those agencies which emerged in the next decade and a half tend to constitute the "second wave," and include such names as Lowe Howard-Spink and Saatchi and Saatchi. Finally, there is the "third wave" which goes back to the mid-1980s and is used to refer to new agencies such as Devito, Butterfield, Day, and Hockney.

Upon the basis of this schema we can make some general comments relating to the likely balance of corporate versus individual influences within the different categories of agency. In the case of the "first wave," for example, their client loyalty will have accrued over a long period of time and will be relatively independent of the qualities and influences of

(continued)

EXHIBIT 3 *(continued)*

---

existing members of staff. This will be less true in the case of the "second wave," since it is likely that their founders will still be in control and will be personally responsible for much of the goodwill enjoyed by the agency. Finally, in the case of the "third wave" agencies their brand value will tend to be heavily skewed towards their high-profile founders and other key personnel.

Following on from the above approach it is clear that the names of the newer agencies tend to be synonymous with the name of their founders or other key personnel. In the event that one of these key personnel leaves the agency, then the agency's own name and state of continuity may be disrupted. In short, this type of agency is extremely susceptible to the mutilation of its brand image.

This will also tend to be the case with the second wave of agencies, although to a lesser extent since their longer existence will have imbued some level of brand value independent of those individuals of whom the agency is the namesake. Nevertheless, it would still be inconceivable to image that the likes of Saatchi and Saatchi could survive the departure of their founders with their reputation intact. Again, to a large extent these agencies are their key personnel.

In the case of the "first wave" agencies such as JWT though, the situation is entirely different. Put simply, the name JWT is not a derivative of any existing individuals within the agency. As such, its future brand value is not contingent upon its continued association with certain high-profile individuals. In discussing brands in general, Professor John Quelch of the Harvard Business School has stated that "brands of the highest stature are likely to be those coincidental with the companies' own name" (e.g., Heinz soup rather than "Head and Shoulders"). Adapting this to the case of advertising agencies, the opposite can seem to be the case; that is, the strongest and most secure brands are those where the product (i.e., the personnel) do not share the company's name.

To conclude then, it appears from this analysis that JWT satisfies all those criteria which would suggest the existence of a strong client loyalty; a loyalty moreover which is grounded upon corporate rather than individual allegiance.

In the case of the United States this strength would seem to be confirmed by the results of the *Advertising Age's* Agency Watch poll which has consistently placed JWT in the number one position in terms of industry perceptions. This consistency, moreover, was not disrupted by the personnel problems experienced by JWT over the last few years: as the *Advertising Age* (May 1988) itself expressed it "JWT seems to be surviving the management turmoil of the past 18 months with its reputation intact."

In the British context this same strength is demonstrated by the high level of continuity of JWT's accounts. In 1986 and 1987, for example, around 96 percent of JWT's clients kept their business with the agency for the following year—an impressive level of retention given the possibility of "one off" campaigns (e.g., government flotations) and the erratic nature of the industry.

As mentioned above, a practical problem with carrying out the brand valuation for an agency in the same way as for a consumer product arises from a lack of data. A more oblique way of approaching the question is required.

An extensive literature exists in economic theory relating to dominant firms and the likelihood of their decline. (See, for example, Geroski in Hay and Vickers (1987), *The Economics of Market Dominance*, for a recent critical survey). In other words, given a firm

EXHIBIT 3

which has a large market share, what is the likelihood of this declining substantially and by what processes will this decline come about? There is a presumption in theory that competitive forces will erode monopoly power and lead to the decline of even the most dominant firm. In practice, the theory is not supported all that well, and powerful firms exercising dominance over markets can persist for a very long time.

Case 8–4

Rossin Greenberg Seronick & Hill Inc. (A)*

Looking through the latest issue of *Computer Reseller News,* Neal Hill, president of the Boston advertising agency Rossin Greenberg Seronick and Hill (RGS&H), came across a story indicating that Microsoft Corporation was conducting an agency review. Two days later, November 5, 1987, Hill wrote to Martin Taucher at Microsoft, Redmond, Washington, suggesting he consider RGS&H. This was an account the agency was keen to secure.

"OUR AMBITION IS YOUR OPPORTUNITY"

RGS&H had been established in 1983. Four years later it had billings of around $25 million and was described in the trade press as the "hottest agency in New England." Yet it was still comparatively small, employing 45 people. Hill would not find it easy to

---

*Professor N. Craig Smith prepared this case with the assistance of Professor John A. Quelch as the basis for class discussion rather than to illustrate either effective or ineffective handling of an administrative situation. Copyright © 1989 by the President and Fellows of Harvard College. Harvard Business School case 9–589–124.

convince the West Coast software company, which had sales of just under $200 million in 1986, that it should transfer its $10 million account to RGS&H. The agency had, however, recently recruited two new creative people, Jamie Mambro and Jay Williams, who had computer industry experience.

In his letter, Hill posed the question: "Why should you even think about an agency in Boston that you've probably never heard of?" He gave four reasons in response:

1. We turn out a wonderful creative product (which has won much more than its share of national and regional awards) and have a tremendous fund of experience in marketing PC-related products, both hardware and software. (That means we do some great advertising, because it's both on target and creatively powerful. *One specific fact:* I've included the recent Lotus insert because *the creative team which produced it and the rest of Lotus' work over the past year joined this agency last Monday.*)

2. We're just under five years old, and billing just over $25 million annually. (Translation: we're old enough to be "real," and large enough to have terrific resources in creative, marketing, media, and production. It also means that we're young enough and small enough to move quickly and intelligently—to still be *very* hungry to do the kind of work that explodes off the page and screen. Just a note: Lotus' agency is just down the road from us in Providence, R.I., and is the same size we are.)

3. We already handle large national accounts—our clients include Hasbro, Dunkin' Donuts, Fidelity Investments, Clarks of England, and British Telecommunications— and have several concrete ideas for eliminating any problems posed by the (perceived) distance between Redmond and Boston. (This demonstrates that we know how to work with advertising needs on the scale of yours . . . and that we'd love to fly out to show you some of our work and explain some of our logistical approaches.)

4. We are intent on becoming a nationally recognized advertising agency—and doing a bang-up job with one or more Microsoft products would take us a good way down that road. (Which means that our ambition is your opportunity.)

A week later, Hill called Taucher and established that his letter should have been sent to Rob Lebow, director of corporate communications, to whom it had been forwarded. On November 16, Hill wrote to Lebow enclosing further samples of work done by the agency's staff: A Lotus direct mail brochure, an advertisement for Charles River Laboratories, and an advertisement for software by a company no longer active in the U.S. market. His key message was: "We are an awfully good agency, with a great deal of knowledge of Microsoft's industry, competition, and products. And we would kill to do even a project for you."

Follow-up calls were not returned, so Hill decided to send a further sample of artwork to Microsoft: a 12 × 9 inch brochure promoting RGS&H and containing a plane ticket for a trip to Boston. This specially produced "flier" was mailed by overnight express to Lebow on November 20. On the front, in white letters against a dark background, it simply stated: "You probably haven't thought about talking to an agency in Boston." The interior of the flier is shown in Exhibit 1.

EXHIBIT 1 Rossin Greenberg Seronick & Hill Inc. (A) RGS&H "Flier"

But, Since We Know Your Competition's Plans, Isn't It Worth Taking A Flier?

Microsoft is in a terrific position right now. Along with the momentum and success of its other products, the company has a fantastic new product—Excel. Its a product that many people feel is the first real threat to the dominance of Lotus 1-2-3.

Interestingly, the people who most strongly share this opinion are the people who *make* Lotus 1-2-3.

We think this fact alone shows just how big an opportunity you have before you. And it's an opportunity we'd like to talk to you about.

You see, the reason we know so much about Lotus is that some of our newest employees just spent the past year and a half working on the Lotus business at another agency. So they are intimately acquainted with Lotus' thoughts about Microsoft—and their plans to deal with the introduction of Excel.

In addition, the rest of our account service, creative and media departments are up to their ears in high tech experience—hardware; software; retail accounts, you name it. And the only thing they know better than the high tech business is the advertising business.

But don't take our word for it. Take this plane ticket and come out and see for yourself. You've got nothing to lose.

And thousands of frequent flier miles to gain.

637

ENCOURAGING NEWS

On November 23, RGS&H received a "no thanks" letter from Lebow. As this was dated November 16, Hill was not too disappointed. A call the following day established that Lebow was out of the office for the next week. On November 30 Hill was told that Lebow "certainly took notice of the mailed piece" and that he should call back December 4, when Lebow would be available. Hill wrote a further letter to Lebow expressing his delight at securing some attention with the flier and explaining "what we wanted to do was to demonstrate simultaneously our creative approach to messaging and our aggressive approach to marketing—in this case, marketing ourselves." He included an extract from *Adweek* (New England) which discussed RGS&H, its commitment to sophisticated office automation and how it pitched against New York agencies for the Playskool print account. Hill also explained that the agency would be interested in a single product or limited-term project instead of the entire account: "We just want a chance to show you what we can do for you."

Social and Ethical Issues

Carnation Infant Formula (A)*

Introduction

John Frank was the category manager for Carnation's two infant formula products: Good Start and Good Nature Follow-up formula. Good Start was a formula for new-born babies, promoted as being nutritionally close to breast milk, while Good Nature Follow-up formula was intended for babies 6 to 12 months of age. In mid-1990, senior management was considering the rather controversial prospect of advertising infant formula directly to mothers. In the face of opposition from such influential quarters as the American Academy of Pediatrics (AAP) and regulatory bodies such as The National Commission for the Prevention of Infant Mortality, John was faced with the task of developing this marketing program. He would be changing the way business had been conducted in the infant formula category, until recently. John had to develop a marketing strategy to present to senior management that reflected the potential reactions of the public, medical community, and competitors, as well as the parent company Nestlé's corporate concerns. The decisions to be made included: whether or not the products should be advertised to the end-user, what communications mix should be used, what media should be used, and what product benefits should be highlighted. This was a major opportunity for the company and for John's career. But it was not without risk.

Was it a food or was it a drug? That seemed to be the key marketing question in the case of infant formula. At least one brand, Gerber, was promoted almost exclusively with a consumer pull strategy. On the other hand, the category leader, Ross Labs (Abbott), argued that infant formula should not be marketed directly to mothers. In the middle, Carnation (Nestlé) was still undecided, and Bristol Myers seemed to have a foot in both doors, selling its own brands (Mead Johnson Group) only through doctors, but also supplying Gerber with their formula. What it all added up to was a potential marketing war brewing in the nation's nurseries.

INDUSTRY STRUCTURE AND MAJOR COMPETITORS

The infant formula industry in the U.S. was dominated by two players. Although there were about five manufacturers, the top two manufacturers accounted for 80 percent of industry sales. (See Exhibit 1). Sales growth was mainly in the form of taking users from

---

*This case was prepared by Assistant Professor Kusum Ailawadi with the assistance of Professor Paul W. Farris, the Darden Graduate School of Business Administration, University of Virginia. Copyright © 1992 by the Darden Graduate Business School Foundation, Charlottesville, Virginia.

EXHIBIT 1 Category Overview

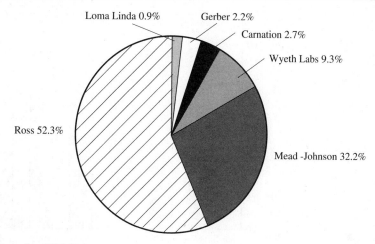

4 weeks ending 12/30/89

Manufacturer's brands/share

	Ross (Abbott Labs) 52.3%	Mead-Johnson (Bristol-Myers) 32.2%	Wyeth (Amer. Home Prod.) 9.3%	Carnation (Nestle) 2.7%	Gerber 2.2%
Cow's milk	Similac	Enfamil	SMA	Good Start Good Nature follow-up	Gerber
Soy	Isomil	Prosobee	Nursoy	- - - -	- - - -
Specialty	Alimentum Advance	Nutramigen Pregestimil	- - - -	- - - -	- - - -

competition, as market growth was limited by birthrate trends. During the last nine months of 1989 (March to December), the category totaled $1.1 billion in retail sales. Projections were for the category to grow 7 percent to 8 percent through 1992 (Exhibit 2).

Traditionally, formula was marketed more like a drug than a consumer product. Manufacturer sales force called on pediatricians and other child-care health professionals—an activity known as "detailing." The salesforce provided the health care professionals with free samples and informational materials in the hope that they would recommend the detailing company's products to their patients. They also provided hospitals with formula samples for their newborn patients. A survey of new mothers, conducted by Carnation, indicated that the hospital sampling method played a large role in formula choice. Pediatricians were very satisfied with this procedure, believing that mothers would

EXHIBIT 2   Projected Size and Growth (in billions of dollars)

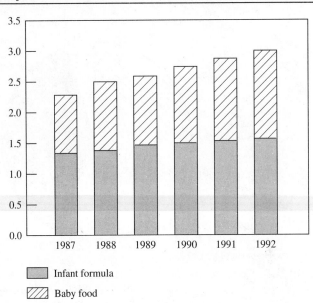

not be discouraged from breast-feeding if their doctor or hospital dispensed the material and samples. Management at Carnation believed that many pediatricians (perhaps 50 percent) recommended a specific brand of infant formula. However, it was not clear whether pediatricians believed that there were important differences in the nutritive value of different formulations. Various brands appeared to be approximately equal in nutritive value (see Exhibit 3).

Abbott Labs

Marketing through doctors was a technique that had worked well for market leader Abbott Laboratories, whose Similac brand controlled about 50 percent of the market. "There are two major reasons behind our decision not to market directly to consumers," said a spokesperson for Abbott Labs. "The first is our commitment to mothers breast-feeding whenever possible. We put right on the label that this is the best thing to do." The second component is that an infant's nutrition during the early stages of life is so critical to brain development that a decision regarding it should only be made in concert with the baby's pediatrician, she said.

Abbott's marketing efforts for Similac were limited to detailing, advertising in professional journals, sponsoring research and symposiums on infant nutrition, and providing product samples to healthcare institutions. It was a marketing strategy that had the approval of the powerful American Academy of Pediatrics (AAP), and it had been standard industry practice in the infant formula category for years. Infant formula was quite an important part of the company's portfolio. In 1988, infant formula accounted for 20 percent of the company's sales and 30.7 percent of its operating profit.

Bristol-Myers Labs

Bristol-Myers Squibb's Mead Johnson subsidiary used the same approach in marketing No. 2 brand Enfamil, Prosobee, and its other formula brands, which had a combined share of about 32 percent. Infant formula accounted for 14.7 percent of the company's sales in 1988, and 24.9 percent of its operating profit.

American Home Products

American Home Products' Wyeth Labs was No. 3 in the market, with two major brands, SMA and Nursoy. The combined share of all infant formula marketed by Wyeth was a little over 9 percent. Like the two market leaders, Wyeth traditionally marketed to doctors. However, Wyeth also provided deals to the trade in order to maintain shelf space in the stores. A large percentage of Wyeth's U.S. sales were presently to the government-subsidized Special Supplemental Food Program for Women, Infants, and Children (WIC), which is discussed later in this case.

Nutricia-Loma Linda

Nutricia was a nutrition company, with emphasis on infant nutrition, that had major operations in the Benelux countries and the United Kingdom, and a minor presence in Southern Europe. Nutricia purchased Loma Linda, thus gaining entry into the U.S. infant formula market, although the company's U.S. market share was only 0.9 percent.

Gerber Products

Bristol-Myers gained another foothold in the infant formula market in August of 1989 when Gerber launched a brand of baby formula. The formula was produced by Bristol-Myers and sold under the Gerber name.

"Research showed that while very few first-time mothers were familiar with the name Similac, most of them were familiar with Gerber," according to a spokesman. So, when Gerber entered the market in 1989, it decided to market directly to the product's consumers. It introduced Gerber Baby Formula with print and broadcast ads as well as a direct-mail program. Its 500-person trade sales force pitched the product to wholesalers and category buyers at big retail accounts. It also had a small medical sales force of about 20 people who promoted it to physicians and other healthcare professionals along with the rest of the Gerber line. By mid-1990, Gerber's dollar share of the infant formula market was 2.9 percent while its unit market share was 3.5 percent.

EXHIBIT 3 Nutrient Comparison—Infant Formulas per 100 Calories*

Nutrient	Units	Breast Milk	Good Start	Similac	Enfamil	SMA	Gerber	Isomil	Pro-Sobee	Nursoy
Protein	g	1.5	2.4	2.22	2.2	2.2	2.2	2.66	3	3.1
Fat	g	5.4	5.1	5.37	5.6	5.3	5.4	5.46	5.3	5.3
Carbohydrate	g	10	11	10.7	10.3	10.6	10.7	10.1	10	10.2
Linoleic acid	mg	540	850	1,300	1,300	500	1,300	1,309	1,200	500
Linolenic acid	mg	75	100	NA	56	69	225	NA	56	69
Cholesterol	mg	20	10	1.6	<1.6	6	NA	0	0	2.3
Calorie/liter		730	670	676	680	676	676	676	780	676
Vitamin A	IU	310	300	300	310	300	300	300	310	300
Vitamin D	IU	3.05	70	60	63	60	60	60	63	60
Vitamin E	IU	0.32(mg)	2.0	3	3.1	1.4	1.4	3	3.1	1.4
Vitamin K	mcg	0.29	8.2	8	8.6	8	8	15	15.6	15
Vitamin B_1	mcg	29	60	100	78	100	100	60	78	100
Vitamin B_2	mcg	49	135	150	150	150	150	90	94	150
Vitamin B_6	mcg	28.5	75	60	63	62.5	60	60	63	63
Vitamin B_{12}	mcg	0.07	0.22	0.25	0.23	0.2	0.25	0.45	0.31	0.3
Niacin	mcg	208	750	1,050	1,250	750	1,050	1,350	1,205	750
Folic acid	mcg	7	9	15	15.6	7.5	15	15	15.6	7.5
Pantothenic acid	mcg	250	450	450	470	315	450	750	470	450
Biotin	mcg	0.6	2.2	4.4	2.3	2.2	4.4	4.5	7.8	5.5
Vitamin C	mg	6	8	9	8.1	8.5	9	9	8.1	8.5
Choline	mg	12.5	12	16	15.6	15	16	8	7.8	13
Inositol	mg	14.9	18	4.7	4.7	4.7	4.7	5	4.7	4.1
Calcium	mg	39	64	75	69	63	75	105	94	90
Phosphoruse	mg	19	36	58	47	42	58	75	74	63
Magnesium	mg	4.9	6.7	6	7.8	7	6	7.5	10.9	10
Iron	mg	0.04	1.5	1.80/0.22	1.80/0.16	1.80/0.2	1.8	1.8	1.88	1.7
Zinc	mg	0.17	0.75	0.75	0.78	0.8	0.75	0.75	0.78	0.8
Manganese	mcg	0.08	7	5	15.6	15	5	30	25	30
Copper	mcg	35	80	90	94	70	90	75	94	70
Iodine	mcg	15.3	8	15	6	9	15	15	10.2	94
Sodium	mg	25	24	28	27	22	33	44	36	30
Potassium	mg	73	98	108	108	83	108	108	122	105
Chloride	mg	58	59	66	63	55.5	70	62	83	56
Taurine	mg	5.6	8	6.7	5.9	5.9	NA	6.7	5.9	5.9
Carnitine	mg	0.95	1.6	NA	5.5	1.88	NA	NA	1.88	1.3

Protein g/100 mL	1.05	1.6	1.5	1.52	1.5	1.5	1.8	2	2.1
Percent soy protein							100	100	100
Percent casein	20		82	40	40	82			
Percent whey protein	80	100	18	60	60	18			
Fat g/100 mL	3.9	3.4	3.6	3.8	3.6	3.6	3.7	3.6	3.6
Percent polyunsaturated	16	22.2	31	28	14.5	37.3	32	28	14.5
Percent monounsaturated	43	33.2	17	15.5	41.3	17.6	17	15.5	41.3
Percent saturated	41	44.6	52	48	44.2	45.1	51	48	44.2
Percent polyunsaturated:saturated	0.39	0.5	0.6	0.58	0.33	0.83	0.63	0.58	0.33
(source)	(Mature-term human milk)	(47% palm olein, 26% soybean, 21% coconut, 6% high-oleic safflower)	(50% corn, 50% coconut)	(55% coconut, 30% corn, 15% soy)	(33% oleo, 27% coconut, 25% high-oleic safflower, 15% soy)	(60% soy, 40% coconut)	(50% corn, 50% coconut)	(55% coconut, 30% corn, 15% soy)	(33% oleo, 27% coconut, 25% high-oleic safflower, 15% soy)
Carbohydrate g/100 mL	7.2	7.4	7.2	7	7.2	7.2	6.8	6.8	6.9
(source)	(lactose)	(lactose and malt odextrin)	(lactose)	(lactose)	(lactose)	(lactose)	(corn syrup solids; sucrose)	(corn syrup)	(sucrose solids)
Renal solute load (mOsm/L)	79	993	99.7	134	91.4	100.3	115.6	178	122
Osmolality (mOsm/kg water)	300	265	300	300	300	290	240	200	296
Canister size (powder) (oz)		12	16	16	16	16	14	14	16
Total fl oz servings†		87.2	116	120	107	118	102	102	107

*Powder formulations; sources of data available upon request. Information on competitive products derived from figures provided by the manufacturers as of February 1991. Similac and Isomil are registered trademarks of Ross Laboratories. Enfamil and ProSobee are registered trademarks of Mead Johnson & Company. SMA and Nursoy are registered trademarks of Wyeth-Ayerst Laboratories. Gerber is a registered trademark of Gerber Products Company.
†Per canister powder, when mixed to standard dilution.
NA = Not available.

Carnation

Nestlé's Carnation company marketed two major brands, Good Start and Good Nature Follow-up formula. In mid-1990, Carnation had a combined unit share of about 2.6 percent, of which 1.8 percent came from the Good Nature Follow-up formula. When the company first entered the U.S. market in 1988, Good Start was launched with the acronym "H.A." (standing for "hypoallergenic") and positioned as a low-cost, good-tasting hypoallergenic cow's milk formula.[1] This claim was made on the package labels and in an informational campaign for parents. Good Nature, on the other hand, was positioned as a regular cow's milk infant formula, and advertised directly to consumers.

According to press reports early in 1989, the company had to reduce consumer advertising under pressure from the AAP, the Food and Drug Administration, and in the face of cases of severe reaction suffered by some infants allergic to cow's milk.[2] The consumer advertising for Good Nature Follow-up formula was reduced to a targeted direct-mail program due to the pressure, while the traditional approach of marketing through detail representatives was taken for Good Start. Also, once Nestle became aware of the potential misunderstanding of the term "hypoallergenic" in the U.S., as "non-allergic," the company voluntarily modified the Good Start label to eliminate "H.A."

In the wake of Gerber's decision to market directly to consumers, however, it was decided that Nestle would monitor the development of Gerber's business and determine if they should return to their consumer marketing strategy. The strong sales results at Gerber encouraged Carnation to reconsider marketing directly to the consumers. Exhibit 4 summarizes the marketing strategies of the major players in the infant formula market.

THE ROLE OF REGULATION AND INFANT FORMULA MARKETING

When it became known that Gerber was marketing its infant formula directly to consumers and Carnation was seriously considering expanding its consumer marketing activities as well, the industry was aghast. A spokesperson for AAP said it was opposed to Gerber's tactics, and Abbott said their company also remained committed to marketing only to healthcare professionals. Opponents of direct consumer marketing of infant formula cited the importance of breast-feeding as a primary reason for their opposition.

The reaction of the market leaders was interesting. Ross Labs (Abbott) continued to decry consumer marketing of infant formula. On the other hand, as was noted earlier in the case, Bristol-Myers was closely involved in Gerber. According to a spokesman for Bristol-Myers, the company was just using up excess manufacturing capacity. Analysts, however, noted that the company was getting a ringside seat for what may well be the

---

[1] Hypoallergenic means a reduced potential to cause an allergic reaction.

[2] "Nestle's Bid to Crash Baby Formula Market in the U.S. Stirs a Row," *The Wall Street Journal*, February 16, 1989.

EXHIBIT 4 Summary of Marketing Strategy: Major Players

Manufacturer	Leading Brand	Position
Ross (Abbott)	Similac Isomil	Category leader 650 medical salesreps Delivers samples through hospitals No advertising direct to consumer
Mead-Johnson (Bristol-Myers)	Enfamil Prosobee	Second in category 535 medical salesreps Delivers samples through hospitals No advertising direct to consumer

	Gerber	Entered category in 1989
		50 medical salesreps
		Mails samples direct to consumer
		TV and print advertising; spent $3.4
		    million on consumer advertising in
		    1989.

Wyeth (AHP)	SMA	Third in category 250 medical salereps Only manufacturer to "deal" at store level to maintain shelf space No advertising direct to consumer
Carnation (Nestlé)	Good Start Follow-up	Entered category in 1988 90 medical salesreps Mails information and coupons direct to consumer Consumer print advertising

first full-scale modern marketing effort in the infant formula category. According to Carnation executives, Bristol-Myers played a major role in the Gerber business. Gerber simply provided marketing support for which Bristol-Myers paid them a royalty and a sales commission. It was also interesting to note that, although the top two manufacturers were strong in the U.S., their worldwide position was reversed, possibly adding fuel to their concern over Carnation/Nestlé's entry (see Exhibit 5).

As a result of the Infant Formula Acts of 1980 and 1986, infant formula was the most strictly regulated food product in the U.S. Although the Act did not address the marketing of infant formula, the AAP, the American Dietetic Association, and the World Health Organization outlined marketing practices that they encourage formula-makers to follow. Exhibit 6 provides a copy of the AAP's policy on direct advertising of infant formula to the public. Exhibit 7 provides excerpts from a letter written to President Timm Crull of Carnation by the chairman of the Subcommittee on Nutrition and Investigations, United States Senate, in 1989, after Carnation first launched its formula products.

According to Carnation executives, the result of marketing through doctors had been a relatively staid $1.6 billion market with nice margins and not too much competition.

EXHIBIT 5   Worldwide Infant Formula Market (excluding U.S.)

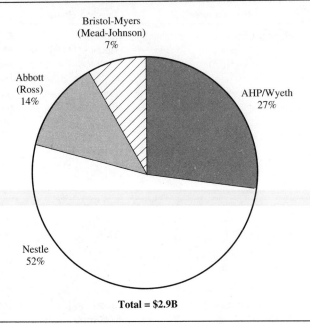

Bristol-Myers
(Mead-Johnson)
7%

Abbott
(Ross)
14%

AHP/Wyeth
27%

Nestle
52%

Total = $2.9B

EXHIBIT 6   American Academy of Pediatrics Policy on Direct Advertising to the Public

Principles for use in response to companies advertising infant formula directly to the public are as
follows:

1. The Academy reaffirms its policy opposing direct advertising of infant formula to the public.
2. If an infant formula company advertises its formula directly to the public, then the Academy will,
   as soon as practical but in no event later than a year from the date on which the direct
   advertising commences, terminate support of Academy programs by that company. If the
   Academy determines that it is necessary or advisable, in support of its policy against the direct
   advertising of infant formula to the public, the Academy will also terminate support of Academy
   programs by companies directly or indirectly involved in or otherwise aiding or abetting a joint
   venture or other endeavor to directly advertise infant formula to the public. If a company does
   not currently provide support for Academy programs, then the Academy will not solicit or
   accept funding from such company for any ongoing or future programs.
3. Advertising in Academy publications directed to the professional and exhibiting at Academy
   meetings will not be impacted by the fact that such company is engaged in direct advertising
   of infant formula to the public.
4. In response to advertising of infant formula to the public, chapters and individual members of
   the Academy must follow their own dictates and make it clear that they are speaking/acting as
   individual persons or chapters and are not representing the Academy.

(Approved by the Executive Board
September 21, 1989

EXHIBIT 7   Excerpts from Letter

To Timm Crull, President, Carnation
From Tom Harkin, Chairman, Subcommittee on Nutrition & Investigations

Dated May 1, 1989

"In recent weeks I have become concerned about reports regarding the marketing techniques being used to market the infant formula, Good Nature. I would like to share with you the reasons for my concern. . . .

"Notwithstanding the Academy's policy, I am told that Good Nature was being marketed directly to mothers using television, direct mail, and ads in parents' magazines. Not only does this appear to violate the Academy's policy, but also the WHO Code of Marketing of Breastmilk Substitutes to which Carnation's parent company, Nestlé, claims to adhere.

"In the United States, the marketing of infant formula has traditionally been directed to health professionals and, in my opinion, it is a tradition that should continue. It is important to promote infant formula through health professionals so that mothers and infants gain access to proper evaluation, support, and care. This position was noted in the policy statement of the American Dietetic Association in September, 1988. In part, the '88 policy reads: "ADA opposes the marketing of infant formula directly to the public. Direct consumer advertising may dissuade women from breast-feeding as well as contribute to the inappropriate formula selection for infants with special needs." . . .

"I would like to hear from you regarding the accuracy of these reports. If they are true, I hope Carnation will reconsider its marketing practices regarding Good Nature. In any event, I would like you to apprise me of your thinking on this matter."

They believed that doctors had a reputation for being resistant to change, and as long as they were the primary focus on infant formula marketing efforts, it would be almost impossible for any newcomers to break into the game.

"In the past, we found it impossible to compete in this category because it was so dominated by the drug companies," said a spokesman for Gerber. "They sold through their detail people who called on doctors, and the market share didn't change for 10 years."

Another major factor in the position of the various formula brands was the Special Supplemental Food Program for Women, Infants and Children (WIC). The WIC was federally financed but run by the states for the benefit of low-income families. It accounted for about one out of every three cans of formula sold. Further, the WIC influence also spilled over to retail sales. The company/brand that was awarded the state WIC contract also tended to increase its shelf space in the supermarket. Until 1987–88, the state WICs paid retail prices for the formula, and operated a system whereby families were issued vouchers for formula that they could exchange for any brand. More often than not, the brand that was chosen was the one recommended by the doctor. In 1987, however, the WIC, under budget pressures and in the face of prices rising at roughly three times the rate of inflation, decided to ask for competitive bids from the formula makers and award their contract to the company offering the highest rebate. According to press reports, the major companies, notably Ross Labs and Mead Johnson, were against competitive bids, and lobbied support from several doctors.[3] They agreed to give rebates if the WICs retained the old open-market system. However, the state WICs were unconvinced, and by 1989, several of them were inviting competitive bids and obtaining significant rebates. Wyeth Labs was one of the manufacturers that gained the most in market share by offering hefty rebates to the WICs.

COMPANY BACKGROUND

Unlike Gerber, Carnation had to deal with more than public, medical, regulatory, and competitor reaction. It carried the additional burden of Nestlé's history of formula marketing in the developing countries during the 1970s. Nestlé and other formula companies advertised and marketed their formulas to mothers in the developing countries, where formula products were often misused. Water was often unavailable or contaminated, and it was difficult to sterilize bottles. Formula tended to be overdiluted. It was charged that Nestlé's marketing policies were unethical and immoral since they discouraged breast-feeding among mothers in developing countries and led to the misuse of the formula products, thus contributing to infant malnutrition and death. The result was a boycott against many Nestlé products, instituted by the Third World Institute. Along with many other world organizations, the institute's successor, Infant Formula Action Coalition (INFACT), also lobbied the World Health Organization to draft a code regulating the advertising and marketing of infant formula in the Third World. The eight-page code, not signed by President Reagan due to a First Amendment conflict, urged a ban on promotion and advertising of baby formula, and called for a halt to distribution of free product samples and/or gifts to physicians.

Thus, when Carnation started selling formula in the U.S. in 1988, it ran into trouble almost immediately. Abbott and Bristol played up Carnation's connection with Nestlé, which had been widely criticized for its methods of selling infant formula in the Third World.

MARKET DEVELOPMENTS

The infant formula category totaled $1.1 billion in U.S. retail sales during the last nine months of 1989. Packaged Facts, a New York based research firm, projected a 7–8.5 percent increase through 1992, to grow the category to approximately $2.1 billion in 1992. Price increases and two trends were responsible for this growth:

1. Birth rates increased 2 percent in 1988 over 1987, and were expected to remain strong throughout the 1990s.
2. More women were returning to the workforce after childbirth, increasing the demand for formula as either a substitute for or supplement to breast milk.

---

[3]*New York Times*, January 9, 1991.

Exhibit 8 summarizes number of births, birthrates, and fertility rates since 1971. Exhibit 9 provides estimates (up to 1989) and projections (1990 onwards) of the number of children under the age of three.

Product, Costs, Margins, and Distribution

Infant formula was sold in three basic forms: concentrate, powder, and ready-to-use. Within each form, there were several formula variations, e.g., (1) regular and with iron; (2) cow's milk and soy-based; and (3) several package sizes. Soy-based products had only 25 percent of the market, while milk-based products accounted for the remaining 75 percent. In addition to these product variations, some premium-priced brands, led by Bristol's Nutramigen, served a special niche in the market—hypoallergenic formula for infants with allergy problems. Abbott's Alimentum was another player in that niche. Carnation also introduced Good Start as a hypoallergenic formula, but one that tasted good and cost no more than ordinary cow's milk infant formula. The claim was modified in the face of opposition from the AAP, contrary data provided by competitors, and instances of severe reactions suffered by some infants allergic to cow's milk. The company's other brand, Good Nature Follow-up was positioned as an ordinary cow's milk formula.

It was not clear whether there were significant differences between the nutritional content and quality of various brands. Gerber advertised the similarity between its own brand and higher-priced market leaders like Similac (see Exhibit 10). On the other hand, Exhibit 11 shows an example of how Abbott advertised a difference between its own and competing brands with a different formulation. The same was true of Carnation. Good

---

EXHIBIT 8 Birth and Fertility Rates in the U.S.: 1971–1990

Year	Number of Births (million)	Birth rate (per 1,000)	Fertility Rate (per 1,000)
1971–1975	3.14–3.56	14.6–17.2	66.0–81.8
1976–1980	3.17–3.61	14.6–15.9	65.0–68.4
1981	3.63	15.8	67.4
1982	3.68	15.9	67.3
1983	3.64	15.5	65.8
1984	3.67	15.5	65.4
1985	3.76	15.8	66.2
1986	3.76	15.6	65.4
1987	3.81	15.7	65.7
1988	3.91	15.9	67.2
1989	4.02	16.2	68.8
1990	4.17	16.7	71.1

Notes: Births are live births. Birth rate is number of births per thousand people, and fertility rate is number of births per thousand women of childbearing age.

Source: FIND/SVP studies by the company.

EXHIBIT 9   Number of Children Under Age Three, by Age: 1980–2000 (in thousands)

Year	Under One	Age One	Age Two	Total
1980	3,561	3,317	3,211	10,089
1981	3,620	3,442	3,318	10,380
1982	3,670	3,495	3,443	10,608
1983	3,684	3,548	3,495	10,727
1984	3,617	3,561	3,548	10,726
1985	3,749	3,496	3,561	10,806
1986	3,728	3,623	3,497	10,848
1987	3,793	3,643	3,611	11,047
1988	3,859	3,668	3,646	11,173
1989	3,945	3,717	3,660	11,322
1990*	3,743	3,636	3,627	11,006
1995*	3,531	3,458	3,504	10,493
2000*	3,388	3,295	3,322	10,005

*Projections.

Source: FIND/SVP Study provided by the company.

Start was promoted as a product with a simpler whey protein that was nutritionally closer to breast milk than competing brands (see Exhibit 12).

There were several sizes and product forms marketed in the infant formula category. In 1989, the number of stock-keeping units (SKUs) for a brand ranged from a low of 1 for a small player called Fearn to a high of 25 for Bristol-Myers' Enfamil. Market shares and the number of SKUs for each of the major brands during 1989 are summarized in Exhibit 13. Exhibit 14 summarizes the percentage of All Commodity Volume (ACV) and retail price data for each brand during the four quarters of 1989.

Although cost and margin data for the individual companies are not available, Exhibit 15 summarizes the variable costs of producing a typical 32-oz. can of standard cow's milk infant formula as of 1989. According to company executives, the costs of producing Carnation infant formula were approximately 5 percent higher because the company was the only U.S. formula maker that utilized a special aseptic processing method. This process yielded a whiter, better smelling and tasting product, since it was cooked outside the can for a short period at a very high temperature.

Eighty percent of all formula sales in the U.S. were made in food stores, while drug stores accounted for only about 8 percent. Exhibit 16 provides a breakdown. The infant formula category does not appear to be very profitable for retailers. According to the "Marsh Super Study" reported in the December 1992 issue of *Progressive Grocer,* baby food and formula accounts for 1.9 percent of the total cubic feet of space in the grocery store, and 0.7 percent of dollar sales and 0.1 percent of gross profit. The average gross profit per unit sold is $0.03, and the average Direct Product Profitability (DPP) per unit sold is actually negative, at − $0.08.

EXHIBIT 10 Copy of a Gerber Infant Formula Advertisement

Caloric Distribution	Gerber Baby Formula	Similac**
Protein, % Calories	9	9
Fat, % Calories	48	48
Carbohydrates, % Calories	43	43
Nutrient Sources		
Protein	Nonfat Milk (18:82 Whey/ Casein)	Nonfat Milk (18:82 Whey/ Casein)
Fat	60% soy** 40% Coconut	60% Soy*** 40% Coconut
Carbohydrates	Lactose	Lactose
Nutrient (Per 100 Calories)		
Protein, g	2.2	2.2
Fat, g	5.4	5.4
Carbohydrates, g	10.7	10.7
Linoleic Acid, mg	1300	1300
Vitamins		
Vitamin A, IU	300	300
Vitamin D, IU	60	60
Vitamin E, IU	3	3
Vitamin K, μg	8	8
Thiamine (B1), μg	100	100
Riboflavin (B2), μg	150	150
Vitamin B6, μg	60	60
Vitamin B12, μg	0.25	0.25
Niacin, μg	1050	1050
Folic Acid, μg	15	15
Pantothenic Acid, μg	450	450
Biotin, μg	4.4	4.4
Vitamin C, mg	9	9
Choline, mg	16	16
Inositol, mg	4.7	4.7
Minerals		
Calcium, mg	75	75
Phosphorus, mg	58	58
Magnesium, mg	6	6
Iron, mg	1.8 (0.16 in low iron)	1.8 (0.22 in low iron)
Zinc, mg	0.75	0.75
Manganese, μg	5	5
Copper, μg	90	90
Iodine, μg	15	15
Sodium, mg	33	28
Potassium, mg	108	108
Chloride, mg	70	66
Price	Compare at your local store . . . you'll be pleasantly surprised!†	

Key g = gram; μg = microgram; mg = milligram; IU = International Units.
*Similac is a registered trademark of Ross Laboratories. **Corn Oil in powder. ***Similac has 50% Corn Oil and 50% Coconut Oil in powder.
†In most stores, Gerber Baby Formula costs less than Similac.

EXHIBIT 11   Copy of a Similac Advertisement

The Difference

Infant Formula

Less Spitting-Up...Less Vomiting

*Mothers reported an
increased percentage of
feedings with spitting-up
or vomiting when infants
were fed a whey-dominant
infant formula compared
with human milk feeding.[1]*

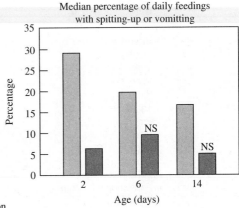

Median percentage of daily feedings
with spitting-up or vomitting

Whey-Dominant Infant Formula With Iron

Human Milk

NS–Not Statistically Significant

*Mothers reported less
 spitting-up or vomiting
with feedings of
casin-dominant
SIMILAC ® WITH IRON
than with a whey-dominant
formula with iron.[1]*

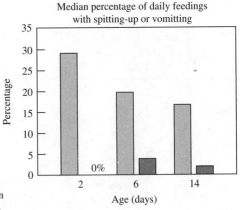

Median percentage of daily feedings
with spitting-up or vomitting

Whey-Dominant Infant Formula With Iron

SIMILAC ® WITH IRON Infant Formula

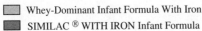

SIMILAC® WITH IRON *is well torated*

EXHIBIT 12

**In answer to your questions
on infant feeding...**

What about a baby's delicate digestive system?

Infants under 6 months old have more delicate digestive systems than older babies, making some of them potentially vulnerable to intolerance of protein molecules that come from most formulas. These protein molecules tend to be large and sometimes difficult to tolerate. Breast milk can help protect a baby's delicate digestive system as it matures. This usually happens by 6 months of age.

Older babies' digestive systems usually let them tolerate large cow's-milk protein molecules found in standard formulas. But some newborns' digestive systems—still immature and vulnerable—may not easily tolerate them.

These large protein molecules can sometimes cause difficulties such as spitting up, diarrhea, or rashes. (Of course, there may be other reasons for such symptoms; so be sure to check with your doctor if they occur.)

Is there a formula for the newborn's digestive system?

The best diet for your new baby is breast milk. However, if you decide to supplement or use a formula, your doctor will help you choose the right formula for your baby.

Standard cow's-milk formulas, such as Similac®, Enfamil®, SMA®, and Gerber®*, have large protein molecules that may sometimes pose difficulties for a newborn's delicate digestive system.

The milk protein in Carnation® GOOD START™ has been specially processed to make it gentle on a newborn's delicate digestive system.[†]

So, if you and your physician are considering formula, Carnation GOOD START is a smart choice.

*Similac, Enfamil, SMA, and Gerber are registered trademarks of Ross Laboratories, Mead Johnson, Wyeth Laboratories, and Gerber Products Company, respectively.   †Like most leading formulas, GOOD START is made with cow's-milk protein. The cow's-milk whey protein in GOOD START is specially processed to be gentle. But if milk allergy is a concern, all formulas, including GOOD START, should be used with caution and only under a doctor's supervision.

GOOD START mixing instructions

Follow all instructions on the GOOD START can carefully.
(Instructions in Spanish can be found on the inside of the can label.)
Instrucciones en Español se encuentran al reverso del cubierto de lata.

Always be sure to use sterilized bottles and nipples. When water is called for, it should be boiled for five minutes, then cooled to a comfortable feeding temperature. Always use formula before the date shown on the can.

To use ready to feed...
1. Clean can top, SHAKE WELL, and open.
2. Pour formula into bottle and feed baby.

To use concentrated liquid...
1. Clean can top, SHAKE WELL, and open.
2. Pour equal amounts of formula and water into sterilized container and stir.
3. Pour formula directly into nursing bottle, test temperature, and feed baby immediately.

To store ready to feed and concentrated liquid...
Discard unused formula left in bottle after feeding. After opening, can should be covered, stored in the refrigerator, and used within 48 hours. Store unopened can at room temperature. Avoid excessive temperatures.

GOOD START™ is nutritionally close to breast milk*

	Breast Milk[†]	GOOD START	Similac®[‡]	Gerber®§
Protein (% whey)	80	100	18	18
Carbohydrate (% lactose)	100	70	100	100
Fat				
% saturated	41.0	44.6	45.1	45.0
% polyunsaturated	16.0	22.2	37.3	37.0
% monounsaturated	43.0	33.2	17.6	18.0

*Comparisons based on liquid formulations.   †Motil KJ. Breast-feeding: Public Health and Clinical Overview: Table 17.2. In: Grand RJ, Sutphen JL, Dietz WH, eds. *Pediatric Nutrition: Theory and Practice.* Boston, Mass: Butterworths, 1987:251–263.   ‡*Composition of Feedings for Infants at Home.* Ross Laboratories, 1989.   §Gerber Products Company, Reference No. 55–148, 1989.   †Lönnerdal B, Forsum E. *Am J Clin Nutr* 41:113–120, 1985.

EXHIBIT 13 1989 SKU and Market Share Data

Brand	Number of SKUs	Unit Share Percent	Unit Share Percent (4 weeks ending 12/30/89)
Ross			
Advance	2	0.1%	0.1%
Isomil	12	15.7	15.0
Similac	24	37.3	37.2
Gerber			
Gerber	17	0.3	2.2
Wyeth Labs			
Nursoy	6	2.6	3.1
SMA	14	6.1	6.2
Carnation			
Good Nature Follow Up	6	1.5	1.8
Good Start	6	0.8	0.9
Mead Johnson			
Nutramigen	6	1.4	0.9
Prosobee	8	7.6	7.0
Enfamil	25	25.5	24.3

Source of data: Nielsen Scantrack.

EXHIBIT 14 1989 ACV and Retail Prices for Concentrate Form

Brand	First Quarter		Second Quarter		Third Quarter		Fourth Quarter	
	Percent ACV	Retail Price	Percent ACV	Retail Price	Percent ACV	Retail Price	Percent ACV	Retail Price
Ross Labs (Abbott)								
Isomil	97%	$0.97	97%	$1.01	97%	$1.02	97%	$1.06
Similac	97	0.95	97	0.99	97	1.00	97	1.04
Gerber								
Gerber	*	*	*	*	12	0.95	59	0.96
Wyeth Labs								
Nursoy	70	0.95	72	0.95	72	0.99	73	0.99
SMA	29	0.94	32	0.95	33	0.98	36	0.99
Nestlé Labs								*
Good Nature Follow Up	*	*	*	*	*	*	*	
Good Start	*	*	*	*	*	*	*	*
Mead Johnson (Bristol-Myers)								
Nutramigen	27	1.86	30	1.87	33	1.87	34	1.87
Prosobee	95	0.97	95	1.00	95	1.01	95	1.06
Enfamil	94	0.95	95	0.98	95	0.98	95	1.02

*Brand had not been introduced at this time.

Source of Data: Nielsen Scantrack. Retail price is for a standard pack size of 8 oz.

EXHIBIT 14 (*continued*)   1989 ACV and Retail Prices for Ready-to-Use Form

Brand	First Quarter		Second Quarter		Third Quarter		Fourth Quarter	
	Percent ACV	Retail Price	Percent ACV	Retail Price	Percent ACV	Retail Price	Percent ACV	Retail Price
				Ross Labs (Abbott)				
Isomil	97%	$1.19	97%	$1.25	97%	$1.27	97%	$1.32
Similac	97	1.17	97	1.22	97	1.25	96	1.30
				Gerber				
Gerber	*	*	*	*	8	1.08	53	1.19
				Wyeth Labs				
Nursoy	51	1.18	53	1.19	55	1.23	55	1.25
SMA	35	1.18	38	1.19	39	1.24	41	1.26
				Nestlé Labs				
Good Nature								1.06
Follow Up	69	1.05	78	1.07	79	1.07	76	
Good Start	*	*	*	*	*	*	*	*
				Mead Johnson (Bristol-Myers)				
Nutramigen	*	*	*	*	*	*	*	*
Prosobee	92	1.20	91	1.24	92	1.25	91	1.30
Enfamil	95	1.18	95	1.22	95	1.23	96	1.28

*Brand had not been introduced at this time.
Retail price is for a standard pack size of 16 oz.

EXHIBIT 14 (*concluded*)   1989 ACV and Retail Prices for Powder Form

Brand	First Quarter		Second Quarter		Third Quarter		Fourth Quarter	
	Percent ACV	Retail Price	Percent ACV	Retail Price	Percent ACV	Retail Price	Percent ACV	Retail Price
				Ross Labs (Abbott)				
Isomil	89%	$ 6.31	89%	$ 6.60	89%	$ 6.73	89%	$ 6.98
Similac	87	6.10	86	6.36	87	6.48	87	6.71
				Gerber				
Gerber	*	*	*	*	7	7.00	44	6.17
				Wyeth Labs				
Nursoy	21	5.30	25	5.28	26	5.39	28	5.40
SMA	10	5.88	13	6.05	14	6.27	16	6.30
				Nestlé Carnation				
Good Nature								5.49
Follow Up	75	5.47	81	5.53	83	5.50	83	
Good Start	78	6.73	83	6.79	85	6.82	82	6.84
				Mead Johnson (Bristol-Myers)				
Nutramigen	39	10.77	40	10.91	42	10.89	43	11.04
Prosobee	80	6.22	79	6.42	80	6.46	80	6.75
Enfamil	82	6.09	82	6.24	83	6.24	83	6.50

*Brand had not been introduced at this time.
Retail price is for a standard pack size of 16 oz.

EXHIBIT 15   Variable Costs for a Regular 32-oz. Can of Cow's Milk Formula

Item	Cost
Packaging:	
Label	$0.02
Case (1/6)	0.06
Can body	0.24
Can end	0.03
Raw material:	
Vegetable oil	0.01
Nonfat dry milk	0.17
Corn syrup	0.02
Vitamin premix	0.01
Other	0.01
Labor and other variable costs:	
Labor	0.04
Utilities	0.05
Total variable costs	0.66

Source: Data provided by the office of Hon. Ron Wyden, Chairman, Small Business Subcommittee on Regulation, Business Opportunities, and Energy, U.S. House of Representatives.

EXHIBIT 16   Formula Sales by Type of Outlet

Outlet	Formula Sales ($000)	Percent Sales ($)	Formula Sales (000 cans)	Percent Sales (units)
Food stores (> $2 mill)	$1,521,780	80.2%	165,036	78.5%
Drug store (> $1 mill)	153,345	8.1	13,626	6.5
Food/drug combination	269,294	14.2	29,752	14.1
Mass merchandiser	302,941	16.0	41,300	19.6
Total*	$1,898,360	100%	$210,310	100%

*Individual figures will not add up to total due to outlet crossovers.

The Role of the Medical Community

Management believed that there was a very strong correlation between the brand of formula that was provided to a new mother as she left the hospital (called a discharge pack) and the brand that she chose when she got home. The case of Marcia Ryles may be fairly typical. When Marcia, a pension fund consultant in Los Angeles, gave birth to her first child in November 1989, her hospital gave her a survival kit before she left for home. With the blanket and toy bear came a large tin of Abbott Labs' powdered Similac, the leading infant formula. When her son, Alex, didn't take to breast feeding, Ryles turned to Similac. She didn't try other brands. Says Ryles: "I just didn't want to risk upsetting him by switching formulas."[4] According to Dr. Lawrence M. Gartner, chairman of the pediatrics department at University of Chicago Hospitals, Abbott, for example, gives the University of Chicago free formula and baby bottles, saving the hospital an estimated $100,000 a year. In return, Gartner's department gives Similac to mothers who don't know which formula to use. "What we give away has a direct influence on what mothers buy," said Dr. Gartner.[5] Exhibit 17 depicts the relationship between the brand of sample received at the hospital and retail market share, according to a survey conducted by Carnation.

The specific brand of formula that a new mother received at the time of hospital discharge depended upon the hospital's procedure. Company executives estimated that there were three basic ways in which the choice of formula was made. In about 75 percent of the instances, the hospital had an exclusive contract with a specific manufacturer. In another 20 percent, some variation of a rotation scheme was employed, e.g., boys got Similac and girls got Enfamil, or Similac was provided from January through June and Enfamil was given out from July through December. In the remaining 5 percent of instances, the choice of formula brand was made by the mother.

EXHIBIT 17   Correlation between Hospital Sampling and Market Share

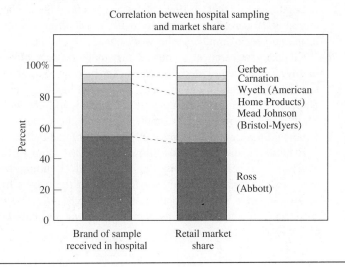

[4]"The Furor Over Formula is Coming to a Boil," *Business Week,* April 9, 1990.
[5]Ibid.

In 1989, when Gerber decided to go directly to the consumer with its new Gerber Baby Formula, reports were that the reaction from the medical community was strong, to say the least. Although the quality of the product was not disputed, many pediatricians and hospitals said that they wouldn't recommend the new formula.[6] Moreover, they stopped recommending the use of other Bristol-Myers formula products as well. One doctor said he was so angry that he kicked the Mead Johnson sales representative out of his hospital and told her not to talk to his residents. Another was also refusing to accept the Bristol-Myers perks—such as providing scholarships for residents—that have earned the infant formula makers a reputation for being the "helpful ally" of the health-care professional. These reports led management to believe that the implications of Carnations' proposed marketing strategy could be serious.

Buyer Behavior

However, the other side of the coin was that the demographics of the market were changing. Bristol-Myers' executives said that the company was simply adapting to a changing marketplace in which mothers are exercising more authority when it comes to infant formula selection.

"Mothers are viewing these products more as consumer-oriented brands," said Don Harris, president of Bristol-Myers's nutritional group. "At this point in time with regard to routine infant formula, there are some mothers and some physicians who are quite willing for the mother to make the decisions in that category," he said.[7]

The debate about consumer advertising came during a decline of breast-feeding. Ross Laboratories said that, in 1989, about 52 percent of the mothers breast-fed their children—a drop of 10 percentage points from 1982. The drop was attributed mostly to the growth in the number of mothers who work outside the home.

Company research also showed that mothers were older, better educated, and more involved with feeding decisions than ever before. More than half of all babies were born to women 25 years of age or older, 78 percent had high school or higher educations, and 50 percent of working mothers returned to the workforce within six weeks of giving birth. More than 80 percent used formula sometime during the first year of the baby's life, and almost 90 percent of working mothers with infants under six months old used formula.

Exhibits 18 and 19 provide information on the labor force participation of mothers of newborns and new first-borns. Exhibits 20 and 21 summarize the company's findings on baby feeding practices during the first year of the baby's life. These findings are based on two separate surveys conducted during 1986–87. The first comprised 598 mothers with babies of age 6–8 months, while the second was based on responses of 593 mothers of babies aged 13–15 months.

---

[6]"Doctors Vow to Proscribe Infant Formula Ad Plans," *The Wall Street Journal,* August 24, 1989.
[7]Ibid.

EXHIBIT 18   Labor Force Participation by Mothers of Newborns

	Age of Mother			
Year	*18–29*	*18–24*	*25–29*	*30–44*
Mothers of newborns in labor force:				
1980	38%	NA	NA	37%
1985	48	47%	49%	50
1988	49	46	52	54
Mothers of new first-borns in labor force:				
1980	46	NA	NA	45
1985	56	53	61	62
1988	55	50	62	68

Notes: Data are limited to women 18–44 years old. Mothers in the labor force are those who had had a child in the 12 months preceding the survey, and were in the labor force at the time of the survey.

Source: FIND/SVP study provided by the company.

EXHIBIT 19   Number of Mothers of Newborns by Labor Force Participation and Educational Attainment

Years of School Completed	Women with Newborns (000)		Share in Labor Force (Percent)	
	1976	*1988*	*1976*	*1988*
Less than high school	783	656	31.0%*	33.7%
High school (4 years)	1,273	1,583	31.6	49.1
College (1–3 years)	413	778	32.1	61.6
College (4 or more years)	328	649	39.0	59.8

*To be read as "In 1976, 31.0 percent of mothers with newborns who had less than a high school education participated in the labor force."

Source: FIND/SVP study provided by the company

The Decision

John Frank had to make the decision about whether or not Carnation should advertise directly to mothers. Further, would this be done in addition to or instead of the traditional marketing to doctors? A marketing plan had to be formulated that specified the total marketing mix and budgets for each element. In addition, it would recommend the specific media to be used and the message that would be communicated. Finally, John also needed to justify his strategy and show how it took into consideration the expected reaction from various stakeholders in the environment.

EXHIBIT 20   Feeding Practices during First Six Months

	Breast Feed Only (Percent)	Formula Only (Percent)	Breast Feed Replaced by Formula (Percent)	Breast Feed Supplemented by Formula (Percent)
Complete sample (N = 598)	12%	35%	9%	44%
By education:				
High school	30%	56%	38%	32%
College	70%	44%	62%	67%
By age of mother:				
25 or under	31%	42%	29%	31%
26–30	35%	35%	52%	41%
Over 30	31%	22%	19%	27%
By employment:				
Full time	10%	28%	35%	31%
Part time	30%	23%	18%	23%
Not employed	60%	49%	48%	46%

Source: Company's study of baby feeding practices, February 1986.

EXHIBIT 21   Total Ounces Used Over One Year

Month	Formula Feeders Only	Supplemental Feeders
First month	$30 \times 6.2 \times 4.1 = 763^*$	$30 \times 1.2 \times 4.0 = 144$
Second month	$30 \times 6.0 \times 4.9 = 883$	$30 \times 1.9 \times 4.8 = 274$
Third month	$30 \times 5.7 \times 5.8 = 992$	$30 \times 2.5 \times 5.8 = 435$
Fourth month	$30 \times 5.2 \times 6.3 = 983$	$30 \times 2.9 \times 6.3 = 548$
Fifth month	$30 \times 4.7 \times 6.9 = 973$	$30 \times 3.2 \times 6.7 = 643$
Sixth month	$30 \times 4.3 \times 7.0 = \underline{903}$	$30 \times 3.4 \times 6.9 = \underline{704}$
Total for first 6 months	5,496 ounces	2,748 ounces
Total for next 6 months	2,410 ounces	2,345 ounces

*To be read: 30 days × 6.2 bottles per day × 4.1 ounces per bottle = 763 ounces.

Source: Company's study of baby feeding practices, February 1986 and June 1987.

Finally, John also had to make some estimates on salesforce requirements, should he decide to market formula in the traditional way, through pediatricians and hospitals. Carnation estimated that there were approximately 33,000 pediatricians in the United States. In addition, there were approximately 4,500 hospitals with birthing centers. A salesperson could reasonably be expected to call on 6–8 pediatricians per day, and it was estimated that a salesperson from Ross Labs typically saw a top pediatrician approximately 26 times per year. Apart from calling on pediatricians, the top salespeople also dealt with neonatologists and hospital administrators to promote the usage of their formula in hospitals. The annual cost per salesperson, including salary, commissions, expenses, etc., was estimated to be approximately $100,000. In addition, supplies, samples, etc., that would have to be provided free to hospitals would cost an extra $25,000 per representative.

Case 9–2

The Massachusetts Lottery*

"It's a chance to make your dreams come true."

The Massachusetts State Lottery was created by a legislative act in September 1971, "to provide a source of revenue for the 351 cities and towns of the Commonwealth." Its first lottery product, a 50-cent weekly game, was introduced the following year and referred to as "The Game" to establish the image of the lottery as being "fun" rather than gambling. The Game realized total revenues of $56 million in 1972, and, in its first full calendar year of operation, $72 million in 1973. In subsequent years, the lottery continued to grow, increasing its revenues and offering a variety of games. By 1988, total revenues were $1,379.2 million, around $235 per capita, generating net revenues distributed to the state of $434.8 million. Chairman Robert Crane, in the lottery's 1987 annual report, commented: "Modern marketing techniques and the most up-to-date electronic equipment enable Massachusetts to be the leader among state lotteries." The lottery had become one of the largest commercial enterprises in the state. Yet state lotteries, and particularly their advertising, were subject to criticism. An editorial in *The Economist*, July 1989, observed:

> Governments have no duty to stop people from spending their money foolishly. But they do have a duty not to encourage people to spend their money in that fashion. On both counts, the role of government in America's current state-lottery frenzy is wrong. Egged on by $400 million a year in fantasy-inducing government-paid advertisements, Americans now spend more than $15 billion a year—up from $2 billion a decade ago—on ever-smaller chances of winning ever-larger sums of money.

---

*Professor N. Craig Smith and Ron Lee prepared this case from public sources with assistance from Professor John A. Quelch as the basis for class discussion. Copyright © 1989 by the President and Fellows of Harvard College. Harvard Business School case 9–590–009.

STATE LOTTERIES

In 1988, 29 states were operating lotteries, generating total revenues of $15.6 billion, or $93.73 per capita; with 48 percent distributed as prizes, 15 percent covering operating costs, and the remaining 37 percent, $5.74 billion, constituting total net revenues to the states. As Table A shows, California had the highest total revenue, with Massachusetts ranked fifth, though having the highest per-capita revenue. On average, 3.3 percent of own-state revenues were generated by lotteries.[1] Half of the states operating lotteries earmarked net revenues entirely for specific public services (education in 50 percent of cases); the remainder added the revenues to general funds.

As well as generating revenue, state lotteries were also intended to provide an alternative to illegal gambling and hence help curb the associated organized crime. A 1972 report by the Fund for the City of New York recommended legalization of the numbers game and betting on sports. Noting that the illegal numbers game was widely played by the poor, the Fund concluded:

1. The primary objective of any legalized gambling should be the elimination of illegal operations;
2. Legal gambling should be seen as a tool of law enforcement rather than a substitute for law enforcement; and
3. The purpose of the legal game should be to attract current players, not to create new players.

Yet in 1989, *The Economist* was urging the privatization of lotteries: "legal private competition would help the consumer. It would quickly drive up the prizes on lottery tickets beyond the current chintzy 48 cents on the dollar. Private lotteries could well put state lotteries out of business completely." Unlike state lotteries, private lotteries and their advertising would also come under Federal Trade Commission jurisdiction.

TABLE A   The Lottery Industry: Leading States, 1988

State/Year Started	1988 Revenues ($ millions)	Percent Change ('88–87)	Revenues per Capita	Prize as Percent of Total Revenues	Operating Expense as Percent of Total Revenues	Net Income ($ millions)	Percent of Revenues to State
California/1985	$2,106.4	$494%	$74.78	49%	13%	$804.0	38%
New York/1967	1,632.0	8	91.17	47	9	725.6	44
Pennsylvania/1972	1,561.0	9	121.48	50	10	725.6	40
Ohio/1974	1,411.0	31	129.78	48	14	545.6	38
Massachusetts/1972	1,379.2	8	234.92	59	10	434.8	31

Source: "Lottomania," *Forbes,* March 6, 1989.

---

[1]Own-state revenues exclude state borrowings and federal grants and reimbursements.

In December 1988, when the prize for the New York Lotto had reached $45 million, the largest in the lottery's history, 80 percent of the state's adult residents bought tickets. Massachusetts claimed more than 60 percent of its adult population regularly bought lottery tickets. Yet research findings suggested a small proportion of participants accounted for most lottery sales. *The Wall Street Journal* cited a study by Duke University economists Charles Clotfelter and Philip Cook which found that the 10 percent betting most frequently accounted for around 50 percent of the total wagered, with the most frequent 20 percent accounting for 65 percent. Characteristics of lottery players and participants in other types of commercial gambling (legal and illegal) were also reported:

- *Sex*: men generally gamble more than women, but almost equal numbers play lotteries;
- *Age*: generally young people gamble the most, but in lotteries the under-25 and over-65 age groups play less frequently and less heavily than the in-between ages;
- *Education*: gambling generally rises with education, but lottery play falls steadily as formal education increases;
- *Occupation*: laborers play the lottery the most and professionals the least;
- *Race*: blacks and Hispanics outplay non-Hispanic whites; and
- *Income*: dollar amount wagered is fairly constant at all income levels, but proportionately higher amounts of household income are therefore wagered by lower-income players.

A California survey reported in *U.S. News and World Report* found that "the poor" wagered 2.1 percent of their income on lotteries, compared with the 0.3 percent expenditure of "the rich." *Money* calculated that the typical player's household income was $25,000. Some poor had become rich, with 800 people winning at least $1 million in 1987, though they represented only 0.0008 percent of the 97 million who played the lottery annually. Sheelah Ryan, a 63-year-old mobile home resident in Florida, won the biggest lottery jackpot in North American history in 1988. She commented: "This is the first time I've ever won $55 million!" However, the odds of winning were greater in other forms of commercial gambling. In comparison to the 50 percent payout in lotteries, prizes averaged 81 percent of the total amount wagered in horse racing, 89 percent in slot machines, and 97 percent in casino table games.

LOTTERY MARKETING[2]

In *Selling Hope*, Clotfelter and Cook questioned whether the businesslike orientation of state lotteries was in the public interest. They attributed much of the success of state lotteries to the use of sophisticated marketing:

> Unlike virtually every other operation of government at any level, but very much like most suppliers of consumer products, lottery agencies pay attention to details of product design, pricing, and promotion. This marketing is motivated by the lotteries' objective of maximizing revenue and made possible by their unusual degree of independence. . . . With the help of . . . specialists and experienced advertising agencies, the lotteries have set about to increase their revenues by stimulating the demand for their products.

---

[2]This section is based on Charles T. Clotfelter and Philip J. Cook, *Selling Hope: State Lotteries in America* (Cambridge: Harvard University Press, 1989).

State lottery marketing was "not as an afterthought but as a deliberate policy." Clotfelter and Cook quote one lottery director as having commented: "To survive and prosper, it is essential that lotteries practice the business technique of the private sector, particularly in the area of marketing."

As monopoly suppliers of legal lottery games, the state lotteries realized their objective of maximizing revenue by strategies of recruiting new users or stimulating increased usage, rather than growing market share. Increasing usage was the dominant strategy, so, for example, Maryland lottery's advertising plan stated: "All advertising programs for the lottery must develop regular participants of the games, not casual impulse sales." Accordingly, target marketing, based on regular marketing research to identify the characteristics and preferences of market segments, was well established. So Arizona, using data collected from winners, found that games involving future drawings were more attractive to older people than to younger ones. Heavy users were targeted in particular, with market segments often geographically defined so that neighborhoods were identified with the highest relative rates of participation for each lottery game. Lottery advertisements in Spanish were commonplace in California and New York, though the targeting of minority groups had become controversial in some states. There had even been a boycott organized of the Illinois lottery, following charges that it devoted special attention to sections of Chicago populated by poor blacks.

According to lottery consultant John Koza, psychographic segmentation as well as demographic segmentation was important. "Belongers," one of nine distinct lifestyle groups in the VALS (Values and Lifestyles) typology, although not inherently attracted to gambling activities, was a substantial group of participants in lotteries because they were government-sanctioned. As Koza put it, for this segment, "If the government says 'it's OK', then it's OK." The "societally conscious" group, however, gambled considerably less than average and, accordingly, was less likely to be targeted. Having segmented the market, lotteries would then put together appropriate marketing mixes.

Product design encompassed play value, prize structure, the variety and complexity of games. Instant "rub-off" games, for example, added play value to an otherwise passive game by incorporating elements of choice and suspense.[3] A mix of prize structures was often used to appeal to different players; though a study showed that neither players nor nonplayers knew the odds of winning the Washington state's lotto game, the awareness of large prizes, rather than the odds, was the overriding concern. Price considerations not only included the ticket price, but also the expected value of prizes. However, lottery managers were often constrained by state legislation specifying payout rates or setting minimum rates, though some states, such as Massachusetts, provided the flexibility to vary the payout rates among games. Yet awareness of this variation was often low, as Clotfelter and Cook conclude, "players generally appear to be ignorant about basic parameters of the lottery games in which they participate."

Convenience of purchase was important in reaching impulse buyers, especially for instant games. Convenience stores, supermarkets, liquor stores, drugstores, newsstands, and lottery ticket kiosks were the main outlets used. Vending machines were sometimes

---

[3]"Rub-off" games had hidden symbols revealed by rubbing a coin over the surface of the card.

utilized in high-traffic areas. Enlisting the support of retail agents was an important place consideration, as Clotfelter and Cook suggest: "A cashier who asks, 'Would you like a lottery ticket with that quart of milk?' may have a significant role in determining a lottery's success in maximizing sales." Promotion considerations encompassed advertising, sales promotions, publicity, and personal selling. Sales promotions included "buy one, get one free" offers; free ticket coupons in newspapers, which achieved high redemption rates; and joint promotions with retailers such as McDonald's. Lottery sales representatives played an important role in dealing with retail agents as well as in favorable publicity. Clotfelter and Cook write: "Imagine how delighted most companies would be if their main product were featured on television news shows and newspaper front pages. For lotteries this kind of publicity has become routine." All lotteries employed public relations specialists.

Advertising was largely on television (an estimated 57 percent of state lottery budgets were allocated to specific media in 1988), but radio (16 percent) was also important, as were point-of-sale advertisements (11 percent), print advertisements (7 percent), and transit signs and billboards (5 percent). Selective data analyzed by Clotfelter and Cook suggested the time devoted to lottery advertising was about three-fourths the total amount for all state advertising, such that "most state citizens see lottery ads far more often than virtually any other message put out by the state." A survey by Maryland found that those most likely to be aware of lottery advertisements were young adults, blacks, television watchers, and lottery players. Attention was paid to the timing of advertising, particularly to coincide with paydays. The advertising plan for Ohio's Super Lotto specified: "Schedule heavier media weight during those times of the month when consumer disposable income peaks."

Clotfelter and Cook's content analysis of a sample of advertisements provided by 13 of the largest lotteries identified eight primary messages, split equally between the "largely informational" and the "basically thematic." Informational advertisements included announcements of a new lottery game; direct appeals to buy tickets (in California: "Watch it grow! Play Lotto 6/49"); information about how to play a lottery game; details about winners; and, notably in brochures, information on rules of the game, prize structures, and the odds of winning. Many advertisements featured a reminder of the lottery's contribution to the state: "Thanks to you, everybody wins" (District of Columbia); "Our schools win, too" (California). Only a few advertisements were devoted to this purpose, though a series on this theme was developed by Maryland:

> One of the most dramatic of these was a television spot depicting a little boy wandering away from his family's campsite in the woods. In the gathering darkness the frightened boy wanders through the woods crying for his mother and father while the worried parents describe their son to police officers. A state police helicopter spots the boy with a searchlight, and a voice-over points out that the state lottery contributed $300 million in funds for public service, part of which was set aside for this police helicopter. As a sobbing mother is notified that her son is safe, the ad intones: "The Maryland state lottery pays off in ways you may not even know about."

Thematic advertisements employed humor and fantasy, with themes of the fun and excitement of the lottery; the dual message that anyone can win and that winning can change your life, such as "before-and-after" advertisements; a focus on wealth and luxury, "The rich. Join them" (Michigan); and a focus on money itself, such as coins being minted. Clotfelter and Cook reported that many advertisements portrayed wealth, leisure, gracious living, excitement, romance, and fame. A California advertisement featured dreams of possibilities created by winning, from a carefree retirement to establishing a father-son business. Advertisements tended to show wholesome surroundings and players younger and more affluent than the typical lottery player. Clotfelter and Cook described lottery advertisements as "among the most clever and appealing shown on television today."

Omissions from lottery advertisements formed the basis of some of the strongest criticisms. A consistent overstatement of the true value of prizes was said to result from not disclosing that large prizes were typically paid out over a 20-year period and that the stated prize was the sum of the payments, not its present value; that large prizes only applied to single winners; and that jackpots were subject to taxation. Clotfelter and Cook found only 20 percent of the advertisements in their sample gave any information on the odds of winning, and usually only the probability of winning any prize as opposed to the grand prize. They suggested that, with over 50 percent of the advertisements mentioning the dollar amount of prizes, there was an emphasis on prizes over probabilities, giving a distorted impression of the probability of winning and increasing players' "subjective probability" of winning.

Missouri, Virginia, and Wisconsin attempted to restrict lottery advertising, viewing it as an inducement to gamble. This was in keeping with a wide-ranging National Association of Broadcasters code of conduct which, if it had not been ruled anti-competitive, would have questioned many lottery advertisements because of specific provisions on lottery advertising practice which, for example, said advertisements should not "indicate what fictitious winners may do, hope to do, or have done with their winnings."

Clotfelter and Cook believed that while those running the lottery were well-intentioned and professional, there were legitimate concerns about their marketing practices, notably the use of misleading advertising and, largely as a consequence, the undermining of the credibility of state government. As California's attorney general commented, "People look to the government to be honest and straightforward and not to be using suckering kinds of techniques."

THE MASSACHUSETTS LOTTERY

The legislation governing the Massachusetts lottery specified revenue distribution such that a minimum of 45 percent was to be paid out in prizes, operating expenses were not to exceed 15 percent (from this amount a 5 percent commission and 1 percent bonus was paid to the sales agents who sold the tickets),, and the balance was to be distributed to the Local Aid Fund for the benefit of the 351 towns and cities of the Commonwealth. The lottery itself assumed no responsibility for determining how much each city or town was to receive. The Department of Revenue was responsible for disbursement of revenue, according to each city or town's population. The cities and towns were then free to use their share of the revenue as they saw fit. The lottery produced around 3.8 percent of Massachusetts revenues generated within the state.

After "The Game" was established in 1972, the Massachusetts State Lottery Commission pioneered the Instant Game. In this game, the player purchased a rub-off ticket with a pre-printed prize structure which allowed the buyer to know immediately if he or she was a winner. Prizes ranged from a free Instant lottery ticket to $100,000 a year for life. Despite its initial success, the Instant Game suffered a decline in popularity in 1977 and 1978. To encourage sales, the prize structure was readjusted to devote a greater portion of the prize money to the lower tier prizes which could be paid "instantly" by the sales agents. In 1987, sales were over $425 million, and the Instant Game became Massachusetts' most popular lottery. In 1976, the Lottery established the Numbers Game in order to allow players to participate more actively through selection of their own four-digit number, type of bet (with variation of the amount and which combination of digits in the four-digit number were bet on), and length of time they wished to play (between one and six days). The second objective of the Numbers Game was to challenge illegal gaming through an attractive and honest numbers game.

Megabucks, a number selection game whose jackpot grew until it was won, was established in 1982. Six numbers were to be chosen from a field of 30 which was later increased to a field of 36. In 1984, three drawings which failed to produce a winner ended by producing a jackpot of $18.2 million. Megabucks was the fastest-growing game in the history of the Massachusetts State Lottery, beginning with weekly sales of $50,000 in 1982 and growing to over $7 million a week in 1987.

Exhibit 1 shows an advertisement for Mass Millions. Launched in 1987, this game was designed to respond to public interest in very large jackpots. Though the Megabucks game routinely produced jackpots of $2 to $6 million, the jackpot did not reach $10 million or more unless no one won the jackpot for three or four drawings. Mass Millions was structured to produce larger but less frequent jackpots than Megabucks. Players selected six numbers out of a field of 46, with each bet costing $1. Players matching all six numbers were guaranteed a minimum jackpot of $1 million. Players who matched five of the six winning numbers plus the "bonus" (or seventh) number won $50,000. The odds of winning the smallest prize ($2) were 1 in 47; the odds of winning the jackpot were 1 in over 9 million.

MASSACHUSETTS LOTTERY ADVERTISING

Massachusetts lottery advertising and promotion expenses in 1988 were just under $11.5 million, with around 38 percent spent on television advertising, 38 percent on radio, 20 percent on press, and 4 percent on point-of-sale materials. Agents selling lottery tickets provided flyers giving information on the odds and prize structures for games. Exhibit 2 shows an example of a flyer for a $1 instant game. Around 250,000 flyers were produced for each instant game (there would typically be seven different games in a year).

Criticism of lottery advertising was not uncommon. Writing in *Adweek* in March 1989, John Carroll suggested the advertising by the Massachusetts lottery "rivals professional wrestling in its egregious manipulation of people's baser instincts." He referred, for example, to the "ESP" campaign:

> Remember the "ESP" campaign? The television spot asked you to pick a number from one to five, then superimposed a number on the screen. (I think there were five versions of the spot.) If you were right, the spot went on to say, you *might* have ESP. Admittedly, that would come in handy when filling out your lottery slip. Unfortunately, though, there are no lottery games in this state that have one-to-five odds. If you really did have ESP, you'd probably have a better chance of making money from the *National Enquirer*.

EXHIBIT 1   Advertisement for Mass Millions

EXHIBIT 2 Instant Game Point-of-Sale Flyer

Rear

With over $66 million in total cash prizes, this game is The New Green Monster.

Play the game like the pros—for money. It's Grand Slam, The Lottery's newest instant game. Scratch out a hit and you could win up to $1,000 instantly.

You could really clean up playing Grand Slam because it's the game of extra winnings—over 16,500 prizes at $500 or more and over $66 million in total cash prizes plus a chance to win up to 4 times on a ticket.

Grand Slam—all the excitement of the big leagues with a chance to come home a winner.

PRIZE STRUCTURE FOR GRAND SLAM

PRIZE AMOUNT	PRIZES IN GAME	PROBABILITY OF WINNING
$1,000	336	1:336,000.0
$1,000 ($500 + $500)	300	1:252,000.0
$1,000	400	1:6,260.9
$500	16,100	1:852.1
$40	118,300	1:423.5
$40 ($10 + $10 + $10 + $10)	238,000	1:900.0
$10	112,000	1:450.0
$10 ($5 + $5)	224,000	1:450.0
$10 ($5 + $4 + $2)	336,000	1:300.0
$10 ($5 + $2 + $2 + $2)	336,000	1:300.0
$5	112,000	1:900.0
$5 ($2 + $1 + $1 + $1)	224,000	1:450.0
$4	336,000	1:300.0
$4 ($2 + $2)	336,000	1:300.0
$4 ($1 + $1 + $1 + $1)	672,000	1:150.0
$4 ($1 + $1 + $1 + $1)	672,000	1:150.0
$2	3,696,000	1:27.3
$2 ($1 + $1)	3,696,000	1:27.3
$1	8,400,000	1:12.0
CASH PRIZES	19,525,100	1:5.2

Prize Structure based on the sale of approximately 100,800,000 tickets.

All winners, tickets and transactions subject to Lottery Commission rules as published in the code of Massachusetts regulations.

THE LOTTERY

Front

671

Case 9–3

*Pepsico and Madonna**

INTRODUCTION

In April 1989, PepsiCo, Inc., the number two soft drink manufacturer in the world announced that it was cancelling a two-minute television commercial starring pop singer Madonna. Pepsi had already paid Madonna close to $5 million for a product endorsement contract that included several advertisements and joint promotion of her upcoming concert tour. A Pepsi executive argued that viewers might confuse the advertisements with a promotional video which first aired the following day and also featured Madonna's new song "Like a Prayer." A Pepsi executive told *The Wall Street Journal*, "We knew she was making a video in a church with a choir. We didn't know the video featured burning crosses, priests, and religious figures."

CELEBRITY ENDORSEMENTS

Pepsi was one of the first companies to use rock stars as commercial endorsers to reach young soft drink consumers. In 1984 and 1987, Pepsi signed multi-million dollar promotional deals with Michael Jackson to support the launch of his *Thriller* and *Bad* albums. Pepsi also signed up rock musicians such as Tina Turner, Lionel Richie, and the Spanish group Menudo to promote its brands.

Pepsi's contract with Madonna was announced in January 1989. Around the same time, Coca Cola signed pop singer George Michael. Some commentators questioned Madonna's appeal. A study released by Marketing Evaluations TVQ Inc. found that Madonna was recognized by 88 percent of respondents but liked by only 25 percent compared to an average of 21 percent for female singers. The corresponding figures for George Michael were 80 percent, 48 percent and 22 percent.

PEPSI VERSUS COKE

Coca Cola's unsuccessful launch of New Coke gave Pepsi an opportunity to strengthen its position as the preferred youth-oriented brand of cola. Coke was forced to drop its popular "Coke Is It" campaign because of consumer confusion between its two brands,

---

*Aimee L. Stern prepared this case from published sources under the supervision of Professors N. Craig Smith and John A. Quelch as the basis for class discussion rather than to illustrate either effective or ineffective handling of an administrative situation. Copyright © 1990 by the President and Fellows of Harvard College. Harvard Business School case 9–590–038.

Classic Coke and New Coke. Coke replaced "Coke Is It" with what some analysts saw as a less appealing slogan, "Can't Beat the Feeling".

In 1988, Pepsi held a 30.7 percent share of overall sales in the $20.7 billion U.S. soft drink market. Coke had a 40.5 percent share. That year, however, Pepsi surpassed Coke in supermarket retail sales for the first time. Industry analysts partially credited Pepsi's advertising for this success.

Between 1985 and 1987, Pepsi increased its U.S. advertising budget from $116.7 million to $135.8 million, while Coke's advertising spending declined from $159 million to $141 million. The vast majority of these budgets were spent on network television.

Pepsi's advertising was considered by analysts to be more creative than Coke's. It consistently outperformed Coke in consumer advertising recall tests. Based on recall scores, Market Facts Inc. calculated that the cost per week of having 1,000 television viewers remember an advertisement was $9.97 for Coke but $8.19 for Pepsi.

"MAKE A WISH"

The two-minute "Make a Wish" advertisement was aired in prime time on March 2, 1989, during the first commercial break of "The Cosby Show". On the same day, the advertisement was shown in 40 countries around the world and viewed by approximately 250 million people. This represented one of the largest single-day media buys in history. Pepsi planned to air 30- and 60-second versions of the advertisement in a continuation of the campaign. A series of additional advertisements with Madonna was also planned.

The advertisement was Madonna's first commercial endorsement. It was described by *Adweek* as a blend of *It's a Wonderful Life* and *Peggy Sue Got Married*. It opened with Madonna watching a black-and-white home movie facsimile of her eighth grade birthday party. The younger version of the singer joined the older Madonna in a song and dance fest. The ad concluded as the older Madonna (in color) viewed her younger self (in black and white) blowing out her birthday candles. She urged the young girl to "Go Ahead, make a Wish". An *Advertising Age* review described the advertisement as "the best commercial of its genre—the perfect balance of entertainment and sell," noting that the Pepsi name was visible eleven times before the closing logo shot.

"LIKE A PRAYER"

The "Like a Prayer" video aired on MTV (Music Television Videos) on March 3. Both the advertisement and video featured Madonna's new song, "Like a Prayer," which was also the theme song for her upcoming concert tour. The video depicted Madonna wearing a black negligee receiving the stigmata of Christ. The commercial contained no footage from the video.

THE REVEREND DONALD WILDMON

American Family Association director Reverend Donald Wildmon was considered the primary reason Pepsi withdrew the advertisement. Wildmon headed a Christian advocacy group with approximately 380,000 members in hundreds of local chapters. In 1989, his organization had a budget of $5 million, funded primarily through small donations. He threatened a boycott of all Pepsi products if the company continued to air the advertisement, and received public support from several individual Catholic bishops. Some Pepsi executives feared that this might be followed by a potentially damaging statement from the U.S. Catholic Conference.

Wildmon's aim was to clear the airwaves of anti-Christian material. His primary targets were not the broadcast networks but the corporations who supported sexually explicit advertisements and television programs. In 1986, he convinced Southland Corp. to remove sexually explicit magazines from its company-owned 7-Eleven stores. In 1989, he convinced General Mills to stop running advertisements on NBC's "Saturday Night Live," a program which Wildmon considered "vulgar".

The association's monthly journal contained headlines such as "Boozing Priest on Show Bought by RJR Nabisco, Pfizer," and "Kellogg, Sara Lee Promote Christian Buffoons on ABC." Wildmon commented that television sex, "done affectionately, with love and within the bonds of marriage, doesn't bother me. But . . . some things you do privately."

PEPSI'S REACTION

Wildmon's first confrontation with Pepsi occurred in the fall of 1988 over its promotional sponsorship of the videocassette release of *ET*. The movie was produced by MCA/Universal, the same studio that had released *The Last Temptation of Christ*. Wildmon asserted that Pepsi's willingness to deal with MCA/Universal implied that the company supported what he viewed as sacrilege in this film. Pepsi refused to cancel the *ET* project.

Wildmon called the Madonna video "one of the most offensive things I've ever seen." Pepsi's initial reaction to Wildmon's threatened boycott was a denial that it would pull the commercial. A few days later, a Pepsi spokesperson announced "a temporary hold on the commercial until we see a reaction to the video." In particular, Pepsi substituted other commercials on MTV after MTV began airing the video. The spokesman said the company was concerned that consumers might confuse the commercial and the video. He stated that Pepsi wanted to see the video gain recognition before it expanded the commercial campaign. Two other religious groups protested, and Pepsi received complaint letters and calls from consumers. A month after the advertisement debuted, Pepsi canceled its affiliation with Madonna in the U.S., including the sponsorship of her U.S. concert tour. However, Pepsi continued to run the advertisements in Europe and Asia. Wildmon then announced an end to the boycott of Pepsi products.

Pepsi executives told reporters that they had not seen the video before it aired and had not been informed that it would air so soon after the commercial. Entertainment marketers speculated that Madonna would not have agreed to any preview even if Pepsi had asked.

Advertising and beverage industry executives expressed outrage that religious groups could pressure Pepsi to censor creative advertising. A Pepsi spokesperson said the Madonna flap generated "a tremendous amount of publicity." However, Russell Klein, senior vice president of Seven-Up Co., told *The Wall Street Journal*, "I find it very difficult to believe Pepsi would find this current mistake acceptable because of the public relations they received. I don't think they're sitting in their offices smiling."

ADVERTISING RECALL

A tracking study by *Advertising Age* and The Gallup Organization found that Pepsi led in unaided advertising recall in March, 1989. One thousand consumers were asked: "Of all the advertising you have seen, heard, or read in the past 30 days, which advertisement first comes to mind?" The three most frequently mentioned advertisers at the end of February and March, 1989, were:

	February Rank	*March Rank*
McDonald's	1	2
Pepsi Cola	2	1
Ford	3	4
Coca Cola	4	3

Pepsi was the most frequently recalled advertiser among all groups except consumers aged 65 or more. The strongest recall was among respondents aged 25–34. When asked "which soft drink advertiser first comes to mind?" the percentages of mentions were:

	February	*March*
Pepsi Cola	37.6%	40.9%
Coca Cola	32.5	29.6
Diet Coke	9.4	8.9

SOURCES

"Soft Drinks: Pepsi's 'New Generation' Takes Over," *Adweek*, March 6, 1989, p. 38.

Bob Garfield, "Pepsi Should Offer Prayer to Madonna," *Advertising Age*, March 6, 1989, p. 76.

Scott Hume, "Pepsi Tops Ad Recall After Madonna Flap," *Advertising Age*, April 24, 1989, p. 12.

Michael J. McCarthy, "Pop Go The Soda Wars: Pepsi Signs Madonna To Appear In Ads," *The Wall Street Journal*, January 26, 1989, pp. B1, B5.

James R. Schiffman, "PepsiCo Cans TV Ads with Madonna, Pointing up Risks of Using Superstars," *The Wall Street Journal*, April 5, 1989, p. B-11.

Scott Ticer, "The Cola Superpowers' Outrageous New Arsenals," *Business Week*, March 20, 1989, pp. 162–163.

Peter Waldman, "This Madonna Isn't What the Reverend Really Had in Mind," *The Wall Street Journal*, April 7, 1989, pp. A1, A8.

Patricia Winters, "Pepsi Won't Cut Ties with Madonna," *Advertising Age*, March 6, 1989, p. 74.

Case 9–4

Audi of America Inc.*

On March 19, 1986, the Center for Auto Safety, a Washington-based group founded by consumer activist Ralph Nader, and the New York state attorney general submitted a petition to the National Highway Traffic Safety Administration (NHTSA) claiming that 1978–86 Audi 5000s equipped with automatic transmissions were unsafe and demanding that they be recalled. A number of incidents involving injury and death had been reported in which Audi 5000s had surged out of control when the drivers shifted from park to drive or reverse. Unintended acceleration problems had been reported on other cars, but not nearly as often as with the Audi 5000. The Audi, like many other European cars, placed the brake and gas pedals closer together than in many American designs so that a driver could move faster between pedals in high-speed emergencies. It was not, however, immediately clear that this was the cause of the problem.

THE RECALL

In July 1986, Audi of America Inc. agreed to recall 132,000 1984–86 models to replace the idle stabilization valve and to relocate the brake and gas pedals. Audi management subsequently decided that installing a shift lock, which required the driver to depress the brake before shifting into gear, would be preferable. The cost of the recall to Audi was estimated at $25 million.

By January 1987, Audi had installed the shift lock in 70,000 cars. In that month, Audi decided to recall another 120,000 Audi 5000s sold between 1978 and 1983 for the same retrofit. Unfortunately for Audi, unintended acceleration incidents began to be reported on cars equipped with the shift locks. By May 1987, the Center for Auto Safety recorded the toll taken by unintended acceleration of Audi 5000s at 1,700 incidents, 1,500 accidents, over 400 injuries, and 7 deaths. In addition to product liability suits filed by victims of unintended acceleration, a class action suit seeking compensation from Audi was initiated on behalf of existing Audi owners whose cars' resale values were depressed by the problem.

---

*This case was prepared by Professor John A. Quelch as the basis for class discussion rather than to illustrate either effective or ineffective handling of an administrative situation. Copyright © 1990 by the President and Fellows of Harvard College. Harvard Business School case 9–590–114.

SALES IMPACT

The unintended acceleration problem had a devastating effect on Audi sales. In 1985, Audi of America enjoyed record sales of 74,000 units. In 1986, sales dropped to 60,000. The rate of decline accelerated following coverage of the Audi safety problem in November 1986 on the CBS Show *60 Minutes*. Audi management complained that reports of unintended acceleration increased dramatically following the broadcast. In January 1987, sales fell to 1.439, or 3.5 units per dealer, from 2.072 the previous year.

By March, Audi management faced a 248-day supply of 5000 models compared to a normal inventory of 60-65 days. Hence, Audi announced a $5,000 rebate from April 1 to June 30, 1987, on the purchase or lease of any 5000-series model. The rebate represented a 23 percent discount off the dealer list price. Close to 120,000 coupons were mailed; 18,000 cars were sold or leased under the program. An Audi survey showed that only 6 percent of coupon recipients would have bought a car had the rebate been $4,000.

In the absence of the promotion, Audi of America sold only 41,300 vehicles in 1987 despite a new advertising campaign launched in the summer with a spending level double that in 1986. In addition, Audi introduced the more aerodynamically styled Audi 80 and 90 to replace the Audi 4000 series, a smaller and less expensive companion line to the 5000. Worldwide Audi sales rose 14 percent in 1987 despite the problem in the United States, which accounted for only 6 percent of the total.

THE VALUE ASSURANCE PLAN

January 1988 sales were only half those in January 1987. The new Audi 80s and 90s were not selling as well as had been expected. Audi management believed that consumer concern over the resale value of the Audis was restraining sales. They, therefore, conceived and launched in February 1988 a value assurance plan on all Audi 80s, 90s, and 5000s.

Under the plan, Audi promised to refund the difference between any new Audi's resale value and the resale value of comparable models sold by BMW, Mercedes-Benz, and Volvo. The Audi had to be resold between two and four years of the purchase date, and the value would be determined by the National Automobile Dealers Association (NADA) used car guide. A hypothetical example was cited in a February 1988 issue of *Automotive News:* assume a 1988 model Audi sold three years after the date of purchase was worth, on average, 56 percent of its $25,000 value. If the average price of the designated competitive models was 60 percent of their original prices, there would be a difference of 4 percent in resale value. Audi would then multiply the $25,000 purchase price by 4 percent—an equation worth $1,000 to the owner. Under the program, the Audi 80 and 90 were considered comparable to the Mercedes Benz 190-E, BMW 325i, and Volvo 740. The Audi 5000S and Quattro were lined up against the Mercedes 269-F, BMW 528e, and the Volvo 760 GLE. The Audi 5000 CS Turbo and Turbo Quattro were compared with the Mercedes 300-E, BMW 535i, and Volvo 760 GLE Turbo.

THE 1988 REBATE

The value assurance plan had a positive but limited impact on retail sales. Frequent media reports on the progress of lawsuits filed against the company by victims of unintended acceleration did not help. Audi management looked forward to September when the 5000 series would be replaced by the new Audi 100 and 200 models that were already sold in Europe. Meanwhile, 1988 sales were still running at only half those in 1987.

Hence, Audi management conceived a second rebate program whereby 400,000 certificates were mailed to current and former Audi owners offering a $4,000 rebate on those Audi 5000s with automatic transmissions still in stock. These vehicles carried a dealer sticker price of $22,180. The rebate offer was good from May 1 through August 31. An existing $2,500 per unit dealer incentive on remaining Audi 5000s was curtailed in favor of the consumer promotion.

It soon became apparent that only 5,500 qualified vehicles were available at Audi dealerships. In June 1988, Costa N. Kensington filed a $76 million class action suit claiming that the Audi promotion represented bait-and-switch advertising with the intent of selling Audi 80s and 90s which, at the time, carried a $2,000-per-unit dealer incentive. Mr. Kensington stated: "It is clear that the plan was not intended to benefit Audi customers but to jump-start sluggish sales of Audi's newly introduced automobiles."

Federal Trade Commission regulations required a retailer to have "a sufficient quantity of the advertised product to meet reasonably anticipated demands unless the advertisement clearly and adequately discloses that the supply is limited." Audi officials pointed to a sentence on the back of the rebate coupon that read "The availability of eligible vehicles is limited." Attorneys general offices in Pennsylvania and Connecticut contended that this warning was inadequate because it did not specify the average number of cars at each dealership.

The Wall Street Journal reported on June 22, 1988, that Audi executives had told their dealers to expect 24,000 interested buyers to visit showrooms as a result of the offer. Responding to a question regarding the gap between supply and demand of the Audi 5000, Audi's general sales manager, Joe Tate, said that the company's projection of 24,000 was inflated in order to generate enthusiasm among dealers and corporate members. "If anything," he said, "we have pulled a bait-and-switch in the minds of our dealers. We may have hyped our numbers to excite a retail organization . . . so we could be certain to sell out the 5000s we had left. It was an attempt to build their confidence." In a memo dated May 2, 1988, Tate told the dealers that the program had been devised "to present attractive purchase alternatives" to coupon holders "who discover that the new 80 and 90 series vehicles may be a better solution to their driving needs." In the company newsletter of the same month, Tate expanded on the company's intentions, pointing out that "Hopefully we can send some of the excess (Audi) 5000 customers toward the 80 and 90 line. What we're trying to do is jump-start Audi sales."

Separately, Dick Mugg, president of Audi America, commented: "In the past, I expected total commitment from the dealer to the product. Now I realize that is a totally unfair expectation. The industry has changed over the years—and probably for the better. We're no different from Procter and Gamble. We've got to earn shelf space; we've got to earn dealer share of mind every day."

Having already suffered allegations of mechanical failure, Audi shuddered at the prospect of a marketing plan which would compound criticism. An unidentified Audi executive commented: "It's frightening to think that just after we've enraged customers with the whole sudden-acceleration issue, we can come back with something that could be construed as bait-and-switch and cause another whole public relations blow up."

FUTURE PLANS

Audi executives were concerned that their plans for launching the Audi 100 and 200 in August 1988 might be derailed by the accusations of bait-and-switch. In addition, Audi of America faced over 100 product liability suits, and the class action suit filed by Audi owners seeking compensation for the loss in resale value of their cars had yet to be resolved. Management planned to launch a new program called the Audi Advantage program that covered almost all normal maintenance and repairs for three years or 50,000 miles on any new Audi. Free roadside assistance was also included. Audi's agency had proposed an advertising campaign that claimed: "Audi introduces a better car to own. And a better way to own a car."

SOURCES

"Audi 5000 Carries Discount of $4000." *Automotive News,* April 18, 1988.

Helen Kahn, "Audi Tries to Settle Class Suit," *Automotive News,* June 13, 1988.

Amal Kumar Naj, "Audi of America Agrees to Recall 5000 Model Cars," *The Wall Street Journal,* January 16, 1987, p. 2.

Bradley A. Schwartz, "Audi Agrees to Give Owners of Its 5000 Rebate Toward Future Audi Purchases," *The Wall Street Journal,* June 8, 1988.

Bradley A. Schwartz, "VW's Audi Unit in the U.S. Draws Fire Over Controversial Incentive Programs," *The Wall Street Journal,* June 22, 1988, p. 7.

Geoff Sundstrom, "NHTSA Won't End Audi Probe," *Automotive News,* June 27, 1988.

David Versical, "An Anatomy," *Automotive News,* May 4, 1987.

David Versical, "Audi Guarantees Resale, Offers Dealer Rebate," *Automotive News,* February 15, 1988.

David Versical, "Mugg—Audi Healer," *Automotive News,* May 30, 1988.

PART 10

Projects and Exercises in Advertising and Promotion Management

Media Planning and
Selection Exercise*

There are many different ways that advertisers can spend their limited budgets. This exercise is intended to introduce you to the problems of evaluating different combinations of media vehicles. The exercise and the model it describes ask the manager to combine "facts" that are available from market research with *quantitative* judgements about the target groups, relative ability of different media to communicate the desired message, and the relative worth of increasing reach versus increasing frequency. Often, going through the exercise makes managers and students painfully aware of the many assumptions that are required to justify one media plan versus alternatives that might be used. Be sure you stay focused on the important questions. An author of several judgmental calculus models, Len Lodish, has said, "it is better to be right than precisely wrong."

This exercise provides an opportunity to apply the concepts of media planning to a variety of situations. The main vehicle of the exercise is a Lotus 1-2-3 model designed to illustrate some of the key decisions involved in developing and evaluating media plans. The model incorporates many of the basic media-planning concepts described in the "Becel Margarine" case (Case 4–1). The Lotus 1-2-3 model, "MEDPLAN," will be distributed by your instructor. See Exhibit 1 for a sample of the key output ("Total Weighted Exposures") and other performance measures, and Exhibit 2 for some examples of the data available in the model.

The first component of the model provides detailed reach and cost data for 22 possible television, print, radio, and outdoor vehicles. This information should be valuable for beginning your analysis of the tradeoffs among various media choices and is the starting point for the Lotus 1-2-3 model you will be using. The remainder of the exercise outlines the steps involved in using the media-planning model and describes what changes you can make to the currently provided inputs so as to build your own media plan.

---

*This exercise and accompanying spreadsheet template were written by Professor Robert Carraway, Professor Paul W. Farris, and Lisa Axel, Research Assistant, and revised by Professors Paul W. Farris and Christopher Gale, and Nischal Rajey, Research Assistant. Copyright © 1990 by the Darden Graduate Business School Foundation, Charlottesville, Virginia.

EXHIBIT 1 Output Computed by the Model

Gross impressions	1,612,968
Total cost	$9,566,848
Budget	$10,000,000
Plan frequency index	0.67
Plan demographic index	0.55
Plan impact index	1.03
Total weighted exposures	616,049
Cost per thousand exposures	$15.53

EXHIBIT 2 Sample of Some Input and Output Displays*

(NOTE: INPUTS CHANGEABLE BY THE USER ARE PRINTED IN BOLD. THESE INPUTS WILL HAVE TO BE SPECIFIED BY USING THE MENU SYSTEM. **DO NOT ENTER THEM DIRECTLY INTO THE MAIN AREA OF THE WORKSHEET.**)

MEDIA PLANNING EXERCISE: **PRESS (ALT-M) TO ACCESS THE MAIN-MENU OPTION.**

DEMOGRAPHIC GROUPS AND WEIGHTS:

Dimensions

	Gender	Age	Income	Education	Size of Household
Category 1	**Male**	**18-24**	**14,999/less**	**College grad**	**1**
Category 2	**Female**	**25-34**	**15-19,999**	**Att'd coll**	**2**
Category 3		**35-44**	**20-29,999**	**Grad HS**	**3-4**
Category 4		**15+**	**30,000+**	**Att'd HS or less**	**5+**

Demographic Weights

	Gender	Age	Income	Education	Size of Household
Category 1	**1.1**	**0.6**	**0.5**	**1.2**	**0.7**
Category 2	**0.9**	**0.9**	**0.8**	**1.0**	**0.9**
Category 3	**0.0**	**1.0**	**1.1**	**0.9**	**1.0**
Category 4	**0.0**	**0.8**	**1.3**	**0.8**	**1.2**

/Note: The inputs shown in this exhibit may not be the same as the ones currently in the MEDPLAN file.

MEDIA INPUT AND
  SCHEDULE:

GROSS IMPRESSIONS	1,528,328		
TOTAL COST	$9,123,678	BUDGET	**$10,000,000**
PLAN FREQUENCY INDEX	0.64	**PRESS (ALT-S) TO PERFORM**	
PLAN DEMOGRAPHIC	0.60	**SENSITIVITY ANALYSIS OF THE**	
PLAN IMPACT INDEX	1.09	**CURRENT SET OF INSERTIONS.**	
TOTAL WEIGHTED EXPOSURES	633,179		
COST PER M EXPOSURES	$14.41		

(continued)

EXHIBIT 2 *(concluded)*

Frequency	Unadjusted Reach (000s)	Percent of Total Population	Frequency Weight	Frequency Index
0	2,993	1.3%	0	0.00
1	8,188	3.5	0	0.00
2	14,800	6.3	0.05	0.00
3	21,091	9.0	0.1	0.01
4	25,645	10.9	0.25	0.03
5	27,719	11.8	0.5	0.06
6	27,306	11.6	0.8	0.09
7	24,930	10.6	0.9	0.10
8+	82,229	35.0	1	0.35
Population (000s)		234,904		0.64

PRESS (ALT-R) TO VIEW THE PERFORMANCE MEASURES.

	Vehicle	Unadjusted Reach (000s)	Average Single-Insertion Audience	Cost per Insertion	Insertions	Total Vehicle Cost	Unadjusted CPM (adults)
1	WCBS News Radio	10,693	0.05	$1,600	6	$9,600	$0.15
2	American Top 40	35,412	0.15	$2,300	4	$9,200	$0.06
3	TODAY Show	4,426	0.02	$69,000	10	$690,000	$15.59
4	All My Children	9,907	0.04	$106,000	15	$1,590,000	$10.70
5	CBS Evening News	15,612	0.07	$145,000	8	$1,160,000	$9.29
6	Cosby Show	32,480	0.14	$215,000	4	$860,000	$6.62
7	Knot's Landing	23,374	0.10	$132,000	2	$264,000	$5.65
8	College football	23,459	0.10	$81,000	6	$486,000	$3.45
9	*Ebony*	7,005	0.03	$31,490	3	$94,470	$4.50
10	*House & Garden*	4,977	0.02	$23,780	2	$47,560	$4.78
11	*Reader's Digest*	39,405	0.17	$115,300	6	$691,800	$2.93
12	*Sports Illust'd*	14,467	0.06	$82,190	8	$657,520	$5.68
13	*Fortune*	2,957	0.01	$41,840	2	$83,680	$14.15
14	*Newsweek*	16,887	0.07	$95,715	4	$382,860	$5.67
15	*Travel & Leisure*	2,177	0.01	$32,040	6	$192,240	$14.72
16	*Rolling Stone*	4,462	0.02	$32,895	2	$65,790	$7.37
17	*Cosmopolitan*	10,172	0.04	$48,195	8	$385,560	$4.74
18	*Gourmet*	2,327	0.01	$18,980	4	$75,920	$8.16
19	*USA Today*	4,193	0.02	$3,295	12	$39,540	$0.79
20	*Wall Street Journal*	4,843	0.02	$95,567	14	$1,337,938	$19.73
21	Your own vehicle		0.00			$0	$0.00
22	Your own vehicle		0.00			$0	$0.00
23	Your own vehicle		0.00			$0	$0.00
	Totals	269,235	0.0573		126	$9,123,678	

EXERCISE OVERVIEW

The following pages describe the judgments and analyses needed to use the media-planning model. Some comments at the end of this exercise may affect your decisions on factors discussed in the earlier sections.

The model's output is controlled almost entirely by your own judgments. Understanding the effect of your judgments on the calculations performed by the model is critical, as is making judgments that are consistent with one another and the advertising and media strategies you have chosen.

An overview of the model's calculation of a plan's "total weighted exposures" is given in Exhibit 3. The model is designed to help you, given your budgetary limitations, to maximize the total weighted exposures to your advertising message.

An intuitive way to think about the media planning problem is the following: advertising exposures are "worth" the most when delivered through powerful media vehicles (high impact weight), to responsive target groups (high target weights), with enough frequency to exceed the threshold (if there is one). Exhibit 3 shows how one might calculate the "worth" of a given media plan in terms of total weighted exposures.

USING THE MEDIA-PLANNING MODEL

Once you have read this exercise and have made some preliminary decisions about the input data you are asked to enter, you will need to access the media-planning spreadsheet on Lotus 1-2-3 software to enter your own data. Simply retrieve the "MEDPLAN.WK1" file—it will be similar to the example printed in this exercise—and begin. Included with this file is a database of 74 generic vehicles from television, radio, print (newspapers and magazines), and outdoor media. This database is contained in the "MEDIADAT.WK1" file, and it needs to be placed in the same drive, directory, or subdirectory of the MEDPLAN file. A printout of this database is included in Appendix 1.

The MEDPLAN file has a menu system that will help you to specify such input data as demographics, frequency response, and choice of vehicles [a user's manual for the menu system is included in Appendix 2]. The menu system (or the main menu) can be accessed by pressing (**ALT-M**). Because of its size, the spreadsheet is designed to operate on "MANUAL CALC"; you will have to press **F9** every time you want the program to calculate new outputs based on the information you enter. Much of the data in the model is "protected" to prevent you from inadvertently typing over formulas that have been built into the program. All the input cells you will vary have been left unprotected and will be easy to alter. However, *none of these inputs should be directly entered into the main area of the worksheet*. Please use the menu system to specify your inputs. The only exceptions are in the case of changing the number of insertions, or the impact weight of the media vehicles. Changing the number of insertions is discussed under the "Sensitivity Analyses" section in Appendix 2. The specification of impact weights is discussed in the "Selection of Media Vehicles" section of this exercise.

The lower half of the spreadsheet calculates the distribution of the total reach and frequency of the exposures generated by the media plan you develop. Note: because of memory limitations, *the maximum number of total insertions that should be entered is*

EXHIBIT 3 Calculation of "Total Weighted Exposures"

Total Weighted Exposures = Gross impressions × plan frequency index × plan demographic index × plan impact index

Gross Impressions as mentioned in the exercise, gives some indication of the volume of exposures your plan achieves.

Plan Frequency Index =

$$\sum_{i=0}^{8} \text{frequency weight}_i \times \text{percent of population}_i$$

where   i = frequency or number of exposures
frequency weights specify the shape of the frequency response function
percent of population = the percent of total U.S. population that receive each given number of exposure (i)

Plan Impact Index =

$$\sum_{i=1}^{\text{No. of Vehicles}} \text{vehicle impact index}_i$$

where   i = the serial number of the vehicle in the model

and, for any vehicle i:

Vehicle Impact Index$_i$ =

$$\left\{ \frac{\text{insertions adjusted reach}_i}{\sum_{\text{all vehicles}} \text{insertions adjusted reach}} \right\} \times \text{vehicle impact weight}_i$$

where   Insertions adjusted reach$_i$ (for vehicle i) = number of insertions$_i$, × unadjusted reach$_i$ (000s), and
The vehicle impact weight is user-specified

Plan Demographic Index =

$$\sum_{i=1}^{\text{No. of Vehicles}} \text{demographic vehicle index}_i$$

where   i = the serial number of the vehicle in the model

and, for any vehicle i:

Demographic Vehicle Index$_i$ =

$$\left\{ \frac{\text{insertions adjusted reach}_i}{\sum_{\text{all vehicles}} \text{insertions adjusted reach}} \right\} \times \text{vehicle demographic weight}_i$$

where   insertions adjusted reach$_i$ (for vehicle i) = number of insertions$_i$ × unadjusted reach$_i$ (000s)

and for any vehicle i:

Vehicle Demographic Weight$_i$ =

$$\left\{ \frac{\sum_{j=1}^{\text{No. of Dimensions}} \text{dimension index}_j}{\text{Total No. of Dimensions}} \right\}$$

EXHIBIT 3   *(concluded)*

where   j = a dimension used in the plan for specifying target groups,

and for any dimension j (like gender, age, etc . . .):

Dimension Index$_j$ =

$$\sum_{k=0}^{4} percent\ of\ vehicle\ i's\ audience\ for\ category\ k \times demographic\ weight\ for\ category\ k$$

where   k = a category within dimension (j)—a maximum of 4 categories per dimension (for example, the categories male and female under the dimension "gender").

and, the demographic weight for category k is user-specified.

170; larger numbers cannot be accommodated by the Lotus 1-2-3 program. Each time you vary the number of insertions required by your media plan, you should update your spreadsheet by recalculating this portion of the spreadsheet. Simply press **F9**, and the computer will calculate the frequency distribution for your media plan.

TARGET-GROUP DEFINITIONS AND WEIGHTS

Before attempting to develop your own target-group weightings, you should review the discussion in the "Becel" case for the calculation of target-group weights and selection of the criteria for defining target groups. The case discussed two possible methods for setting target-group weights. The first method was additive, in the sense that a particular person received "points" or "weights" for a variety of different characteristics. The second method was multiplicative, in the sense that a zero for any characteristic would make the person have a zero weight. A third approach would be to define mutually exclusive and collectively exhaustive subgroups, each of which could then each be given a separate weight. For example, having two levels of income and two levels of family size would enable you to define four groups of consumers. Three levels for each of the criteria would yield nine groups. Obviously, the latter approach would be suitable only for a few different descriptors of target groups and a few levels of each; otherwise, the number of calculations would become too great. Similarly, the second, multiplicative, approach would entail simulations, or a comparable method, to cope with the number of calculations that would be required.

When defining your target-group (category) weights for the various categories, you will need to keep in mind that, in the model, target-group weights are incorporated with the calculation of the "Total Weighted Exposures" in an additive form (see Exhibit 3). The judgments you need to make are the five relevant subgroups you want to study and, then, the relative weights of each demographic category—e.g., male, female, age 18–24, age 25–34, etc. These weights should reflect your best estimates of the relative propensities of these categories to respond to your advertising message (regardless of the vehicle used to convey it). The weights should be specified by accessing the "DEMOS" option under the "INPUTS" sub-menu of the main menu. To provide you with ease in choosing your target groups, the DEMOS option lists eight dimensions (with four categories each), namely, gender, age, income, education, size of household, occupation, geographic region, and neighborhood. However, you are encouraged to use no more than five dimensions (more dimensions would entail a very precise definition of your target group). An empty slot has also been included to let you specify your own dimension (if necessary); however, you will need to be able to specify the demographic distribution (in percentages) under this dimension of the audience of *every vehicle* in the model. For the eight predefined dimensions, commonly used categories have been assigned. Furthermore, for every vehicle in the database the audience composition has been specified according to these categories. If you intend to use different categories for a predefined dimension, you will need to possess the audience composition (in percentages) for *every vehicle* in your media plan.

In Table 1, sample weights have been entered into the spreadsheet to illustrate the index format you should use for your own demographic weightings. Five demographic criteria are identified for you in Table 2, with up to four categories identified within each demographic dimension.

In general, the demographic dimensions you choose to help define your target groups, the number of levels into which you divide each criterion, and the weights you assign to each level should reflect the following:

1. *Sizable categories.* Performing calculations for very small categories makes little sense.
2. *Differences in weights assigned.* Again, dividing the target into categories that will be weighted the same has little purpose.
3. *Criteria that enable you to discriminate among media vehicles.*
4. *Amount of product-class use and probability of choosing the advertised brand.*
5. *Fit with advertising message.* For example, if the message is designed to convince users of competing brands to try your brand, media should be targeted at users of competing brands. If the message merely seeks to reinforce use by current customers, the media should be targeted toward these customers.

The criteria you use should be similar to those used for market-segmentation decisions, in that you will typically want to find segments that are identifiable, have different buying behavior, and are accessible in terms of your marketing strategy. For accuracy, the composition of your target audience should be as similar as possible within groups and as different as possible across groups.

For many categories of products, the number of product-class and/or brand users that are exposed to certain media vehicles can be determined from Simmons (or similar data). If such information is available, you may be able to use product-use indices to weight the media directly and to avoid defining your target groups in terms of demographics or other criteria. The difference between this approach and the one recommended for use with the media-planning model is subtle but important. Demographic definitions presumably reflect some inherent consumer inclination to prefer a product or to be a good prospect for purchasing it. Targeting media toward present users reflects past use, but not necessarily future potential.

This point also bears upon calculations of product use to augment judgments about target-group weighting. A common method is to calculate the percentage of a brand's

TABLE 1   Sample Target-Group Weightings

	Gender	Age	Income	Education	Household
Category 1	1.1	0.6	0.5	1.2	0.7
Category 2	0.9	0.9	0.8	1.0	0.9
Category 3	—	1.0	1.1	0.9	1.0
Category 4	—	0.8	1.3	0.8	1.2

TABLE 2   Demographic Categories and Weights

	Gender	Age	Income	Education	Household Size
Category 1	Male	18–24	14,999 or less	College graduate	1
Category 2	Female	25–34	15–19,999	Attended college	2
Category 3	NA	35–44	20–29,999	Graduated high school	3–4
Category 4	NA	45+	30,000+	Attended high school	5+

sales made to a specific group (say, large families) and divide that by the percentage of the total population in the same group. Thus if large families account for 40 percent of your product's sales but only 10 percent of the total population, you might conclude that large families are four times as likely as the average household to consume your product. Judgment will be needed to assess whether this calculation reflects a historical pattern (perhaps you have advertised only to large families or promoted large sizes of the product in the past) or actual potential for increased sales, and your evaluation must be carefully considered.

For this exercise, you may not need to use geographical location to weight your target group, because the media vehicles initially selected for the model have relatively even viewing/listening/reading frequencies across the United States. With media vehicles with disproportionately high readerships in certain regions (for example, *Southern Living* or *The New York Times*), geographical considerations might come into play.

Check your target-group weightings carefully before moving on to the media-planning portion of the exercise. One worthwhile check is to ask whether the criteria you have chosen are strongly interrelated. If so, you might be overweighting or underweighting certain subgroups of your target audience. If a product manager gave high weights to the following groups of German consumers, for example—Catholics, large families, rural dwellers, and citizens of Bavaria—the same general population would tend to be overweighted, because Bavaria is more rural than the rest of West Germany and has a higher percentage of Catholic residents than Germany as a whole. In this case, the product manager might do well to choose criteria that are not so closely related to one another. Cross-tabulations and/or regression analyses can help you sort out which of the various criteria are really important and which are so closely related that you might as well use only one of them.

A second useful check might be to question the target-group weightings as they relate to one another. For example, do you really consider an ad exposure to a male 1.22 (1.1/.9) times as desirable as one to a female? Or is one advertising exposure to someone with a high income really 2.6 (1.3/.5) times as valuable as an exposure to someone with an income in the Category 1 range? If the answers to questions such as these are yes, then the form reflects your judgments and will guide the media-planning process appropriately.

SELECTION OF VEHICLES

After you have defined your principal target segments, you will be ready to begin the media-selection process. The media-planning model can accommodate 23 vehicles, and it breaks their total reach into categories by the various dimensions. However, you may replace any of these vehicles, or change some of the information on them (like cost per insertion, to change the type of ad). You may also enter in vehicles of your own choosing, provided you have the total costs, reach, and breakdowns of their audience composition. Do not enter the CPM (cost per thousand adults) for your vehicle. The model will calculate it for you. Vehicles can be added or edited in the model by accessing the "VEHICLES" option of the main-menu, which is discussed in more detail in Appendix 2. Based on the weights you assign to each demographic category (e.g., male vs. female, college graduate vs. high school graduate, one-person household vs. household of five or more), the model calculates the adjusted reach of each vehicle. It also provides unadjusted cost information and calculates adjusted costs per thousand exposures based on the demographic- and impact-adjusted reach of each vehicle. All of these variables are incorporated into the calculation of "Total Weighted Exposures" (this calculation is shown in detail in Exhibit 3).

In general, when choosing media vehicles, you will want to choose those with the lowest adjusted cost per thousand. An important exception to this rule, however, is: If other audience characteristics would not be reflected by the weighted cost per thousand, consider audience composition before making your final media selections. The vehicles you choose should represent the best candidates for inclusion in your final media plan.

The model asks you to make several important judgments that will indirectly help determine which vehicles you select for your media plan. The shape of your response function (described in some detail in the "Response Function" section) will ultimately determine whether your plan emphasizes the widest possible reach, the highest possible frequency or, more probably, some combination of the two objectives. Moreover, the impact weights you assign to each vehicle will make vehicles more or less attractive based on your judgment of their effectiveness in conveying advertising messages, viewer involvement and attention, or other factors not accounted for by the target weights. The impact weights can be specified for any vehicle on an individual basis by accessing the "VEHICLES" option, and then *editing* the vehicle for the necessary changes. Alternatively, if you wish to specify the impact weights on a relative basis for all the vehicles, you may do so by viewing the records on the current vehicles in the model, which are listed in cells "O1 . . . AM1" (press F5, and then O1 to access these records). The demographic composition of each vehicle's readership is already specifically accounted for by the vehicle's audience-composition figures and your weights. (Do not double-count by assigning your impact weights on the basis of audience composition.)

The vehicle impact weights you assign are used to calculate each vehicle's adjusted reach and adjusted cost per thousand exposures. These figures, in turn, determine the relative attractiveness of each vehicle and help you select those you wish to incorporate into your media plan.

BUDGET

Your target budget level may be specified under the "CHECK" option of the "MAXES" sub-menu. If you do not intend to use the "optimization" feature of this model (it is recommended that you do not use the optimization feature early in your use of the model), all you need to input is the budget (cell BJ174) and then press **F9** once you are done. *Do not enter the budget directly into the main area of the worksheet.*

If you intend to run the optimization feature, you will also need to specify a flexibility range for your budget. Entering three separate budget levels is often useful: the actual amount expected to be available, a low budget (no less than 80 percent of the expected level), and a high budget (no more than 120 percent of the expected budget). The purpose of having more than one budget level is to provide some flexibility in planning as well as to guide your sensitivity analyses. This flexibility in your budget, in percentage terms $(+/-)$ should be specified along with the budget under the "CHECK" option. Press **F9** once you have specified your budget and its flexibility range. Under the "CHECK" option there is a feature to check for budget feasibility. This feature is not relevant to this exercise. It is used for providing a fail-safe device for running the optimization program. It is left to the instructor's discretion if the optimization is to be included in this exercise.

All budgets are tentative until spent. Media budgets are no exception. If something occurs that makes reducing the advertising budget desirable, a plan selected on the basis of the lower budget can be substituted. Conversely, if more money becomes available than planned, the higher budget can be used. With the media-planning model, you will be able to produce media plans at budget levels that range from your low to your high estimates to cover all eventualities.

You should also carefully consider the time period that corresponds to your budget. The model need not apply only to annual budgets; monthly and quarterly media plans can be prepared as well. Judgments as to the proper choice of response functions are often easier to conceptualize over short periods of time. Changes in media availability, schedules, and costs may also make the use of shorter time periods preferable to the use of long time periods. Besides, the limit of 170 insertions does not allow for advertising campaigns of long time periods.

RESPONSE FUNCTION

The principal purpose of the response function in media planning is to steer the tradeoffs made between selecting plans that yield incremental frequency of exposures to the same individuals vs. those that increase the number of individuals reached. Although it may not be intuitively obvious, a linear response function would probably provide a plan with the greatest frequency. Given such a response function, the media planner would buy as much space in the least expensive media vehicles as possible. On the other hand, S-shaped response functions suggest that increasing the frequency of exposures has a declining impact after a certain level is reached. Given this type of response function, a media planner would aim to maximize the number of individuals exposed to a threshold level of advertisements.

The media-planning spreadsheet allows you to enter your own response function, based on your predictions of the effectiveness of each additional advertising exposure to your target audience. The frequency response function can be entered under the "FREQ" option of the "INPUTS" sub-menu. Each household (or person) must fit into one of the categories of "number of exposures" or "frequency." A gradual "S-curve" response function has been entered in the spreadsheet in the column near the top labeled "frequency weight." Note that this curve attributes no impact to the first exposure, only marginal impact for exposures two and three, more significant impact for exposures four, five, and six, and declining impacts for each additional exposure. The "FREQ" option lets you specify frequency weights for other types of response functions if you so desire. *Do not enter the frequency weights directly into the main area of the worksheet. Use the menu system.* To help you visualize the shape of your chosen response function, the spreadsheet allows you to view the graph of the function simply by pressing **F10** on your computer keypad. Each time you change the numbers in the frequency weight column (and press F9 to recalculate the spreadsheet), a new graph will be displayed. Table 3 gives examples of other response functions.

The step function in Table 3 indicates that advertising is effective only after three exposures for a given individual. Subsequent exposures to the same individual are of no value. The declining response function indicates that each advertising exposure adds less to the total effect than the one before it. The peaked response function is similar to the S-curve up to the fifth exposure, but then the values actually decline. This function, in effect, says that people receiving eight exposures are "worth" the same as those receiving only one. It also implies that advertising frequency has a negative effect after five exposures.

TABLE 3   Sample Response Functions

Exposure Number	Step Function	Declining	S-Curve	Peaked
0	0	0	0	0
1	0	.4	.1	.1
2	0	.7	.3	.3
3	1.0	.85	.7	.7
4	1.0	.95	.95	.95
5	1.0	.99	.99	1.0
6	1.0	1.0	1.0	.7
7	1.0	1.0	1.0	.3
8	1.0	1.0	1.0	.1

While thinking of the response function in terms of probability of purchase for individual consumers is conceptually appealing, care must be taken with this analogy to ensure that the response function is not misunderstood. As it relates to the model, the response function is meant to illustrate only the relative incremental probability of purchase (or other measure of advertising effectiveness) that results from increased advertising exposure to the same individual.

OUTPUT

As you alter your media plan, the model calculates a number of output variables for you. These variables are located together at the top of the spreadsheet below the "Media Input and Schedule" heading. They can be viewed at any time by pressing **Alt-R.** The first key variable is the total number of gross impressions, or unadjusted impacts, your plan achieves. This figure represents the total unadjusted reach of the publications you select times the number of insertions in each publication and gives some indication of the volume of exposures your plan achieves.

The second key variable is the total cost of your plan, which is merely the cost per insertion times the number of insertions in each publication. This figure should be compared with the advertising budget you identified earlier in the process. Once you've identified a plan that maximizes your weighted audience exposures for your expected budget level, you can use sensitivity analyses to help gauge whether additional advertising dollars will have a large or small impact on audience response.

A third output variable is the "Plan Frequency Index." This figure is the sum of the products of the percentages of the total U.S. population that receive each given number of exposures to your advertisements (0–8 +) and the frequency weight you assigned (as part of your response function) to each of these particular exposure levels. An index of 1.0 would mean that no further gains from additional advertising frequency would be possible, as 100 percent of the solution would have received the optimal number of exposures.

The fourth variable is the "Plan Demographic Index," a figure that represents the sum of the products of the gender index, the age index, the income index, the education index, and the household-size index for all vehicles included in your media plan. A demographic index of 1.0 would suggest that, on average, the individuals reached by the vehicles in your media plan rate a 1.0 in terms of their demographic attractiveness.

The fifth variable, and the final key index calculated by the model, is the "Plan Impact Index," which represents the percentage of gross exposures from each vehicle, weighted by the vehicle impact, and summed over all vehicles included in the media plan. This index is meant to adjust your media selections for reader impact so that high-impact vehicles with large readerships receive additional weight in the plan.

The sixth key variable, the "Total Weighted Exposures," is the product of the total gross impressions, the plan frequency index, the plan demographic index, and the plan impact index. This figure is perhaps the most important in the entire spreadsheet. This figure is the one your plan should seek, within your budgetary constraints, to maximize.

The seventh variable, the "Cost Per Thousand Weighted Exposures," represents the advertising dollars spent for every thousand exposures received. This variable should be viewed as a rough guide to the effectiveness of your advertising spending overall. In general, the lower the cost per thousand exposures, the greater the impact of each advertising dollar. Because of the large number of factors combined to arrive at this figure, a plan may be developed that has a low unadjusted cost per thousand exposures but a high cost per thousand exposures.

Below the "Cost/M Exposures" figures is a "reach-frequency" table. It shows the number of households (HH) (in 000's and percent) exposed to various frequency levels; net reach (percent exposed at least once) is equal to 100 less the percent exposed "0" times.

In order to perform sensitivity analyses on the output by changing the number of insertions on the set of media vehicles in the model, you may directly enter the changes under the "insertions" column, by pressing **ALT-S.** This keystroke will take you to an area of the worksheet where you will be able to make these changes. Once you have specified a new set of insertions, press **ALT-R** to view the new output or performance measures.

CONCLUDING NOTE

The media-planning model described here addresses many of the problems in media planning, but it does not obviate the need for experienced and capable media buyers. Buying media exposure requires a great deal of experience and current knowledge of media markets. "Deals" are the rule, not the exception, and published rate cards may be mere starting points for negotiation. Nevertheless, one needs to have a direction and sense of purpose for media buying, which only media planning can provide. Price is only one component of the total package.

Formal media-planning models can be a valuable complement to creativity in selecting and scheduling media, because they challenge media planners to put numbers around their intuitive thinking. Models are enemies of creativity in media planning only if they are allowed to manage the manager.

APPENDIX 1: Printout of the Database of Media Vehicles in the "MEDIADAT.WK1" File

			Weekday Daytime TV			Weekend Daytime TV	
VEHICLES →			1	2	3	4	5
Vehicle ID #:			Drama	News	Quiz	Reg Sports	Sport Spec
Impact:			1.00	1.00	1.00	1.00	1.00
Reach (000s):			5,282	1,888	3,226	1,019	1,419
Cost/insertion:			$17,500	$10,200	$18,500	$9,000	$17,000
CPM (Adults):			$3.31	$5.40	$5.73	$8.83	$11.98
Dimensions	Categories	Demo %ages	%age in population:				
Gender	Male	47	0.17	0.36	0.29	0.73	0.59
	Female	53	0.83	0.64	0.71	0.27	0.41
	N/A	0	0.00	0.00	0.00	0.00	0.00
	N/A	0	0.00	0.00	0.00	0.00	0.00
Age	18-24	17	0.17	0.13	0.14	0.14	0.16
	25-34	24	0.21	0.18	0.17	0.23	0.16
	35-44	18	0.15	0.15	0.12	0.16	0.13
	45+	41	0.47	0.54	0.57	0.47	0.55
HH Income	$25,000+	49	0.34	0.43	0.29	0.45	0.49
	$15-24,999	20	0.20	0.20	0.23	0.23	0.20
	$10-14,999	14	0.16	0.15	0.17	0.15	0.14
	$9,999/less	17	0.30	0.22	0.31	0.17	0.17
Education	College Grad	17	0.09	0.15	0.08	0.18	0.19
	Att'd College	18	0.15	0.15	0.13	0.17	0.15
	Grad H.S.	40	0.41	0.43	0.40	0.39	0.39
	Att'd H.S./Less	25	0.35	0.27	0.39	0.26	0.27
Occupation	Professnl/Mgr.	16	0.07	0.12	0.06	0.15	0.15
	Techn/Clerical	19	0.13	0.15	0.09	0.14	0.13
	Other Employed	26	0.17	0.19	0.18	0.29	0.24
	Not Employed	39	0.63	0.54	0.67	0.42	0.48
Size of HH	1	12	0.14	0.14	0.16	0.13	0.13
	2	31	0.30	0.37	0.35	0.36	0.40
	3-4	40	0.37	0.35	0.33	0.37	0.34
	5+	17	0.19	0.14	0.16	0.14	0.13
Neighborhood	Metro Central City	30	0.31	0.30	0.29	0.35	0.31
	Metro Suburban	46	0.39	0.43	0.42	0.45	0.51
	Non Metro	24	0.30	0.27	0.29	0.20	0.18
	N/A	0	0.00	0.00	0.00	0.00	0.00
Region	Northeast	22	0.20	0.19	0.19	0.24	0.22
	North Central	25	0.23	0.24	0.25	0.23	0.23
	South	34	0.44	0.40	0.38	0.33	0.38
	West	19	0.13	0.17	0.18	0.20	0.17
Empty	N/A	0	0.00	0.00	0.00	0.00	0.00
	N/A	0	0.00	0.00	0.00	0.00	0.00
	N/A	0	0.00	0.00	0.00	0.00	0.00
	N/A	0	0.00	0.00	0.00	0.00	0.00

Total Population: 187,957,000

Early Evening TV   Prime Time TV   TV Specials

	6 Wkdy News	7 WkndNews	8 Adventure	9 FeatrFilm	10 Gen/Drama	11 SitCom	12 SpncMysDr	13 Sports	14 Award/Pag	15 FeatFilm	16 Info
	1.00	1.00	1.00	1.00	1.00	1.00	1.00	1.00	1.00	1.00	1.00
	6,609	3,058	7,543	8,272	11,752	10,057	8,487	1,438	10,148	8,029	4,869
	$36,100	$32,200	$104,700	$119,500	$104,725	$132,000	$98,300	$19,300	$150,000	$102,000	$50,000
	$5.46	$10.53	$13.88	$14.45	$8.91	$13.13	$11.58	$13.42	$14.78	$12.70	$10.27
	0.48	0.52	0.49	0.44	0.36	0.38	0.46	0.59	0.40	0.43	0.44
	0.52	0.48	0.51	0.56	0.64	0.62	0.54	0.41	0.60	0.57	0.56
	0.00	0.00	0.00	0.00	0.00	0.00	0.00	0.00	0.00	0.00	0.00
	0.00	0.00	0.00	0.00	0.00	0.00	0.00	0.00	0.00	0.00	0.00
	0.13	0.13	0.18	0.17	0.15	0.16	0.16	0.16	0.13	0.13	0.15
	0.15	0.13	0.23	0.24	0.22	0.24	0.23	0.15	0.18	0.22	0.22
	0.13	0.11	0.18	0.18	0.16	0.16	0.18	0.13	0.14	0.15	0.16
	0.59	0.63	0.41	0.41	0.47	0.44	0.43	0.56	0.55	0.50	0.47
	0.41	0.40	0.45	0.48	0.42	0.43	0.46	0.50	0.42	0.46	0.44
	0.20	0.21	0.21	0.22	0.21	0.22	0.22	0.20	0.23	0.22	0.22
	0.16	0.16	0.16	0.14	0.16	0.15	0.15	0.13	0.17	0.14	0.16
	0.23	0.23	0.18	0.16	0.21	0.20	0.17	0.17	0.18	0.18	0.18
	0.14	0.15	0.14	0.16	0.14	0.14	0.15	0.20	0.15	0.17	0.16
	0.15	0.14	0.17	0.18	0.16	0.16	0.18	0.16	0.16	0.16	0.16
	0.39	0.38	0.40	0.41	0.40	0.42	0.41	0.40	0.41	0.41	0.42
	0.32	0.33	0.29	0.25	0.30	0.28	0.26	0.24	0.29	0.26	0.26
	0.12	0.12	0.13	0.15	0.12	0.13	0.14	0.15	0.14	0.15	0.13
	0.13	0.13	0.18	0.20	0.17	0.18	0.19	0.14	0.16	0.16	0.17
	0.22	0.19	0.28	0.26	0.23	0.22	0.26	0.23	0.20	0.24	0.25
	0.53	0.57	0.41	0.39	0.48	0.47	0.41	0.48	0.50	0.45	0.45
	0.16	0.17	0.11	0.11	0.13	0.13	0.12	0.13	0.14	0.13	0.13
	0.40	0.42	0.30	0.31	0.34	0.32	0.31	0.39	0.36	0.34	0.33
	0.32	0.30	0.41	0.41	0.38	0.39	0.40	0.35	0.36	0.39	0.39
	0.12	0.11	0.18	0.17	0.15	0.16	0.17	0.13	0.14	0.14	0.15
	0.30	0.32	0.29	0.31	0.31	0.31	0.31	0.31	0.31	0.32	0.29
	0.45	0.45	0.44	0.44	0.44	0.45	0.44	0.52	0.43	0.45	0.46
	0.25	0.23	0.27	0.25	0.25	0.24	0.25	0.17	0.26	0.23	0.25
	0.00	0.00	0.00	0.00	0.00	0.00	0.00	0.00	0.00	0.00	0.00
	0.22	0.24	0.20	0.23	0.21	0.23	0.21	0.23	0.23	0.22	0.24
	0.24	0.23	0.24	0.25	0.24	0.25	0.24	0.23	0.22	0.24	0.27
	0.39	0.35	0.38	0.35	0.38	0.35	0.37	0.37	0.37	0.37	0.34
	0.15	0.18	0.18	0.17	0.17	0.17	0.18	0.17	0.18	0.17	0.15
	0.00	0.00	0.00	0.00	0.00	0.00	0.00	0.00	0.00	0.00	0.00
	0.00	0.00	0.00	0.00	0.00	0.00	0.00	0.00	0.00	0.00	0.00
	0.00	0.00	0.00	0.00	0.00	0.00	0.00	0.00	0.00	0.00	0.00
	0.00	0.00	0.00	0.00	0.00	0.00	0.00	0.00	0.00	0.00	0.00

		Cable			Newspapers			Newspapers			Women's Magazines	
	17 Variety	18 Home Wired	19 Not Wired	20 Pay/View	21 WSJ	22 USA Today	23 NY Times	24 Daily	25 Weekend	26 LHJ	27 Cosmo
	1.00	1.00	1.00	1.00	1.25	1.30	1.00	1.00	1.00	1.00	0.85
	6,227	3,700	5,100	2,000	4,653	34,600	1,306	4,000	5,000	12,450	8,472
	$98,000	$20,000	$25,000	$20,000	$105,352	$215,000	$25,000	$75,000	$90,000	$84,900	$64,045
	$15.74	$5.41	$4.90	$10.00	$22.64	$6.21	$19.14	$18.75	$18.00	$6.82	$7.56
	0.48	0.48	0.46	0.50	0.69	0.71	0.56	0.49	0.48	0.10	0.17
	0.52	0.52	0.54	0.50	0.31	0.29	0.44	0.51	0.52	0.90	0.83
	0.00	0.00	0.00	0.00	0.00	0.00	0.00	0.00	0.00	0.00	0.00
	0.14	0.17	0.17	0.19	0.11	0.20	0.11	0.15	0.15	0.13	0.37
	0.22	0.25	0.23	0.28	0.26	0.26	0.27	0.22	0.23	0.24	0.31
	0.16	0.20	0.16	0.22	0.24	0.21	0.21	0.19	0.19	0.21	0.16
	0.48	0.38	0.44	0.31	0.39	0.33	0.41	0.44	0.43	0.42	0.16
	0.47	0.57	0.43	0.66	0.85	0.66	0.80	0.55	0.57	0.53	0.58
	0.21	0.19	0.21	0.18	0.10	0.15	0.12	0.20	0.20	0.22	0.19
	0.14	0.12	0.16	0.09	0.03	0.12	0.06	0.13	0.12	0.11	0.12
	0.18	0.12	0.20	0.07	0.02	0.07	0.02	0.12	0.11	0.14	0.11
	0.16	0.19	0.15	0.19	0.59	0.28	0.52	0.21	0.21	0.19	0.20
	0.16	0.20	0.16	0.23	0.21	0.27	0.21	0.19	0.19	0.21	0.27
	0.42	0.41	0.39	0.44	0.17	0.35	0.22	0.41	0.41	0.45	0.42
	0.26	0.20	0.30	0.14	0.03	0.10	0.05	0.19	0.19	0.15	0.11
	0.15	0.18	0.13	0.20	0.50	0.25	0.45	0.19	0.19	0.16	0.18
	0.17	0.22	0.17	0.24	0.26	0.24	0.20	0.20	0.20	0.26	0.32
	0.23	0.16	0.26	0.28	0.09	0.24	0.09	0.23	0.24	0.15	0.21
	0.45	0.44	0.44	0.28	0.15	0.27	0.26	0.38	0.37	0.43	0.29
	0.13	0.08	0.15	0.05	0.10	0.10	0.14	0.11	0.10	0.11	0.11
	0.34	0.29	0.32	0.24	0.35	0.27	0.35	0.32	0.32	0.31	0.26
	0.38	0.45	0.37	0.50	0.42	0.45	0.37	0.41	0.41	0.41	0.45
	0.15	0.18	0.16	0.21	0.13	0.18	0.14	0.16	0.17	0.17	0.18
	0.32	0.28	0.31	0.29	0.38	0.34	0.50	0.32	0.33	0.26	0.38
	0.46	0.46	0.45	0.52	0.53	0.50	0.48	0.48	0.50	0.45	0.45
	0.22	0.26	0.24	0.19	0.09	0.16	0.02	0.20	0.17	0.29	0.17
	0.00	0.00	0.00	0.00	0.00	0.00	0.00	0.00	0.00	0.00	0.00
	0.23	0.25	0.20	0.26	0.27	0.25	0.85	0.25	0.26	0.19	0.25
	0.28	0.24	0.26	0.26	0.25	0.28	0.02	0.25	0.26	0.30	0.22
	0.29	0.33	0.34	0.31	0.25	0.32	0.10	0.31	0.30	0.34	0.33
	0.20	0.18	0.20	0.17	0.23	0.15	0.03	0.19	0.18	0.17	0.20
	0.00	0.00	0.00	0.00	0.00	0.00	0.00	0.00	0.00	0.00	0.00
	0.00	0.00	0.00	0.00	0.00	0.00	0.00	0.00	0.00	0.00	0.00
	0.00	0.00	0.00	0.00	0.00	0.00	0.00	0.00	0.00	0.00	0.00

	Shelter Magazines					Sports Magazines			News Magazines		
	28	29	30	31	32	33	34	35	36	37	38
	Mdmslle	McCalls	Cntry Lvg	Hous & Gar	Btr Hms	Sprts Ill	Sprtg Nws	Sport	Newsweek	Time	US News
	1.00	1.00	1.00	0.80	1.00	1.20	1.00	1.00	1.00	1.00	1.00
	4,032	14,272	3,605	3,832	17,299	3,150	625	850	3,100	4,000	2,150
	$39,470	$83,315	$51,920	$35,020	$136,500	$120,950	$18,500	$28,500	$108,050	$128,000	$72,400
	$9.79	$5.84	$14.40	$9.14	$7.89	$38.40	$29.60	$33.53	$34.85	$32.00	$33.67
	0.70	0.13	0.26	0.23	0.21	0.80	0.91	0.86	0.57	0.57	0.63
	0.93	0.87	0.74	0.77	0.79	0.20	0.09	0.14	0.43	0.43	0.37
	0.00	0.00	0.00	0.00	0.00	0.00	0.00	0.00	0.00	0.00	0.00
	0.42	0.12	0.12	0.13	0.12	0.27	0.25	0.29	0.17	0.20	0.16
	0.26	0.22	0.30	0.24	0.24	0.30	0.28	0.35	0.27	0.27	0.23
	0.14	0.20	0.23	0.20	0.20	0.20	0.23	0.14	0.22	0.21	0.19
	0.18	0.46	0.35	0.43	0.44	0.23	0.24	0.22	0.34	0.32	0.42
	0.58	0.53	0.63	0.61	0.56	0.66	0.63	0.50	0.68	0.66	0.66
	0.20	0.22	0.20	0.17	0.20	0.16	0.17	0.21	0.16	0.16	0.15
	0.10	0.12	0.09	0.12	0.12	0.10	0.13	0.16	0.08	0.10	0.10
	0.12	0.13	0.08	0.10	0.12	0.08	0.07	0.13	0.08	0.08	0.09
	0.20	0.16	0.26	0.28	0.18	0.28	0.23	0.14	0.36	0.34	0.35
	0.35	0.19	0.23	0.26	0.19	0.25	0.19	0.20	0.26	0.25	0.25
	0.34	0.48	0.43	0.32	0.44	0.35	0.43	0.43	0.29	0.30	0.28
	0.11	0.17	0.08	0.14	0.19	0.12	0.15	0.23	0.09	0.11	0.12
	0.18	0.14	0.21	0.26	0.17	0.25	0.20	0.17	0.30	0.30	0.25
	0.32	0.25	0.26	0.21	0.22	0.21	0.16	0.13	0.23	0.21	0.21
	0.20	0.17	0.17	0.16	0.18	0.31	0.42	0.43	0.19	0.22	0.24
	0.30	0.44	0.36	0.37	0.43	0.23	0.22	0.27	0.28	0.27	0.30
	0.11	0.11	0.08	0.10	0.09	0.08	0.09	0.07	0.10	0.10	0.10
	0.25	0.30	0.30	0.32	0.31	0.24	0.23	0.23	0.28	0.29	0.32
	0.46	0.42	0.45	0.42	0.41	0.48	0.43	0.44	0.44	0.44	0.41
	0.18	0.17	0.17	0.16	0.19	0.20	0.25	0.26	0.18	0.17	0.17
	0.35	0.27	0.26	0.36	0.27	0.33	0.32	0.36	0.34	0.35	0.32
	0.48	0.44	0.47	0.44	0.47	0.48	0.46	0.41	0.49	0.49	0.49
	0.17	0.29	0.27	0.20	0.26	0.19	0.22	0.23	0.17	0.16	0.19
	0.00	0.00	0.00	0.00	0.00	0.00	0.00	0.00	0.00	0.00	0.00
	0.26	0.21	0.22	0.22	0.20	0.24	0.25	0.20	0.24	0.25	0.18
	0.26	0.30	0.34	0.25	0.32	0.23	0.26	0.27	0.25	0.24	0.24
	0.35	0.34	0.31	0.37	0.32	0.34	0.31	0.40	0.30	0.30	0.35
	0.13	0.15	0.13	0.16	0.16	0.19	0.18	0.13	0.21	0.21	0.23
	0.00	0.00	0.00	0.00	0.00	0.00	0.00	0.00	0.00	0.00	0.00
	0.00	0.00	0.00	0.00	0.00	0.00	0.00	0.00	0.00	0.00	0.00
	0.00	0.00	0.00	0.00	0.00	0.00	0.00	0.00	0.00	0.00	0.00
	0.00	0.00	0.00	0.00	0.00	0.00	0.00	0.00	0.00	0.00	0.00

	Car Magazines				Hobby Magazines			Scientific Magazines			
	39	40	41	42	43	44	45	46	47	48	49
	Car&Drvr	Hot Rod	MtrTrends	Road&Trk	MdrnPhotg	GolfDgst	Fld&Strm	Omni	ScnceDgst	ScntfcAmr	PopScnce
	1.00	1.00	1.00	1.00	1.00	1.00	1.00	1.00	1.00	1.00	1.00
	950	875	850	725	850	1,400	2,000	750	507	572	1,800
	$61,410	$36,750	$55,440	$45,585	$57,920	$64,730	$62,790	$30,165	$32,000	$29,250	$45,400
	$64.64	$42.00	$65.22	$62.88	$68.14	$46.24	$31.40	$40.22	$63.12	$51.14	$25.22
	0.89	0.88	0.90	0.90	0.67	0.76	0.80	0.68	0.67	0.63	0.83
	0.11	0.12	0.10	0.10	0.33	0.24	0.20	0.32	0.33	0.37	0.17
	0.00	0.00	0.00	0.00	0.00	0.00	0.00	0.00	0.00	0.00	0.00
	0.00	0.00	0.00	0.00	0.00	0.00	0.00	0.00	0.18	0.00	0.00
	0.39	0.44	0.30	0.39	0.26	0.90	0.22	0.32	0.27	0.20	0.16
	0.29	0.32	0.30	0.31	0.30	0.23	0.30	0.38	0.27	0.24	0.26
	0.18	0.16	0.15	0.17	0.24	0.21	0.19	0.16	0.28	0.27	0.23
	0.14	0.08	0.25	0.13	0.20	0.47	0.29	0.14	0.66	0.29	0.35
	0.69	0.52	0.68	0.72	0.71	0.75	0.54	0.70	0.13	0.76	0.67
	0.12	0.18	0.18	0.10	0.15	0.11	0.20	0.15	0.12	0.10	0.16
	0.11	0.14	0.06	0.10	0.08	0.11	0.15	0.07	0.09	0.06	0.08
	0.08	0.16	0.08	0.08	0.06	0.03	0.11	0.80	0.32	0.08	0.09
	0.18	0.05	0.19	0.22	0.21	0.34	0.10	0.34	0.29	0.54	0.25
	0.26	0.15	0.23	0.26	0.34	0.26	0.18	0.33	0.27	0.32	0.25
	0.42	0.53	0.42	0.38	0.39	0.33	0.50	0.25	0.12	0.11	0.38
	0.14	0.27	0.16	0.14	0.06	0.07	0.22	0.08	0.24	0.03	0.12
	0.20	0.07	0.17	0.20	0.29	0.31	0.12	0.30	0.24	0.54	0.26
	0.20	0.15	0.21	0.22	0.20	0.23	0.16	0.20	0.25	0.16	0.16
	0.40	0.54	0.36	0.39	0.27	0.19	0.43	0.27	0.27	0.10	0.31
	0.20	0.24	0.26	0.19	0.24	0.27	0.29	0.23	0.10	0.20	0.27
	0.07	0.04	0.08	0.07	0.08	0.08	0.06	0.10	0.28	0.13	0.09
	0.24	0.20	0.28	0.27	0.28	0.37	0.25	0.23	0.41	0.31	0.32
	0.44	0.45	0.39	0.44	0.50	0.44	0.47	0.49	0.21	0.42	0.42
	0.25	0.31	0.25	0.22	0.14	0.11	0.22	0.18	0.41	0.14	0.17
	0.29	0.24	0.28	0.30	0.33	0.26	0.20	0.42	0.17	0.38	0.31
	0.56	0.43	0.54	0.55	0.48	0.54	0.44	0.46	0.00	0.54	0.48
	0.15	0.33	0.18	0.15	0.19	0.20	0.36	0.12	0.18	0.08	0.21
	0.00	0.00	0.00	0.00	0.00	0.00	0.00	0.00	0.28	0.00	0.00
	0.26	0.19	0.27	0.21	0.21	0.30	0.16	0.26	0.34	0.29	0.18
	0.19	0.22	0.26	0.30	0.30	0.20	0.31	0.18	0.20	0.19	0.36
	0.33	0.41	0.29	0.32	0.26	0.31	0.36	0.26	0.00	0.23	0.28
	0.22	0.18	0.18	0.20	0.23	0.19	0.17	0.30	0.00	0.29	0.18
	0.00	0.00	0.00	0.00	0.00	0.00	0.00	0.00	0.00	0.00	0.00
	0.00	0.00	0.00	0.00	0.00	0.00	0.00	0.00	0.00	0.00	0.00
	0.00	0.00	0.00	0.00	0.00	0.00	0.00	0.00	0.00	0.00	0.00

	Mens' Magazines			Ethnic Magazines			Health & Fitness Magazines			Radio Network	
	50	51	52	53	54	55	56	57	58	59	60
	Esquire	Playboy	Penthouse	Ebony	Essence	Jet	Prvention	Shape	Health	Adlt Cntmp	Album/Rock
	1.00	1.00	1.00	0.90	1.00	1.00	1.00	1.00	1.00	1.00	1.00
	997	3,400	2,000	1,750	850	1,800	3,000	2,000	2,232	18,249	4,313
	$35,530	$68,545	$31,355	$38,103	$25,560	$17,544	$36,750	$18,220	$25,110	$18,000	$4,500
	$35.64	$20.16	$15.68	$21.77	$30.07	$9.75	$12.25	$9.11	$11.25	$0.99	$1.04
	0.55	0.79	0.80	0.39	0.27	0.46	0.29	0.21	0.26	0.48	0.64
	0.45	0.21	0.20	0.61	0.73	0.54	0.71	0.79	0.74	0.52	0.36
	0.00	0.00	0.00	0.00	0.00	0.00	0.00	0.00	0.00	0.00	0.00
	0.18	0.24	0.26	0.25	0.28	0.25	0.06	0.35	0.17	0.18	0.37
	0.32	0.39	0.40	0.30	0.37	0.33	0.16	0.43	0.25	0.30	0.38
	0.18	0.19	0.20	0.18	0.17	0.16	0.20	0.15	0.20	0.18	0.12
	0.32	0.18	0.14	0.27	0.18	0.26	0.58	0.07	0.38	0.34	0.13
	0.60	0.58	0.56	0.37	0.42	0.36	0.54	0.61	0.50	0.55	0.60
	0.16	0.19	0.21	0.21	0.18	0.19	0.20	0.19	0.21	0.21	0.17
	0.09	0.12	0.11	0.17	0.16	0.16	0.15	0.09	0.13	0.12	0.12
	0.15	0.11	0.12	0.25	0.24	0.29	0.11	0.11	0.16	0.12	0.11
	0.32	0.22	0.19	0.16	0.18	0.11	0.19	0.28	0.18	0.20	0.20
	0.22	0.22	0.22	0.20	0.26	0.20	0.23	0.29	0.23	0.20	0.23
	0.33	0.38	0.41	0.39	0.40	0.43	0.40	0.36	0.37	0.41	0.41
	0.13	0.18	0.18	0.25	0.16	0.26	0.18	0.07	0.22	0.19	0.16
	0.26	0.21	0.21	0.14	0.17	0.11	0.16	0.28	0.17	0.19	0.20
	0.22	0.19	0.19	0.20	0.30	0.18	0.22	0.29	0.23	0.22	0.24
	0.24	0.38	0.38	0.31	0.23	0.34	0.19	0.22	0.21	0.28	0.35
	0.28	0.22	0.22	0.35	0.30	0.37	0.43	0.21	0.39	0.31	0.21
	0.14	0.10	0.11	0.10	0.09	0.11	0.13	0.11	0.11	0.10	0.10
	0.34	0.27	0.26	0.26	0.27	0.23	0.36	0.35	0.32	0.29	0.26
	0.40	0.45	0.42	0.41	0.43	0.42	0.37	0.47	0.40	0.44	0.45
	0.12	0.18	0.21	0.23	0.21	0.24	0.14	0.07	0.17	0.17	0.19
	0.42	0.32	0.32	0.56	0.60	0.57	0.28	0.39	0.31	0.27	0.32
	0.41	0.46	0.48	0.28	0.29	0.22	0.45	0.41	0.43	0.44	0.54
	0.17	0.22	0.20	0.16	0.11	0.21	0.27	0.20	0.26	0.29	0.14
	0.00	0.00	0.00	0.00	0.00	0.00	0.00	0.00	0.00	0.00	0.00
	0.23	0.22	0.22	0.14	0.17	0.12	0.25	0.15	0.21	0.22	0.31
	0.22	0.22	0.24	0.18	0.21	0.19	0.30	0.21	0.26	0.33	0.16
	0.41	0.33	0.34	0.57	0.51	0.60	0.25	0.33	0.36	0.27	0.27
	0.14	0.24	0.21	0.11	0.11	0.09	0.20	0.31	0.17	0.18	0.26
	0.00	0.00	0.00	0.00	0.00	0.00	0.00	0.00	0.00	0.00	0.00
	0.00	0.00	0.00	0.00	0.00	0.00	0.00	0.00	0.00	0.00	0.00
	0.00	0.00	0.00	0.00	0.00	0.00	0.00	0.00	0.00	0.00	0.00

	Radio Network					Radio						Outdoor (Monthly)		Top Ten Mts
	61	62	63	64	65	66	67	68	69	70	71	72	73	74
	All News	Black	Classical	CHR/Rock	Country	EZListeng	GoldOld	Nostalgia	News/Talk	Religious	UrbCntmpy	100 Shwg	50 Shwg	25 Shwg
	1.00	1.00	1.00	1.00	1.00	1.00	1.00	1.00	1.00	1.00	1.00	1.00	1.00	1.00
	2,663	2,745	1,364	12,572	13,495	5,833	3,000	5,913	4,099	3,511	2,200	78,247	74,241	68,590
	$2,300	$3,500	$3,000	$10,000	$10,000	$7,000	$3,500	$4,000	$2,500	$2,000	$3,000	$1,591,447	$858,143	$429,072
	$0.86	$1.28	$2.20	$0.80	$0.74	$1.20	$1.17	$0.68	$0.61	$0.57	$1.36	$20.34	$11.56	$6.26
	0.61	0.40	0.54	0.45	0.50	0.49	0.51	0.43	0.54	0.39	0.41	0.48	0.48	0.48
	0.39	0.60	0.46	0.55	0.50	0.51	0.49	0.57	0.46	0.61	0.59	0.52	0.52	0.52
	0.00	0.00	0.00	0.00	0.00	0.00	0.00	0.00	0.00	0.00	0.00	0.00	0.00	0.00
	0.10	0.27	0.11	0.28	0.14	0.14	0.13	0.13	0.12	0.16	0.26	0.17	0.17	0.18
	0.16	0.27	0.25	0.34	0.23	0.18	0.36	0.15	0.17	0.29	0.34	0.25	0.25	0.25
	0.22	0.17	0.22	0.19	0.22	0.18	0.26	0.17	0.19	0.21	0.14	0.18	0.18	0.18
	0.52	0.29	0.42	0.19	0.41	0.50	0.25	0.55	0.52	0.34	0.26	0.40	0.40	0.39
	0.61	0.34	0.67	0.57	0.46	0.56	0.49	0.49	0.59	0.47	0.42	0.50	0.50	0.50
	0.12	0.21	0.15	0.21	0.24	0.23	0.31	0.21	0.16	0.23	0.20	0.19	0.20	0.20
	0.11	0.14	0.11	0.11	0.13	0.12	0.11	0.14	0.12	0.12	0.15	0.14	0.14	0.14
	0.16	0.31	0.07	0.17	0.17	0.09	0.09	0.16	0.13	0.18	0.23	0.16	0.16	0.16
	0.24	0.12	0.43	0.23	0.14	0.21	0.19	0.15	0.25	0.17	0.15	0.17	0.17	0.17
	0.15	0.16	0.16	0.42	0.16	0.17	0.19	0.17	0.18	0.18	0.20	0.17	0.17	0.17
	0.39	0.38	0.29	0.18	0.42	0.43	0.42	0.46	0.38	0.42	0.35	0.40	0.40	0.40
	0.22	0.34	0.12	0.18	0.28	0.19	0.20	0.22	0.19	0.23	0.30	0.26	0.26	0.26
	0.23	0.11	0.35	0.25	0.14	0.20	0.15	0.16	0.21	0.13	0.15	0.19	0.20	0.20
	0.16	0.15	0.23	0.28	0.19	0.21	0.28	0.18	0.20	0.22	0.17	0.16	0.16	0.16
	0.20	0.33	0.20	0.29	0.30	0.23	0.32	0.22	0.21	0.26	0.25	0.27	0.26	0.27
	0.41	0.41	0.22	0.07	0.37	0.36	0.25	0.44	0.38	0.39	0.43	0.38	0.38	0.37
	0.13	0.09	0.12	0.25	0.10	0.11	0.09	0.13	0.16	0.10	0.09	0.12	0.12	0.11
	0.34	0.24	0.24	0.47	0.31	0.36	0.23	0.35	0.34	0.27	0.24	0.30	0.30	0.31
	0.39	0.43	0.36	0.21	0.42	0.38	0.41	0.38	0.35	0.39	0.48	0.41	0.41	0.41
	0.14	0.24	0.38	0.33	0.17	0.15	0.27	0.14	0.15	0.24	0.19	0.17	0.17	0.17
	0.43	0.48	0.14	0.49	0.24	0.31	0.31	0.30	0.34	0.29	0.58	0.32	0.32	0.31
	0.54	0.28	0.42	0.18	0.40	0.57	0.47	0.42	0.56	0.46	0.36	0.48	0.47	0.51
	0.03	0.24	0.49	0.27	0.36	0.12	0.22	0.28	0.10	0.25	0.06	0.20	0.21	0.18
	0.52	0.09	0.09	0.23	0.00	0.00	0.00	0.00	0.00	0.00	0.00	0.00	0.00	0.00
	0.15	0.13	0.24	0.34	0.07	0.29	0.28	0.35	0.33	0.18	0.30	0.22	0.22	0.23
	0.14	0.72	0.27	0.16	0.32	0.23	0.18	0.24	0.28	0.25	0.21	0.26	0.26	0.25
	0.19	0.06	0.23	0.00	0.46	0.29	0.44	0.26	0.16	0.38	0.46	0.00	0.00	0.00
	0.00	0.00	0.26	0.00	0.15	0.19	0.10	0.15	0.23	0.19	0.03	0.00	0.00	0.00
	0.00	0.00	0.00	0.00	0.00	0.00	0.00	0.00	0.00	0.00	0.00	0.00	0.00	0.00
	0.00	0.00	0.00	0.00	0.00	0.00	0.00	0.00	0.00	0.00	0.00	0.00	0.00	0.00

APPENDIX 2
User's Manual for the Menu System and the Optimization Feature*

INTRODUCTION

Welcome to the user's manual for the Media Planning Exercise worksheet. It will help you in using the menu system and the optimization feature and in understanding the various options within the menu system. This manual is divided into sections, each representing the options under the main menu. Each of these sections are further divided into sub-sections, representing the options under each sub-menu. For each of these sections and sub-sections there are some explanations and steps (keystrokes) that will help you access or execute necessary options under the menu system. Explanations for important sections have also been included in the worksheet. For each section, the corresponding visual displays of areas within the worksheet have been provided. Please take the time to read through this manual before using the menu system.

> NOTE: DO NOT ENTER ANY OF THE MODEL'S INPUT DATA DIRECTLY INTO THE MAIN AREA OF THE WORKSHEET. USE THE MENU SYSTEM FOR SPECIFYING THE INPUTS, BE IT DEMOGRAPHICS, FREQUENCY WEIGHTS, VEHICLES, BUDGET, ETC.

---

*Developed by Professor Paul W. Farris, Darden Graduate School of Business Administration, and Nischal N. Rajey, Department of Systems Engineering, University of Virginia.

The Main Menu

Once you have loaded the worksheet file "MEDPLAN.WK1" into the 1-2-3 software, you may access the main menu by pressing **ALT-M.** The main menu is divided into five options, namely: INPUTS, VEHICLES, MAXES, OPTIMIZE, and LISTING. Figure 1 shows the main menu display.

To select any of the options within the main menu or the sub-menus:

* *either—press the first letter key of the option* (for example, to choose inputs press I)
* *or—*use the arrow keys to *highlight the option* in the menu bar and then press **ENTER.**

Each of these options are described in more detail below. Once you are in a sub-menu, if you wish to access other options of the main menu, you will need to return to the main menu by pressing **ALT-M.** The **EXIT** option will return you to the main area of the worksheet. In brief, the INPUTS option will let you specify the demographic distribution for your product's target audience, the total population, and the weights for the frequency response function. The VEHICLES option will let you add or edit vehicles that you intend to use in the media planning exercise. The MAXES option will let you specify your budget, its flexibility range, and the maximum insertions per vehicle (which is only necessary if you intend to run the optimization program). The OPTIMIZE option will take you through the optimization feature of the model. Finally, the LISTING option will let you view the macro codes for the various programs that are used in the worksheet. DO NOT CHANGE ANY OF THE MACROS UNLESS ASKED TO DO SO BY THE INSTRUCTOR.

SECTION 1—INPUTS OPTION:

The INPUTS option lets you specify the demographic distribution and the corresponding weights for your target audience, and the weights for the frequency response function. When you access this option under the main menu, you will be shown a sub-menu for this section. Figure 1.1 shows a display of this sub-menu.

FIGURE 1

```
I = = = = = = = = = = = = = = = = = = = = = = = = = = = = = = = = =I
I                    * * * MAIN MENU OPTIONS * * *                  I
I                                                                   I
I    INPUTS:   Lets you specify the global demographics and the     I
I              frequency weights.                                   I
I                                                                   I
I  VEHICLES:   Lets you add or edit a vehicle (ALT-A).              I
I                                                                   I
I     MAXES:   Lets you specify the max insertions per vehicle and check I
I              for its budget feasibility (ALT-B) (also provides an I
I              explanation of this section).                        I
I                                                                   I
I  OPTIMIZE:   Provides an explanation of the simulated annealing   I
I              algorithm, lets you set the parameters and run the   I
I              algorithm (ALT-O).                                   I
I                                                                   I
I   LISTING:   Shows the program listings of macros.                I
I                                                                   I
I      EXIT:   Returns to the media planning model.                 I
I = = = = = = = = = = = = = = = = = = = = = = = = = = = = = = = = =I
```

FIGURE 1.1

```
* * * INPUTS MENU OPTIONS * * *
         (JUDGMENTAL INPUTS)
DEMOS:    Lets you specify the global demographics (i.e., up to 9 dimensions, 4
          categories or target groups each, and the corresponding demographic
          weights). PRESS [F9] WHEN YOU ARE DONE.
FREQS:    Lets you specify the frequency weights for the frequency response
          function. PRESS [F9] WHEN YOU ARE DONE.
MAIN MENU: Returns to the main menu options.
          NOTE: THESE INPUTS ARE GLOBAL AND SHOULD BE SPECIFIED BEFORE
                PERFORMING ANY ANALYSES ON THE MEDIA PLANNING MODEL.
```

As shown in Figure 1.1, the options under this sub-menu are: DEMOS and FREQS. The DEMOS option will let you specify the demographics, and the FREQS option will let you specify the frequency weights. When you are within any of these options, if you wish to proceed to other options either in the main menu or even under this sub-menu, you will need to access the main menu all over again by pressing **ALT-M.** Also, when this sub-menu is displayed to you, and if you wish to return to the main menu, access the MAIN MENU option.

Section 1.1—DEMOS Option

If you access the DEMOS option, you will be taken to an area of the worksheet where you will be able to define the demographic distribution and the demographic weights. Figure 1.1(a) shows a display of that area of the worksheet. You may specify up to nine demographic dimensions (e.g., age, gender, occupation, etc.) with four categories for each, thus defining the distribution within each dimension, and also you will be able to specify judgmental weights to each category showing the importance of each of the categories for the successful marketing of your product to the target audience. It is suggested that you use no more than five dimensions in your plan. Using more than five dimensions will entail a very precise definition of your target group. This option also lets you specify the total population of your target audience. This could be the entire population of the country, or the population of a state, etc. Read through Figure 1.1(a).

The values that you specify in this area of the worksheet will remain global for the entire worksheet. Hence, you will need to go through this process before performing any analyses on the worksheet. Also, if you have less than nine dimensions or four categories, please enter "N/A" to reflect it and enter a weight of zero for the corresponding demographic weight. Once you have finished entering the demographics, press **[F9]** to

FIGURE 1.1(a)

= =

JUDGMENTAL INPUTS—GLOBAL DEMOGRAPHICS

PRESS **ALT-M** TO RETURN TO THE MAIN MENU OPTIONS

In the table below, you may specify the TOTAL POPULATION, the DEMOGRAPHIC DIMENSIONS, each
of their CATEGORIES, and their corresponding DEMOGRAPHIC WEIGHTS.

NOTE: 1) There can only be a maximum of 4 categories for each dimension. If you have
fewer than 9 dimensions or fewer than 4 categories for any dimension, PLEASE
ENTER N/A in the place of the dimensions or categories not used, and ZEROES
for their corresponding demographic weights.

PROCEED
DOWN

2) The values you specify below will remain global for the entire Media Planning
Model. Hence, they should be specified before you perform any operations on
the model, be it adding or editing a vehicle, or running the optimization
program.

	TOTAL POPULATION:		187,957	* * *
	(In thousands)		= = = = =	PRESS [F9]
			Demographic	ONCE YOU
	Dimensions	Categories	Weights	ARE DONE
	= = = = =	= = = = =	= = = = =	* * *
PROCEED	Gender	Male	1.1	
DOWN		Female	0.9	
		N/A	0.0	
		N/A	0.0	
	Age	18-24	0.6	
		25-34	0.9	
		35-44	1.0	
		45+	0.8	
	HH Income	$25,000+	1.3	* * *
		$15-24,999	1.1	PRESS [F9]
		$10-14,999	0.8	ONCE YOU
		$9,999/Less	0.5	ARE DONE
				* * *
	Education	Coll grad	1.2	
		Att'd coll	1.0	
		Grad HS	0.9	
		Att'd HS/Less	0.8	
PROCEED	Occupation	Profssnl/Mgr	0	
DOWN		Techn/Cleric	0	
		Other employd	0	
		Not emplyd	0	

(continued)

FIGURE 1.1(a) *(concluded)*

```
= = = = = = = = = = = = = = = = = = = = = = = = = = = = = = = = = = = :
        Size of HH          1                         0.7        *  *  *
                            2                         0.9
                            3-4                       1.0     PRESS [F9]
                            5+                         1.2     ONCE YOU
                                                             ARE DONE
     - - - - - - - - - - - - - - - - - - - - - - - - -        *  *  *
        Neighbrhood         Metro Ctrl C              0
                            Metro Suburb              0
                            Non Metro                 0
                            N/A                       0

     - - - - - - - - - - - - - - - - - - - - - - - - -
        Region              Northeast                 0
                            N. Central                0
                            South                     0
                            West                      0

     - - - - - - - - - - - - - - - - - - - - - - - - -
        Empty               N/A                       0        *  *  *
                            N/A                       0     PRESS [F9]
                            N/A                       0     ONCE YOU
                            N/A                       0     ARE DONE
                                                      0        *  *  *

     - - - - - - - - - - - - - - - - - - - - - - - - -
        PRESS ALT-M TO RETURN TO THE MAIN MENU OPTIONS

= = = = = = = = = = = = = = = = = = = = = = = = = = = = = = = = = = = =
```

incorporate these values into the model. To get out of this area of the worksheet press **ALT-M** to access the main menu.

> WARNING: DO NOT ENTER THESE VALUES DIRECTLY INTO
> THE MAIN AREA OF THE WORKSHEET, BECAUSE
> ALL AREAS OF THE WORKSHEET REFERENCE THESE
> VALUES. USE THE DEMOS OPTION.

Section 1.2—FREQS Option

The FREQS option will take you to an area of the worksheet where you will be able to specify the frequency weights for the frequency response function. Figure 1.1(b) shows a display of that area of the worksheet. Once you have entered the weights, press **[F9]** to incorporate the function into the model. You can view the shape of your response function by pressing **[F10]**. Again, you will need to access the main menu to get out of this area of the worksheet.

The warning under the section on demographics applies here also.

FIGURE 1.1(b)

= :

JUDGMENTAL INPUTS--FREQUENCY WEIGHTS

PRESS **ALT-M** TO RETURN TO THE MAIN MENU OPTIONS

In the table below you may specify the FREQUENCY WEIGHTS for the frequency response function.

PRESS **[F9]** ONCE YOU ARE DONE.
PRESS **[F10]** TO VIEW THE RESPONSE FUNCTION.

NOTE:

PROCEED
DOWN

1) The values you specify below will remain global for the entire Media Planning Model. Hence, they should be specified before you perform any operations on the model, be it adding or editing a vehicle, or running the optimization program.

Frequency	Frequency Weight	
---= = =	---= = =	* * *
0		PRESS **[F9]**
	0	ONCE YOU
1	0	ARE DONE
2	0.05	* * *
3	0.1	
4	0.25	
5	0.5	
6	0.8	
7	0.9	
8	1	
---= = =	---= = =	

= =

SECTION 2—VEHICLES OPTION

The VEHICLES option under the main menu lets you add or edit vehicles in the model. Once you access this option, you will be shown a list of the current vehicles in the model and their corresponding serial numbers. Figure 2.1 shows a display of this list. To add/replace or edit a vehicle, type in the corresponding serial number of the vehicle's slot at the query and then press **ENTER.** If you wish to edit some attributes (like cost per insertion or impact) of a vehicle currently in the model, type **[e]** at the next query. However, if you wish to replace a vehicle from the model with one from the database or if you wish to add in a vehicle of your own choosing, type **[r]** (the letter's case is not important.

If in the above display you entered an **[e]** for editing a vehicle, then all current records on the vehicle will be accessed. You will then be able to change or enter the required attributes for the vehicle. Figure 2.2 shows a display of the records on a candidate vehicle (#13—*Newsweek*).

FIGURE 2.1

= :

ADDING OR EDITING VEHICLES IN THE MODEL

Given below is a list of the current media vehicles and their serial #s:

(1) Drama	(9) Daily	(17) Playboy
(2) Quiz	(10) Cosmo	(18) Essence
(3) Wkdy News	(11) Cntry Lvg	(19) Shape
(4) FeatrFilm	(12) Sprts Ill	(20) Album/Rock
(5) SpncMysDr	(13) Newsweek	(21) Nostalgia
(6) Info	(14) Car&Drvr	(22) 100 Shwg
(7) Home Wired	(15) Road&Trk	(23) Empty Slot
(8) WSJ	(16) ScntfcAmr	

WHICH VEHICLE DO YOU WISH TO REPLACE/EDIT (ENTER SERIAL #):   13
=======

PLEASE ENTER [R] TO REPLACE/ADD, OR [E] TO EDIT: e
=======

= :

FIGURE 2.2

= =

CURRENT RECORDS ON VEHICLE NO: 13

To add or edit a vehicle, enter in the necessary
changes for it, below. **THEN PRESS ALT-A**

Vehicle Name:	Newsweek
Impact:	1.00
Reach (in 000s):	3,100
Cost per insertion:	$108,050
CPM (Adults):	$34.85

**Table for target group %ages in population
reach:**

Dimensions	Demographic Breakdowns	%age of Population
-----------	------------	----------
Gender	Male	0.57
	Female	0.43
	N/A	0.00
	N/A	0.00
Age	18–24	0.17
	25–34	0.27
	35–44	0.22
	45+	0.34
HH Income	$25,000+	0.68
	$15–24,999	0.16
	$10–14,999	0.08
	$9,999/Less	0.08

FIGURE 2.2 (*concluded*)

= =

Dimensions	Demographic Breakdowns	%age of Population
Education	Coll grad	0.36
	Att'd coll	0.26
	Grad HS	0.29
	Att'd HS/Less	0.09
Occupation	Profssnl/Mgr	0.30
	Techn/Cleric	0.23
	Other emplyd	0.19
	Not emplyd	0.28
Size of HH	1	0.10
	2	0.28
	3–4	0.44
	5+	0.18
Neighbrhood	Metro Ctrl C	0.34
	Metro Suburb	0.49
	Non Metro	0.17
	N/A	0.00
Region	Northeast	0.24
	N. Central	0.25
	South	0.30
	West	0.21
Empty	N/A	0.00
	N/A	0.00
	N/A	0.00
	N/A	0.00

= =

In order to incorporate a vehicle into the model, you will need to specify its name, its impact weight (its communication or persuasion power to the audience), the cost for one insertion, and the population of the vehicle's audience (the reach). The insertion cost can be used as a way to specify the type of ad that you wish to place in the vehicle. For example, you may wish to place a full-page color ad (as opposed to a black-and-white ad) in a magazine. The cost of the insertion will reflect the type of ad. You need not specify the CPM (cost per thousand adults). The model calculates it for you.

In this section you will also have to specify the demographic distribution of the vehicle's audience (the audience composition), i.e., the percentage of the reach for each demographic category. Enter zeroes for non-applicable categories.

Once you have finished with entering in the necessary information on the vehicle, press **ALT-A** to incorporate the vehicle into the model. After the vehicle has been put into the model, you will be given the option to add or edit more vehicles. This option is displayed in Figure 2.2(a). If you choose to add or edit more vehicles, you will revisit the display in Figure 2.1. If you choose not to do so, you will be taken back to the main menu options.

In the display shown in Figure 2.1, if you entered **[r]**, then you will be given the option of either adding a vehicle of your own choosing, or one from the database. This option is shown in Figure 2.2(b).

If for instance you wish to add in your own vehicle, type in **[a]** at the query. You will then be shown the display in Figure 2.2. However, this time there will be no records on any vehicle, i.e., you will be shown a display with blank data fields. This will let you specify the vehicle's name, impact weight, reach, cost/insertion, and the relevant demographic distribution. You may add in your own vehicle only if you have the necessary data (especially the demographic composition of its audience). Press **ALT-A** after having entered in the necessary information.

In the display shown in Figure 2.2(b), if you typed in a **[c]** for replacing the current vehicle in the slot with one from the database in the "MEDIADAT.WK1" file, you will be shown the display in Figure 2.2(c).

To access a vehicle from the database, you will need to perform two steps in series (as shown in Figure 2.2(c)). The first step requires you to enter the ID number of the

FIGURE 2.2(a)

```
MEDIA VEHICLE:     =  Newsweek

HAS BEEN ADDED INTO THE MEDIA PLANNING MODEL


DO YOU WISH TO ADD OR EDIT
ANOTHER VEHICLE?                              (Y/N):  y
```

FIGURE 2.2(b)

```
    ENTER [C] TO COPY A VEHICLE FROM THE MASTER LIST IN THE
    "MEDIADAT.WK1" FILE


            OR


    ENTER [A] TO ADD IN YOUR OWN VEHICLE
    (one that is not in the master list).


    YOUR RESPONSE (C/A)?:   c
```

FIGURE 2.2(c)

```
ENTER THE "ID #" OF THE VEHICLE IN THE CONTROL PANEL
PROMPT ABOVE--which says:
                Enter range name or address:
                THEN

AGAIN AT THE CENTRAL PANEL PROMPT ABOVE, TYPE IN THE
DRIVE, SUBDIRECTORY (IF ANY), AND FILENAME--"MEDIA.WK1",
i.e.,
At the prompt:
         Enter name of file to combine:
Type in:
              [Drive]:\[Subdirectory]\MEDIADAT.WK1
                   THEN PRESS [ENTER]
for example: D:\FARRIS\MEDIADAT.WK1
(See the appendix 1 in the media note for the Database
Printout and hence the Vehicle ID #.)
```

vehicle that you wish to have incorporated in the model. The list of the media vehicles and their corresponding ID numbers can be viewed in Appendix 1 of the media note. In the next step you will need to specify the **"MEDIADAT.WK1"** filename and its location. If both the "MEDPLAN.WK1" file and the "MEDIADAT.WK1" file are in the default directory specified in your LOTUS 1-2-3 software, then at the second prompt of the control panel ("Enter Name of File To Combine") just enter **MEDIADAT.** However, if you are unsure of the default location, type in (to specify the location) the **drive, sub-directory** (if any), and then **"MEDIADAT."** Once the vehicle has been added into the model, you will be given the option of adding more vehicles, like in the editing case.

SECTION 3—MAXES OPTION

The MAXES option under the main menu lets you specify your budget, its flexibility range ($+/-$ X percent), and the maximum insertions for each vehicle. The budget feasibility check defines a solution space of different combinations of vehicle insertions and it will be a critical step since its successful completion will guarantee an error-free run of the optimization algorithm. It requires you to specify maximum insertion on the vehicles such that the total number of maximum insertions does not exceed 170 and also that the total cost of these maximum insertions exceeds the upper bound on the budget flexibility range. This will become clearer later. However, if you do not intend to run the optimization program, the budget feasibility check will have no effect whatsoever on the performance of your plan (you will *not* need to specify maximum insertions). You may enter the insertions manually by pressing **ALT-R,** after which you may view the performance measure by pressing **ALT-S.** DO NOT ENTER YOUR BUDGET OR ITS

FLEXIBILITY RANGE IN THE MAIN AREA OF THE WORKSHEET. DO IT THROUGH THE "CHECK" OPTION UNDER THIS SUB-MENU.

Even if you do not intend to run the optimization program, use the "CHECK" option to specify your budget.

Figure 3.1 shows a display of the MAXES sub-menu. Under this sub-menu the options are: EXPLAIN and CHECK.

Section 3.1—EXPLAIN Option

This option provides an explanation to this section. Basically it describes four scenarios which you could be faced with, given a certain set of maximum insertions, a budget, and its flexibility range. There is a constraint of a maximum of 170 insertions for the model due to computational reasons. Figure 3.1(a) shows a display of this area of the worksheet. Please read through this display very carefully.

For illustration of the four scenarios mentioned above, see Figure 3.1(b). This display is not available in the Media Planning worksheet.

Figure 3.1(b) shows a hypothetical situation of the four scenarios in relation to the upper bound on the budget's flexibility range. The terms "I < = 170" and "I > 170" imply that the total number of maximum insertions is less than 170 and greater than 170, respectively. The scenarios are indicated in parenthesis. Keep in mind that no matter what your media plan consists of, the total number of insertions cannot exceed 170 due to computational reasons. Here the critical relational point is the upper bound on the flexibility range indicated by **[U].** Again, the four scenarios represent the relationship of the total cost of maximum insertions to the upper bound on the flexibility range.

The objective here is to use as much of the budget flexibility range as possible. The optimization algorithm generates test cases comprising different combinations of insertions

---

FIGURE 3.1

```
┌ = = = = = = = = = = = = = = = = = = = = = = = = = = = = = = = = = = = = ┐
│                    * * * MAXES MENU OPTIONS * * *                        │
│                                                                         │
│   EXPLAIN:   Provides an explanation of the reason for specifying the    │
│              maximum insertions per vehicle and checking its budget      │
│              feasibility.                                                │
│                                                                         │
│     CHECK:   Lets you specify the maximum insertions per vehicle, your   │
│              budget and its flexibility range (+/- X percent).           │
│              PRESS ALT-B TO CHECK FOR THE FEASIBILITY OF THE TOTAL COST   │
│              OF MAXIMUM INSERTIONS WITHIN THE FLEXIBILITY RANGE OF YOUR   │
│              BUDGET.                                                     │
│                                                                         │
│  MAIN MENU:  Returns to the main menu options.                          │
│                                                                         │
│              NOTE: YOU SHOULD PERFORM THIS FEASIBILITY CHECK BEFORE THE   │
│                    OPTIMIZATION OF THE MODEL.                            │
│                                                                         │
└ = = = = = = = = = = = = = = = = = = = = = = = = = = = = = = = = = = = = ┘
```

FIGURE 3.1(a)

SPECIFYING MAX INSERTIONS PER VEHICLES AND CHECKING BUDGET
FEASIBILITY

AN EXPLANATION

PRESS ALT-M TO RETURN TO THE MAIN MENU OPTIONS

Due to time constraints (monthly, weekly, advertising), it is
possible that you can have only a limited number of insertions per
vehicle (maximum insertions per vehicle). You can also have a
flexibility of +/−X percent in your budget. This specifies a range
of tolerance of the total cost within your budget. The MAXIMUM
INSERTIONS PER VEHICLE, your BUDGET, and its FLEXIBILITY RANGE can
be entered by accessing CHECK under the MAXES option of the main
menu. You can then check for budget feasibility. NOTE THAT THESE
VALUES SHOULD BE SPECIFIED BEFORE YOU RUN THE OPTIMIZATION
ALGORITHM.

WHY CHECK FOR BUDGET FEASIBILITY?
The optimization algorithm will try to maintain the total cost of
the set of vehicle insertions within the flexibility range of your
budget. **THE MEDIA PLANNING MODEL CAN ONLY HANDLE A TOTAL OF 170
INSERTIONS.** Given these facts, you could be faced with four
scenarios as to how the total number of maximum insertions and its
total cost relates to the flexibility range of your budget. Scenario
4 is the best option.

The four scenarios are:

PROCEED
DOWN

1) **The total number of maximum insertions per vehicle
exceeds 170 and its total cost exceeds the upper bound
for the budget flexibility range.**
Even though the optimization algorithm maintains the
total cost within the budget flexibility range, with the
above scenario you could be faced with one problem while
running the optimization algorithm: i.e., the total
number of insertions for some set of insertions that the
algorithm is analyzing, may exceed 170.
If this situation occurs while checking for budget
feasibility, then you will be given the option of
reducing the maximum number of insertions.
If you opt not to make these changes, then you may be
taking the risk of being asked to reduce the maximum
insertions and running the budget feasibility check all
over again, if the optimization algorithm is analyzing a
solution set for which the total number of insertions
exceeds 170.
By specifying total number of maximum insertions to be
≤=170, you will have the best option, scenario 4.

(continued)

FIGURE 3.1(a)   *(concluded)*

```
┌ = = = = = = = = = = = = = = = = = = = = = = = = = = = = = = ┐
│               2)  The total number of maximum insertions per vehicle     │
│                   exceeds 170 and its total cost lies below the upper    │
│   PROCEED         bound for the budget flexibility range.                │
│   DOWN            This condition implies that the total cost of maximum  │
│     ┊             insertions undershoots the maximum of the flexibility  │
│     ┊             range. In this case, you will not be considering any   │
│     ┊             solutions in the upper region of your budget flexibility│
│     ┊             range. Also, the optimization algorithm may generate a │
│     ▼             solution set with total insertions exceeding 170, in   │
│                   which case the program will crash.                     │
│                   If this situation occurs, then you will be asked to    │
│                   reduce the maximum number of insertions **and** reduce your │
│                   budget or replace some of the vehicles with more       │
│                   expensive ones. Here, it is necessary that you make    │
│                   these changes.                                         │
│                                                                          │
│               3)  The total number of maximum insertions per vehicle is  │
│                   less than 170 and its total cost lies below the upper  │
│   PROCEED         bound for the budget flexibility range.                │
│   DOWN            This case is quite similar to scenario 2. Again, you   │
│     ┊             will not be considering any solutions in the upper     │
│     ┊             region of the budget flexibility range.                │
│     ┊             Here, in addition to the option of reducing your budget│
│     ┊             or replacing some vehicles with more expensive ones, you│
│     ▼             can also increase the maximum number of insertions and │
│                   add more vehicles. It is necessary that you make these │
│                   changes.                                               │
│                                                                          │
│               4)  The total no. of maximum insertions per vehicle is less │
│                   than 170 and its total cost exceeds the upper bound for│
│                   the budget flexibility range.                          │
│                   This is the best option to have for the set of maximum │
│                   insertions and your budget.                            │
│                   In this case the total number of insertions would never│
│                   exceed 170. The optimization algorithm will work down  │
│                   from this point toward the budget for an initial       │
│                   starting solution set.                                 │
│   All of the above scenarios can be checked by accessing CHECK under     │
│   the MAXES option of the main menu.                                     │
│                                                                          │
└ = = = = = = = = = = = = = = = = = = = = = = = = = = = = = = ┘
```

for the vehicles in the model, while maintaining the cost of these test cases within the budget flexibility range. Clearly, scenarios 2 and 3 leave a portion of the range unused (the region to the right of the filled dots). The optimization algorithm will work down from the maximum cost to the budget for an initial feasible solution, by deleting insertions. This is not possible with both scenarios 2 and 3. In the case of scenario 1, it is possible for the optimization algorithm to generate an initial feasible solution set. However, it is also quite possible that the total number of insertions of a certain test case may exceed 170, in which case further computations will be impossible. Scenario 4 will guarantee

---

FIGURE 3.1(a)

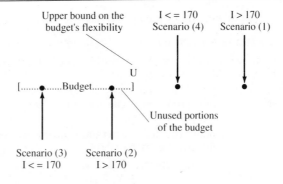

I = Total number of insertions.
● = Total cost of maximum insertions in relation to the budget.

---

that the total number of insertions on any test case will never exceed 170 and also that all the test cases will lie within the budget flexibility range.

Section 3.2—CHECK Option

The CHECK option under the MAXES sub-menu will take you through the process of checking for budget feasibility. Here you will be able to specify your budget, its flexibility range (in percentage), and the maximum insertions for every vehicle in the model, and then run the feasibility check process by pressing **ALT-B.** Again, you will need to access this option for specifying the budget and its flexibility range, even if you do not intend to run the optimization program. When you access this option you will be taken to the corresponding area in the worksheet, as displayed in Figure 3.2(a).

As mentioned in section 3.1 (EXPLAIN option), it is important to maintain the total number of maximum insertions to be less than or equal to 170. Instead of running the budget feasibility check process over and over again to ensure that you are faced with scenario 4, the process can be cut short (but not over with) by making sure that the total insertions are less than or equal to 170. This is done by pressing **[F9]** and checking the sum of the insertions (see Figure 3.2(a)). You are advised to ensure that this sum is as close to 170 as possible.

Once you have entered in the necessary information in the display shown in Figure 3.2(a), you may start the feasibility check process by pressing **ALT-B.** With the information you will have specified, you may be faced with one of the four scenarios. If you are faced with scenario 1, then you will be shown the display in Figure 3.2(b).

Again, although in this scenario it is possible for the optimization algorithm to generate an initial feasible solution, a test case may be produced for which the total number of insertions exceeds 170, in which case no computations will be possible. Hence, here you are given the option of making some recommended changes to the model. If you enter

---

FIGURE 3.2(a)

= =

SPECIFYING MAX INSERTIONS PER VEHICLE AND CHECKING BUDGET FEASIBILITY

PRESS ALT-M TO RETURN TO THE MAIN MENU OPTIONS

For an explanation of this section, please see EXPLAIN under the MAXES
option of the main menu.

PROCEED   You may specify your budget, its flexibility range ($+/-X$
DOWN   percent), and the maximum number of insertions for each
  | vehicle, below.
  |
  | ONCE YOU HAVE FINISHED DOING SO, PRESS ALT-B, TO CHECK FOR
  | BUDGET FEASIBILITY.
  |
  | TOTAL BUDGET: $8,000,000
  V   = = = = = =

FLEXIBILITY RANGE ($+/-X$ percent):   5%   ENTER
                                                    (X/100)

ENTER THE MAXIMUM INSERTIONS PER
VEHICLE BELOW

	Vehicle No.	Vehicle	Max No. of Insertions
	1	Drama	13
	2	Quiz	13
	3	Wkdy News	13
PRESS ALT-B	4	FeatrFilm	13
TO CHECK	5	SpncMysDr	13
FOR			
BUDGET	6	Info	13
FEASIBILITY	7	Home Wired	13
	8	WSJ	12
	9	Daily	12
	10	Cosmo	4
YOU MAY	11	Cntry Lvg	4
PRESS [F9]	12	Sprts Ill	4
TO	13	Newsweek	4
CALCULATE			
THE SUM OF	14	Car&Drvr	4
MAXIMUM	15	Road&Trk	4
INSERTIONS,	16	ScntfcAmr	4
SHOWN BELOW	17	Playboy	4
	18	Essence	4
THIS SUM	19	Shape	4
MUST NOT	20	Album/Rock	4
EXCEED 170	21	Nostalgia	10
	22	100 Shwg	1
	23	Empty Slot	0

SUM: 170

PRESS ALT-B TO CHECK FOR BUDGET FEASIBILITY

= =

[y] for your response in Figure 3.2(b), you will be shown the recommended changes as displayed in Figure 3.2(c).

Now, to incorporate the necessary changes into the model, you will need to return to the section on budget feasibility check. This can be done in two ways:

either press **ALT-C,** or
access the main menu (press **ALT-M**), choose the MAXES option, and then choose the CHECK option.

If you are faced with scenario 2, then you will be shown the display in Figure 3.2(d).

Again, to incorporate the changes follow the steps shown above. The recommendation on including more expensive vehicles in the model also implies that you could add in more expensive ad-types into the media plan. That is, you could replace a black-and-white ad with a color ad, or choose a longer (in terms of time) commercial for TV shows. These features will be reflected in the cost per insertion for the vehicles. To incorporate these changes, access the VEHICLES option under the main menu.

If you are faced with scenario 3, you will be shown the display in Figure 3.2(e) below.

If you are shown the display in Figure 3.2(f), you have successfully completed the budget feasibility check process and you will now be able to run an error-free optimization of the model. The budget feasibility check process may be long and tedious, requiring you to change the maximum insertions on the vehicles, the budget, its flexibility range,

FIGURE 3.2(b)

```
┌ = = = = = = = = = = = = = = = = = = = = = = = = = = = = = = = ┐
│                                                                │
│                   * * * WARNING * * *                (Scenario 1) │
│                                                                │
│   THE TOTAL NO. OF MAXIMUM INSERTIONS HAS EXCEEDED 170 AND ITS TOTAL │
│     COST HAS EXCEEDED THE UPPER BOUND FOR THE BUDGET FLEXIBILITY RANGE │
│   (See Explain under Maxes in the main menu)                   │
│                                                                │
│                                                                │
│   THIS MAY CAUSE SOME PROBLEMS WHILE RUNNING THE OPTIMIZATION  │
│     ALGORITHM.                                                 │
│                                                                │
│                                                                │
│   DO YOU WISH TO MAKE CHANGES ?  (Y/N): Y_____         │
│                                                                │
│   (THE CHANGES ARE STRONGLY RECOMMENDED                        │
│   IF YOU CHOOSE NOT TO MAKE THE CHANGES, THEN YOU MAY FACE THE RISK OF │
│     THE INSERTIONS' CONSTRAINT WHILE RUNNING THE OPTIMIZATION  │
│     ALGORITHM.                                                 │
│                                                                │
└ = = = = = = = = = = = = = = = = = = = = = = = = = = = = = = = ┘
```

FIGURE 3.2(c)

```
┌ = = = = = = = = = = = = = = = = = = = = = = = = = = = = = = = ┐
│                                                                │
│   POSSIBLE CHANGES TO MODIFY SCENARIO 1:                       │
│                                                                │
│                                                                │
│   --DECREASE THE MAXIMUM INSERTIONS ON SOME VEHICLES           │
│                                                                │
│                                                                │
│   PRESS ALT-C, THEN RUN THE BUDGET FEASIBILITY CHECK (ALT-B)   │
│                                                                │
└ = = = = = = = = = = = = = = = = = = = = = = = = = = = = = = = ┘
```

FIGURE 3.2(d)

```
╔ = = = = = = = = = = = = = = = = = = = = = = = = = = = = = = ═╗
│                    * * * WARNING * * *                    (Scenario 2)  │
│                                                                         │
│       THE TOTAL NO. OF MAXIMUM INSERTIONS HAS EXCEEDED 170 AND ITS      │
│          TOTAL COST IS LESS THAN THE UPPER BOUND FOR THE BUDGET         │
│          FLEXIBILITY RANGE                                              │
│       (See Explain under Maxes in the main menu)                        │
│                                                                         │
│       POSSIBLE CHANGES:                                                 │
│                                                                         │
│     1)  REPLACE SOME VEHICLES WITH MORE EXPENSIVE ONES                  │
│         Access Vehicles in the main menu, PRESS ALT-M                   │
│                         AND/OR                                          │
│     2)  DECREASE YOUR BUDGET,  (ALT-C)                                  │
│                         AND/OR                                          │
│     3)  REDUCE THE MAXIMUM NO. OF INSERTIONS,  (ALT-C)                  │
│  NOTE: Check budget feasibility again after having made these changes   │
│                                                                         │
╚ = = = = = = = = = = = = = = = = = = = = = = = = = = = = = = ═╝
```

FIGURE 3.2(e)

```
╔ = = = = = = = = = = = = = = = = = = = = = = = = = = = = = = ═╗
│                    * * * WARNING * * *                    (Scenario 3)  │
│                                                                         │
│       THE TOTAL NO. OF MAXIMUM INSERTIONS IS <= 170 AND ITS TOTAL       │
│          COST IS LESS THAN THE UPPER BOUND OF THE BUDGET FLEXIBILITY     │
│          RANGE                                                          │
│       (See Explain under Maxes in the main menu)                        │
│                                                                         │
│                                                                         │
│       POSSIBLE CHANGES:                                                 │
│                                                                         │
│     1)  ADD MORE VEHICLES OR REPLACE SOME WITH MORE EXPENSIVE ONES      │
│         Access Vehicles in the main menu, PRESS ALT-M                   │
│                                                                         │
│     2)  DECREASE YOUR BUDGET OR RANGE, OR INCREASE THE MAXIMUM          │
│             INSERTIONS ON SOME VEHICLES. PRESS ALT-C                    │
│  NOTE: Check budget feasibility again after having made the changes     │
│                                                                         │
╚ = = = = = = = = = = = = = = = = = = = = = = = = = = = = = = ═╝
```

FIGURE 3.2(f)

```
╔ = = = = = = = = = = = = = = = = = = = = = = = = = = = = = = ═╗
│                    ***GOOD NEWS***                        (Scenario 4)  │
│       THE TOTAL NO. OF MAXIMUM INSERTIONS IS <= 170 AND ITS TOTAL COST  │
│          HAS EXCEEDED THE UPPER BOUND OF THE BUDGET FLEXIBILITY RANGE   │
│       (See Explain under Maxes in the main menu)                        │
│                                                                         │
│                                                                         │
│       YOU MAY NOW PROCEED WITH THE OPTIMIZATION OF THE MEDIA PLANNING   │
│          MODEL                                                          │
│                                                                         │
│       PRESS ALT-M TO ACCESS THE MAIN MENU OPTIONS                       │
╚ = = = = = = = = = = = = = = = = = = = = = = = = = = = = = = ═╝
```

and even adding or editing vehicles to acquire the desired result. Nevertheless, it is still very important that you successfully complete this process if you intend to optimize the model.

SECTION 4—OPTIMIZE OPTION

This option will take you through the optimization of the algorithm. The model is optimized by an algorithm called simulated annealing. The options under the OPTIMIZE sub-menu are displayed in Figure 4.1.

Section 4.1—EXPLAIN Option

The EXPLAIN option provides an explanation of the simulated annealing algorithm, and the key parameters used in the algorithm. The simulated annealing algorithm is a pseudo-random search algorithm. It randomly mutates (alters) solution sets (i.e., the set of insertions) to improve on the objective function while maintaining the total cost within the budget flexibility range. Figure 4.1(a) provides the display for the EXPLAIN option in this sub-menu. READ THROUGH THIS EXPLANATION. IT WILL HELP YOU IN UNDERSTANDING THE PARAMETERS FOR THE ALGORITHM.

Section 4.2—TEST Option

The TEST option helps you design an appropriate cooling schedule for the algorithm. The cooling schedule regulates the rate of decrease in the acceptance probability of a poor solution. The schedule will need to be designed based on how long you wish to run the optimization algorithm. The run-time of the algorithm is directly represented by the number of iterations. Hence, you will need to visually inspect the rate of decrease in the probability with the iteration count. Basically, it is advised that a small probability of 0.05 be reached at around the last iteration as opposed to having such a probability when

FIGURE 4.1

```
 ┌ = = = = = = = = = = = = = = = = = = = = = = = = = = = = = = = ┐
 |                 * * * OPTIMIZE MENU OPTIONS * * *             |
 |                                                               |
 |   EXPLAIN:  Provides an explanation of the simulated annealing|
 |             algorithm and its parameters.                     |
 |                                                               |
 |      TEST:  Lets you experiment with some of the important    |
 |             parameters in the SA algorithm, so as to design an|
 |             appropriate cooling schedule.                     |
 |                                                               |
 |     PARMS:  Lets you set your chosen parameters for the SA    |
 |             algorithm and then run the model optimization by  |
 |             PRESSING ALT-O.                                    |
 |                                                               |
 |  CURR-MAX:  Lets you view the best solution, if you end the   |
 |             algorithm execution, by PRESSING CTRL-BREAK.      |
 |                                                               |
 | MAIN-MENU:  Returns to the main menu option.                  |
 |                                                               |
 └ = = = = = = = = = = = = = = = = = = = = = = = = = = = = = = = ┘
```

FIGURE 4.1(a)

= =

OPTIMIZATION OF THE MEDIA PLANNING MODEL BY SIMULATED ANNEALING
AN EXPLANATION

PRESS ALT-M TO RETURN TO THE MAIN MENU OPTIONS

Simulated annealing is a combinatorial optimization algorithm, which finds near-optimal solutions for different kinds of problems. It is based on the method of cooling/annealing metals. At high temperatures, the molecules in a metal can rearrange themselves fairly easily. But at low temperatures only very limited motion is possible. With a slow and gradual decline in the temperature, the end product is normally a very uniform block of metal with little or no deformations.

In the media planning model, we need to find an optimal set of the number of insertions per media vehicle so as to optimize the OBJECTIVE FUNCTION. In this model, the objective function is given by:

[TOTAL WEIGHTED EXPOSURES/TOTAL COST]

When applying simulated annealing to this optimization problem, we need to change or mutate the set of insertions and then accept those sets that improve the objective function value. However, if we do not allow for the acceptance of a few poor solutions, which may lead us to even better solutions, we may be stuck at a local maximum (like the top of a small hill, rather than the peak in a mountain range). Simulated annealing allows for this kind of a decision process.

Like in the annealing of metals, earlier on in the search (cooling process) we can allow for the acceptance of fairly poor solutions. We accept a poor solution with a certain probability. This probability is fairly high earlier in the process (so as to examine an entire surface of possible solution sets or metal forms), but is steadily decreased as we iterate the process over and over again. An analogy to this would be the search for the summit of a mountain range (the optimum). Earlier in the day, we may be more likely to go downhill, in the hope of finding a higher mountain, because of our fresh energy. But towards the end of the day, after having lost a lot of our energy, we would be less likely to go downhill, and climb another mountain, but rather we would climb to the summit of the mountain we then found ourselves on. We would assume that this summit was the highest point in the mountain range. However, if we kept a record of the highest mountain we had seen thus far, then we would at least have a knowledge of where we had found the highest known mountain. Similarly, simulated annealing keeps a record of the best solution.

In simulated annealing, the probability of accepting a poor solution is given by the function:

p = exp(−(Delta × ScaleFactor)/Temperature)

where,

Delta	**absolute(New Obj. func. − Old Obj. Func.)**
ScaleFactor:	**a factor to regulate the decrease in the prob.**
Temperature:	**a record of the time elapsed since the start of the search**

The main parameters here are Delta, the Scale Factor and the Temperature. Here is the intuition behind the function shown above. The probability (p), being exponentially inverse, is a decreasing function. Keeping the temperature and scale factor constant, if we have a large delta, i.e., the new objective function value is a lot smaller than the previous one, then the probability of accepting this new value and its associated solution set (insertions) will be quite small and vice versa. The scale factor in some sense regulates the rate of decline of the probability, based on the value of delta. In the media planning model the value of delta could be anywhere between 0.5 and 0.000001!!

FIGURE 4.1(a)   (*concluded*)

= =

The scale factor helps to compensate for these wild fluctuations in the value of delta, and hence the value of the acceptance probability. The Temperature in some sense keeps a record of the time that has elapsed since the start of the algorithm. Hence, earlier on in the process, when the Temperature is relatively high, we have a reasonably high probability of accepting a poor solution and vice versa. The Temperature is decreased steadily by a DISCOUNT FACTOR (BETA). This is given by:

$$T(N + 1) = BETA \times T(N)$$

where,

N is the number of iterations done thus far

The value of BETA normally ranges from 0.8 to 0.99. The higher the BETA value, the slower the rate of decrease in temperature, and vice versa.

There are two other important parameters in simulated annealing. They are:

No. of iterations
Max. mutations per iteration.

These two parameters regulate the total runtime of the algorithm. The no. of iterations specifies the time length of searching the entire neighborhood within the budget flexibility range.

The iteration counter is updated only when a set of insertions is accepted, whether it is a good or a poor solution. If the set is rejected, then simulated annealing mutates the set, i.e., adds or subtracts one or two insertions for a random vehicle, depending on the total cost's relation to the budget range. Hence, if we were stuck in a local maximum, then the solution set would keep mutating forever, unless we set a limit to the number of mutations simulated annealing could perform for a given immediate neighborhood (not the entire surface area of feasible solutions).

You may experiment with the parameters: Temperature (also initial temperature), BETA, Scale factor, delta, and no. of iterations, in order to decide upon an appropriate cooling schedule (or decrease in probability), by accessing **TEST** under the **OPTIMIZE** option of the main menu. One way of deciding on the values of these parameters is studying the decrease in probability with the iteration no. and temperature. At the last iteration, the temperature should be close to zero and the probability should be very small (like 0.005).

You can use your discretion on the number of runs, iterations, and mutations. If you specify a new no. of iterations, then you will need to come up with an appropriate cooling schedule.

PRESS ALT-M TO RETURN TO THE MAIN MENU OPTIONS

= =

the iterations have been half-finished. Figure 4.2(a) displays the area of the worksheet where you will be able to design a cooling schedule.

You will need to play around with the parameters to obtain an appropriate cooling schedule, assuming that you have an idea as to how many iterations you wish to have. In the parameters above, only enter more than 100 total number of insertions.

The following table has been developed to aid you in designing cooling schedules based on how long you wish to run the algorithm (in terms of minutes).

Always set Initial Temperature to be 100.

Time in Minutes	Number of Iterations	Number of Mutations	BETA Value	Scale Factor
5	50	25	0.90	300
10	100	50	0.95	300
15	150	75	0.97	700
20	200	100	0.98	1,000

The above cooling schedules are approximates. They are designed to give you a guide in designing a good cooling schedule. Basically, for a larger number of vehicles you will need to run the optimization algorithm for a relatively longer period of time. This allows enough time for the algorithm to search the entire feasible solution space for an optimal solution. Once you have finished designing an appropriate cooling schedule, you may proceed to set the parameters for running the optimization algorithm.

Section 4.3—PARMS Option

This option will let you specify the important parameters in the optimization algorithm and will also let you run the algorithm (by pressing **ALT-O**). Figure 4.3(a) shows this display.

FIGURE 4.2(a)

= =

EXPERIMENTING WITH THE PARAMETERS IN SIMULATED ANNEALING

PRESS ALT-M TO RETURN TO THE MAIN MENU OPTIONS

```
Initial Temperature:        100
BETA:                       0.93
DELTA:                      0.01
ScaleFactor:                1000
Total # of Iterations:      100
```

Iteration	Temperature	Acceptance Probability
1	100.0	0.905
10	65.0	0.857
20	42.3	0.789
30	27.5	0.695
40	17.9	0.571
50	11.6	0.422
60	7.5	0.266
70	4.9	0.130
80	3.2	0.043
90	2.1	0.008
100	1.3	0.001

AFTER HAVING ENTERED IN YOUR NEW PARAMETERS, PRESS [F9] TO RECALCULATE THE VALUES IN THE TABLE

= =

Once you have specified the parameters shown in Figure 4.3(a) you may execute the simulated annealing algorithm by pressing **ALT-O.** Initially, the algorithm will search for an initial feasible solution and you will be shown the display in Figure 4.3(b) below.

When an initial feasible solution has been found, you will then be shown the display in Figure 4.3(c).

FIGURE 4.3(a)

```
╔════════════════════════════════════════════════╗
║  SETTING PARAMETERS FOR THE SIMULATED ANNEALING ALGORITHM      ║
║                                                                ║
║      PRESS ALT-M TO RETURN TO THE MAIN MENU OPTIONS            ║
║                                                                ║
║      PLEASE ENTER THE PARAMETERS FOR THE SIMULATED            ║
║      ANNEALING ALGORITHM BELOW.                               ║
║                                                                ║
║      PRESS ALT-O TO OPTIMIZE THE MEDIA PLANNING MODEL          ║
║                                                                ║
║      TOTAL NUMBER OF MEDIA VEHICLES:          22              ║
║      INITIAL TEMPERATURE:                     100             ║
║      BETA:                                    0.95            ║
║      SCALE FACTOR:                            300             ║
║      TOTAL NUMBER OF ITERATIONS PER RUN:      100             ║
║      MAX MUTATIONS PER ITERATION:             50              ║
║                                                                ║
╚════════════════════════════════════════════════╝
```

FIGURE 4.3(b)

```
╔════════════════════════════════════════════════╗
║         SEARCHING FOR INITIAL FEASIBLE SOLUTION SET           ║
╚════════════════════════════════════════════════╝
```

FIGURE 4.3(c)

```
╔════════════════════════════════════════════════╗
║ THE SIMULATED ANNEALING ALGORITHM IS NOW BEING EXECUTED       ║
║ YOU WILL BE PRESENTED WITH THE FINAL RESULTS OF THE MEDIA PLANNING ║
║ MODEL OPTIMIZATION ONCE THE ALGORITHM HAS FINISHED EXECUTION  ║
║ THE OPTIMIZATION OF THE MEDIA PLANNING MODEL TAKES QUITE A WHILE. ║
║ HENCE, YOU MAY WANT TO TAKE A SMALL BREAK.                    ║
║ IF YOU WISH TO END THE ALGORITHM EXECUTION TO VIEW THE BEST SOLUTION ║
║ FOUND THUS FAR, FIRST PRESS CTRL-BREAK, ESC, AND THEN ALT-D   ║
║ This can also be done by accessing CURR-MAX, under the OPTIMIZE ║
║ option in the main menu                                       ║
║                                                                ║
╚════════════════════════════════════════════════╝
```

If you have *not* successfully completed the budget feasibility check process under the "MAXES" option in the main menu, then the total number of insertions in a certain test case may exceed 170, after which the algorithm will stop execution, and you will be presented with the display in Figure 4.3(d). This will entail performing the budget feasibility check all over again. This situation is most likely to occur if you do not perform the feasibility check or accept scenario 1 (see "EXPLAIN" under "MAXES").

If at any time during the execution of the algorithm you wish to end the execution and see the best solution found thus far, execute the following steps:

- *either*—press **CTRL-BREAK, ESC,** and then **ALT-D,**
- or—press **CTRL-BREAK, ESC, ALT-M** (main menu), and then choose the "OPTIMIZE" option and then the "CURRMAX" option.

If you execute the steps shown above or if you wait until the end of the algorithm execution, you will be presented with the final results of the optimization or the best (hopefully optimal) solution. In the final results you will be presented with the values of some variables of interest (total cost, total weighted exposures), the objective function value, the optimal solution set of insertions, and also the set of maximum insertions. The set of maximum insertions has been provided to help you see how many insertions, of the maximum available, have been utilized. Figure 4.3(e) presents a display of a sample final result.

If you wish to print these results so as to have a hard copy for sensitivity analyses, press **ALT-P.**

SECTION 5—LISTING OPTION

The LISTING option provides a program listing along with comments of the macros used in the model. It has four sub-options: LIB-MENU, ADD-MAC, BUDG-MAC, and SA-LIST. If you choose this option from the main menu you will be shown the display in Figure 5.1.

FIGURE 4.3(d)

```
┌ = = = = = = = = = = = = = = = = = = = = = = = = = = = = = = = = = ┐
│                    * * * WARNING * * *                            │
│                                                                   │
│   THE TOTAL NUMBER OF INSERTIONS HAS EXCEEDED 170                  │
│   YOU WILL NEED TO ENSURE THAT THE TOTAL NO. OF MAXIMUM"           │
│   INSERTIONS IS <= 170                                             │
│   You may make the following changes:                             │
│   -Reduce the maximum insertions on some vehicles                 │
│   PRESS ALT-C TO INCORPORATE THE ABOVE MENTIONED CHANGES          │
│   THEN, RUN THE BUDGET FEASIBILITY CHECK OVER AGAIN               │
│   (BY PRESSING ALT-B)                                             │
│   THESE STEPS MUST BE TAKEN TO SUCCESSFULLY RUN THE OPTIMIZATION  │
│   ALGORITHM                                                       │
│                                                                   │
└ = = = = = = = = = = = = = = = = = = = = = = = = = = = = = = = = = ┘
```

FIGURE 4.3(e)

```
╔═══════════════════════════════════════════════════════════╗
   FINAL RESULTS OF THE OPTIMIZATION OF THE MEDIA PLANNING MODEL
   ------------------------------------------------------------------

             => PRESS ALT-M TO RETURN TO THE MAIN MENU OPTIONS
             => PRESS ALT-P TO PRINT THESE RESULTS
             => PRESS THE [HOME] KEY TO RETURN TO THE MAIN
                   WORKSHEET AREA

                GROSS IMPRESSIONS:                    1,136,261
             (A) TOTAL COST:                         $6,820,508
             (B) TOT WTD EXPOSURES:                     770,945
                 COST/M EXPOSURES:                        $8.85

             THE OPTIMAL OBJECTIVE FUNCTION VALUE (B/A) IS:
                                                           0.118

             OPTIMAL SET OF INSERTIONS:
```

Vehicle No.	Vehicle	Optimal Set Insertions	Max No. of Insertions
1	Drama	10	13
2	Quiz	10	13
3	Wkdy News	12	13
4	FeatrFilm	9	13
5	SpncMysDr	1	13
6	Info	12	13
7	Home Wired	11	13
8	WSJ	3	12
9	Daily	4	12
10	Cosmo	3	4
11	Cntry Lvg	3	4
12	Sprts Ill	4	4
13	Newsweek	3	4
14	Car&Drvr	1	4
15	Road&Trk	1	4
16	ScntfcAmr	3	4
17	Playboy	3	4
18	Essence	1	4
19	Shape	1	4
20	Album/Rock	2	4
21	Nostalgia	10	10
22	100 Shwg	1	1
23	Empty Slot	0	0

FIGURE 5.1

```
┌ = = = = = = = = = = = = = = = = = = = = = = = = = = = = = = = = ┐
|              + + + LISTINGS MENU OPTIONS + + +                  |
|    LIB-MENU: Shows the program listings of the menu macros      |
|    ADD-MAC: Shows the program listings of the macro to add      |
|             or edit vehicles                                    |
|    BUDG-MAC: Shows the budget feasibility check macro           |
|     SA-LIST: Shows the program listing of the simulated         |
|              annealing algorithm                                |
|    MAIN-MENU: Returns to the main menu options                 |
└ = = = = = = = = = = = = = = = = = = = = = = = = = = = = = = = = ┘
```

The LIB-MENU option will let you view the macro code (menu library) for the menu system. The ADD-MAC will display the macro codes for the process of adding or editing a vehicle, and the BUDG-MAC option will let you view the macro code for checking budget feasibility. Finally, the SA-LIST option will provide you with the program listing of the simulated annealing algorithm. All of these programs have documented comments.

You are given access to these program listings in case you are curious about the structuring of the programs, especially the simulated annealing algorithm.

WARNING: DO NOT ALTER ANY OF THE CODE IN THE PRO-
GRAM LISTINGS UNLESS ASKED TO DO SO BY THE
INSTRUCTOR.

PERFORMING SENSITIVITY ANALYSES

Concerning sensitivity analyses on the number of insertions for each, there are two methods at your disposal. The first is more applicable to the case where you have not used the optimization feature. Here, you will need to specify the insertions on each vehicle manually. For this case, the insertions can be directly entered into the main area of the worksheet, by pressing **ALT-S.** This keystroke will show you a portion of the spreadsheet with the name of the vehicles on the left-hand column and the number of insertions on the extreme right-hand column. You may enter in the number of insertions directly in the right hand column. After having specified the insertions, press **ALT-R** to view the output or performance measures.

If, however, you have run the optimization program and have seen the final results of the optimization, then first print out the results by pressing **ALT-P.** Now study the utilization of the insertion from the maximum number available. If, for instance, a vehicle has almost all of its insertions utilized, then it is advisable to relax the constraint of maximum insertions on this vehicle (i.e., increase the maximum number of insertions for the vehicle). This vehicle is supposedly more valuable to the media plan. This increase in the maximum insertions can be counter-balanced by decreasing/tightening the constraint on a less-valuable vehicle (one with hardly any insertions utilized).

The maximum number of insertions can be set through the "CHECK" option under the "MAXES" sub-menu. Please keep in mind that this will entail the running of the budget feasibility check all over again. You may also replace some of the poor vehicles by accessing the "VEHICLES" option in the main-menu.

FINAL COMMENTS

We hope that this user's manual to the menu system and the optimization feature of the Media Planning Model have been helpful to you. If you have any comments regarding this manual or any questions on the use of the menu system and any features within it, please contact your instructor or Professor Paul Farris.

Case 10–2

*Promotion Planning Project**

This note was written to assist students in conducting a computer-based analysis of the Procter & Gamble Co. (B) case (Case 6–4). It describes the assumptions in a worksheet developed to help students support their conclusions on how to promote H-80. It also gives advice on how to input the necessary data. Attached as exhibits are: (1) an *abbreviated* sample of the worksheet output (for the first 3 months of a 12-month plan), (2) a special worksheet to help you think about the effect of your plan on revenue (a sales forecasting worksheet), and (3) a promotional calendar (from Exhibits 3 through 5 in the case).

Although the volume and content of material associated with this case may seem overwhelming at first, take the components one step at a time and the synergistic link between the case and worksheet should become evident. First, read Procter & Gamble Co. (B). This case outlines the problem and describes the promotional alternatives available. Next, scan the worksheet (called "PGPLAN") to get an idea of what is included there. Finally, read through this project with the worksheet displayed in front of you. You can then scroll to the appropriate portion of the worksheet as it is described in this guide.

The worksheet is essentially a computerized version of Exhibit 18 from the case. The last two columns, "Number of Average Weeks Volume" and "Cost," are not included.

---

*This note was prepared by Professor Christopher Gale and John Barrett, research assistant. The Darden Graduate School of Business Administration, University of Virginia. Copyright © 1986 by the Darden Graduate Business School Foundation, Charlottesville, Virginia.

Instead, you will find a summary section that provides total cost by event and total number of units used and/or distributed. A print range called "TOTALS" has already been created that includes this summary section. The print range "TOTALS" is a rectangular block of cells from P20 in the upper left hand corner to R158 in the lower right. In addition, monthly costs of your promotion plan are given at the bottom of the worksheet (in cells D157 to O157).

Several of the assumptions/calculations included in this worksheet may conflict with your interpretation of case facts. Since this worksheet is just one possible version of Exhibit 18, you should understand the implicit assumptions behind the calculations. This document describes the meaning of calculations used in this worksheet.

For simplicity, all dollar figures (except those given in the summary section discussed above) are given in thousands. Numbers (of coupons, refund offers, and so forth) vary in their units. Pay close attention to the magnitude of numbers requested by the worksheet.

A second print range (called "FORECAST" and containing cells U22 to AB87) will print the "Sales Forecasting Worksheet" mentioned above. This is a form to help you quantify the effects of your promotion plan on revenue for H-80. A copy of this print range is attached. Since the assumptions necessary to generate revenue information are numerous, NO FORMULAS ARE INCLUDED IN THIS SECTION. You should carefully consider the effect of your promotional plan on revenue and derive the appropriate formulas and relationships to accurately portray these considerations.

The worksheet is divided into three sections: (1) Determination of Monthly Sales Volume, (2) Calculation of Cost of Promotion, and (3) Consistency Check of Promotional Plan. The first section, Determination of Monthly Sales Volume, contains monthly volume in both physical and statistical cases. The second section, Calculation of Cost of Promotion, includes eight components which determine the total cost of your promotional plan. These eight components are listed along the left side of Exhibit 18 of the case. The last section, Consistency Check of Promotional Plan, will help you to ensure that your model makes sense. These three sections are found in Rows 12 to 34, 37 to 159, and 162 to 203, respectively.

SECTION ONE—DETERMINATION OF MONTHLY SALES VOLUME

Stocking and trade allowances differ in the way in which they are calculated. Stocking allowances are a form of discount given on a per-physical-case (constant size of case) basis. Trade allowances are a similar type of discount but are given on a per-statistical-case (constant number of ounces of product) basis. The number of ounces in a physical case will vary based on the size of the container used (12 oz., 32 oz., and so on), while the number of ounces in a statistical case will be constant across all sizes of container. A statistical case is defined by Procter & Gamble as 310 ounces of product. The first portion of the worksheet asks for some estimates from you and calculates the rest of the information needed for subsequent sections.

You should enter the projected size of the total LDL market and the projected share of market for H-80 in cells D17 and D18, respectively. (Estimates for these figures are given in Table 2 of the case.) The number of statistical cases represented by this market share objective is calculated in cell F18. The number of physical cases sold, by size of container, is given for each month in cells D27 through 030. Calculation of these numbers is based on the size of the market (in F18), the actual/statistical case ratio (from Table 3 and shown in B27 to B30), the historical percentage of volume for each size of container (given in Table 3 and shown in C27 to C30), and market share growth (using Dawn's experience listed in Table 5 and in Row 23).

A few words of warning about these calculations may be in order. First, notice that the Range D27 . . . 030 is unprotected despite the presence of rather lengthy formulas there. This is to allow you to alter the proportions among case sizes (C27 to C30) over time, should you wish to do so. One would reasonably expect that this distribution would change over the course of the year.

Second, you may also wish to change the market share growth in Row 23. If you do so, make sure that the percentages you use total to 1,200 percent over the year (or an average of 100 percent per month).

Last, the share of market in statistical cases (F18) should equal the total number of statistical cases actually distributed (R34). This is automatically checked for you in Section Three of the worksheet, but you will probably want to double-check this correspondence.

SECTION TWO—CALCULATION OF COST OF PROMOTION

Stocking Allowances

Once the numbers of physical cases have either been entered or calculated based on your estimate of the size of the market and determination of a market-share objective, you should enter the stocking allowance you would like to use for each package size in Rows 43 through 46. The monthly totals calculated in Row 48 multiply the number of cases (from Rows 27 to 30) times their respective stocking allowance (in Rows 43 through 46), and sums each of the four terms.

Trade Allowances

The trade allowance (based on *statistical cases,* not physical cases) is calculated based on two additional terms you enter: the dollar amount of the trade allowance in Row 52 and the percentage of cases affected by the allowance in Row 53. Monthly total cost of the trade allowance is calculated in Row 55. The formula simply multiplies the number of statistical cases (calculated in Row 34) by the two figures you entered in Rows 52 and 53.

Sampling

Costs for sampling are easily calculated from the delivered cost per unit figures given in Exhibit 11. Since the cost is not influenced by the number of samples actually used by recipients of the samples, the number of samples distributed is multiplied by the respective delivered cost per unit (from Exhibit 11 and listed in Column C, Rows 61 through 64).

Thus, the monthly totals in Row 66 consist of four terms: the number of 6-ounce samples distributed times their delivered cost per unit ($0.75), plus the number of 3-ounce samples delivered times their respective cost per unit ($0.53), and so forth. The result is further multiplied by 1,000; since the number of samples entered by the user is in millions, multiplication by 1,000 keeps cost figures in thousands of dollars.

Couponing

Couponing costs are a function of the distribution costs, the value of the coupon, the number of coupons distributed, and the number redeemed. Information for these calculations is found in Exhibits 12 and 13. The user enters the coupon value (either $0.20, $0.25, $0.35, $.50, $1.00, or 0 if you are using a "get one free" coupon) in Row 71. Based on this value, the computer calculates the redemption rate compared to a $0.20 coupon (from Exhibit 13). In Column B, Rows 77 through 84, the redemption rates for a new brand are given. These figures are calculated by multiplying the "Estimated Percent Redemption" in Exhibit 12 by 1.5 (since coupons for new brands redeem 50 percent higher than average—see the first footnote). The redemption rate for a new brand is multiplied by the redemption rate compared to a $0.20 coupon, resulting in the effective redemption rate.

The monthly total coupon cost has two components: distribution and fulfillment costs. Distribution costs are calculated in Row 86 by multiplying the number of coupons distributed (in millions) through each method by the cost per thousand of that method. These costs are included in Exhibit 12. The monthly total coupon cost is calculated by multiplying the number of coupons used each month of the promotion times the respective redemption rate for a new brand (Column B, Rows 77 through 84). These eight terms (one for each method of distribution) are further multiplied by the value of the coupon (Row 71) and the redemption rate as a function of the value of the coupon (Row 73). Lastly, the distribution costs from Row 86 are added. The result is the number of coupons actually returned times their value, or the cost of the coupon program, plus the distribution costs.

Misredemption, given as a percentage of coupons redeemed in Exhibit 12, will not affect the calculated cost of your promotion plan. It will overstate the number of bottles of H-80 sold on coupon. This should be taken into account in your volume calculations.

Special Packs

Calculations for the cost of special packs are based on data from Exhibit 14 and Table 3. Calculations proceed based on the cost descriptions given in Exhibit 14. You may change the value for any month of the promotion by entering a 1 (low value), 2 (medium value), or 3 (high value) in Row 93. The numbers of special packs used in each month of the promotion (in thousands) are entered in Rows 95 through 98.

Price packs are available for any size of H-80. Since the worksheet cannot know which size you want to offer the price pack on, you must tell it—by entering the retail unit price in Row 101. The computer will calculate the number of units per statistical case based on the retail price you enter. The normal retail price and the number of units per statistical case are given for each size of H-80 in Table 3 of the case. Be sure to choose from only the four retail prices listed in Table 3.

To avoid division by zero, the formula first checks to see if there is a number entered in Row 95. (If you are not using price packs in your plan, that row will be empty.) If a number is there, the worksheet computes a 30 percent discount for a high-value price pack (a 3 in Row 93), a 20 percent discount for a medium-value price pack (a 2 in Row 93), or a 10 percent discount for a low-value price pack (a 1 in Row 93). The worksheet also adds a $0.50 per statistical case handling charge.

Bonus packs are only available in the 32-oz. size. To calculate the cost of using them, the number of bonus packs used (entered in Row 96) is divided by the number of 32-oz. containers per statistical case (from Table 3: 9.7). This figure is multiplied by the cost per statistical case given in Exhibit 14 for each value of the bonus pack promotion.

Prepriced sizes are also limited to a single size, 12 ounces. The cost of the promotion is very similar to that for price packs: the number of bottles offering the prepriced discount in Row 97 is multiplied by the savings off the regular retail price plus the cost per statistical case for handling. The number of statistical cases represented by the number of bottles in Row 97 is calculated using the figure of 25.8 items per statistical case from Table 3.

Trial size is the simplest of the special pack calculations. The total cost of the promotion is simply the number of units offered times a cost per unit, determined by the value of the promotion.

Monthly total cost for all special pack promotions is given in Row 110 and is simply a sum of the cost of the four possible special pack promotions.

Refunds

Calculations for the cost of a refund program are based on data from Exhibit 15. You are required to enter the number of purchases required before a refund is given in Row 115, and the number of refund offers distributed (in thousands) for each type of distribution vehicle in Rows 117 through 121.

The percent responses, calculated in Rows 123 through 127, are based on the number of purchases required and the method of distribution. These estimates are given in Exhibit 15, part II, under the heading, "Estimated response as percent of offers distributed."

Monthly totals (in Row 129) are then calculated by multiplying the number of offers distributed for each method of distribution by the respective response rate and summing these figures. Thus there are five terms in this equation. This total is then multiplied by $1.34, which is the value of the refund plus a $0.34 handling charge (see the footnote in Exhibit 15).

Calculation of execution costs of a refund promotion are based on the footnote in Exhibit 15. Costs for display/sales aids and print advertising are at your discretion. Direct mail costs are $16.45 per thousand. There are no costs for in/on-pack distribution using other brands; however there is a 3-cent charge per unit for distribution via our own brand. The monthly total given in Row 136 is a sum of all execution costs of refund promotion.

Premiums and Group Promotions

The amount and frequency of premiums and group promotions are both left completely up to the user, although estimated annual costs from Exhibit 16 and the text, respectively, are included in Column C, Rows 142 through 146 and Row 154, for each reference.

The monthly total for all forms of promotion is calculated in Row 157, and the grand total is given in cell P157. Consistent with case facts, this grand total should not exceed $37 million. As mentioned at the beginning of this note, a complete summary is included in cells P20 to R158 and is already set up as a print range called "TOTALS." Please note that the figures reported in these cells are actual units, not thousands or millions. Most of these calculations are sums across all 12 months of the plan.

SECTION THREE—CONSISTENCY CHECK OF PROMOTIONAL PLAN

Target Share of Market

The target market share calculated by multiplying the estimated size of the total LDL market in statistical cases (D17) by the expected percentage SOM (D18) equals the size of the target share of the market, in statistical cases, for H-80 by the end of the first year. This figure should equal the total number of statistical cases in Section One (R34).

Volume Check

This section compares the total number of units sold (in all sizes of containers) with the number of sales caused by promotional activities. The estimated effects of the promotions are contained in the exhibit(s) corresponding to a particular type of promotion. The total number of units sold (Row 183) should be consistent with the total number of customers created (Row 187). Monthly and yearly totals should reflect your assumptions about trade loading, lagged effects of promotions, and so forth.

The results of these two consistency checks are contained in a print range called "CONSISTENCY" and include cells A167 . . . P203. If you are using a standard dot matrix printer and 8½" by 11" paper, this print range is too wide to print without "wrapping." In such a case, dividing the print range into two separate ranges before printing will provide more legible results. The procedure for creating the new ranges employs the following keystrokes:

/RNC   (Range Name Create) to create a new named range.

 1-2-3 will request a name. Type a name of your choosing but not one of the names that appear on the screen.

 1-2-3 will request a range. To divide CONSISTENCY in half, type A167 . . . H203.

Follow the same procedure to create a range name for the other half of CONSISTENCY. Be sure to use a different name and the range I167 . . . P203.

Use the same print procedure outlined on the following page. Five print ranges will be listed (the three original and the two you created).

Finally, the other print range included in this worksheet, called "FORECAST" and including cells U22 to AB87, is for your use as an electronic scratch pad to gauge the effect of your promotion plan on revenue. The only automatic calculation in this portion of the worksheet is a total in cell AB87. All other figures must be entered by you based on your assumptions about the effects of a promotion plan and longevity of those effects.

To use any of the three print ranges included in the worksheet, first make sure the printer you are using is turned on and is on-line, then enter the following keystrokes:

/P   to PRINT a file.

P   to send the file to the PRINTER.

R   to specify a RANGE to send to the printer.

F3   to list the three print ranges already in the worksheet.

You can use the arrow keys to highlight the print range you want to print and then press the **enter** key. Then just press

G   to GO, or print the range.

and the printer will begin printing the range you requested.

COLUMN LETTERS — A B C D E F / P Q R
ROW NUMBERS — 1–55

```
     A            B            C

 8  Print Ranges -> Cost & Volume Summary: "TOTALS"
 9                 Sales Summary: "FORECAST"
10                 Consistency Check: "CONSISTENCY"

14  SECTION ONE -- DETERMINATION OF MONTHLY SALES VOLUME

17  SIZE OF 1983 LDL MARKET: ('000s of stat. cases)        59,800
18      H-80 ESTIMATED 1983 MARKET SHARE:              7%   or  ->   4,186

20                                    Month:     Month 1   Month 2   Month 3

22  NUMBER OF PHYSICAL CASES MOVED: ('000s)
23      % of Estimated Year I Share (Table 5):       30%       30%        80

                    Actual/    % of Stat.
                    Stat. Ratio  Volume:                                        Dollars          TOTALS (actual-numbers)   Volumes
                                                                                -------                                    -------
27  48 oz. Size        1.39        10%        8         8        20            $797,971          Physical Cases: 48 oz. Size   35,045
28  32 oz. Size        1.24        30%       25        25        68          $2,412,837                         32 oz. Size  118,276
29  22 oz. Size        1.14        45%       41        41       111          $3,746,993                         22 oz. Size  193,543
30  12 oz. Size        0.93        15%       17        17        45          $1,324,695                         12 oz. Size   78,851

32  Total Physical Cases per Month:            91        91       243        $8,282,495          Total Phys. Cases          425,715

34  Equivalent Statistical Cases:             105       105       279                            Statistical Cases:         488,367

38  SECTION TWO -- CALCULATION OF COST OF PROMOTION

42  I) STOCKING ALLOWANCE:
43      Dollars / 48 oz. Case               $1.30     $0.00     $1.70
44      Dollars / 32 oz. Case                1.30
45      Dollars / 22 oz. Case                1.30
46      Dollars / 12 oz. Case                1.30
48      Monthly Total ($000s):              $119        $0       $34           $152,636          Stocking Allowance

51  II) TRADE ALLOWANCE:
52      Dollars / Statistical Case          $1.30     $1.30     $0.00
53      Percentage of Cases Affected:       100%       35%       45%
55      Monthly Total ($000s):              $136       $48        $0            $47,616          Trade Allowance
```

III) SAMPLING: (Exhibit 11)

	Delivered Cost/Unit:			--Millions of Samples--				Samples:	
-6 oz	$0.75			0.00	0.00	0.00	$0	6 oz. Samples	0
-3 oz	$0.53			0.00	3.50	3.50	$3,710,000	3 oz. Samples	7,000,000
-1.5 oz	$0.41			0.00	0.00	0.00	$0	1.5 oz. Samples	0
-2 x .75 oz	$0.31			0.00	0.00	0.00	$0	2-.75 oz. Samples	0
Monthly Total ($000s):				$0	$1,855	$1,855	$3,710,000	Sample Total	7,000,000

IV) COUPONING:

				-- Coupon Value: ($0.20)		
Redemption Rate Compared to				$0.35	$0.20	$0.00
$0.20 Coupon: (Exhibit 13) ->				1.25	1.00	0.00

Method of Distr. Redemption Rate for a New
Brand (Exhibit 12)

				------Millions of Coupons------					
-Mail-Single	17.4%			0	100	0	$0	Mail-Single	15,000,000
-Co-op	17.4%	Millions	:	X	X	35	$14,750	-Co-op	35,000,000
-Extended	15.9%	of	:	0	0	100	$22,958	-Extended	8,000,000
-FSI -Single	11.4%	Coupons	:	0	0	0	$0	FSI -Single	
-F Page Co	8.6%	Distrib-	:	0	0	0		-F Page Co	0
-2/5 P Co op	7.7%	uted	:	0	0	0		-2/5 P Co op	0
-BFD	4.7%		:	0	0	0		BFD	0
-Magazine	3.9%		:	0	0	0		Magazine	0
Distribution Cost ($000s):				$0	$14,750	$22,958	$2,525,750	Distribution Cost	58,000,000
Monthly Total ($000s):				$0	$576	$576	$3,529,520	Total Coupon	

V) SPECIAL PACK: Value of Special Pack ->

			------Value of Promotion-----						
			1	1	1	1			
Method: -Price Pack	Thousands	:	25	4,400				# Price	475,000
-Bonus Pack	of Special	:	0	3,200				# Bonus	200,000
-Prepriced	Packs	:	0	4,100				# Prepriced	275,000
-Trial Size		:	0	2,800				# Trial	0
								Total Special Pack	950,000

If you are using price packs,
enter the normal retail price ->   retail price $0.84 $1.46 $2.04
(based on the size of package).   #/stat. case   25.80 14.00 9.70
(Table 3)

		$2.04			
	retail price	$0.84 $1.46 $2.04			
	#/stat. case	25.80 14.00 9.70			

Monthly Cost: -Price Pack	$2.58	$0.00	$1,124.40	$301,180	# Price
(Exhibit 14) -Bonus Pack	0.00	0.00	1,402.06	$125,773	# Bonus
-Prepriced	0.00	0.00	1,112.66	$120,829	# Prepriced
-Trial Size	0.00	0.00	616.00	$0	# Trial
Monthly Total ($000s):	$3	$0	$4,255	$547,783	Special Pack Cost

56
57
58
59
60
61
62
63
64
65
66
67
68
69
70
71
72
73
74
75
76
77
78
79
80
81
82
83
84
85
86
87
88
89
90
91
92
93
94
95
96
97
98
99
100
101
102
103
104
105
106
107
108
109
110
111

COLUMN LETTERS

Row	A	B	C	D (3)	E (2)	F / I (1)	P	Q
113								
114					← Number of →			
115	VI) REFUND:		Number of Purchases Required ->	3	2	1		
116	($1.34/refund)							Refunds:
117		-Print	No. of :	0	5,000			* Print 5,000,000
118		-Point of Sale	Refund !	0	2,500			* Point of Sale 2,500,000
119		-Direct Mail	Offers !	0				* Direct Mail 10,000,000
120		-In/On Pack, Other	Distr. !	0	1,000			* In/On Pack, Other 1,000,000
121		-In/On Pack, Own	(000s) !	0				* In/On Pack, Own 0
122								
123	% response:	-Print		0.3%	0.5%	0.9%		Total Refunds 18,500,000
124	(Exhibit 15)	-Point of Sale		1.8%	3.0%	5.4%		
125		-Direct Mail		1.2%	2.0%	3.6%		
126		-In/On Pack, Other		2.7%	4.5%	8.2%		
127		-In/On Pack, Own		4.2%	7.0%	12.7%		
128								
129			Monthly Total ($000s):	$0	$0	$351	$511,880	Redemption Costs
130								
131	Execution Costs:	-Display/Sales Aids ($000s)	$400.00				$250,000	Display/Sales Aids
132	(Exhibit 15	-Print Advertising ($000s)	120.00				$175,000	Print Advertising
133	footnote)	-Direct Mail		0.00	0.00	0.00	$164,500,000	Direct Mail
134		-In/On Pack, Own		0.00	0.00	0.00	$0	In/On Pack, Own
135								
136			Monthly Total ($000s):	$520	$0	$0	$164,925,000	Execution Costs
137								
138								
139								
140			National					
141	VII) PREMIUM: (Exhibit 16)		Cost:($000s)					Premiums:
142		-Self-Liquidator	$200				$0	On/In Pack 0
143		-Partial Liquid.	$400				$0	Near Pack 0
144		-Free-in-Mail	$2,200				$100,000	Free in Mail 1
145		-Near Pack	$950		100		$0	Self-Liquidator 0
146		-On/In Pack	$950				$0	Partial Liquid. 0
147								
148			Monthly total ($000s):	$0	$100	$0	$100,000	Total Premium 1
149								
150								
151								
152								
153			National					
154	VIII) GROUP PROMOTION: ($000s)		Cost: ($000) $50					Group Promotion 1
155					$50		$50,000	
156								
157			Monthly Total for All Events ($000s):	$777	$25,011	$7,071	$173,574,434	Grand Total 1
158								
159				Month 1	Month 2	Month 3		
160								
161								
162								
163								

SECTION THREE -- CONSISTENCY CHECK OF PROMOTIONAL PLAN

Target SOM (Statistical cases): 4,186,000   should equal: 488,367   the num

Volume Check (000s):	Month 1	Month 2	Month 3	Month 4	Month 5
Total Physical Cases per Month:	91	91	243	0	0
Equivalent Statistical Cases:	105	105	279	0	0
Number of Units Sold: 48 oz.	68	68	180	0	0
(in 000s) 32 oz.	304	304	811	0	0
22 oz.	664	664	1,770	0	0
12 oz.	406	406	1,081	0	0
Total No. of Units Sold: (000s)	1,441	1,441	3,842	---0	0

6,724 Units Sold

Should be consistent with the generated impact of promotions;

No. of Customers Created: (000s)	385	4,572	2,237	0	0

7,194 Customers Created

	Month 1	Month 2	Month 3	Month 4	Month 5
a) . . .from sampling:	0	1,050	1,050	0	0
b) . . .from couponing:	0	3,522	0	0	0
c) . . .from coupons:					
price packs:	25	0	450	0	0
bonus packs:	0	0	200	0	0
prepriced size:	0	0	275	0	0
trial size:	0	0	0	0	0
d) . . .from refunds:					
print:	0	0	45	0	0
point of sale:	0	0	135	0	0
direct mail:	360	0	0	0	0
in/on pack, other:	0	0	82	0	0
in/on pack, own:	0	0	0	0	0
e) . . .from premiums:	0	0	0	0	0
f) . . .from group promotion:	0	0	0	0	0

Source: Procter & Gamble Co. (B) (S84-048) Revised 3/18/86
National Sales Promotion Plan (Exhibit 18-Case B)
Copyright © 1986 by the Colgate Darden Graduate School of Business
Written by John Barrett: based on a Worksheet by Thorn Landers, Darden '86

ROW NUMBERS

737

	Number of Cases Increase	Relative Value of Case	Dollar Value per Case		Resulting Change in Sales
Stocking allowance:					
48-oz. size					
32-oz. size					
22-oz. size					
12-oz. size					
Trade allowance:					
Stat. cases					

	Percent Usage	Percent Repurchase	Decay Rate	Net Annual Effect
Sampling				
6 oz.				
3 oz.				
1.5 oz				
2 × .75 oz.				

	Percent Responding	Change in Volume	Life of Impact	Decay Rate	Net Annual Effect
Couponing:					
Mail:					
Single					
Co-op					
Extended					
FSI:					
Single					
Full page					
$^2/_5$ page					
BFD					
Magazine					
Special pack:					
Price pack					
Bonus pack					
Prepriced					
Trial size					
Refund:					
Print					
Point-of-sale					
Direct mail					
In/on-pack, other					
In/on-pack, own					
Premium:					
On/in pack					
Near pack					
Free in-mail					
Self-liquidator					
Partial liquidator					
Group promotion					
Total					

Ivory, Dawn, and Joy Promotion Calendars: 1981–1983 (from Exhibits 3, 4, and 5 in the case)

Year	Brand	January	February	March	April	May	June	July	August	September	October	November	December
1981	Ivory	20¢ coupon, $1.30 trade allowance	48 oz.: 30¢-off price pack; 22 oz.: $1.30 trade allowance			32 oz.: 20¢-off price pack	22 oz.: $1.30 trade allowance		32 oz.: 20¢-off price pack; 20¢ BFD coupon		20¢-off F.S. coupon; $1.30 trade allowance		
	Dawn	32 oz.: 20¢-off price pack		22 oz.: 13¢-off price pack		32 oz.: $1.30 trade allowance		22 oz.: 13¢-off price pack		48 oz.: 30¢-off price pack	32 oz.: 20¢-off price pack		
	Joy		32 oz. 20¢-off price pack		22 oz.: 13¢-off price pack		20¢ F.S. coupon; $1.30 trade allowance		22 oz.: 13¢-off price pack	20¢ F.S. coupon; $1.30 trade allowance		32 oz.: 20¢-off price pack	
1982	Ivory	48 oz.: Harlequin premium; $1.30 trade allowance	32 oz.: 20¢-off price pack			22 oz.: 13¢-off price pack	32 oz.: 20¢-off price pack			20¢-off F.S. coupon; $1.30 trade allowance			32 oz.: 27¢-off price pack
	Dawn	20¢ PCH coupon; $1.30 trade allowance		32 oz.: 20¢-off price pack		22 oz.: 13¢-off price pack		48 oz.: 30¢-off price pack			22 oz.: 20¢-off price pack	32 oz.: $1.30 trade allowance	

(continued)

Ivory, Dawn, and Joy Promotion Calendars: 1981–1983 (from Exhibits 3, 4, and 5 in the case) (concluded)

Year	Brand	January	February	March	April	May	June	July	August	September	October	November	December
	Joy		48 oz.: 2 40¢ coupons: 22 oz.: 13¢-off price pack		32 oz.: 20¢-off price pack		22 oz.: 13¢-off price pack		20¢ F.S. coupon; $1.30 trade allowance		48 oz. 40¢-off price pack	20¢ mailed coupon; $1.30 trade allowance	
	H-80												
1983 (proposed)	Ivory	20¢-off BFD—any size; $1.80 trade allowance	22 oz.: 20¢-off price pack			32 oz.: 27¢-off price pack		22 oz.: 20¢-off price pack		20¢ F.S. coupon; $1.80 trade allowance		48 oz.: 40¢-off price pack	
	Dawn	20¢ PCH coupon; $1.80 trade allowance		32 oz.: 27¢-off price pack		20¢ F.S. coupon; $1.80 trade allowance		20¢ F.S. coupon; $1.80 trade allowance			22 oz.: 20¢-off price pack		20¢ F.S. coupon; $1.80 trade allowance
	Joy	32 oz.: 27¢-off price pack	20¢ F.S. coupon; $1.80 trade allowance		22 oz.: 20¢-off price pack .		12 oz.: 49¢ prepackaged pack			22 oz.: 20¢-off price pack		20¢ mailed coupon; $1.80 trade allowance	
	H-80												

Case 10–3

Competition-for-Account Project*

Because of a "difference in management philosophy," several of the organizations discussed in the cases contained in this book have decided to select new advertising agencies. (Your instructor will tell you which organization is now a potential client of your agency.) As a member of a six- to eight-person team of specialists from various departments (creative, account management, research, and media), your job is to work with the team to secure the new business for your agency.

Much of the preliminary work has been done. The situation is now one of a choice between your agency and a major competitor. The client has requested (and you have agreed to) a formal presentation of your proposed advertising strategy which will be evaluated in comparison to that of your one remaining competitor.

On the day of the competition, the remainder of the class will serve as the executive task force charged with hiring a new agency.

Company and market information is available for the preparation of the presentation in the case describing the organization, but the client naturally expects you will take advantage of any other published information contained in your library which is relevant to the advertising agency.

Financial arrangements have been worked out already, but you expect a significant amount of time and money will be spent in excess of the compensation received by the losing agency.

The client has expressed a strong preference for a full-service agency that will function as a "partner" in the business. As such, the client has cautioned against mere "dog and pony" examples of creative work but wants a fully integrated advertising strategy. The client still has many unresolved advertising and marketing questions and is looking for your ability to contribute to the solution of strategic as well as executional problems. The following guidelines have been issued to help structure the presentation and ensure comparability.

---

*This case was written by Professor Paul W. Farris, The Darden Graduate School of Business Administration, University of Virginia. Copyright © 1981 by the Sponsors of The Darden Graduate Business School Foundation, Charlottesville, Virginia.

PRESENTATION GUIDELINES

1. Time allotted: 20 minutes presentation (for each team); 10 minutes question-answer.
2. Assume the client is familiar with the agency and individual team-member credentials and has found them impressive.
3. Devote the bulk of your analysis to the problems which you see as critical, but cover the following:
    a. Marketing/advertising objectives.
    b. Models of consumer/buyer behavior relevant to market and advertising decisions.
    c. Issues of segmentation/positioning and competitive analysis.
    d. Message design/copy strategy (roughs are highly desirable).
    e. Media planning and scheduling.
    f. Budgeting for national and regional advertising as well as consumer promotions.
    g. Measurement techniques and approaches which are appropriate for tactical and strategic decisions in this market.
    h. A description of how the various elements fit into a total strategic package.
4. Be prepared to provide back-up analyses/data for questions about your strategy.

While it is unlikely you will be permitted to be present during your competitor's presentation *or* the discussion of the relative merits of the two presentations, you have been promised some client feedback regardless of whether you win or lose. It is expected that individual members of the client's executive task force will submit comments on the strengths and weaknesses of the two presentations and the main reasons they decided to vote for one agency instead of the other. It is also possible that you might be allowed to view a videotape of the presentations (including your own).

Case 10–4

*Media Allocation Exercise**

Advertisers continually confront the decision of how to best allocate their advertising budgets among alternative media. Exhibit 1 presents a percentage breakdown of 1987 media expenditures for each of 10 companies which ranked among the top 100 national advertisers in 1987.

The ten companies are listed below in a different order. See if you can match the

---

**This case was prepared from published sources by Professor John A. Quelch as the basis for class discussion. Copyright © 1982 by the President and Fellows of Harvard College. Harvard Business School case 9–582–120.

EXHIBIT 1   Percentage Breakdown of Measured Media Advertising Expenditures for Ten Leading National Advertisers: 1987

	Newspapers	Supplements	Magazines	Television	Radio	Outdoor	Business Publications
A.	0.0%	0.3%	2.0%	94.4%	1.2%	1.8%	0.3%
B.	4.6	2.3	24.9	47.3	4.5	15.1	0.7
C.	0.7	0.3	10.4	83.7	4.2	0.1	0.5
D.	0.0	2.9	9.8	53.2	33.4	0.3	0.3
E.	65.1	0.4	3.9	12.7	15.1	1.5	1.2
F.	2.5	0.0	27.3	57.9	11.7	0.6	0.0
G.	9.8	0.8	32.4	48.8	5.0	0.1	3.1
H.	15.7	0.2	15.0	63.5	3.9	0.6	0.9
I.	0.1	0.0	5.6	94.2	0.0	0.0	0.1
J.	0.0	0.0	31.0	68.1	0.9	0.0	0.0

Source: *Advertising Age,* September 28, 1988.

profiles in Exhibit 1 with the company names. What factors explain variations in media breakdowns among companies selling different types of products and services?

1. *Hasbro Inc.*: Toys and Milton Bradley games, Playskool.
2. *Time Inc.*: Magazine and book publishing.
3. *Noxell Corp.*: Cover Girl cosmetics and Raintree skin moisturizers.
4. *McDonald's Corp.*: Fast-food restaurants.
5. *Sears, Roebuck & Co.*: Retailing, Kenmore appliances, Craftsman tools, Allstate insurance.
6. *Seagram Co. Ltd.*: Liquor, wine, and Tropicana fruit juices.
7. *Toyota Motor Sales U.S.A. Inc.*: Passenger cars and trucks.
8. *United States Government*: Government-agency services including, for example, postal and travel services and armed forces recruiting.
9. *Procter & Gamble Co.*: Household products, personal-care products, foods, and beverages.
10. *Texas Air*. Passenger and freight air service.

Case 10–5

*Promotion Incentive Allocation Exercise**

Based on responses to an annual reader survey, *Incentive Marketing* magazine estimated that $15,832,382,000 was spent in the United States in 1989 on incentives directed at salespeople, at dealers, and at consumers. This figure included merchandise and travel incentives only. Cash incentives such as salesforce commissions and trade promotion allowances were not included. And, among consumer promotions, only the cost of premiums and sweepstakes were included; the costs of cents-off packs, refunds, coupons, and samples were not covered in the survey.

Despite these omissions, it is clear that the mix of promotion incentives varies widely among industries. Exhibit 1 reports the percentage breakdown of incentive expenditures for each of 8 industries. These 8 were among the top 30 in incentive expenditures in

EXHIBIT 1 Percentage Breakdowns of Promotion Incentive Expenditures for Eight Industries: 1989

	Trade Incentives			Consumer Premiums	
	Sales Force Merchandise and Travel	Dealer Merchandise and Travel	Business Gifts	Mail-In Promotions	Other Premiums
Industry A	19.4%	1.1%	23.3%	9.1%	47.0%
Industry B	38.4	37.6	12.1	9.0	2.8
Industry C	26.2	36.6	6.3	8.4	22.6
Industry D	15.7	8.4	2.8	40.0	33.2
Industry E	66.0	12.3	9.1	11.4	2.3
Industry F	36.5	11.9	8.1	21.1	22.3
Industry G	30.1	27.6	5.1	18.0	19.0
Industry H	39.0	13.3	18.2	14.0	15.7
Average for All U.S. Industry	33.0	18.1	10.3	15.4	23.2

Source: *Incentive Marketing*, December 1989.

*This case was prepared from published sources by Professor John A. Quelch as the basis for class discussion. Copyright © 1982 by the President and Fellows of Harvard College. Harvard Business School case 9–582–120.

1989. Listed below in a different order are the names of the eight industries. Can you determine which profile on Exhibit 1 represents which industry? What factors account for differences in the promotion incentive mix from one industry to another?

1. Food Products
2. Feed, Fertilizer, Farm Supplies
3. Toiletries and Cosmetics
4. Apparel
5. Bank, Savings and Loan
6. Sporting Goods and Toys
7. Insurance
8. Auto Parts, Accessories, Tires

Case 10–6

Advertising/Sales Ratio Exercise*

In 1981, the Federal Trade Commission reported 1975 financial data for each of 261 lines of business, representing the full range of industrial and consumer products manufacturers in the U.S. economy. Each line of business was equivalent to one or a few closely related Standard Industrial Classification (SIC) four-digit product groupings. The 1975 data were gathered from 471 firms, including the 250 largest manufacturers plus a sample of the next 750.

Among other data, the FTC reported for each line of business the advertising expense-to-sales ratio, the total selling expense- (including advertising) to-sales ratio, and the total research and development expense-to-sales ratio. Exhibit 1 presents these three ratios for each of 12 lines of business. Across all 261 lines of business, the weighted average advertising-to-sales ratio was 1.2 percent, while the weighted average total selling expense-to-sales ratio was 6.7 percent.

The 12 lines of business are listed below in a different order. Match the profiles on Exhibit 1 with the lines of business. What factors explain variations in each ratio among the lines of business? What factors explain different combinations of the three ratios?

*Professor John A. Quelch prepared this case from published sources as the basis for classroom discussion. Copyright © 1982 by the President and Fellows of Harvard College. Harvard Business School case 9–582–121.

EXHIBIT 1 Advertising to Sales, Selling Expense to Sales, and R&D to Sales for 12 Lines of Business: 1975

	Media Advertising Expense to Sales		Total Selling Expense to Sales		Total R & D Expense to Sales	
	Percent	Rank[1]	Percent	Rank[1]	Percent	Rank[2]
A.	20.1%	1	35.1%	1	2.8%	17
B.	2.2	51	8.4	100	4.9	7
C.	10.2	7	19.5	22	0.7	73
D.	3.1	32	21.1	13	0.1	131
E.	1.2	78	23.7	8	3.9	12
F.	0.7	113	9.9	77	0.0	135
G.	0.1	198	0.6	229	32.5	1
H.	0.1	210	14.0	40	0.8	56
I.	1.7	63	16.5	28	3.6	13
J.	6.3	15	20.6	17	0.8	55
K.	2.9	36	12.0	50	0.6	78
L.	2.0	54	28.3	3	0.2	117

[1]Rank out of 261 lines of buisness.
[2]Rank out of 135 lines of business for which R&D data were available.

Source: Federal Trade Commission, 1975 Line of Business Survey.

1. Books
2. Guided Missiles, Space Vehicles
3. Manifold Business Forms
4. Pesticides and Agricultural Chemicals
5. Woodworking Machinery
6. Bread, Cake, and Related Products
7. Cereal Breakfast Foods
8. Proprietary Drugs
9. Surgical and Medical Instruments
10. Bottled and Canned Soft Drinks
11. Typewriters and Office Machines
12. Fluid Milk

Index